A COMMUNITY OF WRITERS

A WORKSHOP COURSE
IN WRITING

A COMMUNITY OF WRITERS

A WORKSHOP COURSE IN WRITING

Second Edition

PETER ELBOW
University of Massachusetts at Amherst

PAT BELANOFF
State University of New York at Stony Brook

McGraw-Hill, Inc.
*New York   St. Louis   San Francisco   Auckland   Bogotá
Caracas   Lisbon   London   Madrid   Mexico City   Milan   Montreal
New Delhi   San Juan   Singapore   Sydney   Tokyo   Toronto*

This book was developed by STEVEN PENSINGER, Inc.

This book was set in Caslon Book by The Clarinda Company.
The editors were Steve Pensinger and Scott Amerman;
the designer was Karen K. Quigley;
the production supervisor was Kathryn Porzio.
R. R. Donnelley & Sons Company was printer and binder.

Cover photo credit: "Grandmother's Dream" Amish quilt,
© 1925. Photograph courtesy of Thos. K. Woodard,
American Antiques & Quilts.

A COMMUNITY OF WRITERS
A Workshop Course in Writing

This book is printed on acid-free paper.

67890   DOC   DOC   909876

ISBN 0-07-019693-1

Library of Congress Cataloging-in-Publication Data

Elbow, Peter.
    A community of writers: a workshop course in writing / Peter
Elbow, Pat Belanoff. —2nd ed.
      p.   cm.
    Includes index.
    ISBN 0-07-019693-1
      1. English language—Rhetoric.   2. College readers.   I. Belanoff,
Pat.   II. Title.
PE1408.E38   1995
808'.0427—dc20   94-4027

ABOUT THE AUTHORS

Peter Elbow is Professor of English at the University of Massachusetts at Amherst.

Before writing *A Community of Writers* he wrote two other books about writing: *Writing Without Teachers* and *Writing with Power: Techniques for Mastering the Writing Process.* He is author of a book of essays about learning and teaching: *Embracing Contraries.* He also wrote *Oppositions in Chaucer,* as well as numerous essays about writing and teaching. His most recent book, *What Is English?,* explores current issues in the profession of English.

He has taught at the Massachusetts Institute of Technology, Franconia College, Evergreen State College, and the State University of New York at Stony Brook—where for five years he directed the Writing Program. He served for four years on the Executive Council of the Modern Language Association and is now a member of the Executive Committee of the Conference on College Composition and Communication. He has given talks and workshops at many colleges and universities.

He attended Williams College and Harvard University and has an M.A. from Exeter College, Oxford University, and a Ph.D. from Brandeis University.

Pat Belanoff is Director of Writing Programs at the State University of New York–Stony Brook. She is president of the SUNY Council on Writing and a member of the College Steering Committee of NCTE. Pat is a co-author (with Betsy Rorschach and Mia Oberlink) of *The Right Handbook,* now in its second edition. She has also co-edited (with Marcia Dickson) *Portfolios: Process and Product* and (with Peter Elbow and Sheryl Fontaine) *Nothing Begins With an N: New Investigations of Freewriting.* Pat has a degree in medieval literature from New York University and continues to teach and publish in this area, too.

CONTENTS

Summary Guidelines for MLA Documentation *inside front cover*
More about the Workshops *ix*
Short Essays in "Ruminations and Theory" *xiii*
Readings *xv*
Preface *xix*

Cover Letter 1
Introduction 5

WORKSHOPS
1. An Introduction to the Variety of Writing Processes 11
2. Getting Experience into Words: Image and Story 39
3. Collaborative Writing: Dialogue, Loop Writing, and the Collage 63
4. Private Writing: Finding What You Have to Say 99
5. From Private to Public Writing: Exploring Audience and Genre 121
6. Writing in the World: An Interview about Writing 153
7. Revising 175
8. Persuasion 211
9. The Essay 231
10. Listening, Reading, and Writing in the Disciplines 253
11. Interpretation as Response: Reading as the Creation of Meaning 285
12. Argument 311
13. Research 337
14. Text Analysis through Examining Figurative Language 365
15. Voice 387
16. Revision through Purpose and Audience: Writing as Doing Things to People 419
17. Autobiography and Portfolio 445

MINI-WORKSHOPS
A. Writing Skills Questionnaire 473
B. Double-Entry or Dialectical Notebooks 476
C. Breathing Life into Words: Text Rendering or Reading Out Loud 481
D. Writing with a Word Processor 487
E. Midterm and End-Term Responses to a Writing Course 494
F. The Sentence and End-Stop Punctuation 499
G. Commas 505
H. Apostrophes 509
I. Quotation and the Punctuation of Reported Speech 513
J. Spelling 517
K. Copyediting and Proofreading 523
L. The Difference between Grammatical Correctness and a Formal, Impersonal Voice 526

SHARING AND RESPONDING

Table of Contents   SR-3
Cover Letter   SR-5
Summary of Kinds of Responses   SR-8
Procedures for Giving and Receiving Responses   SR-13
Full Explanations of Kinds of Responses—With Samples   SR-18
    1. Sharing: No Response   SR-18
    2. Pointing and Center of Gravity   SR-19
    3. Summary and Sayback   SR-22
    4. What Is Almost Said? What Do You Want to Hear More About?   SR-25
    5. Reply   SR-27
    6. Voice   SR-29
    7. Movies of the Reader's Mind   SR-31
    8. Metaphorical Descriptions   SR-38
    9. Believing and Doubting   SR-41
   10. Skeleton Feedback and Descriptive Outline   SR-44
   11. Criterion-Based Feedback   SR-50

Sample Essays   SR-57

Works Cited   WC-1
Acknowledgments   A-1
Author/Title Index   I-1
Subject Index   I-6
Guide to Kinds of Responding   inside back cover

MORE ABOUT THE WORKSHOPS

WORKSHOP 1
AN INTRODUCTION TO THE VARIETY OF WRITING PROCESSES   11

- Generating words and ideas, getting started on process writing, practicing a wide variety of kinds of writing
- Creating a collage through cut-and-paste revising

WORKSHOP 2
GETTING EXPERIENCE INTO WORDS: IMAGE AND STORY   39

- Learning to *experience* what you write about, not just understand it
- Moving from description to narrative
- Writing and getting carried away—and then shaping and tightening your words

WORKSHOP 3
COLLABORATIVE WRITING: DIALOGUE, LOOP WRITING, AND THE COLLAGE   63

- Overcoming boring topics and the lack of something to write
- Writing dialogue
- Practicing collaboration in writing

WORKSHOP 4
PRIVATE WRITING: FINDING WHAT YOU HAVE TO SAY   99

- Using strategies that help you discover that you always have lots to say
- Turning process writing into an essay

WORKSHOP 5
FROM PRIVATE TO PUBLIC WRITING: EXPLORING AUDIENCE AND GENRE   121

- Using private writing as a source of public writing
- Practicing writing in a number of genres
- Understanding how both ignoring and heeding audience affects your writing

WORKSHOP 6
WRITING IN THE WORLD: AN INTERVIEW ABOUT WRITING   153

- Getting a sense of the different kinds of writing people do and discovering how varied writing processes are
- Finding a theme in a mass of material and learning to get voice and liveliness into your writing

WORKSHOP 7
REVISING   175

- Revising a paper you wrote for a previous workshop
- Understanding better the nature of revision and its importance for good writing
- Revising at three levels: content, structure, and mechanics and usage

WORKSHOP 8
PERSUASION   211

- Planting seeds so others will be willing to listen to your opinions
- Analyzing how written words cause people to change their thinking or action
- Comparing the use of long, formal arguments and shorter, informal kinds of persuasion

WORKSHOP 9
THE ESSAY   231

- Reading and analyzing essays; seeing them as entries into the workings of the mind
- Writing both a personal and an impersonal essay and coming to grips with the differences between them

WORKSHOP 10
LISTENING, READING, AND WRITING IN THE DISCIPLINES   253

- Exploring how writing differs from one discipline to another
- Using writing as a way to learn
- Writing on the same topic for a general audience and a specialized audience

WORKSHOP 11
INTERPRETATION AS RESPONSE: READING AS THE CREATION OF MEANING   285

- Developing an awareness of the active and exploratory nature of reading and interpreting
- Rendering or performing texts

WORKSHOP 12
ARGUMENT   311

- Learning to see through an essay to the skeleton of reasoning underneath it; evaluating the arguments of others and improving your own
- Thinking about the nature of argument and recognizing that there is no magic *right* way to argue

WORKSHOP 13
RESEARCH   337

- Understanding both personal research and library research and their potential interaction
- Collaborating with others in different times and places
- Documenting material from written and spoken sources

WORKSHOP 14
TEXT ANALYSIS THROUGH EXAMINING FIGURATIVE LANGUAGE   365

- Improving your understanding of hard texts
- Understanding the nature of metaphor, simile, image, and symbol

WORKSHOP 15
VOICE   387

- Understanding what is meant by "voice" in writing
- Practicing a variety of ways of getting voice into your writing

WORKSHOP 16
REVISION THROUGH PURPOSE AND AUDIENCE: WRITING AS DOING THINGS TO PEOPLE   419

- Revising a paper from an earlier workshop by thinking pointedly about what you want words to *do,* and to *whom*
- Thinking about the connections between genre and purpose
- Describing writing goals as expressive, transactional, and poetic

WORKSHOP 17
AUTOBIOGRAPHY AND PORTFOLIO   445

- Improving your writing by becoming a student of your own writing processes
- Looking back over the semester and what you've learned; preparing a portfolio of your writing
- Reflecting on the value of metacognitive thinking

SHORT ESSAYS IN "RUMINATIONS AND THEORY"

WORKSHOP 1

Why We Think Freewriting Is Important   21
Why We Think Process Writing Is Important   23
A Collage about Collages   24

WORKSHOP 2

Writing and Getting Carried Away   47

WORKSHOP 3

Loop Writing and the Dangerous Method   80
"It's Impossible Not to Think of Something"   82

WORKSHOP 4

Private Writing: Why Write It If No One Will See It?   107
What's the Sense in Felt Sense?   110

WORKSHOP 5

About Audience   137
Are Genres Form or Content?   140

WORKSHOP 7

Putting Revising into Perspective   184
Revising and Grammar   186

WORKSHOP 8

Informal Persuasion and Formal Argument   221

WORKSHOP 9

The Essay   239

WORKSHOP 10

Knowledge and Writing within Discipline Communities   261
An Argument for Freshman Composition   263

xiv

SHORT ESSAYS IN
"RUMINATIONS
AND THEORY"

WORKSHOP 11

About the Artificiality of Our Exercise: Repeatedly Interrupting Your
  Reading and Asking You to Write   298

WORKSHOP 12

Nonadversarial Argument   321
Reasoning and Grammar   324

WORKSHOP 13

The Ongoing Conversation   353

WORKSHOP 14

Figurative Language as a Window on the Mind   373

WORKSHOP 16

Purpose, Genre, and an Overview of Rhetorical Terrain   430
Global Goals: Expressive, Transactional, and Poetic   432
Can We Forget about Purpose and Audience?   434

WORKSHOP 17

Autobiography and Metacognition   452

READINGS

WORKSHOP 1
AN INTRODUCTION TO THE VARIETY OF WRITING PROCESSES

"Example of a Student's Freewriting"   27
"Robert Bingham (1925–1982)"   28
"The Feel of Writing—and Teaching Writing," Donald Murray   29
"Collage about Myself as a Writer," with cover letter, Steve Clark   33
"Chronic Releasing: A Collage," with process writing, Matt Ludvino   36

WORKSHOP 2
GETTING EXPERIENCE INTO WORDS: IMAGE AND STORY

"Image of Ice-Cream Man," with process writing, Mitchell Shack   50
"An Ice-Cream Man," Mitchell Shack   51
"Caye Ocho Beach," with cover letter, Isabelle Foucard   53
"A Worn Path," Eudora Welty   55

WORKSHOP 3
COLLABORATIVE WRITING: DIALOGUE, LOOP WRITING,
AND THE COLLAGE

"Loop Writing about Teaching Writing," Lynn Hammond   84
"Loop Writing Collage," Darci Jungwirth   87
"Collage about Human Differences," with process writing, Amy Vignali   90
"Collaborative Collage about Writing a Collage," Laura Corry,
    Elija Goodwin, Matt Ludvino, Denise Morey, Tassie Walsh   92
"Process Notes about Collaborative Writing," Kathy Reckendorf   95

WORKSHOP 4
PRIVATE WRITING: FINDING WHAT YOU HAVE TO SAY

"Example of Open-Ended Writing Process," with cover letter,
    Melissa Fogel   112
"Process Log about Using the Open-Ended Process," Manuel Depina   114
"Process Log about Private Writing," Irene Wong   115
"Example of Writing with the Perl Guidelines," Peter Elbow   116
"Felt Sense," Eugene Gendlin   119

WORKSHOP 5
FROM PRIVATE TO PUBLIC WRITING: EXPLORING AUDIENCE
AND GENRE

"Be Brave Sweet Sister: Essay Developed from Open-Ended Writing,"
    Melissa Fogel   142
"A Letter," Mark Levensky   144
From "Parts of Speech and Punctuation," Gertrude Stein   145
"Autobiography," Nazim Hakmit   146
"About Being a Man: Essay Developed from Private Writing,"
    Charles Miller   148
"What's a Short, Bald-Headed, Potbellied Guy to Do? The List of Risk
    Factors for Heart Disease Grows Even Longer," Michael Lemonick   149
"Meditation," a student   151

WORKSHOP 6
WRITING IN THE WORLD: AN INTERVIEW ABOUT WRITING

"Portrait of My Mother as a Writer," with process writing,
    Kristin Bresnan   166
"Interview," Salvatore Bianco   169
"Tackling Racism in the Mystery Novel: *New York Newsday* Interview with
    Walter Mosley"   170

WORKSHOP 7
REVISING

"The Male Bashing Stereotype" (three drafts), Kimberly Graham   188
"Drafts and Revisions of an Editorial for the *Daily Hampshire Gazette*,"
    with cover letter Kay Moran   193
"Drafts and Revisions of Two Short Book Reviews for *Glamour* Magazine,"
    with cover letter Laura Mathews   197
"Divisible Man" (two drafts), John Edgar Wideman   205

WORKSHOP 8
PERSUASION

"Short Letters," Janine Ramaz   223
"Letter to a Product Producer," with advertisement, Jason Multer   224
"The Great Person-Hole Cover Debate: A Modest Proposal for Anyone Who
    Thinks the Word 'He' Is Just Plain Easier . . . ,"   Lindsy Van Gelder   226
"Some Reflections on Not Voting in Presidential Elections," Meg Hyre   227

WORKSHOP 9
THE ESSAY

"Untitled 1" and "Untitled 2," Eleanor Klinko   242
"The Essay," Edmund Gosse   244
"On Essaying," James Moffett   247
"Essay: What I Think, What I Am," Edward Hoagland   249

WORKSHOP 10
LISTENING, READING, AND WRITING IN THE DISCIPLINES

From "Father–Daughter Incest," Judith Herman and Lisa Hirschman   265
"Reductionism and Biological Determinism," Lynda Birke   269
From "American Experience," Vern L. Bullough   271
"A New World beyond Snow White," Sandra M. Gilbert and
   Susan Gubar   274
"What Keeps an Airplane Up (two versions)," Gary Kolnicki   277

WORKSHOP 11
INTERPRETATION AS RESPONSE: READING AS THE CREATION
OF MEANING

"The Writer," Richard Wilbur   300
"Responses to the 'Writer'"
   "Movies of the Mind While Reading," Elijah Goodwin   301
   "Movies of the Mind While Reading," Tassie Walsh   302
   "Collage Dialogue on 'The Writer'" Barbara Hales and Julie Nelson   302
   "Some Thoughts about 'The Writer' on the Occasion of the Death of
      Isaac Bashevis Singer," Laura Wenk   303
"Quiet until the Thaw," from the Cree Indians   304
"Rain Straight Down," from the Cree Indians   305
"I Am Sorrow," Sindy Cheung   306
"Wishing in the Dark," Bi Chen   306
"Sonnet 3," Burt Hatlen   307
"How Poetry Comes to Me," Gary Snyder   308
"Sliver," Langston Hughes   308
"Analysis of 'Sliver,'" Randie Gay   308

WORKSHOP 12
ARGUMENT

"Letter to the Editor (about Batman)," Nicholas Corwin   327
"Aiming a Cannon at a Mosquito," Mona Charen   328
"Analysis of My Argument in 'Short Letters,'" Janine Ramaz   329
"Too Much for Too Little," with cover letter, a student   330
"Gas Analgesia"   331
"With All Deliberate Speed: What's So Bad about Writing Fast?"
   William F. Buckley, Jr.   332

WORKSHOP 13
RESEARCH

"When a Child Has Cancer," Kymberly Saganski   356
"The Life and Times of Shag," Alan M. Beck   358
"Writing Mathematics," William Zinsser   361

WORKSHOP 14
TEXT ANALYSIS THROUGH EXAMINING FIGURATIVE LANGUAGE

"My Mother, That Feast of Light," Kate Barnes   376
"My Mother, That Beast of Blight," Amber Moltenbrey   376
"Writing Styles in 'My Mother, That Feast of Light,'" Karen Daley   378
"One Art," Elizabeth Bishop   379
"Untitled," Adrienne Rich   380
"Wen-Fu," Lu Chi   380
"The Book of the Grotesque," Sherwood Anderson   382
From *Metaphors We Live By*, George Lakoff and Mark Johnson   384

WORKSHOP 15
VOICE

"A Collage of Passages about Voice"   399
"Speak for Yourself," Susan Faludi   401
"Voices I Hear," Bryant Shea   403
"A Collage of Passages about Split Infinitives from Style Manuals"   404
"Nobody Mean More to Me Than You—And the Future Life of
   Willie Jordan," June Jordan   406

WORKSHOP 16
REVISION THROUGH PURPOSE AND AUDIENCE: WRITING AS DOING
THINGS TO PEOPLE

"Is Phoenix Jackson's Grandson Really Dead?" Eudora Welty   436
"Analysis of Cover Letter for Advertisement"   438
"Revision of Cover Letter"   439
From "A Conversation with My Father," Grace Paley   440

WORKSHOP 17
AUTOBIOGRAPHY AND PORTFOLIO: THE SELF AS WRITER

"Case Study of Myself as Writer," Barbara Smith   455
"Case Study," Mitchell Shack   458
From *Hunger of Memory*, Richard Rodriguez   461
From "A Case Study of Myself as a Writer," Jean Shepherd   464
"A Look Inside: Case Study of Myself as a Writer," Greg Teets   466

PREFACE

We have written *A Community of Writers* for college freshmen and women in a one-semester writing course.[1] We've made our book as practical as we can, with lots of hands-on workshop activities. But we don't hide our interest in theory; our book reflects much recent scholarship in composition. And we push students to become thoughtful about their writing process through regular entries in a writing process diary.

We have structured this second edition of our book into seventeen *workshops*—each consisting of a set of activities and a writing assignment designed to illustrate an important feature of the writing process (and designed to take up one or two weeks). The workshops are arranged in a coherent order that provides plenty of direction for teachers who want to follow our lead. (And we've written an extensive instructor's manual for teachers to consult.) But we've also given teachers great latitude by including far too many workshops for one semester and by making each workshop self-contained—so that teachers can completely rearrange their order to suit their own approaches or priorities.

In addition to the main workshops, there are ten *mini-workshops*—short pieces each devoted to a smaller feature of writing or usage and suitable to be assigned as outside reading or used for a single class meeting.

We've made some changes from the first edition, but the basic orientation and underlying philosophy have not changed. In this revision, we've emphasized collaborative writing, writing in other disciplines, and voice more than we did in the first edition. These emphases grow out of our own teaching interests which, in turn, grow out of what we continue to learn from other researchers and scholars in the field of composition and rhetoric.

The final section of our textbook, *Sharing and Responding,* is an unusual feature we're particularly proud of: a series of graduated activities designed to help students learn to respond usefully to each other's writing. (In the first

---

[1] *The book is also appropriate for a one- or two-quarter course—and perhaps for a full-year course if supplemented with additional readings. A Community of Writers will also be useful for high school seniors or college sophomores or juniors—for we haven't much differentiated our audience in terms of age or skill level. That is, when we work with unskilled or reluctant students, we find they benefit from working on the same interesting, substantive, and sometimes difficult writing tasks we ask of our most skilled students—so long as we explain clearly what we are asking and why we are asking it, and give lots of support. On the other hand, even when we are working with very skilled and experienced students, we give lots of encouragement and take the informal, nontechnical stance you see here. The core of our book is a series of writing activities that we have found appropriate whether we're working with young children or college faculty.*

edition, this section was bound separately, but many teachers asked us for this change.[2]) We've met many teachers who say, "Peer feedback doesn't work." We believe it's really a matter of giving students more guidance; that's what this final section of our book aims to do.

We've tried above all to make a book that is *writerly*. Our overriding principle is that we all learn writing best by writing: writing a great deal, in various modes, to various audiences, and with lots of feedback from diverse readers. This book is not a handbook that lays out rules of grammar or guidelines for good usage—nor even principles of good writing. It is a book of writing activities.

Yet in taking this writerly—even idealistic—approach we have been mindful of the constraints of the classroom setting: grading, time cut up artificially into fifty-minute blocks and into semesters or quarters, and the sometimes vexed authority relationships that grow out of teaching a course which, at many schools, is the only one absolutely required of all students.

We spent more than three years writing the first edition of this book and over a year revising it for this second edition. We and a number of our colleagues tried out drafts of both versions in our classrooms, and we have been able to include samples of student writing derived from these trials or sent to us by teachers who used the first edition. We do not intend these samples as models of excellence to imitate or illustrations of pitfalls to avoid, but simply as *examples:* a range of what students have written in response to these tasks. We like these pieces—just as we also like the examples of professional writing that we include with them in the readings. We have purposely mingled the student and professional writing together without differentiation in order to emphasize that we don't think there is anything *different in kind* that distinguishes student writing from professional writing.

For it is a point of principle with us to treat students as writers: people who deserve to be in charge of what they write, who already know a lot about discourse (even when it doesn't look like it)—and whose greatest need is *readers*. Feeling ourselves speaking to students as other writers, we have tried to speak honestly about our own writing in a series of boxes scattered throughout the book—excerpts from our own process writing diaries. We've also collected apt pieces of students' and professionals' process writing for these boxes.

Although each workshop is self-contained, we encourage linkage between them, particularly because we want to emphasize revision. After all, most writers can wait a few weeks or even months before revising something they care about. Thus we have designed many workshops in such a way that students can fulfill the assignment by revising or transforming a piece they did for an earlier workshop.

---

[2]Sharing and Responding *is available separately also.*

When Peter Elbow published *Writing Without Teachers* in 1973, peer response groups were little known and the idea of students working by themselves to give feedback to each other's writing tended to be dismissed as "the blind leading the blind." Since that time, however, peer response has come to be accepted by most writing teachers and theorists as useful and important to the teaching of writing. Yet even now textbooks don't give much specific and detailed help to students for engaging in this complex activity. And students sometimes think of peer feedback as merely an idiosyncratic, experimental activity that their particular teacher happens to like.

Countless teachers have learned that it's no good saying blithely, "Okay. Now get into groups and give feedback to each other." Trying it this way—without preparation and sustained help—has lead many teachers to announce, "I tried peer response groups and they just don't work!"

We've written the *Sharing and Responding* section to remedy these problems. Students can give each other remarkably useful and productive feedback on their writing. But most of them need substantive help and instruction. And they usually take the process more seriously and do a better job when they see this help laid out carefully in a published book—not just in teacher handouts and oral instructions.

In this section of our text, then, we have gathered together a full and detailed sequence of suggestions for students to use in sharing their writing with each other and giving and receiving useful feedback. We've learned that teachers with the widest range of diverse styles and approaches to the teaching of writing often want their students to learn to use peer response.

We found that our first edition tempted some teachers to try peer responding who had been reluctant to do so—or who had had unfortunate experiences with it. For there is often something messy and potentially chaotic about using peer groups. One is always trying to shout one last suggestion while students are moving into pairs or groups, and chairs are scraping, and the hubbub of talk is taking over. *"Oh yes, and don't forget. . ."*—but they don't hear. And one is always running to the photocopy machine at the last minute to copy directions and suggestions. Of course nothing will ever make peer response groups tidy and quiet (we wouldn't want to), but these published suggestions are a good way to give students more specific help: explanations, examples, guidelines, and principles for the complex feedback process. In particular, we like being able to ask students to read about a feedback process *for homework* before we practice it in class.

Sharing and Responding contains many more techniques than a student or teacher could use all the time. Our principle in writing the book (and in our teaching) is this: that students need to *try out* a wide spectrum of ways to respond to a text in order to end up finally in the best position to *choose,* on any particular occasion, what kind of feedback to ask for or to give. Different kinds of response are suitable for different writers, different kinds of writing, and for different audience situations. But even though we are presenting a wide array of techniques, we have made the sequence clearer and simpler than in the first edition.

When we use these techniques for peer responding, we sometimes ask students to work in pairs, sometimes in small groups. We sometimes change groups during the semester; often we stick with stable pairs or groups so that students can build up safety by coming to trust each other. We sometimes try for both goals by keeping permanent pairs throughout the semester, yet sometimes shifting the *pairings* of pairs to make new groups of four. Before sending students into pairs or groups for peer response, we tend to illustrate and practice each response technique in the whole class on one or two sample texts.

 ## ACKNOWLEDGMENTS

We are greatful for help in what (like all writing and revising tasks) has proved to be a bigger job than we expected. We thank our numerous friends and colleagues who tried out early drafts and used the first edition, and we thank the students in their classes and in our own. These students and teachers have given us many good comments that have guided us during this revision. We particularly thank those students and professionals who have allowed us to use their pieces in the readings. We feel lucky to have worked with editors Steve Pensinger and Scott Amerman and to have gotten such helpful and detailed feedback from our original reviewers: Richard L. Larson, Carol Singley, Michael Steinberg, and John Trimbur, and from those who reviewed the text in preparation for the second edition: Maureen Hoag, Susan Kirschner, Jane Terry Lee, Ben W. McClelland, M. Terry Mitze, Betty P. Pytlik, Nancy L. Schultz, and Pia S. Walters.

We also thank Doris Alkon, Paul Connolly, Gene Doty, Cami Elbow, Claire Frost, Mara Holt, Roni Keane, Laurie Kutchins, Glen Klopfenstein, Irene Papoulis, Marlene Perl, Pat Perry, Debrah Raschke, Valerie Reimers, Barbara Rhodes, John Wright, and Frances Zak.

Peter Elbow
Pat Belanoff

A COMMUNITY OF WRITERS

A WORKSHOP COURSE
IN WRITING

COVER LETTER

Dear Student:

Our goal in this book is to help you write better. This main goal breaks down into several smaller goals: to show you a variety of *ways* to get writing done, to get you to do a variety of *kinds* of writing, and to give you a bit of background theory to help you understand that writing can produce ideas and experiences as well as record them. But our main subsidiary goal—in fact, it's almost synonymous with our main goal—is to help you see that writing can be enjoyable as well as useful, fun as well as frustrating.

We enjoyed writing the first edition of this book and revising it for this second edition. Our collaboration started when we were both teaching and directing a writing program at the same school (Stony Brook). As we worked together and talked through classroom activities and theories about them, we found ourselves agreeing. In particular, we discovered that both of us wanted some way to make peer feedback and interaction more official and more integral to our classrooms. What was most exciting, though, was our growing recognition that our talk and sharing was leading us to ideas neither of us would have come to alone. This excitement led to the first edition of this textbook.

As we wrote that first edition of this book, we continued to talk over our ideas about teaching writing with each other and with other colleagues and friends. It was a challenging task to get what we believed about teaching writing into concrete activities. When one of us moved to another school (University of Massachusetts), our collaboration continued in visits, at conferences, and in hours of phone conversations. All of the revised edition came about that way.

But writing and revising this book was also frustrating and hard at times. Deadlines to meet. Ideas that just wouldn't come out as good on paper as they seemed in our conversations. Struggling to get our words to sound right to us. Getting fed up with the whole project and how much time it was taking. Proofreading to do. Decisions on readings and on the order of workshops. Little things such as deciding on size of type and where process boxes should go. But it *was* a pleasure to see that first edition: finished and printed with all our writing between its covers. We think that seeing the finished second edition may be even more rewarding.

The hardest part about the revision was deciding what to throw out from the first edition. We knew we wanted to add some new things—collaborative writing, a workshop on voice, something about portfolios, and more about writing in other classes—but adding meant leaving out some of what

1

was in that first edition. Otherwise the text would just be unmanageable. To keep that from happening, we combined some of the units (that's what we called them in the first edition) into single workshops. Some things we just discarded.

We think this edition is a better book than the first edition. We've added much more on collaborative writing: we know that such writing is becoming more and more important in schools as well as in the business and work world. We've cut back on the number of questions about process writing since both teachers and students told us there were too many. The workshop on voice introduces techniques which are not much a part of contemporary writing classes, but which we think should be. We also think we've tightened up the writing—another thing we got feedback on from teachers and students.

But we didn't follow all the feedback we got. Some teachers wanted us to include more on current cultural and political issues and do less with personal writing. We did add some readings on current social issues, but we did not cut back on personal, exploratory writing because we think that it's such writing that helps us connect to subjects—even social, cultural, and political subjects. Some students told us they wanted us to be more directive, to give more clear-cut assignments, and to devote more space to issues of grammar and form. We did tighten up some of the assignments, but we left most of them pretty open-ended because we think that deciding on an exact topic is part of the whole writing process. We think you need to wrestle with it.

We don't talk much in the textbook itself about one of our obvious beliefs: that writing classes are an important part of every student's education. Obviously we wouldn't write a textbook if we didn't think so. Nor do we want to dwell on it much here. But there are many in the field of writing, teaching writing, and rhetoric who think that all writing should occur in subject-area classes, that no classes should be specifically devoted to writing as a subject. We disagree. In our way of seeing it, students need space and time to work directly on writing. To think about how you go about writing. To try out—with some degree of safety—new approaches, new styles, new forms. To spend time on sharing and responding to writing.

One thing we have not changed is the title of our textbook: *A Community of Writers: A Workshop Course in Writing*. That title expressed then and continues to express now some of our major thoughts about writing and teaching writing. The key words in it for us are *community, workshop,* and *writer.* Here's why:

Community. Language is social and socializing. It's possible for us to write just for ourselves and throw it away—in fact, we're going to try to get you to do that at times in this book. But if you had never had anyone to *talk* to, you would never have developed any language at all—and therefore wouldn't be able to talk or write even to yourself. And the benefits of social language continue throughout our lives. The more we experience the pleasure that comes from communication—listening to others, reading to them, writing to them, talking to them—the better we get at all these skills.

Workshop.   The only way to learn to write is by writing. No one can teach you how to write; they can only create situations in which you learn for yourself from what you're doing. Our text suggests a classroom where students do things under the guidance of a teacher who is a master at writing because she has done more of it and thought more about it than students. But she isn't a person who does it in some special, magical way any more than a master carpenter works in a magical way.

Thus the heart of this book is a series of writing situations and assignments. We know that if you can enter into them, you will teach yourself writing. We believe that deep down, most students want to work on their writing, though some of them will resent being made to do so; on some campuses, freshman writing is the only course students have no choice about. If you're one of these resentful students, we ask you to put your resentment on the back burner and enter into our assignments. Give us a chance. We think we can help you teach yourself. In truth, the most important piece you'll write in this course may well be the biography of yourself-as-writer which comes at the end of the book. It should contain *what you've learned* and *how you've learned it.* It will be a useful document, particularly if you include advice for yourself for future writing: sort of a little individualized textbook.

Writer.   We assume that all students—including you—profit from being treated as writers. A writer isn't some peculiar absent-minded genius who goes into a trance and magically produces good writing. A writer is someone who writes a lot and who cares a lot about it. The best writers struggle. You may well already *be* a writer. If not, we can help you become one in this non-magical sense of the word—someone who enjoys writing, cares about writing, and struggles but gets satisfaction from the struggle. Our first step is to start right off *treating* you like a writer.

Here are the things we assume when we treat you like a writer:

- Like all writers, you have lots of words and ideas in you. If it feels as though you *don't,* that's just a sign that you haven't put down enough words and ideas yet. The more you put down, the more you'll have left. We'll get you started.
- Like all writers, you own your writing. Only you can know when the words you put on paper fulfill the intentions toward meaning you started with. Others—your classmates, friends, teacher, tutors in your school's writing center—can help you see how your words work, but it is you who must decide what suggestions are important and what changes to make (if any). Some pieces you won't want to revise; others—once you try them out on readers—you will have a greater incentive to work on.
- Like all writers, you need to share your writing with others. Only by sharing your writing, getting the feeling of what it's like to have an audience by actually reading to one—only in this way will you begin to know what it means to communicate through writing. Part of the problem in schools and colleges is that you often write only for a teacher—and write about topics the teacher knows more about than you do—and write only for a grade. We

can't totally eliminate these problems, but we can get you to write for more people than your teacher. After all, writers don't write for just one person. Thus they learn that different people have different reactions to the same piece of writing. That's something you'll discover too from listening to various classmates' reactions to your writing. You may even learn that the grade on the paper is not as valuable in the long run as the reactions of these other readers.

■ Like all writers, you're already a sophisticated user of your native language. When you speak, you don't consciously think about words; you think about meaning and the words tend to come out correctly. Unless you are scared, subjects and verbs usually agree, sentence structures work, vocabulary is appropriate. In addition to that, you also react almost intuitively to your social situation—where you are and who you're talking to. Therefore when you concentrate on your meaning as you write, all these natural language abilities will function in the same way to produce mostly correct language. This natural language ability will also help you make judgments about your writing and the writing of your classmates. You may need to learn to trust these natural abilities more and to think consciously about them so as to learn from them.

But it's just as well to acknowledge a difficulty on this score. We say we want you to *own* your writing and to take responsibility for your own choices. But here is a book full of "orders" for you to follow—used in a course where your teacher will also give you "orders." It's easy to feel like you are just doing "our" writing or "your teacher's" writing.

It might seem as though the definition of a good student is someone who's good at following orders. But that's not quite right. The definition of a good student is someone who can *learn the most,* and what makes you learn the most is the ability to *own* even what you are stuck with—to take over or internalize what comes from outside. This is a difficult and paradoxical skill. Sometimes in order to learn to internalize, you need to be able to resist. Thus it might happen that we tell you to do X, and your teacher compounds it by requiring Y in addition, but *you* realize that you will learn the most if you do Z. If you get a lower mark for it, well, you decide that's worth the price—because it's your learning.

We would like feedback on our book. Sometimes we fear we get too preachy. Sometimes we get carried away with our own ideas. Sometimes we go on about them too long. We want to sound like we're issuing invitations to write rather than orders to write. But we may not always get that tone exactly right. We welcome your feedback about all this as well as about individual workshops and assignments. Maybe someday we'll revise this book again, but our main feeling now is one we're sure you often feel about a writing task: relief at calling it done—at least for now.

Peter Elbow
Pat Belanoff

INTRODUCTION

This book has two main messages: Writing is hard. Writing is easy. It is obvious that writing is hard—or at least that writing *well* is hard. But it helps to understand where the difficulty comes from.

Imagine you are having a relaxed, interesting conversation with your best friend. You're in a comfortable room where you both feel right at home. You are both talking away and having a wonderful time. You find you have lots to say because you like talking to this person who likes you and is interested in what you have to say.

Then someone else comes into the room and starts listening to the conversation. A friend. But quickly you feel that something is peculiar because this friend doesn't say anything, doesn't join in, only listens. It makes you feel a little funny, but you keep up the conversation.

Then more people start coming in. Some of them are strangers and they don't say anything either: they just listen.

Then your friend stops talking altogether and asks you just to do all the talking yourself.

Then someone pulls out a tape recorder and starts recording what you say.

Finally your friend, even though she won't join in the conversation, starts quizzing you as you are talking and asks:

- "Are you really sure that what you are saying is interesting?"
- "Are you sure that what you are saying is right?"
- "Are you sure you understand what you are saying?"

And she doesn't just ask questions, she gives "helpful suggestions":

- "Make sure that what you say is well organized."
- "Think carefully about who is listening. Are you speaking in a way that suits these listeners?"
- "Watch your language; don't make any mistakes in grammar; don't sound dumb."

This is an allegory of writing. In writing, you must keep on putting out words, but no one answers or responds. You are putting out words for an audience but you don't know how they are reacting. You may know who the intended reader is (probably someone who will *grade* it), but you don't really know who else *might* read it: who the reader might show it to or who might find it lying around. You are trying to get your thinking right, your organization right, and your language right—all at the same time. And there's spelling and punctuation to worry about too.

No wonder writing is hard.

But we have another message: writing is easy. Writing is easier than talking because it's safer than talking. For you can "say" something on

5

paper and no one has to see it. If you've ever blurted out something wrong to the wrong person and wanted to bite your tongue off as soon as the words came out of your mouth, you know that you can never undo what you've spoken. But in writing you can blurt out anything and see what it looks like on paper and no one need ever see it. You can even keep yourself from ever seeing it again. In short, writing is much more flexible and private than talking.

People expect you to make some sort of sense when you talk—otherwise, they'll stop listening or think you're odd. But you don't *have* to make any sense when you write. You can go on and on forever when you write; you can't do that in speech because people will stop listening after a while no matter how much they like you.

Writing lets you "talk" about any topic to all, even if you don't know anyone who is interested enough to listen. And there are certain things it's hard to talk to anyone about. Writing lets you "talk" to anyone and tell them anything—and you can decide later whether to show it to them.

Admittedly, in describing how easy writing is, we're talking about writing in itself—not about *good writing*. It gets harder when "good" enters the picture or when you're writing for a tough reader, particularly a tough reader who will judge the writing. But even when your goal is to produce good writing for a harsh judge, you can *start out* this way, just writing for yourself. Afterwards it turns out to be *much* easier to make it good than you might have thought. For one thing, when you do all that easy writing, surprising amounts of it are in fact already pretty good. Those parts that are *potentially good* but badly written are often easy to fix up once you've got them down in one form or another. What's really hard about writing is unnecessary: trying to get it right the *first time.*

Behind what we've just said is the fact that writing requires two mental abilities that are so different that they usually conflict with each other: the ability to *create* an abundance of words and ideas; and the ability to *criticize* and discard words and ideas. To write well we need to be both generative and cutthroat. We all know the awful feeling of trying to use both "muscles" at once: trying to come up with words and ideas and at the same time seeing how nothing is good enough. We get stuck. But we can get unstuck by separating the mental processes: we can think of more words and ideas if we hold off all criticism (as in brainstorming); and we can be more critical and tough-minded if we have already piled up more material than we need.

In short, even though writing gets most of us into the pickle of trying to use two muscles that get in each other's way, it is writing that creates the ideal ground for using those muscles one at a time.

 ## ABOUT THE STRUCTURE OF THIS BOOK

There are three separate sections: the workshops, the mini-workshops, and sharing and responding.

Workshops

These make up the main part of the book. They contain the main activities and writing assignments (one major assignment per workshop). We believe that most of the learning will come from these activities and assignments, not from any ideas or information we give. We assume that most teachers will spend a week on each workshop (though longer would make sense too). There are too many workshops for one semester, so teachers will have to leave some out. Many of the workshops ask you to write something that builds upon what you wrote for a previous one, but despite these potential sequences, all the workshops can stand on their own. Thus teachers can use the workshops in whatever order suits them. However your teacher arranges the workshops, you'll want to keep all your writing for possible later use.

At the end of most workshops, we have included a section titled "Ruminations and Theory." To "ruminate" is, literally, to "chew the cud." In these sections we share some of the thinking we've done that lies behind the workshop. We are wrapped up in these explorations; we think the issues are important. But we have no doubt that the main way you learn is by doing the workshop's activities, not by reading theory. So if you don't feel that these explorations are helping you, skip them (unless your teacher says otherwise).

Mini-Workshops

These short sections can be read or studied on your own or used as the basis of single class sessions. Mini-workshops seldom involve writing assignments.

Sharing and Responding

We've put into one section all the good methods we know for getting feedback from classmates on your writing. You can use these in pairs or in small groups. The ability to give responses to your classmates' writing and to get their responses to your own writing may be the most important thing you learn from this book. We talk more about this in a separate introduction to that section.

In the first edition, we did not include the *Sharing and Responding* section; it was a separate booklet. It's still available that way because many teachers use it and don't use the textbook. But those teachers who did use it with the textbook told us that they wanted it bound into the book itself. We took that advice.

Actually, we hope *Sharing and Responding* will become the most useful part of our textbook to you during the course and afterwards too. You can use it for all writing tasks, in school and out.

WORKSHOPS

WORKSHOP

1

AN INTRODUCTION TO THE VARIETY OF WRITING PROCESSES

We have two related goals for this first workshop. First, we want to show you how to get words and thoughts on paper quickly, easily, and productively, and thus show you that there are always lots more where they came from. We can help you build a foundation of confidence in the face of a blank page—confidence you can draw on later when writing tasks get harder. Our emphasis here is on *generating* words and ideas. Second, we want to introduce you to a wide variety of kinds of writing—to show you that there is no one thing, "writing," but rather different kinds of writing for different situations.

The heart of this workshop is a series of short writing tasks which involve different writing processes. Some of the pieces will be for others to read and some only for yourself; some pieces will have a specified topic and some will not. Your teacher will probably ask you to do some of this writing in class and some of it at home.

Through these short writing assignments, we are introducing a major goal of the whole book: for you to become more aware of what is going on as you write so that you can take more control of your writing process. By trying out different kinds of writing and reflecting on what is happening each time, you will get over something that causes many people trouble: the tendency to use just one "writing gear" for every writing task.

We won't work much with revising in this workshop, but we'll introduce cut-and-paste revising to help you end up with a *final assignment:* a "collage" of good passages that will be a mini-portrait of yourself as a writer at this point. This will be a piece of finished writing that you can share with others and with your teacher.

 ## A SPECTRUM OF WRITING TASKS

1. Freewriting. Freewriting means private, nonstop writing about whatever is on your mind or whatever you want to explore. Don't worry about whether your writing is any good or even whether it makes sense. Don't worry about spelling or grammar. If you can't think of the word you want, put in a squiggle. Just keep writing and see what comes. Changing topics is fine. Try to follow the writing where it wants to go. If you run out of something to say, just write "I have nothing to say," or write about how you feel at the moment, or keep repeating the last word or the last sentence. More will come. And don't worry about trying to write down *everything* that comes to mind. The main thing in freewriting is trusting yourself and your words: taking a spirit of adventure. Try to let the no-stopping rule get you more involved, more steamed up, more energized. Allow for risks. Remember, you don't have to show freewriting to anyone. There is an example of a student's freewriting in the "Readings" at the end of the workshop. (We talk about why freewriting is so important to us in the final, optional section of the workshop, "Ruminations and Theory.")

2. Focused freewriting. This is freewriting where you stay on one topic. It har-

There seems to be a sort of fatality in my mind leading me to put at first my statement and proposition in a wrong or awkward form. Formerly I used to think about my sentences before writing them down; but for several years I have found that it saves time to scribble in a vile hand whole pages as quickly as I possibly can, contracting half the words; and then correct deliberately. Sentences thus scribbled down are often better ones than I could have written deliberately.

Charles Darwin

nesses the "freewriting muscle"—the muscle that enables you to allow the words to go down on paper quickly without planning or worrying about quality—for the sake of exploring one subject. Focused freewriting is especially useful for the hardest thing about writing: getting started. Try ten minutes of focused freewriting on one of these topics:

- Tell about a time when writing went particularly well or badly. What was the topic, and who was the audience? Try to tell in detail how you went about writing and what happened. What can you learn from this example?
- Tell about someone who was important to your writing: a teacher or someone else who was helpful or harmful.

3. Clustering or mapping. Try a cluster diagram on this topic: "What does writing mean to you?" (Or if you prefer: "What is a writer? Do you think of yourself as a writer?") Put the word "writing" (or "writer") in the middle of a sheet of paper and draw a circle around it. Then jot down all around it as many words and concepts as you can think of that you associate with writing. The ones that seem most important you can write closest to your central word; if they seem less important, write them farther away. Try to keep related ones more or less together, but this isn't always possible. But you can draw connecting lines between concepts that seem related. Thus, you will make a trial "map" of the possible lines of thinking and connection. Cluster diagrams are often messy; sometimes you end up with a kind of spider's web of relations. But such diagrams are a good means for quickly getting down lots of possible subtopics and connections and also for giving a quick overview of a large conceptual territory. (You might think of traditional outlines as a more orderly form of clustering or mapping, but they aren't so visual or spatial. For more about using outlines, see pages 346–347.)

4. Invisible writing. This is a variation on focused freewriting. This means writing in such a way that you can't see the words. This odd situation is very easy to achieve if you write on a word processor: just turn down the screen. You can also do this by writing with an empty ballpoint pen on a sheet of paper and putting carbon paper and another sheet underneath. Invisible writing is confusing at first, but most people get used to it quickly and then find it surprisingly useful. It makes you write *more* because you can't pause at all or else you lose track of what you're saying. What's more important is how invisible writing increases your *concentration*. It does wonders when your mind is

13

wandering too much. It forces you to focus better on what you have in mind—on the emerging meaning in your head. Invisible writing makes most people realize how often in their normal writing they let their mind get distracted from what they are writing about: either because something else is on their mind or just because they stop too often and look back at what they have already written. Try invisible writing—especially if you write on a word processor. Possible topic:

- Write about the *physical conditions* for your writing. Where and when do you like to write? What implements do you use and why: pen, pencil, typewriter, computer? What kind of pad or paper? Do you need silence and solitude, or do you prefer to have music on or other people around?

5. Public informal writing. Here is a piece of writing to share with others (in this case with your classmates), but it is not for evaluation—only for the sake of communicating with them. Because it is public writing, you may find yourself pausing and thinking and perhaps changing some things as you go along (as opposed to freewriting, where you never stop but put down whatever comes to mind). Since you probably don't yet know the others in your class, give yourself time at the end to look over what you've written and see whether you want to cross out or change anything.

- Introduce yourself as a writer. What are your strengths as a writer and learner? What are you proud of? What do you most want to learn? What do you need from others in order to do your best as a student and writer? What can you contribute to a learning community?
- Write an introduction of yourself for others in this course. You choose the form and the length: don't tell more than you feel comfortable telling.

The sharing will help everyone in the class learn more about the writing process and about each other. When you read your short piece out loud to others—whether to one person, to a small group, or to the whole class—make sure you don't sabotage it by mumbling or reading too quickly. Please read slowly, loudly, and distinctly.

6. Letter. Letters are partly public and partly private. That is, they go to a reader, but usually only to one or two readers. (Of course there are "open letters" or "letters to the editor," but they feel different from most letters precisely because they are so much more public.) Letters to friends and family are often informal and casual. Sometimes we don't even look them over before mailing them. But letters can be just as formal as any writing, if they are to strangers or for business purposes. Still, even in the most formal letter, we usually write directly *to* the receiver—addressing her in the second person—which is rare in any other kind of writing.*

- Try using the letter form in a way that is probably new to you: write a letter to your teacher introducing yourself. Say as much or as little as you

---

*You'll notice that sometimes we refer to people in general as he *and* him, *and sometimes as* she *and* her.

want at this point. We suggest that you talk about your goals, hopes, and needs for this class: what you want to get out of it, what you can contribute, what you hope will not happen, and what makes you nervous or anxious about the class. This is not writing for a grade; it is writing just to communicate. We teachers can teach better if we know more about our students and what they want and need from the course.

7. Collaborative writing. Much of the world's writing is done collaboratively. We collaborated to write this book. Probably most writing in business and government and research is done collaboratively. There is often a collaborative element even in "individual writing" (such as when "your" ideas become different as a result of discussing them with others or getting feedback). Collaboration is more companionable, but it can be more complicated to have to work things out together. The task now is to work with one or two others to produce a paragraph or more on one of these topics. Together you can work your way to agreement on what you write (or perhaps you already agree) or write a piece that describes differences of opinion and experience. (See Workshop 3 for more about collaboration.)

■ What are some of the most helpful and least helpful things that teachers have done in assisting you with your writing?
■ What makes a good teacher of writing?

8. Careful writing to be evaluated by a teacher. Many students have never written except for a teacher, and the teacher has always noted mistakes or given some kind of evaluative comment or even a grade. Have you, like many students, fallen into assuming that writing *means* writing for evaluation by a teacher? We will try to convince you that this is not the most useful way to think about writing. Yet of course much of your school writing will be evaluated by your teacher. After all the informal writing you have done, see what it feels like to write something that your teacher will evaluate in some way.
    Possible topics:
■ Briefly describe the differences between speaking and writing.
■ Write a short summary of one of our pieces in "Ruminations and Theory," in this workshop (pages 21–24), or of something else your teacher may suggest. This is a test of careful reading as well as careful writing.

9. Revising. In this workshop we are not asking for what may be the hardest task in writing: to revise a long piece. But try revising one of the shorter pieces you have written so far. For now we won't talk about techniques for revising (we will in some later workshops). Just pick a short piece that interests you but dissatisfies you—perhaps one that you have read aloud. Don't just change a word here and there; try wading in and making substantive changes—changes even in what it says. Experiment; make it different. Notice that "revising" doesn't necessarily mean making something better: it means making it different. You won't learn the difficult skill of making things better unless you are adventuresome about making them different and perhaps worse.

10. Process writing. Much of what we've asked for in this workshop has already been process writing: an exploration of what happens when you write, that is, an exploration of your writing process. But so far we've asked you to explore the writing you've done in the past, whereas it is particularly useful to do process writing about only one piece—right after you complete it, so that what happened is still fresh in your mind. What usually works best for process writing is simply to tell the story of what actually happened, with as much honesty and detail as possible, not in order to judge or even necessarily to figure things out: just to notice in a spirit of calm, benign acceptance. The goal is not to *judge* yourself or prove anything or reach big conclusions. You can be sure that if you do process writing regularly (and we will try to twist your arm to make that happen!), you *will* reach plenty of interesting conclusions. You don't have to *try* for them. If you are like most people, you'll have to give some effort to trying to remember some of the steps you went through, the feelings and thoughts that occurred, and so forth. It's usually easier to remember and write down what happened if you write it in the form of a story. For example,

> First I thought of my brother and the words tumbled onto the paper as fast as I could write. Time went by faster than I expected. I came up with some thoughts that were new to me. Then when I wrote about my mother I began to feel mixed up and I slowed down and I couldn't figure out what I wanted to say. I knew what I felt about my brother; I wasn't sure of my feelings when I came to my mother. I stopped for a long time and walked around feeling stuck. Then . . . [and so forth].

Sometimes process writing is easier if you do it after *two* writing sessions and compare what happened in the two. Remember that process writing is not just about the act of writing itself, but also about everything that goes into writing: thoughts about your topic way before you start to write, collecting material to use, talks with others, feedback, daydreaming, false starts.

■ Do a ten-minute process writing about what was happening as you wrote one of the preceding tasks or assignments. Look for the details or specifics of what you did or what happened.

You'll see many pieces of process writing in this book: lots of short "process boxes" scattered throughout, and some in the "Readings" sections. Some are written by students, some by published writers, and some by us. We've put in so many pieces because we're fascinated by what a wide range of events and feelings go on when people write. (We speak more about process writing in the "Ruminations" section at the end of this workshop.)

11. Cover letter. When writers send their manuscript to a publisher or magazine or editor, they always include a letter introducing it. Cover letters for finished papers you're handing in to your teacher can serve similar purposes: to explain things that you think will make your teacher a better and more useful reader of your work. Many teachers ask for cover letters with all major assignments. There are various issues that students and writers like to address—and that teachers like to ask for—in cover letters. Throughout a semester we try to ask students to consider questions like these:

PROCESS BOX

Cover Letter

I had a very good idea of what I wanted to write about the song I picked. This is one of my favorite songs that I listen to. I like it because of the meaning it has and because of its great rhythm. In starting to write this, the inflow of information just flooded the paper. I kept putting down the things that I felt were trying to be said. After I analyzed almost every detail and every line of the song, I began to question where is this song leading and what is he really trying to say. I began with the idea that this song was about suicide in general and in the end I ended up contradicting that idea and finding a new meaning to this song. I was very surprised at finding this new meaning just from this analysis. I now listen to the song in a different light.

I have to credit a friend of mine who brought out the idea of the threat of nuclear war as the major idea in the song. If he didn't point it out to me then I really wouldn't have been so interested in trying to find out the deeper meanings of this song.

I wrote this paper with an analytical point of view. The views I expressed are through my own interpretation of the lines and verses. I was very lucky to find that the interpretation I had was coherent to the major point of the song. This song was as hard as many of the poems I have read and analyzed in my other classes. It showed me that things aren't always as they appear to be and everything has a deeper context. I am glad I was able to find that this song was more than it seems because now every time I hear this song I will enjoy it all the more.

Student

- What was your purpose? What effect were you trying to achieve?
- What was interesting about the process you went through in writing this paper, and what did you learn from it?
- What was most difficult about this paper, and what did you learn from the attempt?
- What do you see as the strengths of the paper, and what would you try to do if you were to revise it some more?
- What's not a part of your paper that you think might help a reader understand or appreciate it more? What didn't you put in? Are there certain events or feelings or memories that led you to write on this topic or to take this approach?
- What feedback or reactions did you get at various times in this paper, and how much did you make use of them, if at all? Any other kinds of help— from classmates? teacher? others?
- What kind of feedback or response would you like from your reader?

It's difficult to hand in a paper you've worked hard on and not say a few words about it. When students come to our offices and hand in a paper, they almost always say something about it. Almost everyone who reads a paper at a professional conference or a story or poem at a reading says something before she starts to read in order to create some link between herself and her audience. We find that cover letters can serve as this kind of link too.

Obviously you can't answer more than two or three of these questions thoughtfully in any one cover letter, but you will be able to consult this list of questions in later assignments.

MAIN ASSIGNMENT: A COLLAGE ABOUT YOU AS WRITER AND HOW YOU WRITE

A "collage" in the original sense, as used by artists, is a picture produced not by painting or drawing but by pasting actual objects on the canvas—objects such as theater tickets, bits of colored paper or cardboard or metal. A written collage consists of separate, disconnected bits of writing rather than one continuous piece. Usually there are spaces or asterisks at the "joints" between the pieces of writing.

A collage can serve as a "quick-and-dirty" way to produce a finished piece of writing. That is, you can just pick out the passages you like best and put them together in whatever order strikes you as best or most interesting. It is traditional in collages to organize the bits intuitively.

In effect, a collage allows you simply to *skip* what are often the hardest parts of the writing process: revising weak passages (you just throw them away); getting the whole piece unified (all the bits are *related,* but there may not be an exact center); figuring out the best order (you settle for what seems fun or interesting); and making transitions between sections (there are none). And yet the finished collage is often a remarkably satisfying and effective piece of writing. We've provided a number of examples of the collage. The third section of "Ruminations and Theory" is a collage. In the "Readings" for this workshop there are several more.

Since the collage we ask you to produce is a portrait of yourself and your experiences in writing, think of your audience for this assignment as your teacher and your classmates: you are introducing that side of yourself to these relative strangers and also helping them learn about how writing is for different people. But think also of *yourself* as your audience: you will manage to tell yourself things about yourself that you didn't know before.

Perhaps the best way to explain a collage further is simply to give you the minimal directions you need for doing the main assignment for this workshop:

- Look through all the pieces you have written so far and choose the ones you like best for giving a picture of how you write.
- Spread them out so you can see them all and then arrange them in what seems the best order.
- Feel free to make all these decisions by instinct or intuition.
- Write one or two more sections if you wish. Perhaps other experiences or thoughts come to mind. Perhaps you now see how you can write something for an opening or closing piece.
- Next, revise it all, but in a minimal and purely "negative" way. That is, don't rewrite (unless there's some particular section you really want to rework). Just *leave out* words, phrases, sentences, or passages that don't work. And instead of trying to make nice connections or transitions between the remaining passages, just leave spaces or put in asterisks.
- Copyedit your collage carefully and type it so that it looks its best when your friends and classmates see it. You may need help with copyediting from a classmate, family member, or roommate. You can return the favor by carefully proofreading something of theirs, since most of us have an eas-

ier time seeing mistakes or usage problems in someone else's writing than in our own.

In the "Ruminations and Theory" section at the end of the workshop, we have written a collage that explains collages.

Possibility for Collaboration

You can fairly easily produce a collaborative collage. You can take passages from each of several writers and decide collaboratively on which pieces to choose and which order to put them in. This would then become a group portrait. It is not necessary to look for agreement: your collaborative collage will probably be even stronger if it shows sharp contrasts between people's experiences and feelings and conclusions. It becomes a kind of dialogue or conversation, not a monologue.

Possibility for Sharing

We are not suggesting feedback or revising for this first workshop, but sharing is definitely in order: reading your piece to listeners for the sake of communication and enjoyment, not for reactions. You have probably already shared some of the short pieces. It will be a pleasure now to share the whole collage. You will get the most benefit and enjoyment from reading it out loud—perhaps in small groups. It is fun to share a collaborative collage by having different parts read by different people. But remember, no feedback at this point, just communication and enjoyment.

If you are not used to reading things out loud to others, you may find it embarrassing or difficult. Timidity and fear get in the way. The trick is to read it as though you *mean* it, as though you *respect* your own words, as though you want to *give* the words to your listeners. Listeners are not supposed to give feedback, but they should stop you and tell you if they can't hear you well. It's all right for them to pester you on this matter. Listen to your voice and enjoy it. Learning to read your writing out loud so others *get it* will, in fact, help your writing. By the way, it can also be useful and enjoyable to trade papers and have people read each other's papers out loud.

 KEEPING A PROCESS JOURNAL

We ask you to keep a process journal for this course. It might be a whole notebook, a section of a larger notebook, or a folder where you keep separate pieces of process writing. Your teacher may make this process journal a requirement for the course, and perhaps even end the course with Workshop 17, which asks for a full case study of your writing and writing process throughout the semester. For this case study you can draw heavily on your process journal.

The best time to do process writing is right after you have been writing. The goal is to find out what really happens—the facts of what occurred on that particular occasion. Don't struggle for conclusions; trust that they'll come.

We spoke earlier of doing process writing in the form of a *story* of your writing session. Another good approach is to plunge into an exploration of what was most *difficult* or *frustrating* for you in that session. Explore what happened: what led to this difficulty? how did you deal with it? Tell everything you can. Interesting insights often come. In short, you can use process writing as a way to try to get some power over what is difficult for you in your writing. As you do this over a number of sessions, you will begin to figure out how to avoid trouble.

Try to make at least one short entry in your process journal whenever you do a significant piece of writing, keeping an eye out especially for clues about what helps you and what hinders you in your writing. Remember that "writing" doesn't just mean "school writing." You are also writing when you leave a note for someone or write a letter or fill out an application—even when you make a list of things to do or buy. Compare these "unnoticed" kinds of writing to "serious" or school writing.

(By the way, in scientific or technical writing, the term "process writing" sometimes refers to writing that describes some particular and often technical process, for example, how blood samples are analyzed in a lab or how to construct a piece of equipment.)

In each workshop we'll give you a few questions to help you remember and notice your writing process. (You might find these questions also helpful for writing cover letters.) If you can remember what is useful and interesting without our questions, feel free to ignore them unless your teacher asks for answers to specific ones. Here are some questions for this workshop:

- What did you notice about trying to write without stopping when you freewrote?
- What did you notice about writing privately and writing for an audience? Were there differences in writing to different audiences?
- Sharing. What was it like reading your words to others? listening to theirs? having your collage distributed?

 ## RUMINATIONS AND THEORY

It has become clear to us from our teaching that students learn most by doing the activities of a workshop, not by reading our thinking in these ruminatory sections. Still, we've met many students who do want to know why we recommend certain activities or make certain assignments. Frankly, we enjoy trying to explain. But if you don't feel that these explorations at the end of each workshop are helping you (and if your teacher doesn't say otherwise), feel free to skip them.

There are three pieces here:

Why We Think Freewriting Is Important

Why We Think Process Writing Is Important

A Collage about Collages

Why We Think Freewriting Is Important

Why should freewriting be so helpful if it is so easy and invites such carelessness in writing and thinking? And why does it also invite some of our best writing and thinking?

First, let's look at the easiness—in comparison with the difficulty of regular writing:

■ Writing is usually judged or even graded, but freewriting is not.

■ Writing usually means thinking about spelling and grammar, but in freewriting you can put all that out of mind.

■ Writing is supposed to make sense, but freewriting can be incoherent or nonsensical.

■ Writing is supposed to stay on one topic and be organized, but freewriting can jump all over the place.

■ Writing is usually for an audience, but freewriting is private. Thus freewriting is even *safer* than speaking, since we almost never speak except when someone's listening.

■ Writing is usually supposed to be more important and dignified and "better" than speech. (Why take the time to write something out unless you are going to try to get it right?) But freewriting is an invitation to let words be *less* important and careful than speech—and to see what you can learn from them.

Thus freewriting removes all the difficulties of regular writing. But freewriting is not just easy. It is also *more demanding* than regular writing. For it insists on the hardest but most important thing of all: writing. But it makes that demand in a context of high safety. Thus freewriting gets us going, gets us rolling. The hardest thing about writing is making oneself keep putting words down on paper, and freewriting makes that happen.

In addition, even though freewriting allows you to be careless or relax, it almost always heightens your thinking. That is, freewriting allows us to stop thinking about the *medium* of writing—about spelling and grammar and forming letters with our hand and choosing words; it makes writing as easy as

---

PROCESS BOX

My free writing is less presentable in handwriting than the public writing. My free writing is a bit more imaginative than the public writing. The public writing seems more formal than the personal writing done in the free writing exercise. I tried to cut down the sentences in my public writing to a shorter type rather than the possible run ons in the long sentences found most presently in the free writing exercise. I seem to be preoccupied with the fact that I have problems with writing. This is reflected in my public writing. I am not at ease with writing publicly and tend to be very formal toward the audience or the reader. New or more complex words tend to pop into my head easier than when I am intent on trying to deal with grammatical problems in my writing. I do understand that shorter and briefer sentences are the best but I like to make my sentences a little more extravagant.

Student

speaking. And therefore it helps us devote *all our thinking* to what we are trying to say. We need no longer be distracted by the process of writing.

Regular careful writing requires us to take the chaos inside our head and turn it into coherence on paper. But this is too hard for most of us to do in one step. Freewriting provides a helpful middle step: getting the chaos in our head *on paper*. This frightens some people at first, but it turns out to be helpful to discover that it's not so hard to get down on paper what's going on in your head—and not so hard to improve it once it's down on paper. What's hard about writing comes from trying to *improve* what's in your head in the act of writing it down. With freewriting you have two steps to produce coherence instead of struggling to produce it all in one.

When you try to avoid bad writing, you write careful, planned sentences. In doing so, almost inevitably—despite your best efforts—you produce some sentences that are tangled, unclear, wooden, or hard to read. This happens because in careful writing you keep stopping when you are bothered by something. You try to figure out what's wrong and try to make some change or adjustment. In all this stopping and fixing, you often lose the thread of your thought and your syntax—and you certainly lose concentration and energy. But when you freewrite, you almost *never* produce a wooden, tangled sentence. We have virtually never seen a passage of freewriting that we couldn't understand easily—while we've seen many passages of careful writing that we couldn't make head or tail of. And most passages of freewriting have a voice and energy and life to them.

It's not that freewriting is always *good*. Far from it. But interestingly enough, it's easier to tighten and clarify bad freewriting than bad careful writing. Try it. Find a long stretch of bad freewriting, and also a piece of careful writing that you struggled over but which is still weak or problematic. Now try to clean up both passages. You'll discover that the careless writing is easier to fix. The careful writing, on the other hand, is sort of delicately glued together and therefore hard to re-glue.

Freewriting is full of "wrong words." You are writing along and get to a word and have a feeling it's the wrong word but you haven't got time to find a better one so you put it down. But because freewriting follows your thinking, putting down the *wrong* word often leads you naturally to the right word. ("I dislike him. No, it's not that I *dislike* him, it's that I'm always uncomfortable around him.") For some mysterious reason, it helps many people to write down that wrong word rather than to stop their writing and search mentally for a better one.

Sometimes a skilled student objects, "But freewriting is for blocked beginners, and I'm a fluent, skilled writer already." It's true that freewriting is good for unskilled students, but we find that *skilled, experienced* writers and teachers get the most out of freewriting. It's an exercise whose payoff increases with the expertise of the writer.

You can't predict how freewriting will work for you. Some people start off with coherent freewriting, but as they use it, they gradually drift into freewriting that's more jumpy and surprising. Some people start off jumpy. It seems as though better writers allow more shifts and jumps into their freewriting—

and more talking to themselves. We sense that people go through stages: perhaps a stage where you write only, "Nothing today, nothing, nothing," over and over—or some other kind of refusal to make meaning. It is important to give yourself permission for this and not measure freewriting by the *quality* of what you turn out. We sense that freewriting "works" in an underground way on what the writer needs to work on—but obviously that's a statement of faith. (We first heard of freewriting from an important pioneer teacher of writing, Ken Macrorie. We've listed a couple of good books by him in the "Works Cited" section at the end of this book. We've also cited a book of essays about freewriting, edited by Belanoff, Elbow, and Fontaine.)

Why We Think Process Writing Is Important

Writing usually seems a mystery: sometimes you slave over something and it comes out awful, and sometimes you dash something off and it comes out good. And yet, of course, dashing things off is no answer either. Thus it is common to feel frustrated and even helpless about writing. But regular process writing can give you power and control over yourself as a writer. You can figure out what specific procedures work for you, under what kinds of conditions, and for what kinds of tasks; and what kinds of procedures undermine your thinking or tend to get you stuck.

If someone asks you out of the blue to tell how you *usually* write, you are very apt to tell lies. For example, you might say, "It always helps me to write an outline first." But what about that assignment when you didn't have time and produced a well-organized piece without an outline? Or that time when you got stuck trying to keep to an outline, which you eventually abandoned anyway? "Words always come slowly and with effort. Writing always discourages me." But what about that time when a whole train of thought bubbled up into your mind as you were writing, and you felt confident as you were writing? How could you make that happen more often?

People's memories play tricks on them, and they succumb to thinking there is one neat pattern to their writing. But if you do regular process writing, you'll discover that the truth is more complicated, and usually much more interesting. And more useful.

But it feels odd to some students to write about their writing. It makes them feel self-conscious. "It's hard enough to think about *what* I'm writing without also trying to think about *how* I'm writing." It often confuses us if we try to analyze our tennis stroke *as* we are trying to hit the ball. But process writing doesn't require you to watch yourself writing while you write, only to think back afterward to what happened.

A sports metaphor is instructive here. Think of process writing as taking an "instant TV replay" of your writing. Videotaping is crucial for tennis, football, baseball, and basketball players. In every sport, serious players and coaches carefully watch tapes of themselves in order to reflect at leisure on matters of technique they cannot give full attention to while playing. Teachers and psychiatrists watch tapes of themselves on the job to try to see what works and doesn't work.

Elbow got interested in writing because he went through a long period when he couldn't get things written. He had to quit graduate school because he couldn't do his papers. The way he got himself going again (five years later) was by doing process writing about almost every writing session—and discovering what was getting in his way. This process writing grew into his first book, *Writing without Teachers*. But neither of us thought about using this kind of writing as a teaching tool until we learned about it from Sondra Perl in the New York City Writing Project.

The most important thinking is *about* thinking. The most important kind of learning is *about* learning. Psychologists call these activities "metacognition." Metacognition gives you more power over your future learning and over yourself. By the same token, the most important writing you do in this course may be about writing. Process writing is what will give you the most control over your future writing and over yourself. It's simple. Just tell what happened. Yet because it consists of self-reflective thinking, it is also the most cognitively sophisticated writing.

A Collage about Collages

I sit here with seven short pieces of writing scattered around me on the sofa and the floor. Some are in pen; some in pencil. A couple of the "pieces" consist of two smaller pieces taped together. The shortest is only two sentences long; the longest is three paragraphs. The miracle is that I *like* it all. I want to show all these blips to readers. But how am I going to put them all together?

□ □ □ □ □

How could I like all this writing when I didn't feel I was doing anything particularly good this week—just churning stuff out, writing fast, producing assorted blips and pieces? And I didn't make *any* changes in what I wrote—or hardly any. (I changed six words, two phrases, and I more or less rewrote one short paragraph.)

The secret weapon was simply to choose bits I like and cross out and throw away everything I don't like—and not feel bad that I wrote lots that I don't like.

I didn't change a word. Yet my pile of writing feels completely different because of all that I left out.

□ □ □ □ □

The collage is cheating, but it works. That's why so many professionals write collages. I see them everywhere now that I've got my eye cocked for them. The collage stresses what is easy and finesses what is hard.

What makes good writing good? Details. Lively, human, clear language—words that sound like someone talking. Surprises. The sense that the writer cared and was involved. Not hitting the reader over the head. If I write fast and with confidence or in a good mood, I get plenty of details and lively language—so long as I pick out the good pieces and throw the rest away. Thus I get good writing. (Or at least writing that's better than most of my labored writing.)

What makes good writing difficult? Sitting down and planning and then producing a complete piece of writing; trying to know where I'm going and trying to get it right as I go; getting the connections or transitions right; figuring out the right organization; working out my train of thought fully and avoiding contradictions. If I just pick out the good pieces and make a collage, *I get to skip all those difficulties*—and still get good writing.

Surprise. I am surprised by what I find in the words I've already written. Here's that experience again: finding something rolling off my pen that I hadn't planned on writing or couldn't have planned on writing. This is the most important writing experience for me. I'll bet not many people write by choice unless they have tasted this pleasure of surprise and are hungry for more of it.

□ □ □ □ □

A TV documentary on cancer. It's really a collage. It opens with shots of a funeral—people standing around the side of a grave: close up of a widow and then down to the coffin being lowered. Cut to a sequence of cells under a high-powered microscope—time-lapse so that we see the cells multiplying and going crazy; a voice is telling us about how cancer cells behave. Then a sequence of a man in the doctor's office—getting the verdict. Then Ronald Reagan making a joke about his cancer. Then a young medical student talking about wanting to go into cancer research—why she finds it exciting and all the progress that's being made. We cut from her, bursting with enthusiasm and health, back to the victim, balding and emaciated from the therapy, but walking in the woods—obviously drinking in the scene as though he can't get enough. Then a sequence of someone earnestly giving us statistics: how many cases of this and that, how much more than in the past, but also how there are more successful treatments and cures. Back now to Reagan going about his work. Then the victim trying to explain things to his child. Finally a sequence of advice about how to avoid cancer.

It's all a hodgepodge—completely "disorganized"—no connectives. But it works.

□ □ □ □ □

Advice:
- Write on only one side of the paper—so you can cut out pieces you want to use.
- You can even write a collage without knowing what it's going to be about. Just do a lot of sessions of writing about whatever comes up. Use all kinds of prompts for writing: hunches, instinct, snippets of overheard conversation, street signs—anything at all. Then look through it for what seems to be the main thing on your mind and make a collage. The human mind is not random; it is coherent. As Chaucer said, "The tongue returns to the aching tooth."
- Try for little stories, moments, snapshots, portraits, dialogues—perhaps even a bit of ranting. This makes your writing alive and experiential, not

An Introduction to the Variety of Writing Processes

just expository or explaining. Take your reader there. (See the prompts or kinds of writing listed for the loop writing process in Workshop 3.)

- After a while, look for the good passages. Sometimes it helps to try reading raw writing to friends. That is, sometimes you don't like something when you just look it over, but you realize it's lively and good when you hear how it sounds or when a friend likes it.

- Save those pieces. Don't revise or change—just cross out and carve away what isn't so good. Work entirely by cutting rather than adding or changing—so you don't lose the life that comes from writing without being "careful."

- Put all the pieces you come up with on the floor and live with them a bit, contemplate them, walk around, and see what they are about. Perhaps forget about them for a while. Then put them in whatever order that pleases you. Trust your intuition. No transitions or connections. In the final copy, just mark transitions with spaces or asterisks.

- Clean it up. Fix mistakes in spelling and grammar and figure out how to punctuate or rearrange the words you like. It's legal to change a few words or phrases, even to add a new blip or a title to make things hang together more.

□ □ □ □ □

The principle of negativity: absence. What makes writing good is not what you put in but what you take out. The mark of old-timers and seasoned professionals. The old tennis pro who never moves but makes his opponent scramble. Line drawings by Picasso as an old man. If everything there is strong, the reader will put in what's not there. Silence is what's most powerful in music; space in art.

□ □ □ □ □

I read my collage out loud to a friend. He ended up thinking I had the opposite opinion from the opinion I really have. Is it because I wrote so badly? No, it's not badly written. It's because, as a collage, it doesn't try to *say* anything: it just *presents* material. Yes. And I like that about collages. They can settle for throwing lots of material at readers and asking them to *experience* it and make up their *own* minds.

But his "misreading" leads to a subversive thought. Perhaps he's right. Perhaps, now that I look at my collage again, I don't think what I thought I thought. Perhaps my collage allowed me to find words for what I didn't know. My collage—and my reading it out loud to my friend—are making me start to disagree with my old self.

Readings

EXAMPLE OF A STUDENT'S FREEWRITING

There we go again—am I back in Ms. Wendell's class? freewritg, freewritg, freewritg—freewriting up to my ears—never did learn how to write an essay. I should really learn to write out my ings—I feel like I write like John Madden talks—slow at first, then speeding up the end to a point that one can't even understand what he's says, or with me, what I'm writg. I dont do this as well as I used to. Forget that. I do this better than I used to. I have such a cold—if I dare get any sicker I'll die. I weighed myself today & almost fainted!!! I'll be eatg oranges for months! There is this cute middle-aged woman sittg next to me who looks at us all as if we are in a ecological study—look at this speciment, semi shaved heard—North Edgewick's only punk—but wait—she wears wool sweaters and skirts—ala Princeton Prep! But that must be the influence of livg so near there. Princeton means Bruce—that little park by the Nassau Inn—getting lost in the campus—could always find my way in, could never get out. PRB—Owen's radio show—fallg asleep on this filthy vinyl couch in that creepy dank cellar—listeng to the death of Suzzy Rocke.—Of course Martini. There is no fall in New York City—There were no leaves to kick around like there are in Princeton!! I missed fall. At least I don't sneeze anymore like I used to when the two oak trees would drop leaves in great big piles in my back yard & I'd fall asleep in them & the dust and dirt would make me sneeze until my mother forbade me to romp in the leaves—we used to play that spider game in Elinor's backyard—she had little skinny trees—I had great big oak trees—Sam is sittg next to me as usual—I can't decide whether or not I should put him on my roster. I miss the cats. I know they must be so adorable by now—so fat & stupid—they surely did take my place—when I left. My poor guilty mother over Thanksgiving battling over her love for the cats & her love for me—would she let me die from my allergy from them—or let them all freeze to death out in the cold! didn't the air filter work? Finally the stupid cat had more kittens in the cellar—three more— longhairs too—the father wooed her away for three weeks—what a romance—she finally came back and then had them. I saw him once, he was huge & longhaired, pale yellow—sort of champagne.

ROBERT BINGHAM (1925–1982)

Published in The New Yorker

He was a tall man of swift humor whose generally instant responses reached far into memory and wide for analogy. Not much missed the attention of his remarkably luminous and steady eyes. He carried with him an education from the Boston Latin School, Phillips Exeter Academy, Harvard College—and a full year under the sky with no shelter as an infantryman in France in the Second World War. Arriving there, he left his rifle on the boat.

One of his lifelong friends, a popular novelist, once asked him why he had given up work as a reporter in order to become an editor.

"I decided that I would rather be a first-rate editor than a second-rate writer," he answered.

The novelist, drawing himself up indignantly, said, "And what is the matter with being a second-rate writer?"

Nothing, of course. But it is given to few people to be a Robert Bingham.

To our considerable good fortune, for nearly twenty years he was a part of *The New Yorker,* primarily as an editor of factual writing. In that time, he addressed millions of words with individual attention, giving each a whisk on the shoulders before sending it into print. He worked closely with many writers and, by their testimony, he may have been the most resonant sounding board any sounder ever had. Adroit as he was in reacting to sentences before him, most of his practice was a subtle form of catalysis done before he saw a manuscript.

Talking on the telephone with a writer in the slough of despond, he would say, "Come, now, it can't be that bad. Nothing could be *that* bad. Why don't you try it on me?"

"But you don't have time to listen to it."

"We'll make time. I'll call you back after I finish this proof."

"Will you?"

"Certainly."

□ □ □ □ □

"In the winter and spring of 1970, I read sixty thousand words to him over the telephone."

□ □ □ □ □

"If you were in his presence, he could edit with the corners of his mouth. Just by angling them down a bit, he could erase something upon which you might otherwise try to insist. If you saw that look, you would be in a hurry to delete the cause of his disdain. In some years, he had a mustache. When he had a mustache, he was a little less effective with that method of editing, but effective nonetheless."

□ □ □ □ □

"I turned in a story that contained a fetid pun. He said we should take that out. He said it was a terrible line. I said, 'A person has a right to make a pun once in a while, and even to be a little coarse.' He said, 'The line is not on the level of the rest of the piece and therefore seems out of place.' I said, 'That may be, but I want it in there.' He said, 'Very well. It's your piece.' Next day, he said, 'I think I ought to tell you I haven't changed my mind about that. It's an unfortunate line.' I said, 'Listen, Bobby. We discussed that. It's funny. I want to use it. If I'm embarrassing anybody, I'm embarrassing myself.' He said, 'O.K. I just work here.' The day after that, I came in and said to him, 'That joke. Let's take that out. I think that ought to come out.' 'Very well,' he said, with no hint of triumph in his eye."

□   □   □   □   □

"As an editor, he wanted to keep his tabula rasa. He was mindful of his presence between writer and reader, and he wished to remain invisible while representing each. He deliberately made no move to join the journeys of research. His writers travelled to interesting places. He might have gone, too. But he never did, because he would not have been able to see the written story from a reader's point of view."

□   □   □   □   □

"Frequently, he wrote me the same note. The note said, 'Mr. _____, my patience is not inexhaustible.' But his patience *was* inexhaustible. When a piece was going to press, he stayed long into the evening while I fumbled with prose under correction. He had pointed out some unarguable flaw. The fabric of the writing needed invisible mending, and I was trying to do it with him in a way satisfactory to him and to the over-all story. He waited because he respected the fact that the writing had taken as much as five months, or even five years, and now he was giving this or that part of it just another five minutes."

□   □   □   □   □

"Edmund Wilson once said that a writer can sometimes be made effective 'only by the intervention of one who is guileless enough and human enough to treat him, not as a monster, nor yet as a mere magical property which is wanted for accomplishing some end, but simply as another man, whose sufferings elicit his sympathy and whose courage and pride he admires.' When writers are said to be gifted, possibly such intervention has been the foremost of the gifts."

THE FEEL OF WRITING—AND TEACHING WRITING

Donald Murray

Emptiness. There will be no more words. Blackness. No, white without color. Silence.

I have not put down any words all day. It is late, and I am tired in the bone. I sit on the edge of the bed, open the notebook, uncap the pen. Nothing.

Or.

Everything has gone well this morning. I wake from sleep, not dreams, the car does not have a flat tire, I do not spill the coffee grounds, I do not turn the shower to cold instead of hot. The telephone does not ring, and I sit at the typewriter with a clean piece of white paper twirled into the machine. Nothing.

If I can make myself wait, remain calm, ready to write but not forcing writing, then words come out of silence. Out of nothing comes writing.

Now it is hard to keep up with the words which write what I did not intend, do not expect. Often this is the best writing, and I know it, but I never welcome that emptiness, that terrible feeling that there will be no more words.

□ □ □ □ □

The student sits in my conference chair, a Van Gogh miner, his hands clasped and hanging down between his legs near the floor, his head slumped forward. He mumbles. "I didn't write nothing." His head rolls up, his face defiant, and then angry when he sees me smiling at him. "What's the matter?" he snarls.

"You look like me, sound like me this morning. Nothing happened."

"What d'ya do?"

"I wanted to kick the cat, but I don't have a cat, and I couldn't pick a fight with my wife. She was out shopping. So I had to sit there and wait."

"And?"

"The words came. Not what I expected. But words. You want to read them?"

I wait while he reads my uneven, early morning draft. I can see him getting interested and suspect he's saying to himself that he could do as good, or perhaps a bit better.

"You just wait?"

"Yes, it isn't easy though."

"Will it work for me?"

"I don't know. Sometimes it works for me and sometimes it doesn't."

□ □ □ □ □

The writing is going well. Everything is connecting. I need a word, and it is in my ear; I need a fact, and it flows out of my fingers; I need a more effective order, and my eye watches sentences as they rearrange themselves on the page. I think this is what writing should be like, and then I stop. I go for another mug of coffee, visit the bathroom, check the mail.

I wonder about this compulsion to interrupt writing which is going well. I see my students do it in the writing workshop. It's so much of a pattern there must be a reason for it. Sometimes I think it is the workman's need to stand back to get distance; other times I think it is simple Calvinist distrust—when everything's going well something must be wrong.

My students arrive in class just at the bell, as if they were hurled there by some gleeful giant. They are rushed, harried, driven. They remind me of me. I barely made it myself. How am I going to create a quiet space around us within which we can listen to writing trying to find its voice?

This is the writer's problem: take all the energy you have to fight your way to the writing desk: reject wife, child, friend, colleague, neighbor; refuse to carry out the trash, take the car to the garage, transplant the blueberry bush; leave the mail unopened and the opened mail unanswered; let the telephone ring; do not answer the knock on the door or prepare for class; ignore the message on your desk to call somebody back; do not rehearse the speech that will impress at the afternoon meeting; do not remember, do not plan; use all your energy to get to your desk, and then try to sit there, calmly, serenely, listening for writing.

I hear a teacher asking a student who has just begun to write. "What is your purpose?"

I hope the teacher will not come to my door when I have just begun to write. What, indeed, is my purpose? To make it through the day? To get tenure? (I already have tenure.) To become rich? (I will not eat on this article.) To impress my parents? (That sounds more like it, but they are dead, and would not read what I wrote when they were alive because, true Scots, they knew they would be disappointed.)

I hear more of the teacher's questions. "What is your purpose in this piece? What do you intend to say in the piece you are writing? Who is your audience?" They may be good questions but it's the first week of the semester and the student has passed in his first tentative draft.

He'd better not ask me. If I knew all those things—my purpose, my content, my reader—I wouldn't have to write this. Well, that's not really true. Perhaps I know my audience in a sort of general way, and perhaps I know what I'm going to say. And that worries me, because I want to write to surprise myself. It would be terrible if I knew my purpose, if I knew what I was doing, how it would all come out. That's when I'll know I'm finished. There are few things more dangerous in writing than too much purpose. . . .

☐ ☐ ☐ ☐ ☐

My father died with a machine plugged into his chest and a small smile on his face. The police found my mother on the floor of her apartment in a nest of covers tugged from the bed. My daughter, Lee, stands always at the corner of my eye, but at twenty she lay in a hospital bed, a beautiful woman without brainwaves. I made the decision to kill my father, to kill my mother, to kill my daughter, to let them go. I hope they have found more peace than I.

I have never said these words until this moment. I did not know I would say these words. They came out of silence. I heard them and I believe them.

Facing their own silences, my students write of death, of hate, of love, of living, of loss. They put down words which reveal a mother plunging a knife into a father while a girl looks on; a student tells of a failure—to kill herself; another student carries her father in her arms, rocking him, trying to comfort him against the pain of cancer in the night.

I tell them that they do not have to write of these things. I tell them they should write of such matters if it bothers them. They tell me it feels good, and then look guilty. I tell them I know. It helps, somehow, to put words on paper. I tell them it gives me distance, in a way, it makes what cannot be believed, a fact. I tell them I cannot understand why it feels good to write of such terrible things, but I confess it does feel good; that is my way of achieving a kind of sanity.

□ □ □ □ □

A student comes to conference and shows me her new notebook. We marvel over it—a looseleaf notebook has a third arm with a clipboard on it which folds over the notebook. We share our wonder at it, for we share the thrill of writing and know the importance of tools. We are always trying out each other's pens or feeling the texture of a new kind of paper between our fingers. We are writers and we know that there is writing in the paper if we know how to let it out.

□ □ □ □ □

Often I write by not writing. I assign a task to my subconscious, then take a nap or go for a walk, do errands, and let my mind work on the problem. It doesn't do much good for me to think thinking.

I tell my students to write every day, for a short time, going away from it and coming back. The going away is as important as coming back. Read, stare out the window, jog, watch a ballgame, eat, go to bed. Sometimes I feel I have to make a note. It's too bad; for what can be forgotten usually should be forgotten. Writing surfaces from my subconscious, but I push it away, the way I shove an over-friendly puppy from my knee. Go away and work by yourself, writing, and come back when I'm at my desk.

□ □ □ □ □

I can recognize my students' papers without looking at their names. I hope they hear their own voices as clearly as I do, for writing is mostly a matter of listening. I sit at my desk listening to hear what my voice says within my head. Sometimes it speaks so clearly I feel I am taking down dictation while I write.

Voice gives writing the sense of an individual speaking to an individual. The reader wants to hear a voice. Voice carries the piece of writing forward; it glues the piece of writing together. Voice gives writing intensity and rhythm and humor and anger and sincerity and sadness. It is often the voice of a piece of writing that tells the writer what the writing means.

COLLAGE ABOUT MYSELF AS A WRITER

Steve Clark

Some teachers require outlines, but outlines just don't work for everyone. In fifth grade I had a strict teacher who declared that anything that wasn't written in outline form first was trash. However, he never required outlines for assignments, so I never wrote any. I encountered further resistance from a high school teacher who tried to argue that papers couldn't be written without outlines. I still didn't agree, but I never actually told him that: my grade was at stake. I would have said that the writing actually writes itself, and that it's a process that outlines can't replace.

I would outline more if I thought my organization needed it. But no one should be telling me how I'm going to write at this stage; it would be best for me to discover things on my own. I don't want to preplan every little detail. Instead, I think, writing should be exciting. There should be some adventure involved.

□ □ □ □ □

It's always nice to work on a word processor. You don't have to worry about poor penmanship, and you don't ever waste any paper (unless the printer messes up). When you type something, authoritative characters appear on the screen in front of you; the shape of the characters looks official and important. I guess it's a little ridiculous to think like that—it seems to be the same way a little kid would react to a typewriter, with all its fancy machinery—but maybe that's all it is. I think there's a little kid in me who can't get enough of all the high-tech wizardry involved with typing.

□ □ □ □

Even though teachers often tell me to write for a specific audience, I find it useful not to worry too much about who's going to read it. If I'm trying to write an essay about anything, it's counterproductive for me to stop at every sentence and say to myself, "Oh, man, what will my friend Bill think of this?" It's easier, and healthier, not to be too self-conscious when you write.

Don't get me wrong: there's no denying the fact that the audience is important. I have to know who I'm writing for at the outset. If I want to write a paper for classmates to read in an English class, I have to try to write something that they can understand on some level beyond spelling and punctuation. I need to take the audience into consideration, yet not be overly cautious about what I write, otherwise I'll have nothing.

□ □ □ □

My first writing assignment in the English language was to write my name seven times on a piece of paper. I found this quite simple, and still do.

□ □ □ □

There's a big difference for me between writing and speaking. When I write, a whole new personality can be evoked that never shows up at any other time. When I'm asked to write a paper for a class—say, for example, a history paper—I am also being asked to communicate with words I never use in speech.

When the papers are handed in, the teacher sees sentences starting with words such as "moreover" and "subsequently." Sure, some people actually speak those words. But I suspect an enormous amount of students in high school and college write those words every day, but wouldn't be caught *dead* saying them out loud. I'm not exempt from this rule, either. I've written the word "indeed" dozens of times in my papers, but you'd have to pay me to use that word in a serious conversation. Indeed, words that seem normal and appropriate for the page can appear pompous when spoken.

☐ ☐ ☐ ☐ ☐

It is common in English classes not to be given a specific assignment, but instead to be told to come up with an assignment for yourself. A professor might say, "Do something with this novel. Submit an idea to me by Wednesday." Having an assignment like this—to come up with an assignment of your own—is perhaps the most challenging and productive kind of schoolwork. It's always hard to come up with a good idea to present to the professor, but the nature of the assignment allows me to do something that really interests me. When I present an idea to the professor, he or she will see my interest, and will be able to see that I'm doing my work. There's much more potential here for exciting ideas, as well as collaboration with other students, than there is for written-in-stone, specific assignments.

☐ ☐ ☐ ☐ ☐

I have a weakness for writing bizarre, abstract short stories. I enjoy writing unconventionally, so much that I sometimes feel tempted to make even the simplest book report a far-flung anomaly that no one in their right mind could ever expect to read. I do not, however, even want to try poetry; I just don't think I'm cut out for it at all. To me, poetry is the strangest kind of writing there is. It usually lacks a plot, as well as characters; often I find myself wondering what the *subject* of a poem is. After I read a poem that I just can't understand, I want to outdo the poet and write something in prose that is even stranger. Strangeness, however, is not my main priority in my writing: instead, I like to take risks and see what happens. It's boring, in any case, for anyone to write exactly what others are expecting all along, so I think everyone should try to write something that's just a little unusual—all the time.

☐ ☐ ☐ ☐ ☐

Writing is extremely unpredictable for me. I never know whether I'm going to come up with a good sentence or idea. Writing is a trial-and-error process; it's experimentation, really. A lot depends on what kind of writing I'm trying to do: if I write some kind of analytical essay, for example, I spend what seems like an infinite amount of time trying to come up with the right thesis statement and introductory paragraph. If I'm trying to write a short story, that infinite amount of time is dedicated simply to coming up with a good plotline. In every case, however, regardless of the style of writing, I always have to experiment, and eventually—with patience—I'll stumble upon something good.

□ □ □ □ □

I can be having an extraordinarily dull, uninspiring day, and within five minutes of walking into a classroom, find myself writing something vital and interesting.

One day my English teacher said, out of the blue, "I'm a prisoner. Write your thoughts on that." Everyone in the class stared at him for a moment, and one girl raised her hand.

"You're a prisoner of work?" she asked.

"Yes," the T.A. replied. "But I'm also an inmate at Walpole State Prison. I've committed more felonies than I can count, and I've been in jail for 22 years. I'm on a work release program."

It was true. We were supposed to write out our reactions to this incredible news, and with incredulous gazes on our faces, we did. Everyone had to write something; everyone wanted to write something because no one was supposed to respond verbally. The written responses reflected feelings of hysteria ("My teacher's an inmate!"), overwhelming curiosity ("What the hell did he do!?"), and even a little fear ("I'm wondering now if this guy is crazy!"). The result was some of the most honest and vivid writing of the whole semester, and it was certainly good practice for all of us. I never knew what I'd be writing next, but that was part of the fun.

□ □ □ □ □

I was never a very good reader or writer until sometime in the middle of fifth grade. I was on a vacation with my family, halfway through that year, and found myself on a sailboat with nothing much to do except get a little seasick. There were a few books lying around, however, and one day, I started to look over one. It was *The Shining* by Stephen King. I'd never read a novel before, but I'd heard that it was quite entertaining, so I tried to read it.

Before I knew it, I'd read the whole book, and was trying to imitate it for an assignment. Our whole class had been asked to write a short story during the vacation, and I decided to do something different, right there on the boat. I actually wanted my story to be special—something no one had seen before, especially from a fifth-grader. I started with "Chapter One," and began to write a novel of epic proportions. After five pages were written, I realized it was probably going to be a little too long; "Chapter One" was still unfinished. After a while I decided to call it quits, and write something shorter, something that was more expected from a fifth-grader. It was a little disappointing.

□ □ □ □ □

Cover Letter

Dear Peter,

Everything I wrote about came upon me unexpectedly, and the results were certainly mixed. Writing about the differences between speech and writing was enjoyable, because I think it's especially true for high school and college students. I think pompousness is a big factor, but I don't know if that fit in with the overall paragraph.

I enjoyed writing about the teachers I've had. When any of these blurbs (is that the right word?) concerned a teacher, a story would pop into my head. The last one was fun to write because it's a mini-story, and something I love to talk about. The blurb about outlines was also enjoyable because I was remembering some of my more, well, demanding teachers.

What seemed to be at the heart of this process for me was not so much a continuity of thought, but instead a feeling of trying to outdo myself. If I didn't like one idea that was already written that much, I left it in and tried to do better the next time. It makes the whole thing a little more real and alive. I'd come up with a new idea every few minutes, completely randomly, and try to jot it down as quickly as possible. The order of the blurbs has no external logic; I tried hard to keep everything fresh and new, and not to stay on one subject for too long. It's a little strange to actually attempt choppiness in a piece of writing when the usual focus is to keep things smooth. I guess I'm still learning.

Steve

CHRONIC RELEASING: A COLLAGE

Matt Ludvino

There were six of us, wandering physically and mentally, feeling discontent and restless, looking for anything tangible. My own thoughts were broken and scattered with the first weeks of college already behind me, a feeling of oppression. This was an inner feeling though, there were no outside pressures or influences other than ones created by myself.

We had been walking around Campus late at night, when we came upon the outskirts of the Fine Arts Center where days earlier someone had been creating a junk sculpture. Various bits and pieces of metal, plastic and wood congealed along with other odd pieces of junk to form unidentifiable art. The sculpture had been dismantled, and various pieces left over were tossed in the bushes alongside the building.

It began simply at first, grabbing various pieces, banging them together, or on the ground, or against the building. Making rhythmic beats, with the most basic, hardcore, industrial instrument—anything we could find. The beats grew louder and faster by the minute. I had found a large metal pole, and began swinging it against the railing that lined the walkway. At intervals I hammered out a beautiful, ear shattering gong, or I would progress to letting the pole reverberate causing it to make one large clang, echoed by four or five smaller ones. Others were banging buckets, using short pieces of wood as drumsticks, and large plastic tubes that made a clacking sound when hit. The rhythms grew more complex. Vocals were added, yelling anything that came to mind, running, jumping, dancing, releasing. People passing through the center stopped to stare for a minute, then promptly turned around and left in the direction they came. This was a full energy release in the purest form imaginable, all the pent up anger, pressure, and confusion we felt that day was vanquished in a glorious display of noise, aggression, and harmless violence.

□ □ □ □ □

They sat in a circle in the small room lit only with a black light. I sat outside the circle feeling dislocated and claustrophobic. They passed the bong around, opening their mouths wide over it so as to take in every bit of the precious smoke that held them together. They knew how I felt about it so they didn't even offer. I became oblivious to them as I watched them crumble. I felt no curiosity, no urge to join them as they coughed and gagged for a trendy meaningless high they didn't need. The room was filled with that sweet smell as they began to feel the effects. I just shook my head in amusement as their manner and mindset changed to become either laid back and uncaring, or agitated and restless, depending on the person. As their circle continued, I looked at myself and a feeling of power washed over me because of self control, because I stayed an observer.

□ □ □ □ □

The sun went down at 5:30 as it always did, casting long shadows along the campus. I was just walking home after checking out the library for the first time, cutting through the campus center towards the Worcester Dining Commons. As I reached the walkway that ran in between Northeast and Worcester, I saw the outline of someone I thought I knew. I was staring from a distance trying to figure out if it was him or not, before yelling to him, when I heard a slurred voice yell, "What are you looking at?" Instantly I felt anger surge through me, and yelled back "You, fucker!" I tried to keep from laughing at my response. When I noticed the figure rushing towards me in the darkness, I envisioned myself hitting him as soon as he came near my arms' reach, seeing him fall, satisfying my most primitive aggressive urge. I hesitated though. He got right up in my face, and the stench of alcohol filled my nostrils, as he asked over and over again, "Who are you looking at, huh, who are you looking at?" This was depressing; it was 5:30 maybe 6:00 and this boy was already out of his skull. That feeling of tension hit me, creeping up from my toes up through my spine to my brain; I wanted to hit him bad. But I didn't. I repressed my violent urges, began talking, telling him to just let it go. Meanwhile I heard another screechy voice yelling to him, probably his girlfriend, to come back. Then suddenly for apparently no reason, the intoxicated man jumped suddenly and ran behind a bush. I just shook my head and left the man to his brainless evening activities.

Process Writing

Writing down experience pieces is often hard, and sometimes uncomfortable. This case was quite the opposite for me. I think it is mostly due to the fact that I don't mind writing personal things in situations where other people read them. The more personal the subject, the more feeling can be put into the writing.

This particular piece contains three experiences, varying in how personal each was. When this project was assigned [write about memorable moments from being at school], these three experiences came to mind instantly. It was only a matter of making the time to write them down.

At first I thought this piece would seem kind of erratic in thought, but when I began actually writing these experiences down, I realized they definitely had a common theme—release. What do I mean by release? A release can be mental or physical; it transcends reality. In actuality, it is a way of going beyond reality. In this piece I subconsciously chose an experience showing a way in which I released, and two others showing how other people often do it. This is where the title, "Chronic Releasing," originates.

WORKSHOP

2

GETTING EXPERIENCE INTO WORDS: IMAGE AND STORY

Your poetry issues of its own accord when you and the object become one.

(Bashō)

Our goal in this workshop is to help you make readers *experience* what you are writing about—not just understand it. We're after words that don't just *describe* the tree outside the window, but make your reader *see* it. This means using words that somehow carry some of the life or energy of that tree. This is a magical way of putting things, but in fact it's not so hard to get this valuable quality into your writing if you take the right approach.

The basic principle here—getting experience into words—applies to all kinds of writing, including essays. But it is easier to learn it with descriptive and narrative writing. That is, it's easier to learn how to get visual and sensory experience into words, and see when you have succeeded, than to get intellectual experience into words. When you learn the principle, you'll be able to apply it to essays.

The crux is this: if you want to get your reader to experience something, *you* must experience it. If you want your reader to see something, then put all your effort into *seeing it.* For your reader to hear or smell something, you must hear or smell it. Put all your effort into having a hallucination. Don't worry about words; worry about seeing. When you can finally see it and hear it and smell it, just open your mouth or start the pen moving and let the words take care of themselves. They may not yet be elegant or well-organized words; you can take care of that problem later. But if you are actually seeing and hearing, your words will have some of that special quality that gives your experience to the reader. If you don't see what you are describing, you may find very nice words but they are less apt to make the reader *see* what you are talking about.

Your main assignment for this workshop will be to develop an image into a story. Your teacher will let you know whether he wants you to save this piece for revision later in the semester or do an extensive revision immediately.

 ## LETTING WORDS GROW OUT OF SEEING

Think of some small object—for now something simple that you know well. For example, you might think of your favorite mug or coffee cup on the kitchen counter. The goal is to describe your mug in spoken words so as to make your listeners *see* it.

The trick is to take your time and not utter a word until *after* you close your eyes and put all your effort into *seeing* that mug on the counter. Don't try to see the whole kitchen or even the whole crowded counter. Focus all your energy on seeing that mug—hallucinating, if you will. Take your time. Don't worry about words or about classmates listening. The important thing is to wait with your eyes closed until you can really see what you are going to describe. When you are finally having that actual experience inside your head, open your mouth and say what you are seeing, letting the words take care of themselves.

Perhaps your speech is halting and full of pauses as you struggle to see and hear inside your head—not "literary" or even grammatical. Perhaps you wander around in your description, changing focus as you pause. Perhaps you talk about the mug, then about the flower pattern, then the light on the surface, then the crumbs on the counter, the half-eaten bit of toast right next to the mug. There's nothing wrong with this: it often results from the effort to see. But now pause a moment and look for the center of gravity, the most important point in your scene, and give your description again, trying to get it whole and into one piece of energy. For example, you might end up with:

> I see my mug. It's white with a blue pattern of flowers. Narrow, small mug, but thick sides. I look inside. Dull gleam on the side of it from the fluorescent light. A few sips of cold black coffee left.

Listeners should just listen. No response. This is their chance to enjoy and to get better at listening. Then the next person gets a turn to describe her object. Make sure she too takes plenty of time to *see* it before talking.

This procedure should take just a few minutes for each person: a minute or so for going inside your head and trying to see, a minute or so for saying what you see. Short descriptions, no more than four or five sentences. If it starts to take longer, that probably means that the speaker is falling into some common traps. If so, interrupt him and remind him of these guidelines:

- *No people or big scenes.* People are too big and complicated to describe at this point. (But you might describe the *hand* holding the mug.) For now, keep it to more or less one object with no more than those few things that are near it or interact with it, such as a spoon standing in the mug, or the page of newspaper underneath the mug. The point of this exercise is *real* description: transporting the thing itself inside readers' minds. (Sometimes readers say, "What a good describer she is: she told me about *fifteen* things in the kitchen." But those fifteen items were often just mentioned or verbally described, not really *conveyed into* the reader's head.)

PROCESS BOX

I didn't even want to do this exercise but felt I had to. Yoon's image was Oriental, although I think I de-Orientalized it as I wrote. I saw the road going down into the woods and I knew at some level that it was only one fork of the road because I seemed to be standing just before the break—but I saw that road more and more, twisting and winding (it was dust-colored) into the trees and forest surrounding it and disappearing into the dark.

But then the leader suggested looking at different parts of the image. I did. And there was the other fork going up a sloping grass-covered hillside toward an open blue sky. Why did I see the "half-empty glass" first? That open blue beckoning sky was there all along.

I was floored by what such a simple game led me to. I certainly won't listen when someone says it's stupid. Is it possible my resistance led me into the forest and obscured the blue sky and when I stopped resisting I saw the blue sky? It was even a different bodily sensation. The tension left my bones and muscles. Wow! And that's an understatement.

Pat Belanoff

■ *Go easy on feelings.* It's a good skill to describe feelings well, but the goal for this exercise is to present the mug, not your feelings about it. Yes, you can describe the mug "through the lens of your feelings"—how the light was twilight dim and the smell of lilacs drifted in the window—but tell what you see and smell, not your feelings.

■ *No stories.* Again, it's tempting to tell the story of who gave you the mug and how you once knocked it off the counter and slopped coffee all over the linoleum. Of course these memories *are* part of the mug for you, but skip them for now.

Story is tempting because it's the most captivating form of discourse. Everyone feels the basic tug of plot: "and next . . . and next . . . and next." But for this foundation exercise, we outlaw stories in order to concentrate on the central task of really seeing—not settling for the easy momentum of "and then . . . and then . . . and then." In effect, this exercise asks you to stick to one instant of time, to what could fit in one still photograph. It's fine to describe the one instant of spilt-coffee-and-mug-fragments on the floor—but only that single snapshot/instant. In a little while we'll get to story or moving pictures.

Can Listeners See It?

After everyone has had one turn at describing, go around again, but this time let listeners give a tiny bit of feedback: have them tell you which parts, if any, they could see (or hear, smell, taste, feel). This is a difficult test. Don't despair if at first listeners can't see *anything* of what you described. It happens frequently. Words that carry real experience are rare. Don't give up; don't assume you are incapable. Everyone is capable of seeing what's in mind and describing it so that others will see it too. But it's a slippery skill. And some listeners are harder to get through to than others. Try to notice which details *did* get through.

The main thing to remember is that if they can't see or hear what you describe, it's probably not a problem of words—wrong words or lack of words; it's a problem of you *not experiencing* your object. You may have interesting ideas or words about your object; you may have strong feelings about it. But if listeners aren't seeing it, *you're* probably not really seeing it either.

Letting Listeners Give an Impetus

Now give listeners a bigger role. Get them to ask you about details you may not have thought of. For example:

■ Tell me about the handle on the mug.
■ Tell me about the surface of the counter.

Then listeners can introduce other senses:

■ What do you hear?
■ What does the surface of the mug *feel* like?
■ What do you smell?

Don't "think up" or "make up" answers to these questions. Just wait for answers to come. Keep the image in mind, look at it inside your head and make *it* give you the new answers.

Letting an Image Move toward Story

Now invite the germ of story or narrative by having a listener ask, "What happens next?" But don't move too fast. Your story will be better if you don't try to "tell a story" but just try to "enrich an image." Above all, avoid the temptation to jump into a long story, especially a corny story. "A hand drops a poison tablet into the mug!" No. The point is to let the next event be small and real—*generated by the image* rather than *imposed on the image by you.* The image must be in charge, not the event. This exercise is practice in standing out of the way, not steering but letting the image steer: letting reality be generated *by reality,* not imposed by a creator.

So when someone asks you "What happens next?" your job is easy. Just close your eyes, go back inside your head, and look at the mug and *wait.* Wait to see what *does* happen next. Don't be in a hurry. Some events may come to your mind that are fake or corny. You'll usually be able to tell that they are manipulations of your mind, not products of the mug. They'll be too contrived or phony. Let them go. Wait for the event that really happens or really could happen. Perhaps it will just be:

> The rock song on the radio ends and a man's voice—fake-cheerful—announces the time, "It's eight forty-seven now, folks. Maybe you should be leaving for work."

For your listeners, the question is always, "Do you believe it? Did it really happen, or was it just made up?" Again it is a matter of *experiencing*—applied this time to an event, not just an image: did you give the experience of the event to the listeners?

Extending the Story through Collaboration

Now your group or pair is ready to try collaborating to develop one image and help it grow into a story.
- One person starts by suggesting a time of day.
- The next person provides an image occurring at that time of day.
- The next person adds a *detail,* but from a different sense modality.
- The following person tells what happens next.
- Another person gives another detail or tells what happens next.

And so on, as far as you care to carry it. Make your own variations. This sequence of tasks works with a small group or even a pair: simply go around and around the circle or take turns.

Remember all the things you worked on above: concentrate on having an experience, not on finding words; wait and look; let your image be in charge, don't impose on the image. If you collaborate, you'll all have to hold the same image in mind even as it develops. In a sense you are working on a collaborative hallucination.

It's helpful at certain points to stop talking and give everyone time to continue developing the image *in writing*. You can compare what people write and maybe even practice collaboratively producing just one version. (We are grateful for having learned about these seeing activities from John Schultz's work. See his name in the "Works Cited" section at the end of this book.)

From Talking to Writing

So far, this has been mostly talking, and we've described it as one long session. But it could be two or more sessions (or perhaps your teacher will suggest leaving out some small steps). Each session should end with some writing. For it's important to start a piece of writing right away when all this experiencing is still alive in your head—when you have been exercising your skill at internal seeing. You need at least fifteen minutes for this writing, more if possible. (Your teacher may take charge of the timing.)

When you are ready to write, we suggest choosing someone else's image. Choose an image which somehow feels interesting to you, which somehow intrigues you or resonates or feels perplexing. It's sometimes better if you don't even know why the image or description feels right or clicks for you. Writing from someone else's image often liberates your imagination. It gives you practice in relinquishing control and letting the image generate material. It's not *your* image and so you'll have less need to own it or control it, and you'll have fewer preconceptions about it.

Start by putting the image into words. But then keep going and see where it leads. Carry it further by asking, "And then what happened? And then

---

PROCESS BOX

My task which I am trying to achieve is, by the power of the written word to make you hear, to make you feel—it is, before all, to make you *see*. That—and no more, and it is everything. If I succeed, you shall find there according to your deserts: encouragement, consolation, fear, charm—all you demand—and, perhaps, also that glimpse of truth for which you have forgotten to ask. . . .

To arrest, for the space of a breath, the hands busy about the work of the earth, and compel men entranced by the sight of distant goals to glance for a moment at the surrounding vision of form and colour, of sunshine and shadows; to make them pause for a look, for a sigh, for a smile—such is the aim, difficult and evanescent, and reserved only for a very few to achieve. But sometimes, by the deserving and the fortunate, even that task is accomplished. And when it is accomplished—behold!—all the truth of life is there: a moment of vision, a sigh, a smile—and the return to an eternal rest.

Joseph Conrad

what?" Let it develop into a story. Don't plan; don't decide where it should go. Just start by re-creating the image and events you remember, and then continually asking, "Then what?" Better yet, ask the question of your developing *story:* ask *it* "What next?" Trust the image to be in charge and trust yourself by standing out of the way. Allow yourself to be surprised. And just as you try not to impose events on the image, try not to impose a meaning on the story. Let the story choose or find its own meaning.

If you have more than one session, it can be helpful to start the later sessions by hearing each other's rough exploratory writing based on images from the previous session. It needn't take much time if you quickly read in pairs or small groups. No need for response. Listen for how the images you heard in the previous session have been enriched and transformed in the writing.

 ## MAIN ASSIGNMENT: FROM IMAGE TO STORY

You may want to base your draft for this workshop on one of the images you've worked on in class, developing it into a full story. But if you prefer, you could start fresh on some new image since this is your chance to do some of what we tried to stop you from doing during the exercises: to describe a person or a large scene or your feelings.

But as you do this more ambitious writing, make sure to rely on the techniques we've been emphasizing in this workshop. Above all, don't fall back on old habits of searching out words and making up stories instead of having experiences. When you feel stymied, stop, close your eyes, look inside, listen. Go through this root experience again and again, as often as you need to. It is a foundation for good writing, writing that conveys an experience to readers.

Don't worry if this approach leads you to write down words that seem jumbled or awkward: not as nice or polished as the writing you usually do. Trust the words that come. You can take time later, as you revise, to clean them up—to cut, rearrange, and add. This way, you'll be working with language that has more life to it.

When you write your story, you may want to make it "say" something to the reader; you may have a "message" you are trying to send. But we would warn you against this impulse. If you start out with a meaning or moral in mind, the story often comes across heavy-handed or preachy. Almost always you do best to concentrate on what might be called "letting the story tell itself," or "letting the meaning take care of itself." You always have chances later, during revising, to spell out meanings more clearly if it seems necessary. Better yet, a chance to help the events *imply* the meaning more clearly. Have faith in the materials you choose, in your vision, and in the power of a story once you set it loose. In fact *you* don't even need to know what a story "means." If you have a strong urge to tell a story, fictional or real, that shows that it means something to you, and often that meaning will be more powerful if you leave it unstated.

Collaborative Option

A group or pair of you who collaborated on an image and story-germ might want to continue together and write a story collaboratively. In collaborating, you can divide the task by *sections:* where each of you writes a different part of the story. Or you can divide the task by *stages:* where one person starts by doing a rough draft, and each succeeding person takes the draft through the next stage. (We've used both of these techniques in collaborating on this book.) If you collaborate, you may have to give special attention to the problem of making the writing consistent, especially if different members write different sections.

SHARING AND RESPONDING

Feedback should focus on the main thing we are working on in this workshop, namely, the ability to make readers and listeners *experience* what you're describing. "Summary and Sayback" will be helpful (in *Sharing and Responding,* Section 3), but perhaps the following pointed questions, addressed to your audience, will also help:

- "Which parts do you see most? Tell me in your own words what you see."
- "Where do you feel the most energy, voice, and life in my writing?"
- "Which parts are the most believable?"
- "Are there places where you feel me trying to take the image where it doesn't want to go?"
- "What does the story mean to you?"

After you've gotten feedback on your draft, your teacher may ask you to revise it now. Or she may ask you to set it aside for revision later.

PROCESS WRITING OR COVER LETTER

The mental process we emphasize in this workshop may be new and difficult for you. But it's a vital process for all writing and thus useful to reflect on.

- Was it hard for you to see your object and stay focused on it? Could you

---

PROCESS BOX

I began writing about a woman whom I remember from my early childhood and soon realized that I really wanted to write about my grandmother. I was remembering her in the detail it takes to make a reader see a character, and it was a very pleasant experience. She hadn't been that clear to me in years. Even if the piece goes nowhere else, the writing of it was a pleasurable reliving of a long buried time of my life. It was important that I cared for the character I was writing about.

Jo Ferrell

get the *seeing* or *experience* to lead to words—instead of your having to look for words? What helped?

■ Could you let the image lead to a story instead of your having to make up a story? What helped?

■ Were these processes easier in speaking or writing?

■ Did you know the meaning the story had for you from the start, or did it sneak up on you—or are you still not sure?

(For more cover letter questions, see Workshop 1, pages 16–17.)

 RUMINATIONS AND THEORY

In these final sections we share some of our thinking and theorizing. If these explorations don't help you do the activities, skip them (unless your teacher directs otherwise).

Writing and Getting Carried Away

Have you sometimes had the experience of getting excited with what you are writing, getting carried away, and later discovering that the writing you produced in that excitement was terrible? Or at least discovering that others thought your writing was terrible? We've certainly had this experience ourselves.

Being carried away can lead to writing that is jumbled or disorganized. The excitement we feel in writing removes all sense of perspective and control and produces a mess—a rich mess, perhaps, but still a mess. "What is your thesis?" "No focus here!" "Sloppy!" are some comments that you might have gotten. Because of this experience, some people try to *avoid* getting carried away. And some teachers warn against it. They conclude that you should write only when you are cool and in control. And yet in this workshop we seem to be advocating getting carried away.

But you don't have to make an either/or choice between being excited and being cool. You can be excited or caught up in your meaning when you are writing *drafts*—and we think you should. Then when you *revise,* you can be coolly controlled and tough. Each of these opposite moods or frames of mind helps enhance the other. That is, if you know you will be tough and controlled as you revise, you'll feel safer about letting yourself get carried away at the earlier stages. And if you know you've let yourself get carried away as you generate, you'll feel tougher about revising, more willing to wield the knife.

So the control problem is solvable if you allow a period for being excited and a period for being cool. But there is another problem with being "carried away." You can get so caught up with your *feelings* that you lose sight of what you are writing about—lose sight of the coffee mug, when the whole point is to see the mug even better.

We're not trying to argue against having feelings as you write; we're not trying to insist on the idea of the artist as coolly detached and paring his fingernails as he looks down on life from a distance. (This image of the artist was

The most difficult part of your assignment (for me) was the imagined object. My mind just wandered from place to place, trying to think of a simple yet interesting object to describe. Perhaps in the next edition of this text you could include a few examples.

The actual object section gave me hope—some focus. You were right about the urges to wander! I am a storyteller. Fortunately I can work these descriptions into my stories to make them more vivid. Thank you for *making* us stop to focus as this will help us produce better writing.

The problem with having listeners see it is that some people have no "pictures" in their head. My fiancé for example has difficulty imagining anything. It doesn't mean it's a bad description; he just can't engage his imagination at will. Perhaps I need to spend more time forming a "focus," before writing or speaking. Did you know it's harder to imagine one particular small thing than it is to picture an entire beach scene? It seemed *too* focused for me.

Danielle

classically expressed by Stephen Dedalus in James Joyce's *Portrait of the Artist as a Young Man.* Wordsworth talks about emotion recollected in tranquillity as the source of poetry. This is *one* good way to go at writing.) But you need to use those feelings to "carry you away" *to the coffee mug* or to the ideas in your essay—to help you see the images and experience the ideas more vividly. If you only get carried away *to your feelings* about the image or idea, readers will get very little. Here's how the Japanese poet Bashō put this idea (in the passage from which we took our opening epigraph, or quotation):

> Go to the pine if you want to learn about the pine, or to the bamboo if you want to learn about the bamboo. And in doing so, you must leave your subjective preoccupation with yourself. Otherwise you impose yourself on the object and do not learn. Your poetry issues of its own accord when you and the object have become one. . . .
> (Bashō, quoted by Balaban 33. See Balaban in "Works Cited.")

Once you get clear about what "being carried away" means—being carried into greater *contact* with what you are writing about—it makes writing much easier and more enjoyable. We suspect that few writers would continue writing unless they were granted the excitement of this experience. This is the excitement of "inspiration," which means literally "a breathing into." In your process writing, you might notice the occasions when you feel excitement: try to notice whether you are excited at seeing and experiencing your subject better, or just excited with feelings and thus losing sight of your subject.

Jonathan Swift, the eighteenth-century author of *Gulliver's Travels,* said that good writing is nothing but finding the right words and putting them in the right places. In a sense, of course, he's right; and it's a fine way to describe good *revising.* But for *producing* or *generating* good writing, you'll find it helpful to think of writing just the other way around (as Bashō does). Don't seek words or worry about where to put them. Put all your energy into "becoming one" with what you are writing about. This principle works for any kind of writing, but it is most obvious and easiest to practice in descriptive writing.

It is a relief to take this approach to writing. It means that you don't need a fancy vocabulary or syntactic complexity to write well. Plenty of good words and good syntax will come of their own accord. Writing turns out to be a richer and more interesting experience this way, less dry or tense because it isn't so much a struggle to find words or correct words, as a struggle to have or relive or enter into experiences. Interestingly enough, some experienced and skilled writers have the hardest time taking this approach. They pay more attention to fancy words and elegant phrasing as they write than to the experience they are writing about. As we read their writing, we are more aware of their nice words than of the meaning or experience of what they are saying.

Readings

IMAGE OF ICE-CREAM MAN

Mitchell Shack

My image of an ice-cream man starting as I hear the ice-cream bells ringing
the next block away. As he comes closer, he puts on his blinking red lights
and his sign, Watch-children, comes out on the driver's side of the truck. I go
around the opposite side and find a window about 3 feet square. Around the
outside of the window are pictures of bomb-pops, snow-cones, chocolate bar
pops, ice-cream cones, shakes, hot fudge sundaes and a bunch of other treats.
Next to each of these items is the price, usually about 20 or 30 cents higher
than the same item bought in the supermarket. There is a little ledge where
the ice-cream man puts down the various items and counts the pennies,
dimes, and nickels the children give him. He places the change in a chrome
change dispenser he wears on his waist. Inside the truck I see a metal
freezer—actually it looks sort of like a refrigerator placed on its back. On
shelves over the freezer are boxes of gum, candy, baseball cards and other
sweets. The outside of the truck is mostly white, except for the area I
mentioned earlier around the window. The shape of the truck reminds one of
a modified bread delivery truck. Next to the window is a little cutout where
there lies a garbage can on the other side so the kids can dispose of the
wrappers. Towards the front of the truck on the passenger's side is a door
similar to the kind you find on a school bus. Looking into the truck from the
doorway, you can see the driver's seat—it's worn in with a jacket hanging
over the chair. There's a big steering wheel and a little metal fan aimed at the
seat. There are great big rear view mirrors outside of the window next to the
seat and door. Above the front windshield are the big letters spelling ICE-
CREAM, and next to it is the infamous bell the kids can hear for five blocks
away.

Process Writing

I had to think of vivid images of what I see when I think of the ice-cream man.
Since there was no ice-cream truck in front of me, I had to rely totally on the
images I had from my memory. Since it had been awhile since my last
encounter with an ice-cream truck, I had trouble remembering some of the
details. I found that I could remember more when I closed my eyes and
concentrated on what I saw when I looked at the ice-cream man. As I started
writing down the major things, more detail popped into my head. I kept on

remembering more things as I kept thinking and my picture in my mind became much more vivid. I could remember myself studying the pictures of the various ice-cream cones and figuring out what I could get with the money I had. I remember racing into the house when I heard the bells and running upstairs to get the money.

I tried to remember the most minute details like getting Italian ices with the little wooden spoon and turning over the Italian ice to get to the bottom which was the best part. It almost seemed as if the ice-cream truck was there—too bad I was getting hungry and would have loved a hot fudge sundae. Anyway, by creating this image in my mind all the details and little things I forgot over the years came back to me as clear as ever.

Mitchell Shack

AN ICE-CREAM MAN*

Mitchell Shack

It was a scorching hot day in the middle of July, almost 100 degrees outside. I was playing football with a bunch of kids from my neighborhood. We were playing ball for almost an hour and I had worked up a good sweat. My throat was dry and I was in desperate need of an ice-cold glass of iced tea. We went into a huddle and I started daydreaming about jumping into a cold pool. The score was tied at twenty-one apiece and we all agreed that the next team that scores wins the game. We were about fifteen yards out from the end zone, actually the area between my friend's mail box and the pine tree across the street. Our team discussed our options and decided we were going to play on fourth down instead of kicking.

We lined up at the line of scrimmage and I was ready to start the down when I heart a faint sound. It sounded like a mixture between the fire bells in school and the bell I used to ring on my tricycle. I stepped back to throw the ball when I heard the noise again. This time it clicked in my head that what I was hearing was the ice-cream man the next block away. I dropped the ball and announced, "I forfeit! The ice-cream man is coming." I reached into my pockets in search of a few coins, but to my dismay they were empty. "Darn," I thought to myself, "I must have left my money in my pants in my room." I started to run toward my house and looked back to see my friends doing the same. The long game and the excessive heat seemed to have little effect on me, for I was running as fast as I ever had. I turned the corner and started running down my block. I could see my house at the end and it seemed as if I was never going to reach it. I ran and ran and then sprinted up the driveway. I reached out for the doorknob to open the door and tried to turn it, but it

---

Shack developed this story from his description printed above.

didn't budge an inch. I started banging on my door and ringing the doorbell, hoping my mom would hear.

My mom came to the door and I was halfway up the stairs before she had a chance to yell at me for almost breaking down the door. I ran into my room in search of my pants containing my allowance money. I checked my floor, under my bed, my closet, my hamper, and behind my dresser, but the pants were nowhere to be found. "Mom! Mom! Where are my pants?" I screamed down to her. "I just took the laundry from your room—check the laundry basket," she replied. So downstairs I ran and grabbed the basket from atop the washing machine. I dumped the laundry on the floor and searched for my pants. I threw socks and shirts all over the place before I found what I was looking for. I reached into my pockets, grabbed the change, and flew out the door. Again I ran down the block, huffing and puffing all the way. I turned onto the street where I was playing and saw the truck in the distance. "Oh no, I better hurry—I think he's getting ready to leave," I thought to myself. The truck from far away looked like an old bread truck, but it would not have mattered one bit if it looked like a garbage truck, just as long as it sold ice cream.

I started getting close to it, when the red blinking sign WATCH—CHILDREN went on and the truck began to move. "Stop! Stop!" I yelled as I ran holding up both my hands. I put on my afterburners and ran in hot pursuit of that beat-up white truck. "Stop! Stop!" I continued to scream, but it had no effect and the truck kept on driving. I ran past my friends who were hysterically laughing as they watched me run while they unwrapped the ice cream they had just bought. The ice-cream truck stopped at a stop sign then turned the corner without noticing me at all. I figured I had better take a short cut so I ran through my friend's back yard, hopped a fence and sprinted through a little patch of woods. I noticed that I had ripped the pocket of my pants, probably while climbing over the fence. I was too concerned about intercepting the ice-cream truck to worry about my pants and I came out of the woods and ran in the middle of the street so I could flag down the truck. I held out both hands and screamed, "Stop!" as I saw the truck approaching, but I noticed something looked different. The truck came to an abrupt halt and I ran alongside it. I looked up but instead of a window, I found a sign reading "Bob's bread delivery service." "Oh no, I stopped the wrong truck," I thought to myself as the driver stepped out and asked me what's wrong. "Oh, nothing. Forget it," I said to the driver, "I just thought you were the ice-cream man." He started laughing and pulled away. I felt like an idiot and just sat there on the curb and tried to catch my breath.

I figured I had better get home and clean up the mess I made out of the laundry. I walked about two blocks, when I turned the corner and saw the ice-cream truck on the side of the road. I couldn't believe my eyes. I thought he was gone for good. I ran alongside the truck and knocked on the closed window. I looked at the pictures next to the window and wanted to buy everything he had. The man came to the window and said. "I'm sorry—we're closed. I'm just packing up a few things before I go home." "Oh please," I pleaded with him. "I ran two blocks home, my house was locked. I couldn't find my pants, I wrecked my mom's laundry, I chased after you another three blocks, ran through my friend's woods and ripped my pants, stopped the wrong truck and when I finally catch up with you, you tell me you're closed!" "You did all that just to buy an ice-cream cone—I think we can make an exception," he said as he smiled at me. I said I wanted a hot fudge sundae and he turned around and started to make it.

I watched him as he was making it, and my mouth watered just looking at all the ice cream, lollipops, bubble gum, chocolate bars, Italian ices, and other candy I saw inside the truck. He reached into the freezer to scoop out some ice cream and I started counting my change as I placed the coins on the little ledge outside of the window. He finished making the sundae and handed it to me along with a plastic spoon. I went to hand him my money when he said, "Forget about the money. This treat is on me." "Thanks a lot! Thank you, Thank you very much!" I blurted out. He closed the window and drove off. I just sat there eating my ice cream, watching the truck fade away into the distance. I was the happiest kid alive.*

CAYE OCHO BEACH

Isabelle Foucard

Caye Ocho beach in Haiti is a beautiful sight. The sand is pure white with little particles shining like diamonds under the reflection of the sun. There are thousands of colorful shells in many different sizes, dispersed all over the sand, which makes the beach look extremely rich. Sometimes there are a few shells moving around which may astonish you but when you lift them, you realize that they are only Hermit crabs that are trying to get on their way. The water is lusciously blue and crystal clear. You can easily see everything through it. Very often, you can see a group of colorful fish swimming peacefully and when you get closer, they disperse so rapidly that you can't tell which way they went. Across the surface of the water, there are little boats with men pulling long fishnets. Some of the fishermen fall asleep in their boats and many others row to different places in the water where they can find more fish.

Lying on the beach, you develop a visual image of the scenery within your head by just listening to the sounds of the environment around you. You feel a peaceful lightness, like being in another world and that nothing else matters. You hear the waves crashing back and forth and you can also smell the sea water. When you feel the dry sand against your back, the cool wind caressing your face, and the hot rays of the sun on your cheeks, a warm feeling of satisfaction comes over you.

---

*See the Readings for Workshop 17 for Mitchell Shack's case study of himself as a writer.

Looking across the water, there are little houses made of palm trees which are surrounded by coconut trees. People are usually drinking coconut milk out of coconut shells while others are sleeping under the shade of trees. A small group of children, sweating from the heat of the sun, confidently climb up the trees to pluck out the coconuts. Laughing all the while, they playfully throw them at their friends. Along the beach quite a distance from the water, there are merchants selling all sorts of seafood. They sit on the sand with piles of leaves before them and large varieties of delicious seafood. Some of the merchants have their kids sitting on their laps and other kids are running around, disturbing the merchants from their work. When they have a customer, they usually pull out a clean leaf from a bag and use it as a plate to serve the food. Sometimes they cook the food on a grill. Most of the time, however, a Haitian peasant likes his raw.

When looking around, you realize that the landscape of the beach is surrounded by the mountains, which resemble the lace train of a wedding gown. They are so gigantic that they make you feel insignificant. The mountains are green, covered with countless growing trees. The few houses that are up there put different colors in between the trees. Further up, there are only trees which give the mountain a mysterious look, as if there's something hidden there. It could excite your curiosity to the point that you would be willing to walk all that distance to discover the mystery. But when you look in the bottom of the mountain, there are people riding donkeys back and forth, and women carrying large baskets of fruits or other merchandise on top of their heads, walking so quickly and without any fear of dropping the baskets. Other women are wearing huge hats to protect themselves from the hot sun.

As you go up in the mountain, you see green lizards sprinting across the dirt path, gaudy butterflies dancing around each other in the hot air, goats eating plants, chickens running around, pigs sleeping and cows tied to trees. Looking up at these trees, there are birds flying from one tree to another. There are male peacocks everywhere opening up their tails in a fan-shape with colorful feathers. The lakes are filled with ducks and geese and horses; mules are drinking the water alongside them. On the other side of the lake, there are people washing their clothes and a few naked kids playing in the water, singing voodoo songs.

Papa Guede, kote ou ye
Mouen leve gran matin-a
Pou mouin ka jouin ou, mais
Mouen paka pab jouin ou
Mouin besoin louange ou
Pou tout sa ou ban nou
Pitit cherie ou, rinmin ou
e nou vle adore ou
Kite mouin jouin ou
Kite mouin jouin ou

Father Guede, where are you?
I woke up early in the morning

Looking for you
But I still can't find you
I want to praise you
For all the things that you had given us
Your dear children, love you
And we want to adore you
Let us find you
Let us find you

While standing on the mountain looking at the scenery during the sunset, you wonder to yourself whether or not you're dreaming.

Cover Letter

I always loved nature and when I used to live in Haiti, which is a beautiful country, I was exposed to different sceneries. Caye Ocho beach is one of them. Caye Ocho beach always made me feel so good. So, when I was assigned to describe scenery, I was so happy to be able to put on paper how I visualize and feel about this beach.

The message that I am trying to send to my readers is to appreciate the beauty of nature. Don't take it for granted because it is there. Also, try to keep it as clean as it is because we are sharing it with different creatures.

When I was writing my paper, I wasn't thinking about any imaginary audience; I was just reliving how I used to feel and how I observed everything about this beach. But I also wanted to share my feelings with someone, with whoever would be reading my paper.

Hopefully, if I described everything well, anyone should enjoy the scenery because it is a beautiful sight. Especially living in New York City, you don't get exposed to these kinds of sights.

I'm not really satisfied with my paper because I feel that I'll never be able to describe everything properly. This is because English isn't my native language and the words don't come easily.

Isabelle Foucard

A WORN PATH*

Eudora Welty

It was December—a bright frozen day in the early morning. Far out in the country there was an old Negro woman with her head tied in a red rag, coming along a path through the pinewoods. Her name was Phoenix Jackson. She was very old and small and she walked slowly in the dark pine shadows, moving a little from side to side in her steps, with the balanced heaviness and

*For Welty's comments about her writing process, and especially about the central role of the image in creating this story, see her essay in the "Readings" for Workshop 16.

lightness of a pendulum in a grandfather clock. She carried a thin, small cane made from an umbrella, and with this she kept tapping the frozen earth in front of her. This made a grave and persistent noise in the still air, that seemed meditative like the chirping of a solitary little bird.

She wore a dark striped dress reaching down to her shoe tops, and an equally long apron of bleached sugar sacks, with a full pocket: all neat and tidy, but every time she took a step she might have fallen over her shoe-laces, which dragged from her unlaced shoes. She looked straight ahead. Her eyes were blue with age. Her skin had a pattern all its own of numberless branching wrinkles and as though a whole little tree stood in the middle of her forehead, but a golden color ran underneath, and the two knobs of her cheeks were illuminated by a yellow burning under the dark. Under the red rag her hair came down on her neck in the frailest of ringlets, still black, and with an odor like copper.

Now and then there was a quivering in the thicket. Old Phoenix said, "Out of my way, all you foxes, owls, beetles, jack rabbits, coons, and wild animals! . . . Keep out from under these feet, little bob-whites. . . . Keep the big wild hogs out of my path. Don't let none of those come running my direction. I got a long way." Under her small black-freckled hand her cane, limber as a buggy whip, would switch at the brush as if to rouse up any hiding things.

On she went. The woods were deep and still. The sun made the pine needles almost too bright to look at, up where the wind rocked. The cones dropped as light as feathers. Down in the hollow was the mourning dove—it was not too late for him.

The path ran up a hill. "Seem like there is chains about my feet, time I get this far," she said, in the voice of argument old people keep to use with themselves. "Something always take a hold of me on this hill—pleads I should stay."

After she got to the top she turned and gave a full, severe look behind her where she had come. "Up through pines," she said at length. "Now down through oaks."

Her eyes opened their widest, and she started down gently. But before she got to the bottom of the hill a bush caught her dress.

Her fingers were busy and intent, but her skirts were full and long, so that before she could pull them free in one place they were caught in another. It was not possible to allow the dress to tear. "I in the thorny bush," she said. "Thorns, you doing your appointed work. Never want to let folks pass—no sir. Old eyes thought you was a pretty little *green* bush."

Finally, trembling all over, she stood free, and after a moment dared to stoop for her cane.

"Sun so high!" she cried, leaning back and looking, while the thick tears went over her eyes. "The time getting all gone here."

At the foot of this hill was a place where a log was laid across the creek.

"Now comes the trial," said Phoenix.

Putting her right foot out, she mounted the log and shut her eyes. Lifting her skirt, levelling her cane fiercely before her, like a festival figure in some parade, she began to march across. Then she opened her eyes and she was safe on the other side.

"I wasn't as old as I thought," she said.

But she sat down to rest. She spread her skirts on the banks around her and folded her hands over her knees. Up above her was a tree in a pearly cloud of mistletoe. She did not dare to close her eyes, and when a little boy brought her a little plate with a slice of marble-cake on it she spoke to him. "That would be acceptable," she said. But when she went to take it there was just her own hand in the air.

So she left that tree, and had to go through a barbed-wire fence. There she had to creep and crawl, spreading her knees and stretching her fingers like a baby trying to climb the steps. But she talked loudly to herself: she could not let her dress be torn now, so late in the day, and she could not pay for having her arm or her leg sawed off if she got caught fast where she was.

At last she was safe through the fence and risen up out in the clearing. Big dead trees, like black men with one arm, were standing in the purple stalks of the withered cotton field. There sat a buzzard.

"Who you watching?"

In the furrow she made her way along.

"Glad this not the season for bulls," she said, looking sideways, "and the good Lord made his snakes to curl up and sleep in the winter. A pleasure I don't see no two-headed snake coming around that tree, where it come once. It took a while to get by him, back in the summer."

She passed through the old cotton and went into a field of dead corn. It whispered and shook and was taller than her head. "Through the maze now," she said, for there was no path.

Then there was something tall, black, and skinny there, moving before her.

At first she took it for a man. It could have been a man dancing in the field. But she stood still and listened, and it did not make a sound. It was as silent as a ghost.

"Ghost," she said sharply, "who be you the ghost of? For I have heard of nary death close by."

But there was no answer—only the ragged dancing in the wind.

She shut her eyes, reached out her hand, and touched a sleeve. She found a coat and inside that an emptiness, cold as ice.

"You scarecrow," she said. Her face lighted. "I ought to be shut up for good," she said with laughter. "My senses is gone. I too old. I the oldest people I ever know. Dance, old scarecrow," she said, "while I dancing with you."

She kicked her foot over the furrow, and with mouth drawn down, shook her head once or twice in a little strutting way. Some husks blew down and whirled in streamers about her skirts.

Then she went on, parting her way from side to side with the cane, through the whispering field. At last she came to the end, to a wagon track where the silver grass blew between the red ruts. The quail were walking around like pullets, seeming all dainty and unseen.

"Walk pretty," she said. "This the easy place. This the easy going."

She followed the track, swaying through the quiet bare fields, through the little strings of trees silver in their dead leaves, past cabins silver from weather, with the doors and windows boarded shut, all like old women under a spell sitting there. "I walking in their sleep," she said, nodding her head vigorously.

In a ravine she went where a spring was silently flowing through a hollow log. Old Phoenix bent and drank. "Sweet-gum makes the water sweet," she said, and drank more. "Nobody know who made this well, for it was here when I was born."

The track crossed a swampy part where the moss hung as white as lace from every limb. "Sleep on, alligators, and blow your bubbles." Then the track went into the road.

Deep, deep the road went down between the high green-colored banks. Overhead the live-oaks met, and it was as dark as a cave.

A black dog with a lolling tongue came up out of the weeds by the ditch. She was meditating, and not ready, and when he came at her she only hit him a little with her cane. Over she went in the ditch, like a little puff of milk-weed.

Down there, her senses drifted away. A dream visited her, and she reached her hand up, but nothing reached down and gave her a pull. So she lay there and presently went to talking. "Old woman," she said to herself, "that black dog come up out of the weeds to stall you off, and now there he sitting on his fine tail, smiling at you."

A white man finally came along and found her—a hunter, a young man, with his dog on a chain.

"Well, Granny!" he laughed. "What are you doing there?"

"Lying on my back like a June-bug waiting to be turned over, mister," she said, reaching up her hand.

He lifted her up, gave her a swing in the air, and set her down, "Anything broken, Granny?"

"No sir, them old dead weeds is springy enough," said Phoenix, when she had got her breath. "I thank you for your trouble."

"Where do you live, Granny?" he asked, while the two dogs were growling at each other.

"Away back yonder sir, behind the ridge. You can't even see it from here."

"On your way home?"

"No, sir, I going to town."

"Why, that's too far! That's as far as I walk when I come out myself, and I get something for my trouble." He patted the stuffed bag he carried, and there hung down a little closed claw. It was one of the bob-whites, with its beak hooked bitterly to show it was dead. "Now you go on home, Granny!"

"I bound to go to town, mister," said Phoenix. "The time come around."

He gave another laugh, filling the whole landscape. "I know you old colored people! Wouldn't miss going to town to see Santa Claus!"

But something held Old Phoenix very still. The deep lines in her face went into a fierce and different radiation. Without warning, she had seen with her own eyes a flashing nickel fall out of the man's pocket onto the ground.

"How old are you, Granny?" he was saying.

"There is no telling, mister," she said, "no telling."

Then she gave a little cry and clapped her hands and said, "Git on away from here, dog! Look! Look at that dog!" She laughed as if in admiration. "He ain't scared of nobody. He a big black dog." She whispered, "Sic him!"

"Watch me get rid of that cur," said the man. "Sic him, Pete! Sic him!"

Phoenix heard the dogs fighting, and heard the man running and throwing sticks. She even heard a gunshot. But she was slowly bending forward by that time, further and further forward, the lids stretched down over her eyes, as if she were doing this in her sleep. Her chin was lowered almost to her knees. The yellow palm of her hand came out from the fold of her apron. Her fingers slid down and along the ground under the piece of money with the grace and care they would have in lifting an egg from under a sitting hen. Then she slowly straightened up, she stood erect, and the nickel was in her apron pocket. A bird flew by. Her lips moved. "God watching me the whole time. I come to stealing."

The man came back, and his own dog panted about them. "Well, I scared him off that time," he said, and then he laughed and lifted his gun and pointed it at Phoenix.

She stood straight and faced him.

"Doesn't the gun scare you?" he said, still pointing it.

"No, sir, I seen plenty go off closer by, in my day, and for less than what I done," she said, holding utterly still.

He smiled, and shouldered the gun. "Well, Granny," he said, "you must be a hundred years old, and scared of nothing. I'd give you a dime if I had any money with me. But you take my advice and stay home, and nothing will happen to you."

"I bound to go on my way, mister," said Phoenix. She inclined her head in the red rag. Then they went in different directions, but she could hear the gun shooting again and again over the hill.

She walked on. The shadows hung from the oak trees to the road like curtains. Then she smelled wood-smoke, and smelled the river, and she saw a steeple and the cabins on their steep steps. Dozens of little black children whirled around her. There ahead was Natchez shining. Bells were ringing. She walked on.

In the paved city it was Christmas time. There were red and green electric lights strung and crisscrossed everywhere, and all turned on in the daytime. Old Phoenix would have been lost if she had not distrusted her eyesight and depended on her feet to know where to take her.

She paused quietly on the sidewalk where people were passing by. A lady came along in the crowd, carrying an armful of red-, green-, and silver-wrapped presents: she gave off perfume like the red roses in hot summer, and Phoenix stopped her.

"Please, missy, will you lace up my shoe?" She held up her foot.

"What do you want, Grandma?"

"See my shoe," said Phoenix. "Do all right for out in the country, but wouldn't look right to go in a big building."

"Stand still then, Grandma," said the lady. She put her packages down on the sidewalk beside her and laced and tied both shoes tightly.

"Can't lace 'em with a cane," said Phoenix. "Thank you, missy. I doesn't mind asking a nice lady to tie up my shoe, when I gets out on the street."

Moving slowly and from side to side, she went into the big building and into a tower of steps, where she walked up and around and around until her feet knew to stop.

She entered a door, and there she saw nailed up on the wall the document that had been stamped with the gold seal and framed in the gold frame, which matched the dream that was hung up in her head.

"Here I be," she said. There was a fixed and ceremonial stiffness over her body.

"A charity case, I suppose," said an attendant who sat at the desk before her.

But Phoenix only looked above her head. There was sweat on her face, the wrinkles in her skin shone like a bright net.

"Speak up, Grandma," the woman said. "What's your name? We must have your history, you know. Have you been here before? What seems to be the trouble with you?"

Old Phoenix only gave a twitch to her face as if a fly were bothering her.

"Are you deaf?" cried the attendant.

But then the nurse came in.

"Oh, that's just old Aunt Phoenix," she said. "She doesn't come for herself—she has a little grandson. She makes these trips just as regular as clockwork. She lives away back off the Old Natchez Trace." She bent down. "Well, Aunt Phoenix, why don't you just take a seat? We won't keep you standing after your long trip." She pointed.

The old woman sat down, bolt upright in the chair.

"Now, how is the boy?" asked the nurse.

Old Phoenix did not speak.

"I said, how is the boy?"

But Phoenix only waited and stared straight ahead, her face very solemn and withdrawn into rigidity.

"Is his throat any better?" asked the nurse. "Aunt Phoenix, don't you hear me? Is your grandson's throat any better since the last time you came for the medicine?"

With her hands on her knees, the woman waited, silent, erect and motionless, just as if she were in armour.

"You mustn't take up our time this way, Aunt Phoenix," the nurse said. "Tell us quickly about your grandson, and get it over. He isn't dead, is he?"

At last there came a flicker and then a flame of comprehension across her face, and she spoke.

"My grandson. It was my memory had left me. There I sat and forgot why I made my long trip."

"Forgot?" The nurse frowned. "After you came so far?"

Then Phoenix was like an old woman begging a dignified forgiveness for waking up frightened in the night. "I never did go to school, I was too old at the Surrender," she said in a soft voice. "I'm an old woman without an education. It was my memory fail me. My little grandson, he is just the same, and I forgot it in the coming."

"Throat never heals, does it?" said the nurse, speaking in a loud sure voice to Old Phoenix. By now she had a card with something written on it, a little list. "Yes. Swallowed lye. When was it—January—two-three years ago—"

Phoenix spoke unasked now. "No, missy, he not dead, he just the same. Every little while his throat begin to close up again, and he not able to swallow. He not get his breath. He not able to help himself. So the time come around, and I go on another trip for the soothing medicine."

"All right. The doctor said as long as you came to get it, you could have it," said the nurse. "But it's an obstinate case."

"My little grandson, he sit up there in the house all wrapped up, waiting by himself," Phoenix went on. "We is the only two left in the world. He suffer and it don't seem to put him back at all. He got a sweet look. He going to last. He wear a little patch quilt and peep out holding his mouth open like a little bird. I remembers so plain now. I not going to forget him again, no, the whole enduring time. I could tell him from all the others in creation."

"All right." The nurse was trying to hush her now. She brought her a bottle of medicine. "Charity," she said, making a check mark in a book.

Old Phoenix held the bottle close to her eyes and then carefully put it into her pocket.

"I thank you," she said.

"It's Christmas time, Grandma," said the attendant. "Could I give you a few pennies out of my purse?"

"Five pennies is a nickel," said Phoenix stiffly.

"Here's a nickel," said the attendant.

Phoenix rose carefully and held out her hand. She received the nickel and then fished the other nickel out of her pocket and laid it beside the new one. She stared at her palm closely, with her head on one side.

Then she gave a tap with her cane on the floor.

"This is what come to me to do," she said. "I going to the store and buy my child a little windmill they sells, made out of paper. He going to find it hard to believe there such a thing in the world. I'll march myself back where he waiting, holding it straight up in this hand."

She lifted her free hand, gave a little nod, turned round, and walked out of the doctor's office. Then her slow step began on the stairs, going down.

WORKSHOP

3

COLLABORATIVE WRITING:
DIALOGUE,
LOOP WRITING,
AND THE COLLAGE

Students often point to two main problems in dealing with school writing assignments: not being interested in the topic *("boorrrring")* and not having enough to say. The activities in this workshop—collaborative writing, dialogue, and loop writing—are all powerful ways to overcome these two problems.

Collaborative writing can be difficult, but we can show you some interesting and productive ways to start: ways to learn collaboration and get many of its benefits, yet avoid many of the difficulties. At the same time, you'll learn two other techniques for expanding your thinking about any topic: dialogue and the loop process. You can use these techniques by yourself even if it is not feasible to collaborate with others.

There are two assignments for this workshop. The first and smaller assignment is to write a dialogue with a partner. The main assignment is to write a collage with one or more partners. (These writing activities are also beneficial if done alone, and perhaps your teacher will ask you to do one or both of them that way.)

 ## WRITING A DIALOGUE

The dialogue is a venerable form of writing. The most famous dialogues were written by Plato, and they recount philosophical conversations between Socrates and some of his fellow Athenians. But Plato got to write both sides of these dialogues (though he is said to have based them on real conversations). We're asking for something more genuinely collaborative from you and your partner: a dialogue in which each of you writes one voice. Your dialogue can be as short or as long and ambitious as you want to make it. Either way, it will serve as a warm-up for the main assignment.

Here's what we suggest. With a partner, decide on a topic that you are both interested in or that you would like to explore through "talking on paper." Perhaps your teacher will suggest a topic. One suggestion is to write about your thoughts and feelings and experiences in cooperative or collaborative activities.

Starting the Dialogue

Writing a dialogue may sound difficult, but you won't have trouble if you realize you are just "having a conversation on paper." After you have chosen your topic, one of you simply starts. Think about how actual conversations start. Someone just *says* something. One of you might just write, "Hi. What do you think about collaborating?" Or "I hate collaborating." Or "I liked social studies group reports. We got together at someone's house and had a lot of fun while we were getting the work done. It was more fun and less lonely." Or "When I was a kid, I always had to do the dishes with my brother and sister. We could never divide up the jobs evenly. We spent more time fighting than doing the dishes. Why did we do this night after night? You'd think we'd have figured out some system." (Also, remember that what you write here is only a rough draft. Before you show it to anyone, you will have a chance to delete and add and change things.)

After one person writes the opening remark, the sheet of paper goes to the other person and she writes her reply: whatever the opening remark leads her to say. (With a computer, you just take turns or pass the keyboard back and forth. If you have networked computers, then you can each sit at your own terminal and write the dialogue "on line.")

It's all right to let the written conversation wander around a bit—just as spoken conversations do. Sometimes one person just says, "Yes, I agree." Fine; the other can reply, "What makes you agree? What is your experience?" And in conversations we often say, "No, I disagree" and then say why. This is fine in writing too, and then the two of you can go on to have an argument. Sometimes there's a kind of pause, when a thread of thought has come to an end, and it's up to the next person to start off a new thread—for example, "Well, I can't think of anything more to say about this point. But here's another point I'd like to know your thoughts about."

Full-scale collaboration can be difficult, but every conversation is really a form of collaboration. We are all practiced at simply *replying* to what someone says and carrying on with an exploration of a topic through talk.

You can go on this way anywhere from three to twenty-three pages—depending on how much time you have and how long a piece your teacher asks for. Some of the Socratic dialogues are more than fifty pages long; in fact Plato's *Republic* is a long book in the form of a dialogue. Just make sure you write more in your first draft than you need for your final version. If your teacher asks for a three-page dialogue, make sure you have written four or more pages.

Here's another way to produce a dialogue on paper. Hold off writing and just start by talking. Simply *have* that conversation with your partner, but take notes as you go along to record the most interesting issues and points that came up. Then reconstruct the best parts of your conversation on paper. (This may be what Plato did with the Socratic dialogues.)

Revising the Dialogue

The next step is to look over what you have and decide together how to make a finished product. Remember that dialogues are naturally informal and conversational in tone, as you'll see from the dialogues in the "Readings." There's no conflict between an informal tone and tough, careful philosophic thinking. What you want to end up with is a conversation on paper that throws light on a subject—and is also interesting to read because it captures on paper the liveliness and voice of conversation. Your conversation might record a disagreement, even a fight; or you might trade your thoughts and ideas and not disagree at all. There is a whole range of possibilities: the full range of ways that people talk to each other in conversation. Conversations and dialogues are particularly satisfying if you can zero in on an issue or a question that you disagree about or want to understand better. The conversation helps you figure things out.

Your teacher might ask you to revise your rough draft carefully and extensively in order to get it as good as you can make it; she may ask you just to clean it up quickly for sharing and then go on; or she might even ask you to treat it as an exercise and leave it unchanged—as a private conversation between the two of you.

If you revise, whether quickly or carefully, you'll want to consider these questions:

- What are the most interesting parts?
- What is the focus, the emphasis? Have you figured anything out or reached a conclusion? You may have to write a bit more to give some focus or closure.
- Which parts will you rearrange or discard?

It's interesting to share dialogues, whether for feedback or just for learning. It's particularly interesting to read them aloud, that is, to "stage" or "perform" the dialogue for a couple of other pairs or perhaps for the whole class. That helps you notice where you've managed to get your written language to sound natural and where it comes out stilted or awkward.

Take a moment, finally, to notice the nature of the collaboration you've just engaged in. You produced a genuinely collaborative piece of writing, yet you avoided most of the difficulties of collaboration. That is, you collaborated to agree on a topic and on which parts of the dialogue to cut and keep and what to add or change. But you didn't have to agree on any ideas or write sentences together or find a common voice or style. And you probably produced a lively, useful, and interesting piece of writing. (If not, you can see now what got in the way and how to do it better next time.)

 ## THE LOOP WRITING PROCESS

Loop writing consists of a series of short pieces of writing that help you think more productively and write more interestingly. It is called a "loop" process because as you do many of these short pieces, you allow your mind to slide away somewhat from full concentration on the topic. While doing these loops, you don't have to worry about the final product and continually ask, "But what will I have to show for this writing?" The loop process works best when you trust that the pieces will be productive and yield good insight in the end. By turning slightly away from the topic and writing little stories, portraits, or even lies, your mind tends to find insights that it can't find otherwise. (In the dark we can sometimes see a faint star or the hands of a clock from the corner of our eye that we cannot see head on.) But these insights are often *implied,* not directly expressed. So you often have to look back on what you wrote and reflect on what it is telling you about your topic. (More about how this works in "Ruminations and Theory.")

Your teacher may invite you or your group to choose your own topic, or she may set a topic. Here are a couple of topics we consider useful to work on as you begin a new writing course and a new stage in your schooling.

- Explore the relationship between speaking and writing. What's useful and problematic about each of them? Are there differences between how your mind works in speaking and writing? Is your language different? Is the "talking on paper" that you are engaged in as you write a dialogue more like writing or talking? What roles do speaking and writing play in your life?

- Consider your gender or race or religion or class or cultural background (or perhaps more than one) in order to explore three things:
  - The strengths and virtues they have given you (i.e., what are you proud of in your inheritance?)
  - The ways they have made people tend to stereotype you or even be prejudiced against you
  - The ways they might have led you to stereotype or even be prejudiced against other people

These are not easy topics. They might seem too large or too personal or too academic. We think they are important in themselves, but we also chose them because we want to show you how the techniques of this workshop—dialogue, loop writing, and collaboration—are all helpful when you are faced with a complex topic you didn't choose.

You can use the loop writing whether you are writing collaboratively or alone—and whether you want to produce an essay or a collage. For this workshop, we are suggesting that you write a collaborative collage. The loop writing process will be the same in any case.

We'll show you five loop processes:

1. First thoughts, prejudices, preconceptions
2. Moments, stories, portraits
3. Dialogue
4. Variations on audience, writer, and time
5. Lies, errors, sayings

You probably can't use all of the loop processes on one writing task, but it's worth learning them and becoming comfortable with them. That's why we're asking you to try them all out for this workshop. If you are writing collaboratively, make sure that, between you and your partner, you use all the varieties (even the subvarieties like moments, stories, portraits). In the readings you'll find examples of loop writing and collages made from loop writing. (By the way, when writing loops, it's best to write only on one side of the paper, so you can cut and paste and rearrange later.)

1. First Thoughts, Prejudices, Preconceptions

You have already sampled this kind of writing if you did focused freewriting in Workshop 1. It is a matter of putting down whatever first comes to your mind about your topic. Focused freewriting might have felt like a "mere exercise," but writing first thoughts is in fact a good way to start out writing a serious essay: you always know more about a topic than you realize. The important thing is to jump in and keep on writing and let yourself get past what you already "have in mind."

I just figured out what it is I'm trying to say—found my point or assertion. I've been wrestling for three days and unable to figure it out—knowing that I've been saying good stuff—knowing that long passages I've been writing are good (some as long as 3–4 pages)—but unable to *say* exactly what it is I'm really trying to say.

I found it when I started to write out a slightly tangential thought. I realized this was a side thought and started writing the sentence as a parenthesis. In mid-sentence I recognized it was even more tangential than I had realized and almost just stopped and crossed the whole thing out as an unhelpful side road. And then I just said what the heck and kept going, and all of a sudden it led to a sentence that zeroed in on and specified *exactly* the precise issue that was at the heart of the 15–20 pages I'd so far written but been unable to sum up.

It's simple and clear once it's said. (And perhaps some person who reads my 15–20 pages would impatiently see my point as obvious and say, "Why don't you just *say* what you're trying to say—and say it in the beginning—instead of meandering all over the place making a mess.") But *I* couldn't see it. Or I couldn't see it till late in the game—and not till I let myself ride on this digression.

Peter Elbow

A helpful way to write first thoughts is to use what might be called "narrative thinking." Simply write your thoughts in the form of a story *as* you're thinking them: "When I think of this topic, what happens first is that I remember _____. Then I think of _____. Then it occurs to me that _____. And then I wonder about _____," and so on. Putting your writing in the form of a story about what's happening in your head from moment to moment takes the emphasis away from the question of whether your thinking is true or right or sensible. It puts the emphasis instead on a different kind of truth and validity: that these thoughts, feelings, images, hunches, and wishes are going on in your mind; that these are snapshots of what *you bring* to the topic. This approach adds to the sense of adventure in the process and often encourages more exploration.

You might worry that this acceptance of prejudices will lead you to wrong ideas or bad thinking. Remember that you're treating this writing not as "the answer" but as exploration. If you want to do good thinking on a topic, you need to understand your own prejudices and preconceptions. The best way to understand them—and to prevent them from infecting your *careful writing*—is to get these candid snapshots of what your mind brings to the topic and how your mind works.

For example, let's say you've decided to focus on the relationship between speaking and writing. Let's say further that you're sick of writing and tired of people (like us) *glorifying* it. You could call this a first thought or preconception. Take it seriously. Explore it; it may lead you somewhere useful. Why are you sick of writing? What about it has been glorified too much? What happens to you when you write? Why do teachers, textbook writers, and journalists glorify writing so much? We think you're more likely to understand writing this way—by acknowledging and exploring your first thoughts—than by either pushing those thoughts aside or defending them as gospel.

Give yourself permission to go along with your preconceptions—even to exaggerate your prejudices. You might want to start off by saying something as extreme as "There is no longer any need to teach students to write now that we have telephones." Once you've written this, you may react so strongly against its absoluteness that you'll want to cross it out. But we suggest that you follow through, push it, nurture it a bit, and protect it from your own criticism for a while. As you allow yourself to get carried away by your extreme idea, you may discover some unexpected problems with writing—or why writing *has* been so important to humankind. You'll begin to understand some of the significant differences between talking on the telephone and writing things down. Almost invariably there are good ideas and interesting insights tangled up in the worst thinking. People seldom come up with good new thinking except through some obsession or exaggeration.

(If you are doing a research project and have to do a lot of reading or research before you can write, use first thoughts and prejudices *before* you do that reading and research. By putting on paper all the ideas you already have—even writing out a quick twenty-minute fantasy of what you *hope* your research will show—you'll find that your reading and research become far more interesting and productive. You'll already have ideas of your own to compare with what "authorities" say: you won't be reading with a blank mind. You're more likely to remember what you read and have more reactions to it.)

2. Moments, Stories, Portraits

You sampled this kind of loop writing in Workshop 1 when you wrote moments, stories, and portraits from your past writing experiences. Just sketch in whatever moments, events, and people you can think of that somehow seem connected to your topic or that come to mind. At this point don't spend any time trying to connect separate pieces to one another or to elaborate on the significance of them unless that just happens while you're writing.

The cognitive power here comes from using *experiential* writing (description and storytelling) for the sake of *expository* writing or thinking. Most of us have had more practice with describing and storytelling than with abstract and inferential writing, so we are often *smarter* when we tell stories than when we give ideas and reasons.

Try testing this idea sometime by asking someone his ideas about the differences and similarities between speaking and writing. After he has said a few things, ask him to tell you moments, incidents, and people that come to mind when he thinks about speaking and writing. After he's talked some more, ask him to reflect on these moments, stories, and portraits to find insights or implications about speaking and writing in each of them.

Usually people come up with more and better thinking by means of this roundabout loop path than by means of careful thinking. Often they'll surprise themselves with new views and realize that they now disagree with some things they'd always thought they believed. The person you tested this idea on may be surprised to discover that what he said about speaking and

writing when you first questioned him is different and not as valid as the reflections he had *after* telling stories. Loop thinking is concrete and specific
thinking that cuts a path around generalities, pieties, and prejudices. Thus
writing up remembered moments sometimes works *against* first thoughts in a
productive way.

3. Dialogue

Describing and storytelling seem more natural than abstract or expository
kinds of discourse like *explaining, giving reasons,* and *making inferences*
because all of us have been describing and telling stories since infancy. Describing lets us just close our eyes and *see* what to say; storytelling carries us
along on a stream of "and then, and then, and then."

But there's an important exception here, because ever since we could talk
we've engaged in *dialogue* too, and dialogue tends to consist of explaining,
giving reasons, and making inferences. When someone told us that we
couldn't have ice cream before lunch or that we had to go to sleep after our
snack or asked us why we thought the flower was "sad," we fell naturally into
giving reasons, explaining, and making inferences. We've been doing it ever
since. That is, dialogue pops us right into the kind of conceptual rather than
experiential language that we need for essays. (Of course, it doesn't *organize*
that conceptual language and thinking into an essaylike form.)

There are other powerful advantages to dialogue. A dialogue injects unusually strong energy into language and thinking. A dialogue makes you speak
and think from your own point of view and yet forces you to imagine another
point of view at the same time. (See the dialogues on pages 88 and 91 of the
readings for this workshop to get a sense of how this works in practice.) A dialogue leads you to the very stuff of essays: assertions, summings-up, reasons,
arguments, examples, counter examples—and probably all in down-to-earth,
clear language.

Thus one of the most powerful ways to do exploratory writing for essays is
simply to write a dialogue with someone. Choose someone who, for whatever
reason, seems important to the topic you want to explore. The person can be
real or fictitious, live or dead, someone you know well or someone you've

---

PROCESS BOX

What you finally read in the published text is
what's been collaged and montaged (can one use
these words like this?) from all my various
improvisations. In other words, writing for me is
also a way of splicing stuff together. That's real
writing for me, and not that initial spontaneous
flow of words. That's in the final text too, but
buried inside the other levels of improvisation.
It's in the various *re*-workings and *re*-writing
sessions that the real elements of improvisation
(and not inspiration) come, because improvisation is always something that builds on something else.

Raymond Federman

never met. And as we mentioned earlier, you can have a productive dialogue with entities other than persons. You've probably already written a dialogue for this workshop, but if you haven't written one on the *topic* you are now exploring, it's worth doing so.

4. Variations on Audience, Writer, and Time

It is classic advice to write to someone who doesn't understand your topic, even if you are really writing something for experts. Writers have traditionally benefited from writing their technical material as though to children; Dr. Samuel Johnson, one of the most prolific and popular writers of the eighteenth century, used to read his writing to his uneducated servant and not stop revising till it was clear to her. It's not just that this process forces you to be clear. The more important effect is that you *see* your topic differently when you direct your thinking to a different audience—and this process gives you new perspectives and new ideas.

You can achieve comparable benefits by varying the *time*. Write about learning and teaching as though you were living in the future or during some period in the past. You will notice many things about teaching and learning that you wouldn't otherwise notice.

Varying the *writer* will even more directly change your perspective and give you new insights. Pretend *you* are that best or worst teacher of yours—step into her shoes—and then try writing from her point of view about you and your learning. How do you suppose she saw you as a student or even as a small child? See, in other words, what that teacher might write about you. Or write in the voice of some famous teacher or thinker you admire.

If you want to end up with something fair and judiciously detached, spend some time writing from the point of view of someone who is very biased and involved in the subject. Then write as someone with the opposite bias. (Obviously this category can merge into a dialogue.)

This mode is good for experimenting: start out writing to various audiences and at various times and as various people. See which are most fruitful to continue with.

5. Lies, Errors, Sayings

These are just sentences or phrases, not extended pieces of writing. Therefore lies, errors, and sayings have a kind of coiled up cognitive power, a lurking energy. They imply more than they state. Afterward you can explore the implications of your lies, errors, and sayings. You'll find much more meaning than you expected.

With *lies* it's fine just to write single sentences, but now and then let yourself spin one out a bit more if it intrigues you. Be bold in your lies: "I *never* remember anything I read." "All teachers are dumb."

By *errors* we mean ideas that are almost right—assertions that are wrong but tempting. Write down things that many people believe, or things you're not sure of, or things you wish were true but might not be: "Careful study always helps me remember better." "Obviously I know more than I used to." "Most students learn to read more easily than they learn to write."

Sayings tend to carry "folk wisdom"; they are worth exploring *and* questioning. They teach you to squeeze a lot of meaning into a pithy and memorable chunk of language. You can use sayings that already exist: "A little learning is a dangerous thing." "All work and no play makes Jack a dull boy." But get yourself to make up your own sayings: "When the student is big, the teacher shrinks." "A triangle is the most stable figure: teacher, student, and book. Take away the book and the figure becomes unstable." You don't always have to know exactly what you mean by sayings you make up. Playing with "proverb syntax" will lead you to formulations that are interesting to explore: "A little danger is a learning thing." "Where there's milk there's money."

If it sounds merely foolish or game playing to write lies, errors, and sayings, try pondering their implications especially in conjunction with each other. Ask yourself questions like these:

- In what respect is this lie true?
- Why do some people think this idea is true?
- Are there times when this is true and times when it's not?
- What would follow if this were true?
- What is it that makes this untrue?

Discussing lies, errors, and sayings with your partner or group is particularly fruitful. You can also make up good ones collaboratively with them.

USING LOOP WRITING FOR YOUR MAIN ASSIGNMENT

Our suggestion for this workshop is to produce a collaborative collage. But it's easier for us to describe how to use loop writing if we start with directions for a solo collage (and we also want to emphasize how these techniques are not just for collaborative writing).

Read through all the pieces you've written. As you read, decide which ones are the most interesting and successful. Which ones throw the most light on the topic? Keep these good ones and arrange them in whatever order seems most interesting and effective. (If you remembered to write on only one side, you can simply cut out the good ones with a scissors, spread them on the floor, and play with various arrangements.)

If you want to produce an *open collage,* you can move at this point toward a final version. Just edit your pieces by making minor revisions: cuts, tightenings, changes. Then proofread. Your collage will be an interesting and lively piece of writing which will throw good light on the topic. That is, an open collage doesn't have to be completely unified with a clear conclusion. It doesn't have to state explicitly what it is "saying." It can plant seeds in the reader's mind. When such seeds bear fruit, the effect on readers is usually more powerful than if you had told them exactly what you want them to think.

But you can work a bit more with your material and produce a *focused collage* rather than an open one. A focused collage is also made up of interesting

and diverse short pieces, but it is more clearly unified and has a conclusion: it *says* what it is saying. For this you need to carry your thinking further and force yourself to figure out what all these pieces of loop writing *mean*. Thus you would have to write one or more additional passages that tell what all the others add up to. These pieces would answer the question "So what?" and would probably come near the beginning or the end. A focused collage is more carefully *framed;* it doesn't leave quite so much up to the reader.

Either way, however, a successful collage gives its pieces to the reader in intuitive order and lets the reader enter into a kind of interaction or collaboration with the piece to make sense out of it. That is one of the advantages and pleasures of the collage for readers: it's a more participatory form. (Actually, of course, all language has gaps and ambiguity and requires the participation of the reader. The collage highlights this quality of all language.) There are collages in the "Readings" for Workshop 1 and a collaborative collage in the "Readings" for this workshop.

Essay. You can also use loop writing to produce an essay rather than a collage. Indeed, one of the best ways to understand the nature of the essay as a form is to explore how it differs from a collage. The essay asks for two things that you don't always need in a collage: full unity and full coherence. Unity: a collage invites you to explore a general territory, and it can be successful if it is "sort of unified"—that is, if all the parts are *related* yet don't all connect perfectly to one precise center. But an essay insists that you work out what the *center* is and keep everything related to it. Coherence: a collage invites you to jump from point to point with no connective passages, and sometimes to jump quite a distance. But an essay insists that you work out your train of thought so that each part follows smoothly, logically, and with connective tissue.

To produce an essay, then, you have to push your thinking harder: work out exactly what you want to say and make sure all the parts really fit it; work out your train of thought and make sure all the parts follow. The crucial process will probably be to look back over all the pieces of loop writing you did and figure out more clearly in your mind what each of them is telling you. This is more work of course, but the benefit is that your thinking is more developed and careful. In other words, the collage is best for *throwing light on* an issue and making people think; the essay is best for *working out your thinking* and reaching a conclusion with as much validity as you can get.

Using Loop Writing for Collaborative Writing

It will probably be obvious by now how to make a collaborative collage from your loop writing, and why a collage is such a helpful way to get used to collaborative writing. First, just get together and listen to each other's loop writing, or share it on paper. Then decide together which pieces seem most interesting and successful, which ones you want to choose for your group collage. The pieces don't need to agree with each other or fit each other in voice or tone. In a collage, contrasts are a benefit: a source of energy that stimulates thinking in readers. In effect, you are putting together a collection of pieces, each written from an "I" point of view, for the sake of a "we" enterprise: a gathering of individuals toward a collaborative purpose. (Whether or not you actually use the first person singular in these pieces doesn't matter.)

Of course you don't want to confuse readers as you jump from one person's writing to another's, but when you make it clear to readers on the title page that this work was written by multiple authors and that it is a collage consisting of individual and distinct passages separated by asterisks rather than smoothly connected, readers will understand what's going on when different "I's" say conflicting things or tell conflicting stories in different voices.

If you want an *open collage,* you can now move to completion: agree on an order for your pieces; work collaboratively to edit, tighten, and proofread. If you want a *focused collage,* you'll have to collaborate a bit further in your thinking. That is, after listening to everyone's loop writing, you need to decide more explicitly on your topic or focus, *and* decide more clearly how your pieces hang together or relate to each other. You don't necessarily have to agree with each other on a conclusion; it's fine to disagree completely. But you do need to agree on your disagreement. That is, you'll have to agree on how to describe *the relationship* between your conflicting opinions, and on that basis write a few *collaborative passages* that represent your *larger collaborative or joint view* of your disagreements. These collaborative passages would probably occur near the opening and/or the closing. In effect, then, the focused collage might be a collection of "I" pieces, but they would be framed by some crucial "we" pieces that express joint or collaborative thinking in order to focus the whole thing better.

If you want to increase the degree of collaboration, you can write a *collaborative essay.* It would consist not of separate blips in separate voices, but an extended piece of writing that readers would feel as more or less connected and single. That is, it needs to consist mostly of "we" thinking and writing, not "I" thinking and writing. Thus when you are writing a collaborative essay, you have to keep discussing your individual loop writing and what it all points to until you can *pretty much* come to some agreement.

But even in this connected essay, you can use quite a few of the "I" passages from your loop writing—transforming them into examples or "points" for your essay. That is, you might frame some of these passages with wording like this: "One of us had the following experience that illustrates what we are saying here: . . . ." Or "One of the authors, however, points out a difficulty with the idea we have just explained: . . . ." In short, it would be an essay from the "we" point of view that represents corporate agreement, yet it would have some genuine diversity of thinking and perhaps even plurality of voice. In fact you could even have an essay that clearly explains and explores a *disagreement:* it would be a case of agreement about the terms of disagreement.

About Collaboration and Agreement

Notice how we are introducing you to collaboration by suggesting a progression from less agreement to more. The dialogue and the open collage provide good starting places because, on the one hand, they require *some* agreement: on which pieces to choose and how to arrange and edit them. But on the other hand, they spare you the two hardest forms of collaboration: reaching full agreement in your thinking and finding a common voice. The focused collage pushes you a bit further into collaboration by asking you to agree in your thinking and find a common voice, but only for a *few* short passages. Finally comes the essay which asks for *full* agreement.

Or does it? Even for the essay, don't struggle for more agreement than you really need. What we consider the most important point in this workshop lies here. When you are trying to write a single and coherent essay—a "seamless" piece—you don't have to make it *too* seamless. You can leave some of those conflicting ideas and voices in there. It's fine in an essay to "break out" at various points with passages that might start like this: "But wait a minute. Let's look at this issue from a contrasting point of view." Or, "Notice what follows, however, when we consider what an opposing voice might say." Or, "There are some serious objections, however, to what we have just been saying." In each case, you can go on for a paragraph or even a long section stating this contrasting idea or arguing this conflicting point of view. And the conflicting point of view can even be in a contrasting voice—either with or without quotation marks. Many readers would consider these "breaks" or this internally "dialogic" quality a *strength* rather than a weakness in an essay.

Thus we are not introducing these easy forms of collaboration (the dialogue and the collage) just because they are easy, though that's a big benefit too. These easy forms bring in a dimension that is often missing in much collaborative writing. Much collaborative writing is weak in its thinking because the writers settle for the *few things they could agree on.* And much collaborative writing has a weak or fake voice because the writers hid their individual voices. The collage may be easy, but it shows you a way to bring to essay writing what is rare and precious and often lacking: some internal *drama of thinking and voice.*

In fact the collage will have the same benefit on your solo writing if you let it. For much solo writing—especially by inexperienced writers—suffers in the same way we just described. The thinking is dull and obvious because the writer latched too soon onto one idea or "thesis" and timidly backed away whenever he felt perplexed or came across a conflicting view; he nervously swept the complication under the rug and hoped no one would notice. And the writer tried to use a "proper" or "impressive" voice and came out with something completely fake and stilted. Most *good* solo writing represents a single writer having some internal dialogue with himself—having more than one point of view and using more than one voice.

So if your teacher asks you to turn your collage into a "single and coherent" piece of writing, don't make things too "single" or one-dimensional. Look for ways to save as much of the dialogical drama of thinking as you can—even the drama of voices—while still getting it all to hang together: rich thinking and complex voices harnessed to a single and coherent task. Therefore, any piece of *good* loop writing that fits your topic probably belongs in your essay. It might have to be moved, reshaped, or reframed; but good thinking and lively voices are what most people are looking for in essays.

(Some colleagues tell us that this is dangerous advice, so perhaps you should take it with a large grain of salt. They would argue that one of the main problems with inexperienced writers is their tendency to save too much—to be too scared to throw things away. But we'd reply that the other main problem with inexperienced writers is their tendency to throw away the lively, perky stuff in their rough writing and replace it with "proper writing"— smooth writing from which all the mistakes have been removed, but writing that is too dull and timid and that no one would ever read by choice.)

"But damn it! You guys keep putting off the question of how to actually reach agreement and find a common voice. You keep giving us ways to avoid it and telling us it's no problem. But we've suffered in collaborative groups that break down because people couldn't agree. We've been forced to work with people we don't want to work with. We've been taken advantage of by loafers. We've had our time wasted when we could have done a better job alone—and quicker too."

Yes, this is a valid objection. There's no getting away from the nuts and bolts of reaching agreement and finding a common voice: it can be hard. For the nitty-gritty difficulty, we offer some nitty-gritty rules of thumb:

- Never try to generate actual prose together. It drives you crazy. One person suggests a sentence; the person with the pencil writes it down; someone else objects; the writer erases and writes something different; someone else tries. And so on until everyone is crabby. Don't argue about or even discuss actual wording until you have some rough drafts to work from. Here are some methods of avoiding this killing situation:
    - Use something like the loop process so that everyone produces prose (everyone takes the risk). Then people can proceed positively rather

than negatively: choose the bits they mostly like rather than criticize what doesn't work.

- Brainstorm. Encourage and accept all ideas and have someone take them down. No criticism. Then hear them and discuss and pick the ones that appeal. Have one person take notes on the agreements and then write up a very rough draft. Share it; hear some general kibitzing as to strengths and weaknesses of this general approach. No arguments about wording yet! Have another person take notes on that discussion and write up a slightly better draft. Now you can start to discuss wording. And so on.

- Meet and discuss the topic and reach general agreement on certain points. But then each person writes up one *section*. Come together to hear the sections; discuss the strengths and weaknesses of the thinking and voice. Then one person does a quick rewrite of the whole thing. Hear it and get feedback. Someone else does the final write up.

- Here's a risky, difficult method, but it can work well if you have the right mix of people. After only a bit of discussion, one person writes a *very* rough *discussion draft*. This must be a brave and nondefensive person who can write quickly with very little effort, for much of what she writes will be rejected and virtually all of it changed.

■ When hard choices have to be made, of course you will sometimes have to argue against each other's thinking. What helps most is a spirit of supportive cooperation. And one concrete technique is helpful: avoid "God statements" and stress "I statements." That is, avoid saying, "This is clearly wrong for the following reasons," and instead say, "This doesn't *seem* right *to me* because I had the following reactions." In short, remember that you are seeing things from only one point of view and you *may be wrong*. Be prepared to change your mind. Someone has to change his or her mind or you won't get the job done. But if you are supportive of each other and creative, it won't be fighting where one person "wins" and the other "loses." It will be a process of collaboratively figuring out *new ideas* that are *better* than those held by any of you individually.

■ When you get close to a final draft and are trying to think about a voice, make sure to read things *out loud*. Get different members to read. Try to hear the different voices in the pieced-together writing. Try reading with exaggeration or parody in order to bring out different possibilities of voice. Then you can decide which voice (more or less) is the one you want to try for. The person who can "do" that voice is probably the one who should do the final polishing version.

■ Be concrete and assertive about spelling out everyone's task. Write it down. Collaboration almost never works without an explicit *schedule*. Be tough-minded about insisting that people fulfill their responsibilities, and on schedule. If you are doing more than your fair share, maybe it's because you haven't insisted that others do *their* fair share: Be tough and expect others to be tough about this.

But Take Hope

Despite the real difficulties, we still think you will do best if you realize that collaboration is not really so hard. It's all a question of getting the right attitude, or spirit, or feeling among you. And that's exactly what our introductory dialogue and collage activity—the "easy collaboration"—will do for you: give you practice and experience working together and reaching agreements.

Attitude. If collaborative writing feels weird, stop a moment and reflect on the fact that it is the most common kind of writing in the world. In business and industry and government, most writing is collaborative. Most research in the hard sciences and social sciences is written collaboratively. And it helps to notice the collaborative dimension even in most "regular" solo writing. Whenever you write something "yourself," you tend to use the ideas and voices that you have absorbed from those around you. Collaboration is the natural thing that humans do. It's only in school that people tend to say, "Make sure you don't get any help from others."

It's helpful to realize, by the way, that we all *learned* collaboration before we learned to do things by ourselves. The collaborative use of language *precedes* the solo use of language. Babies learn to speak by first having dialogues with parents. Only by means of the language learning they get through these dialogues do they gradually learn to "internalize" language enough to speak or think extended strings of language on their own.

Realize too that moving from difference to agreement is not just a *difficulty;* it is also an opportunity. If you have to struggle to work out some agreements, that very process will carry your thinking and analysis further. It will help you find weaknesses in your present views and lead you to new ideas that none of you could find alone. Collaboration is the most powerful way to expand your thinking about something because it brings multiple minds to bear on it.

 SHARING AND RESPONDING

If you are writing collaboratively, you will probably do most of your sharing among yourselves in the process. In particular, as you read over your dialogue in order to edit it and as you share your loop pieces in the first steps toward the collage, remember this: mostly listen; listen for what is good. Put your effort into picking out the good bits and see if that process will show you what to use—so you don't have to spend much time criticizing the ones you don't like. The *spirit* of collaboration is best served if you can make your choices by means of positive enthusiasm rather than by means of negative criticism.

If you want to get responses from others on your dialogue or collage, some of the main questions would be these:

- "Which words or sections or pieces are strongest?"
- "What do you hear the main sections saying?"

■ "What do you hear the whole piece saying?"
■ "What happens as you listen? What are the steps or stages in your response? That is, tell us how the sequencing of pieces in our collage works for you."

 ## PROCESS WRITING OR COVER LETTER

You have probably tried more *processes* here than in most workshops—and some of the most unusual and perhaps difficult processes too: dialogue, loop writing, collage, collaboration. You will have your hands full simply talking about the ones that were most important to you: what was helpful and not helpful, difficult and easy, surprising or interesting.

But for future writing decisions it will be helpful to answer these questions:

■ Which loop processes did you find the most helpful for getting involved in the topic and expanding your thinking? Are there other loop processes that you sense *will* be helpful for you if you get more familiar with them?
■ Describe the collaboration or collaborations you engaged in. What were the sticky points, and how could you deal with them better next time?
■ How can you get more of the drama of thinking and of voice into your future solo writing?

For more cover letter questions, see Workshop 1, pages 16–17.

 ## RUMINATIONS AND THEORY

Loop Writing and the Dangerous Method

"It's Impossible *Not* to Think of Something"

Loop Writing and the Dangerous Method

The loop process is most useful if you want to do a lot of thinking about your topic; if you are having trouble finding things to say; or if you feel bored, unconnected, or alienated from what you have to write about. It is probably *least* useful if you already know what you want to say or are in a hurry for a final draft. The loop process does make a mess.

Many teachers and textbooks say that in order to produce a "good" piece of writing, you must figure out what you want to say *before you start writing:* "Think before you write," they say. Once you've done that, they suggest that you make an outline of your whole paper. Only then are you to start actual writing in the sense of producing a connected series of sentences and paragraphs.

This advice sounds sensible. But trying to begin by getting your meaning clear in your mind—so that you can write something right the first time—is what we call "the dangerous method." It's dangerous because it leads to various writing difficulties that most of us are familiar with.

I enjoyed the loop writing. When I first saw the assignment, I thought it would be easy to complete because I had been thinking about how and why I learned to write on and off since this summer. I'd had to write a paper about it last year. I figured I'd be able to use whole chunks of it for this assignment. Once you explained how you wanted us to approach it, though, and after I read the description of it, I decided not to even look at the other paper. The process sounded like fun; I just dove right in.

For the most part it *was* fun. Being compulsive in my fear that I'd forget something important, I began with the instant first draft to get all the "important" details down. Then I felt relaxed enough to do some of the more creative loops and dives. I particularly liked speaking in other voices to myself. I do a lot of talking to myself anyway and this seemed to legitimize the process.

After I finished looping, I went back using the cut and rearrange function on the computer and put everything in chronological order. Another compulsion: somehow things don't seem right to me unless they're in time sequence. And it seemed to work here.

Kathy Reckendorf

- You find yourself procrastinating: "I can't start writing yet. I haven't thought this through well enough. My outline isn't right. I've got to do more reading and studying and thinking."
- You spend hours trying to figure out what you want to say—perhaps even making a very careful outline—but you don't really come up with much that's interesting.
- Even when you *do* figure out much to say beforehand and get it neatly outlined, as you try to write from your outline you feel constrained. You start to wander away from the outline, which makes you feel guilty. You think of a new idea you love, but it doesn't fit. Or worse yet, your planning starts to unravel as you write: you think of new problems or objections to something in your outline, or you can't quite explain the idea or the transition that seemed so right when it was in outline form.
- You agonize over every sentence in an effort to get it right. You constantly cross out, change, revise, start over.
- When you finally get it written, you can't bring yourself to make major revisions—or throw even a sentence away—because you've poured so much agonizing effort into writing it.

Perhaps you are not troubled by these difficulties. Perhaps you are actually *good* at the dangerous method of getting everything clear before you start writing. If so, by all means write in that way. And of course there are a few writing tasks where you must get your meaning clear before writing—such as for exams with no revising time.

But usually when we write we *need* to do more thinking about our topic. Even if we believe we understand quite well what we want to say, our thinking can benefit from exploratory writing: we find new thoughts and new ways of talking about our old thoughts. It's as though we cannot see the full implications of our thoughts until we see them concretized in writing.

Loop writing is also useful because it stimulates fluency and makes you feel freer as you write. Since the process is a bit unusual, it jogs you out of any writing rut you may be in. One of the main reasons people don't write better is that whenever they write, they unthinkingly slip into their habitual gear. Our goal in this book is to get you to experience an array of *different* processes for getting things written so that you have more options. With more options you can choose the writing process that's best for you and for the particular writing task you face.

Of course writing *does* require getting your meaning clear in your mind, often even making an outline. And writing certainly means communicating to others what you've *already* figured out. But these processes usually work best *after* you've already done enough exploratory writing to produce good raw material—and if possible after you've felt the mental click that tells you, "Ah! That's it! *Now* I see exactly what I want to say." This insight is often accompanied by some clues about organization.

"It's Impossible Not to Think of Something"

So wrote the poet William Stafford. Whenever we pay attention to our mind, we find words there; we may not always be satisfied with those words, but they're there nevertheless. If we put these words on paper, other words take their place inside our heads. By definition this process is infinite. But we're quite likely not to believe in it until it is proved to us; we need to record the words we find in our head and realize for ourselves that others take their place. This new set of words may or may not have an obvious connection to the old set of words. And the same may be said for each succeeding set of words. Consequently, the only limit to what we can write comes from our muscles: how long we can sit up, hold a pen, type.

When we write something down and don't stop to look back inside our heads, more words come anyway, and these words begin to appear on the page. If we continue to write, we become conscious of new sets of words only as they appear on paper. This gives us the sense that the words are writing themselves. In truth almost all writing happens this way, whether it's exploratory or not. We rarely plan any written sentence out entirely in our heads. We start off a sentence with an intention to go somewhere with it and with the faith that we can do that. And we continue the same way when we've finished that sentence.

This is not to say that we don't get stuck. We do. Think of yourself, if you will, as being in a maze. You come to a junction and are baffled. You could just sit and try to reason through the alternatives, but if you've never been in this maze before, that's hopeless. Your best chance of getting to the end is just to try every possibility. Since every piece of writing is unique, you can think of each one as a maze you've never been in—even though you may know something about mazes in general. When you're stuck, it isn't because you don't have words; it's because you're trying to figure out *in advance* whether they're the right words. But the only way to know that is to write them out.

At first they may seem as though they're "wrong" words, but if you keep writing, you may arrive at some good ideas that you would never have gotten to otherwise. And even if you come to a dead end or become irreversibly discouraged, you can always return to the point in the maze where you were stuck in the first place and take a different path. And remember: if your *aim* is to learn more about mazes themselves, you would deliberately take as many routes as possible.

This, of course, is analogous to loop writing. You start off a certain way, a way that seems to be heading where you want to go, and travel wherever that takes you. If you are blocked in some way or don't like what you're doing, you can return to your original subject and start off from it again in another way. You may well discover that there are quite a few effective approaches to your topic. Once you know that, you have choices. And—if your aim is just to learn more about writing—you can explore every approach to maximize that learning.

Readings

LOOP WRITING ABOUT TEACHING WRITING

Lynn Hammond

[First Thoughts]

"I don't want to teach 75 students. I can't reach 25 in a class, I can't keep track of 75 individual progresses. In fact, I'm not sure I have enough caring in me to muster up for 75 students every 10 weeks."

"Yep. That's a problem."

[Moments; Portraits]

Henry who said he'd get his paper to my door by 6:30 am yesterday before I left for my 8:00 plane. It wasn't there. He gives great feedback but can't ask for help when he needs it, I think. I missed him in some way this quarter. Didn't know he was in trouble until his last papers didn't arrive. One of the silent lost in a crowd of 75 students.

Vincent. Tall black, very slow of speech, not a speaker much less a writer of standard English. I told him at the beginning of the quarter he would have to work very hard to pass this course.

"I'm not stupid," he said, "but I'm not a good writer."

He was right on both counts, though many would have taken his slow speech for slow brain power. Somehow I liked him from the beginning. He knew it and I knew that he knew it in the way that dogs know who isn't afraid of them. In other classes (overgeneralizing: in many other classes) I think kids would have derided him. In my class we listened supportively. His big breakthrough came after a conference in which I told him that his topic seemed to be "why he hated writing."

He wrote it, and he even shared it in class. A torrent of experiences roaring out of him in a totally new, angry, authoritative voice. He was writing about something he knew about and had strong feelings about. After that, he became a writer. He still doesn't speak a standard dialect, but we understood him, and he has a lot to say to us.

[Sayings; So What?]

Teachers should be caring. Teachers should be encouraging. Teachers shouldn't have to grade. Teaching works best in small groups. Teaching works best when there's a caring (engaged?) relationship between students and teachers. Teachers have to be generous, to give more sometimes than can be reasonably expected. Teachers can therefore burn out. I think some of this is overload with papers, etc., but I think even more it has to do with so much *giving* usually with little recognition from colleagues or superiors. Students respond enthusiastically sometimes but not always, and you can't always either predict or remedy. You can try to be a researcher in your classroom. An important way, I think, to keep yourself alive and improve your teaching, and if you can share this in a writing group with peers, so much the better.

I.e., I think we have to form communities among ourselves to help us keep writing, keep investigating and learning, and to give each other support.

A wonderful part of being a member of this Institute has been having a writing group of fellow teachers who are genuinely dedicated to helping me, each other, our students move in our thinking. People who are genuinely interested in what I have to say who have given me permission to write in my own idiosyncratic ways.

So that has been enormously empowering and has helped me want to write.

[Stories]

Janet reminded me of Donna, a little black girl in my class this fall who asked the first thing in her first conference:

"You aren't married?"

"No," I answered.

"How do you stand it?"

I don't know what I answered. It was clear that she came from a culture in which this was not an offensive question and I didn't take offense. She picked up the ball again soon.

"I'm going to be married by the time I graduate so my boy . . . husband can give me a car for graduation."

"I find it easier to buy my own cars and have the resulting freedom," I said, perhaps a little too aggressively, but I felt a need to burst her secure sense of being able to predict these things so clearly when I wasn't even sure she was going to be able to pass my course. I wondered as she left how large a role intention plays in outcome. Maybe she will be married by the time she graduates.

I'm surprised in other ways by their insularity. They thought the reason [the black writer James] Baldwin encountered racial prejudice in NJ was that when he moved from Harlem to NJ he had moved "down South."

[So What? What's the Assertion?]

What concerns me about teaching writing? With 25 students in a classroom, I simply can't keep track of them all, can't keep them all engaged. At least, not in the big group. If I break them into small groups, I can keep them mostly all engaged, but then I have so little sense of what's going on, and I don't get to know them and their writing so well.

[Stories]

Landau, tall, black, sexy, shy, towering over everyone. Hard to get him to sit down. Introduced himself as "Lazy Landau" [in an introducing game in the first class where you have to put an adjective with your name].

"Is that a warning?" I asked. No. He let me in little by little. He wouldn't come to conferences but would always see me far off on campus and stop to talk. He asked if this course was supposed to be personal, and I said he didn't want people to get to know him that well.

Eventually he finally came to a conference and said, "I probably shouldn't admit this to you, but I don't need to learn how to write. I'm going to be a naval aviator."

I struggled to keep myself from pointing out all the ways he might need writing in his adult life, from being an aviator to writing love letters. I tried to be with him, to hear what he was saying. I sensed that if I prescribed, I'd lose him. I said, "OK. Write about that. That's what's on your mind."

He did. I don't remember that paper too well, but as I recall, before it was finished, he allowed that there might be reasons to write. More importantly, he had written.

Then we read James Baldwin. He kept saying he had nothing to write about. Finally I said, "Why don't you write about being black in America today. From your experience, is Baldwin dated or not?"

"OK," he said.

Next class, nothing. "What's going on?" I asked.

"I'll write something for you, but I won't share it in my writing group."

"OK," I said.

He came in the next time and handed me 10 pages. He had grown up in a white neighborhood. He could pal around with white kids, but it was understood that he couldn't go out with white girls. His mother had warned him about that as Baldwin's father had warned him.

Then Sheri, a white girl, convinced him that she wanted to be his girlfriend and that it would be OK. He hesitated, but he got along with her family, she with his. They became very involved. One day Sheri said since he'd be going off to college soon, she wanted their relationship to cool down. After dealing with a lot of evasion he learned that her parents couldn't stand the pressure from neighbors at letting her go out with a black guy, and her grandmother had written her out of her will.

"I don't see how you can keep from smashing things," I said.

"It's hard," he said calmly, "but you learn. I play a lot of soccer."

After we talked about his experiences for a while I asked, "How can you turn this into a 'paper' about Baldwin?"

"I don't know."

"Landau, I think this is a powerful piece of writing. As a letter to me, it's finished. But I need to be moving you toward writing an essay about Baldwin. Can you compare and contrast other experiences you've had with Baldwin's and make it more a public document? Can you write something to show my all-white class? They think Baldwin is too extreme and that no prejudice exists today."

The next day I had conferences until five. At five, Landau danced in and handed me a paper. "Is this long enough?" he asked, not sitting down. "How would I know?" I ask.

I read it while he danced nervously around the room. It was full of one detail after another. All fraternities on campus—all black and all white: no mixtures. No black head basketball coaches in the US. All kinds of personal anecdotes written with voice and conviction.

"It's wonderful," I said. "Can I read it to my 9:00 class? They need to know this."

"That's why I wrote it," he said, looking down at me straight, finally standing still for the first time.

The next day I asked students who I thought had written the best papers to read theirs out loud. Then I read Landau's. They were all riveted, stunned, moved. They knew it was much more powerful than anything they had written. This was writing with a mission.

[So What?]

What am I trying to say with this story? And with Vincent too? Kind of what I wrote last night about other teachers as an audience? That for people to see themselves as writers, they need real audiences, not graders, but people who want to hear what they *really* want to say and who have the skills to help them find out what that is and how to do it. I think anything less isn't really teaching, and trying to do it with 75 students is crazy.

Maybe I also need to acknowledge that I wrote only about my minority students.

LOOP WRITING COLLAGE

Darci Jungwirth

Sara was afraid to come home at night. When she got there she would always find the same thing: her father with a beer in his hand and his breath smelling of alcohol. His hair was all messed up and he was sitting in the brown recliner with the ripped seat that he never bothered to get patched after an incident with a cigarette left burning. He always greeted her the same way. "Hi darling, how was your day?" He would try to be nice first but always ended up getting out of control or going off the handle over nothing. She would end up huddled on her bed, both her body and soul wincing in pain from this man, her father. She lay on her soft old bed with the dusty pink comforter for hours. When she could finally get her strength up she did her homework that had to be completed adequately to avoid another beating.

□ □ □ □ □

Child: Dad, why do you hit me?

Dad: Son, I don't know why. I had a bad day at work and bills are due to-morrow. I had so much tension and anger built up inside me that I was just mad at the world and you happened to be there.

Child: But Dad, you do it all the time; don't you realize that you make me scared to be around you at all. I'm always worried that you are going to haul off and hit me at any moment. You say things that make me feel bad too. I don't think that you love me. I feel like everything that goes wrong in your life is my fault and that I am worth nothing.

Dad: I don't mean to be mad at you son; it is just that I feel so bad myself and then I see you and it makes me feel even worse that you are not happy either. I don't want the responsibility to feed you all the time and to keep you entertained—it all adds pressure to the stress I have already.

Child: What would you do if you didn't have me Dad? Who would you take your anger out on then? You already went through Mom; that was why she left. You make me feel like the lowest piece of garbage on the whole earth and you made her feel that way too. You need to realize that it is you who needs to deal with your problem first. I am only a child and I should not have to deal with your frustration—it is not my fault. The bruises I get from your beatings will go away on the outside but inside they just keep getting bigger and bigger. They will never heal. The panic and fear I feel when you go off on me cannot be erased from my memory—how can you forget that kind of terror? It is like watching a horror movie. I am watching but there is nothing I can do to help.

□ □ □ □ □

The abuser who comes to mind is about 35 to 40 years of age; he has painful eyes and dark hair. He stands nearly six feet tall, average build. He is your average guy; he does not look like he could ever hurt anyone but after you've seen his anger you can. He is not really a bad person but he has had a hard life. When he was a child the same kind of father did the same kinds of things to him. He always vowed never to turn out like him but for some ironic reason he is the mirror image of that man he hated, the same looks, the same eyes.

He walks a tad bowlegged and seems to have self-confidence. He wears nice business clothes to work and casual clothes at home. On the weekends he takes care of the house and mows the yard. He lives alone with his daughter now. She does all the household chores while he does all the "men's work." He does not lay a hand on the dishes or a pan.

□ □ □ □ □

Your Daddy does not hurt you because he hates you. He loves you very much. He does not want to hit you and say mean things but he is very sad. Since your Mommy left he has been very unhappy and he wishes she would come back. Do you know how you feel when you go to school and the teacher tells you that you have to come inside because recess is over; sometimes you get mad at her because you are having such a good time playing on the playground. You get mad at your teacher but it is not her fault that recess is over. You are not really mad at the teacher but you act like you are mad at her. Well, when your daddy hurts you, it is the same thing. Your Daddy is not really mad at you; he is just angry about other things that are happening in his life.

You are not being a bad girl or doing anything wrong when your daddy hits you. When your Daddy does this to you, you need to go tell someone so that your daddy can get help from the doctor. The doctor will help your daddy get all better and then he will not hit you anymore. He will be the daddy you remember who used to take you to the playground and play catch with you in the front yard. You are a very good girl and I am very proud of you.

□ □ □ □ □

The children are victims; they are the ones who have to live with the torture for the rest of their lives and try to deal with an abusive parent along with all the other growing up they are doing that is tough enough already.

The line between spankings as punishment and when they turn into beatings is a very fine line that is difficult to draw. Many people receive spankings in childhood for getting out of line or doing something that is not acceptable to their parents.

□ □ □ □ □

LIES—OPPOSITE VIEWPOINT: The parents are right; there is no such thing as child abuse. It is all a misconception and the people who try so hard to put child abusers behind bars are all people who should mind their own business. They should worry about their own families. The kids were being brats so they deserved to get a good whipping. They are at fault and they can be blamed for everything. Kids are worth nothing and they should be treated like they are nothing. Parents are always right and never do anything wrong. The parents who abuse their children should not be punished; they should be rewarded for doing justice to the whole society. It was the kids' fault that the dog came and wet on the rug and that they did not get A's in every subject at school. It was the kids' fault that their mother ran out and is never coming back; they made her cry and leave. I never hurt her; it was just the damn kids, always screaming and yelling. I was right to hit them. Parents are too lenient on their kids these days. There is nothing like a good whipping to leave purple marks all over their puny little bodies to teach them a good lesson. They will thank me for it when they are older. I hope that they can beat their kids too, or else they will never learn discipline. All the anger I feel right now is because of them. If I did not have the kids in my life everything would be perfect. Kids cause all the problems. Nothing is my fault; it is all theirs. I know I am right.

□ □ □ □ □

They are not just beating their children for the fun of it. The children are scapegoats for their parents' frustration. They need to get help for the sources of the anger that cause abuse in the first place.

□ □ □ □ □

They are still to be held responsible for their acts and it is never acceptable to beat a child.

□ □ □ □ □

Almost more important than counseling for the parents is counseling for the children who actually have to go through this hell. They feel trapped, unable to get out, and helpless. They need a hand to grasp, a person to talk to.

COLLAGE ABOUT HUMAN DIFFERENCES

Amy Vignali

I grew up in a fairly small town in southeastern Massachusetts; middle class is definitely a word you could use to describe it. Most of the kids I went to school with had the same basic middle-class background. But working in a jewelry factory in East Providence this past summer gave me a chance to be exposed to people very different from me in many ways such as education, home life, morals, etc.

At first, I was stared at constantly as every newcomer is, and I'm sure I was viewed as a college snob by many. But as they got to know me, I was accepted by the people I worked closely with. I was known as the little freckle-faced white girl. I didn't mind the name because I knew they didn't mean any harm by it. I became particularly friendly with a black guy named Paul. By talking to him I really began to realize a lot of misconceptions people had about me. He truly believed that my parents gave me money whenever I wanted and that all white people did this. I almost laughed in his face because this is something my parents would never do. My mother once told me she'd choke on the words if she told me not to get a job. Since leaving that job, although we still keep in touch, I haven't had a chance to see Paul again. He believes that this is because he's black and I think that makes him only good enough to talk to at work. He'll never know how mad that makes me when he says that.

□ □ □ □ □

Because I've grown up in the middle class I've always believed in the American dream. I believed that everyone had the chance to be successful and there was a solution to every problem. I remember reading *Native Son* last year and not being able to believe that Bigger could not have straightened himself out. He was given a chance and he blew it, and he would blow every chance he ever had because of the circumstances of his life; he was a born loser.

One day while working at my job in the jewelry factory this summer, I found myself in a conversation with a guy named Bob. I discovered, much to my surprise, that he was well educated and had at one time shared my ambition of law school. But in his last year of school, his father became very ill and Bob was forced to quit school and get a job in order to support his family. I thought it was such a pity that he was wasting his brain doing manual labor. So a few days later I went to Bob to encourage him to finish his education and earn his law degree. But he told me that it was impossible now, he had his own family to support and could never take the time out of work. What a tragedy! Even though Bob wasn't a born loser like Bigger he had also suffered an unfortunate twist of fate and would never be able to realize his dream. I can't imagine what I would do if my life's dreams were dashed apart before my eyes.

□ □ □ □ □

"Hi Bigger!"

"Hi Amy!"

"Bigger, why couldn't you behave when you got that job for the white family?"

"I did behave. It was Mary and Jan who couldn't leave me alone. I just wanted to be left alone."

"Why did you have to go and kill Mary?"

"I didn't want to, I just wanted her to be quiet so her mother wouldn't find me in her room. I did not want to get in no trouble."

"Her mother was a good woman, she would have understood."

"You're stupid if you think that way, especially when it comes to a daughter. I don't trust no white folks."

"I guess I really don't know how you feel. I've always been among mostly whites, and I don't know how it feels to be outnumbered. But I still don't understand."

"There's nothing to understand; that's just the way things are. You can't change them."

□ □ □ □ □

Our similarities as human beings far outweigh our differences.

□ □ □ □ □

Differences. I think they're important. I love to talk to people from different places. I mean, imagine what a boring place the world would be if we all were 5'8", had blond hair and blue eyes, played racquetball on Tuesdays, ate at 6:00 every night, etc. And if everyone would view these differences as enriching aspects rather than negative ones, I think the world would be a much better place. Furthermore, I feel that everyone has prejudices even if they keep them well hidden. Although I won't deny my own feelings against certain people and things, I must admit that I had never experienced prejudiced feelings toward me until I came to U. Mass. I think it's ironic that a place that's supposed to be teaching open-mindedness is home to some of the worst discrimination.

Process Writing

Peter,

I had a lot of trouble with this assignment at every step. I have no idea what you wanted. Everything I write sounds terrible. I especially had trouble with the dialogue because every time I began a conversation in my head it sounded so predictable. I couldn't think of anyone I could have a conversation with naturally. I revised it as best I could. For some reason I concentrated mostly on the differences between whites and blacks, although I don't consider myself prejudiced.

I really wanted to write the story about Bob no matter what because that really bothered me. I also wanted to include Bigger from *Native Son* because the two circumstances were similar: people being trapped into a pattern they just can't break free from.

I found the stories and prejudices to be easier even though they blended together a lot. I find that I'm even having trouble writing this. I'm putting a lot of time and effort in, but I don't feel that it's showing. I wrote the two articles on the jewelry factory for Tuesday, and although they seemed bad to me, they sounded better when I read them to Karen. I was afraid they would be too boring, but Karen said they really made her think. I guess if I can't make people laugh, I can make them think. I sometimes think of things to write about my boyfriend, but I don't like to mention him too much and have you and the class saying, "Not another Jim story." All my roommate wrote about last semester in her class was her boyfriend, and that's still all she talks about. I'd hate to have my life depending on one thing. Sorry I got off the subject.

I think it sounded better when I read my collage out loud—I guess because I could let my voice help the words. On my second blip I had to explain a lot about what I meant concerning differences. Basically I meant that although I have the chance to go to college and succeed, not everyone else can, and therefore we are different. There are so many different factors that contribute to it. Also I had a lot of trouble deciding on how to label my town's size. I mean it's small, but not that small. About 12,000 people. It all depends on the size of the town that the person reading it comes from.

Amy Vignali

COLLABORATIVE COLLAGE ABOUT
WRITING A COLLAGE

Laura Corry, Elija Goodwin, Matt Ludvino, Denise Morey, Tassie Walsh

□ □ □ □ □

We sat around the table hearing the audible roar of gun blasts and explosions from the video games over at one end of the cafeteria. Several conversations went on at once. We spoke about anything. The work was the last thing on our mind. We were just getting to know each other.

□ □ □ □ □

The first day that we met together as a group alone, I felt kind of awkward. I didn't really know these people. Would I want to spend the semester working with them or would things be strained? I worried that perhaps there might be some kind of "impenetrable barrier" between us. However, as we sat down and began the process of getting to know each other, I began to feel more at ease and comfortable. We talked for quite a while and there was really no awkwardness, no strained moments, no long periods of quiet. As a group we seemed to hit it off. I did not feel shy about saying what I really felt.

□ □ □ □ □

When five people, different in every way, share experiences with each other, there is going to be something there. Different ideas and opinions, mannerisms, and mind-sets, sharing different pieces of themselves with each other. There is something to be learned there. Something intangible will be received whether anyone wants to or not. The ideas were already out there for everyone to see. Something will be absorbed. I have a yearning for knowledge and I have a problem with understanding people: any insight gained is definitely appreciated.

□ □ □ □ □

I think working as a group was hard because no one wanted to. No one wanted to meet for a long time and try to figure out something to write and then sit and write it. We seemed to want to find something we could do on our own and yet put it together as a group. I think part of why this happened is because we did not fully trust each other. Time is very hard for all of us, and it always seems that one person does not show up or cannot stay. How can we put our grade in the hands of a group of peers yet strangers?

□ □ □ □ □

The situation was strange. We all had ideals with no way to express them. Well, maybe it's just me. This group project really brought me down in the beginning. I've never written with anyone else before. I tried to be reasonable but no ideas would come.

□ □ □ □ □

As I sat down at the computer my mind froze up. I had had all these ideas running around in my head and now nothing. I stared at a blank screen. The hum of the computer lulling me asleep at this late hour. I started to write just to get anything down. What came out wasn't what I wanted, but it was a start. I think just the thought of writing with a theme, a topic, for the group was stifling my thoughts and creativity. Suddenly, an inspiration hit me. Yes, that was more like it. But it still needed work and more added. So I saved and shut the computer off to let the ideas ferment a little bit.

□ □ □ □ □

It was a couple of Thursdays ago; we were all determined to figure out what our group project was going to be. We thought about reviewing a book or movie. This was not a unique enough idea. We then as a group talked about writing a play. "Yea, that's it; write a play." "How will we approach it?" Yes, this would be very creative, but as a group we felt that there was a lack of time to challenge ourselves and make this work. After just telling the group that my brain was dead (mental block), I had an idea.

□ □ □ □ □

I remember when we decided on our collaborative project. Suddenly the mood changed. We all had smiles on our faces and our body movements became more relaxed. It's amazing how decision-making can cause such stress and how the larger the group the harder it is to make a decision.

□ □ □ □ □

It is harder to write in a group. I feel like these writing exercises are helpful, but each time that we are asked to do them I wonder about the content of my writing compared to the others'. I feel like I have a responsibility to the group to write well and please them.

□ □ □ □ □

We shared the writing we did by reading it out loud. This was almost ritualistic when the group met.

□ □ □ □ □

Even in a small group, it is hard to get together at a set time. Everyone is so busy. It got easier when the group got comfortable with each other because we realized that we would do fine even with the absence of one person.

□ □ □ □ □

Everyone must be there and contributing. When one person doesn't show or can't make it, like when I had exams, it really seems to disrupt the group. It is hard to make decisions, and you miss that person's input to bounce off of. Once a group is formed, each piece is sort of essential for it to work. When someone has another obligation, things really seem to fall apart.

□ □ □ □ □

When I work in a group I get very nervous. There have been too many times when I have had to do more work than others and yet we get the same grade. Or, because of something someone else did, I did not get as good a grade as I should have. Because of this, I don't like working in groups. If I have to, I am always the one asking if people have finished their part and making sure that they know exactly what they should do.

□ □ □ □ □

Here I am again, back at the Newman Center, staring mindlessly at the grain of the table top. I can barely hear the others' discussion over the bang of my thoughts. It's not that I don't care; it's just that after a while you get burnt out and need to drain the cluttered pool in your head. I sometimes feel a little suffocated this semester. Not because of this class alone, but because of the combined workload of all my classes. It seems like I'm being held underwater for two minutes at a time. I thrash at the invisible hands until they let me go, but only long enough to catch a gasping breath. Then I'm submerged again in a block of water looking up as the sun's rays hit the surface, distorting the skyline.

□ □ □ □ □

Whenever the group found itself confused about something, I always tried to give my best input and knowledge. In the group, I always made sure that I knew what the assignment was, when it was due, and so on. Knowing myself, I am aware that when I am involved in any group I like to participate in this way. Yet I am shy and I feel timid when I have to speak aloud. This weakness became less noticeable as I became more comfortable with the group.

□ □ □ □ □

When I work in a group I am sort of on the outskirts. I stay fairly quiet, occasionally voice ideas when I feel they are important, support others' ideas when I feel they are good. But when it comes down to making decisions, I usually can be happy and work with any decision that is made, so I let others battle it out while I watch.

□ □ □ □ □

The best part of working in a group is being able to bounce off each other's ideas. When we start talking, even about seemingly unrelated topics, we start identifying with each other or disagreeing, and that makes us think about things in ways we hadn't before. Soon we are coming up with a pretty good description of school and how we have reacted to it. Problems we've had in the past and why. It starts off pretty informally and soon we have a wealth of learning and potential papers.

PROCESS NOTES ABOUT COLLABORATIVE WRITING (EXCERPTS)

Kathy Reckendorf

Well, the book review is finished and Deb, Tracey and I are still friends. I wonder, however, how we'd feel after yesterday's marathon session if we hadn't started out as friends. If I'd been with "strangers" for this project, I'm afraid it would have been quite painful at times. So anyhow, here's the process (or *my* version of it) that we used.

As you know, we began with a dialogue on the computer. We took turns writing observations and responses about our books over the course of a week or so during our free periods and after school. We didn't talk to each other in person about what we were writing; we just wrote and responded on the computer. This was fun for me. I felt Deb and Tracey were a "safe" audience and I knew much of what I was writing was going to be scrapped, so I felt free to just ramble on about whatever happened to come to mind.

The next step was to print out a hard copy which we then went over in class last week. We made a list of what seemed to be the most important points we wanted to cover in the actual book review. We came up with a total of six points which we divided between the three of us. Once we had our assignments, we worked individually on them, then brought our work together and merged it onto one disk.

□ □ □ □ □

All this made me think about my style of writing and question whether it was OK to take the long, rambling route so often. Up until this assignment, it never occurred to me that I should give it up and *try* to get to the point more directly. I *like* taking the longer scenic route both when I read and when I write. Unfortunately, I found with this assignment that you can't always have your druthers, especially in a collaborative setting.

□ □ □ □ □

Back to the group process. With a little bit of cutting and moving on the computer, we had our "first draft." We printed out a hard copy for each of us to look over, and planned to meet for the heavy duty editing Friday after school. After reading the whole document, Deb went back in and changed her introduction before we got together, and we each read and made marginal comments in preparation for our editing session. I found myself feeling awkward about editing Tracey and Deb's sections; I only picked out typos and usage problems. With my own stuff, I felt more secure in making initial changes in wording.

□ □ □ □ □

Once we retyped and printed, we decided to read each paragraph out loud and edit on the hard copy if necessary. The author of each paragraph did the reading. We commented mostly on stylistic issues—things that were too wordy or imprecisely written. No comments on content though. That's quite interesting, actually. For the main part of the paper, we didn't change anyone's ideas/thoughts/content. . . . As I had expected, my sections also had to be majorly redone because of their excessive wordiness; most of the time it was a simple matter of crossing out unnecessary words and phrases, and in some cases, combining ideas more precisely.

□ □ □ □ □

This is one of the reasons that working with friends seems better. "Sublimely suitable" didn't seem all that foolish when I wrote it, but I knew beyond a doubt that it was *awful* in the split second before it came out of my mouth. I started laughing before I ever got the line out, and then, when Deb and Tracey read ahead, they joined me. I don't know if it was exhaustion, frustration, embarrassment or what, but I couldn't stop laughing and before long all three of us were looking for Kleenex. It took a good ten minutes before we could continue. If I had been among strangers I would have been mortified. With Deb and Tracey it ended up being a few minutes of comic relief.

□ □ □ □ □

Maybe the most important part of our collaboration was the conclusion, since it is the only part of the paper that we truly wrote together. Tracey and I had each written a paragraph that would have served as a conclusion. . . . Deb and Tracey experimented with brand new conclusions for 15 to 20 minutes while I typed. They were both getting frustrated, so I joined them when I finished. I suggested we make a list of what points we wanted to make in the conclusion, so we brainstormed for five minutes. Then we all started throwing out lines and writing down the ones we liked. After we had a few of them, I moved over to the computer and asked them to read back what we had come up with so far. I typed it in and they looked over my shoulder. We read it out loud and spent about twenty minutes changing a word here, a phrase there, trying to tie our points together.

□   □   □   □   □

WORKSHOP

4

PRIVATE WRITING: FINDING WHAT YOU HAVE TO SAY

In this workshop we want to teach you that you always have lots to write about and that you can always get it on paper without agony. We will show you two processes for using private writing to find things to say: Sondra Perl's guidelines for composing and the open-ended writing process. Most important of all, we want to convince you that your best writing may consist of material you didn't know you had in mind.

Think of this workshop as a presentation of the basic *foundation* for writing: learning how to keep on writing after you run out of things "in mind." Once you learn to do this, you'll realize that you can always keep going even when you feel stuck. You can apply this basic ability to all writing occasions. Often textbooks tell students: "Think before you write." Here we are trying to show you the reverse: how writing can *lead* to thinking.

Just as important, we hope you will discover the benefits of *private writing.* In this workshop you will produce a lot of private writing. In the next workshop, you'll learn ways to make use of private writing for producing public writings. If you're interested in reading more about the theory behind these practices, you can turn to "Ruminations and Theory" at the end of this workshop.

 MAIN ASSIGNMENT

1. Produce at least ten pages of private writing by using the Perl guidelines and/or the open-ended process. Thus we're asking for a considerable amount of writing with no assigned topic: you work with whatever topics are most important for you. No one but you will see this writing (though your teacher might insist that you flash an impressive wad of pages to show that you have done this exploratory writing at home as well as in class). You can emphasize one method or the other in your private writing, depending on which one is more helpful to you. There are samples of both kinds of writing at the end of the workshop.

2. Write two to three pages of process writing about what happens when you work on the Perl guidelines and the open-ended process. Your teacher may ask you to build a genuine essay or draft out of this process writing—unified and reaching some definite conclusions. Or she may ask for a collage. Or she may invite this writing to be rough—just two or three pages of the best bits of your process writing slightly cleaned up but not shaped into a unified, connected essay. At the end of the workshop, you'll find some samples of process writing about the private writing. Remember that there are many different, equally valid ways of making an essay from process writing.

 SONDRA PERL'S COMPOSING GUIDELINES

The writing guidelines will help you discover what is on your mind and *almost* on your mind. If they seem artificial, think of them as "exercises." But they are exercises that will help you to perform certain subtle but crucial mental operations that most skilled and experienced writers do naturally:

I got out this diary, & read as one always does read one's own writing, with a kind of guilty intensity. I confess that the rough & random style of it, often so ungrammatical, & crying for a word altered, afflicted me somewhat. I am trying to tell whichever self it is that reads this hereafter that I can write very much better; & take no time over this; & forbid her to let the eye of man behold it. . . . But what is more to the point is my belief that the habit of writing thus for my own eye only is good practise. It loosens the ligaments. Never mind the misses & the stumbles. Going at such a pace as I do I must make the most direct & instant shots at my object, & thus have to lay hands on words, choose them, & shoot them with no more pause than is needed to put my pen in the ink. I believe that during the past year I can trace some increase of ease in my professional writing which I attribute to my casual half hours after tea.

Virginia Woolf

- Continue writing, even when you don't know where you're going.
- Periodically pause and ask, "What's this all about?"
- Periodically check what you have written against your *internal* sense of where you're going or what you want to say—your "felt sense."

Your teacher may guide you by reading the guidelines out loud, or else ask you to guide yourself by following the guidelines from the book. You need at least thirty or forty minutes. If it feels mechanical to follow them in a group setting, remember that the goal is to teach you a procedure you can use on your own. Trying them out in class is a way to give you a taste of the experience. After some practice with the directives or questions that follow, you'll be able to sense how to distribute your time yourself.*

Remember that this is private writing. You don't have to show it to anyone. You may end up with pieces you want to share, but that's a decision for later.

1. Find a way to get comfortable. Shake out your hand. Take some slow, deep breaths and settle into your chair. Close your eyes if you'd like to. Relax. Find a way to be quietly and comfortably aware of your inner state. Try to let go of any tension by slow breathing.

2. Ask yourself, "What's going on with me right now? Is there anything in the way of my writing today?" When you hear yourself answering, take a minute to jot down a list of any distractions or impediments that come to mind. If there are noises or other distractions, notice them, and then bring your attention back to yourself.

3. Now ask yourself, "What's on my mind? Of all the things I know about, what might I like to write about now?" When you hear yourself answering, jot down what comes. Maybe you get one thing; maybe a list. If you feel totally

---

We thank Perl for permission to copy these guidelines. We have made tiny modifications—mostly just some cutting. Sondra Perl is a professor of English at Herbert H. Lehman College and founder of the New York City Writing Project.

blocked, you may write down "Nothing." Even this can be taken further by asking yourself, "What is this 'Nothing' all about?"

4. Ask yourself, "Now that I have a list—long or short—is there anything I've left out, any other piece I'm overlooking, maybe even a word I like, something else I might want to write about sometime that I can add to this list?" Add anything that comes to mind.

5. Whether you have one definite idea or a whole list of things, look over what you have and ask, "What here draws my attention right now? What could I begin to write about, even if I'm not certain where it will lead?" Take the idea, word, or item and put it at the top of a new page. (Save the first page for another time.)

6. Now—taking a deep breath and settling comfortably into your chair—ask yourself, "What are all the things I know about this topic and all the associations I have with it? What can I say about it now?" Spend as long as you need writing down these responses. Perhaps it will be a sustained piece of freewriting or stream of consciousness, or perhaps separate bits, or notes to yourself.

7. Now having written for a good while, interrupt yourself, set aside all the writing you've done, and take a fresh look at this topic or issue. Grab hold of the *whole* topic—not the bits and pieces—and ask yourself, "What makes this topic interesting to me? What's *important* about this that I haven't said yet? What's the *heart* of this issue for me?" Wait quietly for a *word, image,* or *phrase* to arise from your "felt sense" of the topic. Write whatever comes. (For more on "felt sense," see "Ruminations and Theory" at the end of this workshop.)

8. Take this word, image, or phrase, and use it to explore further. Ask yourself, "What's this all about?" As you write, let the "felt sense" deepen. Where do you feel that "felt sense"? Where in your body does it seem centered? Ask yourself, "Is this right? Am I getting closer? Am I saying it?" If not, ask yourself, "What is wrong or missing?" and keep writing. See if you can feel when you're on the right track. See if you can feel the shift or click inside when you get close: "Oh yes, this says it."

9. If you're at a dead end, you can ask yourself, "What makes this topic hard for me?" Again pause and see if a word, image, or phrase comes to you that captures this difficulty in a fresh way—and if it will lead you to some more writing.

10. When you find yourself stopping, ask, "What's missing? What hasn't yet gotten down on paper?" and again look to your "felt sense" for a word or an image. Write what comes to mind.

11. When again you find yourself stopping, ask yourelf, "Where is this leading? What's the point I'm trying to make?" Again write down whatever comes to mind.

12. Once you feel you're near or at the end, ask yourself, "Does this feel complete?" Look to your "felt sense," your gut reaction, even to your body, for the answer. Again write down whatever answer comes to you. If the answer is "No," pause and ask yourself, "What's missing?" and continue writing.

These guidelines work differently for different people—and even differently for you on different occasions. The main thing to remember is that they are meant for you to use on your own, flexibly, in your own way. There is nothing sacred about the exact format or wording. They are not meant to be a strait-jacket. To help you in adapting them to your own needs, here is a list of what are probably the four pivotal moments:

- Relax, stretch, clear your mind, try to attend quietly to what's inside—and note any distractions or feelings that may be preventing you from writing. Allow yourself to be aware of your body and your physical surroundings.

- Start with a list of things you *could* write about. Often we can't find what we really want to write about until the third or fourth item—or not until that subtle after-question, "Is there something else I might have forgotten?"

- As you are writing, periodically pause and look to that felt sense somewhere inside you—that feeling, image, or word that somehow represents what you are trying to get at—and ask whether your writing is really getting at it. This comparing or checking back ("Is this it?") will often lead to a productive "shift" in your mind ("Oh, now I see what it is I want to say").

- Finally, toward the end, ask, "What's this all about? Where does this writing seem to be trying to go?" And especially ask, "What's missing? What *haven't* I written about?"

The specific details of the procedure are much less important than the charitable, supportive, and generative spirit behind the whole thing. (In the "Readings" at the end of the workshop, we have printed the writing Peter

---

PROCESS BOX

On Writing When Using Perl Guidelines

Didn't write what I intended to write—intended to be pragmatic—write out what I *needed* to write out. But someway the other topic forced itself on me and became too exciting to ignore. Topic appeared on paper when I searched my head for something I really wanted to write about. Found all the prompts helpful except one.

The nonhelpful one was, "Use image, idea, phrase, and keep trying to get it right"—because it felt right to me already. The spot when I started on metaphor and metonomy. Don't know why I got on that. Doesn't connect in very well—and yet I know there's a connection, and I guess I saw it as relevant. But I did drop it when Peter said, "Where is this going?"

While writing, I found pleasant revelings coming forth and thought, "Gee! These are good ideas!" Thought of typing it up and giving copies to Peter and Don for comment—not sure I was thinking of them as audiences. Didn't really feel I was writing for them as I wrote—they came to mind because I know they have thoughts on these subjects. I'd like them both to think I'm on to something good—but I'm really wanting this idea worked out for myself. Believe they could help me do that.

I did have some feeling of going around in circles, not putting things together into one Bingo result—but I do think there's stuff there to explore. I'm glad I wrote this.

Pat Belanoff

Elbow did using the Perl guidelines—writing that formed the basis of Mini-workshop D, "Writing with a Word Processor.")

 THE OPEN-ENDED WRITING PROCESS

The open-ended process is another way to encourage exploratory, private writing. Where the Perl guidelines help you find words for what is sort of in your mind but not in words, the open-ended process pushes you to figure out entirely new thoughts and ideas that are as yet nowhere near your mind.

The open-ended process consists of a simple movement back and forth between two basic activities: *freewriting* and *summing-up.*

Start by freewriting. (Or, start by listing things you *might* write about and then start freewriting.) Simply explore whatever topics emerge for you *while* you're doing this unfocused freewriting.

After ten or fifteen minutes of freewriting, stop and look back or think over what you've written. (Pause, take a deep breath, stretch, look around.) Then write down a sentence, phrase, or image to summarize the most interesting or important thing you find in your freewriting. Look for a center of gravity: that piece of your writing that seems to pull on you the most strongly. You don't have to try for an accurate or objective summary of your freewriting. You might focus on some small detail from your freewriting if that seems the most important to you now. You might even write down a thought that didn't occur in your freewriting but occurs to you now as you pause. The point of these summings-up is to provide a springboard for your next piece of freewriting, your next dive into language.

For that's the next step: more freewriting. As you write, learn to keep on writing even if you don't know where you are going. Learn to ride waves of writing for longer and longer periods of time. When words start to run out after only five minutes, force yourself to keep going. Remember, you don't have to stay on the same subject. Write "What else could I write about?" and "What else?" and keep on writing to see what comes. The goal is to lose yourself in language, to lose perspective.

Then stop again to sum up. And so on.

Follow this back-and-forth chain of freewriting and summing-up wherever it leads you.

The open-ended process gets its power from alternating two contrary kinds of mentality or two opposed ways of producing language. During the freewriting you are *immersed* in your words: your head is down and you are tumbling along in an underbrush of language; you tend to be working more in words than in thoughts. Indeed the *goal* is to get lost in the words and not worry about the thoughts or where they are going.

When you pause and sum up, you use a completely different mentality or way of producing language. You extricate yourself from the underbrush of words and, as it were, climb up a tall tree to see where you have gotten yourself: you seek perspective and detachment. In this process you are trying to work more in thoughts than in words. These summing-up sentences or phrases help keep your freewriting productive. For if you do nothing but freewrite for hours and never stop to climb a tree, you sometimes just go in circles.

As you move back and forth between the two activities, sometimes your writing will change: in subject, in mode, or in style. For example, having written the story of what happened to you, your pausing and summing-up may lead you to see that you now need to write about the *person* who was involved in that event. Let these changes occur. Perhaps you've been writing to yourself, and now you realize you want to write to someone else—a letter, perhaps. You may even want to write a poem or a prayer or a dialogue. Sometimes the open-ended writing will lead you closer and closer to what you were trying to get at from the beginning; but sometimes it takes you far afield to something new that surprises you.

Your teacher may well introduce the open-ended process in class. Sitting and writing privately in a public group might seem odd at first—just as it did with the Perl guidelines. But again, we want you to practice this new procedure *once* with some direction. Otherwise you tend to drift into your usual writing habits. The goal is to learn a *new* writing process so that you can then use it flexibly by yourself.

 ## PROCESS WRITING ASSIGNMENT

Make sure to do process writing each time you use each method, whether in or out of class. Here are some questions or prompts that might help you notice and describe more of what happens:

- What happened in using the Perl process? In particular:
  - When finding or choosing your original topic?
  - When pausing to sum up in a phrase or image or to get yourself focused on your chosen topic?
  - When seeking your "felt sense" and checking your writing against it?
- What happened in using the open-ended process? In particular:
  - When finding or choosing the idea you started with?
  - When summing up or finding a center of gravity?
  - What about the overall path or progression? Where did it take you?
- What did you notice about the difference between doing these processes in class and at home? In what ways did the teacher's prompts help? get in the way?
- So much of this week's writing is *private.* How did this affect *what* you wrote and *how* you wrote?
- What did you learn about your writing? language? thinking? And what did you learn about writing, language, and thinking in general by comparing your experience with that of your classmates?

In order to produce your piece of writing for sharing with your teacher and probably with other students, read through all of your process writing and decide which events and moments and themes seem the most important. Your teacher will tell you whether she wants you to produce a collage or an essay. For a collage you can obviously select from the pieces you have already writ-

In the freewriting we did today, I see some possibilities for subjects to write about. What interested me was that I didn't feel compelled to put the ideas into the final form I intend to use. In the light of this, I was more able to get the flood of thoughts out on paper for observation. I can see what I think and am able to discard things that don't hold my interest longer than a few seconds. There are lots of germs in my open writing. It is a road for me to wander along and maybe pick up bits of dried grass, some flowers, shells and a few rocks.

Jo Ferrell

ten, using the procedures we described in Workshop 1 for cleaning them up and arranging them. For an essay, you may need to make more changes and do more thinking or writing to figure out a main point or main conclusion. But you will obviously be able to use a number of passages from the process writing you've already done. Consult your teacher for how much revising she wants on this assignment—how polished a draft you should turn in.

 ## POSSIBILITIES FOR COLLABORATION

If your teacher invites or asks for collaboration, there are various possibilities. Two or three of you could write a *dialogue* about your experiences with the Perl guidelines and the open-ended process. One person might start the conversation with a question or an observation or a description of something that happened to her as she was writing. Then the next person takes the paper and writes a response. Then the third person, and so on. If there are more than two people, you can get everyone to write in the same order, or invite the conversation to jump around according to who most wants to make the next entry. But don't let one or two people hog the conversation. (A dialogue works well on a computer: people take turns with the keyboard. If you have linked or networked computers, you can create the dialogue with all participants writing from their own terminal. You can even create a class dialogue.)

Collages lend themselves to collaboration. Two to four of you can produce a group portrait by creating a longer collage out of pieces drawn from all your process writing. You can also collaborate more closely and produce a co-written essay. This will take more planning and discussing. See Workshop 3 for more about collaborating.

 ## SHARING AND RESPONDING

Of course you will not get any response to your exploratory writing since it is all private. But you might want some responses on your process writing, either at an early or late stage. "Summary and Sayback," "Pointing and Center of Gravity," and "Metaphorical Descriptions" in *Sharing and Responding* at the end of the book, will give you helpful methods for feedback. Here are a few additional questions for you to ask when you share your process writing:

- "Which parts interest you the most or stick the most in your mind?"
- "What do you hear me *saying* in my process writing? Not saying?"
- "What aspects of the writing process do I seem the most interested in and the least interested in?"
- "What did you learn from my process writing that could be useful to you?"

 RUMINATIONS AND THEORY

Private Writing: Why Write It If No One Will See It?

What's the Sense in Felt Sense?

Private Writing: Why Write It If No One Will See It?

We tend to assume that the goal of writing is to end up with words on paper for others to see. Usually that is our goal, but sometimes we get better words for readers in the long run if we start out writing *not* for readers.

And *sometimes* our goal is not even to produce words for readers. More often than you might realize, the goal of writing is to end up with some new *understanding* or *thinking* or *feeling*. The writing that led to it may be unimportant or can even be thrown away. Most teachers collect and read all the writing they assign, but if you really ask them, most of them would admit that the writing isn't what's most important or valuable: it's the students' new knowledge and understanding.

Of course readers are helpful. Sometimes it's hard to get yourself to write unless you have a reader. But private writing has special power to lead you to new insight. It's only when writing is private that you can take the biggest risks, or explore thoughts that others might think are wrong or dumb, or explore feelings that others might think are weird or wrong. It's hard to really explore what is happening in your mind if you have to let someone else see your words straight off. Privacy can help you feel safer to explore what readers might not like. Private writing reduces the pervasive pressure of the social context around us. A traditional form of private writing—the diary or journal—has long given people a chance to feel what they want to feel, and even *be* what they want to be, apart from how others want them to feel or be. Private writing gives *space*.

Some of you may find private writing difficult at first. You may scarcely have written anything except what you hand in to a teacher. "Why write it if she's not going to read it?" you may feel. But this is exactly the feeling we want to help you get past. You can't write well until you really *own* your writing—yet how can you really own it if you always have to check it with someone else?

But if you haven't done much private writing, you may find that it's hard to get "energized" for it; you miss a kind of alertness or pressure that an audi-

From a Student Journal

B.S. the ability to write in length and say little. It's easy to say nothing and fill up space. If I wanted to, I could fill up this page and the next, without saying a thing about myself. That was an example of B.S., a writing form that's in very low standing, I'm sure, in many English classes. For some students it's easier to fill a page with nonsense, that doesn't seem like nonsense, than to fulfill their requirements of writing about themselves. Again this is an example of going around in circles to fill space and to make it look like a person has done their work when in reality they haven't. The ability to do this over a long period is not hard for some people; for others it's hard to think of what to say, or write next. Like me for instance I had trouble with that last line; it took me five minutes to think of something to say. That, again, is an example of writing anything to fill space. I lied; it didn't take five minutes to write down those sentences; I had them planned out ahead of time. I also had the confession thought of before I got to it. It was a way to fill space, to tell you I lied, then to tell you I didn't, then to tell you about the whole thing. Just to fill space. Going around and around to fill space can get the reader and the writer confused. As you can see, I spent the whole page trying to explain about writing to fill space; if you do it long enough it's hard to stop. Again, I'm telling you I should stop, to fill these last few lines. The best way to stop, when you've tried your best to fill up the space is to just, STOP! (Because if you don't you'll just keep going & going & going & going. . . .)

---

ence puts on you to stay on your toes. Talking to listeners can get your juices flowing. But you can always show your writing to an audience later: we're just asking you to assume it's private *while* writing and not let yourself show it to readers except as a later separate step (and then only if you want to).

You may even find it slightly scary to be invited to write privately about "whatever comes": you may have some unpleasant thoughts or feelings—some piece of unhappiness or fear—that you know will come up but which you don't want to deal with.

It's true that these thoughts and feelings will come: anything that's important will come. But it turns out that private writing gives you a chance to *let go* of thoughts and feelings that are clogging up your head and getting in your way. Oddly enough, once you write things down, you can more easily move beyond them and not feel their pressure. Writing is a way to let something go.

For a striking example of using private writing to let go of what is unhelpful, consider Ray Knight's private writing. Here we have a successful major league baseball player who was dropped from his team and then made a strong comeback. What follows is from an interview with him after his comeback:

RESURRECTING A CAREER

The test for him came last fall when he went home to Albany, Ga., and considered that he was standing at the crossroads of his career.

"Your physical ability gets you to the big leagues," he reasoned. . . . "Your mental ability keeps you there. And I knew I had the mental ability."

"So, I got very strong physically. I lifted weights for the first time in three or four years. I built a batting cage. . . . But the key was that I made up my mind I was going to show Dave [Johnson, the coach] I could do it."

"I started writing down my thoughts in a book—my notes. If I had a positive thought, I'd write it down at once. If I had a negative thought, I'd write it down and scratch it out." (Durso 53)

We have met teachers who think that their students have nothing to write about because they are "too young" or have led "sheltered lives" or "can't think"—or have such inferior writing skills that they should not be invited to write about whatever is on their minds. It's not surprising that some students and teachers have been fooled into thinking this way because of the following experience. The teacher says, "OK, now you can write about whatever you want to write about." But the student, given complete choice, can't think of anything to write; she goes blank, feels empty or bored. Or else she starts off strong but runs out of things to say after only a short burst of writing. After this experience even the student may be tricked into feeling, "Oh dear, I have *nothing* to write about."

But to engage in private writing for extended stretches as in this workshop is to discover that this experience is misleading. You discover that at any moment of the day or night, even if you are completely bored and out of the mood for writing, your head is nevertheless full of rich material to write about. It is this confidence in having *plenty* to say—in inner fecundity—that provides an important foundation for *all* future writing.

Here is an eloquent personal statement by a distinguished writer about private writing for exploring:

> I am following a process that leads so wildly and originally into new territory that no judgment can at the moment be made about values, significance, and so on. I am making something new, something that has not been judged before. Later others—and maybe I myself—will make judgments. Now, I am headlong to discover. Any distraction may harm the creating.
>
> So, receptive, careless of failure, I spin out things on the page. And a wonderful freedom comes. If something occurs to me, it is all right to accept it. It has one justification: it occurs to me. No one else can guide me. I must follow my own weak, wandering diffident impulses.
>
> A strange bonus happens. At times, without my insisting on it, my writings become coherent: the successive elements that occur to me are clearly related. They lead by themselves to new connections. Sometimes the language, even the syllables that happen along, may start a trend. Sometimes the materials alert me to something waiting in my mind, ready for sustained attention. (Stafford 18–19)

We know all of you can discover what William Stafford discovered, but no one discovers it unless she gives herself the freedom to risk, and perhaps to try out new ways of writing privately (such as the Perl guidelines, the open-ended process, and the loop writing you did in Workshop 3). For more perspective on private writing and its relation to writing for different kinds of audiences, see "About Audience" in "Ruminations and Theory," Workshop 5.

What's the Sense in Felt Sense?

In one sense, of course, we *don't* know something until we have it in words. But in another sense we do indeed know quite a lot, and it's a question of learning how to tap it better.

Why does Sondra Perl ask us about something as vague as felt sense? and ask us where we feel it *in our body?* Why such a nutty approach? The answer to the question leads us to one of the most important issues in writing—both practically and theoretically. The issue is this: What do we have "in mind" before we have words for it? Is it some set of different words farther inside our head—fainter or in smaller print? If so, what lies behind *them* to guide or produce them? Behind our words, then, inevitably, must be some *non*verbal feeling or "sense."

You can easily prove this mysterious phenomenon by asking yourself, after you've been writing a while, the crucial question: "Is this what I've been wanting to say?" What's interesting is that we can almost always answer this question. So then we need to ask, "What is the *basis* for our answer—for our being able to say, 'Yes, this really *is* what I was wanting to say,' or 'No, that's not it,' or 'Sort of, but not quite'?" We haven't got *words* for what's in mind, but we have *something* against which we can match the words we've used—in order to see whether they are adequate to our intention. We may not have the *right* words to say what we want to say, but we do know what we want to say well enough to recognize when our words are right or wrong, closer or farther away.

"Felt sense" is what Eugene Gendlin has named this internal knowledge or awareness that we call on. And his point—which we too want to emphasize—is that we can learn to call on it better. It may seem odd or unfashionable to suggest that our felt sense of what we're writing about might be located in a part of the body. But many people experience what's "in mind" not just "in the head" but also—as they say—"in the gut."

The crucial operation in the Perl process is when you pause and attend to that felt sense—pause and say, "What's my *feeling* for what I'm getting at?" (or "What's my image or word?"). You *then* ask yourself, "Have I managed to *say* what I'm getting at?" The most productive situation, ironically, is when you answer "No." For in that moment of experiencing a *mis*match or *non*fit between your words and your felt sense, *you tend to experience a click or shift that moves you closer to knowing this thing that you can't yet say.* In short, pausing, checking, and saying "No" usually lead you to better words.

One reason people don't pause and check their words against their felt sense often enough is that they get too discouraged about the mismatch. They think that the question is a test and that "No" means they've failed the test. ("*Again* I've proved that I'm no good at finding words!") They don't realize that if you ask the question of yourself in the right way—in a charitable and constructive spirit—"No" is the better answer: it can always lead you to a better understanding of what you are trying to get at.

Remember, however, that when we urge you to attend more to your felt sense and then pause and check your words against it, we're *not* saying that thing that perhaps you've heard too often: "Stop! What is your *thesis?*" That's not our question. We're asking instead: "What is the physical feeling or image you have that somehow *stands for* what you're wanting to say?" You haven't got a thesis yet—haven't *got* the right words yet—but you do have a genuinely available felt knowledge for what you're trying to get at. If you check any trial set of words against that feeling, you can tell whether or not they are what you were trying to say.

For a concrete and vivid example of how this works—this recurrent process of checking your words against a felt sense in order to gradually figure out what you really mean—see the short passage written by Eugene Gendlin in the "Readings" for this workshop.

Readings

EXAMPLE OF OPEN-ENDED WRITING*

Melissa Fogel

Alienation . . . like being alone, like feeling shut out, with no friends, no one to turn to. then there is a light, somewhere down that halll, of someone who feels the same someone who shares in the utter feeling of alone. shes warm and kind and she knows how to feel.

□ □ □ □ □

    I called, he was warm and sharing the way he said I love you last noght was with care, like he was beginning to know what it means to say those words, to say them and to mean them. sometimes I feel like I don't have a problem sometimes I feel like my only friend is the city we live in the city of angels lonely as I am together we cry. so becky banged andy. so I have Jeff. I cant wait fgor the dream sequence its so beautiful and lovely, lovely what a cheesy word, its white and red and everything is like the dawn, foggy yet glissening. I cant wait, only a couple of more days. The times I feel alone, are sometimes truthful other times they are brought on by my own anxieties, and that scares me more than being alone. Today is blue and blue, ironic I wear those colors right now. The banquet is tonight. and that horrible horrible neophite ceremony. Why scare others. I don't want others to feel the fear I experience so often. Expose them to sunshine, not thunder storms. The rain was coming down hard, and the crash of thunder was so monstrous, I thought I would hide my head under the pillow. I remember the raccoon, it just jumped right out at me. Initiation is a time to reflect on the meaning of Kappa, it is a time to recognize all the good of sisterhood, I look forward to experiencing the other side of the beauty. Oh joy another hour and a half.

□ □ □ □ □

    Who am I? Where do I go from here?

□ □ □ □ □

How is it that we can print this private writing in public? Peter Elbow used the open-ended writing process with a class and went through the whole cycle: from doing private writing to producing a public piece. After all this, he asked whether any students would be willing to let him see their private writing. He thought Melissa Fogel's was interesting and would serve as a good example for the book, and he asked her permission to use it. You'll see her public writing in the next workshop. We have not corrected any of Melissa's typing mistakes (it was a computer classroom) since we want to highlight the fact that this is informal private writing where there is no concern for mechanics.

I am Melissa the great the wonderful, with a face of anger, sometimes happiness, I guess it depends on the mood my life has. The tone of the day almost like writing, whats the tone melissa, why I do not know, the tone today is fun, happy, get it done, eat and merry, be loyal to kappa. Its blue day for gods sake, your favorite color in the world, Jeff's too. Is he far away thinking of me now. I am so shungry right now I wish I had finished that slim fast shake, since we will be here for the entire time. now that I am totally off track. I wonder if I am the only sophomore that is taking this class. Good thing I took, that horrible typing class in the eleventh grade. Well lets try to get deeper . . . If I stay and let myself be subject to the life I create for myself, I accept without hesitation or sigh that life, the one where I stay in Mass. and live on expressing myself through friends and family, that family I call Kappa. If I go I delete that, its just not worth it today anyway, tomorrow ask me again. When I think about jeff he scares me, not because he scares me physically, not even him. Its the idea of having a boyfriend again that scares me. falling in love again means sacrificing my feelings for another, it means taking the risk of somehow being left, being alone again and learning to cope all over again. Danny left me high and dry, now I cant stand him, but I'm over him. gone. Jeff is the sweetest, he's everything a girl could ask for and the physical is slowly slipping into place, which might be better for me, who knows. All I know right now is that I miss him, miss him to death.

□ □ □ □ □

Our hearts meet somewhere along a sea of lonliness, somewhere among the vast mountains of trust. Then my hand grabs his, and we walk the path I call life.

□ □ □ □ □

And so this class drags on. . and on. . Maybe if I try to save her I can. No she is brain washed, lost in the crowd of men who want to take her away from our family. for so long it was tight, together we shared not always with words but with actions and he the masked ass of the century destroyed that closeness in one fell swoop. She is only a child looking for some attention, he could see that in her lost eyes of a sea of blue. See that she was crying out of the term middle, he seized her while she cried, and gave her a shoulder to lean on, why did she fall. Because we all looked away for a split second and she was gone. Now we all pay. . . I just want her to be happy. She wont with him, even though he was there when we were busy, he is a do nothing a go nowhere. and she lives with that, nothing else. Can I stop and help you little girl. Do you need my shoulder to cry on, I won't hurt you in the end, I am sister I will not leave. I am sister, trust me please. My little brat from behind, catch up come play in the yard with us, no I want to swing, swing in the rain. It feels good on my tongue. But it is not safe little girl, don't you see it's not safe. She falls quick, hard under the swing set, we don't see her. Wait I see her. She lies in a pool of mud and blood. Someone help her she is falling. Now she is falling again into another pool of mud and blood. This time the consequences more than a couple of stitches. but wait do you remember sister? The stitces did not hurt the little girl, she asked for a piece of gum, maybe there is hope, maybe she will survive with a smile left on her time beaten face. Maybe she will live and live long with the family, the ones who forgive and forget, nomatter what you do or say, or who you go out with.

□ □ □ □ □

So I am alone and afraid of feeling alone. Should I go and do something about this, or work through it, like so many other times, by myself. I also look forward to the end of this week with all the beauty it possesses. The song the laughter and the fun at the end of it all. I am also fearing the closeness I have with Jeff. It scares me, to think I fall again. Then there is my sister, Will she be o.k. boy you have a lot to think about!!!!

Cover Letter

Dear Peter,

I have participated in this exercise before. The amount of freedom is so amazing. The feeling of writing whatever your mind may find deep within its core allows the writer to express herself without any fear of denial. I do believe some of our writing in this fine University of ours is extremely narrow and limited. One has guidelines and rules and finds oneself lacking creativity. This type of writing had me smiling again, with my fingers typing away, yearning for more and more. However, because I am so used to being confined in my writing, my thoughts did not wander as much as they used to. I found myself staying on one topic very diligently. With more practice I could probably find creative aspects of writing lurking behind the closed doorway.

I found that a bunch of my underlying fears of whatever seemed deep in my thoughts, would surface, no matter how hard I tried to retain them. Maybe this sort of writing is a release from the everyday tensions. It did remind me of diary writing: the kind of writing that enables you to let go of your anxieties and fears, to come up with solutions to the problems you write about.

The honesty of my writing today was present. There was a lack of superficial qualities in my writing. I wasn't putting up a front for a professor, or running for a thesaurus to help improve my wording. I was me, a horrible speller and a not-so-great writer. I was creative and I enjoyed the writing experience.

My heart and soul was in this writing today, something I haven't felt in years!!!

Sincerely,
Melissa Fogel

PROCESS LOG ABOUT USING THE OPEN-ENDED PROCESS

Manuel Depina

As I was doing the private writing, I struggled tremendously, especially with the open-ended process. I went through the open-ended guidelines. I read them about twenty-five times, and still couldn't come up with anything. I couldn't figure out how to do the mechanics and compose it in a way which I would feel most comfortable with.

I followed everything that was in the guidelines. I shook off my hands, took a deep breath, closed my eyes, and still the paper in front of me was blank. I couldn't get myself to relax and concentrate like I usually do. This was probably due to the different method and procedure that I would normally follow.

Believe it or not, reading the guidelines for the twenty-sixth time. I finally got something down. The word *pressure* came to my mind, and I wrote it down as soon as I could, fearing I might forget it.

After I wrote the first word, it seemed like a bomb waiting to explode. Afterward my pen couldn't keep up with my brain, and the words seemed to fall into their proper places. Meanwhile I felt a pleasant feeling of relief and comfort which propelled me and made me want to write more.

The thing that contributes most to my technique is the listing process. After I had that part done, I simply followed the guidelines. And I must admit it was very helpful.

PROCESS LOG ABOUT PRIVATE WRITING

Irene Wong

When I began my diary writing, I wrote about how I felt about writing on my problem, "Can I write ten pages about this?" But after I stated my issue, it just started to roll. Thoughts which at first came out randomly began to get thought out, and detailed discussions emerged. I found myself debating ideas and reasons that I had never before discussed at such lengths.

It surprised me when I came to realize just how much the people in my life play on the decision I must make. It surprised me many a time when I wrote down things that were in the back of my mind but that I had never taken the time out to analyze. Some other times, I found out those things were points I was afraid to look at in the eye. But by writing it out, I was able to partially explain the reason why I felt that way. Seeing my hostilities or fears written out made them seem less ominous and much easier to extinguish. It also enabled me to distinguish exactly the size of this problem, and I felt a little more secure after knowing how big it was. It's ironic, but although now I realize how big this problem is, it was better than when it was an unpredictable problem lurking in the dark. I can't say I figured much out. The solution is there; it's the outcome of my solution that scares me. It's something I have to do, and I can't bear the consequences. I tried to trick my mind by writing things that are "logical," but my mind clicked right back into the "illogical" track.

I learned a lot through this assignment. As I said, it cleared up a few important things for me. The ultimate answer lies ominously in its sleep.

EXAMPLE OF WRITING WITH THE PERL GUIDELINES

Peter Elbow

Note on this text. *This was Perl writing I did during a workshop—about an hour and a half—demonstrating the Perl process to teachers. I emphasized to everyone that the writing would be private and that they could use it for whatever kind of writing they wanted or needed to do. When I started listing things I could write about (I didn't save my list), I was hit hardest by my need to get going on the job currently staring me in the face: writing a piece for this textbook about writing on a word processor. Most of my previous Perl writing had been personal and exploratory—about some strong feelings or event in my life. Once I even tried writing a story. And usually I don't have much sense of audience during Perl writing. But on that morning I gave myself permission to work on this piece of public, pragmatic, "duty" writing for our textbook.*

Because I was leading the workshop and my mind was somewhat occupied by that role, I didn't have as much concentration for my own work as I would have had if someone else had been in charge. I didn't get so much written. I remember feeling distracted. (Also slightly guilty, for as it were, "doing my homework in class.")

I give here what I wrote that morning—as I wrote it (except for correcting some spelling and filling in some missing punctuation and making a couple of other minor corrections so it's readable). In several places I insert, in capital letters, the Perl questions that my writing is responding to (e.g., WHAT'S THIS ALL ABOUT?)

See the mini-workshop entitled "Writing with a Word Processor" for a revision of what I wrote here.

I'm sitting here writing with my pen. About writing with a word processor. Seems odd. I normally write <u>on</u> my WP, but today I'm in a workshop with other teachers and we have a chance to write together about whatever we need to write.

The two main skills in writing are <u>making a mess</u> and cleaning up the mess.

That is, it's hard to write well unless we are inventive and fecund—open to lots of words and ideas. That means being open and accepting to the words and ideas which come. Not being too quick to reject and say no. When we do that, we make a mess. We write down (or at least consider) too much. ~~We~~ Too many words; we start down too many paths. Branching and complex. We need that mess.

Yet in order to write well we also need to do just the opposite: we need to ~~say no and~~ be skeptical and rejecting—to throw away or change everything that's not the best; to reject what <u>looks</u> or <u>sounds</u> nice but isn't really, in the end, up to snuff.

It turns out that the WP is ideal for both these mental operations. ~~It helps~~

It ~~helps in make~~ makes it easier than with pen and paper to make <u>more</u> of a mess. We can throw down everything to the screen easily in more [I left a few blank lines; I think I assumed I'd come back and say more.]

Yet it also makes it easier than with pen and paper to clean up that mess. It's so easy to throw away what's discarded, fix words and spellings—and come up with neat copy.

Indeed, I would say that the main <u>psychological</u> danger in writing with a WP is that its fixing and cleaning up is so easy—indeed so fun—that it's tempting to stop every time you mistype or misspell a word or change your mind about a word and go back and fix it.

Learn to block that impulse. Learn to sustain your generating. Learn to keep on writing—as though it were pen and ink or typewriter and it were too hard to make a change. Otherwise you will distract yourself from your generating. Learn, in short, to <u>make</u> a mess.

You can let yourself write notes to yourself <u>in</u> your text when you're not sure. Instead of stopping and scratching your head and thinking when you become puzzled, you can <u>keep on</u> writing about your puzzlement. (Because it's so easy to erase them later.) I tend to put these remarks in CAPS—or indent them 5 spaces [in a block that's all indented]. So I can see later that they're not part of the text.

Why that's useful. When you keep writing

But—edit on screen/paper.

~~Start anywhere—cause you can move it around~~

WHAT'S IT ALL ABOUT?

—new power

—new relationship to words

—addiction

—my duty

—new horizons

WHERE DO YOU FEEL IT?

I feel it in my upper stomach.

WHAT'S THE PHRASE?

<u>new power</u>

<u>It's scary: but it leads to addiction. It can change your relationship to writing.</u>

<u>click</u> [I felt a click here; a shift of felt sense. Asking myself what it's about, what's the phrase, and where I feel it—these acts led me closer to what seemed interesting and important. Leading to what follows.]

<u>Screen is something half way between mind and paper.</u>

Mind is a mess: paper is supposed to be neat. When I'm writing on screen. it feels like it's sort of—half—still in my mind. It's a second mind. It's ~~not~~ still partly <u>in</u> me.

Like my mind I can't look at all of it at once, I can only put my attention on one bit at a time. I don't yet have complete detachment from it till I print it out.

It gives me a second mind.

WHAT'S LEFT OUT?

Techniques.

—How to adopt right attitude.

—Not be scared. You can't hurt the machine.

—You <u>can</u> get into trouble by losing text if you aren't careful to back up—but don't be worried.

—Writing as play.

What do I love about it?

—That it lets me get so much down.

—When I have a new idea, I just start writing it (using a carriage return to start a new line). I don't have to worry about putting it in the right order. I can jump back from idea to idea.

—<u>Because</u> you know you can correct, you have <u>permission</u> to write a messier way.

—You can start anywhere, in the middle, add late idea—cause you can move things around.

—It's so easy to revise. I suddenly see a new idea or new arrangement after I'm almost done—and I can wade in and do it—and print out clean copy.

—I can experiment. Leave one version as it is. <u>Copy.</u> Start revising but leave the old one. In case I lose good aspects of the old one in the revising process.

—I can print out 3–4 copies—at middle stage—and give' em to someone else. And they'll be neat and easy to read.

—Spelling and grammar checker. Handwriting and spelling have always been superficials of writing, but they've influenced readers more than anything else. Form of snobbery. If your spelling and handwriting and grammar are bad, I won't take you seriously. Now anyone can turn out professional copy.

What's hard/Don't like

Another mind. Sometimes I make such a mess that I feel in a swamp. Too many options. Once I remember feeling. "Oh, I wish I were writing in ink on expensive velum so that I would just choose a word and be done. Not feel like I have to keep revising and changing. I want something <u>final</u> (I must find that process piece I wrote when I was in that situation).

Sometimes I try to revise too much on screen. Too much chaos in the mind.

It's an enharmonic, changeable medium: it's a mind <u>or</u> it's paper—and it moves back and forth. If on screen, it's fluid—it's my mind; if I print it out, it stops being fluid and changing and I get it still and quiet where I can deal with it. I can take a mind scan.

Need it.

One can move back and forth.

It's like a brain photograph.

FELT SENSE*

Eugene Gendlin

You say that I am tired. If you consider your statement to be phenomenological, you will consider your statement wrong if I do not feel tired.

Your statement invites me to see if I am tired. How would I do that? Not by reviewing how long I have worked, and not by looking in the mirror. I can attend to my body directly and see if I find there what is called "tired." That is direct reference. Until you asked me, I paid no attention. Now, in reaction to your words, I seek to set up such "an" experience as we call "tired." If I cannot do so (and, note, this is not a matter of choice), your statement was wrong. Let us suppose that I agree I am "sort of tired."

Let me show how much further we can go than when we first considered this example.

Now suppose I say, "I am not exactly tired, but I am getting a little weary." It is clear that here you were definitely right in some way. Your words succeeded in "directly referring." They were also close in what they conveyed; they were pointing in the right direction. (I might have said, "No, I have a slight toothache.") We do not know as yet why I prefer "weary" to "tired"—they seem to be indistinguishable. "Weary" might perhaps include along with "tired" some sense of some long, drawnout cause for being tired, and indeed we have been working all day and all evening. (It is this sort of experiential sense of how a word is used which the linguistic analysts explicate.)

We must note that I probably did not feel tired until you said so. Your saying it made it true by leading me to create, specify, set out, distinguish (these words are equivalent here) "an" experience. Before I tried to refer to it, it wasn't there; now that I do, it is.

Yet, the feeling must be there; I do not just make it. Trying to refer to it, trying to see if I am tired, doesn't always make that feeling. Since now it did, for me, I would want to say that it was there before only I didn't notice it. Of course, as a "this feeling" it certainly was not there before. (Yet the case is different than if you had suddenly made me tired, perhaps by telling me some heavy news. There is a continuity between how I remember being before, and my direct reference now to this tired feeling: thus the tired feeling is a newly set-out aspect of the over-all experience I was attending to.)

Suppose I now continue to explicate why "weary" seems to be true for me, and "tired" doesn't. I may say next, "Well, it's sort of not tired, but tired-of. That's why I said 'weary.' I don't feel like going on to this next job we have to tackle now. It's too tough."

---

*You may want to read an analysis of this piece, which we include in the readings for Workshop 11.

Having said this, which is a more exact version of how I feel (as well as an explication of the use of the word I preferred), I might say, a moment or two later, "I feel like going out and having a good time. I am not at all tired—just so we don't have to get into this next job, it's too hard to do."

Now I am actually denying flatly what seemed above to be "in the right direction," though I really feel no different. I am still talking about "the same thing," and, despite the flat denial of what I said, I hold that what I say now is what my feeling really "was."

As I continue now to say just what it is about the next job that seems so tough, I may say, "Well, it isn't exactly hard to do, but what is hard is that I know they won't like how I'll do it." And then, "The job is really easy." And, again, further, "It isn't so much that I care what they think of it; it's just this one way I care, and that's a way that they're right, really. Gee, I don't care at all what they think! But this one criticism they'll make, I know they're right about that. It's really what I think that I care about." And, further, "I could help it, but I would have to take a day off to study up on how to do it right, and I don't want to do that."

And, again, "Really, I do want to. Every time I hit this sort of thing I wish so much that I could take the time off to learn how to do it, but I just can't give myself the time off. It would seem like a whole day with nothing done. I don't feel any trust in myself if I go and do something that isn't a part of the routine we call work, just doing something because I'd like to do it." And, later, "Hell, I'll do it tomorrow."

This aspect of experience—its vast capacity to be further schematized and unitized in relation to verbalization, and thereby revealing aspects which, we now say, it most truly "was," has not been recognized at all in philosophy until now. Therefore no systematic method has been devised for the various kinds of steps involved in explication.

It is clear from the example that one's own feelings can be stated falsely by oneself, and later corrected. There can be several steps in such correcting.

WORKSHOP
5

FROM PRIVATE TO PUBLIC WRITING: EXPLORING AUDIENCE AND GENRE

In this workshop we will ask you to use your private exploratory writing from Workshop 4 as seeds or raw material for a piece of public writing. The main workshop activity will be a series of short writing exercises to explore the possibilities for developing your private writing into a public piece: to develop it in terms of different *audiences,* and to develop it in terms of different *genres* (or forms or types) of writing. We'll ask you to explore by doing a number of ten- to fifteen-minute sketches. In each sketch you'll try writing to a different audience or in a different genre.

The main assignment will be to choose an audience or genre you want to use, and write a full draft of a public piece for sharing with others.

In this workshop, you'll get a feeling for different audiences and genres, and how you can make choices about audience and genre to help you take a piece of writing where you want it to go. In the process, you will come away with a better understanding of the tricky relationship between form and content. Sometimes you will feel yourself (putting it crudely) pouring existing content into new containers, and sometimes you will feel that the containers are helping you think of new content. That is, sometimes the exercises will lead you to "revise" or "shape" the content or ideas from your private writing to fit different audiences or genres. But sometimes the process of thinking in terms of an audience or genre will make you think of *new* content or ideas that weren't even in your private writing.

 ## LOOKING BACK OVER YOUR PRIVATE WRITING

Some theorists think that we haven't, in a sense, *finished* expressing any thought until we finally make it public in some form: without communication, a natural cycle isn't complete. We disagree. We think it's perfectly natural to express some thoughts and feelings and keep them to ourselves. Some speak of this as being our *own* audience. We often need privacy in order to explore our thinking and feeling without nervousness or fear. You may well not want to share much of what you got on paper in the previous workshop.

But of course we often *do* want to communicate to others what is private inside our heads. If we've written our thoughts and feelings down on paper, sometimes we can simply hand it over unchanged to readers. For language itself is a public medium. But private writing often needs to be transformed in order to communicate its sense to others. Depending on the audience, we can modify it only slightly (perhaps for a good friend) or else modify it extensively (perhaps for strangers). (There's more on audience and its effect on writing in "Ruminations and Theory" at the end of this workshop.)

The first step is to look back over the private writing you did in Workshop 4, just to get it fresh in mind. As you look back, you're likely to have mixed feelings about it. You may feel good about how much you wrote, about how diverse it is, and about how you were able to record your thinking and feeling in a way you'd never done before. As you read it over, part of it will probably re-match with the "felt sense" of it still in your head, and the match will feel gratifying to you. Or perhaps you'll be pleased because this "private ex-

I find it is so much easier to say something to a person when, instead of saying it face-to-face, I am able to write the message down. In fact I tried that system just today. I had a problem with my friend, but when I tried to speak to him about it, I just could not find the words, even though I knew exactly what I wanted to say. I complained about the situation to another friend who gave me the suggestion that I write a letter. Even if I didn't give it to him, I would at least have my thoughts expressed on paper. I tried the advice and, believe it or not, it worked. I believe that I got everything down that I wanted to say, completely and honestly. When I didn't have to look at his face and know that he was listening to me at that very moment, I felt so free at the thought of expressing my emotions. I did end up giving the letter to him, but that's another story.

Katie Houston

ploratory" writing is not very much of a mess at all: some of it may well be clear, shaped, and strong.

But you may also react negatively, at least to part of it: "*Yuk.* What a mess! What drivel my mind is full of." This reaction often occurs when people first try out private exploratory writing. It's important to remember that you weren't trying to produce good, well-organized writing; you were trying to give yourself the safety to produce an accurate mind-scan or brain x-ray, as it were. Minds are messy. When you produce messy writing, that's not a problem—indeed, in a way it's a *good* sign.

For the mess means not only that you were able to trust yourself enough to record what was actually going on in your mind. It also means that you have begun to learn a powerful way to find things to write (a powerful heuristic). For if you read through that mess in the proper spirit of noncritical inquiry, you will find *more* possible topics and potential trains of thought for writing than if you had written something careful and well-organized. Messiness means that you didn't keep just to one neat path but let your writing record the many diverse side paths that every mind inevitably considers. You might want to explore some of these paths further now.

We suspect your private writing has some or all of these characteristics:

- *Contradictions.* You thought or felt X at one point, but then later on you wandered into thinking or feeling Not-X. If you are going to engage in good thinking, you *need* contradiction; you need to wrestle with both sides or get both sides to wrestle with each other. In this way you'll come up with *new* thinking, not just a restatement of your old thoughts.
- *Changes of topic and digressions.* Your writing was going in one direction but suddenly it veered off or changed direction completely. There's cognitive power in this jumpy diversity: there are seeds for different pieces of writing. But even more interesting than that, *there are important unstated insights implied at every jump or point of change or digression.* Look closely at each jump or shift in your writing. Pause and ask yourself: "How did my mind make that jump? What is the connection?" Even if there is no "real" or "rational" connection (say you jumped from radios to swim-

ming), there was always something *in your mind* that served as a bridge between radios and swimming. Noticing that bridge will throw some light on both of them. The mind is incapable of pure randomness.

■ *Obsessions.* Your writing seemed to be in a rut, grinding over and over again in a tiresome or depressing way about the same event or the same feelings. Some people who have not done this kind of private exploratory writing before say, "How depressing!" or "How childish!" or "How irrational!" But remember: if this material came out on paper, it's in your head. You can't get rid of it by *not* writing it down. Writing it down is usually the best way to get rid of it: perhaps by giving you enough perspective on it to work through it, or perhaps only by giving you a place to "put it down" so you know it's there. You don't have to "carry it" any more in your head so you can stop thinking about it. Everyone obsesses sometimes. You'll find you can learn things and get perspective on yourself by reading through the obsessions. If they really bother you or get in the way of functioning at your best, you may decide you want to talk to someone you trust about them. And there may well be things in the obsession that you would enjoy communicating even to people you don't know well.

 TRYING OUT AUDIENCES

After you've read through your private writing, think of an audience that you would like to write to and communicate some part of what's in your private writing. That is, choose a specific person or group of people that somehow *fit* a theme or feeling or passage in your private writing. Perhaps there is someone who doesn't seem to understand an experience you've had or your reaction to an experience, and you particularly want them to finally "get it." Perhaps you need to tell someone how much they helped or hurt you, how much you admire them, or what has been happening to you since they last heard from you.

Now take eight to ten minutes and explore what it would be like to direct this material from your private writing to this person or group. We're not asking you to write the whole piece in this short time; just sketch it out.

What you write might naturally take the form of a letter; perhaps not. Don't worry about that yet. Just say what you want to say to that audience. So it's fine as you write your sketch to skip around a bit as ideas strike you. The goal is to notice what it is like writing to this audience.

For the next step is to choose a *different* audience to whom you could write about the same material. Do another eight- to ten-minute exploration of what it's like writing to them. For of course we often talk differently to different people. (Sometimes you can tell whom someone is talking to on the phone just by listening to how they talk to them.) The change in audience may also change *what* you say, not just *how* you say it. For example, we know a student who decided to drop out of college for a while and wrote entirely different reasons for her decision to her friends, to her parents, and to school officials. A letter can be very personal and private (to a close friend) or more public and formal (to an organization or a newspaper editor). Besides, you may not find yourself writing in the form of a letter: you may decide to write something like an op-ed piece for a certain newspaper, a children's story for certain young children you know and love, a proposal to a certain school organization or administrator, or a kind of personal essay to members of your class. Just write. The goal here is to focus on audience and write in whatever genre or not-genre comes along. In the next section we'll focus on genre.

Here is an example of Melissa Fogel experimenting with two different audiences for her private, open-ended writing (which is printed in the "Readings" for the last workshop). First she decided to try writing to her roommate:

> Roommates are hard to come by. Some are dirty and never clean up their mess; some are noisy and never let a person get to sleep at night. However sometimes people are blessed with a "roomie" that is not only respectful, but dependable—a companion a person can always count on. In times of trouble you helped me see things a little more clearly. You stood by my side when I needed the support and you gave sound advice to one who usually gets too emotionally wrapped in a situation.
>
> There were times when your help was indispensible. When my family seemed to tear from the seams, you sat me down and saw me through. You helped me remember the good in every person, and made me realize that troubled times are like clouds. For even the clouds linger for a long time, but they always clear up and let the sun shine through. When I felt my sister and I would never be close again, you taught me to fight and continue my hike up the enormous mountain. Along that hike I often needed times of encouragement, or sips of water. Sometimes I needed an actual push. Always, you were there, smiling and pushing.
>
> Of all the roommates I could of ended up with, I am pretty lucky to room with a best friend. Thank you for your time and patience and understanding. It's not everyday one comes across a good-hearted friend that will listen with such a caring ear.

Then she decided to try writing to her own boyfriend (about her first encounter with her sister's boyfriend):

> Our eyes met from across the room. I knew I needed to speak to him, to say my piece, to untangle the knot that keeps us from understanding each other. I wanted to tell him how I felt. How he hurt me, indirectly of course. I wanted to explain my reasons for disapproval, and my feelings of anger toward a complete stranger to me. How could he be so blind, and not see my sister's suffering? Maybe he thinks he is helping her in some way. He changed her in the time they were together. Into a meek soul, who doesn't have the courage to walk away from this relationship. I just want him to see a different perspective. Want him to realize the pain he has caused my family. Whether it be because of worry or sorrow, we can hardly bear to see them together. If only he could sacrifice his needs for just one moment and give to her. She has given so much to him. She has given to him materialistic items, emotional outpourings, and a love that some will never find no matter how hard they search. He has given her nothing except a sense of security. So do I beg him to change, or do I yell at him and cause a scene? Or should I simply let time take its toll, and wait for the day when my strong little sister breaks from her shell to a better place for her mind and soul?

For another interesting example to illustrate focus on audience, consider the letter by Mark Levensky in the "Readings" for this workshop. He is a college professor and he wrote to the teachers at his old elementary school about his dismal experiences trying to learn spelling from them. You might argue that those teachers weren't really his audience, and that he was actually writing to *all* elementary teachers since he published this letter in the major national publication for elementary English teachers. Yet as you read his piece, we think you'll sense that he was genuinely directing his words to that small audience of his own teachers—really "taking on" that audience in his head. He might well have started out trying to write an essay about spelling to *all* elementary teachers, but then found he could say what he wanted better when he changed audiences and directed his thoughts to his old teachers. It certainly sounds as though this audience "clicked" for Levensky. This is a common experience of writers, and there is an important general principle here. Look for an audience that clicks. If you find it, you can often write something more easily and something that will then work for a larger, different, or more problematic audience.

For your main assignment you'll be able to choose one of these audience sketches—and/or a genre sketch—to develop into a full piece.

 TRYING OUT GENRES

A genre is a widely recognized *form* of writing. Some genres are large, inclusive, and loosely defined—such as *poetry* and *prose*. Some genres are smaller and less inclusive—such as *essay* and *fiction*. Then there are even smaller, more specific genres—which are the ones we will ask you to try out in this workshop: (1) description or portrait, (2) narrative or story, (3) dialogue, (4) persuasive essay, (5) expository essay, (6) satire or parody, (7) meditation or personal essay, and (8) poetry (we leave this one broad).

You probably won't have time to try out all these genres. Your teacher will give you direction as to how many and perhaps which ones to try. As you try them out, notice when you find yourself pouring existing content into various containers and when the containers make you think of new content. (By the way, we could put "letter" in this list, but we assume that most of you probably explored the possibility of this genre in the last section.)

(1) Description or Portrait

Read through or think back over your private writing to find a *scene, object,* or *person* that feels important but is perhaps not much developed. Do eight to ten minutes of descriptive writing. First, close your eyes and try to experience your subject using your eyes, ears, nose, and touch (as we suggested in Workshop 2). Then go on to describe it in writing.

Obviously you can't complete a large scene in this short time. But take a minute or two at the end to make a note to yourself about how you'd shape it or organize it if you were to finish it. As with audiences, these are sketches.

The goal is simply to get a start—to test how fruitful it might be to write a longer piece of public writing in this genre of description.

If your private writing is already mostly descriptive, or already contains a very full description or portrait, you might skip this exercise. In effect, your private writing already led you to use the genre of description or portrait. Just take a moment more to write about what changes you would consider, if any, to focus on the description and make your piece *public:* Would you shape it any differently? What would be the center? Are there any changes in style or approach you would want to make?

Melissa Fogel discovered that her private, open-ended writing (in the "Readings" for the last workshop) led her finally to an image of her sister swinging on a swing and then falling off—and indeed this image became the germ of her revised public piece of writing. (Just as Eudora Welty's image served as the germ that led her to write 'A Worn Path." The story is printed in the "Readings" for Workshop 2, and she describes how it grew from an image in a piece we've printed in the "Readings" for Workshop 16.)

Peter Elbow tried out a fast sketch of an image of himself at the computer:

His shoulders began to hunch more as he got more frustrated with the computer. He was sitting forward on his chair, his eyes as though drawn toward the screen. Periodically he would stop, lean back, try to take a deep breath and relax, but then as he struggled more, he would hunch again and you could see his muscles gradually become tense. On one side of the computer were papers and notes he was trying to write from. On the other side and on the floor around him were the computer manuals—propped open to various pages with random objects: books, pencils, boxes of floppy disks. Behind him a window showed clear, bright blue sky, but he was oblivious to it. At this point, he didn't even live in the same universe with that blue sky.

(2) Narrative or story

Where are the potential *stories* in what you wrote? Look for crucial events, moments, turning points. These points might not even be *in* what you wrote, but only implied. For example, perhaps your writing is nothing but your feelings about a certain person or your thoughts about a certain issue. But there are stories that could be *found* or *made* that relate to that person or issue.

PROCESS BOX

I noticed that during the assigned periods of writing I still felt pressure to get things right. So words and ideas came hard. But when the assigned times ended, a flood of ideas and approaches came. . . . I do a lot of thinking before I write. I need time to mull it over before I put words on paper. So the assigned times were hard for doing this.

A revelation. I never thought of leaving works unfinished. I began a bunch of writings now—to work on later—like a real writer.

Gene Gramarossa

Start at an important moment in that story—not necessarily the beginning—and just write for eight to ten minutes to get the feel for the shifts that would happen if you made a story. This may lead you to new material or new insights.

If your private writing is already mostly story, or has an extended narrative in it, just take a couple of moments and jot down what adjusting you'd do to focus on it and make it public. Would you heighten or play with the plot? the mood? the narrator or that narrator's point of view?

Melissa Fogel tried using her private writing for narrative:

> Once upon a time, in a fast-paced city of lights, action, and turmoil, there lived a family. This family wasn't an average family. For in the big city it is hard to find average families. This family, like every other family in the big city, had problems. These problems had nothing to do with money or violence, like most in the city. This family struggled with emotional stress that revolved around one of the family members, the middle child. This middle child was a beautiful girl, for she had eyes the color of the sky and skin that only a china doll could retain. She had long brown locks of curls, and in the sun you could see the gold highlights glowing. She had unique style and sensitivity, and she would share the world with you if she could. There were other children in the family, an older sister and two younger brothers. They all went about their own lives, sometimes fighting, like normal adolescents. But under the surface fights about clothes and the car, they shared a love and respect that isn't easy to come by in the big city. One day the middle child announced that she had a new love. Everyone was happy for the girl. They knew this boy was a very lucky person. But as time went on, problems with this boy began to appear. Changes in the middle child began to take place, changes that no one could understand, not even the sister and brothers that loved her more than the world itself.

(3) Dialogue

You may not think of yourself as naturally writing "dialogue," but there may well be *germs* of dialogue in your private writing: places where you said "No" or "But wait a minute" or "I agree" or "Here's one thing for sure." In passages like that, you are really *speaking to* another voice—even if that other voice is just another feeling or opinion in your own head. And there are even more passages that imply a dialogue—such as if you wrote about someone who disagrees with you. And if you wrote, "Then we got into a fight" or "She asked him out for a date," it would be a natural thing to break that out into an actual dialogue or conversation of what they said to each other.

Take eight to ten minutes and start a dialogue: perhaps with that person you disagree with, perhaps between two conflicting feelings. Perhaps there are two people in your private writing who had an interchange or who disagree with each other; get them talking. But it's not necessary that people disagree. If they simply have different temperaments, any dialogue they have will be fruitful. Start the conversation and just see where it goes.

And don't forget that you can easily write productive dialogues with *objects* or *ideas*: with a house, a book, a place, a piece of clothing. You can have a fruitful dialogue with anything that is important to you in your exploratory writing. The trick is simply to have one member of the dialogue say something to start off. As little as "Hello"—or, "What was it like being the house we've all lived in, and seeing and hearing everything we've all said to each other?" Just see what answer comes; let the conversation proceed. Get your pen moving and the dialogue will unfold and create new material: new ideas that are not part of your original exploratory writing. The dialogue may affect or even change the views or feelings you had when doing your exploratory writing.

Examples: Look at Michael Lemonick's *Time* magazine dialogue (in the "Readings" for this workshop) to see how the dialogue form is a lively way to present technical information.

When Peter Elbow looked back over his private Perl writing (printed in the "Readings" for the last workshop), he realized that he could start a dialogue between himself and the computer.

Peter:	Why do you always give me such trouble? Why do you so often mess me up or not do what I want you to do? I paid a lot of money for you. I got instructions. Most of all, why won't you *talk* to me when I need you?
Computer:	Actually, I talk to you quite often.
Peter:	Yes, you send me messages—"bad command," "insert target disk in Drive B"—worse yet, "FATAL ERROR"—but when I'm really in trouble, you just sit there silent and refuse to do what I want you to do.
Computer:	Unfortunately it's you who gives me trouble: you refuse to do what's needed. But I don't hold it against you. I just wait for you to catch on. I do everything you ask me to—no matter how many times you ask me to do it; I never forget anything; I'm never bored or impatient. There's only a problem when you don't know my language or you ask me to do something that is impossible. I'm not programmed to know your language perfectly. It's your job to learn mine. As soon as you speak meaningfully to me, I'll speak meaningfully to you.
Peter:	Don't take that superior tone with me! "I never make a mistake. I never make a mistake." Why do you keep saying that to me?
Computer:	I didn't say that; I never have. But in fact I never do make a mistake. In our dealings, I'm sorry to say that it's only you who makes mistakes.
Peter:	*SEE!* I won't put up with this arrogance. (Wait a minute; let me get a hold of myself. It's only a machine. Calm myself.) OK, I'll be more reasonable with you. I admit it. Of course I make mistakes. But I'm doing the best I can. I try to do things right; and when something doesn't work, I look at the manual; I go over my steps one at a time and try it again and again. But still it doesn't work. Sometimes I get so mad I want to hurl you across the room. And you just sit there silent, superior, condescending.

Computer:	But that's it, don't you see? You are so irrational. Why do you give me the same order again and again when you see it's not working? And then you get so *angry* because *you're* doing something irrational.
Peter:	But I can't help it.
Computer:	Yes, that's what perplexes me. Why do I bring out irrationality in you? I've been watching you these months. I've never seen you as furious and fuming—as close to violence—with anyone else as with me. Not with your wife or children or students or coworkers. What do I do that brings out your irrationality?
Peter:	That's a good question.

(4) Persuasive Essay

What are some of the important *opinions* or *beliefs* in your exploratory writing? What if you tried to persuade people to agree with you? Are there certain people you particularly want to persuade? You'll find that the persuasive essay as a genre will often serve as a means of "rhetorical invention": that is, the process of trying to persuade will often bring up reasons or arguments that you didn't think of earlier when you were just expressing or exploring your opinion for yourself.

Take eight or ten minutes now and start the germ of a persuasive essay, beginning perhaps with summing up your point as briefly as possible. Before you stop, try quickly to jot down as many reasons as you can think of that you might use; and try to sketch out a possible organization for the essay. If what you wrote privately was already more or less in a persuasive mode (or a big chunk of it was), just write for a few moments about what changes you would make to shape it or make it stronger. (Workshop 8 deals more fully with persuasion.)

Melissa Fogel tried using her private writing for a persuasive essay:

I of all people know what it's like to use a boyfriend for a sense of security and escape. I also know what the consequences are for doing such a thing. Relationships these days are under tremendous stress. The problems one of us decides to take on become a problem for the couple. Sometimes even the smallest problems cause the largest rifts between two people. However to stay involved with someone because it is the easiest thing to do, or because of the fear of being on your own, produces a strain no other problem can compare to. When hiding behind someone, you can lose a sense of identity and pride. You can become so wrapped up in the lie that you can't see the truth, even when people are trying to tell you so. The lie can fester and create long-term disaster. After a while, you can't see the trouble brewing. This trouble can come in all forms. It can cause fighting between those who are trying to make you see the truth, it can hurt the people that care about you, and most of all it can hurt you. You may give up on yourself—decide that you're not good enough for others. You may stop caring for your health and your appearance. You may even lose the qualities you had when you began the relationship. Sometimes when you're unsure if you are falling into this trap, you should break off the relationship for a while and try to regain your life and self once again. You may find that liking you is more important than whether or not someone else likes you.

(5) Expository Essay

What's the most interesting *question, issue,* or *concept* in your exploratory writing? Most people think of an essay as *explaining* something that they understand. That approach is common, but if you want the most interesting essay—and want to have the most interesting time writing it—don't look for answers or conclusions or explanations; look for questions or perplexity. What do you need to understand better? You'll discover that you can produce good writing even though you don't yet really understand the issue you are trying to write about. Remember that many good published essays don't give solutions: they clarify or analyze a question so that others can understand it better and go to work on it.

So sniff out the issue of greatest interest to you and take eight to ten minutes to start exploring it. You can think of what you are writing as an example of the general form known as "expository essay": an essay which explains. But if you wish, you can think of different subgenres which represent different *ways* of explaining—each of which could give a slightly different shape to your writing. (Workshops 9 through 11 and 13 through 14 explore different kinds of essays.)

- *Analysis.* Perhaps your private writing talks about lots of things that are all *connected* to an incident or *related* to a topic or feeling, but it's not clear how it all adds up or what the main point is. The basic question is the one that lies behind all thinking and writing: "What does all this mean?" or "So what?" In the end, most essay assignments in most disciplines ask this same question: "What sense can you make of this tangled pile of data?" Analysis means untangling a tangle.

- *Definition.* Perhaps your private writing leads to some complex or slippery concept you want to figure out (e.g., selfishness). The clearest and most down-to-earth way to define is "ostensive"—that is, pointing or giving examples. (X and Y are examples of selfishness, but Z is not, and here's why.) This isn't so different from the technique in classical rhetoric of "defining by collection and division": "collecting" *selfishness* together with all the things that are like it to see why they are alike, and then "dividing" them to see how *selfishness* differs from them. And it's really the same approach used in zoological definition: *genus* tells how something is like its cousins; *species* tells how it differs from its cousins. Thus the essay of definition is closely related to the next form.

- *Compare-contrast.* It's often hard to define or figure out things to say about one thing by itself. It's much easier when you can relate it to one or more others—continually holding them up against each other to find similarities and differences. This gives mental leverage. And your private writing may well suggest two or more people, places, or ideas that invite comparison.

- *"Process essay."* In scientific or technical writing, a "process essay" explains how to do something (e.g., how to go about making water from hydrogen and oxygen). But process essays are not limited to these disciplines. You can write about the steps you go through, for example, to cook a particular meal or prepare a garden plot in the spring—or to do something less concrete such as convincing a parent or teacher of something. We asked for a process essay about private exploratory writing in the last workshop.

■ *Research essay.* Of course it's not feasible for this ten-minute sketch to do any interviewing or library research, but if your private writing suggests some areas you'd like to study more, you can now write out some of the questions you would pursue. You could then take up the issue again in Workshop 13 about research essays.

■ *Five-paragraph essay.* This is a school-invented genre, and unfortunately, it is the only genre that some students are taught. The first paragraph introduces the thesis, the three "body paragraphs" each give a reason and an example, and the last paragraph gives a conclusion that restates the thesis. The five-paragraph essay limits thinking because it is so rigid about form. But it is a handy formula in certain conditions where you don't want to think an issue through—either for lack of time or because you've already worked it out. Thus, it is a handy genre for timed exams: "In twenty minutes, explain the importance of the Civil War."

Select one or more of these essay subgenres and write for at least ten minutes on each one you pick.

Examples. Peter Elbow used his private Perl writing (in the "Readings" for the last workshop) as the basis for an expository essay which is printed as the mini-workshop "Writing with a Word Processor." The piece by Gertrude Stein in this workshop's "Readings" is a small essay of definition—but in parody form.

(6) Satire or Parody

There might well be germs of satire or parody in your private writing: moments where you make fun of something or someone. If not, what could your private exploratory writing *lead you* to make fun of? A person you'd like to show as silly? An opinion or view that needs puncturing? Yourself when you realize you did something silly? A situation or "scene" that is on the brink of the ridiculous (e.g., people who show off)?

The essence of satire is to exaggerate or distort. Thus you could satirize someone in your exploratory writing (or yourself) by simply describing—but exaggerating certain traits. Or you could put down the thoughts and feelings that run through the person's head (a monologue) but overdo it—carry the thoughts and feelings beyond the plausible, exaggerate the manner of talking. Or you can make fun of an *opinion* or *view* by stating it and even arguing for it, but pushing it a bit too far. Or you can create a tone or voice which is off: be highly dignified about something trivial, or very flippant about something serious.

Gertrude Stein's treatment of commas in the readings parodies a process or "how to" essay and an essay of definition. For another example, notice the passage from an essay printed on page 181 of Workshop 7. The writer makes fun of the disco scene and uses some satiric language. She chose to make fun of them by looking accurately at them and using her own voice; she could have made fun of them by using an exaggerated or distorted view or using a different voice.

(7) Meditation or Personal Essay

These are particularly interesting public forms because they often function as a somewhat *private* genre turned public: an invitation to others to overhear our transaction with ourselves. It might well be that a portion of your private exploratory writing could be turned into a meditation or personal essay without having to make many changes at all.

Examples. Melissa Fogel's private writing was already meditative and personal. By focusing on one topic, she made a meditative personal essay.

Peter Elbow began to write a brief meditative piece, building on some of his private Perl writing, but also reflecting on ideas he generated in his dialogue. (You may find, as he did, that one genre exploration sometimes prompts or speaks to another.) Here is part of what he wrote:

He's right. (Or is it she? It?) I do get madder at that machine than at anyone else in my life. Why should that be?

Is it because it's a machine and I *can* get mad at it? I can't let myself get so mad at people? That's a nice thought—me as sensible and rational: that I don't act irrationally toward people since it would hurt them and instead I save it for a machine which can never be hurt by my feelings. That's like the dog who moderates his roughness when playing with a tiny toddler. It's like the toddler who hits his parent as hard as he can in blissful faith that anything he puts out, they can deal with. Can I remember when I first realized I could *hurt* my parents? No; but it must have been an awful realization.

But somehow that's too pretty a story: me as purely sensible and rational. There's undeniably something disturbing about getting so heated up at a machine. Is it that I want to kick it because it's helpless? Little kids often seem to pick on the weak one.

133

But in a way it's not weak at all. It's so powerful; so much more powerful than I. It can do all these things I can't do. And my frustration mounts because I know what's happening is not its fault. *And* if I harm it, *I* would be the one to suffer and would have to pay to have it fixed.

But that reminds me of other occasions when I feel that way. It's true that I never seem to get as mad at people but I do get almost as mad and frustrated when I'm trying to *fix* some object or machine and cannot do it. It makes me want to cry with frustration.

Perhaps I was getting at something important in my dialogue earlier: the fact that the damn thing won't *talk* to me. I guess that's the hardest thing for me to bear: it's certainly the best way for someone to torture me—not to talk to me. I need a response from creatures around me. Without that, I find existence intolerable.

(8) Poetry

Young children seem to be naturally drawn to poetry, but most of us become somewhat intimidated by it as we grow older and as teachers talk to us about the richness and intricacy of great poetry. We know that some of you have continued to write poetry since childhood—or have perhaps come back to it. We will attempt no formal definition of poetry here; we'll just say that for us, poetry is utterance where the language is special or the voice particularly matters; it is discourse or language one wants to savor. We find that most people can write poetry with a little encouragement if they know they don't have to show it to anyone else. We also believe that the very process of writing poetry brings us to a richer understanding of the potential in all language—including even the language of formal essays.

As you read back over your private writing, you may find language that already seems somehow resonant—words that feel right on your tongue or phrases that recur in your ear. Perhaps you can shape some of this into poetry. Remember that poetry does not have to rhyme or even have a formal design; much modern poetry has neither, at least not in a strictly patterned way. You may find that you can create poetry out of some of your private writing with minimal changes. Or you may want to extract some passages—lines and phrases—and build a poem on them.

Examples. Peter Elbow extracted the lines that had resonance for him and played with them and came up with this. He realized in the middle of it that it was also a dialogue.

Don't make a mess.
    No.

Clean it up.
    I don't want to. I refuse. I love throwing things down.

Throw it away.
    I won't. It's mine. I like it that way.

Make a mess.
    No.

Wait a minute. What? Don't confuse me.
What if I don't want to?

Make a mess.
 I'm in a swamp. I'm on the kitchen floor.
 It's slimy with spilled food.
 I'll never get clean.
 Too much chaos.

Change your mind.
 My mind is a mess.
 I'm half in my mind—half out.
 How do I get permission to do it differently?
 Will you make it all right?
 I feel it in my stomach.
 I want a guarantee.

Good luck.

See the poem "Autobiography" by the Turkish poet Nazim Hakmit in the "Readings" for an example of how good published poetry can use the plainest everyday language.

 ## MAIN ASSIGNMENT

For your main assignment, take one of the quick sketches you have made and develop it into a full draft. It could be an audience sketch or a genre sketch. Perhaps your teacher will direct you. (You could also develop two sketches into two drafts so that you can compare more fully the effects of varying the audience or genre. If you do two drafts, they will probably be rougher.)

The simplest way to decide which sketch to work on is to think back and decide which one brought out a "click"—a feeling, even if faint, that tells you that this is an interesting direction (or "container") in which to develop some of your private writing. By writing the trial sketches, you may discover that your mind was unconsciously working mostly in terms of one genre, for example, by telling a story or analyzing a problem.

Reading the sketches out loud can help you decide which to use. Or listeners can help you. (Your teacher may want to emphasize practice with somewhat more formal or school genres and ask you to restrict yourself to some form of *essay* for your main assignment.)

After you choose a sketch—that is, choose a genre or audience—look back over all your private writing and take a few quick notes on what you want to include in your first draft. Sometimes you need to do a genuine rewriting: the private writing puts you in a position where you can now start fresh and say clearly and exactly what you want to say. But don't change more than is necessary. It's amazing, sometimes, how little has to be changed from messy, rough private writing to make it polished and ordered. Inexperienced writers sometimes write lively and interesting rough private writing, but in revision they throw away or ruin the most lively, perky, and individual language and the most adventuresome, powerful thinking and instead go for what is safe and "nice" and conventional. So don't be timid. Look for what has energy and juice and life and find a way to use it.

Once you have a draft of your major assignment for this workshop, your teacher will either give you an opportunity for more feedback and revision or ask you to set it aside to work on later—perhaps for another workshop in this book.

Possibilities for Collaboration

Full collaboration is probably harder here than in many other workshops, since you are starting from private writing. Still, some of you might find that you have similar themes or even stories in your private writing and would like to write something together. Here are two likely routes toward collaborative collages. (1) Choose the same theme or issue and produce a group of short pieces that are addressed to various audiences and that use various genres. This will yield you a collage that explores a theme or issue in a rich and interesting way. (2) Choose the same audience or genre and let the themes or issues vary. This will yield a more unusual, experimental piece, but one that will throw interesting light on the audience or genre.

 ### POSSIBLE QUESTIONS FOR SHARING AND RESPONDING

Since you and your classmates are likely to end up with a wide range of diverse kinds of writing—to different audiences and in different genres—there are no common feedback questions to suggest. But perhaps you would find it useful to read your pieces to listeners with no overt cues as to audience or genre and ask them what they feel the audience and genre to be—and the degree to which they feel the piece is a common or an unusual treatment of that audience and genre. For of course a piece can work well even if it is unusual and violates some readers' expectations.

Perhaps it will be most useful just to get movies of the readers' minds—to find out what is going on moment by moment as they read or listen to your work (see "Movies of the Reader's Mind," Section 7 of *Sharing and Responding* at the end of the book, page SR31). Toward this goal, it helps to pause two or three times as you are reading to them (or make them pause as they are reading), and have them tell you what is going on in their minds at that moment.

 ### PROCESS WRITING AND COVER LETTER

- What did you notice and feel looking back over your private writing? Encouraged, discouraged, bothered? Why?
- Talk about the differences between thinking in terms of audience and thinking in terms of genre.

- What was it like moving from private to public? Did it make a big difference in how you wrote?
- What was it like doing all those short sketches or trial starts. Could you get yourself to jump in and do one burst of writing and then move on to another? If you found it hard, what would it take to become more comfortable with it?
- How did you decide which genre or audience to use?

 RUMINATIONS AND THEORY

About Audience

Are Genres Form or Content?

About Audience

Most teachers and theorists of rhetoric say that you should think about your audience before you write and keep audience in mind while you are writing. Yet we find that it often helps our writing to forget about audience as we write.

When you write, do you prefer to plunge in, exploring your topic on paper without any regard to the readers, and then revise later to fit the readers? Or do you prefer to think about whom you are writing to from the start and as you write?

Your answer may well depend on your temperament. Or it may be that keeping readers in mind is better for certain writing *tasks* (or for certain readers) than for other tasks or readers. The issue of audience is a complex tangle, but an important one. We are going to work toward untangling it here and end up with some practical advice for how to make audience work *for* you and prevent it from working against you.

A Balance among the Four Possible Relations to an Audience

Many students have never written except in school: all their writing has been assigned, read, and evaluated or graded by a teacher. If you never write except for evaluation by teachers, you can drift into unconsciously feeling as though that's what writing *is:* performing for someone in authority in order to be judged. Many students have no sense of writing as a way to *communicate* with real readers. And they may lack any sense of writing as a way to communicate privately with themselves, to explore thoughts and feelings on paper just for the sake of exploring. It is useful to become more conscious of the four main ways of relating to or using an audience in writing:

1. ***Keeping your writing to yourself.*** This is a case of *not* using an audience—keeping readers out of your way, out of your hair. We hope you have already learned how fruitful it can be not to worry or even think about readers as you write. Many people who were blocked in their writing and then learn the knack of private writing say: "I discovered that the problem wasn't

writing: it was writing for an audience." If you have kept a diary which you don't intend to share, you have participated in a venerable and traditional form of writing for no audience other than oneself. But of course you can also use private writing to help you produce material which is *eventually* intended for an audience.

2. Giving your writing to an audience but getting no feedback or response from them: sharing. Here, too, we hope we have already shown you how much you can learn from this simple, quick, and satisfying way of relating to an audience. When you share but don't get feedback, it emphasizes writing to *communicate* rather than writing to perform or be judged. Obviously communication is the most common and natural way to use words—the way we are most skilled at.

3. Giving your writing to an audience for NONEVALUATIVE feedback or response. Sometimes in school we fall into assuming that the only thing to do with a piece of writing is to try to talk about how good or bad it is or diagnose its strengths and weaknesses or give suggestions for improvement. It is crucial to realize that we can get lots of really helpful responses to our writing without any of that. And we can get it from readers other than a teacher: from peers, friends, parents, and any others who might be interested in us or what we write. Really, one of the least interesting things we can ask about any piece of writing is how good or bad it is. It's usually much more interesting and fruitful to ask questions like these: "What does it seem to be saying? Does it say different things to different readers? Why did the writer write it? Why should we read it, or what can we get out of it or apply to our experience? How is it put together, and how does it function?" We have plenty of suggestions for useful nonevaluative response in the "Sharing and Responding" section of each workshop and in *Sharing and Responding* at the end of the book.

4. Giving your writing to an audience for EVALUATIVE response. When we use readers in the other three ways just described, then it makes good sense sometimes to get evaluative response from them. Evaluative response is only a problem if that's all you ever get; or if you trust it too much—forgetting that even the best professional critics cannot agree in their evaluations.

Audience as a Focusing Force on Our Minds

Think of audience as exerting a kind of magnetism or focusing force on our minds. The closer we are to our listeners or readers and the more we think about them, the more influence they have on our thoughts and feelings. That is, when we are with people or very aware of them in our minds, we are more likely to feel their concerns or see their point of view. When we go off by ourselves or forget them, we ignore their point of view. Both these situations have harmful and helpful outcomes.

Some audiences are helpful because they make it easier to write. Such an audience usually consists of a person or a group who likes us and respects us and is interested in what we are interested in. People who want to hear what we have to say tend to make us think of more things to say and to write more fluently. Their receptivity opens our minds. And the act of writing to such readers tends to shape and focus what we are thinking about—even if we had been confused before sitting down to write.

But other audiences are unhelpful or problematic because they make it harder to write. Certain audiences intimidate us or make us nervous. Most of us have had the experience of finding it harder and harder to write for a teacher because the teacher did nothing but criticize what we wrote. We may actually find ourselves *unable* to write for this type of person no matter how hard we try. (This happened to Peter Elbow and forced him to drop out of graduate school. It was this experience that got him interested in the writing process.) There are other kinds of problem audiences too. If an audience is completely unknown (for example, an admissions committee or a prospective employer you've never met or someone from another culture) or vague ("the general public"), you may find it hard to write for them.

The trick then is to notice when an audience is being helpful or not helpful so you can decide whether to think about them or forget about them as you write. Occasionally, a frightening or difficult audience is helpful to keep in mind right from the start. They energize us and lead us to be brave. We look them in the eye, and doing so empowers us and clears our minds: we suddenly find exactly the words and thoughts we need to say to them.

Even though audience is a tricky theoretical issue, the practical answer is simple if you think in terms of a little three-step dance with readers: first a step *toward* readers, then *away from* them, and finally *back toward* them.

- Toward your audience. Start by bringing your readers to mind. Imagine them; see them. Doing so may help you focus your thinking and your approach to your topic. By bringing readers consciously into your mind, you may well find more to say, just as you would naturally find things to say if you were standing there in front of them and they asked you what was on your mind. If things go well, you simply keep this first relationship to the audience for the whole writing process.

- Away from your audience. *If* you have any difficulty with your writing, it may be because your audience is getting in your way: because they are unknown or intimidating or because thinking about them makes you worry too much about trying to get your writing right. Try putting them out of mind and writing for yourself: get your thoughts straight in your *own* mind—even if you know that this process is leading you to write things that are not right for your intended audience. If you can once put clearly on paper what *you* think, then it's not so hard afterward to make changes or adjustments to suit your words to the audience.

- Finally, back again *toward* readers. No matter how clear you see things for *yourself,* you must consciously bring your audience to mind again—as a central part of your *revising* process. In doing so you may realize that what is clear for you is not clear for them unless you explain something they may not know about; or you may realize that for them you need a change in approach. You may even decide you need to *hide* some of your own ideas or feelings when writing to them. This would have been hard earlier, for it's hard to hide something while you are in the act of working it out.

Do you usually start writing by thinking mainly about *what* you want to say or *how* you want to say it? That is, are you thinking about content or form?

Starting with Content

In this textbook we often suggest doing freewriting or exploratory writing without worrying about organization. "Invite chaos," we say; "Worry later about organization or form." In making this suggestion we might seem to be making an interesting (and arguable) theoretical assumption: that first you create "content" (pure content-without-form, as it were) and then you give it "form."

Even though Genesis tells us that God took this approach when He created the heavens and the earth (starting out with "formless" matter), it is only one way to talk about the process of creation. Yet the approach is remarkably helpful to many people in their writing. Whether skilled or unskilled, many people find it a relief when they allow themselves to produce "raw content-without-form"—find it *enabling* to turn out pages and pages of writing without worrying about whether it's organized or fits a certain form.

In Workshops 4 and 5 we may seem even to have *exaggerated* this one-sided approach. In Workshop 4 we asked you to produce, as it were, gallons of formless *content,* and now in this workshop we ask you to pour those gallons into various bottles or forms.

Let us now turn around and look at the *other* way of talking about form and content in the process of creation. In the first place, strictly speaking *all* writing has form: there's no such thing as content-without-form. All that writing you produced in Workshop 4 cannot but have *some* form. Perhaps the form is mixed or messy, but that's form too. Besides, what looks messy at first glance is often quite patterned. What you wrote may have a large coherent pattern which is obscured by local clutter, digressions, and interruptions.

For example, if you look carefully at your seemingly chaotic private, exploratory writing, you may see that it is shaped by a single narrative flow—or even by a clever flashback narrative pattern. Or perhaps your exploratory writing has a three-step pattern of moving from *event* to *reactions* to the event to *reflective thoughts* about that event and your reactions. Or maybe you'll find the opposite pattern: a movement from reflective thoughts back to the events behind those thoughts. The point is that if you manage to record what's going on in your mind, you are almost certainly recording patterns. Our minds operate by patterns even when we are confused. The human mind is incapable of pure randomness or chaos. Therefore when you look at your private exploratory writing, don't just respect the chaos as useful and valid (which it is); keep an eye out also for the *order* hiding behind the seeming chaos.

This realization leads to a very practical consequence: there are always organizations and genres *already lurking* in your seemingly messy exploratory writing—organizations and genres that you can discover and prune into shape (like recovering a shapely tree that has become overgrown). Just because you weren't *aware* of writing within a particular genre doesn't mean that you wrote genreless material. When you "organize" your chaotic private writing, you probably don't have to *create* organization from scratch; you can clarify the latent organization that's already there. Or more likely you can choose and develop one of the two or three overlapping organizations that are operating—like overlapping wave patterns caused by two or three pebbles dropped in a pond.

In sum, there's no such thing as "starting with content only"; you can't have a smidgen of content that is not fully formed. But you can *pretend* to start with content. That is, you can put all your attention on following a train of words or thoughts where they lead and totally ignore consideration of form.

Starting with Form

So too, it's possible to *pretend* to start with form. And this too is a very practical approach that can help in writing. That is, it can be helpful to *start with an organization or genre* and look to content afterward. For a genre isn't just a mold to pour unformed raw writing into or a sewing pattern to lay on top of whole cloth to show us where to cut. A genre can serve as a way to *generate* or invent content: choosing a genre will make you think of words and ideas that you might not think of otherwise. For example, if you decide to use narrative as a form, you will not just *arrange* your material in terms of time; you will almost certainly *think of* certain connecting or even causal events you had forgotten. If you are vacillating between a persuasive and an analytic essay, the persuasive genre will cause you to think of reasons and arguments; the analytic genre will cause you to think of hypotheses and causal relationships.

Of course it's common to start by choosing a genre. For example, we may decide to write a letter to someone and not be sure yet what we'll say. Or we may decide to write an essay with a certain organization (for example, a point-by-point refutation of someone else's view). Or someone may choose a genre for us: "Write a persuasive essay on any topic." In Workshop 2, we specified description and narration as the starting points for writing. In loop writing we started with mini-genres (portrait, narrative, letter, and so forth). In this workshop, however, we ask you to think about these genres or types *after* you have done lots of writing.

Because language is inherently both form and content, we can never really have pure content or pure form. It is only *our* consciousness which tends, at any given moment, to emphasize one more than the other. If we use process writing to study our tendencies of mind when we write, we will gradually learn when it's helpful to put more attention on form as we write, and when it's helpful to put more attention on content. In this way we can take better control of our writing process.

Readings

BE BRAVE SWEET SISTER: ESSAY DEVELOPED FROM OPEN-ENDED WRITING

Melissa Fogel

My sister Jennifer and I were the closest two sisters could be. We were not abnormal, we had our fights, yet they were fights you'd have with any life-long roommate. All of my childhood memories are filled with her face. Her baby blue eyes, her long curly brown hair and of course her chubby little cheeks. Our days were spent torturing our little brother, playing dress up with mom's clothes, climbing trees, sledding down the back of our yard, riding bikes until we couldn't walk, or just singing along to the radio in our make-believe band. I die a little each time I think that the laughter left our family, or my sweet little sister has vanished from my life.

Jennifer has been dating a man our family has trouble relating to. Although she would love to blame it on the color of his skin, this is far from the truth. My family has trouble relating to his ten year leap over her age, his twenty two arrests, and his three times in jail serving longer than six months. Take all the legal problems away and my family will not relinquish their problem with this man. My sister is young, beautiful, and intelligent; however she has very little self esteem, and seems to let herself get lost in the crowd. The man she dates does not help in this situation; he only lets her hide under his arms. Jennifer needs someone to motivate her in school and life—to show the world that she is an incredible woman with enormous gifts to give. He just hides her, and feeds her fear.

The days without her now are almost empty, almost depressing. She and I fight on the subject whenever one of us can muster up the energy. Some days I want to reach for her thin little neck and start strangling. For her path down this life time she has chosen will only break the rope that ties our hearts together. The anger I feel rises inside of me until I can hardly see straight. My nails bury themselves into my skin and tears cascade down the pale cheeks of my pain ridden face. I can see the anger in Jennifer as well. Her blue eyes become black and there is no reflection of the sister she once loved staring back at her. I am the enemy, with a black heart and red horns that stick strangely towards the sky. Our clashes have become so ugly, that I began to fear seeing her in the halls of the house—the same halls we used to bang into while playing a fast paced game of tag. Now these halls are empty, lonely, and ugly.

The pain of losing her is harder to describe than the anger. The pain gnaws on the inside of my heart, making it slowly bleed to death into a sea some call the soul. I have painful reminders of what our relationship used to be like in the back of my mind trying to break free and huddle over the mess we have now. My days at home are so dark. The rooms seem so cloudy, even when the sun peers through the hazy windows. The cloud seems to follow me into every sphere of my life, hanging over my head and gliding along the paths I choose to follow. It shadows my every move and makes others aware through the ugly darkness that covers my face. It seems as if this cloud will never let me free, until I confront the pain that steals my body from a happier existence.

That is where the fear becomes effervescent in the scope of my life. This confrontation that seems inevitable pulls at my sleeve as a nagging child does to her mother. In every scenario I play on the record player of my mind, Jennifer either wins the war, or drives off for good. I can't lose her entirely, I would die without my sister. Yet I can't see her with someone who does not bring out the Jennifer I know and love. I fear the loneliness I will experience without her. I fear the pain she will have to endure in a life under his wing, and I fear the guilt that will creep into my heart if I make her leave him for a life of loneliness.

I remember one rainy afternoon, despite the warnings we heard from our parents, my sister, brother and I went out to play. We ran over to our neighbor John's house, because he had the coolest swing set. It was wet and I had a really eerie feeling about the day. My sister ran over to the swing set to a bench where four people could sit and began to swing really high. She called me over but I couldn't do it; I didn't feel right about it. So I called her over to come play with me. To no avail: she wouldn't stop swinging. About ten minutes later I heard a scream. I ran over to find my little sister underneath that swing laying in a pool of blood. She was crying. The rest is memory to the adults, because they took over from there. Jennifer was rushed to the hospital where she was given fifteen stitches in the top of her head. I remember waiting by the window, so scared I would never see her again. Well she came home with a goofy story about how she was very brave, didn't cry and asked the doctor for gum while he was sewing her up.

The story seems ironic to me now. I'm calling out to my sister, for I have this awful feeling about this boyfriend of hers. Yet she doesn't hear me; she keeps on swinging. I keep calling; she keeps swinging. I want her to come home and every day I wait by the window of fear for her to come back to her big sister. Maybe one day she will come home with a new story of how she let him go, was very brave, didn't even cry and asked for a piece of gum.

A LETTER

Published in Elementary English

Teachers
Perkins School
43 & College
Des Moines, Iowa 50311

Dear Teachers:

This morning, just as I woke up, I remembered something that I have thought about off and on for years. I remembered taking spelling tests when I was in grade school at Perkins. As I remembered this, I experienced some of the feelings that I experienced when I prepared for these tests, took them, and got them back. I experienced fear, anxiety and humiliation.

I remember the spelling books that we used. The color, size and shape of the books. How the words to be learned were grouped on the page. And I can remember how hard I tried to learn these words. Doing just what my teachers said. Printing the words over and over again. Spelling a word to myself with my eyes closed and then opening my eyes to check if I was right. Spelling the words for my parents before bed. Going over them again and again right before the test. I can also remember what it was like to take the spelling tests. A piece of wide margined paper and a pencil. The teacher saying the words aloud. Fear and anxiety. I struggled to remember how to spell each word. Erase. No matter how I spelled a word, it looked wrong. Fear. I crossed out, printed over, went back, tried again. "One minute left." Anxiety. When my spelling papers came back they were covered with red marks, blue marks, check marks, correction marks, and poor grades. It was so humiliating. And it was always the same. No matter how much I prepared or how hard I tried, I couldn't spell most of the words. And no matter how many spelling tests I took and failed, there were always more spelling tests to take and fail. We got a new book of spelling words at the beginning of each term.

At the time my teachers tried to help me. They told me what I had to do in order to improve: "Print the words over and over again. Spell a word to yourself with your eyes closed and then open your eyes to check if you are right. Spell the words for your parents before bed. Go over them again and again right before the test." My teachers also said that unless I learned to spell I would never get into high school, or out of high school, or into college, or out of college. And the last thing that they always told me was that I couldn't spell.

What I want to say to you teachers now is this. I couldn't spell very well then, and I still can't. I got into high school, and out of high school, and into college, and out of college. While my teachers at Perkins didn't teach me to spell, they did manage to have an effect on me. For example, this morning, twenty five years later, I woke up and remembered their spelling tests, and experienced the fear, anxiety and humiliation that I felt when I prepared for these tests, took them, and got them back. If you are still giving children these spelling tests, please stop doing so at once.

Sincerely yours,

Mark Levensky
Associate Professor
Department of Humanities
Massachusetts Institute of Technology
Cambridge, Massachusetts

From PARTS OF SPEECH AND PUNCTUATION

Gertrude Stein

What does a comma do.

I have refused them so often and left them out so much and did without them so continually that I have come finally to be indifferent to them. I do not now care whether you put them in or not but for a long time I felt very definitely about them and would have nothing to do with them.

As I say commas are servile and they have no life of their own, and their use is not a use, it is a way of replacing one's own interest and I do decidedly like to like my own interest my own interest in what I am doing. A comma by helping you along holding your coat for you and putting on your shoes keeps you from living your life as actively as you should lead it and to me for many years and I still do feel that way about it only now I do not pay as much attention to them, the use of them was positively degrading. Let me tell you what I feel and what I mean and what I felt and what I meant.

When I was writing those long sentences of The Making of Americans verbs active present verbs with long dependent adverbial clauses became a passion with me. I have told you that I recognize verbs and adverbs aided by prepositions and conjunctions with pronouns as possessing the whole of the active life of writing.

Complications make eventually for simplicity and therefore I have always liked dependent adverbial clauses. I have liked dependent adverbial clauses because of their variety of dependence and independence. You can see how loving the intensity of complication of these things that commas would be degrading. Why if you want the pleasure of concentrating on the final simplicity of excessive complication would you want any artificial aid to bring about that simplicity. Do you see now why I feel about the comma as I did and as I do.

Think about anything you really like to do and you will see what I mean.

When it gets really difficult you want to disentangle rather than to cut the knot, at least so anybody feels who is working with any thread, so anybody feels who is working with any tool so anybody feels who is writing any sentence or reading it after it has been written. And what does a comma do, a comma does nothing but make easy a thing that if you like it enough is easy enough without the comma. A long complicated sentence should force itself upon you, make you know yourself knowing it and the comma, well at the most a comma is a poor period that it lets you stop and take a breath but if you want to take a breath you ought to know yourself that you want to take a breath. It is not like stopping altogether which is what a period does stopping altogether has something to do with going on, but taking a breath well you are always taking a breath and why emphasize one breath rather than another breath. Anyway that is the way I felt about it and I felt that about it very very strongly. And so I almost never used a comma. The longer, the more complicated the sentence the greater the number of the same kinds of words I had following one after another, the more the very many more I had of them the more I felt the passionate need of their taking care of themselves by themselves and not helping them, and thereby enfeebling them by putting in a comma.

So that is the way I felt punctuation in prose, in poetry it is a little different but more so and later I will go into that. But that is the way I felt about punctuation in prose.

AUTOBIOGRAPHY

Nazim Hakmit

I was born in 1902
I never once went back to my birthplace
I don't like to turn back
at three I served as a pasha's grandson in Aleppo
at nineteen as a student at Moscow Communist University
at forty-nine I was back in Moscow as a guest of the Tcheka Party
and I've been a poet since I was fourteen
some people know all about plants some about fish
                                      I know separation
some people know the names of the stars by heart
                                      I recite absences

I've slept in prisons and in grand hotels
I've known hunger even a hunger strike and there's almost no food
   I haven't tasted
at thirty they wanted to hang me

at forty-eight to give me the Peace Medal
                         which they did
at thirty-six I covered four square meters of concrete in half a year
at fifty-nine I flew from Prague to Havana in eighteen hours
I never saw Lenin I stood watch at his coffin in '24
in '61 the tomb that I visit is his books
they tried to tear me away from my party
                         it didn't work
nor was I crushed under falling idols
in '51 I sailed with a young friend into the teeth of death
in '52 I spent four months flat on my back with a broken heart
    waiting for death
I was jealous of the women I loved
I didn't envy Charlie Chaplin one bit
I deceived my women
I never talked behind my friends' backs
I drank but not every day
I earned my bread money honestly what happiness
out of embarrassment for another I lied
I lied so as not to hurt someone else
    but I also lied for no reason at all
I've ridden in trains planes and cars
most people don't get the chance
I went to the opera
    most people can't go they haven't even heard of the opera
and since '21 I haven't been to the places that most people visit
    mosques churches temples synagogues sorcerers
    but I've had my coffee grounds read
my writings are published in thirty forty languages
    in my Turkey in my Turkish they're banned
cancer hasn't caught up with me yet
and nothing says that it has to
I'll never be a prime minister or anything like that
and I'm not interested in such a life
nor did I go to war
or burrow in bomb shelters in the bottom of the night
and I never had to take to the roads under diving planes
but I fell in love at close to sixty
in short comrades
even if today in Berlin I'm *croaking* of grief
        I can say that I've lived like a human being
and who knows
    how much longer I'll live
        what else will happen to me.

ABOUT BEING A MAN: ESSAY DEVELOPED FROM
PRIVATE WRITING

Charles Miller

In this paper I will discuss, through personal experience, what it is to grow up male and all that is expected of a "man" and why we exhibit these traits.

It all begins as a child. My father treated my older brother and me more like his buddies than his sons. He would be gone for sometimes weeks at a time on a flight and when he would come home, even though we missed him, there were no hugs and kisses. He'd walk through the door and say, very unenthusiastically, "Hello boys" and give us a swift slap on the back or shoulder. Or shake our hands, clenching tightly, making us squeeze back as hard as possible. This was followed by some sort of strength test to see if we had gotten any stronger while he had been away.

We were never allowed to cry in my house: "Men don't cry." Believe me having an older brother around to beat the hell out of you, it was extremely hard not to cry occasionally. If my father saw us crying he would say "What the hell are you crying for, go outside!" Or if we were already outside it was "Go see your mother!"

Then there was sibling rivalry. My brother and I were constantly getting into fights and I had my share of getting beaten up, and if I ever cried the taunting from him and his friends was worse than the black and blues. To be called a sissy or a wimp was the worst torture and embarrassment possible. So you learned not to cry, show no pain, "suck it up," be a man about it.

Then there were times on the schoolyard when I found myself walking up to another male classmate and punching him in the gut as hard as I possibly could, only because he may have called me a name or maybe it was because his mom dressed him funny or he had a "girly" lunchbox. All the boys were so hostile towards one another at that age: it seems so horrible now.

And then there was proving oneself. You always had to prove yourself as a young boy. Climb the highest tree, jump the widest stream, ride your bike down the steepest hill, or hold your breath the longest. You always accepted the challenge. Even if you didn't want to, you had to. Otherwise you would be called a wimp and society turned their backs on you. So you go through with it, and if you didn't make it you do it again no matter how bad your knees were scraped from the first try. If you challenged that test of "manhood" and beat it, then you would gain status in this society and become a leader, and it felt pretty good, until someone did something better.

This competition among peers carried on into high-school. But for some odd reason it became even more important. When playing sports you were never allowed to show or at least permit yourself to show any pain, no matter how bad you were hurt. "Suck it up. Don't be a candy ass." Sometimes you would be in so much pain you didn't want to move, but you would get up and get back into it. You felt more like a man playing with the pain than to sit out

149

Readings
What's a Short,
Bald-headed Pot-
bellied Guy to Do?

like a wimp. All I got from that manly bull was an unbelievably painful knee reconstruction operation, over a year of therapy, and years of knee problems to look forward to. All for the image I, as a male, am supposed to portray.

I realize now that trying to portray that image is foolish. There is no reason to harm oneself in an effort to be manly. Helpless and in pain is all I felt lying in that hospital bed. With a group of therapists standing around you urging you to move your leg just the slightest bit and struggling to the point of exhaustion without success you feel anything but manly. If I could go back in time I would stop myself at the first sign of any knee problems and gladly accept being a wimp for awhile, rather than screw up my knee permanently.

If I have a son, just like any other father, I want him to be tough and brave to all challenges. But I will not force these ideals of manliness on him. If he wants to take on a challenge it should be for himself and not to impress me or anyone else. It is far better for him to achieve something for himself rather than do something against his will merely to impress other males and hold true to that portrait of being male.

WHAT'S A SHORT, BALD-HEADED, POTBELLIED GUY TO DO?
The List of Risk Factors for Heart Disease Grows Even Longer

By Michael D. Lemonick, Published in Time *Magazine*

Well-Informed Barber: I've noticed your hair is thinning quite a bit on top.
Borscht Belt Comedian: So? Who wants fat hair?
Barber: Very funny. But I guess you haven't read the latest issue of the *Journal of the American Medical Association.* A study out of the Boston University School of Public Health shows that men with bald spots can have more than three times the risk of heart attack as guys with a full head of hair.
Comic: You should talk. If your hairline recedes any more, you'll have to start buying floor wax instead of Brylcreem.
Barber: Ah, but the study also says that only a bald spot on top—so-called vertex baldness—is the problem. If you're losing hair in front or on the sides, you're probably O.K.
Comic: You've got to be kidding. How can baldness have anything to do with the heart?
Barber: The researchers don't know. It could be that both are related to a common factor—a high level of the male hormone dihydrotestos-terone is one plausible culprit. In any case, an editorial in *JAMA* says the correlation between baldness and heart disease is statisti-cally sound.
Comic: I'm not going to worry; I'm only 50.
Barber: The men in the study were all under 55.

Comic: I want a second opinion.

Barber: O.K., you're short too. You know, of course, that a 1991 study at the Harvard Medical School showed that men under 5 ft. 7 in. have a 60% greater risk of a first heart attack than tall men do.

Comic: Watch it, you're starting to get on my nerves! I don't want to blow my stack; I hear that anger is bad for your heart too.

Barber: Don't bet on it. A new study at the Mayo Clinic has failed to show any relationship between hostility and heart disease. Nervousness, though . . . well, the latest thinking is that emotional stress is not so good.

Comic: Listen, I try to take care of my heart. I take my blood-pressure pills religiously. My pressure has dropped way down. Don't tell me *that* isn't good.

Barber: Well, maybe not. Medical researchers at Albert Einstein Medical College demonstrated a few years ago that while a moderate drop in blood pressure can reduce heart-attack risk, a large drop can actually increase it.

Comic: At least I've got my weight down.

Barber: You're slimmer in the thighs and rear, but you've still got a big potbelly. Yours is the body type associated with a higher risk of heart disease.

Comic: O.K., killjoy, how about this? I switched from caffeinated coffee to decaf.

Barber: Out of the frying pan, into the fire. Yes, some people say drinking more than five cups of regular coffee can raise your risk of dying from heart disease, but decaf may raise your blood levels of LDL cholesterol, which is bad for the arteries.

Comic: Hey, but I've improved my diet: I gave up high-fat liver pâté and wine.

Barber: Gave them up? Don't you know that people in the south of France eat twice as much pâté as anyone else in the country but have the lowest rates of fatal heart disease? The French in general have less heart disease than Americans, though they eat lots of fat and cholesterol. Red wine could be part of the reason.

Comic: O.K., O.K., but at least I get a good night's sleep, more than I could say for some of the French.

Barber: Sleep's not so safe either. Just last month the *New England Journal of Medicine* reported that when you're dreaming, the sympathetic nervous system, which helps the body react to emergencies, is twice as active as it is when you're awake. Your heart beats faster, your blood pressure goes up, and your blood can get stickier, so it can clot and cause a heart attack. On the other hand, waking up isn't so great either. Heart attacks occur more often in the morning than at any other time of the day.

Comic: Boy, you're a real barrel of laughs. Got any other good news?

Barber: You see that crease in your earlobes? A kind of diagonal wrinkle? A University of Chicago physician did a study showing that such a crease may be associated with—you guessed it—an increased risk of heart disease.

Comic: Enough, already. I get it. I'm as good as dead. I might as well give up salad and fish and start eating pastrami and French fries again. I'll cut out my daily three-mile walk. I might as well go back to cigarettes too.

Barber: What's that? You say you get moderate exercise, eat a low-fat diet and don't smoke? Well, that's another story. Those things make more of a difference to your cardiovascular health than any of the things I was talking about. And besides, most of the studies I mentioned are considered suggestive but not definitive. They could even be wrong. Forget everything I said. Let's try combing some hair over from the side to hide that bald spot.

Comic: Now you're talking. I was beginning to think I'd have to see my doctor for a haircut.

MEDITATION

A Student

I enter the store and quietly take a seat, while music fills the air. Sitting in here, I can hear a piano melody drifting on by, and the screeching of a trumpet being played out of tune. Endless time passes by, and then my teacher clomps on in, venerable in wisdom if not in age. He shoots a smile, and we begin a new lesson on how to play music.

We enter a stuffy little room and talk a while about how things are going, and we tell a few jokes. Eventually we decide that it's time to play some music, so I take out my guitar. It's an electric, so we plug it into the amp and make some adjustments. We play some jazz tunes for a while, and I crack up because the B string keeps on going out of tune. All of my strings are dead as a doornail and need to be replaced badly. A little light is being reflected back from the black finish—the way the light is reflected off a car's hood. This looks really impressive, but I really wouldn't want to be caught in the glare. It is great though, and the whole thing has a lot of sentimental value for me.

My guitar in general is great—if you ignore some minor imperfections. While we're playing I can see a clear reflection of the opposite wall in its finish. I also begin to notice the thing's general condition. There's a little bit of dust and grime accumulating on the finish, but it's nothing that a little polish couldn't take care of. I've gotten it scratched up a bit—not too badly, but just enough to notice at a certain angle. The pick guard is scratched up pretty badly too, but I can't complain, because that's what it's there for. These things don't really detract from its appearance, though; they're just my mark on the instrument. I use it on a regular basis, and if it wasn't a little worn, I'd be pretty upset.

After my teacher tells me that I have got to get new strings (ha ha), we go on to play a few more songs. We play lots of good music in the process—the fretboard action is great, and I manage to keep the thing relatively in tune. The music is a little too loud at first, but we adjust the volume a bit to fix that. First, I play harmony, and my teacher plays melody, and then after a while we switch parts. The harmony is a kind of structure to build the melody around, the melody gives definition to the music. The music has many dimensions to it, and different groups of notes change and flow, transmogrifying into new things as they move through time. Then I make a mistake, and we laugh as the whole thing falls down like a house of cards. We try again. The music floats, soars, and dives—it stops and starts again and shudders with a kind of life of its own. It becomes one big cohesive thing, a whole somehow bigger than its component parts, a kind of thing in itself. And ultimately it ends.

And when the music's over, I pack away the guitar in a black hard-shell case and say good-by. We tell a few more jokes and go our separate ways—until next week. . . .

□ □ □ □ □

There won't be a "next week" for lessons, though I can't hold onto the past. I'll always remember the people, though, and what they stood for—their hopes, their dreams, and their fears. And they'll always be a part of me. Forever.

Just like my guitar.

Process Note

In this essay, I wasn't just describing a guitar—I was describing much more. I was describing my feelings toward musicianship in general, and toward some of the most important people in my life—my guitar teachers. I think and feel very much like they do, and I'll be in debt to them forever. This is a kind of tribute to them.

WORKSHOP
6

WRITING IN THE
WORLD: AN INTERVIEW
ABOUT WRITING

For this workshop you will be asked to conduct and write up an interview with someone about how they write. Our goal is for you to learn about the great diversity of kinds of writing and ways of writing in the world so that you'll see more options when you approach a writing task. As you hear the interviews written by your classmates, you will get much more perspective and awareness about all the things writing can do.

But we also have other goals for this workshop:

- As you work through this assignment, you'll get practice in how to find or carve out a theme or develop a conclusion from a mass of diverse material.
- You'll also learn to conduct interviews: to hear what another person is saying but also "hear" what's behind what she is saying.
- School writing and academic essay writing are always in danger of going dead. The interview is good for helping you get lively speech-qualities and "voice" into your writing because you will use lots of quoted speech.
- You'll get the chance to begin to think about how writing is often the blending together of your own ideas and the ideas of others into a text you can call your own.

 MAIN ASSIGNMENT

Your main assignment is to conduct and write up an interview and to include in your write-up some conclusions you've drawn about writing as the result of your interview.

Choosing Someone to Interview

Pick someone who writes a significant amount and cares about writing. Four possibilities suggest themselves:

- An adult professional: either a professional writer or someone who has to write for her job. You might even want to use this assignment as an opportunity to talk to someone in a field you are considering for yourself. (You may be surprised how much people have to write in fields that seem distant from writing. Recent research shows that engineers, for example, spend an average of 25 percent of their week writing.)
- An adult who is devoted to writing though it is not part of his job. This might be someone who writes fiction or poetry or does research in his free time.
- A junior, senior, or graduate student who is majoring in a subject you would like to explore.
- A member of your writing class. (Probably you'll want to pick someone who is particularly interested in writing, though it could also be useful to interview someone who particularly hates writing in order to learn how that can happen to people and what the effects are.)

If you are working in groups, you'll all learn the most if you each choose a different kind of person to interview. Adult subjects make the most sense for students who live at home or nearby, since they can pick an adult from their home environment. But of course there are adults on any campus—not just faculty—who write seriously, whether or not it is part of their job.

It's best to have *two* interviews with your subject (about three hours in all). Set up these interviews early and follow through to make them happen. (Busy people sometimes have to change appointments, so you may need to push to get your interviews.) The important thing is to make sure the person has enough interest in writing to give you the time you need.

Collaborative Options

This is a good workshop for collaborative writing. You can interview with one or more partners and then write up the interview and your conclusions collaboratively. Another approach is for each of you to interview different people, but then join with one or two other classmates to write a comparison of your interviewees, including some conclusions all of you arrive at collaboratively.

A Practice Interview with a Classmate

Some of you may have done some interviewing in the past, perhaps as a reporter for a school newspaper, perhaps as part of an assignment for a particular class. If so, you can help others in the class who haven't had this experience. Interviews can be fun, but they do take some practice and skill, especially if the process makes you nervous. We suggest here a quick practice session with a classmate.

Before your interview, you need to have some questions to ask. Either in class (if your teacher provides time) or prior to class, jot down some things you would like to know about how other people write. Shape these into questions, but beware of making these questions too abstract or general. Otherwise you'll learn only people's *theories* about writing, not how they actually go about writing. You can't trust people's theories. For example, a person might say, "I always start with an outline" or "I always use 3 × 5 cards," but if you can get them to tell some stories and incidents from memory in detail, they will often realize (perhaps for the first time) that some of their best writing *didn't* involve outlines or 3 × 5 cards. Or sometimes people say that writing is always agony for them, but if you can get them to ramble honestly, they'll come upon times when they were genuinely enjoying themselves.

Together with your classmates, you'll probably come up with questions useful for both your in-class practice interview and your "real" interview. Here are some questions we've found useful:

- *Kinds.* "Tell me what kinds of writing you do. Don't leave out things like list-making or writing checks."
  - "Tell me about important writing times or incidents in your life."
    - Good times
    - Bad times
    - Especially perplexing times
    - An occasion when something unexpected happened

- Some situation where you had to write in a completely different way
- "What I find hardest in writing is_____; is that hard for you too?"
- *Mini-case study.* "Please show me something you wrote and just tell me the whole story of how it got written. Reflect on whether this mini-case is representative of how you usually write."
- *Conditions.* "Tell me something about where and when you usually write and what you usually use: pencil, pen, paper, computer. Do you think any of this makes a difference in your writing?"
- *Functions.* "What does most of your writing 'do'? Entertain? Inform? Persuade? Present experience? Earn money? Help you feel fulfilled? Get you a grade? Help you think? Get emotions out so you can go on?"

Suggestions for Your Practice Session

Interview a classmate for ten minutes. Take notes, and don't be nervous or furtive or self-conscious about doing so either now or in your longer interviews. Be proud of it. Most people are flattered that you care enough about what they are saying to get it right.

For this practice interview, it's best not to use a tape recorder; you'll benefit from being forced to listen closely to your interviewee. Some interviewers take full notes; some take sparse notes. Obviously you can't take down all the words and listen at the same time. Try jotting down a running list of interesting key words and phrases. You need words that *sound* like the person talking and words that will help you recapture actual words, phrases, and whole sentences when you go over your notes right after the interview. Put your main energy during the interview into listening, being interested, asking questions out of your genuine curiosity, and jotting down that rich list of actual spoken words and phrases. These notes will serve as memory jogs later. And remember that this is just practice; try out different strategies to see what works best for you.

Stop after ten minutes. Go over your notes immediately: that's crucial. They'll help you reconstruct the interview in your own words. But if you've been good at jotting down rich words and phrases, and if you don't let too much time go by, your notes will also help you reconstruct the person's actual words, phrases, and sentences. These will give energy and richness to your interview.

If this were your longer interview, you would be going over your notes alone. But for this exercise, do this reconstructing aloud in front of your subject. As you go through your notes repeating and reconstructing, she can help by making corrections of wording. And after you finish, she can mention things that *she* thought important or interesting that you didn't mention—just to give you another perspective on what you recorded.

If this were your longer interview, you would also be jotting down some of *your* thoughts and observations and trains of thought as you reconstruct the interview. But for this quick in-class exercise, simply *say* some of these observations after you have reconstructed your subject's words. After this inter-

Interviewing made me sort of nervous because I just didn't know whether she wanted to talk to me about this or was just being nice or polite. I took some notes at the beginning but they didn't mean much; when I tried to figure them out I couldn't even remember talking about those things. I was just too nervous. When she started talking about trying to write a novel and how her daughter knocked milk on the pages and then the dog sat on them I just laughed. I remember that and I didn't even take notes. I remember so clearly that she said "My dog's an author!" Then I wasn't so nervous anymore.

Marsha Koons

view-and-reporting-back, switch places and give your classmate a chance to interview you and report back.

You and your partner will also find it valuable to talk about what it was like being interviewed: what approaches made you feel most comfortable and which questions proved to be the most effective prompts for stimulating memory and thoughts.

Option in Threes. This same interviewing exercise can be rich and interesting in groups of three. One person interviews another for ten minutes, as before, but with the third person as onlooker, either just listening or also taking notes (for practice). Then when the interviewer reconstructs his notes, the onlooker can chime in to help capture the words actually spoken or to comment on things he would have tried to record that the interviewer omitted. Or they can both reconstruct notes, compare them, and learn from each other—with, of course, the help of the interviewee.

 ## YOUR REAL INTERVIEW

Once you've selected a person to interview, you may want to prepare additional specific questions. Notice how the reporter who interviewed Walter Mosley (see "Readings" at the end of this workshop) asked questions directly relevant to the kind of writing the interviewee does. Look over your questions just before the interview.

Otherwise, what we've said about your practice interview applies to your real interview. You may be nervous as you start, but once you relax, you'll enjoy the process. Remember to be open about taking notes—your interviewee will probably expect it—but don't get so caught up in note taking that you can't get involved in the conversation. Jot down key words, actual spoken words or phrases that capture your subject's way of talking. When you get involved and listen attentively, your natural curiosity will begin to direct the questions you ask. And the fact that you become genuinely engaged in what your subject says will increase your ability to remember it.

If you are not going to be able to arrange a second interview, you'll also want to look at the elaborations on the basic questions we suggest for that second interview (page 159–160). You may want to write out some of these questions for yourself—perhaps on large index cards to take to the interview. Then you can jot down words from your subject's reply on each card with the question that evoked those words. But remember not to stick slavishly to these questions; let your interviewee guide the direction of the conversation. Use your prepared questions when you seem to have reached the end of a line of thought.

What's important is to give your subject enough freedom to get involved in what she's saying. If she doesn't seem to want to talk and just gives short answers—if you feel your interview falling into a lifeless question-and-answer pattern—try to use more open-ended questions, such as "Tell me a story about a time when you were really pleased (disappointed) with . . ." or "Tell me more about that" or "How did you feel about that?" and so forth. And don't be afraid to wait a bit at the end of an answer; be willing to leave long silences hanging in the air. People often give their best answers after a long pause for reflection. Remember that one of the best things you can say is simply, "That sounds interesting; talk some more about that."

Once your subject gets going, you can intervene with clarifying questions, for example, "What were you writing with? How were you feeling at that point? Did that take a long time? Were you thinking about your audience at that point or just steaming along suiting yourself?"

Tape Recorder. You might use a tape recorder for your interview if you prefer, and if you have one available and your subject doesn't object. It will let you quote your subject's words exactly. Most people don't mind being recorded and soon get over being self-conscious. You won't have to take notes during the interview (except perhaps to record your own thoughts and reactions). But a tape recorder doesn't solve your interviewing problems. You'll still have to take notes *as you listen to the tape.* And taping can deceive you into becoming a lazy listener. You can capture much more in notes than you might expect, and note taking is an important skill to develop.

Reconstructing Your Notes after the Interview

We said this about your practice interview and we repeat it here for emphasis: it's crucial to make time right after the interview to go over your sketchy notes.

- Reconstruct and write out in more detail your subject's most interesting or striking words.
- Write out some of your *own* observations, reactions, questions, and trains of thought about what the person has said.
- If you had to decide now on a "moral of the story," what would it be? You don't have to settle it yet, but what's the most interesting conclusion you could draw at this point?
- Don't forget to include some *physical* details such as the setting (the room and the atmosphere), the person's appearance (how she was dressed, how she spoke and moved), what her pieces of writing actually looked like

(whether drafts or final copies). Such details don't just "add color"; they often help tell the story and convey the ideas you are trying to get across.

■ Work out some new questions for a second interview, questions which follow up on ideas generated as you reconstruct your notes.

If you delay going over your notes for even three or four hours, you will lose many crucial details. Remember that for right now you are not trying even for a draft of your interview; all you're doing is going over and adding to your notes.

Questions for Your Thinking and for the Second Interview

Before you go to your second interview, try sharing what you've done so far with others in your class. You can read them your rough write-up of the first interview, the questions you have come up with, and the tentative conclusions you've drawn. You may even want to try role-playing your interviewee; it's surprising what such a strategy can make you and others realize.

You'll particularly want to ask others if they see implications in your material which you haven't noted, or if there are certain issues which they think you need to follow up on during the second interview. In this way everyone gets practice looking through rough material and speculating about conclusions or inferences: practice with "So what?" or "What's interesting here?" or "What bears pursuing here?" In the interview of Walter Mosley in the "Readings," the interviewer does not include implications he drew. You and your classmates might want to practice drawing implications by using this interview as material.

Besides helping you see and do more with your material, there is another goal in this sharing: to help you learn more about interviewing and what kinds of questions to ask. The sharing will make you more skilled when you come to your second interview.

Here are some elaborations of our previous questions and a few additional ones you might want to keep in mind as you flesh out your notes from your first interview—trying to get straight what you have already found out and what you still need to ask at a second interview. These questions may also be helpful in writing the essay itself.

■ *Kinds.* Make sure you covered all the possibilities. For example, if your interviewee is a reporter and if she says she writes nothing but news stories, ask her to explore differences between *kinds* of news stories.

■ *Processes.* Make sure you have lots of details here: what happens in your interviewee's mind before she does any writing—during the hours or days *before* she puts a word on paper? What are her first words on paper? notes? outline? or just random jottings? Or does she go right to written-out drafts or perhaps even directly to final drafts? What are her feelings throughout the whole process? What about the role of other people? What kinds of feedback help her? And don't settle for a "general story of how I *always* or *usually* write." Probe for differences and exceptions.

■ *Audience.* If your first interview didn't touch on this, ask her about her important readers, past and present: former teachers, present friends, supervisors. Get her to talk about what makes an audience helpful or not helpful for her. (Audience is a complicated issue because often, especially on the job, there is more than one audience: the news story may be for people who buy the paper, but the editor sees it first and has to like it; the memo may be for the clients or buyers, but it has to work for the writer's immediate supervisor too.) Does she think a lot or not so much about audience when writing? At which points in the writing process does she think about audience most?

- *Changes.* What important changes have occurred in how she writes and feels about writing? Does she see other changes in the future? Does she have writing goals she hasn't yet met? What are her hopes about these?
- *Functions.* If your interviewee says that the function of her writing is just to make money, ask her to think about subsidiary functions within that main function. Does her writing persuade, give orders, explain things, give information? Ask her to think about function in connection with audience.
- *Conclusions.* These can be tentative for now, but if you figure out some now, it will help you set up additional questions for your second interview.

The Second Interview

You may want to start off the second interview by asking whether the person herself thought of things she'd like to add to the previous interview. Then you can go on to your prepared questions, but don't feel tied to them. In fact, you may want to star those which you consider essential and use the others only if you have time.

Before the interview is over, try out a few of your conclusions and see what her response is. You can state these as only tentative: "As I was looking over my notes, it struck me that you seem to get the ideas that matter to you when you are *not* writing. Am I right?" Or, "I got the sense that your writing process is changing—that you now take more chances. Do you feel that's so?" Your subject should do most of the *talking,* but you should probably give more *direction* this time than with the first interview: there are things you need to find out, and this is your last chance.

 WRITING UP THE INTERVIEW

The easiest way to get a draft is to make a collage. Using your intuition, simply choose the most interesting bits from your notes from both of the interviews: quotations that best recall the person's voice, pieces from your own reflections and explanations, and observations that capture essential points particularly well.

As you pick bits, keep in mind that the final version of your interview should include—at a minimum—discussion of these four elements: (1) the *kinds* of writing the person does; (2) the *ways* in which the person writes; (3) the *functions* of the writing the person does; and most important, (4) something *you* conclude. Notice that the interview of Mosley does not include any of the interviewer's conclusions. The student samples in the "Readings" do, however.

Perhaps you don't yet have any conclusions—any "so what's?" But this is the time to dream some up, even if they are very speculative or uncertain. It will hasten your thinking process and stimulate more useful feedback on your draft. (Someone in disagreeing with your crazy idea may give you a genuinely good one.)

For now let your collage be a bit too long: leave too much there and allow it to be a bit of an "everything-but-the-kitchen-sink collage." Your teacher will let you know whether you should polish up your interview, turn it into an essay rather than a collage, or leave it in its rough form as mainly a source for a comparative analysis you will write with a classmate.

Revision: Moving toward a Polished Finished Interview

(If your teacher does not expect a polished interview, you can skip this section for now. At some later time, you may want to polish your interview; then you can come back to this section.)

Read the rough draft of your interview aloud to your classmates or a classroom group, or to some friends. Don't ask them for a *critique* but rather for collaborative help. Then take the plunge into creating a strong, coherent, and more definite draft. At this stage, you have to be firm about cutting and figuring out what you are really trying to show and say.

Audience. You might assume your audience to be your classmates and your teacher. Admittedly this is a "school assignment" and may even be graded. But remember that you are the expert on your topic: you are telling your audience things that they don't know, things that will be helpful to them. And your classmates and teacher are not the only likely audience. This kind of interview is frequently published in local newspapers, campus newspapers, and magazines—especially magazines that writers read. You might choose this interview to revise during one of the later revising workshops—and then send it off to see if it could be published.

You will need to make some important decisions:

■ What will your main thought be? Perhaps you know already, but perhaps you haven't figured it out yet. Look back over everything and struggle with it. It's a good sign when your "point" arrives late in this way; it means you didn't close off possibilities.

- On the basis of your main thought, which bits will you keep and which leave out?
- Are the four crucial ingredients here: *kinds* of writing, *ways* of writing, *functions* of writing, and *your* conclusions?
- How will you structure your piece so it doesn't seem too jumpy or collage-like (unless, of course, your teacher has asked for a collage)? Find some way to connect all the parts into a coherent sequence—with a sense of beginning, middle, and end. You could structure it as a narrative, simply reporting the most interesting things that were said in the actual order they occurred and putting your conclusions at the end or interspersed throughout. But this is dangerous since the interview itself may well have been *un*-structured or wandering; you probably invited the subject to follow her digressions. Therefore you'll probably have to figure out a focus and arrange your material to fit it.

It's a struggle to take a lot of rough writing and turn it into something organized, coherent, and effective for readers. You will have to work at standing back, choosing the best parts, and figuring out the best order—and then tightening sentences and polishing grammar, punctuation, and usage.

As a step toward revising, either now or later in the semester, you can send your good draft to the person you interviewed. Ask her to correct quotations and respond to the portrait you created and to the observations and conclusions you have made. This response will be particularly important if you had only one interview. You may even be able to incorporate parts of her response in a final version if you revise several weeks later.

Your Words and the Words of the Person You Interview

Some interviewers use only their subject's words and none of their own. Though these "modest" interviewers do not *say* anything explicitly about their subject, they *imply* a great deal by the way they arrange the quoted material. Other interviewers include many of their own words, but none of their own ideas or conclusions—just summaries and explanations of what was said by the person interviewed.

In this assignment, however, we are asking you not just to portray the person you are interviewing but also to "say" something: to figure out some conclusion and say it instead of just implying it. Notice how both of the student samples at the end of this workshop say something that they have concluded about their interviewees. Nevertheless, interview essays are intriguingly different from most other writing in that you can get the person you interview to do much of your "writing" for you. If you interview thoughtfully, take good notes, and choose from them well, a substantial part of "your" piece will consist of your subject's words.

About Accuracy in Quotation. If you used a tape recorder, you can note somewhere that you did so and that your quoted passages are the actual words spoken by your subject. Even so, however, it is customary when transcribing someone's casual speech to do minor cleaning up: leaving out "um's" and "er's" and digressive phrases, and fixing grammar and the like. If you didn't use a tape recorder, do your best to find and reconstruct some actual words, phrases, and sentences and put them in quotation marks, for actual quotations are the lifeblood of an interview. But acknowledge that you were working from notes and therefore might not have gotten some of the quotations *exactly* right. (For help with the mechanics of quoting, see Mini-Workshop I.)

Collaborative Option

If you have selected or been assigned to write a collaborative comparison essay, do five or ten minutes of focused freewriting about what you see as the conclusions you can draw about your writer on the basis of your interview. Then get together with your partner(s) and trade freewritings as a way to get started on your collaborative analysis. You may want to extend this written conversation through several interchanges as you did in Workshop 3.

Here are some possible areas to consider jointly.

1. How alike or different are the kinds of writing our interviewees do?
2. In what ways are our interviewees' writing habits alike or different?
3. What can we say about each of our interviewees' attitudes toward writing? What effects do these attitudes seem to have?
4. How does the writing our interviewees do relate to the writing they did while in school? to the writing we do in school?
5. What conclusions can we draw from each of the interviews? Are these conclusions consistent, or do we seem to draw very different conclusions from each of the interviews? If so, what does this suggest?
6. What can we learn about our own writing processes from studying these two interviews?

Once you and your partner have discussed or written about these and other issues, you can begin to draft your collaborative essay. (You might want to look back at Workshop 3 for guidelines for collaborative writing.) Remember that the most important element of your collaborative essay is the *conclusion you and your partner have reached about writing or thinking*. Perhaps it will be a conclusion about why people write well or with satisfaction—or why they have difficulty—or about the nature of writing or language or readers. Perhaps it will be something the two of you conclude about *your own* writing on the basis of comparing your interviews and reflecting on them. Figure out something that is interesting to the two of you and it will almost certainly be interesting to readers.

As you work toward your final draft, don't let the liveliness of your interviews evaporate; you can quote short revealing phrases or longer statements which illustrate important points. Juxtaposing the voices of the two interviewees is one way to get a significant idea across to your readers.

Once you have an organized draft which makes the points you and your partner have agreed to include, you can share it with your classmates or other valued readers. Keep in mind that you and your partner don't have to agree on every statement you make. Disagreements can be thought-provoking for readers. The more significant the disagreement, the more urgent it is to present it to others.

 ## SUGGESTIONS FOR SHARING AND RESPONDING

If you are doing this workshop early in the semester, the main benefit from readers will come from "Sharing: No Response" in *Sharing and Responding* at the end of this book. We recommend staying away from judgment or advice. You could also use "Pointing and Center of Gravity," "Summary and Sayback," and "What Is Almost Said? What Do You Want to Hear More About?" in *Sharing and Responding.* Here are some other questions that are particularly appropriate to this workshop.
- "What themes or conclusions do you see in my material?"
- "What lessons about your own writing do you learn from my interview?"
- "How would you describe the voice you hear in my interviewee? How does her way of talking paint a picture of the kind of person she is?"

If you did a collaborative essay, you may want to use the following questions also:
- "Does our collaborative writing sound like it alternates between two different styles? Do you find this useful or distracting? Point to places where you see the style shift. Are there places where our agreement seems forced and unconvincing?"

 ## PROCESS JOURNAL AND
COVER LETTER QUESTIONS

You won't need the questions that follow if you can just write about moments in this week's writing when things went well and badly—and surprisingly.

What was going on for you: in your thinking and feeling? How did words behave for you? These stories will build a powerful foundation for growth in your writing.

- How did your note taking go? What was it like reconstructing your notes?

- When did your conclusion or main point come to you? Was it a struggle to find one, or did it just seem to appear? Finding the *point* in a great mass of messy material is one of the main cognitive skills involved in learning. On the basis of this workshop's assignment, give yourself advice on ways to develop this skill in the future.

- Compare the goals or functions your interviewee was trying to achieve in her writings and the goals or functions you try to achieve in the various writings you do. How often do you actually think about what your writing *does* (other than fulfill an assignment)?

Readings

PORTRAIT OF MY MOTHER AS A WRITER

Kristin Bresnan

My mother was a writer? The thought made me laugh when I first considered it, but as I sat at the kitchen table with her that Sunday evening, sharing a bottle of wine and listening to her talk, that silly thought I had quickly diminished.

I have to admit now that I wasn't very excited about doing the interview, just because I didn't think that my mother would have anything interesting to say about writing. Wrong again. My mother's always been one who loves to talk, so it turned out that I'd ask a simple question, and she'd go on supplying me with such a long, elaborate answer that I couldn't keep up with her!

I started off by asking my mother what kinds of writing she does at this point in her life. She then proceeded to tell me that most of the writing she does now is for her job; it's not private writing. She finds this unfortunate because she loves writing poetry, but she just doesn't seem to have the time for it lately. My mother develops corporate training programs, and it takes up a lot of her time. She's not afraid to admit that she doesn't find it very exciting, and she's looking for something new. At the present time she is also designing a user's manual for a hotel reservations computer software system that my father is developing. She says sarcastically that this is the only spark of excitement in her job right now.

I find it interesting that she doesn't like to write for business, because she also has her Ph.D. I asked her, "How could someone who doesn't enjoy writing for business ever desire to get their Ph.D., which requires such a great deal of writing?" Well, in her opinion, writing her doctoral dissertation was a great experience. She started with a very clear idea of what she wanted to accomplish. It was all very organized. "The fact that it was so organized made the scientific aspect of it a little easier for me to deal with." Overall it ended up being an enjoyable experience and made her learn a lot about herself. She finds that when she writes now, whether it's private writing or business writing, she has a lot of pre-organization. "I'm clear about what I'm going to write; it doesn't unfold as I write, it's already there to begin with."

Even before high school my mother was told that she had writing talent. It was this talent that won her a writing contest which made her the editor of her high-school yearbook. While in college she continued and was frequently published in the college paper.

When I asked how she felt about herself personally as a writer, she replied, "I take pride in the quality of my writing. When I write I have a whole choice of possibilities of how I'm going to write something and I like to make sure that I make the best choice. I'm gifted in that way. It's like I have an internal computer. I automatically choose what's best, and if I can't do it right away, I elaborate on it for a while until I do get it right." I then thought to myself how nice it must be to have so much self-confidence about your writing.

I then asked my mother if there was any particular person or experience that influenced her as far as her writing skills and techniques were concerned. In other words, was she born with it or did it slowly develop with the help of some outside influence? I'm always wondering why some people have it and others don't. My mother then laughed and told me that the best thing that ever happened to her as far as writing is concerned was that she was raised as a product of the Catholic school system. She says, "I never thought I'd be saying anything positive about going to Catholic school, but I do have to admit that they really helped me develop my talent. They were so scrupulous about writing skills that students would strive for perfection in their writing. To them it was a special craft. I was always told that I had talent and I was encouraged to go on further with my writing. So this was where my self-confidence first developed, and I then had the incentive to move on and write more. For this I am very thankful."

Assuming that that was enough said on that subject, I then switched the topic a little bit and asked my mother if she ever thinks about an audience when she writes. After a long pause, she decided that she doesn't think about one at all because "I have a lot of confidence in my writing ability. I feel that I'm the best one to evaluate my writing, so I usually don't even think about an audience. The only time I might is if I was going to write fiction."

This coincidentally led us into talking about her hopes and fears about writing in the future. More than anything my mother would like to write a novel. Something along the lines of a Danielle Steele novel. Well, for those of you who don't know who Danielle Steele is, she writes tasteful, classy, "trashy" novels, not cheap Harlequin Romance stories. I found this amusing simply because I could actually picture my mother, the nine-to-five business woman with the Ph.D., writing a soap-opera story!

For now she only has time to write her poetry once a month or so. "When I do get the chance to write, I get an idea and it doubles. I become the vehicle for the poem and it flows through me. The words seem to have a life of their own."

I told her that with a tacky statement like that, she ought to be writing more than once every month or so just to get it out of her system! She laughed at that, a little. I asked her if she ever felt frustrated because she didn't get the chance to write very often. She explained to me that she doesn't really get frustrated but when she does get the chance to write her poetry, it seems to "explode out onto the page."

"What's your one biggest regret about writing?" I then asked. She replied, "I mainly regret the fact that I haven't kept a steady diary over the years. Writing a diary would serve a great purpose to me because then I could see how my attitudes and opinions have changed over the years. I've never given my writing the credit that it deserves by keeping and storing it all in one place—it's all kind of spread out all over the place."

I then decided to wrap things up by asking her what her overall view was on writing. Was there any sort of moral to the story? She started off by saying that different circumstances provide different ways of writing. Obviously this is easy to agree with. My mother explained that "Sometimes writing can be emotional, as with a poet, and other times writing can be more intellectual and logical, as with a scientist. There is more of a set process with a scientist than there is with a poet."

I thought about the differences for a minute and then decided that one thing that they share is the importance of clarity. Whether it's one or the other, the message has to be clear. That's where the audience comes in. My mother agreed with me. She said, "That's why poetry is more exciting to me. I want them to understand and feel the same emotion." We both agreed that the main point is that the audience has to feel what one is saying. A person can't relate to your writing unless they feel what you're saying.

I came out of the interview with a more positive attitude than when we began. I realized that my mother and I agreed on a lot of the same things. It's not so much your skill that matters when writing, it's the feeling and desire that you put into it.

The one thing that we didn't agree on was the audience aspect. According to my mother, the audience only matters in some kinds of writing, like fiction and poetry. For me the audience plays a large role all of the time. I find it impossible not to think about who will be reading my paper and what they will think. Can they relate to it? Do they feel what I'm trying to say? For me that's always the number one concern.

Process Writing

I was dreading this assignment but when I was actually writing the final draft I found myself enjoying it. I liked the way it was all fitting together. But at the end I realized that this was probably because of the fact that almost the entire thing is made up of direct quotes from my mother! It's her stuff that sounds nice, not mine! This upset me, but then I realized that it wasn't totally true—only partially. Oh well, I'm sure I'll never be 100 percent satisfied with anything I write.

I learned a lot about my mother that I didn't know to begin with. We don't get to spend much time together and this gave us a chance to sit down and have a nice talk. It turned out to be fun.

I found myself kind of turning it into a parody while I was writing the final draft. I could've stuck in a few really good one-liners but then I immediately remembered that I'd be reading it out loud to the class, so I decided not to stick them in. I *hate* reading out loud. It unfortunately influenced the way I wrote, but not much.

INTERVIEW

Salvatore Bianco

I conducted my interview with my brother, Anthony Bianco. I interviewed him as a person who greatly dislikes writing. Our conversation took place in my bedroom, and it lasted about an hour and fifteen minutes. The atmosphere was a very relaxed, casual one, and, because of this, my brother's opinions were both open and honest.

Anthony is a sophomore in high school and feels that he has had his share of writing assignments. I asked him how he felt about writing, and he said that he disliked it so much to the point where he actually hated it. The main question that I wanted answered was—Why?

My brother told me many reasons for his attitude toward writing. The primary reason, according to him, is that, "I never get the grade I feel I deserve. I've put a lot of effort into some assignments, and they were given bad grades." He told me about the time he was working on a biography about Edgar Allan Poe. Anthony stayed up most of the night, dedicating a great deal of time and effort to it, but all he received for it was a C−. "I did all that work for nothing! I don't even like writing; it's just a waste of my time." He also told me that he does not like writing book reports which have to be due at a certain date because he feels they take up too much of his time, and he does not like having these things on his mind. When he does do poorly on reports that he knows he has put time and effort into, it comes back to him with comments and question marks written all over them. "That gets me annoyed because the way I wrote the sentences seemed right to me; I don't understand what the teachers want from me!"

The actual writing of an essay seems to be a problem for my brother. He finds it difficult to write proper introductions and conclusions. Also, he is unable to recognize when new paragraphs should be started. He is easily at a loss for ideas, and he feels that his vocabulary is very limited. Because of this last problem, Anthony usually cannot find the proper words to express his ideas. "I know what I want to say, but I just don't know how to say it."

I then asked my brother what thoughts run through his mind just prior to writing. He often wonders about the length of the essay, what it will be about, when he will finish it, if he will be satisfied with it, and how the teacher will grade it. When he writes, he finds that he really does not concentrate on what he is doing. This is especially true during essay exams. "When I'm being rushed, I can't think straight!"

I thought it was necessary to find out just how he goes about writing something. Anthony told me that if his grades were borderline, he would take "very short" notes on his subject. Then he would write his rough draft before actually writing the final version. If, however, his grades were not borderline, he would just write the essay straight through and only recopy it if the first one was totally illegible.

Although Anthony hates to write, he does prefer some aspects of it to others. He would rather write a composition than, for example, a biography because he feels biographies are boring, yet finds it easy to make up stories and exaggerate them when possible. He also likes writing at home more than in school because there is hardly any pressure for him to deal with at home. When at home, Anthony prefers to write in either the kitchen during the evening or in the backyard on the picnic table during the late afternoon hours. Noise does not seem to bother my brother's concentration. Yet he does feel that he writes better when there is little noise. But he does not care about writing enough to worry about finding a place to work where it is quiet. Anthony seems to write only for himself, unless grades are involved. He says he does not write for the class because "the teacher doesn't make us get involved with discussing each other's essays." And he does not write for the teacher because "no matter how much I work on my essay, it won't meet my teacher's standards anyway."

In conducting this interview on my brother, I feel that I have learned some things about him and myself as well. I never realized how much my brother was so dead set against writing. I can understand how trying one's best but failing to be rewarded for it is enough to discourage most people. I have also learned that no matter how many times he is forced to write, and no matter what grades he receives for his writing, my brother is not going to change his attitude toward writing. What I learned about myself from this interview was that I value writing more than I previously thought I did. Of course, I have had my share of disappointments. But I am glad that I have been able to push myself to do better because writing can very well be an extremely pleasurable experience.

TACKLING RACISM IN THE MYSTERY NOVEL

The New York Newsday *Interview with Walter Mosley*

Q.   Why aren't there many black writers of mysteries?
A.   There are maybe five or six. The first contemporary writer of black mysteries, in the late '80s, was Gar Anthony Haywood. After him, me. Then Barbara Neely, and there's another four or five since I started writing. There are more black fiction writers.

In the white publishing world there's been a kind of prejudice that black people don't read. And if they do read, they read what white people read— therefore there's not a great interest [in publishing black writers]. But indeed there is this great interest among black people to read stories and fiction about black people—about their lives, about what's going on in their world. Also, a lot of white readers are very interested, and this is kind of a stunning thing to the publishing world. Of course, after Terry McMillan [author of "Waiting to Exhale"] started making millions of dollars, they said, *"Hmmm."*

Q.   Do you think about a specific audience, black or white, when you write your books?

A.   My understanding of fiction is, it's like you're on a train, and there are two people sitting behind you having a terribly interesting conversation that completely captivates you as you overhear it. With these books, the conversation is going on between me and a group of people from my father's generation who are either still down in Texas or migrated from Texas to Los Angeles. My audience is anyone who wants to overhear that conversation.

Q.   Why did you set your three mysteries in South Central Los Angeles in the late 1940s and early '50s?

A.   One of the things I'm trying to do is map the development of Los Angeles from a kind of a sleepy place to the sprawling metropolis it is today. And also map the black influx, which happened after World War II, from the deep South into Southern California. I was born in 1952, and all the stories I heard when I was a kid were about the deep South starting in maybe the mid-'30s, and going up until the '50s. The stories I tell start with that sensibility.

Q.   How did you create your main character, Easy Rawlins?

A.   I originally wrote a book called "Gone Fishin'," about Easy and his friend Mouse. But it wasn't a mystery. They were young black men searching out their fathers in the swamps of southeastern Texas. And, of course, the publishing world said, "Very interesting, but who's going to read this?" So it never got published.

Still, while writing that book, I was so excited about Easy; I loved his story, I loved his life. In the [mystery] genre, publishers and writers make the most money if they write a series, using the same characters again and again. The problem with writing a series is that if you take a character who's already fully developed, which is one of the easiest things to do, you can write a very good story, but the next story is going to be similar—the guy's the same person. By the time you get to the fifth and sixth story, it's stale—in your own mind at least, because you've done it.

Easy will be at least five years older every time I write a book, and different things will be going on in his life: His children will be older, they'll be having different problems, his relationship to them will be different. The whole political and social climate will be different.

Q.   It's interesting to think how South Central L.A. has changed . . .

A.   And hasn't. I was born in South Central, in the projects, in Watts. We moved when I was pretty young to another part of South Central outside of Watts, on Central Avenue.

I went back to L.A in December. While I was there, people started calling me. One guy was doing a film—I'm not sure what it was—but he wanted me to go back to my old house at 76th and Central and my old elementary school, Victory Baptist Day School. The people I knew when I lived there 30 years ago are still on that block. The houses are the same. It's very poor; I didn't even realize how poor I was when I was a kid. And when I went to my old school, it was exactly the same: They have the same merry-go-round, the same buildings, the same desks. Nothing had changed. One of the things about poverty is that it's like being in amber. The street I grew up on was a mixture of black people and Chicanos, and it's *still* a mixture of black people and Chicanos.

The community has evolved less than the communities around it. But South Central still lives under the same pressure; what happens is that every once in a while people become aware of it and go, "Wow!"

Q.   When you began writing seriously, you were a computer programer.
A.   Yes. I was working for Mobil Oil as a consultant. I wasn't doing anything in particular, just writing for the job. I wrote a sentence—I'll always remember it: "On hot, sticky days in southern Louisiana the fire ants swarm." I thought, That's interesting. I wonder what happened next? And I just started writing. It was so much fun. I took a class from a guy in his house, and when I outgrew that I went to City College and studied there for a while. And I just kept writing.

Q.   How did you get sidetracked into computer programing?
A.   I teach writing, and one of the things I recognize is that you can have very talented people, very facile with words and use of language, but who are young and don't really understand life. And so when they write there's something not quite true about it. For me, for a long time, it just never seemed right to become a writer because I really didn't know what I had to say. And indeed I don't think I had anything to say until I was in my thirties.

Q.   Which crime writers influenced you?
A.   My early influences there were Dashiell Hammett, Raymond Chandler, and Ross MacDonald. They were all impressive writers who were not only writing mysteries, they were writing about the world in a certain way. They were writing about the society—criticizing the society and moving all through it—which is the great thing you can do with crime fiction. You can go anywhere. You can be with kings and the next thing you know, you're in a hobo jungle down in southeast L.A.

Q.   Do you feel an obligation to deal specifically with race in your books?
A.   One of the big issues in black life in America is racism. So [many of] the best writers have taken on the issues of black life in racist America. That's one of the reasons so few black people have gone into the genres—not only mysteries, but westerns, romances, etc. I'm a little uncomfortable writing like that, because I hate giving racism that much purchase. If I write about a character, then that character is going to say the truth from his point of view. I try to make every character fully realized as themselves, so the issues of their lives should come out, as far as my talent allows, and I shouldn't have to worry about what I should or shouldn't be saying.

Q. Some people would say that some of the characters Easy deals with are stereotypes of black people.

A. I try my best to create a full milieu for Easy, so he has people who would never commit a crime, or Quinten Naylor, the policeman, who is completely straitlaced. There are a lot of white people who are criminals in these books. I'm writing crime novels; they are about crimes. They're about people who are committing crimes, who are involved in crime. I'm talking about the whole milieu, not about some person who just happened to come to a moment of crime.

I create complex characters, and I think their motivations are clear. Most of them don't consider themselves criminals, but once you get involved in Easy's world, it's hard to stay out of trouble.

WORKSHOP

7

REVISING

If you did the preceding workshops, you've already done a lot of revising. In Workshop 1 you did quick revising (but nevertheless major revising) by simply cutting heavily to make a collage. In Workshops 3 and 6 (loop writing and the interview) you were faced with a mass of disorganized, rough, exploratory material from which to produce a coherent draft: you had to go through and choose, discard, shape, and rewrite. *All* the activity in Workshop 5 was revising: a series of quick transformations of parts of your private writing to try out audiences and genres, and then a sustained transformation and rewriting as you worked on your main piece of public writing. (Even your story in Workshop 2 probably involved a bit of revision of the image writing you started with.)

Thus we've already asked for lots of revising—just treating it for what it is, namely, an inherent part of the whole writing process. But at some point it's worth making revising the main focus of a workshop's work. (Your teacher may decide to use this workshop earlier or later in the sequence.) In this workshop the whole assignment is to work on revising something you've written earlier.

Many people believe that good writers write something and send it off to a publisher, who prints it exactly as it's written. That's not how it works. When we read something published, we have no way of knowing what it first looked like and what changes the author made—first on his own and then on the advice of editors. But many writers testify to how much they revise and what a struggle revision can be. Here are two writers talking about revision:

> I am a witness to the lateness of my own vocation, the hesitations and terrors that still haunt all my beginnings, the painful slowness with which I proceed through a minimum of four drafts in both fiction and nonfiction.
>
> —Francine du Plessix Gray

> I had a difficult time revising this piece. I was never sure if my ideas made sense. I wasn't sure of what I really wanted to say. My feedback groups helped a lot by offering opinions on different directions my original paper seemed to be taking. They helped me to see where my thoughts got hidden somewhere in the words I used. After a lot of rethinking and reorganizing (and also with the help of a classmate's "literary analysis" on my paper), I found my way through my thoughts and realized where my paper should go. The revision process was long and difficult, but I feel it did a lot of good.
>
> —Stephanie Curcio (student, process writing)

Our goals in the workshop are to help you understand better the nature of revising and its importance for good writing, and most of all to be better at doing it. We will show you a number of useful revision strategies.

You will have noticed the note of pain and struggle in the preceding quotations, and you may have painful revising memories yourself. There's no way to make revising easy or fun: inherently it involves going over work again and again, evaluating, criticizing, and throwing away what sometimes seems like part of yourself.

Nevertheless we hope to counteract the tendency to be too grim or tense about revising and show that, like generating, it benefits from a spirit of playfulness. And, when finished, revision can generate immense satisfaction.

 THREE LEVELS OF REVISING

Many students equate revision with "correcting mechanics" or copyediting. Experienced writers never confuse the two. For them, revision means entering into a conversation with their previous thoughts. They match what they have already written against what they *now* wish to say, and create out of the two a new piece which suits their present purpose. What this implies is that revision never stops. But of course writers need to finish things for particular deadlines, and so they revise what they have and submit it—usually with the recognition that if they submitted it later, they'd make additional changes.

Since this is how revision actually works, no one can say exactly what revising is. Probably the best definition is this: revising is whatever a writer does to change a piece of writing for a particular reader or readers—whoever they may be (e.g., friends, colleagues, an editor at a publishing house, the general reading public of a particular publication, a teacher, or even oneself). But to help us talk about revision, we're going to distinguish three levels:

1. Reseeing or rethinking: changing what a piece says, or its "bones"
2. Reworking or reshaping: changing how a piece says it, or changing its "muscles"
3. Copyediting or proofreading for mechanics and usage: checking for deviations from standard conventions, or changing the writing's "skin"

1. *Reseeing or rethinking: changing the bones.* When you read over something you've written, you often realize that it doesn't say what you now want it to say: you now see you were wrong, or you've changed your mind, or you need more, or you left something out, or you didn't understand the full implications of what you were saying. The process of writing and rereading *changes* you (changes *you*). At its most extreme, this level of revising may mean that you crumple up what you've written and aim it toward the trash basket: the cartoon image of a writer surrounded by wads of discarded paper is not far from the truth. Most writers feel they have to discard lots before they come up with something they can use. When this textbook first came

---

PROCESS BOX

I just figured out that all this stuff about revising is simply "man-talk" for changing your mind— which I have done and been made fun of for my whole life.

Andrea Warren

out, Workshop 3, which is now all about collaboration—using the loop process and the collage as methods—had no mention of collaboration. It was only about the loop process. In the intervening years we got more and more interested in collaboration. As we were revising, we saw we could change the whole emphasis of Workshop 3.

2. *Reworking or reshaping: changing the muscles.* This second level of revising means that you're satisfied with *what* you are saying (or trying to say), but not with *how* you've said it. Working on "how" tends to mean thinking about readers: thinking about how your thoughts will be read or understood by people other than yourself. Thus feedback from readers is particularly useful for this level of revising. One of the most common kinds of reworking is to improve clarity. Perhaps you realize you need to change the order you present things in; or you need an introduction, conclusion, and some transitions; or you've implied ideas or suggested attitudes that you don't want there.* Most common of all, you simply need to leave out parts that may be OK in themselves (or even precious to you) but that don't quite belong now that you've finally figured out what the piece of writing is really saying. These passages clog your piece and will distract or tire readers. (You may not believe we left out a lot of the first draft of this book, but we did.)

3. *Copyediting or proofreading: changing the skin.* This third level of revising is usually what you do right before you hand something in or send it to its most important readers. At its simplest, it means finding typographical errors. At a level slightly above that, it means fixing sentence structure and checking spelling, punctuation, subject-verb agreement, and other features of usage.

A writer needs to do all three kinds of revising and ideally in the order we've described them. After all, there's no point in fixing the spelling of a word or the style of a sentence if you're going to cut it, and no point struggling to reword the presentation of an idea until you know you're going to keep it. But of course writing activities don't always stay in a neat order. Sometimes it's not until you rework the presentation of an idea that you realize that it needs to be cut.

 MAIN ASSIGNMENT

Choose a piece of your writing that you want to revise at all three levels. It probably makes the most sense to pick something that you feel dissatisfied with so that you know you won't mind doing extensive work on it.

---

* In our reworking level of revising this book, we found ourselves giving a good deal of attention to the subtitles scattered throughout the workshops: adding some and clarifying many. Having finally figured out what we were trying to say—where we were going—we were now trying to improve the road signs others would try to follow.

Share your piece with your group and use them to help you discover aspects of your subject which you have neglected or explore possible major revisions: ways in which you might change your mind or disagree with your earlier draft or reach different conclusions. Or perhaps it's a descriptive piece or story, and you want to change the whole approach. Here are two suggestions to guide your group work:

1. When you've finished reading your piece (and before oral discussion), allow a few minutes for freewriting. You can write down any additional thoughts you have on your topic or story, any doubts you now have about what you've written—anything at all about what the piece says. Those who have been listening to you should simply pretend that they've been assigned your subject and write their thoughts about it. At the end of this freewriting period, each group member can read what he's written. All this can serve as starters for discussion, but since this is your paper, you should guide the discussion and follow up on what is particularly interesting to you. (The others will have this same chance to be in charge when they read their papers.) You may want to ask your group members to give you their copies of what they've written so that you can reread them at your leisure.

2. Another way to approach this level of revision is to ask each group member (including yourself) to pick out the most interesting sentences and freewrite about why they are interesting, what they mean, and so forth. For this exercise you'll have to read your paper twice to your group—but reading twice is always a good idea. (It's best *not* to provide copies for your group since you want them to focus on your ideas, not on specific wording.) While doing this, it isn't necessary or even advisable for any of you to try to stick to what your main idea is. Remember, you're trying to explore all aspects of a topic no matter how unrelated they might seem at first. Try to make an inner act of *letting go* of the thinking you did—of embarking on an adventure to see things differently.

PROCESS BOX

In most of my freewriting the aim has been to open up my thinking—let those centrifugal forces go. In this one my problem was the centrifugal forces had taken over too much and I couldn't work because of the chaos. So this freewriting—less interesting in many ways—was an attempt to get the centripetal forces AND to pull things together so I could see them more clearly and see where to go next. I'm still frightened of it, though.

Erika Scheurer

On the basis of your group's discussion, decide what you now want to say; then rewrite your paper. Don't be surprised if you find yourself doing more revising than you expected. You may even discard the ideas you started to revise with. That's part of what should happen.

If you find this difficult—for example, if you find you don't want to change what you've said or what the story deals with—do some experimenting anyway. Play with your ideas or story. Revision is usually done in a spirit of clenched teeth and duty, but it can be done better in a spirit of play or even fooling around. The most reliable (and enjoyable) technique for changing the bones of your writing is to role-play. Pretend to be someone else who has a different view or outlook on your topic or issue: a real person you know or an imagined person. Then rewrite or rethink your piece from this person's point of view. It's fine to use their voice too.

Another technique is to pick a paragraph (or even a sentence or image) and build a whole new essay or story around it. In other words, deliberately try to write something different even if you're satisfied with what your original piece says. It helps to start with a fresh sheet of paper or computer file to free you from the original way you developed your ideas.

If you give it half a chance, you can let yourself get caught up in this kind of play. The words you produce will create their own complex of ideas, which in turn will lead to other words, sentences, and paragraphs. Let the process change your mind-set so that you are no longer striving to write something different from the original version; you're working toward fulfilling some new goal or purpose, one that has grown out of the writing itself.

Once you've made your revision, you can decide whether you want to use it or your original for the remainder of the work in this workshop. Remember: revisions aren't necessarily better; they're different. Once you understand this, you'll be willing to take risks as you revise: changing everything almost totally, exploring something which seems at first odd or silly to you, trying new approaches, developing some ideas that you don't even agree with. You can throw it all away if you want to. Almost invariably, though, you discover something substantial that you like—something that you'll want to incorporate into your original. Whatever happens, there's no reason to use a revision just because it's a revision. And of course you may now decide you've got two pieces you want to finish up.

SECOND-LEVEL REVISING: USING OTHERS TO REWORK, RESHAPE, OR CHANGE THE MUSCLES

When you've decided which version of your essay to use, you're ready to practice the second level of revision—reworking. For this, prepare a good legible copy of the version you've selected and use very wide left- or right-hand margins—say, about 3 inches. Make copies for your group. Before going to class, write a brief paragraph just for yourself which states briefly your purpose for writing the paper and the reasons why you chose to accomplish your purpose in the way you did. Then, on your copy of the essay, write in the margin some notes on each paragraph. These notes should include a *summary* of what the paragraph says and a statement of its *purpose* and how it fits in where it is. Purposes can include introducing, restating, giving examples, setting a scene, building suspense, giving your opinion(s), describing, moving to another aspect of your paper, concluding, and so forth. (See "Skeleton Feedback and Descriptive Outline" in *Sharing and Responding* for more about this powerful activity.) Here's how one student writer summarized the purpose of a paper she planned to revise at the second level:

> I wanted to make readers see the disco scene, so I describe it. But I also wanted to show how silly it is—poke fun at the people in it.

And here are the marginal summaries she wrote about the first few paragraphs of her essay (you'll notice that she had already begun to think of possible changes):

Outside the crowd waits. Guys clad in their outermost layer of skins, their pants, are nervously looking for their "Id's" within their wallets. Of course they make sure every girl sees the big wad of bills. What they don't know is that there is always a girl in the crowd who decides to light a cigarette and upon doing this sees that the big wad of bills is in fact one dollar bills. News travels fast and soon everyone is laughing at the guys. Then there are the young enticing girls. They look about twenty with their make-up caked upon their faces (you'd need a Brillo pad to scrub it all off), skin-tight Spandex and heels. These "women" are in actuality fourteen or fifteen years old; what gives them away is the way they smoke. They simply don't inhale. The drag of smoke enters and exits in the same dense cloud; they need to fan the air with their hands so as not to die of suffocation.

Introducing, setting the scene, describing people.

Also trying to set the tone—being sarcastic. I'd like readers to wonder what's going to happen.

The tension is building, and it seems to hang in the air like a low-lying cloud. The people are moving closer and closer to the entrance as if stalking prey. The doors open and everyone pushes in. Suddenly a pink Cadillac screeches to a halt and the driver gets out. The multitude of people stop! It's as if a spell were cast upon them. "It's him!" a young girl cries.

Showing what happens right before the doors open, maybe try to get suspense going. Also introduce Mr. Big—be sarcastic about him too.

He is tall, dark, and rich! He is wearing a white suit (polyester of course) with a black "silk" shirt. His shirt was, of course, opened to his naval displaying the jewelry. His jewelry consisted of three rope chains, each varying in length and width, and the fourth was an inch-thick rope chain exposing

Describes and makes fun of Mr. Big. Moves the story ahead a bit. Shows how people react to him and how phony everything is.

the Italian phallic symbol, the horn. The crowd, still mystified, parted like the Red Sea, allowing Mr. Big to enter the disco. The two-ton bouncers who were once mountains of malice became little pups when greeting him. "Can I help you, Mr. Big?" "Your table is waiting for you, Mr. Big." "You look very nice today, Mr. Big," and so on.

Once that awesome happening settled and passed, the crowd went back to pushing and shoving through the doors. It's really ridiculous to see people, who are supposed to be grown-ups, react like little children when they see a circus for the first time. If they only realized that the circus they're watching (Mr. Big) gets his ears boxed by his mother if he comes home too late.

Gives my opinion about all this, although I'm not sure why I put it here—maybe because I'm now going to move the scene inside.

Once inside, the eardrums shatter like a drinking glass does when a high-pitched voice is applied to it. This calamity happens because of the booming music which seems to vibrate the entire building. Ah, there's Mr. Big and his harem. All the women flock around him as if he were a mirror. He'll make his grand entrance on the dance floor later on.

Describing the scene inside, including Mr. Big. I'm making fun of the women who hang around him. I want to describe everything step by step as someone would see it when they went in.

Upon entering, the bar is to the person's left, and a few steps below is the dance floor. By the way, the steps are notorious killers since many, under the influence of alcohol, forget they exist. On the other side there is the seating area consisting of dozens of tables and black velvety, cushiony, re-cliner-type chairs. They are the type of chairs you lose yourself in.

This is more description of the inside. The thing about the steps is something I always think about when I look down at the dance floor because I fell on them once. Maybe this should all be added to the paragraph before since it's all description.

Ask your group members to write the same kind of margin notes on their copies of your essay. Also ask them to jot down a few words specifying any emotional reaction they may have to each paragraph: are they curious, bored, annoyed, offended, excited, informed, hostile or so forth, and can they pinpoint the words or phrases that cause their reaction? They can do all this at home or in class. If this work is done at home, your teacher will probably give you some time in class to share and get clarification.

Assignment for Second-Level Revising

Using the feedback you've gotten, decide what changes, if any, you want to make. Most of your changes will probably be aimed at making your meaning clearer. This can include restructuring (reordering paragraphs, adding transitions, providing or reworking introductions and conclusions, adding background information), *rewriting* (reworking sentences or phrases to alter their emotional impact or clarify their meaning), and *adding* (everything from new

I've just written and revised a paper about freewriting I was writing for a conference.

I procrastinated, as I always do, waiting for special inspiration—it didn't come (usually it doesn't). So I forced it, felt like I was stammering on paper. After ten minutes, though, I was rolling.

After about thirty minutes of this nonstop writing, I had a good amount of stuff on paper, although I still wasn't particularly pleased with what I had come up with. Still, I had to get it done, so I started working with it. As I did that, more and more came out. Soon I had a rough draft of my paper. But I didn't particularly like it, so I fiddled with it some more. Since I had agreed to read it at a get-together of a group of us who meet about once a month to work on our writing, I had to get it in some sort of presentable form.

I told everyone before I started reading it that it sort of did what I wanted it to do; I just didn't think it did it very well. After I finished reading, the members of the group started talking about the ideas in it—not criticizing anything and not giving me many suggestions, just talking about it.

As I drove home that night, it came to me—I knew what I had to do. I had to reorganize, present what I wanted to say as a story of an intellectual quest, what started me on the quest, what I found along the way, and what I concluded when I finished the quest. I don't know why I hadn't seen this before, but I hadn't. Something about sitting in the group and reading it, hearing it discussed a bit, made it (my text) into an object I could look at from a greater distance and shape in a more logical way. The next day I made these revisions with very little effort.

Pat Belanoff

---

points, to examples, to clarifying phrases). If, while doing this, you find yourself moving back to the first level of revision (altering *what* you say), don't be surprised. We told you that the three levels of revision cannot be fully compartmentalized. You need to keep in mind too that form and content are inextricably linked; changing *how* something is said almost always affects *what* is said.

One final note about this level of revising. Your paper is yours and you need to trust your own instincts about how you say something. We think that, before ideas get into words, there is always an impulse toward meaning, a "felt sense." Once we put an idea into words, we test it against that original impulse; and when the words and the impulse match, we know it—we know we've got the idea right for ourselves. Sometimes this felt sense of "rightness" comes immediately, sometimes we have to rewrite several times before we feel it, and sometimes we just give up and recognize that, for the moment, we can't achieve it. Our point is that only you know exactly when you've said what you want to say. Someone else may suggest a very nice sentence, but it's no good if it's not what you are trying to say.

In the readings at the end of the workshop we have included drafts and revisions of two essays. As you read them, you may want to jot down a list of the changes each author makes. For another example of revising, compare Peter Elbow's Perl writing (Workshop 4, "Readings") and his revision of it in Mini-Workshop D, "Writing with a Word Processor."

When you've finished this second level of revision, type up a final, clean copy of your paper—double- or even triple-spaced. This can be the copy you hand in to your teacher if she uses the proofreading procedure we suggest in Mini-Workshop K ("Copyediting and Proofreading"). Make at least two copies of this final version. It is these copies which you will use for copyediting and proofreading, the final level of revision. For suggestions on this final, third level of revision, see Mini-Workshop K.

 ## PROCESS JOURNAL AND COVER LETTER QUESTIONS

You've probably done *some* process writing in previous workshops about the revising you did there. But since we haven't until now made revising the focus of a workshop, it's important to try to learn as much as you can about what happens for you in this slippery process. Try to re-create and describe as much as you can of what you did in all the revising activities of this workshop: feelings, thoughts, reactions, things you can learn. If you need help, these prompts may be of use:

- Simply gather as many memories and reactions as you can under the three stages:
    - First-level revising of "bones," or what you said
    - Second-level revising of "muscles," or how you said it
    - Third-level "skin-deep" copyediting or proofreading
- Freewrite about your own revision processes in the past and about how you feel about revision. Do you revise a great deal? If so, why? What writings of your own are you the most reluctant to revise? Why? When you revise, which level do you most tend to work at?
- At what points in your writing do you tend to stop and fix things? Is it frequent? What triggers you to stop the flow of words and go back to change something?

 ## RUMINATIONS AND THEORY

Putting Revising into Perspective

Revising and Grammar

Putting Revising into Perspective

There are two principal resources for good revision: time and new eyes. The best source of new eyes is other people; but if you let time go by, *you've* changed since you did your last draft, and so in a sense your eyes are different. You don't see things the same way you did. This is why it's so important to try to put something aside for a while and do your serious reviewing after a week or more has passed. This is why we've arranged this text so that you revise something a week or more after you first explored and wrote it.

Revision for the sake of revision can be a deadening chore. That's why we ask you to practice first-level revision as a game. "What would I say *if* I were so-and-so and I saw things differently?" (Of course, you don't need the game if you discover you actually do see your subject differently.) Playing the game may lead you to new insights about your subject which you'll want to incorporate into what you're writing.

We know that much revision in the working world is probably reworking, not reseeing. If your boss tells you to write a report on a meeting of a special planning group, you can hardly revise it into suggestions for improving company management even if that's what you'd rather write. Still, if you learn that you don't have to stick slavishly to what you've already written, you can free yourself to use the first drafts as seeds rather than constraints. There are always deadlines, of course, and so at some point we have to stop new thinking about our subject and focus instead on refining what we've already said. We think that most students, however, get to this second step too soon; they don't recognize the power and pleasure of the prior step. That is why, in this workshop, we require you to do first-level revision even if you are satisfied with what you've already said.

Revising Isn't Everything. Almost everything we write needs revision of some kind, but often not much. Perhaps you knew ahead of time what you needed to say and you more or less said it. You don't need to change what you've said, only how you say it. *Or*—and don't forget this—the piece is rough but not *important* enough to revise: better to start over or even to write something entirely different.

Sometimes revising can squeeze the life out of language. Our original impulse to communicate often injects a particular and unique energy into the words we use. Revising can drive us farther and farther from that impulse and deaden what we write.

The message in all this is that revising is important, but you don't have to revise everything, and revising doesn't have to be a quest for perfection. Otherwise writing is too much of a chore. Choose pieces that are good or that you love; learn to let other pieces go. Learn to do superficial revising when you just want to make something presentable and aren't trying to make it the greatest thing you've ever written. Some people say we learn most by revising. Perhaps. But we learn just as much by writing more new pieces.

Another important lesson is that deep revision of *what* you say does not necessarily produce a better piece of writing. It produces a different piece of writing which you or your reader may or may not like better. *And yet* . . . revision is *almost* always necessary to produce a good piece of writing. We've revised the workshops of this textbook over and over. A few parts of it have changed very little from the first time we wrote them, but most have changed a lot, and some are unrecognizable. We've added much and discarded almost as much. We've struggled with ways of saying things and even more with what is necessary to say at all. And through all this revising, we've tried to keep the language alive.

Ultimately there are rewards for this hard work: the feeling that we've gotten something the way we wanted it, the feeling that by working so hard we've actually realized for the first time the fullness of some idea lurking just below words.

Revising and Grammar

Many people think that learning to write means learning grammar. When we ask students at the beginning of a semester what they expect from our course, many say they expect to be taught grammar. They rarely understand that "grammar mistakes" (deviations from standard usage such as subject-verb agreement, spelling, tense forms, and so forth) do not usually lead to a distortion of meaning—though, of course, they can. But deviations from standard usage can be quite *distracting* for many readers. Each of us can probably tolerate a different level of deviation. Some people can read a whole paper in which the final "s" is missing from present-tense verbs and not react. Others will react to even one missing "s."

The real problem with errors in usage is that they force the reader into giving attention to the words instead of the meaning. If a reader is continually distracted in this way, she begins to believe that the author's meaning is unclear, the organization is poor, or the quality of thinking is mediocre. Or she'll think that the writer is not very committed to the ideas he's presenting; and if that's the case, why should she as a reader give them much attention?

There is a continuing debate in scholarly and pedagogical journals about whether to teach grammar and usage in writing courses. Here is our position:

- Instruction in grammar cannot serve as a substitute for instruction in writing.
- What students learn from doing grammar exercises rarely transfers to their writing.
- There is a need for discussion about what people mean by "standard usage"—along with its function in society and its relation to nonstandard dialects.
- Elimination of certain usage errors (particularly the dropping of "s"—as in *she see*—and the use of nonstandard verb forms—*she could of done it*) is a slow process. We cannot expect students to alter very quickly something so basic to their natural language.
- Instruction in standard usage should focus on the errors students actually make and the contexts in which they make them.
- Students should be forced to articulate for themselves the reasons why they use nonstandard forms. Only in this way can they begin to build different rules into their personal language.
- Students should be required to submit final copies of their revised pieces that are free from errors in typing and usage. We believe in giving students some help in achieving this, but what's most important is making them realize that they have to find whatever help they need. Students who are poor spellers, for instance, may always have to find someone who is willing to check their papers for all misspelled words. Spelling checkers on computers are a godsend for such students. Remember, however, that a checker cannot tell you that "there" should be "their." It may well be that com-

puters will soon be supplied with easy programs for checking some other aspects of usage. In any event, we believe students must find ways to write Standard English whenever they want or need to. This does not mean we consider Standard English superior to other varieties; in fact, we encourage students to hold on to their native dialects, whatever they may be. Such dialects give language life and often gradually serve to renew Standard English. Nevertheless, students need to be proficient in Standard English if they want to avoid being discriminated against and having certain doors slammed in their faces.

Readings

THE MALE BASHING STEREOTYPE—EARLY DRAFT

Kimberly Graham

Why did we, as a society, need to create a term such as "male bashing"? What is it? Who is guilty of it?

Many women are now feeling dissatisfied with aspects of their lives that they once accepted. They want to be more than housewives. Some want to go back to school in the pursuit of an education and a better job. Many that are in the work force want more power and prestige. Some of these women believe that men are to blame for their dissatisfaction; it was men, after all, that controlled most parts of their lives. They married men and became housewives. Most of their bosses are men. Women needing a scapegoat? Women are very demanding; they like to intimidate men, and if they do not get what they want, they do not see a future in their relationship with him. To vent their frustrations they resort to male bashing. They blame men for everything. If their car wasn't fixed right, it was because the mechanic is a man. When a crime is committed against a woman, they blame all men. If a female co-worker was sexually harassed by her boss, they assume all male bosses would do the same thing. Male bashing is an overgrown tendency to blame men for every dissatisfaction and to assume all men are alike. It's too bad that we had to come up with this term because it is dangerous and self-destructive.

The media and certain medical circles played a big part in the creation of the term "male bashing." Almost every week on either *The Oprah Winfrey Show* or *Donahue,* there is one segment on the state of male-female relationships. Most of the segments include panelists who have just written a "revolutionary" new book, or a group of women (or men) talking about their problems. Inevitably one show turns into a male bash event because of either a panelist's views or the comments from a participant in the studio audience. One *O.W.S.* was originally about why women marry men that are less financially successful or intelligent than they are. The view at the end of the show turned out to be that women were sick of the games men usually play and they wanted someone they had control over. Men they were used to going out with were egotistical, selfish, cruel, stupid, immature, afraid of commitment, and the list continued. Phil Donahue presented one panel of all men that had formed a "men's club," and the women in the audience felt that they were weak and immature for wanting to be with each other instead of women. There has also been a rapid flow of books written by psychologists and therapists on the state of the sexes. *Men That Hate Women and the Women Who Love Them* was a best seller in hardcover and paperback. *Women That Men Love, Women That Men Leave* is a fairly recent one describing types of women and why men leave them. Books like these give male bashers fuel for their arguments because, as the titles suggest, they put men in a bad light.

One of the most controversial books of late is Shere Hite's new one titled: *Women and Love: A Cultural Revolution in Progress.* It presents the views of 4500 women and Hite's conclusions from those views. Critics of the book called it inaccurate and false and also think Hite is guilty of male bashing. She based her report on findings from only 4500 women when the number should have been much larger. She assumed that the views of the participating women were also those of the rest of the female population. For instance, she has concluded that about ninety-three percent of all women are unhappy with their current relationships and about seventy percent are unfaithful but believe in monogamy. It's inaccurate to judge for the many with data from only the few. The book is presented as a testament to the unhappiness of women because of men, and it should be presented more objectively.

The first draft ended here. Following, in boldface type, are questions the writer's group members asked and the writer's responses to them.

Do women have a reason to bash and holler?   I have to admit—I have met some stupid, immature, egotistical men. But I don't think that all men are alike and I haven't blamed all my frustrations on them. Why do some women resort to mental violence? The media has provided many groupings for men and women. There are the "men afraid of commitment," "the older men only interested in younger women," "the men obsessed with getting ahead in their careers," and "all men in their twenties."

Many women tend to find one fault in a man and turn it into a basis for criticism of all men who have the same fault.   Then they find a media grouping and conclude that all men are alike. There are also slots for women: "tired housewives and mothers not wanting sex," "women only interested in having a career," "women living off the men who marry them," and "all women in their forties." If we stopped creating these groupings maybe there would not be bashing against anybody because people would be judged as individuals.

Male bashing is dangerous because it gives men the idea that all women are out to get them.   That's not true. Yes, some are, but not all of us are violent militant feminists. It gives society the impression that feminism is to blame and that things were fine before it started. Women guilty of male bashing also put down the concept of feminism. They are fighting for equality, yet they are discriminating against all men for the actions of a few of them. We seem to be going backward in our struggle.

THE GRAHAM REPORT—MIDDLE DRAFT

Kimberly Graham

What women want—recently there has been a lot of publicity on what women were not getting. And who do we point our lotioned, perfumed hands at? MEN—who else? If we are unhappy, then men, as a race in themselves, are to blame, right? We don't have anyone else to blame. The whole female population is unmistakably guiltless. Why the propensity to turn men into scapegoats?

Him: (while watching the Minnesota Twins win the World Series): Yeah!!!
          GO, GO, GO!!!
Her: Let's go to a movie or something. Do you want to talk?
Him: Umm.
Her: Was that a yes or a no?
Him: Umm.
Her: Why don't you ever want to talk?

Now, there is a definite problem going on there. The woman (we'll call her June) obviously wanted to talk about something, and she tried to communicate her desire to the man (he's Ward). But her timing was off. Asking her husband, or boyfriend, if he wanted to talk while the World Series was on is like asking her to meet his mother-in-law while she is applying a deep-cleaning, pore-rejuvenating, look-twenty-years-younger facial mask. Neither the game nor the mask are necessarily important things, but to the person involved, they constitute a sort of livelihood. June could have waited until Ward was done watching the game to ask him to go out. It's common courtesy. Just because it was a man (inarticulately) refusing to talk does not mean that all men would do the same thing. If June had realized how she would feel if Ward did the same to her, then she might have understood his grumbling disinterest. Many frustrated women today are trying to pin the source of their dissatisfaction onto men only, when a more constructive activity would be to look inside themselves and find the core of their pain. It is a difficult thing to do when the easy way out is to blame, accuse, and complain.

A spotlight has been lit on one woman of the last few turbulent decades who has analyzed the state of relationships in the horrendous romantic environment of the eighties: Shere Hite. Her new book, entitled *Women and Love: A Cultural Revolution in Progress,* is fast on its way to becoming a very controversial bestseller. In it she explores the mentality of dissatisfied women and concludes that men play a large, if not total, role in the creation of female frustration.

I say: poop on her. Yes there are some disgusting examples of the male species, for example: men that proudly and continuously examine just how many decibels their next belch can create (and whether it will crack the tempered glass of their bathroom windows); blind dates that show up displaying their impressionist renditions of nine tattoos scattered extremely artistically upon their mud-splattered arms; college letches that, when confronted with a group of two women and seventeen inebriated fraternity brothers, suggest consuming and emptying all the bottles of Rolling Rock Beer to start a game of strip spin-the-bottle; polyester-clad barflies ambling up to a woman and, in not so much as two steps, managing to regurgitate the evening's content of alcohol consumed into her lap. . . . Need I go on? But it is very important to remember (I know . . . even I am having a hard time after the last paragraph) that not all men are responsible for women's anguish. Many people search for scapegoats because they are afraid to admit that they might have made a mistake. A lot of women find it easy to blame men because they know they will receive sympathy from many other women. Ms. Hite has perpetuated the myth of male-created frustration by presenting the views of 4500 women and applying them to the national population. She has not stated what women want—she has stated what *unhappy* women want.

Why are we bringing up the question of what women want, anyway? Why now? Don't get me wrong; it's not that I think the question is not an important one. On the contrary; I consider it crucial. But why all the clamor now?

I think I have an answer. Now that women have gone out and "done it all"—worked, had babies, entered politics, entered space, developed an argument supporting the metaphysical qualities and the transcendental properties of the color black, drunk a six-pack of Jolt—they are beginning to realize that maybe they overdid it. Stress and burnout are beginning to catch up. In their struggle to prove themselves to society, some women went too far and are now afraid to say, "Hey, I made a mistake. This isn't what I wanted." I can understand why they would be afraid to admit it. Some men would turn around and reply, "You should have stayed in the kitchen where the little woman belongs!!" They have also seen many stressed-out men continue with their struggles, and the women do not want to be the ones to quit. Women have had to prove themselves to society by going beyond what men have done, and for that reason they find a purpose to voice their unhappiness to their boyfriends, husbands, lovers, and so on.

This society would not have to wonder what women (or men) wanted if there were no sexual barriers. Just suppose that there were no physical differences between the male and female bodies. Yes folks, it would be mighty boring, but for the sake of argument, imagine. (Here comes another scenario.)

Ward: Hello Ms. Flintstone. How did the reports on juvenile penguins in the South Antarctic come out on the IBM/PC with color graphics?

Wilma: Just fine, Mr. Cleaver, but I had problems in the area of young penguin street gangs terrorizing the arctic corners.

Ward: Well, why don't you work on it some more and I will get back to you.

Neither Ward nor Wilma has any distinguishing sexual characteristics, so Ward is not wondering what color Wilma's lingerie is while he curses her feminine lack of computer literacy, and Wilma is not wondering if Ward wears boxers or jockeys as she tears apart his masculine egocentricity. Without sexual characteristics people would not be considered men and women separately, but people . . . just people. Then our society would wonder about the wants of everybody as a whole. Definition of this fantasy land: UTOPIA.

THE GRAHAM REPORT—FINAL DRAFT

Kimberly Graham

What women want—recently there has been a lot of publicity on what women were not getting. WHAT DO WE WANT?? Who has the answers?? Shere Hite? Oprah Winfrey? Ronald Reagan? My plumber? I don't know if I even understand the question.

The statement—what women want—has turned into the question: What kind of men do women want? I cannot speak for the whole female population, but I know what I want in a man; or rather, what I don't want.

I do not desire any man that proudly and continuously examines just how many decibels his next belch can create (and whether it will crack the tempered glass of his bathroom windows). So he drank sixteen cases of Ballantine Ale—big deal! He must be able to control his bodily functions among mixed company. Besides, I do not appreciate his friends' attempting to grade the intensity of the belch by holding up their callused fingers.

Nor do I remain at my door, awaiting blind dates that show up displaying their impressionist renditions of nine tattoos scattered extremely artistically upon their mud-splattered arms. A date is an occasion for which one showers, washes, scrubs, DISINFECTS, FUMIGATES!! And I am not the least bit interested in hearing that the tattoo "artist's" name was Anthony "Michelangelo" Giancanna.

Since I am a female University of Massachusetts student, this next type of man particularly makes me ill. College letches that, when confronted with a group of two women and seventeen inebriated fraternity brothers, suggest consuming and emptying all the bottles of Rolling Rock Beer to start a game of strip spin-the-bottle. What's even more terrifying is when one of them shows up with a Twister mat and a bottle of Mazola. I'm just as fun and exciting as the next person, but hey, public displays of sweltering lust just aren't my style.

The least desirable of this lengthening list of odd personas is the pseudo-feminist pig who claims to respect Gloria Steinem's every word, while secretly wondering if there exists a small, white, cotton flower embroidered in the center of her brassiere. It is this same sad excuse for a man who, after suggesting an evening at the Four Seasons, thinks convincing a date to pay for a thirteen-course dinner with raspberry crepes and two orders of baked Alaska constitutes a feminist attitude. After all, if she wants to be equal then she should pay for his dinner, theater tickets, Brooks Brothers' suits, IBM/PC with full-color graphics, diamond-blue metallic Porsche, fifty-three-room chateau in the Swiss Alps, etc. The pseudo-feminist pig is also very articulate concerning women's issues and proves it with a phone bill of $3,975.87 to Dial-a-Porn. He is the most dangerous of the undesirables since he has the ability to con unknowing women into thinking that he is compassionate and charming, while secretly wanting to cover them with instant banana Jell-O pudding while handcuffed in the back seat of a mint-green 1974 Chevy Impala.

I do not want to dwell on the above descriptions because, as a feminist, my imagination concerning the various mutant abnormalities of the male species may . . . how can I say it subtly . . . run rampant through the hellish field of sarcastic literary discourse. I have determined what kind of men I don't want. Hopefully these caustic exaggerations will not offend any male egos. As unbelievable as it may seem, I do have a glimmer of hope in the existence of desirable men. But where are they? Do I have to travel to southwest Kansas to find an underpaid tractor salesman who loves to wear the color pink? I suppose there is an Antarctican ice fisherman who is more than willing to relax and enjoy the benefits of my making fifty times more income than he would ever make. Maybe there is a Holiday Inn pool maintenance staff person, living in Acapulco, Mexico, who knows how to cook homemade turkey soup and double German chocolate cake while diapering an infant. WHERE ARE THEY?

So what does this paper prove? I have come up with an answer to what women want. Or have I? No, the statement is too vague. Society should not generalize—it's an emotional question. I do know what qualities I like in a man: compassion, sense of humor, intelligence, sense of equality toward women, respect for the human race, the ability to read aloud the works of D. H. Lawrence while stirring instant banana Jell-O pudding. . . .

DRAFTS AND REVISIONS OF AN EDITORIAL FOR THE *DAILY HAMPSHIRE GAZETTE*

Kay J. Moran, Editorial Page/Business Editor

We see here the role of substantial revising—if not always total rethinking—even in writing that is done fast under a tight deadline. Moran went from her first start to her final version in only a few minutes more than an hour. Normally she works entirely on screen and never prints out copy, but at our request, she pushed the print button periodically and gave us eleven stages to look at. See her cover letter for more about how she works. Here is her first start—which printed out at 9:39 a.m.:

```
David K. Scott, who grew up on a cold, rocky

island off the northern coast of Scotland, was
```

chosen last week as chancellor of the University of Massachusetts Amherst campus.

In July he'll take over at the campus which has made national headlines for its cultural diversity and incidents of racial friction.

Here is what she had a couple of printouts and 15 minutes later (9:54 a.m.)

Many on campus were enthusiastic when David K. Scott was chosen last week as chancellor of the University of Massachusetts at Amherst.

He comes with high qualifications. As a former provost and vice president for academic affairs at Michigan State University in East Lansing, he understands the strengths and problems of a large land grant institution. As a nuclear physicist he can talk to scientists as well as humanists. UMass President Michael Hooker cited as Scott's particular strengths a keen understanding of the role a university can play in economic development, and his knowledge of the emerging world community.

stRon

Story says and humility, honesty and eloquence

to On July 1 he'll take over

who grew up on a cold, rocky island off the

northern coast of Scotland, at the campus which has made national headlines for its cultural diversity and incidents of racial friction. Though announcement of his appointment was greeted by many at UMass with enthusiasm, others expressed disappointment and doubt he would be able to improve the racial climate.

He said he believes that, while a public university should reflect the diversity of the whole state, the Amherst campus does not, and he intends to take action after the large

Here is her near-to-final version (10:20 a.m.)—with handwritten changes to show the final version—which was printed at 10:52 a.m.:

A NEW CHANCELLOR

Many on campus were enthusiastic when David K. Scott was chosen last week as chancellor of the University of Massachusetts at Amherst, ~~a post~~ *beginning* ∧ ~~he'll assume~~ July 1.

He comes with strong qualifications. As a former provost and vice president for academic affairs at Michigan State University in East Lansing, he understands the mission of a large land grant institution. As a nuclear physicist he can talk to scientists as well as humanists.

"Scott's particular strengths, said UMass President Michael Hooker, are a keen understanding of the role such a university can play in regional economic development, and his knowledge of the emerging world community. ¶Ronald Story, UMass vice president for academic affairs and chair of the chancellor search committee, cited Scott's humility, honesty and eloquence.

Both are important to the state's—and the campus'—future prosperity.

Some on the UMass-Amherst campus, ~~which has made national headlines for its cultural diversity and~~ *where* incidents of racial friction, *have made national headlines* expressed disappointment and doubt last week that Scott, who grew up on a cold, rocky island off the northern coast of Scotland, would be able to improve the campus racial climate.

We urge the doubters to give him a chance. He said last week that racism is an issue which must be discussed; then action should be taken. Furthermore, he said that the Amherst Campus does not now reflect the diversity of the whole state, as a large public university ought to.

For his part, Scott should be careful not to react defensively when he is criticized by those disappointed with his choice, but listen to them carefully. His comment to a reporter last Thursday was a good start: "Those who do not support me remind me of what some of my weaknesses are—and what areas I need to improve."

My duties at a small daily afternoon newspaper in Massachusetts include the editorial page and writing editorials four days a week. Editorials are unsigned. I write with a police-fire-radio scanner at my elbow, at a desk surrounded by the desks of other editors working on deadline, in a wide-open newsroom. We have to work fast to produce a daily paper. We talk constantly among each other and with reporters. That's part of the job.

You can see on the printout the times various versions of this editorial were printed out. In between, I also edited a page-1 news story for that day's paper, opened mail, took several phone calls and discussed a letter to the editor with a woman who brought it in person. An average morning.

Usually, I think about and research possible editorial topics on weekends and discuss them with the editor-in-chief on Mondays. Research involves reading the news, talking with reporters and others. Hardest are the days I start off with no good ideas, because I still have to produce an editorial.

All writing and editing at the newspaper is done on a computer terminal; I revise and improvise as I go along, as does everybody. The editorial or story develops and is refined as it grows. When it's finished, after a quick final read, I send it (electronically) to the publisher. He reads it, and if he has questions or doubts, we discuss it. Sometimes the discussions get heated, but his is the final decision. In the editorial printed here, he thought describing Scott's island as "cold, rocky" was irrelevant, so he took out those words. I think he was right.

Next, the editorial gets read by two copy editors. Then it is printed out and put on the page.

Kay J. Moran, Editorial Page/Business Editor

DRAFTS AND REVISIONS OF TWO SHORT BOOK REVIEWS FOR *GLAMOUR* MAGAZINE

Laura Mathews, Book Review Editor

What follows is only a small selection from a dozen or more drafts which show a succession of changes—large and small—over a period of a few days.

Drafts of the Review of *A Season in Purgatory*

Figure 1 is a page or so of Mathews' first, handwritten, exploratory writing. You can see her crossings-out and writings-in. (And what we provide here is neater than her actual page of explorations.)

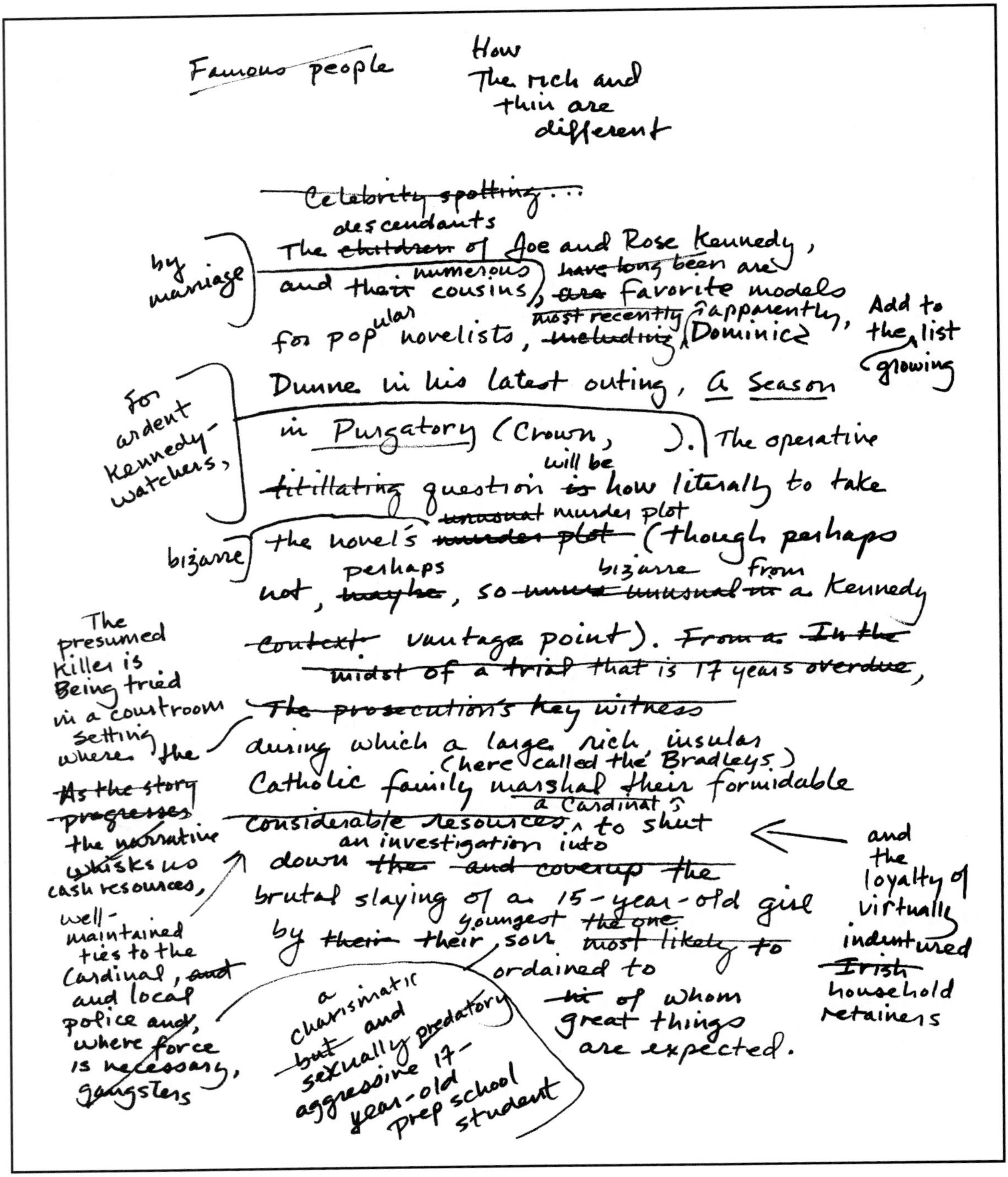

Famous people

How
The rich and
thin are
different

~~Celebrity spotting...~~

descendants
by marriage) The ~~children~~ of Joe and Rose Kennedy,
numerous
and their cousins, ~~have long been~~ are ~~are~~ favorite models
ular   most recently ; apparently,   Add to
for pop novelists, ~~including~~ Dominick ",   the list
growing
for ardent Kennedy-watchers,) Dunne in his latest outing, A Season

in Purgatory (Crown,   ). The operative
will be
~~titillating~~ question ~~is~~ how literally to take
unusual murder plot
bizarre) the novel's ~~murder plot~~ (though perhaps
perhaps   bizarre   from
not, ~~maybe~~, so ~~much~~ ~~unusual or~~ a Kennedy

~~context~~ vantage point). ~~From a~~ ~~In the~~
The   ~~midst of a trial~~ that is 17 years overdue,
presumed
killer is
Being tried   ~~The prosecution's key witness~~
in a courtroom
setting
where, the   during which a large, rich, insular
(here called the Bradleys.)
~~As the story~~   Catholic family marshal their formidable
~~progresses~~   a Cardinal s
the narrative   ~~considerable resources~~ ^ to shut   and
~~whisks us~~   an investigation into   the
cash resources, down ~~the~~ ~~and coverup the~~   ← loyalty of
well-   virtually
maintained   brutal slaying of a 15-year-old girl   indentured
ties to the   youngest   the one
Cardinal, ~~and~~ by ~~their~~ their , son ~~most likely to~~   ~~Irish~~
and local   ordained to   household
police and,   ~~in~~ of whom   retainers
where force   a charismatic   great things
is necessary, but and   are expected.
gangsters   sexually predatory
               aggressive 17-
               year-old
               prep school
               student

Figure 1
Mathews' first handwritten, exploratory writing for review of *A Season in Purgatory*.

The first typed draft, which really consists of two "draft starts" in the same writing session, follows:

HOW THE RICH GET AWAY WITH MURDER . . . With a daringly identifiable cast of characters, Dominick Dunne's *A Season in Purgatory* (Crown $) informs on a rich and charismatic Catholic family and the murder of a young debutante by one of its wayward sons. Prime witness to the coverup, Harrison Burns is a relatively impoverished prep school classmate of the son's, whom the family plies with hush money in the form of a full scholarship to Yale.

FUN FAKES . . .

Novels inspired by the Kennedys are as commonplace as imitation designer handbags. Titillating in their disclosures, the plots often pass for genuine *romans a clef,* as do *faux* Chanel or Hermes to the undiscriminating eye.

A bright red dustjacket evoking Catholic cardinals, blood and flames of damnation announces the arrival of Dominick Dunne's *A Season in Purgatory* (Crown $tk).

The hero is a solemn, fallen saint sort of guy who has carried a burdensome secret since adolescence.

Solemn in his disgust, yet transfixed by people
whose privilege extends to committing crimes
"without consequence."

The typed version that follows is a middle-stage draft. The handwritten additions and changes show how Mathews moved from her middle-stage draft to her final draft. Keep in mind, however, that what you see written by hand is not really one revision; it is the sum of five or six more drafts. Note too that we have not been able to give any indication here of the many scrawled comments and questions from fellow editors that sometimes led Mathews to make some of her changes. That is, the collaborative dimension of writing with fellow editors is invisible here.

■**Rich and Thin . . .** In the "easy [reading] but not totally

~~sinful~~ [junk] category," ~~there is~~ A Season in Purgatory

(Crown, $tk), [is] the latest outing by Dominick Dunne

(~~An Inconvenient Woman~~). Kennedy-watchers will

wonder how literally to ~~take the~~ [interpret] ~~bizarre~~ [the] murder

plot, in which a [the Bradley's,] rich Catholic clan ~~of sprawling~~

~~ambition and brawling manners (here called the~~

~~Bradleys)~~ deals with the mess created by the

family's favorite son: ~~Inconveniently~~ [Inauspiciously] enough,

this future presidential hopeful has smashed the

skull of a 15-year-old girl. ~~His weapon:~~ [with] a

baseball bat, ~~identifiable as Bradley property.~~ [then dragged the body into the woods near the family home.]

With the help of a [visiting] prepschool friend ~~who is~~

[What follows is a behind the scenes primer on the exertion of influence.]

~~visiting the Bradley home that same weekend, he~~

~~has dragged the body into the surrounding woods.~~

What does it take, exactly, to silence witnesses

and shut down a police inquiry? ~~And how do those~~

~~in the know live with themselves afterward?~~ The

answer comes _{via} ~~in the person of~~ narrator/hero

Harrison Burns--the prep school accomplice who, 17

years after watching his friend _{confidently deny and} get away with

murder, _{decides} ~~has decided~~ to break his vow of silence.

And talk he does. Writing in his most _{entertaining} ~~mea culpa~~,

Graham-Gree_{e-}nish voice, Dunne smoothes any ~~plot~~

raggedness _{of plot} with cunning _{insights about} ~~descriptions of all~~ the

little conveniences of ~~being worth~~ _{having} a lot of money

_{and zero integrity.} ~~including the privilege of "crime without~~

~~consequence."~~

The following is the final, printed version:

■ **RICH AND THIN** . . . In the "easy reading but not totally junk" category, *A Season in Purgatory* (Crown Publishers, $22) is the latest outing by **Dominick Dunne** (*The Two Mrs. Grenvilles*). Kennedy watchers will wonder how literally to interpret the murder plot, in which the Bradleys, a rich Catholic clan, deal with the mess created by the family's favorite son. Inauspiciously enough, this future presidential hopeful has smashed the skull of a 15-year-old girl with a baseball bat, then dragged the body into the woods near the family home with the help of a visiting prep-school friend. What follows is a behind-the-scenes primer on the exertion of influence. What does it take, exactly, to silence witnesses and shut down a police inquiry? The answer comes via narrator-hero Harrison Burns, the prep-school accomplice who, 17 years after watching his friend confidently deny and get away with murder, decides to break his vow of silence. And talk he does. Writing in his most entertaining, Graham Greene-ish voice, Dunne smoothes any raggedness of plot with cunning insights about the little conveniences of having a lot of money and zero integrity.

Drafts of Review of *The Road to Wellville*

Figure 2 is a page or so of Mathews' first, handwritten, exploratory writing. You can see her crossings-out and writings-in. (And what we provide here is neater than her actual page of explorations.)

T.C. Boyle   The Road to Wellville

In a story so focussed on gross anatomy
(the grosser, the more ~~so~~ explicit) ~~focussed~~
~~the woman's organ most conspicuously~~
~~neglected is the breast~~   ~~emotions are~~
feelings elicited are disgust and
a kind of grade school snickering

Lots of emetic, stingy on the tenderness

Too   ungenial, mocking
often his → disdain + cynicism
~~Contempt~~ for what his characters are up to,
rubs off on them. Then again it's
~~Cardboard~~   hard to love cardboard.

~~white~~ Though he redeems them in a final twist
        spate of ~~selfs~~ ~~discoveries~~
                    self=discoveries,
                        unmaskings
        and paybacks
Farcical, but not always likable:
            lively
A novel destined for the big screen—
where casting may add some flesh +
                              warmth to
these ~~bare-boned~~ characters
        ~~cardboard~~
        ~~dry as~~
Emotionally dry as
~~Dry as~~ cornflakes eaten straight from the box

~~His subject~~   ~~whether~~
                        seem to
American pieties ~~have always~~ fascinated
+ incense T.C. Boyle, ~~and bring out~~
"clean living" being foremost

A familiar complement of Boyle characters:
a batty authority figure, a ~~renegade~~ prodigal
son, ~~and the~~ a much-put-upon
~~bystander~~ reluctant mediator

Garrison
Keillor
without
geniality,
Twain
without
lovable
character
(but maybe
Huck grew
on us over
time)

their
~~they're~~
naivete
and
self-
delusions

Caricature
without
much
insight or
subtlety
regarding
motive:
People
act
basically
out of
greed,
lust,
vanity or fear

The typed version that follows is a middle-stage draft. The handwritten additions and changes show how Mathews moved from her middle-stage draft to her final draft. Keep in mind that here too we cannot see all the stages or the comments by others.

Cereal Murder . . . In the early 1900s, fashionable Americans flocked to a famous spa in Battle Creek, Michigan founded by John Harvey Kellogg (inventor of the corn flake ~~and peanut butter~~), to have their colons massaged [by day] and their ears burned [by night] as Dr. Kellogg [delivered his famous vegetarian] ~~exhorted them to renounce beef in~~ ~~his mandatory evening~~ lecture ~~series~~ ("Of Steak and Sin"). Oddly, **T. Coraghessan Boyle** (<u>World's End</u>), seems to be the first ~~novelist~~ to explore the satirical potential of this footnote [to] ~~in~~ America's long obsession with health cures. [His new novel] ~~In the tradition of Ragtime~~, <u>The Road to Wellville</u> (Viking, $22.50), [is paved with allusions to quack therapies as the story] entwines the quests of three sets of characters: Will and Eleanor Lightbody, a naive young couple ~~from New York~~ who are seeking a cure for Will's indigestion and Eleanor's (unacknowledged) frigidity; the autocratic Dr. Kellogg, [whose adopted] ~~who is tormented by~~ ~~his degenerate~~ son, George [is a meat-eating ingrate] ~~the only one of~~ [in cahoots with Ossining.] ~~Kellogg's numerous foster children to reject~~

~~the benefits of five enemas a day; and~~ Charley

Ossining, an ~~inept~~ confidence man ~~interested~~ ^who hopes to secure^

~~in securing~~ the Lightbodys' financial backing

^to launch^ ~~for a new cereal called~~ "Per-Fo." ^a nutritionally perfect cereal; and^ Some

readers may find Boyle's ~~comic sensibility~~ ^humor^

too disdainful ^and the story's surprise murder too silly.^ ~~to hold them in thrall~~. But

^at its best, his sending up of^ ^fanaticism cleverly reminds us of the extremes^ ~~if~~ dietary ~~lunacy and medical quackery~~

^to which Americans will go in pursuit of perfection.^ ~~fascinate you, this novel is a health~~

~~cynic's feast.~~

The following is the final, printed version:

■ **CEREAL MURDER . . .** In the early 1900s, fashionable Americans flocked to a spa in Battle Creek, Michigan, founded by John Harvey Kellogg (inventor of the corn flake), to have their colons massaged by day and their ears burned by night as Dr. Kellogg delivered his famous vegetarian lecture, "Of Steak and Sin." Oddly, **T. Coraghessan Boyle** (*World's End*) seems to be the first to exploit the satirical potential of this footnote to America's long obsession with health cures. His new novel, *The Road to Wellville* (Viking, $22.50), is paved with allusions to quack therapies as the story entwines the quests of three sets of characters: Will and Eleanor Lightbody, a naive young couple who are seeking a cure for Will's indigestion and Eleanor's (unacknowledged) frigidity; Charlie Ossining, a confidence man who hopes to secure the Lightbodys' financial backing to launch Per-Fo, a nutritionally perfect cereal; and the autocratic Kellogg, whose adopted son, George, is a meat-eating ingrate in cahoots with Ossining. Some readers may find Boyle's humor too disdainful and the story's surprise murder too silly. But at its best, his send-up of dietary fanaticism cleverly reminds us of the extremes to which Americans will go in pursuit of perfection.

Cover Letter from Laura Mathews

Dear Peter,

Glamour Book Editor Tells All

Here it is—chaos to column, arranged chronologically back to front. If you'd asked to see my drafts from 3 years ago, you'd have received a carton-load. I no longer feel the need to print out every revision I make during the drafting stage. The "hard copy" marked "draft" or "revise" represents the stage of writing where I stop hating my own phrases and feel both focussed and productive. I know at that point that the column will get written in a matter of days (or hours) and am willing to let my editor (not the copy editor, but the editor with whom I discuss the month's review choices and my take on them) see a draft. I should point out that, as a writer on staff, I am greatly indulged in terms of deadlines and post put-through revising [revising after going to the printer]. I'm like an addict who'll take advantage of anyone who raises a query: e.g., if the managing editor puts one mark on her galley, I'll answer her question but also use it as an excuse to diddle with other sentences. The point is that there's a great deal more collaboration involved than if I were a free-lancer sending in a monthly dispatch. On the one hand, I have more control over the editing; on the other hand, I'm not as efficient as I'd have to be working on my own (or I suspect that's the case).

One final observation about "voice." When I pick up the issue and turn to the book page to read the final product, what I hear is <u>Glamour</u>'s voice, not Laura's.

Love,
Laura

DIVISIBLE MAN—EARLY DRAFT

John Edgar Wideman

In 1968 when I first read Daniel Patrick Moynihan's *The Negro Family: The Case for National Action,* I was teaching English at the University of Pennsylvania. Nearly all my students were white, most from well to do families and they came to me, a black man, born "disadvantaged" and poor, to learn to read and write, I was an outsider. The only black associate professor in the college of Arts and Sciences, the youngest member by at least a decade of the tenured faculty, and for three years, 1963–66—the tumultuous summers of freedom rides, urban riots, voter registration drives, the march on Washington, JFK assassination—I'd been living in another country, gaining advanced training at Oxford University in the art of being an anomaly. The fiction written by my Penn students revealed their fears, ambitions and frustrations. I was positioned in an ideal place to hear the intimate histories of a generation. Because I'd been conditioned since childhood to pay close attention to the ways of white folk who held the power of life or death over me, and because my decision to be a writer obliged me to cultivate a curiosity and sensitivity to other people's lives, I listened closely to my students. Clearly, they weren't very happy. Though they were the natural inheritors of America's vast postwar prosperity and power, the prospect of stepping into their mothers' and fathers' shoes did not enthrall them. A counter culture was forming. How and why is a fascinating story but not one I want to tell here. The point here is that I understood beyond a doubt that the American Dream, the American family Mr. Moynihan was prescribing as an antidote to black family breakdown and social delinquency was itself compromised, in dire need of revitalization and redefinition.

I'd been raised in the briar patch Mr. Moynihan was attempting to describe with his statistics, categories and comparisons, so I dismissed much of what he said as inessential and misguided, the kind of response to me and mine I'd been warding off all my life, a part standing for the whole, my color or poverty or speech or hair or anger, anything different, distinctive about me used to explain me, contain me. Bits and pieces of me all my fellow Americans across the racial chasm cared to acknowledge. Hadn't black Americans always been a divisible people: Africans doomed to slavery by arguments claiming they were less than human, the slave defined by the Constitution as 3/5's of a person, and now the urban underclass perceived not as people but a threatening swarm of cripples, criminals, and misfits? So Mr. Moynihan's failure to see me whole came as less of a surprise than his acceptance of white American family life as a solid, enduring model for blacks to emulate. . . .

Blacks remain clustered at the bottom of the economic ladder so the plight of the underclass appears to have something to do with color. Look again. The exit doors are crowded and all the faces are not black. Are we in the midst of another experiment, testing with black shock troops whether in times of shrinking economic resources we can expel the poor and dependent from the social compact?

The real voodoo economics works something like this. Take a black doll. Stick a pin in its breast. See if it cringes, hollers, cries; see if anybody notices or cares. Then you know how much you can get away with. How much of the White Man's burden can be borne by the Black man, and vice versa.

There are no black people or white people in America. There are Americans of countless colors. And fear. And confusion. And a history compounded of fear, confusion, violence, lies, a past so terrible we cannot behold it without resorting to the myths of blackness and whiteness in order to explain, justify and perpetuate a way of being that denies the evidence of our eyes, our hearts and minds. . . .

A color jones rides us. We're addicted. The habit of perceiving people as black or white feeds upon itself. Consumes us. We are the junky who wakes up each morning in hell, reeking, crusty, who promises himself no more. For a clear moment he sees the terrible shape he's in and knows he must stop his death dance with the drug. But he's so deep into his habit that he depends on it to get himself started. To move he needs a hit. And then another. He's gone again till another morning when he awakens, wallowing in his filth, stunned that things are a little worse than the last time he looked around. And so on. . . .

Because the concept of a White American is meaningless, the way White Italian or White Hungarian would be meaningless without Black Italians or Black Hungarians, the very terms of separation have become terms of mutual dependency. If we are not black or white, what are we? Though biologists and geneticists have discredited the notion of race as a significant measure of difference among the world's peoples, the world goes on punishing people for skin color, hair texture, the absence or presence of epicanthic folds in the eyes. Culture, the play of man's biological imperatives within the threshing round of space/time and physical environment, creates the evaluative frame that gives meaning to individual lives. To paraphrase an Ibo proverb, a man without a culture is like a butterfly without wings. I'm intensely proud of my Afro-American heritage. But color can also be a cage. Culture provides terms of reference for making sense of the world; color-consciousness leads to color itself becoming a terminal condition. For over 350 years Americans identified as black have been hammering away at the cage of color, using black to deny and affirm, to elaborate a culture, to refuse a culture.

> Whither shall I go from thy Spirit
> Or whither shall I flee from thy presence?

I still teach creative writing to mostly white students at the University of Massachusetts now. I remain an outsider. By choice. By necessity. The sixties are being re-invented. Mr. Moynihan's report is exhumed and vindicated as prophetic. The story of the sixties is being packaged in—surprise, surprise—black and white: good whites helping downtrodden blacks out of the darkness into the light. A noble effort that failed because a handful of evil whites and a horde of unreconstructable blacks weren't ready for the great leap forward. Old business recycled as new business as it's business as usual. An old man is fired because he trots out biological inferiority or superiority (it's not exactly clear which) to justify the status quo in professional sports: black players, white coaches, managers. CBS disassociates itself from the commentator's racist remarks, then broadcasts without apology the game between the Redskins and Vikings he was scheduled to cover. Redskins? Washington *Redskins?*

I remember a time when Americans all across this remarkable land were awakening to a sense that something drastic was wrong, that our history burdened us with failures and responsibilities, that we might hold in our hands the power to change what worried us. I remember entertaining the possibility of a better life. Really better. A life in which words like *freedom, justice, conscience* had a place. I recall Martin Luther King exhorting us to imagine ourselves as participants in the ancient drama of sacrifice, redemption and salvation. A dream of better, not more. Really better. Not more pigs slopping at the trough, not a larger bite of a rotten pie, not more but better. For everyone, and everyone meaning really everyone.

The Sunday morning of the Washington-Minnesota game I went with my son, Dan, for breakfast at the Classe Cafe in Amherst, Massachusetts, and a young guy and his lady friend sit down at the next table. As he undrapes the oversize, forties, street-person-look overcoat in which he's swaddled, the guy complains to his companion, "It's white, it's so white, everybody in here's so white. I mean white white. Geez. They're just so white." I can't tell you for whose benefit he's speaking but I overhear him without much effort and wonder as I look at his "whiteness," what color he thinks he is and whether or not he counts Danny and me as allies or if in some way we'd been subtly incorporated into the white, white everywhere the young man found so discouraging.

We returned home for a double-header of play-off games. As a kid I always rooted for the underdog. One of the worst sounds in the world was the cavalry bugle in the Saturday matinee signaling that John Wayne was coming to kick the Indians' behinds. That Sunday Minnesota was the underdog so I couldn't help rooting for them, even though the possibility of a black quarterback in the Super Bowl squeezed me inside Doug Williams's jersey, a second heart pumping, urging him to excel. I was a divisible man. As homework for this essay, I'd promised myself I'd keep track of how and when racial issues entered into an ordinary All-American orgy of football on the tube. Very quickly I gave up the project. Race was implicated so much, in so many ways, that my choice was either watch or write and that one was easy.

Can a black in America ever be a whole person in the eyes of his countrymen? In the phrase "black man" the adjective subdivides the man before man ever arrives on the scene. Metonymy—a part signifies the whole. A black athlete may have super thighs sure enough but why should that attribute imply, as it does, the absence of dedication, practice, willpower, a brain. Doesn't everybody have a brain? Why must each part be attested, proved, explicitly cataloged again and again to guarantee a black athlete, any of us, the harmony, integrity of a human being. Consider the reams of statistics accumulated about black people. Why all the numbers and tables and graphs? What they produce are fragmentary people, abstractions, stereotypes that the media solemnly report, then transform, by way of countless TV cop shows, into a violent fantasy that has come to stand for black life in the national consciousness. Are the people who claim to be trying to put Humpty-Dumpty together again, the same ones who keep pushing him off the wall?

Redskins, Blackskins. Minstrels. Beasts in the Jungle. Superstars. Our fear of being what we could be rather than what we are causes us to invent labels, to resist as long as we're able that moment when we must stare at the Other and see ourselves. But the road home leads home, and home is where we all must live and if that road's not taken, no one ever gets there.

THE DIVISIBLE MAN—AS PUBLISHED IN
LIFE MAGAZINE

John Edgar Wideman

Valentine's Day, 1988, sun shining, sky blue and I find myself climbing the stairs outside New Africa House, where the Afro-American Studies Department of the University of Massachusetts, Amherst, is located. Black students, outraged by racial attacks and harassment, have occupied New Africa House and sent out word they aren't leaving until changes are made. This quiet Sunday afternoon no barricades, no cop cars yet, or milling crowds, no gaggle of TV trucks, but trouble's here sure enough, trouble with explosive potential, the recurring national nightmare—restless natives, the never-ending business of pacification, reassertion of hegemony and preservation of the natural order, white over black.

Mounting those steps I begin to visualize the faces inside the building. Their youth, vulnerability, beauty, righteous anger, and I want to scream, shout, tear down that building and lots more. I've been here before. Oh, yes. Twenty years before, when I was a professor at the University of Pennsylvania, black students had taken over Penn's College Hall. Then as now most of my colleagues and students were white. Then as now I was a man in the middle, witness, victim, protester, tenured faces, anticipating faces. Not white or black, but real colors, real faces, like my children's. Yours. The inheritors of our racial confusions and hate. What hurt me in 1968 and lacerates me again is that I have much to say that will confirm and almost nothing to offer that will alleviate the problems driving these young people to the edge of despair.

Why are students still locking themselves within walls, forced by the very form of their protest to reproduce the segregated society they cannot abide? Where are the alternative institutions—educational, economic, political—we dreamed of creating in the '60s? Wouldn't this student demonstration be followed by a flood of apologies, promises, the inevitable backsliding and backlash, leaving the circle of racism unbroken? I recalled the publication nearly 25 years ago of Daniel Patrick Moynihan's *The Negro Family: The Case for National Action.* Didn't it confuse the nature of race relations? It took the view that the American Dream was not failing, it was failing only for blacks. A false description leading to false remedies: Let's determine what's wrong with blacks so we can cure them, bring them, or some of them, aboard our Good Ship Lollipop. Hadn't Mr. Moynihan heard James Baldwin's eloquent refusal to be integrated into a burning house? The plethora of Great Society social programs that perpetuated a doctor-patient, patron-client, master-slave relationship between whites and blacks remains a withering testament to a failure of vision.

I'd been raised in the briar patch Mr. Moynihan attempted to describe with his statistics, categories and comparisons, so I could dismiss many of his conclusions as nonessential and misguided, the kind of response to me and mine I'd been warding off all my life. Metonymy: a part signifies the whole. My color, poverty, hair, speech, anger, anything different about me used to explain me. In the phrase "black man," *black* subdivides *man* long before *man* ever arrives on the scene. Hadn't Afro-Americans always been a divisible people: Africans doomed to slavery by arguments claiming they were less than human, the slave defined by the Constitution as three fifths of a person, the urban poor perceived not as people but as a threatening swarm of cripples, criminals and misfits?

Conditioned to treating us as Other, the majority doesn't react to atrocities visited upon the black community as if those horrors are happening to fellow Americans and ultimately, inevitably, to themselves. We are shock troops, guinea pigs. Blacks remain clustered at the bottom of the economic ladder, so the plight of the underclass appears to have something to do with color. Check it out. The exit doors of industry are crowded with people being pushed out of jobs, and not all the faces are black.

The original voodoo economics works something like this. Take a black doll. Stick a pin in its chest. See if it cringes, hollers, cries; see if anybody notices, if anybody cares. Then you know how much you can get away with. How much of the white man's burden can be borne by the black man, and vice versa.

There are not black people or white people in America. There are Americans of countless colors. The wrong questions are always the ones we ask about ourselves. Wrong because they are framed in terms of black and white. A color jones rides us. We're addicted. The terms of separation are the terms of our dependency. If we are not black or white, what are we? Though biologists and geneticists have discredited the notion of race as a significant measure of difference among the world's peoples, the world goes on punishing people for skin color, hair texture and the absence or presence of epicanthic folds in the eyes. It is culture that creates the evaluative frame that gives meaning to individual lives. To paraphrase a Kongo proverb, a man without a culture is like a grasshopper without wings.

I am intensely proud of my Afro-American heritage and of my color. But color can also be a cage and color consciousness can become a terminal condition. For more than 350 years Americans identified as black have been using the cage of color to deny and affirm, to elaborate one culture, to refuse another.

I remember a time when Americans all across this remarkable land were awakening to a sense that something was drastically wrong, that our history burdened us with failures and responsibilities, that we might hold in our hands the power to change what it was that worried us. I remember entertaining the possibility of a better life. Really better. A life in which words like *freedom, justice, conscience* had a place. I recall Martin Luther King exhorting us to imagine ourselves as participants in the ancient drama of sacrifice, redemption and salvation. A dream of better, not more. Truly better. Not more pigs slopping at the trough, not a larger bite of a rotten pie, not more, but better. For everyone, and everyone meaning really everyone.

I reach out to the door of the New Africa House.

WORKSHOP

8

PERSUASION

The emphasis in this workshop is on writing persuasively: how can *written words* cause people to listen and then change their thinking or behavior? Your assignment is twofold: (1) a persuasive letter to be mailed to an appropriate audience/publication and (2) an explanation of the persuasive qualities of that letter.

We'd like your thinking on persuasion to be grounded in your own experience—not just in theories. Therefore, please stop now and freewrite (this will remain private writing) about an occasion in your own life when someone's words played a big role in affecting how you felt or thought about something—or even changed your action. Or write about an occasion when *your* words affected someone else's thinking, feeling, or behavior. Tell the story of this event in some detail. What really happened? And then speculate about how or why these words managed to be persuasive. If something else besides logic and hard evidence was important, what was this something else?

 PERSUASION AS INFORMAL ARGUMENT

Sometimes people are persuaded by long, formal arguments that somehow "prove" or "settle" an issue by means of incisive reasoning and evidence. But sometimes these good arguments don't work; that is, the reader is somehow not persuaded even though the argument is impressive. (In fact there is no such thing as pure logic except in closed systems like mathematics or symbolic logic. As soon as you apply logic to real events and natural language, there is always slippage because premises are debatable and situations are never static.) Persuasion always depends on the context: what is persuasive to what audience when. Worse yet, there is always the question of whether a given audience will "listen": *take seriously* or *try on* what you present. No logic or information can be effective if people have closed their minds to what you are saying or showing them. So at the heart of persuasion is the ability to get someone to *listen* to you.

The focus for this workshop, then, is the process of how people's minds are affected by informal, often short pieces of writing, and by the words and graphics (pictures, spacing, size and color of letters, and so forth) of advertisements. To get someone else to really take in or absorb an opinion that differs from his own—to feel it as "interesting," to swallow an advertising claim just a bit even if not actually believing it—that is a huge accomplishment. In this workshop we will consider persuasion not as the formal problem of argument and logic but as the human problem of getting someone to *listen* to your opinion. (In Workshop 12, we focus on more formal, longer pieces of argument.)

At first glance it might seem discouraging that "good" arguments often don't work. It means that if you take your goal to be the complete persuasion of "the enemy," you are almost bound to fail, for people seldom change their minds all at once. Complete arguments which "prove" that *our side* is right and *their side* is wrong are usually effective only for our side: for gatherings of our team to help us clarify our thinking, to help us remember why we believe what we believe, and to make us feel better about our position. They are seldom read by the other team (except when they are doing research about why we are wrong).

But this view is not so discouraging if you look closely at how words affect people. After all, it would be odd if people changed their minds all at once. And we see that though progress in persuasion is always slow, and we may not be good at creating airtight arguments, the *main* act in persuasion is something we *are* all good at: sensing the other person and somehow reaching out and getting the other person to *listen*. Best of all, persuasion doesn't require length. The main task is to get readers to open the door; too many words only make resistant readers close the door tighter.

Consider the fact that more people read letters to the editor in the newspaper than read the news or editorials or even sports. What distinguishes these published letters is that they are short, and they consist of people speaking out to others. If you want the quickest and best way to affect the thinking of the community you are part of, get a good letter published in your student or city newspaper or in a magazine that publishes letters. In this way you can be *published* and *read*.

Here are some examples:

To the Editor:

The women's magazine editors whose Sept. 25 letters criticize Elizabeth Whelan's Sept. 8 Op-Ed article on their health reporting ignore the main point: it is contradictory for magazines presumably concerned about women's health to carry advertising for a product, namely, cigarettes, that brings disease, miscarriages, premature widowhood or death to women.

They declare "we have cautioned women repeatedly about the hazards of smoking," but how can anyone take them seriously when their advertising promotes smoking? If these magazines have women's best interests at heart, they will drop their cigarette ads.

—Louise P. Dudley, *New York Times*, October 12, 1992

To the Editor:

(A previous letter writer) feels women with children should be prohibited from going on spaceflights. If there is to be such a rule, it should also prohibit men with children from going on spaceflights. The loss of a father is just as bad as the loss of a mother.

—*The Daily News*, March 20, 1986

To the Editor:

The Oct. 17 killing of a Japanese exchange student in Baton Rouge, La., described in "Another Magnum, Another Victim" (Op-Ed, Oct. 31) could not have been prevented by restricting the Second Amendment rights of Americans to ownership of hunting weapons alone, as the authors recommend. Hunting arms are intended to kill with a single shot, and the .44 Magnum round used in this killing is widely used in low-power hunting rifles. It is unproductive to blame American attitudes about guns for a problem that is rooted in white American attitudes toward members of other races.

I have little doubt that the young victim, Yoshihiro Hattori, would still be alive today had he been as white as his companion the evening of his murder. The white friend of the victim was alongside Hr. Hattori the instant the victim was gunned down, and so gives witness to the murder.

Deterring bias crime by vigorously prosecuting gross incidents such as this one will save more lives than restricting a homeowner's right of self-defense.

—Ludwig R. Vogel, *New York Times,* Nov. 1, 1992
(The writer is chairman of the New York State Libertarian Party.)

To the Editor:

My father read to me today the article about Batman, "Batman and the Jewish Question" (Op-Ed, July 2).

It made me very surprised when they said that the Penguin had to be Jewish because of his nose and his fondness for herring. For Pete's sake, he's a penguin; give him a break.

—Rebecca Stokes, *New York Times,* July 20, 1992
(For a longer, more argumentlike letter on this same subject, see the readings at the end of Workshop 12.)

The essence of persuasion in today's world is often embodied in advertisements—in magazines, newspapers, on billboards, radio, and television. Advertisers to the general public usually have only one goal: to get you to buy their product. We admit that some advertisements have a heavy informational component (see Workshop 12). But most advertisements are more persuasion than argument. We've included one here for you to react to, for the Land Rover Defender 110 (see the facing page).

EVALUATING SHORT PIECES OF PERSUASION

By yourself—or better yet with your group—answer as many of the following questions as possible.

For both letters and ad:

1. *Most persuasive.* Which letter/advertisement persuaded you the most? the least? Answer the question using quick intuitive judgment. After answering the following questions, come back to this one. You may discover you've changed your mind.
2. *Your position.* What was your position on the topic of the letter/advertisement *before* reading it? For each piece, how much did it *change* your thinking or feeling?

Own one of these legendary forms of jungle transportation.

Many consider it the most exotic vehicle on earth.

It's survived safaris through the jungles of Sulawesi. Madagascar. And the Amazon. Treks across the Wahiba Sands of Oman. The Rub al Khali. Even the Great Rift Valley of Kenya.

It's the Land Rover Defender 110. World renowned for wading through swamps. Crossing savannahs. Venturing deep into kingdoms of the wild.

And even better. Out of them.

There are 500 Land Rover Defender 110s now available in America, more than ready to handle everything the country has to offer.

Including roads.

You can see one of these nearly indestructible vehicles at select Range Rover dealers. For the one nearest you, call 1-800-FINE 4WD.

We realize, of course, that at around $40,000*, it's hardly a frivolous investment. But considering how it's built, it's likely the most solid one you'll ever make.

Because unlike a vine, you won't have to go from one to the next.

LAND ROVER **DEFENDER 110**

3. *Listening and trust.* Which one made you *listen/look* most—even if it didn't change your thoughts or feelings? Why? Was it because you trusted the writer/advertiser?

4. *Assumptions.* What did each author/advertiser seem to be assuming as true? Do you agree with these assumptions? What does that have to do with your reactions?

5. *Audience.* For each letter/advertisement, do you think you're the audience the writer had in mind? How does that affect whether or not you're persuaded? If you're the wrong audience, what sort of audience do you think the writers had in mind?

6. *Voice.* Go around the circle in your group and read each of the letters aloud at least twice—and also the words in the advertisements. Does hearing the words change your reactions? "Put on" or "enter into" the voice you hear, and write as though you were that person.

For the letters:

7. *Claim.* For each letter, state the claim in as short a sentence as possible.

8. *Support.* For each letter, what is the support for its claim? Try to summarize it in a sentence. What would you say the writer was relying on: logic, information, example, emotion, language, or something else?

9. *Language.* In each case, did the language add to or detract from the writer's presentation? Try to be specific about exactly which pieces of language had what effect on you.

For the ad:*

10. *Purpose.* What is the ad trying to do? All ads are selling something: some a tangible product, others an intangible service or idea. Determine what your particular ad is selling or advocating.

11. *Focus.* Locate the focal point of the ad. Where do your eyes go to first when you look at the ad?

12. *Visual.* Identify the place and objects in the ad and explain the purpose of each. Does color play a role in the ad at all? Explain. Does the picture illustrate the copy?

13. *Language.* Consider first the headline or "grabber"—the big print that gets your attention first. What does it say, and how does it say it? Next, examine the blurb, or the more detailed written content, and consider (a) the language—the words used and why (pay particular attention to *adjectives* here); and (b) the type of approach used—is it description, comparison, definition, exemplification, testimonial, or something else? Does the written part complement the picture?

These questions are based on an exercise developed at Arizona State University by Alice Robertson, now at SUNY—Stony Brook.

I got the idea for the topic for this piece from something my brother said the last time I saw him. When I first wrote this piece on my brother, I truly loved the way the experience just rolled off my tongue. Yet I knew I needed to work on the grammar. When I read it to the small group in class, I realized that I didn't want to really share this experience with others. But the group had no criticism of my paper at all; they just loved it which really wasn't helpful.

So my next step was I went to the Writing Center and made an appointment with a tutor. She told me that I needed to continue the psychoanalysis of the main character and be more definite in my writing. She also suggested to change the order of the paper. Start with setting the scene of the barbecue and then lower the boom on my brother's dropping out of medical school.

So I revised the paper then making it more descriptive and analyzing the character. At this point I really disliked the whole paper. I believe this is because I enjoyed writing the paper from the point of view of a child rather than an adult. I thought for quite a long time after writing this paper about how to improve it, but I was unable to do so.

Finally after making many appointments at the Writing Center, I truly became disgusted with the paper. The appointments were canceled because of the weather, but at that point I didn't care anymore because I no longer wanted to improve a paper that in the beginning I really loved.

Student

For both letters and ad:

14. *Conclusion.* On the basis of these examples and questions, can you reach some tentative conclusions about what is most helpful and least helpful in short informal persuasion—in trying to get readers who disagree to *listen* to you? in trying to get an audience to look and buy? What do you see as the chief difference between how these letters and ads persuade?

 WRITING A LETTER TO THE EDITOR

Spend some time reading and scanning newspapers: neighborhood papers, local papers, school newspapers. Pick several issues out of these newspapers which you feel strongly about and begin freewriting, telling *why* you feel strongly about them and why you think others ought to as well. In your freewriting, concentrate on *your* reasons for your strong feelings on your topic. Don't think yet about persuading others. It's your own emotional and intellectual commitment that you need to tap now.

One approach here is to think back to when you first became aware of how you felt about the issue you want to write on. Describe the experience that led to your stance. Writing out this experience will help you get a firm grip on why *you* believe as you do.

Push yourself to write at least ten or fifteen minutes on each topic you select. You might even want to "rant and rave" about your topics a bit—no harm done; this is not what you're actually going to send off, and the ranting will help you get at the core of your feelings and thoughts. After you've done this exploratory private writing, set it aside for a bit—even an hour helps. Read it over when you come back and decide which issue now appeals to you the most, the one you want to use for your final letter. Isolate for yourself the point you want to make about this issue, and state it as directly and concisely as possible so that you can incorporate it into a letter.

Now you're ready to write a first draft for sharing with your classmates. And now you must begin to think about your audience. Chances are you may want to address the same audience as the one addressed by the article you're reacting to. Other students in the class can help you characterize this audience on the basis of the original article.

Another good way to approach this first draft is to try to come up with possible objections to your views. You may or may not have done this as you were freewriting. But now you can make a list of all the reasons that might keep people from accepting your assertions. To get these clear, try writing a dialogue with yourself where you speak on both sides of your issue. You can, of course, enlist a classmate to write out the opposing side. (For more on the specifics of writing collaborative dialogues, see Workshop 3.)

Writing out an internal dialogue or a dialogue with a classmate is even more useful when you know that you care about a particular issue but you haven't gotten clear for yourself exactly what your position is. For example, you may think the issue of whether or not campus police should carry guns is crucial, but still not be exactly sure of where you stand.

You may wonder why we suggest writing a dialogue instead of just talking through issues and differences. Talking about your issue is, of course, a good thing to do, but producing a written dialogue requires you to spell things out more concretely. That's good for seeing your issue clearly.

After you've done your freewriting or dialogue, decide on your focus and whether or not you want to take objections into consideration. For it's not *necessarily* a good idea to answer opposing opinions: sometimes too much answering-of-objections can make your piece sound defensive and you are better off with a piece that is shorter and more direct.

Collaborative Option with Advertisements

With your classroom group, select (or invent) a product to write an advertisement for, and produce the advertisement collaboratively. Obviously, in doing so, you'll want to consider visual qualities too: color, pictures, size of letters, and so forth. You should also decide where your advertisement should be placed (newspaper, general-audience magazines, specialty magazine, and so forth) to generate the most business. In the readings, we've included a classroom-designed advertisement.

Other Options

As your main assignment for this workshop, rather than producing a letter or advertisement of your own, you can expand on your analysis of one of the letters or ads from the first part of this workshop. You could write on just one let-

Professors' grades even had the power to change my own opinion about what I'd written. For example, last semester I wrote a nice paper on *The Faerie Queene*. I put a lot of effort into it and really cared about the subject matter. . . . However, I received a fairly mediocre grade, the same grade I received on a previous paper that I had spent much less time on. I thought to myself, "Well all that work went for nothin'." Immediately, I negated the paper just because of the grade I received on it. I started to believe that my paper was worthless. However, looking back on it, I now realize that the paper helped me appreciate *The Faerie Queene*. I don't believe that I would have read it as closely, cared about what the story was telling me, if I hadn't been writing a paper on the poem. In short, I took ownership of the work and I made sure that the paper remained mine as well. I did not let my professor kidnap my paper by putting a grade on it. The paper was important to me, the writer, and that's what matters.

Jerry Boyd

ter or ad, or do a comparison of two or more. This too could be a collaborative project. Or you might want to base your main assignment on an analysis of the persuasiveness of Lindsy Van Gelder's "The Great Person-Hole Cover Debate" in the "Readings" of this workshop. Or, finally, you might decide to tape and analyze a TV ad. (Don't forget to consider why the ad was featured within a particular program and at a particular time.) Your task is the same regardless of your subject: how does the writer/advertiser get an audience to listen?

 WRITING YOUR EXPLANATION

The second part of the assignment for this workshop is the explanatory piece for your teacher and classmates about the purpose and audience of your letter. After reading your letter to your group and perhaps discussing it with them, try freewriting answers to the following questions:

■ What is my purpose in writing this piece?
■ Who is my audience? How do I expect them to react? Why would they react this way?
■ What am I assuming to be true? How does that work for my piece?
■ What sort of voice have I embedded in my letter? Why did I choose this voice? (We suggest you read your piece aloud and exaggerate the voice you think is there.)
■ What is the claim I'm making? How am I supporting it?
■ What decisions did I make about the language of my letter? What was the basis for these decisions?

You may also want to look ahead at our exploration of our own purposes in writing this book (printed in Workshop 16; see pages 425–426).

On the basis of your reflections on all these questions, you should be able to produce a solid first draft to share with your classmates.

Publication. Your class may want to keep a folder or notebook with copies of all the letters after they've been mailed to the chosen publications. To this folder, everyone can add copies of letters that *do* get published plus any responses to them. This will make interesting reading for everyone.

Collaborative Option

Do a bit of role-playing and assume that you are an advertising copywriter who wishes to sell the advertisement you and your group designed to the company which produces the product being advertised. Write a persuasive letter to the president of the company explaining why your advertisement is an effective one: who its audience is, what its purpose is, and how it works. Naturally you will include a copy of the advertisement itself. This assignment leads realistically to collaboration since almost all work in advertising agencies *is* collaborative. Two or three of you could thus undertake this assignment jointly.

PROCESS BOX

Cover Letter

I am, without a doubt, a writer in transition; and this assignment made me painfully aware of this fact. I sat down on Saturday night and wrote 2 pages in the style that I have grown accustomed to; but I was growing more and more uncomfortable with the way it sounded as I went along. At about 1:00 a.m. I threw it all away and went to bed. On Sunday I experienced the worst writer's block that I have ever encountered, writing a paragraph or two and then throwing it away—again and again. This was made all the more frustrating by the fact that I knew exactly what I wanted to say, I just couldn't organize it in a way that "felt" right. I tried freewriting and that went great, but when I tried to take what I'd put down and organize it I found that I couldn't. I spent 12 hrs on the computer (on and off) on Sunday and ended up with *nothing*.

At this point I was panicking. I began to think that maybe I'd jumped out of the leaky boat of my old writing style, and into the water: wasn't it better to have a leaky boat than no boat at all? With this happy thought in mind I went to bed.

On Monday morning I decided that I would take a deep breath, lighten up on my self-criticism, and plow through it, so that at least I would have something completed that I could work with. By 3:00 when I left for class, to my great surprise, I was more than half done and I liked the way it sounded.

I guess what I was really looking for was a paper that was less uptight than my usual work, and something that had a bit of myself in it. Even though it is really only the introduction of my final paper which is "personal" I feel more like I'm "in there" throughout the paper than I ever have before. The rest of the paper came very easily after I got through the assumptions—it almost wrote itself in response to them.

I'm optimistic and I feel that I have some clear goals to work towards.

Bill Brown

With persuasive texts in particular, we need to see how they work with readers. Thus it is important to get the kind of feedback you need using techniques from *Sharing and Responding* at the end of this book. The main feedback technique might be "Movies of the Reader's Mind" (Section 7), which encourages readers to start by telling you their original opinion on your topic. You can even ask readers to talk about your topic before you show them your piece, and then have them tell you what went on in their minds *as* they were listening to it. The early forms of feedback (Sections 1 through 5) are useful for an early draft—helping you develop your own thinking. Getting people to describe your voice tells you how trustworthy you sound (Section 6). "Believing" feedback can help you develop your argument further; "doubting" can help you see what objections readers *could* raise (Section 9).

And, of course, you can use the questions we presented earlier in this workshop as strategies for analyzing persuasive letters and ads. Be sure you get your classmates to talk about whom they see as the audience for your letter or ad and what they see you trying to get them to think or do. You can take notes on this to help you with the accompanying explanatory writing.

PROCESS JOURNAL AND COVER LETTER QUESTIONS

- How did you choose your topic for the letter assignment? Did you find yourself believing your assertions more and more as you wrote—or less and less?
- About audience. You were probably very aware of audience when writing your short letters to actual newspapers. Then we advised you not to worry about who your audience might be when you started to revise the short letter into a longer letter. Reflect a bit on what happened and what you came to notice about you and audience awareness. Did we give you bad advice?
- About working in groups. What did you do that helped the group work better? What did others do that helped? Were there things that you or others did that seemed harmful? What would it take to avoid such words or actions next time?
- How would you compare writing an advertisement with most of the school writing you do? Are there ways these two kinds of writing could help one another?

RUMINATIONS AND THEORY

Informal Persuasion and Formal Argument

We find it useful to lay out two opposite answers to the question of how words can persuade. At one extreme is the *extended, formal argument*—the careful, elaborated "proof"—in which you are as logical as possible and you don't re-sort at all to feelings or emotional "persuasive language." At the other extreme is *informal persuasion*—more intuitive and experiential. This kind of persuasion doesn't try to mount a full argument; in fact it may not use an "argument" at all. It may just convey an important piece of information or tell a story.

Extended formal argument requires readers to read carefully and at length. They've got to be interested enough in you or in what you are saying to give you lots of time and attention. Extended, careful argument is what you might be expected to write for an audience that is *expert* or *professional*—for example, if you were writing a report for a college task force about the location of a new building or about a particular health-care plan. Such an audience isn't interested in emotional arguments or in being "persuaded." You don't have to coax them to read and to think carefully about the matter; they're already interested in figuring out what's the best view. It's their job to read with care. They want good analysis and good reasons. If they find you trying to persuade them with an emotional appeal rather than reasons and evidence, they'll likely start to distrust you and say, "What is this pesky writer trying to hide? What are the 'real' reasons he's covering up?" Clever persuasion gets in their way.

Informal persuasion, at the other extreme, is the kind of thing you find in editorials, leaflets, advertisements, short spoken interchanges, and—of course—letters to the editor in newspapers. It's usually shorter than formal argument, settling for making a couple of the best points—perhaps giving a reason and some information and some personal experience all wrapped up together. Often this kind of argument doesn't try to *change* someone's think-ing but rather just to plant a seed. This is the kind of piece you need to write if you are trying to reach readers who have no special reason or commitment to read what you've written.

Brevity is the most common solution to the problem of readers who are li-able to wander away at any moment. Whatever you want to say to such an audience, you have to say it fast. You can't take it as your goal to completely change their thinking. Planting a seed or opening a door is probably the best you can hope for.

But informal arguments aren't always short. The crucial thing that marks informal argument is a decision to forgo full argument and instead to *reach* or *interest* readers—perhaps by getting them to experience something or by telling a story. For example, *Uncle Tom's Cabin* is a story—a novel—but it functions as a piece of persuasion, and it had a powerful effect on national sentiment about slavery before the Civil War. Informal persuasion may make "points," but more often it succeeds by conveying *experience* or affecting feelings. We will wait until Workshop 12, "Argument," to concentrate on for-mal arguments.

Readings

SHORT LETTERS

Janine Ramaz

People who write short letters to the editors of their local newspapers know that they have to make their points briefly and clearly. Readers of newspaper "Letters to the Editor" sections are mainly interested in knowing what their fellow citizens think on issues the newspaper has printed articles on. If they want to read long, detailed arguments, they will look for them elsewhere in the paper. So letter writers must use few words to get across their opinions. In this paper, I'm going to look at how three short letters do this.

All the letter writers know that they have to say right away what letter or article they're writing about. So they identify that in the very first sentence. This is good because then people who aren't interested in these particular subjects will probably go on and read something else. But then when the letter writer says also briefly what the content is, readers who missed the other letter or the article but are interested will go ahead and read the letter. So every one of the writers of the letters I'm looking at says quickly what the issue is.

This issue is the subject of the letter. The issues of my three letters are: advertising cigarettes in a woman's magazine, parents on spaceflights, and owning guns. I believe that the most effective of these three letters is the one about spaceflight.

The first of the letters I read, the one about women's smoking, was really too long. The writer of this letter made the same point twice. Furthermore, the second time she says it she uses the words "but how can anyone take them seriously." I hear a whiny voice here which makes the whole letter less strong.

The third of these three letters is criticizing those who are using a particular unfortunate incident to argue against gun ownership. To me, the argument is weak because the writer avoids the whole issue of banning all kinds of guns which might have saved the young man's life. Since I was sure the writer would not approve of banning all guns, his point got weaker for me. And, too, not all accidental gun shootings involve people of different races.

The letter I thought most effective was also the shortest. The writer made his point (I'm not really sure if the writer was male or female because there was no name) in plain simple language: "The loss of a father is just as bad as the loss of a mother." Furthermore I think this letter will have a broader appeal than the other two because the first one would appeal mostly to women and perhaps turn men and non-feminist women off. The third letter appeals mainly to gun lovers, though it would also have some appeal to those with strong beliefs in good racial relations.

The letter about spaceflights really made me think about something I hadn't thought of before and even to come to a new conclusion that parents shouldn't go on spaceflights. It should just be single people or married people with no children. That's the main reason I consider this letter the best: it made me do some thinking after I read it and didn't burden me with unnecessary words.

□ □ □ □ □

LETTER TO A PRODUCT PRODUCER

January 8, 1994

Mr. John Jones, President
Wilton Products
5555 Fifth Avenue
American City, American State 55555

Dear Mr. Jones:

We read in *Advertising World* that your company is seeking a vibrant new team to design ads for Wilton's new breakfast cereal, Designer Breakfast. We're enclosing an ad which demonstrates our ability to produce ads for this exciting new product.

Our chief appeal in this ad is to ambitious young men and women who pride themselves in creating unique styles and images for themselves—young people who are already on the road to success. You will notice that we have put the name of the cereal across the top of the page to show how superior it is. The words "You design your outfit every day / why not design your breakfast?" at the top of the page and "You wouldn't wear the same outfit every day / Why eat the same breakfast every day?" come together because they are the same type and echoing structures. The questions challenge readers to participate in the ad itself.

You will note that both figures are stylish in different ways and that both are looking directly at the reader. These are young people secure in their identities. Readers will want to emulate them. The male figure is looking back as though satisfied with the way his day starts. The female figure is moving forward energetically; she has had a nutritious, filling breakfast which gives her the energy she needs to be successful. We also want our ad to appeal to young people who believe both men and women should have careers. We don't really think this is a family cereal.

We've kept the words to a minimum. Readers will want to know what the ingredients are and how the whole idea works. So we've given that

Designer Breakfast

You design your outfit every day, why not *design your breakfast?*

corn chips? nuts? raisins?
dried fruit? crisp rice?
bran flakes? mini-
marshmallows? granola?
wheat germ? honey kernels?

Our packaging allows you
to combine any or all of
these ingredients to produce
*a different breakfast
every morning.*

You wouldn't wear the same outfit every day.

Why eat the same breakfast every day?

Each DESIGNER BREAKFAST box contains ten separate packages of each of the ingredients. Open and combine different ones every day.

And don't worry about the environment, because we have. Our packages are all made out of recycled newsprint.

information twice. And we added the environment tag at the bottom because again we think that today's young career-oriented people care about the environment. We envision this ad in magazines such as *Newsweek* and *Time,* but also in style publications such as *Vogue* and *Country Gentlemen.*

We believe that this ad and others like it will sell this exciting new product. If you would like to see more of what we can do, please call.

Sincerely,

Jason Multer
Antoinette Jajee
Martine Oxenham
Ngoyen Nong
Alex Ujibwa

THE GREAT PERSON-HOLE COVER DEBATE
A Modest Proposal for Anyone Who Thinks the Word "He"
Is Just Plain Easier . . .

Lindsy Van Gelder

I wasn't looking for trouble. What I was looking for, actually, was a little tourist information to help me plan a camping trip to New England.

But there it was, on the first page of the 1979 edition of the State of Vermont *Digest of Fish and Game Laws and Regulations:* a special message of welcome from one Edward F. Kehoe, commissioner of the Vermont Fish and Game Department, to the reader and would-be camper, *i.e.,* me.

This person (*i.e.,* me) is called "the sportsman."

"We have no 'sportswomen, sportspersons, sportsboys, or sportsgirls,' " Commissioner Kehoe hastened to explain, obviously anticipating that some of us sportsfeminists might feel a bit overlooked. "But," he added, "we are pleased to report that we do have many great sportsmen who are women, as well as young people of both sexes."

It's just that the Fish and Game Department is trying to keep things "simple and forthright" and to respect "long-standing tradition." And anyway, we really ought to be flattered, "sportsman" being "a meaningful title being earned by a special kind of dedicated man, woman, or young person, as opposed to just any hunter, fisherman, or trapper."

I have heard this particular line of reasoning before. In fact, I've heard it so often that I've come to think of it as The Great Person-Hole Cover Debate, since gender-neutral manholes are invariably brought into the argument as evidence of the lengths to which humorless, Newspeak-spouting feminists will go to destroy their mother tongue.

Consternation about woman-handling the language comes from all sides. Sexual conservatives who see the feminist movement as a unisex plot and who long for the good old days of *vive la différence,* when men were men and women were women, nonetheless do not rally behind the notion that the term "mankind" excludes women.

But most of the people who choke on expressions like "spokesperson" aren't right-wing misogynists, and this is what troubles me. Like the undoubtedly well-meaning folks at the Vermont Fish and Game Department, they tend to reassure you right up front that they're only trying to keep things "simple" and to follow "tradition," and that some of their best men are women, anyway.

Usually they wind up warning you, with great sincerity, that you're jeopardizing the worthy cause of women's rights by focusing on "trivial" side issues. I would like to know how anything that gets people so defensive and resistant can possibly be called "trivial," whatever else it might be.

The English language is alive and constantly changing. Progress—both scientific and social—is reflected in our language, or should be.

Not too long ago, there was a product called "flesh-colored" Band-Aids. The flesh in question was colored Caucasian. Once the civil rights movement pointed out the racism inherent in the name, it was dropped. I cannot imagine reading a thoughtful, well-intentioned company policy statement explaining that while the Band-Aids would continue to be called "flesh-colored" for old time's sake, black and brown people would now be considered honorary whites and were perfectly welcome to use them.

Most sensitive people manage to describe our national religious traditions as "Judeo-Christian," even though it takes a few seconds longer to say than "Christian." So why is it such a hardship to say "he or she" instead of "he"?

I have a modest proposal for anyone who maintains that "he" is just plain easier: since "he" has been the style for several centuries now—and since it really includes everybody anyway, right?—it seems only fair to give "she" a turn. Instead of having to ponder over the intricacies of, say, "Congressman" versus "Congressperson" versus "Representative," we can simplify things by calling them all "Congresswomen."

Other clarifications will follow: "a woman's home is her castle" . . . "a giant step for all womankind" . . . "all women are created equal" . . . "Fisherwoman's Wharf." . . .

And don't be upset by the business letter that begins "Dear Madam," fellas. It means you, too.

SOME REFLECTIONS ON NOT VOTING IN PRESIDENTIAL ELECTIONS

Meg Hyre, published in The Catholic Worker

I voted in the last two presidential elections, but I intend not to do it again. Each time previously I lost my nerve: Was my wish to withdraw from electoral politics not, perhaps, too cynical? Could I honestly say that I thought it made *no* difference who won the election? These doubts finally drew me to the voting booth but, as with many a dubious enterprise, I didn't like myself very much the next morning! For the last four years, I have asked my friends to remind me not to vote in 1992.

This resolution not to vote is perhaps best described as an "experiment in truth" or an effort in the clarification of thought. One principle I am sure of. The character of the Catholic Worker's anarchism and decentralism requires that whatever action we take be rooted (first and last) in hope, not in despair. Thus informed, the decision not to vote is only a step on the way to seeking (and helping to make) something better.

Nonetheless, as a Catholic, I do not take lightly this abandonment of the established political avenues, however faulty they may be. Henri de Lubac has said that the true character of Catholicism will always be one of synthesis. As Jesus was pleased to share in our humanity, we ourselves must embrace that humanity even as we "partake of His divinity." Our natures are social and political, as well as emotional and intellectual. And in any case, it is not ours to reject our share in the common life or the common condition.

Our end is given to us—fullness of life in God. But we must choose this end for ourselves, and then find the best means to the end. This is our freedom, and it is profound. All other things being equal, says St. Augustine, we may choose our vocations—for instance, the active or contemplative lives—simply from love or sheer preference. Beyond this, our use of the things of this world must depend on our very best judgment, exercised in the light of faith. That's what prudence is, and as Robert Ludlow noted many years ago, that leaves us as Catholics a very broad field in which to exercise our political responsibilities.

You could say that my theory of politics has evolved along much the same lines as my theory of romance. If you keep settling for less than what you really hope for in love, while waiting for the right one to come along, all the really honorable ones will pass you by, because they see that you are already attached! At some point you've got to go for broke where matters of the heart are concerned. Well, it's the same for politics. How can you expect to find a really worthwhile political involvement if you keep believing the same old party promises, and agreeing to give it yet another try? In fact, until you make that clean break, you won't be in a truly free position to discover the possibilities!

So much of what we need to accomplish in ourselves and in our society is breaking the hold of the many "necessities" we imagine ourselves to be at the mercy of. This is as true with regard to the state as it is with regard to our creature comforts (and these are not incidentally related). We must always ask ourselves, do things *have* to be this way? Such changes in understanding and action are not easy, quick, or painless, but one must start somewhere.

A book I highly recommend in helping to see things a different way is *Anarchy in Action* by Colin Ward, (Freedom Press). One need not agree with Colin Ward's approach entirely to appreciate his key insights. Chief among these are his explanations of *what* government (in our case, the state) is, and *how* its power can be actually lessened.

On government, he quotes Martin Buber: "All forms of government have this in common: Each possesses more power than is required by the given conditions; in fact, this excess in the capacity for making dispositions is actually what we understand by political power. The measure of this excess, which cannot, of course, be computed precisely, represents the exact difference between administration and government." Government derives its authority from the threat of internal and external instability, but always demands for itself more power than is actually necessary for the task. The disparity existing today between the power of the state and its execution of its lawful functions is great indeed.

But how can this arrangement be changed? On this question, Colin Ward cites Gustav Landauer, German anarchist and close friend of Martin Buber's: "The state is not something which can be destroyed by a revolution, but is a condition, a certain relationship between human beings, a mode of human behavior; we destroy it by contracting other relationships, by behaving differently." It is we who actively make the social and political order, Landauer reminds us. This is a potent reminder, but it is hard to keep in view unless it is somehow lived.

That is why I am not voting. I have decided that it is time to contract new, and more honorable, ties. What do I have to go on? My own days are now engaged in the domestic sphere that my marriage has created, as well as with my study of philosophy and preparation to teach. It is hard to think of two more politically abused notions today than "vision" and "the family." But my instinct and experience tell me that the home life and the thinking life are radical and political vocations in this world, when they are faithfully lived, when they are the foundation of a common life open to the stranger and those in need. These are the means that I see open to me—means for resistance and means for hope. I'm sure you know ways of your own.

229

Readings
Some Reflections
on Not Voting in
Presidential
Elections

WORKSHOP
9

THE ESSAY

Our aim in this workshop is to introduce you to the essay both as a literary form and as a school form. Along the way, we're going to talk about the difference between personal and impersonal writing and get you to do some thinking about what it means to write "expository" essays in academic language. In Workshop 10, we'll give you another chance to practice the typical language of academic writing.

The main assignment for this workshop will be to draft two essays, one personal, one impersonal, based on the subject matter of some other course you're taking, and revise at least one of them into a final version.

We've sequenced this workshop by asking you first to write your own essays and then read and think about the three published essays at the end of the workshop. You or your teacher may want to rearrange this sequence by reading the published essays either at the very beginning of the workshop or at some point in the middle. The essay is such a flexible form that no one example can be considered an ideal representation.

 ## THE ESSAY

The essay is a slithery form; perhaps (notice we only say *perhaps*) we all recognize an essay when we see one, but few of us could actually define the form. That may well be its strength: it permits much; its outlines are pliable. To help you understand the essay better, we present some of our thoughts about it in "Theory and Ruminations" at the conclusion of this workshop and some essays about it in the "Readings" section.

We haven't used the word *essay* much in this textbook; we usually call what you're asked to do "papers" or "writing." "Composition" is a word we also tend to avoid because it's almost always used for writing done only in school—or only in English classes. We're hoping we can get you to see that writing is writing: it isn't something you do just for English classes or just for school. Nor are we teaching a way of going about writing which is applicable only to school writing.

"Expository" has come to be the term used in schools and in academic discourse for essays that *explain*. Expository writing thus tends toward the impersonal more than toward the personal. Many of your teachers would probably describe the papers they ask you to do by the adjective "expository." We use the word in Workshop 5 to categorize one of the genres you might use to reshape your private writing into public writing. This workshop will ask you to do some variant of that transformation.

First Round of Freewriting: Private Freewriting

Your purpose in this first session of exploratory writing will be to come up with a topic which grows out of something you're studying in another class. This topic or subject should be one you have personal opinions about that you haven't been able to express in that other class. Perhaps you're learning about stages of adolescent growth or about gender roles and your teacher hasn't asked you how you connect or don't connect to any of this. Perhaps you're taking a geology class and have strong feelings about the environment and business growth which you haven't been able to express. Or maybe your teacher has a particular bias which you find irritating: gives you feminist interpretations of everything you read or (the opposite) seems to slight women in general.

Everything you learn in school has some relevance to what happens outside of school—though we admit that those connections are sometimes hard to uncover. We believe that if you *do* uncover these connections, you'll learn more in the class. That's part of our goal for the activities of this workshop.

If you have difficulties coming up with a topic, think about the following possibilities:

- If you're taking a sociology or psychology course, how do the theories presented by the teacher and the textbook relate to you, your particular generation, and its interests: for example, to music, clothes, sports, media? How do these theories relate to problems such as excessive drug and alcohol use and changing family structures?

- If you're taking a philosophy course, how does what you're learning there connect to your values, for example about religion, sexual mores, and gender roles? Does your approach to these issues differ from that of your parents? your grandparents? Do you know people whom you or others describe as "philosophical"? What does that mean? How does that connect (or not connect) to your philosophy course?

- If you're taking an education course, what does that course say about the role of education in *your* life and in the current life of our country? Does it connect to what we so often hear and read about today's young people being less intelligent, poorer writers and thinkers, less prepared for college work than before? Do you see any evidence that the theories presented in the class have functioned in your education—either now or in the past?

PROCESS BOX

Curiously, when I am involved in the actual process of writing, I find myself intensely dissatisfied with the act itself—my inability to find the words I want, to visualize a scene, to make it sound smooth enough. For this reason I am almost constantly revising as I go along, sometimes reworking a sentence two or three times before I can go on to the next one. (Though this is almost always at the level of syntax rather than thought. That is, I tend to play with the wording and hardly ever touch the structure or function of the sentence within my argument or development: once something has been written down, even if only partially, I tend to feel committed to the *essence* of that thought and unable to change direction.)

I think this approach is usually a bad one, especially for expository or simple functional writing. Yet it is one I find myself unable to easily discard. The other side of this way of working is that after I've finished even a small section—let's say a paragraph or so—I feel immensely pleased with what I've put down, often more so than I should be. Because of this, it usually takes me at least several days after the fact to recognize that something I've written is not up to snuff.

J. A. Iovine

■ If you're taking a botany or geology course, what has it made you think about with regard to issues like the environment, waste disposal, the diminishing rain forests? Do these scientific fields tend to rely on "facts" and leave little room for intuition and feelings? Where do you run into this fact-feeling difference in your own life?

■ If you're taking a math course, how applicable are the problems you confront to issues in your own everyday life? Math anxiety is said to be prevalent in our society. Do you or others you know suffer from that anxiety? Why do you think American students on average are poorer math students than students in Japan and China? Is there room for creativity and intuition in the solution of math problems? How do you feel about that? Why?

Basically what we're asking you to reflect on as you freewrite is how some idea you're confronting in one of your classes is important beyond the confines of the class and how it relates to your own life and experience and to the lives of others you know.

Second Round: Public Freewriting

Assume that you've been asked to write on your subject by the teacher of the other class: specifically, your assignment is to relate the ideas, concepts, facts, and so forth, embodied in your topic to some interest of yours outside the classroom. You will be expected to share most of this second round of freewriting—however, as with all public freewriting, you always have the option of withholding pieces of it.

See what you end up saying about your topic when you are addressing your words to fellow students and to your teacher.

You may also profit from seeking out others in the class you're writing about. Ask them to respond to what you've written after they read it or listen to you read it. Perhaps they'll lend you their notes. Once you've done this, write out what you've learned as a result and add it to the collection of writing on your ideas.

If you actually have a writing assignment for this class, you have a good reason to go see the professor during her office hours. But even if you don't, she'll probably be interested in what you're doing for the writing class. Maybe you'd like to ask her to help you design a topic which she would consider appropriate for the class, if she did assign a paper asking you to connect the subject matter of her course to aspects of your own life. Or if you have established a topic, do some writing and thinking on it first and then ask her for some response. After you've talked to the teacher, you can do some more freewriting based on her response.

Personal and Impersonal

Now we ask you to think about the difference between personal and impersonal writing. We think that you'll discover that this difference is not always the same as the difference between private and public writing. *Some* of what you wrote privately will be impersonal and some of what you wrote publicly will be personal. Keep in mind that it isn't subject matter that determines whether an essay is personal or impersonal: it's the way you approach that subject matter. When you approach a subject personally, you focus more on your own thoughts and reactions to your subject. When you approach a subject impersonally, you focus more on information as a way of "informing" your readers about it, not about you. In personal writing, who you are comes across more; in impersonal writing, your subject matter comes across more.

Of course there's no absolute difference between personal and impersonal writing. There's almost always both some information and some of you in anything you write. Even when you write what seems like "pure" information, your selection of it was a personal selection. But once you've selected information, you can present it more *as information* or more as *your personal slant* on that information.

Look back now over your two pieces of freewriting and try as well as you can to mark what is personal and impersonal. You might try using a straight line to mark what seems definitely impersonal and a wavy line to mark what seems definitely personal. Leave unmarked what seems ambiguous.

You may not find neat separations between whole sections of personal or impersonal writing—or even between sentences. Sometimes you will find a phrase or even a single word that is personal within a passage that is largely impersonal—or vice-versa. (You can draw a line under just a word or phrase, or draw a line alongside a longer passage.) You can often get a strong sense of the difference between personal and impersonal tone by reading over sentences or passages and *omitting* words or phrases or sentences you've marked as personal. It's surprising what a difference a word or two can make.

Bring this material to class and try sharing whatever you are willing to share with your partner or group—to see if they agree with your distinctions between personal and impersonal. (Also, they might have suggestions for enriching both kinds of writing.) But let us stress that we're not asking you to share anything you don't want to share.

Keep in mind that your assignment is to discuss your topic's relevance to the world outside the classroom in which you're studying it. In one version you'll be seeing this connection in personal terms; in the other version you'll be seeing this same connection impersonally. Your task is to come to terms with this distinction.

Revision

Now you're ready to build the personal elements of your freewriting into one essay and the impersonal elements into another essay. Certain parts of these two essays may be almost identical. Which essay (personal or impersonal) you develop into a final version will depend on your writing teacher's instructions.

It's probably not fair to ask the teacher of the other course to read two versions. But perhaps she will be willing to read and respond to one version if you show her the questions in the box at the very end of this workshop (page 251) and assure her they are designed to help her comment *quickly* and without having to become a "writing teacher." You'll probably want to give her the impersonal version, but don't automatically assume she wouldn't want to respond to the more personal version.

If you can't get comments from the teacher of the subject-matter course, perhaps you can find one or more students in that class who are willing to read your version(s) and give their reactions as readers with some knowledge of the field.

Collaborative Option

The ideal collaboration for this project would be with someone or some others who are in both of the classes you're writing for in this workshop. The impersonal essay could be a traditional expository essay, written collaboratively, with an emphasis on demonstrating an understanding of your subject as it connects to the world outside the classroom. But the personal essay could grow out of a written dialogue, which would allow each (or all) of you the opportunity to describe your experiences and express opinions. The final paper could even *be* this dialogue with collaboratively written concluding remarks.

But, of course, another student doesn't have to be in this other class to have personal reactions to its subject matter. You could work with a partner and each of you write up an impersonal essay which you share with one another. You can then invite your partner to engage in a dialogue about the implications of the information and concepts in your paper; you, in turn, would engage in a dialogue about the subject of his paper. These dialogues could then be collaboratively smoothed out and transformed into personal essays, or they could remain as dialogues.

Alternative Assignment

Rather than actually producing a personal or impersonal essay for this workshop, your teacher might ask you to write an analysis of the two kinds of writing you've produced for this workshop: personal and impersonal. If you ended up with a fair amount of private writing while you were freewriting, you might want to include an analysis of the differences between private and public writing also—and even some thoughts about how the personal/impersonal dichotomy differs from (or is the same as) the private/public dichotomy. The freewritings you've done, the drafts you produce, and the conversations you've had can serve as data for your analysis.

 READING ESSAYS

We selected the three essays at the end of this workshop because they represent a mix of styles and purposes. Another factor in our choice, which will become obvious as soon as you start reading them, is their subject matter.

Earlier we suggested that you read both versions of your essay aloud in order to see how the voice in each creates meaning and tone. You can do the same exercise with these published essays. Choose typical passages from each and do readings. Get more than one person's reading of a passage so that you can talk about the differences in voice you hear. But you'll want to talk about the similarities too so that you can discuss whether or not there are voices actually "in" the essays themselves. If you decide what voice an essay is written in, does that tell you any other things about the essay?

You can do some writing in response to these essays also. You may want to use the writing-while-reading strategies we set out in Workshops 10, 11, 14, and in the mini-workshops on dialectical notebooks and text rendering. You can, of course, use some combination of these.

After you've done some reading aloud and some writing on all three essays, do some focused freewriting in answer to the following questions:

■ Which would you describe as the most personal? the most impersonal? Point to specific features that lead you to these conclusions.

■ In which essay does the author seem to speak to you most directly? Which essay do you feel least like an audience for? Why?

■ Which essay seems to you most like literature? Why? Again, point to specific features.

■ From which essay did you learn the most? the least?

■ As you were reading, which essay made you feel most like you were inside the author's mind?

■ Which essay was the most interesting to you? the least? Why? How do your answers to these questions relate to the questions you've already answered?

After you've answered the above questions, pretend that each of the essays is the only true representative of the essay form and write three separate, brief definitions of the genre. Then write one definition which covers all three of the essays. Think about this definition: what's in it that surprises you? What's not there that you think is important? Or do you think your definition is adequate as a general definition of the genre?

SUGGESTIONS FOR SHARING AND RESPONDING

When you share your exploratory rough writing (with the exception of those parts you consider private), you'll find the techniques in Sections 2 and 3 of *Sharing and Responding* ("Summary and Sayback" and "Pointing and Center of Gravity") particularly productive. Additionally, here are some questions you'll find helpful:

■ "Point to specific spots where the way I think and the kind of person I am is most evident. Least evident."

■ "What would I need to do to this rough writing to make it more personal? more impersonal?"

When you share drafts of your essays, read aloud passages from both the personal and the impersonal versions. Get others to read them too. Talk about the voice in them. Think about the gestures that go with each reading. What makes a voice personal or impersonal? Is an impersonal voice the same as a distant, stuffy voice? Is a personal voice the same as a conversational one? Do you want to make any changes in voice?

Additionally, when sharing and responding to these drafts, you'll find these sections of *Sharing and Responding* most useful: "Criterion-Based Feedback," Section 11; and "Movies of the Reader's Mind," Section 7. But you may also want to consider the following questions:

■ "For each essay draft, are there spots where it drifts too far from its basic orientation: either personal or impersonal? Point to specific spots."

■ "Are the ideas and concepts clear? Point to spots where they are the most and the least clear."

Two drafts by everyone in the class create a mountain of writing to respond to; there probably won't be time enough to read and discuss all of it. Early freewriting can be discussed in pairs. For more finished drafts, you may need to bring in copies so that others can take your work home for commenting. Everyone in the group can read all the papers, but write comments on only one set of two drafts. Then when the group meets, each person's writing gets discussed, but the main comments are by the person(s) who wrote comments, and others chime in briefly based on their reading at home.

 PROCESS JOURNAL AND COVER LETTER QUESTIONS

If you need some help retrieving from memory your experiences and reactions while doing the writing for this workshop, you can use the following questions:

■ What did you learn from bringing your writing course to bear on another course? from writing about that subject for this class? from seeing that teacher for help and feedback?

■ In what ways did reading aloud help you sense the differences between a personal and impersonal voice?

■ What did you learn from sharing readings of the published essays with your classmates?

Remember that, for a cover letter, you can almost always use most of the questions we listed in Workshop 1 on page 17.

 ## RUMINATIONS AND THEORY

The Essay

Historically, the essay as an individual form was born in the sixteenth century. Its birth occurred during the Renaissance, a time we think of as an age of individualism and new discovery. Thus it is a true child of its times. The Frenchman Michel de Montaigne, who initiated the form, named it *essai,* a French word having its roots in the Latin words *exagium,* meaning a weighing or balancing, and *exigere,* meaning to examine. For Montaigne, the "essai" was "a try," or a kind of "go at" something. In writing about this new form he was developing, Montaigne says that its purposes are deeply personal.

> I desire therein to be delineated in mine own genuine, simple and ordinary fashion, without contention, art or study; for it is myself I portray. . . . Myself am the groundwork of my book.

Francis Bacon was the first English writer of essays. His essays are quite different from Montaigne's; the first ones, in fact, are more like notes. It is probably Abraham Cowley who should be considered the father of the English essay, but it wasn't until the eighteenth century that the essay became a dominant form in English literature. We won't go on with this history, here, but we do hope you noticed that in our last sentence we spoke of the essay as "literature."

We invite you to read the essay in the "Readings" section entitled "What I Think, What I Am" by Edward Hoagland. In it he notes that "essays . . . hang somewhere on a line between two sturdy poles: this is what I think, and this is what I am." The conclusion of his essay merits repetition.

> A personal essay frequently is not autobiographical at all, but what it does keep in common with autobiography is that, through its tone and tumbling progression, it conveys the quality of the author's mind. Nothing gets in the way. Because essays are directly concerned with the mind and its idiosyncrasy, the very freedom the mind possesses is bestowed on this branch of literature that does honor to it, and the fascination of the mind is the fascination of the essay.

What's so fascinating about the personal essay is that we can find it engaging even when the subject doesn't interest us at all. What engages us is the workings of a human mind. When an essayist gives us that, the subject takes a backseat: it is merely the way of getting into another's mind.

You'll notice that the above quotation begins with the words "a personal essay." But there is also something known as the "impersonal essay," an essay which is focused more on *what* is said than on the qualities of the writer's mind. Yet even that is only a relative alteration of the form. Perhaps it's best to think of essays along a continuum from personal to impersonal: each essay blends these two in its own way.

As you have already realized by reading this far, the personal essay is not usually a school-assigned form. Most teachers are mainly interested in what you know and tend to judge your writing on that basis. There are, of course, classes in which teachers want you to assess the information you present and come to conclusions of your own; but this usually means they're interested in seeing how intelligently you can think about your material.

Changes are appearing, however—particularly at schools and in programs where multicultural and feminist theory is urging teachers not to reject the personal out of hand. It is mainly western culture which values the detached intellectual stance and prefers that the personal not muddle up the impersonal. Other cultures don't always make such a division. Feminist theorists take a slightly different tack: they stress the impossibility of separating the personal and the impersonal and the relevance of the context (including the stance of an author) for full understanding of any written text. Teachers guided by these theories might require you to include the personal in papers written for them.

Nonetheless, we still think that the primary interest of most teachers is the substance of your writing, not your mind as it engages the task of thinking about the material. Consequently, you may well write impersonal essays to fulfill school assignments, but you'll not often write a personal essay to do so. The one place where you're likely to write personal essays (other than in a course like this one) is in an advanced composition course. Such courses are often rightly grouped with courses in writing fiction and poetry—because the essay is a literary genre.

Another way we can talk about the essay is in terms we use in Workshop 16, where we briefly present James Britton's taxonomy of types of writing: expressive, transactional, and poetic. The personal essay lies in the expressive camp, moving perhaps toward the poetic; the impersonal essay lies within the transactional field with some nods toward the expressive.

The impersonal essay moves toward the "article" or "paper." We often speak of newspaper "articles" or "professional articles": articles which usually appear in the periodicals of a particular discipline and manifest the language features of that discipline. But professionals also write articles directed toward a general public; such articles or "essays" are often more personal than purely professional articles.

In an essay in *The New York Times Book Review*, Elizabeth Hardwick writes:

> William Gass, in what must be called an essay, a brilliant one, about Emerson, an essayist destined from the cradle, makes a distinction between the article and the essay. Having been employed by the university and having heard so many of his colleagues "doing an article on," Mr. Gass has come to think of the article as "that awful object" because it is under the command of defensiveness in footnote, reference, coverage, and would also pretend that all must be useful and certain, even if it is "very likely a veritable Michelin of misdirections." If the article has a certain

sheen and professional polish, it is the polish of "the scrubbed step"—practical economy and neatness. The essay, in Mr. Gass's view, is a great meadow of style and personal manner, freed from the need for defense except that provided by an individual intelligence and sparkle. We consent to watch a mind at work, without agreement often, but only for pleasure. Knowledge hereby attained, great indeed, is again wanted for the pleasure of itself. (44)

And one more quote. In a review of a collection of essays by Italo Calvino, the reviewer, Christopher Lehmann-Haupt concludes:

These essays are instructive and often arresting, but it is the responsive play of Mr. Calvino's mind that seduces us. We are invited into a circle that includes the work, its creators and Mr. Calvino as observer.

Readings

UNTITLED 1

Eleanor Klinko

I had an inkling of what was going on but when the words were stated to my face it was like an earthquake shattering my world into tiny pieces. My very close friend, the one with whom I have shared so many wonderful times, just told me she was gay.

It was a balmy Wednesday afternoon and my friend and I were driving down my street headed for an exotic boutique. Sitting next to me she seemed jumpy, her hands moving as she talked. I only remember jumbles of what she said about girls and feelings. These words led up to one word that I do remember. I only heard it after I daringly asked, "Are you gay?" I choked on my words.

She replied, "Yes." We were looking at each other face to face. My mind was not controlling my foot on the brake. Realizing this I quickly pressed the pedal to the floor, jerking the car to a stop before hitting the car in front of mine.

I was stunned. The words were a slap across my face. My cheek stung as my mind was bombarded with flashbacks of our days spent together. We would play the guitar, play basketball, go to concerts, listen to music, study history, shuffle through leaves, and shoot coconuts at each other in the snow. These are the activities of two energetic high school girls.

She talked about a young English teacher she liked in school. She had seen her at a gay bar and they danced together. This conversation was awkward, probably because I never had one like it before and never expected to. Weren't two girls supposed to be talking about guys? But I didn't go against her; I actually tried to help her figure a strategy to be with this woman. I don't know why I didn't start yelling and bombard her with questions. I was stunned, a little scared, confused, and really didn't want to accept what she was saying.

There she sat, my friend, in the passenger seat of my car. Her soft pale skin and long thin blonde hair did not coincide with her tall muscular body. She really didn't have any feminine features except for her fair complexion and soft hair. She dressed in faded jeans and ripped concert T-shirts. Studded black leather dressed her waist and wrists. Maybe I should have known from her appearance but I didn't. She had masculine features. She used a trucker's wallet which attached to her pants by a chain, sewed a Harley Davidson patch on her leather jacket, wore black leather motorcycle boots, and had four tattoos on her body. She smoked cigarettes and drank beer like a guy. She did not hold and puff on a cigarette the way a woman does.

What do I do now? I loved her and would do almost anything for her, but how could I feel this way now? She might think that I wanted to be more than a friend. But I didn't want to lose her friendship because I didn't want to lose the good times we shared.

I couldn't tell anyone about my situation. I was embarrassed to talk to my father about the subject. He would not tell me to stop my friendship with her because he allows me to choose my own friends. But he would prefer I spent less time with her so my feelings wouldn't be influenced by hers. I didn't tell any other people, partly because it wouldn't be fair to my friend and partly because I feared the rumors that might start about her and me being more than just friends. People in high school love to start rumors especially if they're not true. People who knew that she and I were close friends might assume that I was like her. And if guys thought I was gay then I would never get asked for a date by a male.

I was in a state of confusion. I wanted to continue with our regular friendship but it felt as if a cloud hung over us. I needed time to think about the situation. Although I liked her for what she was and for being open with me, I didn't like her any more than a friend, and I knew I could never have a relationship with a girl. I told her all this. She accepted. I didn't hold anything against her because I had no right to. She didn't hurt me; she just made me think about a reality of life.

UNTITLED 2

Eleanor Klinko

Three years ago my best friend told me she was gay. We had been friends for over ten years and I had never even suspected it. Perhaps I should have because her soft pale skin and long thin blonde hair did not coincide with her tall muscular body. She really didn't have any feminine features except for her fair complexion and soft hair. She dressed in faded jeans and ripped concert T-shirts. Studded black leather dressed her waist and wrists. Maybe I should have known from her appearance but I didn't. She had masculine features. She used a trucker's wallet which attached to her pants by a chain, sewed a Harley Davidson patch on her leather jacket, wore black leather motorcycle boots, and had four tattoos on her body. She smoked cigarettes and drank beer like a guy. She did not hold and puff on a cigarette the way a woman does.

Certainly others have faced this situation, but I didn't know personally anyone who had. I can remember seeing a segment of "Love Boat," where one of the crew member's friends had had a sex change. Part of the story was how the crew member adjusted to that. I also remember that on one of the soap operas there was a family who had to deal with the discovery that the son was gay. I had known about homosexuals for years; in fact, I remember when I thought I could recognize gay men as I walked around the streets of the

Village. But later I realized from some reading I did that gays are not identifiable according to some stereotypical image. Gay men can be short or tall, fat or thin, muscular or not. They can be construction workers, truckers, or ballet dancers. They can prefer baseball to cooking. I now know one cannot tell if a man is gay by looking at him. But I didn't know that at the time my friend confided in me.

I knew far less about gay women. My experience suggests that gay women are less likely to "come out of the closet" than gay men. Many of my male friends are sure that they know what a gay woman looks like—and their descriptions are not very flattering. And even though my friend, I now realize, has masculine traits, I suspect that gay women can look as feminine in the traditional sense as straight women. And, also, I know many women who wear just as much leather as my friend does and are *not* gay.

I now realize that when my friend told me about herself, I had three choices. I could accept her and continue our friendship. I could reject her, which I suspect is what my father would have wanted me to do had he known. Or I could simply act as though I didn't know and continue our friendship just as it was. I knew the latter was not really possible since I suspected the lack of honesty between us would kill our relationship. I couldn't reject her because she had been and still was my friend. So I accepted her and was able to tell her how I felt. She, in turn, was able to accept that.

One thing I have learned from this experience is that gay people are more like the rest of us than unlike us. My girlfriend loves her parents, curses her car when it won't start, values honest relationships, wants to do well in school, get a good job, and make a fair amount of money. The biggest difference between us, I guess, is that I want to get married and have a family. Even so, my friend and I still have enough in common to spend hours talking.

THE ESSAY*

Edmund Gosse

ESSAY, ESSAYIST (Fr. *essai,* Late Lat. *exagium,* a weighing or balance; *exigere,* to examine; the term in general meaning any trial or effort). As a form of literature, the essay is a composition of moderate length, usually in prose, which deals in an easy, cursory way with the external conditions of a subject, and, in strictness, with that subject only as it affects the writer. Dr. Johnson, himself an eminent essayist, defines an essay as "an irregular, undigested piece"; the irregularity may perhaps be admitted, but want of thought, that is to say lack of proper mental digestion, is certainly not

---

From an entry in the famous eleventh edition of the Encyclopaedia Britannica, 1910.

characteristic of a fine example. It should, on the contrary, always be the brief and light result of experience and profound meditation, while "undigested" is the last epithet to be applied to the essays of Montaigne, Addison or Lamb. Bacon said that the Epistles of Seneca were "essays," but this can hardly be allowed. Bacon himself goes on to admit that "the word is late, though the thing is ancient." The word, in fact, was invented for this species of writing by Montaigne, who merely meant that these were experiments in a new kind of literature. This original meaning, namely that these pieces were attempts or endeavours, feeling their way towards the expression of what would need a far wider space to exhaust, was lost in England in the course of the eighteenth century. This is seen by the various attempts made in the nineteenth century to coin a word which should express a still smaller work, as distinctive in comparison with the essay as the essay is by the side of the monograph: none of these linguistic experiments, such as *essayette, essaykin* (Thackeray) and *essaylet* (Helps) have taken hold of the language. As a matter of fact, the journalistic word *article* covers the lesser form of essay, although not exhaustively, since the essays in the monthly and quarterly reviews, which are fully as extended as an essay should ever be, are frequently termed "articles," while many "articles" in newspapers, dictionaries and encyclopaedias are in no sense essays. It may be said that the idea of a detached work is combined with the word "essay," which should be neither a section of a disquisition nor a chapter in a book which aims at the systematic development of a story. Locke's *Essay on the Human Understanding* is not an essay at all, or cluster of essays, in this technical sense, but refers to the experimental and tentative nature of the inquiry which the philosopher was undertaking. Of the curious use of the word so repeatedly made by Pope mention will be made below.

The essay, as a species of literature, was invented by Montaigne, who had probably little suspicion of the far-reaching importance of what he had created. In his dejected moments, he turned to rail at what he had written, and to call his essays "inepties" and "sottises." But in his own heart he must have been well satisfied with the new and beautiful form which he had added to literary tradition. He was perfectly aware that he had devised a new thing; that he had invented a way of communicating himself to the world as a type of human nature. He designed it to carry out his peculiar object, which was to produce an accurate portrait of his own soul, not as it was yesterday or will be to-morrow, but as it is to-day. It is not often that we can date with any approach to accuracy the arrival of a new class of literature into the world, but it was in the month of March 1571 that the essay was invented. It was started in the second story of the old tower of the castle of Montaigne, in a study to which the philosopher withdrew for that purpose, surrounded by his books, close to his chapel, sheltered from the excesses of a fatiguing world. He wrote slowly, not systematically; it took nine years to finish the two first books of the essays. In 1574 the manuscript of the work, so far as it was then completed, was nearly lost, for it was confiscated by the pontifical police in Rome, where Montaigne was residing, and was not returned to the author for four months. The earliest imprint saw the light in 1580, at Bordeaux, and the

Paris edition of 1588, which is the fifth, contains the final text of the great author. These dates are not negligible in the briefest history of the essay, for they are those of its revelation to the world of readers. It was in the delightful chapters of his new, strange book that Montaigne introduced the fashion of writing briefly, irregularly, with constant digressions and interruptions, about the world as it appears to the individual who writes. The *Essais* were instantly welcomed, and few writers of the Renaissance had so instant and so vast a popularity as Montaigne. But while the philosophy, and above all the graceful stoicism, of the great master were admired and copied in France, the exact shape in which he had put down his thoughts, in the exquisite negligence of a series of essays, was too delicate to tempt an imitator. It is to be noted that neither Charron, nor Mlle de Gournay, his most immediate disciples, tried to write essays. But Montaigne, who liked to fancy that the Eyquem family was of English extraction, had spoken affably of the English people as his "cousins," and it has always been admitted that his genius has an affinity with the English. He was early read in England, and certainly by Bacon, whose is the second great name connected with this form of literature. It was in 1597, only five years after the death of Montaigne, that Bacon published in a small octavo the first ten of his essays. These he increased to 38 in 1612 and to 68 in 1625. In their first form, the essays of Bacon had nothing of the fulness or grace of Montaigne's; they are meagre notes; scarcely more than the headings for discourses. It is possible that when he wrote them he was not yet familiar with the style of his predecessor, which was first made popular in England, in 1603, when Florio published that translation of the *Essais* which Shakespeare unquestionably read. In the later editions Bacon greatly expanded his theme, but he never reached, or but seldom, the freedom and ease, the seeming formlessness held in by an invisible chain, which are the glory of Montaigne, and distinguish the typical essayist. It would seem that at first, in England, as in France, no lesser writer was willing to adopt a title which belonged to so great a presence as that of Bacon or Montaigne. . . . [Gosse continues by speaking of a variety of English essays, including those of Lamb and Macaulay.] Nothing can be more remarkable than the difference . . . between Lamb and Macaulay, the former for ever demanding, even cajoling, the sympathy of the reader, the latter scanning the horizon for an enemy to controvert. In later times the essay in England has been cultivated in each of these ways, by a thousand journalists and authors. The "leaders" of a daily newspaper are examples of the popularization of the essay, and they point to the danger which now attacks it, that of producing a purely ephemeral or even momentary species of effect. The essay, in its best days, was intended to be as lasting as a poem or a historical monograph; it aimed at being one of the most durable and precious departments of literature. . . .

ON ESSAYING

James Moffett

College composition instructors and anthologists of essays have doted for
years on George Orwell's "Shooting an Elephant," which they hold up to
students as a model of essay or "expository writing." Please look closely at it
even if you think you know it well; if a student wrote it, it would be called
"personal writing," that is, soft and nonintellectual. Orwell narrated in first
person how as a British civil servant in Burma he was intimidated by villagers
into shooting an elephant against his will. But so effectively does he say what
happens by telling what happened that the force of his theme—the
individual's moral choice whether or not to conform to the group—leaves us
with the impression that the memoir is "expository,"—that is chiefly cast in
the present tense of generalization and in third person. What we really want
to help youngsters learn is how to express ideas of universal value in a
personal voice. Fables, parables, poems and songs, fiction and memoir may
convey ideas as well as or better than editorials and critiques. Orwell does
indeed provide a fine model, but teachers should not let prejudice fool them
into misunderstanding the actual kind of discourse in which he wrote
"Shooting an Elephant" and other excellent essays, for this leads to a
confusing double standard whereby we ask students to emulate a great writer
but to do it in another form.

The Essay: An Attempt

Orwell wrote deep in a tradition of English letters, honoring the essay as a
candid blend of personal and universal. It was resurrected if not invented
during the Renaissance by Montaigne, who coined the term *essai* from
essayer, to attempt. From his position of philosophical skepticism ("What do
I know?") he saw his writing as personal attempts to discover truth, what he
thought and what could be thought, in exactly the same sense that Donald
Murray or Janet Emig or I myself might speak of writing as discovery. From
Burton's *Anatomy of Melancholy* and Browne's *Urn Burial;* Addison's and
Steele's *Spectator* articles; through the essays of Swift, Lamb, Hazlitt, and
DeQuincey to those of Orwell, Virginia Woolf, Joan Didion, and Norman
Mailer, English literature has maintained a marvelous tradition, fusing
personal experience, private vision, and downright eccentricity, with
intellectual vigor and verbal objectification. In color, depth, and stylistic
originality it rivals some of our best poetry. Look back over Hazlitt's "The
Fight" and compare it with Mailer's intellectual reportage of the Ali-Frazier
fight in *King of the Hill* or "On the Feeling of Immortality in Youth" or "On
Familiar Style"; DeQuincey's "Confessions of an Opium Eater" or "On the
Knocking at the Gate in *Macbeth*," which begins: "From my boyish days I had
always felt a great perplexity on one point in *Macbeth*"; or Lamb's "The Two
Races of Men," "Poor Relations," or "On Sanity of True Genius." Consider too

a book like Henry Adams's *Education of Henry Adams* for its simultaneous treatment of personal and national or historical.

Some essayists, like Montaigne and Emerson, tend toward generality, as reflected in titles like "Friendship" or "Self-Reliance," but tone and source are personal, and we cannot doubt the clear kinship between essays featuring memoir or eyewitness reportage and those of generality, for the same writers do both, sometimes in a single essay, sometimes in separate pieces; and Lamb and Thoreau stand in the same relation to Montaigne and Emerson as fable to moral or parable to proverb. The difference lies not in the fundamental approach, which is in any case personal, but in the degree of explicitness of the theme. "I bear within me the exemplar of the human condition," said Montaigne. Descending deep enough within, the essayist links up personal with universal, self with self.

Transpersonal, Not Impersonal

Schools mistreat writing because the society suffers at the moment from drastic misunderstandings about the nature of knowledge. Applying "scientific" criteria that would be unacceptable to most real scientists making the breakthroughs out there on the frontier, many people have come to think that subtracting the self makes for objectivity and validity. But depersonalization is not impartiality. It is, quite literally, madness. Einstein said, "The observer is the essence of the situation." It is not by abandoning the self but by developing it that we achieve impartiality and validity. The deeper we go consciously into ourselves, the better chance we have of reaching universality, as Montaigne knew so well. Transpersonal, not impersonal. It is an undeterred faith in this that makes a great writer cultivate his individuality until others feel he speaks for them better than they do themselves. Teachers should be the first to understand this misunderstanding and to start undoing it, so that schooling in general and writing in particular can offset rather than reinforce the problem.

Here are two examples of what we're up against—one from a famous current encyclopedia and one from a leading publisher, typical and telling symptoms. Most English majors probably sampled or at least heard of Sir Thomas Browne, a very individualistic seventeenth-century master of an original prose style, a writer's writer much admired by successors. Of his *Pseudodoxia Epidemica* Funk and Wagnalls *Standard Reference Encyclopedia* says, "Its unscientific approach and odd assemblage of obscure facts typify his haphazard erudition," and then concludes the entry: "Despite Browne's deficiencies as a thinker his style entitles him to high rank among the masters of English prose." What this verdict tells me is that the writer of that entry felt overwhelmed by all the books Browne had read that he had not and that he knew far less than he should have known about the enormously important and complex networks of thought and knowledge, called esoteric, that after several millenia of evolution still had great influence on Newton, Bacon, and Descartes (who displayed at times equally "irrational" intellectual behavior). The encyclopedist's judgment on such a writer as Browne is nothing but smart-ass chauvinism: permitted to poison basic information sources, it makes "science" as deadly a censor as ever the Church was during its Inquisition.

We can avoid producing Brownes in our school system by having all youngsters read and write the same things—a goal we have closely approximated—and then their approach will not be unscientific, their assemblage odd, their facts obscure, nor their erudition haphazard. And we will have ensured that no one will be able to emulate the great essayists we hold up as models (or even read them with any comprehension). Real essaying cannot thrive without cultivation of the individual. Who would have any reason to read anyone else? (And I want to know how Browne's style could be worth so much if he were merely raving.)

The second example is personal. When I received the edited manuscript of the original edition of *Student-Centered Language Arts and Reading, K-13* back from the publisher, I was aghast. "My" editor had rewritten sentences throughout the whole book to eliminate first-person references and other elements of the author's presence and voice. This included altering diction and sentence structure at times to get a more anonymous or distanced effect. Faced with the appalling labor of restoring all those sentences, I called the editor, furious. She said righteously, "But we always do that—it's policy." It never occurred to her to exempt, or even to warn, an author who wouldn't be publishing the book in the first place if he weren't regarded as some kind of expert in writing.

Remove the Double Standard

You can't trust your encyclopedia, your publisher, your school administration. And you can't trust yourself until you learn to spot how you too may be spreading the plague, as Camus calls it. The double standard in "Look at the greats, but don't do what they did" naturally goes along with our era of Scientific Inquisition, which is really technocratic plague. Teachers stand in a fine position to spread infection. If you let yourself be convinced that "personal" or "creative" writing is merely narcissistic, self-indulgent, and weak-minded, then you have just removed your own first person.

ESSAY: WHAT I THINK, WHAT I AM

Edward Hoagland

Our loneliness makes us avid column readers these days. The personalities in The New York Post, Chicago Daily News, San Francisco Chronicle constitute our neighbors now, some of them local characters but also the opinionated national stars. And movie reviewers thrive on our need for somebody emotional who is willing to pay attention to us and return week after week, year after year, through all the to-and-fro of other friends to flatter us by pouring out his (her) heart. They are essayists, as Elizabeth Hardwick is,

James Baldwin was. We sometimes hear that essays are an old-fashioned form, that so-and-so is the "last essayist," but the facts of the marketplace argue quite otherwise. Essays of almost any kind are so much easier for a writer to sell now than short stories, so many more see print, it's odd that though two fine anthologies remain which publish the year's best stories, no comparable collection exists for essays.* Such changes in the reading public's taste aren't always to the good, needless to say. The art of telling stories predated even cave-painting, surely; and if we ever find ourselves living in caves again, it (with painting) will be the only art left, after movies, novels, essays, photography, biography and all the rest have gone down the drain—the art to build from.

One has the sense with the short story form that while everything may have been done, nothing has been overdone: it has a permanence. Essays, if a comparison is to be made, although they go back 400 years to Montaigne, seem a newfangled, mercurial, sometimes hokey sort of affair which has lent itself to many of the excesses of the age from spurious autobiography to spurious hallucination, as well as the shabby careerism of traditional journalism. It's a greased pig. Essays are associated with the way young writers fashion a name—on plain crowded newsprint in hybrid vehicles like The Village Voice, Rolling Stone, The Soho Weekly News (also Fiction magazine), instead of the thick paper stock and thin readership of Partisan Review.

Essays, however, hang somewhere on a line between two sturdy poles: this is what I think, and this is what I am. Autobiographies which aren't novels are generally extended essays, indeed. A personal essay is like the human voice talking, its order the mind's natural flow, instead of a systematized outline of ideas. Though more wayward or informal than an article or treatise, somewhere it contains a point which is its real center, even if the point couldn't be expressed in fewer words than the essayist has employed. Essays don't usually "boil down" to a summary, as articles do, but on the other hand they have fewer "levels" than first-rate fiction—a flatter surface—because we aren't supposed to argue about their meaning. In the old distinction between teaching versus story-telling—however cleverly the author muddles it up—an essay is intended to convey the same point to each of us.

This emphasis upon mind speaking to mind is what makes essays less universal in their appeal than stories. They are addressed to an educated, perhaps a middle-class, reader, with certain presuppositions shared, a frame of reference, even a commitment to civility—not the grand and golden empathy inherent in every man which the story-teller has a chance to tap. At the same time, of course, the artful "I" of an essay can be as chameleon as any narrator in fiction: and essays do tell a story just as often as a short story stakes a claim to a particular viewpoint.

Mark Twain's piece called "Corn-pone Opinions," for example, which is about public opinion, begins with a vignette as vivid as any in "Huckleberry

---

This is no longer true. See the yearly publication, Best American Essays, published by Ticknor and Fields.

Finn." When he was a boy of 15, Twain says, he used to hang out a back window and listen to the sermons preached by a neighbor's slave standing on top of a woodpile. The fellow "imitated the pulpit style of the several clergymen of the village, and did it well and with fine passion and energy. To me he was a wonder. I believed he was the greatest orator in the United States and would some day be heard from. But it did not happen; in the distribution of rewards he was overlooked. . . . He interrupted his preaching now and then to saw a stick of wood, but the sawing was a pretense—he did it with his mouth, exactly imitating the sound the bucksaw makes in shrieking its way through the wood. But it served its purpose, it kept his master from coming out to see how the work was getting along."

The extraordinary flexibility of essays is what has enabled them to ride out rough weather and hybridize into forms to suit the times. And just as one of the first things a fiction writer learns is that he needn't actually be writing fiction to write a short story—he can tell his own history or anyone else's as exactly as he remembers it and it will still be "fiction" if it remains primarily a story—an essayist soon discovers that he doesn't have to tell the whole truth and nothing but the truth, he can shape or shave his memories as long as the purpose is served of elucidating a truthful point. A personal essay frequently is not autobiographical at all, but what it does keep in common with autobiography is that, through its tone and tumbling progression, it conveys the quality of the author's mind. Nothing gets in the way. Because essays are directly concerned with the mind and its idiosyncrasy, the very freedom the mind possesses is bestowed on this branch of literature that does honor to it, and the fascination of the mind is the fascination of the essay.

QUESTIONS TO HELP SUBJECT-MATTER TEACHERS GIVE FEEDBACK MORE QUICKLY AND EASILY

You can give me very helpful feedback if you would please just *note* certain passages in my paper:

- Please use a checkmark to indicate phrases or passages where I've got the idea or concept right, and a cross where I seem to be misunderstanding the idea or concept or getting it wrong.
- Please use a straight line below phrases and passages that are clear and effective for you, and a wavy line below phrases and passages that are unclear.
- Please circle words or passages where the language, style, discourse, or approach seems inappropriate for you as a teacher and reader in this field.

If you have time: Are there any other comments you would like to make to me—either orally or in writing?

The assignment from my writing course is: (1) to explain how a concept or issue in one of my other courses relates to my own life and experience outside that course; (2) to experiment with the difference between making that explanation in personal terms and making it in impersonal terms.

WORKSHOP

10

LISTENING, READING, AND WRITING IN THE DISCIPLINES

Our aim in this workshop is to get you to do some thinking about the differences between writing for a general audience and writing within a specific discipline. We also hope you'll begin to understand the importance of learning to write within your chosen discipline and the ways writing differs from one discipline to another.

But this workshop is a bit different from most of the others in our book because we have an important goal apart from completion of the main assignment itself: we want to get you to practice some writing techniques which will help you become a better learner. That is, we want to show you how you can use informal writing to *learn* subject matter, not just to demonstrate that you know it. (In the "Readings" for Workshop 13, there's an excerpt from William Zinsser's *Writing to Learn* which presents the results of some of his research on using writing to learn mathematics.)

Your main assignment will be to draft two pieces with the same subject: something you are studying in another class. One piece will be written for members of your writing class; the other for members of the other class (including the teacher). For each finished piece, you will be expected to prepare a cover letter explaining why you consider the piece appropriate for the class for which it was written.

In Workshop 9 we asked you to write about connections between your school work and nonschool life for two different audiences. Our aim there was for you to begin to understand that it's possible to take both a personal and an impersonal stance toward connections between school and your experience outside of school. We also encouraged you to do some audience analysis, especially as a guide to revision.

This workshop is similar to Workshop 9 in that we're asking you again to draft papers for two different audiences: one which is studying the subject you are writing about and one which isn't. But here we emphasize the subject itself. Your main purpose is not to connect the subject with your experiences out of school but to pick out a difficult or interesting concept and explain it to a general and a professional audience.

In the "Readings" at the end of this workshop, there are several pieces on the same subject written within varying disciplines. And on page 259 there are suggestions to help you analyze these readings and to help you revise your assignment for this workshop. Your teacher may ask you to do this reading and analysis before you begin any work on the assignment itself.

 GETTING STARTED

Probably the chief task in most of your college classes is to sift through a great deal of material and single out what's most important from what's less important. There's no way any of us can remember *everything* we hear and read; we're always involved in selecting. This assignment foregrounds that whole process.

From the outset of this course, we've been asking you to listen to your classmates and others who hear or read your papers. The more carefully you listen, the more resources you'll have for revision. And the more carefully you listen to others read their pieces, the more likely it will be that you'll give them good advice for revision—if that's what they're seeking.

But we've also stressed reading aloud to others from whom you ask *no* response because we think that having an audience physically present and listening somehow enables you to view your paper differently. Having a listener can be powerful: we're sure you've said or heard others say something like: "I like to talk to her because she's a good listener."

You've done a lot of listening to teachers in the past twelve years of your life. Taking notes in class seems to come naturally to some students, while others struggle. Your writing teacher may decide to give you practice in taking notes by giving a short lecture on some subject relevant to the class and then asking you to write out your notes as fully as you can and discuss the whole process. This will give you a chance to see how others take notes and how all of you can give one another tips. Here's some of what you might discover:

- It isn't wise to try to write down "word for word" what your teacher says. You usually end up losing track of the main thrust of the lecture.
- It's usually better to put things down in your own words if you can, since your teacher's words may not mean much to you when you reread your notes.
- If you've been given a reading assignment in preparation for a teacher's lecture, it's useful to read the assignment both before and after the lecture. You'll be surprised to discover that the "after" reading often produces different understandings than the "before" reading. But doing the "before" reading almost always makes the lecture more comprehensible and the note-taking easier.
- It helps as you're taking notes to put question marks next to facts and concepts you don't "get." This will allow you to keep going and yet know where you had troubles. This will help you focus your second reading and will also pinpoint what to ask questions about. And if the teacher doesn't

---

PROCESS BOX

For a term paper in another class I experimented with different ways of writing. I became very excited when after a long afternoon of writing and looking for my paper in the massive outpouring of words, I found myself instead. I found myself at the bottom of a mountain. I felt the mountain, I saw it, I knew that I was there. The exhilaration of this discovery faded when I realized I'd have to ascend up "Revising Notch" if I wanted to reach the summit.

Frank Massey

allow for questions, you can write up some questions based on these pinpointed spots and ask them during the professor's office hours.

■ Perhaps the most important thing a good note taker does is sit down and flesh out or rewrite notes as soon as possible after class. You'll recall that we gave you this same advice for the interview workshop. The general ideas are still in your head to help you put together what might lose meaning in the following hours. Being forced to write out ideas has a way of making them stick.

You may want to add to this list what you've learned about yourself as a note taker and talk about that with your classmates too.

In the Other Class

Choose a class for this assignment; we suggest you choose the class you're having the most difficulties with because what we're asking for will help you learn the material better. But perhaps you'd rather choose a class you really enjoy and want to get even more out of. It needs to be a class in which the teacher lectures quite a bit or our assignment won't work out.

Take notes in the class as you usually do. Rewrite those notes as soon as you can after the class is over. Read your notes aloud to your partner or group members and ask them to tell you what they "hear" as the main ideas of the class.

We know students (especially students whose first language is not English) who tape classroom lectures and then study from the tapes. If you do this, here are a couple of suggestions:

■ Keep your notebook and pencil handy while listening to the original lecture. Not having to catch everything frees you to pick out and jot down what comes through as particularly important.

■ *Take your notes from the lecture tape:* you can listen to it as many times as possible. But writing up the notes will help you learn and remember the material as well as prepare you to write short-answer exam responses and papers. Remember what we said earlier: you can't remember everything; the effort to take notes will force you to separate what is most important from what is least important.

Next, take notes on the chapter or unit in the textbook (or other reading material) which the teacher assigned as preparatory or follow-up reading for the lecture you took notes on. (See Mini-Workshop B for a good technique for note-taking, the "double-entry" process.)

Collaborative Option

This is a good assignment for working collaboratively. The ideal collaboration, of course, would be to find one or two students from this writing class who are also in the other class. Then both or all of you can take notes and compare them. You can each read your notes to the same audience and ask that audience to tell you what they "hear" as the same in your notes and what they "hear" as different.

(One nice side effect of this collaborative work is that you'll discover the benefits of working in small study groups with others in your classes. Research has demonstrated that students who participate in informal study groups usually do better in school.)

There are a number of ways you could take the assignment from this point, including writing collaborative drafts and final papers. Or you might want to produce either collaboratively or individually a comparison of how two (or possibly even three) of you take notes and read textbooks.

 ## MOVING TO DRAFTS

During the course of this workshop, you've collected a wealth of data to use in completing your assignment. You should have the following:

- Rough and written-up notes taken during a lecture and during your reading
- Responses to these notes from classmates

Before you actually start writing your drafts, you may need to do some exploratory freewriting to settle on your topic. In contrast to your task for Workshop 9, your main purpose here is not to connect what you're learning to your own life; your purpose is to pick out a difficult or interesting concept from your freewriting and dialectical notebook and explain it to two different audiences. Once you've picked it out, it may help to discuss it directly with these two audiences—and perhaps later to write directly *to* them. The goal is to heighten your sense of contact or relationship with these two audiences so that your thinking and language will relate well to each of them.

The audience for one of your drafts will be the teacher and classmates of your writing class. You can think of them as equivalent to a general or lay audience. The audience for the other draft will be the teacher of the other class. This is a more specialized audience. We suggest that you talk to this other teacher during her office hours, tell her what you're doing, and ask her if she would be willing to read a draft of the paper which you consider appropriate

---

PROCESS BOX

I was surprised that Professor _____ said he'd read my paper on the problems of Marxism because there are so many students in that class. Guess it's good they aren't all doing a 101 paper on economics! He seemed to think he had to point out grammar errors even though I'd told him he didn't have to. But I'm not sure some of those were really grammar mistakes. Oh well. I fixed them up anyway. He seemed to be kind of a rough grader so I'm glad in a way that I wasn't writing it for him.

Now I have to revise and I don't know which paper I want to revise. Somehow it did feel different writing the two papers because I worried more about *what* I was saying in the paper for Professor _____. But I think when all is said and done I care more about the paper for this class—so guess I'll revise that one—maybe get more of the "facts" in there.

Jonah Swartz

for her class. If she agrees (and even if she seems reluctant), show her the form we included at the very end of the previous workshop (page 251) as a possible guide to her response.

Your teacher may ask you to polish both drafts or only one. Another option is for you to polish neither of these drafts but instead write an essay which analyzes the differences between the two drafts. The questions you use to analyze the readings at the end of this workshop will be helpful here. These appear further on in this workshop on pages 259 and 260. If this alternative were pursued collaboratively, you and your partner(s) could analyze more than one set of drafts.

Preparing Your Cover Letter

Your teacher may have asked you to add cover letters to every assignment you hand in to her. If not, you may want to look back at our discussion about these in Workshop 1. We're putting a bit more emphasis on cover letters in this workshop, but we think they're important for all assignments. Your particular purpose for this cover letter will be to reflect on how the two different audiences influenced

1. Your stance toward your subject and the organization, method of reasoning, vocabulary, and style of the paper
2. The thinking, drafting, writing, and revision of the final paper(s)

Obviously you can't cover all this in the 200 words or so that fit on one cover page. If you find you have too much to say, select what seems the most interesting to you and save the rest for your process journal.

 EXAMINING DIFFERENCES

A good way to begin to understand differences between the discourses of various disciplines (as well as differences between language directed at specialists and nonspecialists within a discipline) is to look at several pieces of writing on the same subject. Included in "Readings" at the end of this workshop are four pieces about women and gender differences. The first one, an excerpt from "Father-Daughter Incest," is by two psychotherapists, Judith Herman and Lisa Hirschman; the second one, an excerpt from "Reducing Women: Feminism and Reductionism," is by a biologist, Lynda Burke; the third one, an excerpt from "American Experience," is by an historian, Vern L. Bullough; and the fourth one, "A New World beyond Snow White," is a newspaper article written by two literary theorists, Sandra M. Gilbert and Susan Gubar. The "Readings" end with a student essay, "What Keeps an Airplane Up"—in two versions. Gary Kolnicki wrote one version for general readers and the other for readers in physics.

As you read through the four professional articles, record your reactions in your process journal. Don't edit these reactions; put down whatever comes into your head as you read, just as you do when you give a "Movies of the Reader's Mind" response to a classmate's paper (see *Sharing and Responding,* Section 7). Another way to analyze each piece is to put down in semi-outline form what each paragraph or small section *says* and *does,* a strategy we describe in Section 10 of *Sharing and Responding.* Some of you may prefer to use the double-entry notebook approach described in Mini-Workshop B.

Using the thinking and writing generated by these ways of responding, do some freewriting about all four pieces. Your teacher may suggest that you do this work collaboratively in groups of four; all of you would read all the pieces, but each of you would freewrite about only one. Then you can pool your observations and discuss the differences you've observed. Focus your freewriting on the following topics:

- *Comprehension.* What is particularly puzzling for you: the language and vocabulary, your lack of background knowledge, an inability to understand the underlying assumptions or the purpose?

- *Reasoning or thinking.* What kinds of reasons or arguments does the author use? What sort of information does the author give to back up what she or he is saying? Do specific examples or personal experience count as evidence? What assumptions is this author making?

- *Structure.* How does the writer organize material? Perhaps deductively (starting with a stated position and then giving reasons, evidence, and examples)? Perhaps inductively (starting with reasons, evidence, and examples, and then stating a conclusion)? Perhaps musing on a theme in a more meditative, wondering way? Perhaps there is a narrative structure. Does she or he tend to use partial summaries at the end of segments of the writing? How does the author use formatting to structure material: subheads, bullets, indenting, and so forth.

- *Purpose.* Why is the author writing this piece? To explain? To persuade? To express himself?

- *Audience.* Do you feel like an audience for the piece? If so, is the author addressing you as a colleague, as a friend, as an educated layperson? And if not, who do you think the piece is written for?

- *Personal and impersonal.* How personal is the writer in the presentation of material? Is the writing completely impersonal, or can you identify spots where the writer becomes more personal—and figure out why? How does the personal or impersonal quality of the writing affect your response?

- *Writer.* What kind of person do you think the writer is? This question doesn't mean that you should go out and try to find out about the author. What we're asking is that you try to characterize the writer on the basis of the piece of writing itself. Starting with an imagined physical description helps.

- *Language.* Are sentences complex in structure? Do they tend to be long or short? Does the author use straightforward language? Does the author use specialized vocabulary? How would you characterize the language in general?

- *Feelings.* What kinds of emotional reactions do you feel yourself having as you read the piece? Do you think these are the feelings the writer wanted you to have? How do these reactions influence your reading?

PROCESS BOX

The "problems" of my country [South Africa] did not set me writing; on the contrary, it was learn- ing to write that set me falling, falling through the surface of "the South African Way of life."

Nadine Gordimer,

■ *Evaluation.* How would you describe the strengths and weaknesses of this piece of writing? Would people in all fields call these strengths and weaknesses?

What we're asking you to do is difficult; it will require time and considerable thought on your part. We suggest that you not try to do it all at once, but rather use several sessions to give yourself some breathing space.

In addition to thinking about how these four pieces differ, we also want you to think about how they're alike: much of what makes for good sociological writing also makes for good natural science writing. Nor can we say that a particular discipline has only one form of writing associated with it. Within each discipline there is a formal and an informal style (at the very least) and a style used for those in the field and for those out of the field. After all, it is important for specialists in any field to be able to talk to nonspecialists too. Yet common to those different styles (or "registers," to use a piece of jargon from linguistics) within each discipline is a *way of thinking* that is characteristic of that discipline: a way of arguing or an agreement about what counts as reasons and evidence. If you're interested in the theory behind our aims, you can turn to the "Ruminations and Theory" section at the end of this workshop.

We need to put in here a disclaimer. We've picked the four essays to be analyzed and have specified the fields in which they're written. You must realize, however, that there is plenty of variation *within* discourses in any one field.

 ## SUGGESTIONS FOR SHARING AND RESPONDING

Because there's so much to share in this workshop, your teacher will probably not be able to give time for all of it during class. Perhaps she'll suggest that all group members exchange drafts, but that each person in the group be given chief responsibility for responding to one other person's two drafts. This way, each writer will get some written response. If everyone reads everyone else's drafts, though, all can participate in the discussion of each paper. Focused freewriting in response to questions about the published pieces can be exchanged in class and read outside of class. Or your teacher may decide to devote extra time to this workshop so that much of the work *can* be done in class.

You'll find "Skeleton Feedback and Descriptive Outline," "Criterion-Based Feedback," and "Pointing and Center of Gravity" (*Sharing and Responding*

Sections 10, 11, and 2) most valuable for this workshop. Following are two more questions which you can address to your group members:

- "What do you see as the main point of my paper(s)? Does it get lost? Does it have enough support?"
- "Are you clear about the subject matter of the lecture and reading I used for this workshop? Do you agree with me about what seems the most significant? What parts need more explanation?"

PROCESS JOURNAL AND COVER LETTER QUESTIONS

- How did you experience the writing out of your lecture notes? Were you able to make everything clear for yourself?
- How has this assignment affected (if at all) your work in other classes? How might it affect that work in the future?
- What makes an audience easy or hard to write for?

RUMINATIONS AND THEORY

Knowledge and Writing within Discipline Communities

An Argument for Freshman Composition

Knowledge and Writing within Discipline Communities

One of the most important things you learn while you're in college is to speak and write in new ways. You've undoubtedly noticed already that the language of your readings and the language of your professors' lectures are different from the language you're accustomed to. You may have noticed too that the way people write about poems and stories is usually different from the way they write about atomic particles. It isn't just that the subject matter of the writing is different or even that the style is different. It's that the *kind* of writing is different because of differences in *thinking* itself: how the writer presents material differs from one subject to the next.

You need to learn to write in ways acceptable within various fields—particularly within the field of your chosen major. Learning to do this requires, of course, that you learn the subject matter: if you're majoring in physics, you have to learn a lot of physics. But in the process of doing that learning, you'll absorb almost unconsciously the language and ways of thinking of physicists. You'll begin to use that language and thinking when you're talking about subjects within the field. You'll also begin to use them when you write about such subjects. A large part of being a good physicist is being comfortable with the *way* physicists talk and write about their subject. If this seems like a strange idea to you, we hope this workshop will help you begin to understand what we're saying.

All this doesn't mean that you'll write *exactly* like other physicists; some of your personal ways of putting words and ideas together will stay with you. Even within physics—often considered one of the least subjective of sciences—writers often have an individual style, and others within the field can often identify a writer by that style.

Most of your learning about how to use the methods of different academic disciplines may not occur until after your freshman year. But all of you take courses in some of these disciplines during your first year in college; perhaps now you're taking a math course or an introductory psychology or sociology course. If so, you're already absorbing the language and thinking of these disciplines along with the knowledge. The real and essential "knowledge" *is* the language and thinking—not just some list of facts. If you write papers for the course, your professor will expect you to demonstrate not only what you know but also how skilled you are in the ways of writing in that discipline.

You needn't actually worry about acquiring the language of a particular field: that happens gradually and usually imperceptibly. But you do need practice at it. That's why it's important for writing and speaking to be a part of all disciplines—from engineering to philosophy. If, when you reach your senior year, you were to compare papers written in an advanced course in your major with papers you wrote in an introductory course in the same discipline, you'd probably be startled at the differences—differences which have been produced by small changes throughout your college years. You'll realize that you now sound more "academic" than you used to.

But even in your senior year in your major—as a "member" of the field—you will still find yourself making adjustments in your writing (after you've clarified ideas for yourself on paper): one set of adjustments for people in your field and another set of adjustments for nonacademics or for academics not in your field. Given the increasing isolation of specialties in our society, we believe strongly that academics need to develop language that is accessible and comfortable for those not in their fields. Some of the very *best* scholars in a discipline often write in the most accessible way.

Within our field (the teaching of composition), we have a special language too—our own jargon. We've tried not to use too much of it in this book because it requires explanation. Also, if you're like us, you find it annoying when people in a particular field—one you're *not* in—use the language of that field in their conversations with you. But in this workshop, we do need to rely on one word which is often heard within our field: "discourse." One of the ways this word is used is to designate the language of a particular discipline; you'll hear us and our cohorts talking about "the discourse features of sociological writing" or, more succinctly, "the discourse of sociology." "Discourse" means both written and spoken language *and* ways of thinking.

It may sound as though we're saying that first you get facts or ideas (about some subject, economics for example) and then you make them conform to some artificial form deemed acceptable by economists. But this is far too simple a conclusion. In a very important sense, the way economists talk and write *creates* economic knowledge. Just as we saw in Workshop 5 that a genre can lead you to see *new* facts and ideas, not just shape ideas you already have, so too a particular discourse can lead you to see *new* facts and ideas, not just shape ones you already have. Think of it this way: economists, psychologists, and mathematicians can all look at the same phenomena—for example, a space shuttle disaster—and come up with different knowledge. That knowledge is a product of their particular angle of vision, their kind of language and thinking, and their kind of questions. Consequently you can never truly write appropriately within a discipline until you have become immersed in its ways of perceiving, thinking, and constructing knowledge.

One further caveat: The modern university or college with its various departments is a fairly recent creation—at least viewed against hundreds of previous years of formal education. Dividing knowledge up into segments—calling some physics, some philosophy, and so forth—is a human act. Since that's so, we need to leave room for the possibility of segmenting knowledge into different categories from the ones we now use. If all of us get locked into the language of our own fields, we're not so likely to see possibilities in the interaction of disciplines or for the creation of new disciplines, new ways of thinking, new ways of seeing.

Another problem with this strict departmentalization is one you may be experiencing: it's often difficult for you to integrate the separate pieces of your education. What you learn in one class often seems to have little relevance to what you learn in another class. This outcome has led many universities and colleges to set up interdisciplinary courses where the interaction of science, art, religion, and history, for example, becomes evident.

An Argument for Freshman Composition

Because of the close marriage between language and knowledge in any discourse field, many experts in the teaching of writing advocate abolishing freshman composition and having all writing occur within disciplinary or subject-matter classes. We don't agree. We think there are certain things common to all writing. Chief among these is the process of writing things out for oneself—for *one's own* purposes before adjusting that writing to others. How you go about doing this constitutes your personal writing process. But no matter what you're writing and for whom, you'll benefit from going through both of these steps. It's too difficult to work things out for yourself and for others at the same time.

In the previous paragraph we spoke of writing for *one's own purposes*. The truth about school writing is that you are often writing to get a good grade; the subject matter can be secondary. And the truth is that it's hard to write well when your subject is not important to you. In subject-area classes, you may have to write papers on topics that have little interest for you. This can be true in your writing class too. One of the things a writing class can do (that there isn't time for in most other classes) is help you find ways to make a subject your own in some way, find some angle on an assigned subject that grabs you. Freewriting, Perl writing, and open-ended writing can all help here. But you'll never believe that unless it actually happens for you. A writing class can provide that opportunity.

Thus, attention to your writing process as *process* is essential. Perhaps you work things out best for yourself by freewriting (we do); but perhaps you find list-making more productive or drawing cluster diagrams or outlining or meditating. Perhaps you use several of these on the same task. Perhaps you alter your ways of working out ideas according to what you're writing. Maybe you always do it the same way regardless of your subject. No matter. There's always a process of some kind. And when you actually sit down to make something clear for yourself, it doesn't matter much if the stuff in your head comes from your personal experience, from reading in a textbook or professional magazine, or from lectures by your professor. What you've learned must still *pass through you* somehow and come out on the page in words chosen and ordered by you.

Once you've worked out something for yourself by whatever process you prefer, you need to have processes to check for audience. Maybe you cut and paste, maybe you put aside what you've done for hours or days, maybe you read it or give it to someone for feedback, maybe you make one draft, maybe you make three or more. Again, whatever you do may be invariable—not dependent at all on your subject or audience. Or maybe you vary this part of your process according to what you're writing and for whom. As you become a better observer of your own writing and revising processes, you'll probably be fairly certain about some things you need to do: make sentences and paragraphs longer or shorter, keep an eagle eye out for repetitions and slips in logic, check to see if you have too many or not enough examples, and so forth. How much of each of these you do may depend on whether your way of writing for yourself is closer to an academic style or closer to a casual style. Thus, depending on your audience, you may need to "academize" your writing or "unacademize" it. Our point is that attention to process is important. (If you've gotten this far in our textbook, we really didn't have to tell you that!)

This is what we believe to be common to all writing. Whether all writing shares certain features such as clarity, logic, voice, and so forth, is a debate we're not entering at this point (though we think there are features all good writing has). The existence of language universals—truths which underlie *all* languages—has been debated for centuries. Do all languages have ways of expressing subjects or agents of action? Do all languages have ways of expressing action apart from the agents of action? Do all languages have expressive, communicative, persuasive, and poetic capabilities? That's another debate we hardly have room for. Here we're arguing something much less broad: that underlying any writing one does is a process for getting that writing done. Our aim in this book is to help you find *your* best processes.

What a writing class can do for you is help you discover your own best writing processes, modify them if necessary, and become adept at using them. Subject-matter classes and teachers don't, and some teachers say they can't, devote time to this often messy task. You'll need to make changes in your writing processes as you move through your college years and out into a career, but your writing class can help establish a firm foundation for doing that.

We have another reason for advocating separate writing classes: they give you the opportunity to do a kind of writing you won't be doing in subject classes. In subject classes, you do writing connected with those subjects. But lots of writing in the world is not specifically categorizable on the basis of the way universities have divided up knowledge. Lots of writing in the world doesn't have anything to do with school at all. Writing classes can give you the chance to do this sort of writing; in the long run, it may be the kind of writing that matters to you the most and that you do the most of for the rest of your life.

Readings

From FATHER-DAUGHTER INCEST
A Clinical Report

Judith Herman and Lisa Hirschman

A Feminist Theoretical Perspective

The incest taboo is universal in human culture. Though it varies from one culture to another, it is generally considered by anthropologists to be the foundation of all kinship structures. Lévi-Strauss describes it as the basic social contract; Mead says its purpose is the preservation of the human social order.[1] All cultures, including our own, regard violations of the taboo with horror and dread. Death has not been considered too extreme a punishment in many societies. In our laws, some states punish incest by up to twenty years' imprisonment.[2]

In spite of the strength of the prohibition on incest, sexual relations between family members do occur. Because of the extreme secrecy which surrounds the violation of our most basic sexual taboo, we have little clinical literature and no accurate statistics on the prevalence of incest. This paper attempts to review what is known about the occurrence of incest between parents and children, to discuss common social attitudes which pervade the existing clinical literature, and to offer a theoretical perspective which locates the incest taboo and its violations within the structure of patriarchy.

The Occurrence of Incest

The Children's Division of the American Humane Association estimates that a minimum of 80,000–100,000 children are sexually molested each year.[3] In the majority of these cases the offender is well known to the child, and in

The authors gratefully acknowledge the contributions of the incest victims themselves and of the therapists who shared their experience with us. For reasons of confidentiality, we cannot thank them by name.

[1]*Claude Lévi-Strauss,* The Elementary Structures of Kinship *(Boston: Beacon Press, 1969), p. 481; Margaret Mead, "Incest," in* International Encyclopedia of the Social Sciences, *ed. David L. Sills (New York: Crowell, Collier & Macmillan, 1968).*

[2]*Herbert Maisch,* Incest *(London: André Deutsch, 1973), p. 69.*

[3]*Vincent De Francis, ed.,* Sexual Abuse of Children *(Denver: Children's Division of the American Humane Association, 1967).*

about 25 percent of them, a relative. These estimates are based on New York City police records and the experience of social workers in a child protection agency. They are, therefore, projections based on observing poor and disorganized families who lack the resources to preserve secrecy. There is reason to believe, however, that most incest in fact occurs in intact families and entirely escapes the attention of social agencies. One in sixteen of the 8,000 white, middle-class women surveyed by Kinsey et al. reported sexual contact with an adult relative during childhood.[4] In the vast majority of these cases, the incident remained a secret.

A constant finding in all existing surveys is the overwhelming predominance of father-daughter incest. Weinberg, in a study of 200 court cases in the Chicago area, found 164 cases of father-daughter incest, compared with two cases of mother-son incest. . . .[5]

Common Attitudes toward Incest in the Professional Literature

Because the subject of incest inspires such strong emotional responses, few authors have even attempted a dispassionate examination of its actual occurrence and effects. Those who have approached the subject have often been unable to avoid defensive reactions such as denial, distancing, or blaming. We undertake this discussion with the full recognition that we ourselves are not immune to these reactions, which may be far more apparent to our readers than to ourselves.

Undoubtedly the most famous and consequential instance of denial of the reality of incest occurs in Freud's 1897 letter to Fliess. In it, Freud reveals the process by which he came to disbelieve the reports of his female patients and develop his concepts of infantile sexuality and the infantile neurosis: "Then there was the astonishing thing that in every case blame was laid on perverse acts by the father, and realization of the unexpected frequency of hysteria, in every case of which the same thing applied, though it was hardly credible that perverted acts against children were so general."[6]

□ □ □ □ □

Even those investigators who have paid attention to cases of acutal incest have often shown a tendency to comment or make judgments concerning the guilt or innocence of the participants. An example:

These children undoubtedly do not deserve completely the cloak of innocence with which they have been endowed by moralists, social reformers, and legislators. The

---

[4]*Alfred Kinsey, W. B. Pomeroy, C. E. Martin, and P. Gebhard. Sexual Behavior in the Human Female (Philadelphia: Saunders & Co., 1953), pp. 116–122.*

[5]*S. Kirson Weinberg,* Incest Behavior *(New York: Citadel Press, 1955).*

[6]*Freud,* The Origins of Psychoanalysis: Letters to Wilhelm Fliess, Drafts and Notes: 1887–1902 *(New York: Basic Books, 1954), p. 215.*

history of the relationship in our cases usually suggests at least some cooperation of the child in the activity, and in some cases the child assumed an active role in initiating the relationship. . . . It is true that the child often rationalized with excuses of fear of physical harm or the enticement of gifts, but there were obviously secondary reasons. Even in the cases where physical force may have been applied by the adult, this did not wholly account for the frequent repetition of the practice.

Finally, a most striking feature was that these children were distinguished as unusually charming and attractive in their outward personalities. Thus, it was not remarkable that frequently we considered the possibility that the child might have been the actual seducer, rather than the one innocently seduced.[7]

□ □ □ □ □

A few investigators, however, have testified to the destructive effects of the incest experience on the development of the child. Sloane and Karpinski, who studied five incestuous families in rural Pennsylvania, conclude: "Indulgence in incest in the post-adolescent period leads to serious repercussions in the girl, even in an environment where the moral standards are relaxed."[8] Kaufman, Peck, and Tagiuri, in a thorough study of eleven victims and their families who were seen at a Boston clinic, report: "Depression and guilt were universal as clinical findings. . . . The underlying craving for an adequate parent . . . dominated the lives of these girls."[9]

Several retrospective studies, including a recent report by Benward and Densen-Gerber, document a strong association between reported incest history and the later development of promiscuity or prostitution.[10] In fact, failure to marry or promiscuity seems to be the only criterion generally accepted in the literature as conclusive evidence that the victim has been harmed.[11] We believe that this finding in itself testifies to the traditional bias which pervades the incest literature.

Our survey of what has been written about incest, then, raises several questions. Why does incest between fathers and daughters occur so much more frequently than incest between mothers and sons? Why, though this finding has been consistently documented in all available sources, has no previous attempt been made to explain it? Why does the incest victim find so little attention or compassion in the literature, while she finds so many authorities who are willing to assert either that the incest did not happen, that it did not harm her, or that she was to blame for it? We

---

[7]*L. Bender and A. Blau, "The Reaction of Children to Sexual Relations with Adults,"* American Journal of Orthopsychiatry *7 (1937): 500–518.*

[8]*P. Sloane and E. Karpinski, "Effects of Incest on the Participants,"* American Journal of Orthopsychiatry *12 (1942): 666–673.*

[9]*I. Kaufman, A. Peck, and L. Tagiuri, "The Family Constellation and Overt Incestuous Relations between Father and Daughter,"* American Journal of Orthopsychiatry *24 (1954): 266–69.*

[10]*J. Benward and J. Densen-Gerber,* Incest as a Causative Factor in Anti-social Behavior: An Exploratory Study *(New York: Odyssey Institute, 1975).*

[11]*Weinberg.*

believe that a feminist perspective must be invoked in order to address these questions.

Beyond Therapy

For both social and psychological reasons, therapy alone seems to be an insufficient response to the situation of the incest victim. Because of its confidential nature, the therapy relationship does not lend itself to a full resolution of the issue of secrecy. The woman who feels herself to be the guardian of a terrible, almost magical secret may find considerable relief from her shame after sharing the secret with another person. However, the shared secrecy then recreates a situation similar to the original incestuous relationship. Instead of the victim alone against the world, there is the special dyad of the victim and her confidant. This, in fact, was a difficult issue for all the participants in our study, since the victims once again were the subject of special interest because of their sexual history.

The women's liberation movement has demonstrated repeatedly to the mental health profession that consciousness raising has often been more beneficial and empowering to women than psychotherapy. In particular, the public revelation of the many and ancient sexual secrets of women (orgasm, rape, abortion) may have contributed far more toward the liberation of women than the attempt to heal individual wounds through a restorative therapeutic relationship.

The same should be true for incest. The victims who feel like bitches, whores, and witches might feel greatly relieved if they felt less lonely, if their identities as the special guardians of a dreadful secret could be shed. Incest will begin to lose its devastating magic power when women begin to speak out about it publicly and realize how common it is.

We know that most cases do not come to the attention of therapists, and those that do, come years after the fact. Thus, as a social problem incest is clearly not amenable to a purely psychotherapeutic approach. Prevention, rather than treatment, seems to be indicated. On the basis of our study and the testimony of these victims, we favor all measures which strengthen and support the mother's role within the family, for it is clear that these daughters feel prey to their fathers' abuse when their mothers are too ill, weak, or downtrodden to protect them. We favor the strengthening of protective services for women and children, including adequate and dignified financial support for mothers, irrespective of their marital status; free, public, round-the-clock child care, and refuge facilities for women in crisis. We favor the vigorous enforcement (by female officials) of laws prohibiting the sexual abuse of children. Offenders should be isolated and reeducated. We see efforts to reintegrate fathers into the world of children as a positive development, but only on the condition that they learn more appropriate parental behavior. A seductive father is not much of an improvement over an abandoning or distant one.

As both Shulamith Firestone and Florence Rush have pointed out, the liberation of children is inseparable from our own.[12] In particular, as long as daughters are subject to seduction in childhood, no adult woman is free. Like prostitution and rape, we believe father-daughter incest will disappear only when male supremacy is ended.

Cambridgeport Problem Center (Hirschman)
Somerville Women's Mental Health Collective (Herman)

REDUCTIONISM AND BIOLOGICAL DETERMINISM

Lynda Birke

Reductionism's hierarchy of levels and associated causes carries with it an implied biological determinism. To take an example used in earlier chapters, a complex social phenomenon, such as violence, towards women, is said to be associated with hormonal abnormality. It is clearly implied that this is seen to be causal (hence the suggestion that we might give appropriate drugs to cure it; these would alter the biochemistry, and hence shift the causality). *Even if* it could be shown that there was indeed a hormonal change associated with the violence (which is doubtful), then to assume that this is causal is to imply that other possible factors are less important. And that, as I have argued, is what biological determinism does; it assumes that the biology is primary, thus having a far greater determining role than any other, social, factor.

What I did not do in the previous discussion, however, was to consider the question of the time-scale over which the determinism is assumed to operate. Since it does influence the nature of the reductionist assumptions made, it is important to consider it further here. Put roughly, there are three kinds of time-scales in biological explanations. First, there is a time-scale that operates in terms of immediately preceding causes—the kind of reductionism that I have discussed above. That is, it assumes that event A at a lower level precedes event B at the next level, and so on. The actual time-scale may be milliseconds, as in the case of nervous transmission, or it may be days or weeks, as in the case of hormonal control systems. The second sense of time-scale concerns the individual development of the organism. Here, causes are seen to operate over a rather longer period. One example of this kind of explanation would be the suggestion that exposure to particular hormones

---

[12]*Shulamith Firestone*, The Dialectic of Sex: The Case for Feminist Revolution *(New York: Bantam Books, 1970); Florence Rush, "The Sexual Abuse of Children: A Feminist Point of View," in Connell and Wilson.*

the violence (which is doubtful), then to assume that this is causal is to imply that other possible factors are less important. And that, as I have argued, is what biological determinism does; it assumes that the biology is primary, thus having a far greater determining role than any other, social, factor.

What I did not do in the previous discussion, however, was to consider the question of the time-scale over which the determinism is assumed to operate. Since it does influence the nature of the reductionist assumptions made, it is important to consider it further here. Put roughly, there are three kinds of time-scales in biological explanations. First, there is a time-scale that operates in terms of immediately preceding causes—the kind of reductionism that I have discussed above. That is, it assumes that event A at a lower level precedes event B at the next level, and so on. The actual time-scale may be milliseconds, as in the case of nervous transmission, or it may be days or weeks, as in the case of hormonal control systems. The second sense of time-scale concerns the individual development of the organism. Here, causes are seen to operate over a rather longer period. One example of this kind of explanation would be the suggestion that exposure to particular hormones during early (foetal or neonatal) life will effectively "switch off" the parts of the brain that control cyclicity in female mammals.[1] This is what is assumed to happen during the normal development of male mammals, with the result that their hormone output as adults is more or less constant. So here events during foetal life are thought to cause irreversible changes in the brain of the animal that are only manifest much later in life (i.e. after puberty). The third sense of time-scale in biology is of course, evolutionary time. Here, the causes are seen to be changes in the genetic material, which may occur for a variety of reasons. These occur in, say, a few individuals, and might confer some advantage to these over the rest of the population, so that these individuals survive and breed better than others. The change then spreads through the population, over a very much longer time-scale than the two previously considered.

Now although the time-scales are vastly different, what these different types of explanation share is an assumption of the *priority* of the lower levels in the explanation. Thus within the literature on hormones and development it is widely assumed that the hormones are prior, and causal to, the changes in later life. On the evolutionary time-scale, it is the *individuals* and their changed genetic complements, that are assumed to be more significant, prior to the population as a whole. The assumptions made about the causal chain are illustrated graphically in Figure 1.

Let me bring this rather abstract discussion back to some of the explanations that have concerned feminists. In doing so I hope to show why reductionism can be criticised at more overtly political levels. The first example is premenstrual tension. A prevalent view of premenstrual tension (PMT) is that it is caused by a hormonal imbalance, particularly of the

---

[1]Paul Weiss, *"The Living System: Determinism Stratified,"* Koestler and Smythies (eds.), Hutchinson, London, 1968, p. 10.

changes of which women have complained are determined by these abnormal hormone levels. So strong is the determinancy assumed to be that hormone abnormalities have successfully been used as grounds for defence in court cases, and the women involved have been acquitted of manslaughter.[3]

This is an example of the first kind of reductionism. It assumes immediately prior causes, running up the reductionist hierarchy. Thus, deranged hormones are said to cause changes in fluid balance which cause changes in the brain which cause mood swings which cause social unrest. No consideration is made—or indeed was made in the court's interpretation of events—of the other contributory factors, such as diet, anxiety, sleep patterns, drug use, income, housing, and many more. If any of these are held to contribute, it is only in a peripheral way; the central culprit is the hormone. And no consideration is given, either, to the possibility that the hormone production itself might be altered by other factors, such as life-style, or diet.

Apart from its reductionist assumptions, this story is an example of what Georgio Bignami has called "ex juvantibus" logic—arguing backwards from that which helps.[4] Although the evidence that progesterone levels in PMT sufferers is deranged is, to say the very least, equivocal, some advocates of the hormonal theory have found that progesterone administration does sometimes help sufferers. The logic then runs: if progesterone helps some sufferers, then it must be a deficiency of progesterone that caused the problem in the first place. This is rather like arguing, Bignami points out, that if a blow on the head stops complaints about an ingrowing toenail, then brain hyperactivity caused the complaints (or perhaps even the ingrowing toenail!)[5] Arguing backwards, however, does not prove the case.

From AMERICAN EXPERIENCE

Vern L. Bullough

When the wife of Governor Hopkins of Connecticut . . . became mentally ill, her insanity was blamed upon the fact that she had spent so much time in

---

[3]See *Katharina Dalton,* Once A Month, *Harvester Press, Brighton and Hunter House, Pomona, California.*

[4]*Dr. Dalton was the expert witness for these court cases and argued her progesterone theory. It has provoked feminist concern on the grounds that PMT could become an excuse for overt discrimination.*

[5]*Georgia Bignami, "Disease Models and Reductionist Thinking in the Biomedical Sciences," in* Against Biological Determinism, *The Dialectics of Biology Group, Allison and Busby, London, 1982.*

reading and writing. "If she had attended her household affairs, and such things as belong to women, and not gone out of her way and calling to meddle in such things as are proper for men, whose minds are stronger, etc., she had kept her wits, and might have improved them usefully and honorably in the place God had set her."[1] Those women who attempted to exceed their assigned role usually found themselves in hot water. A good illustration of this is Anne Hutchinson (1591 to 1643), who was banned from Massachusetts because she had exceeded "woman's place" by holding informal weekly meetings of women to discuss the sermons of the previous Sunday and to interpret them for her listeners. Such activity was held to be "a thing not tolerable nor comely in the sight of God nor fitting" for a woman to do. When Mrs. Hutchinson retorted that the Bible gave permission for women to teach the young (Titus 2:3–5), she was warned that such teachings were to be restricted to teaching young women "about their business to love their husbands," not religious views that differed from the majority.[2]

The Puritans in New England found biblical justification for their subjugation of women in the fifth commandment and its reference to honoring a father and mother. Though both sexes were clearly mentioned in the commandment it was held that "father and mother" were to be interpreted as meaning not only parents but all superiors and since the husband was the superior of the wife by the law of conjugal subjection, as well as by nature, she had no choice but to respect his wishes.[3] When one New England woman wrote a book her brother publicly rebuked her by stating that your "printing of a Book beyond the custom of your sex, doth rankly smell."[4] Anne Bradstreet (1612 to 1672), America's first woman poet, conscious of the male hostility to the educated female, prefaced her book:

I am obnoxious to each carping tongue
Who says my hand a needle better fits.
A poets pen all scorn I should thus wrong,
For such despite they caste on Female wits:
If what I do prove well, it won't advance,
They'l say it's stoln, or else it was by chance.[5]

Even when women went to school they often read special textbooks prepared for them in order to limit the strain on their faculties. Such titles as *Newton's Ladies Philosophy, The Lady's Geography, The Female Academy, The Ladies Complete Letter Writer,* and the *Female Miscellany* were often

[1]*John Winthrop,* The History of New England 1630–1649 *(2 vols., Boston: Thomas B. Wait, 1826), vol. 2, p. 216.*

[2]*David Hall, ed.,* The Antinomian Controversy, 1636–1638 *(Middleton, Conn.: Wesleyan University Press, 1968), pp. 312, 315–316.*

[3]*For a discussion of this see Thomas Cobbet,* A Fruitful and Useful Discourse Touching the Honour Due from Children to Parents *(London, 1656), p. 18.*

[4]*Thomas Parker,* The Copy of a Letter Written to His Sister *(London, 1650), p. 13.*

[5]*Anne Bradstreet,* The Works of Anne Bradstreet, *ed. by John Harvard Ellis (New York: Peter Smith, 1932), p. 101.*

advertised.[6] Women were not always happy with such restrictions and Anne Bradstreet was one of those who protested against the generalizations about female inferiority. She pointed to Queen Elizabeth as an example of a woman who had made considerable contributions to civilization and concluded:

> Now say, have women worth or have they none?
> Or have they some, but with our Queen is't gone?
> Nay Masculines, you have thus taxt us long,
> But she, though dead, will vindicate our wrong.
> Let such as say our Sex is void of Reason,
> Know tis a Slander now, but once was Treason.[7]

Women of course were invaluable as economic adjuncts to their husbands and they did other jobs which either required no formal education or little technical knowledge. Others served in more skilled capacities as private tutors, as school mistresses, or as midwives and herb doctors. Many served as nurses but usually as a sideline rather than a real occupation. Women were also shopkeepers, although their shops were usually run from their own homes. Maria Provost, wife of James Alexander, kept one of the largest shops in New York City. One evening in 1721 she gave birth to a daughter after having spent the day behind the counter and the next day with the help of her sixteen-year-old apprentice she opened the shop and sold thirty pounds worth of merchandise from her bed. Her husband bragged that he was very lucky to have such a good wife who "alone would make a man easy and happy had he nothing else to depend on."[8] Women, of course, served as seamstresses, milliners, laundresses, dyers, and stay-makers, but they also had other occupations; Jane Inch of Maryland was a silversmith, while Mary Willet took over her husband's pewter business after his death. In South Carolina Anna Maria Hoyland advertised that she would do any kind of "braziery and tinwork" as her mother had done. Maria Warwell mended china and Cassandra Ducker of Maryland owned and ran a fulling mill.[9] It was only when cities grew larger and occupations more specialized and professionalized that women were cut out of most jobs. This was because as cities became larger the business districts centralized and it became much more difficult for women to run a store from their home or to compete with the specialized stores. As specialization increased in importance, more training was required and women were denied the opportunity to be apprentices or in the cases of the professions to attend the necessary colleges or universities. Continental ideas about what constituted the fashionable woman also exercised more influence as Americans reached higher levels of prosperity. Increasingly those women who pretended to any culture or status imitated their English cousins in their ideas about women's role.

---

[6]*Julia Cherry Spruill,* Women's Life and Work in the Southern Colonies *(Chapel Hill: University of North Carolina Press, 1938), p. 202.*
[7]*Bradstreet,* Works, *p. 361.*
[8]*Alice Morse Earle,* Colonial Days in Old New York *(Port Washington, N.Y.: Friedman, 1962), p. 163.*
[9]*Spruill,* Women's Life, *p. 288.*

had other occupations; Jane Inch of Maryland was a silversmith, while Mary Willet took over her husband's pewter business after his death. In South Carolina Anna Maria Hoyland advertised that she would do any kind of "braziery and tinwork" as her mother had done. Maria Warwell mended china and Cassandra Ducker of Maryland owned and ran a fulling mill.[9] It was only when cities grew larger and occupations more specialized and professionalized that women were cut out of most jobs. This was because as cities became larger the business districts centralized and it became much more difficult for women to run a store from their home or to compete with the specialized stores. As specialization increased in importance, more training was required and women were denied the opportunity to be apprentices or in the cases of the professions to attend the necessary colleges or universities. Continental ideas about what constituted the fashionable woman also exercised more influence as Americans reached higher levels of prosperity. Increasingly those women who pretended to any culture or status imitated their English cousins in their ideas about women's role.

Still the vastness of America often allowed different norms to be followed. On Nantucket Island, for example, the whaling fleets kept the men away from home on voyages from two to five years in length, with the result that much of the island's business was handled by the women. Status for such a woman came from her ability to best make or protect her husband's money during his absence. Under such conditions it was very difficult for a woman to be a "clinging vine," if only because as one islander remarked, there were "no sturdy oaks" for her to cling to. Though mainlanders characterized Nantucket women as "homely and ungenteel," and their Quakerism kept their dress plain, they performed many of the tasks reserved for men in other parts of America. One preserved anecdote, perhaps apocryphal, tells the tale of a good wife who while at a store decided to buy a whole barrel of flour rather than make several trips to the store, and then to save delivery time, picked up the barrel and carried it home.[10] It was perhaps no accident that women from Nantucket contributed out of proportion to the leaders of the women's rights movement in the nineteenth century. Lucretia Mott, one of the early feminists, and Maria Mitchell, professor of astronomy at Vassar and militant champion of a new place for women, were both natives of the island.

---

[9]*Spruill*, Women's Life, *p. 288.*
[10]*William Oliver Steven,* Nantucket, the Far Away Island *(New York: Dodd, Mead, 1966), p. 103.*

A NEW WORLD BEYOND SNOW WHITE*

Sandra M. Gilbert and Susan Gubar

New York—In 1979 we dramatized the dilemma of 19th century women, especially women writers, through a discussion of "Snow White." There was a good queen who pricked her finger with a needle, watched blood fall on snow, gave birth to a girl, died and was replaced by a wicked queen, who became stepmother to Snow White.

When a mother figure becomes self-assertive in a society that discourages independence, we suggested in our analysis of the story, it is as if the good mother dies and is replaced by a wicked stepmother. Thus, the tale illuminates the conflict between socially prescribed femininity and the rebellious woman artist's desire for power.

But now too much has happened for the story of sexuality and its discontents to be summarized along the classic lines of "Snow White." Increasing numbers of women have entered the workplace. They have been through the sex wars associated with the modern liberation movement. And many American families have been transformed by a second wave of feminism.

If a '90s storyteller, a contemporary Scheherazade, were to meditate on the story of "Snow White," then, what new plots might she weave?

She might continue the story like this:

"Who is the most powerful of them all?" the queen asked her husband, resenting his smug sense of superiority. The king quickly answered that he was 10 times more powerful than she and her stepdaughter Snow White put together. So she and the lovely girl plotted to kill him.

They lured the king into a dark forest, planning to tear out his heart. But a passing huntsman rescued the majestic man and brought him to a male sanctuary where seven dwarfs and a prince disguised him as a statue of God in a glass coffin.

Meanwhile

What the reader imagines as an outcome of this revision clearly depends on which side he or she is on in the battle between the sexes.

Can the king and the queen make love, not war? Another rewriting might focus on current controversies about the erotic, and in particular on recent re-imaginings of women's desire.

"Who is the fairest of them all?" the queen asked, and her mirror said Snow White was the sexiest girl in the realm. So the queen set out to perfect

---

The writers are authors of The Mad-woman in the Attic *and the forthcoming* Letters from the Front, *third volume of* No Man's Land: The Place of the Woman Writer in the 20th Century. *They contributed this comment to* The New York Times.

the child's charms. She hired a huntsman to take the girl to a finishing school run by dwarfs where she would be taught costuming, hairdressing and how to stay on a diet. The queen hoped her stepdaughter might become Miss Dark Forest of 1992.

But en route to the school the handsome huntsman seduced Snow White. By the time she finally arrived at the mansion of the dwarfs, she was quite adept in the arts of love. Indeed, she was ready to teach the dwarfs a thing or two.

As this version suggests, changes in sexual standards have a double meaning for women: On the one hand, our heroine's erotic urges have been liberated; on the other, she risks becoming no more than a marketable commodity.

Because heterosexuality is so problematic here, our Scheherazade might want to use the old tale to explore alternative sexualities. "Who is the fairest of them all?" the queen asked, and when the mirror said Snow White was the most beautiful, the queen realized that she loved the girl with a love surpassing the love of man.

But as the two grew closer, the king became suspicious and plotted to kill Snow White. He hired a huntsman to take the girl into a forest and tear out her heart. The queen, though, got wind of his plans and arranged for Snow White to hide in a commune run by kindly dwarfs, where she could study her maternal heritage and receive nocturnal visits from the queen (disguised as a huntsman).

But the king, determined to stop these unnatural activities, arranged for a mercenary prince to capture the girl. This clever fellow disguised himself as a medical man and offered her three gifts to heal her of what he asserted was a neurosis: a feminine costume, a new hairdo and the fruit of his knowledge.

Depending on our storyteller's views about alternative sexualities, this third revision might result in a blissful union between the queen and Snow White (or maybe a happy-ever-after pairing of the king and the prince).

But given the increasing indeterminacy of our plot, the final retelling of the story could well represent many recent speculations about the artificiality of such traditional categories as gender, race and identity.

"Who is the fairest of them all?" the queen asked her mirror, for she realized that she was a mere mask. So were Snow White and the king. Who and what were they all, anyway? Merely signifiers, signifying nothing—or so she thought in her bleakest moments.

Or were those her wisest moments? Because everything seemed so indeterminate to the royal couple, they decided to send their brilliant daughter to a seminar run by bookish dwarfs who pondered the riddle of gender identity. Accompanied only by a philosophical huntsman, the girl made her way through circuitous paths into a bewildering forest of no names. "Am I no more than a glass coffin?" she wondered aloud.

Despite the tales our modern Scheherazade might produce, there is one constant: Snow White is of woman born and, even in an age of in vitro fertilization and surrogate motherhood, she would still be of woman born. What sort of woman could be her mother now, though? Mightn't Snow White as easily be born to the ambitious second queen as to the more dutiful first?

Because contemporary women are no longer inevitably silenced and domesticated, perhaps there need be no murderous conflict between Snow White and the second queen. And because women can negotiate between procreativity and creativity more easily today than they could 50 years ago, perhaps there need be no split between Snow White's biological mother and her rebellious stepmother.

In fact, many of the women poets and novelists who came to prominence after World War II were mothers—as were a great many other postwar women professionals—and these writers frequently focused on maternity. How might one of these mother-writers tell the old story of "Snow White"? Would she tell it all, or would the major cultural changes she represents so transform the basic outlines of the tale that its plot would no longer be recognizable?

There was a good queen who pricked her finger with a needle, watched blood fall on snow, gave birth to a girl named Snow White and lived to rear her. Sometimes when this queen looked into the mirror of her mind, she passed in her thoughts through the looking glass into a forest of stories so new that only she and her daughter could tell them.

WHAT KEEPS AN AIRPLANE UP?
Version for General Readers or Students in the Writing Class

Gary Kolnicki

At least once in the course of your life while sitting in an airplane, you must have asked yourself, "What keeps this thing from falling out of the sky?" You may think you understand. You've probably studied it or had it explained to you. But ask yourself, as you sit there looking out at nothing but clouds, if you can explain it to yourself and the answer will probably be No.

Two dynamic effects supply the lift for an airplane in flight. The simplest and most obvious source is what is called "the kite effect." Because the wing of the plane is slightly tipped upwards like a kite (see Figure 1), and because the plane is moving forward through the air, molecules slam with high speed into the *bottom* surface of the wing, pushing it upwards. Clearly there would be no kite effect if the plane were not moving forward. (It's true that the kite may not seem to be moving forward, but in fact it is moving forward with respect to the air around it—for the kite only flies if there is a good breeze.)

But the kite effect supplies only about one-third of the lift in an airplane. Two-thirds of the lift comes from what is called the "dynamic lift effect." This

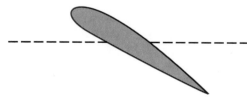

Figure 1
Cross section of a wing.

effect also depends upon the plane moving forward very fast. (Thus planes don't try to take off till they have a good velocity.) But to understand the dynamic lift effect, the major source of support for an airplane, you need to understand how gas particles exert pressure at a microscopic level.

Air is a gas that consists of a very large number of particles or molecules in high-speed motion. These molecules travel in straight lines in all directions. Because air is so dense, these molecules continuously collide with one another, bouncing off in all directions in zigzag paths. But because there are so *many* molecules moving randomly in this way, it turns out that at any given moment about the same number of particles are moving in all directions—with a result that there is no net movement of air. There's lots of motion, but as a whole it's getting nowhere.

But these molecules do exert pressure on any surface that they run into (and the more molecules, the more pressure). For when the randomly moving molecules hit the wall, they transfer their momentum to the wall—causing pressure. In an air-filled box, for example, an empty cigarette box on the table, the air exerts an *equal* pressure on all the walls since there are an equal number of particles bouncing off each wall. Thus the box stays where it is on the table: all those molecules are hitting on all walls equally.

An airplane wing is shaped in such a way as to make an "airfoil." It is rounded in the front, and arches to a point in the back. Because of this airfoil shape (and because it is somewhat tipped upward) there is an *imbalance* of pressure as the wing passes through the air.

As the wing passes through the air, the air takes two distinct paths across the wing: above and below (see Figure 2). Since the upper stream travels a longer path than the lower stream, the lower stream reaches the back of the wing first.

Because the upper stream hasn't yet reached the back, the air above the rear of the wing has lower pressure, causing the lower stream to curl up and back rather than to continue in the same direction. The upper stream meets this curling stream and forces it in a circular flow, called a vortex (see Figure 3). The upper stream is accelerated due to the lower pressure under the vortex.

The Bernoulli principle predicts dynamic lift under these conditions. According to this principle, a higher speed results in lower pressure. The stream above the wing has a higher velocity and produces a lower pressure—thus a net upward force or lift. Remember that this effect is all being produced by molecular collisions at the microscopic level.

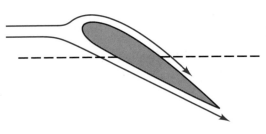

Figure 2
Path difference.

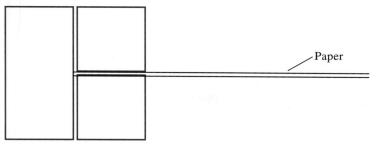

Figure 4
Small volumes of air.

This picture describes a case in which no motion results. Look now at Figure 5 with the top box moving to the right. The force which moves the upper box must result from an imbalance in pressure between it and the larger box in front. Since the large box's pressure hasn't changed, the upper box must have a lower pressure in order to be moved to the right. It follows that the faster the motion, the lower the pressure. The lower pressure above results in a net force upwards, or lift.

Flaps, moveable deflectors at the trailing edge of the wing, control the amount of lift. If a flap is in a downward position, it increases the curvature of the wing and thus makes the path difference between upper and lower flows even greater. This results in a process similar to the one just described and lift increases. The opposite occurs if the flap is in an upward position.

Of course, more can be explained about the complicated subject of flight. Basically, however, the physical processes described above prevent an airplane's falling out of the sky. Though not magical, the effects which describe the way air alone can hold up a jumbo jet are quite fascinating, complicated, and unexpected. Even a person with basic physics knowledge may not be aware of the sources of an airplane's lift on a fundamental level.

Figure 5
Motion from pressure imbalance.

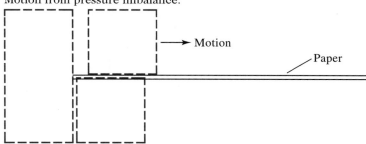

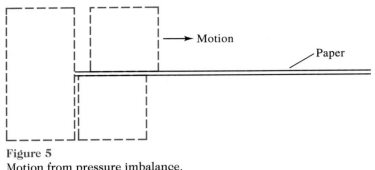

Figure 5
Motion from pressure imbalance.

WHAT KEEPS AN AIRPLANE UP?
Version for Teachers or for People Who Know a Bit about Physics

Gary Kolnicki

Even though many people believe they understand the way an airplane flies, very few truly know the physical processes which occur.

Two dynamic effects join to supply nearly all the support, or lift, for an airplane in flight. For an airfoil or wing, dynamic lift and the kite effect provide nearly all the lift.

Instrumental in understanding dynamic lift and the kite effect is a fundamental understanding of the gas particle theory along with a concept of pressure at a microscopic level. The Bernoulli equation predicts that these two effects will bring lift but does not aid in explaining them.

Air, a gas, consists of a very large number of particles in high-speed motion which travel in straight lines in all directions. Because air is so dense, particles continually collide with one another, bouncing off into other directions, in zig-zag paths. Since there are a large number of particles in this random motion at any one time, about the same number of particles move in all directions causing no net movement of air.

Pressure of a gas on a surface is a force due to collisions of molecules of the gas with that surface. As the molecules in random motion move in a way so that they hit the wall and transfer their momentum, pressure results. Therefore, the more particles in the gas, the more particles that will be moving in that certain direction, colliding with the wall, and putting more pressure on it. In an air-filled box, the air exerts an equal pressure on each wall, since there are an equal number of particles bouncing off each wall.

An airfoil is shaped and oriented so that an imbalance in pressure results as the wing passes through the air. The following effect accounts for the majority of this pressure imbalance. It is called dynamic lift.

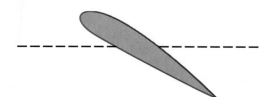

Figure 1
Cross section of a wing.

A wing's cross section appears in Figure 1. It is rounded in the front and arches to a point in the back. Figure 1 also illustrates the upward direction in which the wing points.

As the wing passes through the air, air takes two distinct paths across the wing: above and below. Since the upper stream travels a longer path than the lower stream, the lower stream reaches the back of the wing first. This is illustrated in Figure 2. Because the upper stream hasn't yet reached the back, the air above the rear of the wing has lower pressure, causing the lower stream to curl up and back rather than to continue in the same direction. The upper stream meets this curling stream and forces it into a circular flow, called a vortex. Figure 3 shows this flow. The upper stream is accelerated due to the lower pressure under the vortex. Once the upper stream has reached a velocity so that the upper and lower streams simultaneously reach the trail end of the wing, a pressure difference will no longer exist to curl up and back the lower stream. The vortex then moves away and dissipates, leaving this continuous flow of air above the wing.

The Bernoulli principle predicts dynamic lift under these conditions. A higher velocity results in lower pressure, according to this principle. Above, a stream with higher velocity than the lower produces lower pressure. Therefore, a net upward force, lift, results.

Microscopically, this effect is caused by molecular collisions.

Consider a piece of paper in a horizontal position with three volumes of air: one below, one above, and one in front (see Figure 4). This picture describes a case in which no motion results. Focus now on Figure 5 with the top box now moving to the right. The force which moves the upper box must result from an imbalance in pressure between it and the larger box in front. Since the large box's pressure hasn't changed, the upper box must have a lower pressure in order to be moved to the right. It follows that the faster the motion, the lower the pressure.

Now, think of air passing across a wing in steady flight. As shown earlier, the upper stream has a higher velocity than the lower stream. Since the air in

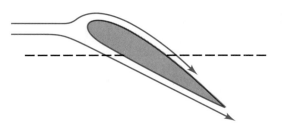

Figure 2
Path difference.

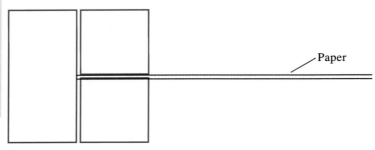

Figure 4
Small volumes of air.

stream. The greater velocity is the result of a larger force, or greater pressure imbalance. The lower pressure above results in a net force upward, or lift.

The kite effect is also described in a microscopic way. This effect occurs due to the upward orientation of the aircraft's wing. As the wing proceeds through the air, molecules slam with high speed into the slightly upturned bottom giving more lift to the plane.

The kite effect accounts for about one-third of total lift. Dynamic lift claims the majority of lift—almost two-thirds. Aircraft velocity is necessary for both these effects, and, therefore, thrust must be supplied. For this reason, aircrafts are designed to minimize friction. In some ways, an airplane is designed to slip through the air like a paper airplane.

Flaps, moveable deflectors at the trailing edge of the wing, control the amount of lift. If a flap is in a downward position, it increases the curvature of the wing and thus makes the path difference between upper and lower flows even greater. This results in a process similar to the one just described and lift increases. The opposite occurs if the flap is in an upward position.

Of course, more can be explained about the complicated subject of flight. Basically, however, the physical processes described above prevent

Figure 5
Motion from pressure imbalance.

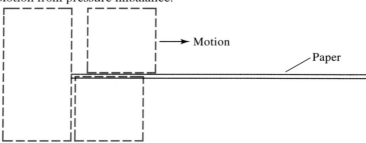

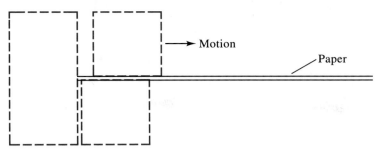

Figure 5
Motion from pressure imbalance.

Bibliography

"Aerodynamics." *Encyclopedia Britannica*. 1970, I, 205–214.

HALLIDAY, DAVID, AND RESNICK, ROBERT. *Fundamentals of Physics*. New York: John Wiley & Sons, Inc., 1974.

"Airplane." *Compton's Encyclopedia*. 1944, I, 90–110.

WORKSHOP

11

INTERPRETATION AS RESPONSE: READING AS THE CREATION OF MEANING

Reading may *look* passive: we sit quietly and let the image of the words print itself on our retina and thus pass inwards to our brain. But the point we want to stress in this workshop is that reading—indeed all meaning-making—is a deeply *active* process of exploration. In fact, when we have trouble reading it's often because we've been mistakenly *trying* to be passive—trying to make ourselves like good cameras, that is, trying to become perfect little photographic plates on which the meanings on the page *print themselves* with photographic accuracy. But since reading doesn't work that way, our performance suffers when we try to operate on that model. Even the "simple" act of seeing is exploratory and active. Though the eye is like a camera, the brain cannot "take in" retinal images, only electric impulses.

The important thing to realize, then, is that seeing or "making sense" of what is around us is always a process that occurs in stages—through the passage of time—not instantaneously like an image passing through a lens. In the first stage, our mind takes in the first pieces of information—the first trickles of electrical impulses—and quickly makes a guess or a hypothesis about what we might be looking at. Then the mind repeatedly checks this guess against further information that comes in. Often we have to change our guess or hypothesis as new information comes in—before we "see what's really there."

Because normal perception occurs so quickly, we seldom realize that this process of first-guessing-and-then-checking is going on. Especially since we don't think of vision in these terms. But if you will keep this explanation in mind in the days and weeks ahead and watch yourself in the act of seeing—particularly when you are trying to see something obscure or something you've never seen before—you'll catch yourself in the act of making these visual guesses or hypotheses: "Sure, that's a yellow car going down the highway," but then in a second, "Oh no, wait. Why is a yellow tractor coming up the highway?" In short we tend to *see what we expect to see*—till evidence forces us to revise our expectation.

If seeing and hearing are such active exploratory processes, so much the more so for reading: it's exactly the same process. When we read words or hear them, we *understand what we expect to understand*—till evidence forces us to revise our expectation. Even in the process of reading individual words, research shows that as soon as we see a few letters (or the shape of the whole word or the phrase that it's part of) we *guess* what the word is and then, as we get more data—or as our guess doesn't seem to fit—we revise our guess. And so the same constructive process goes on in all reading—whether for words, phrases, sentences, paragraphs, chapters or whole books.

Consider this simple opening sentence: "All the long afternoon, I worked in the windowless office, shivering from the air-conditioning, trying to find the mistake I'd made that morning as a bank clerk." We get a *bit* of meaning from the phrase "all the long afternoon," but for most readers, that meaning gets slightly modified and reinterpreted when we discover what kind of afternoon it was. "I" gets stashed away with *some* meaning, but it waits to find out what kind of "I" it is—even what age and gender. "Worked" gives us a meaning, but it too gets a bit of reinterpretation later in the sentence when we discover what kind of work it is.

In this workshop we will show you three different ways of interpreting a poem by *responding* and actively creating meaning—three different activities or exercises. There's quite a lot to do here; if your teacher has to skip an activity, we hope you'll experiment with it anyway.

We have two other goals in exploring the reading or interpreting process: helping you do better with hard texts, and helping you use the collaborative dimension of reading.

For the *main assignment* in this workshop, your teacher might simply ask for the writing you produce as the third response. Or the main assignment might be an essay explaining what you've figured out about the poem using all three responses.

1. MOVIES OF THE READER'S MIND: INTERRUPTING YOUR READING TO CAPTURE RESPONSES ON THE FLY

This activity is a kind of mini-laboratory in the reading process: an exercise to help you become more aware of your conscious and unconscious reactions as you read. In this exercise we interrupt you as you read a poem—we stop you in midpoem and ask you what's going on in your mind—so that you can notice your responses and reactions and interpretations as they are in the process of happening. The poem we're using has four stanzas (of different lengths), and we've broken it up and printed each stanza in a box on separate pages starting on page 288 and continuing on the following three left-hand pages (290, 292, and 294). We've done this so that you can notice and write down your reactions to each stanza before you see the rest of the poem. If this strikes you as highly artificial, you are right. But it is a valuable way to help you capture some of the mental events in your reading and meaning-making that you usually don't see.

Capturing Reactions on the Fly

Start, then, and read the first stanza of the poem in the box on page 288. Read it through once—reading however you normally read. There's no hurry. But when you finish, do a couple of minutes of freewriting to get down on

PROCESS BOX

As for inspiration, I've come to believe in it again, after years of devaluing it. But I know that it occurs as much for me in the course of a poem, spurred by the words I didn't know I was going to use, as much as it occurs by events that might precede the poem. . . . After I write a lit- tle while I have some sense of what I'm doing, so I'm going toward something, but I always want that thing I'm going towards to be a surprise for me. Frost says "no surprise in the poet, no sur- prise in the reader. . . ."

Stephen Dunn

Audre Lorde

For those of us who live at the shoreline
standing upon the constant edges of decision
crucial and alone
for those of us who cannot indulge
the passing dreams of choice
who love in doorways coming and going
in the hours between dawns
looking inward and outward
at once before and after
seeking a now that can breed
futures
like bread in our children's mouths
so their dreams will not reflect
the death of ours;

paper what happened in your mind as you were reading the stanza, and after you finished it and were trying to make sense of the words. What meanings or partial meanings came to mind? What did it make you think of, feel, remember? What words linger in your head?

Of course sometimes we read something and our only reaction is, "Huh???" That's fine. Write it down. But try to write a few more words about what *kind* of "Huh?" this was: frustrated? bored? angry? In any event you'll probably want to read the stanza again and see what sense you make this time and what goes on in your mind and feelings. Jot down some notes on this too.

Then go on and do the same with the following stanzas on the following three left-hand pages. Just make sure to keep stopping now and then to freewrite for a couple of minutes and record the mental events as you go. You could do this whole exercise with a tape recorder, speaking your reactions as you go rather than writing. You might capture more that way.

Should you try to "finish" or "master" one stanza before going on to read the next one? There's no right answer. We all read in different ways—and differently for different pieces of writing. Do what you normally do. However, it's worth pointing out here that one of the biggest problems some people have in reading is a tendency to spend too long trying to master one part before moving on. This usually gives you needless frustration since there's often no way to really find out what an early part means until you see a later part. That's how language works. Notice how there's an interesting correlation here between the reading and the writing process—that is, a similar problem in both realms: *trying to do it right the first time.* It's an impossible goal. Most people read better and write better when they let go a bit and learn *not* to work so hard to get it right each time—but to come back again and again, that is, to revise.

Before you have finished, make sure you have read all the parts of the poem at least four or five times—*and* that at least two of those readings involve reading the poem as a whole, from start to finish rather than in bits. When you read it straight through, you may well have new thoughts about what it means, new feelings, memories, frustrations, associations. Or you may simply become more convinced of what you saw before. (But even "becoming more convinced" is "something going on in your mind.") So make sure you stop after these read-throughs and freewrite for a few minutes to record what is going on in your thoughts and feelings.

What we are asking for is really "process writing"—but about your *reading* process. It will help you get a better sense of how your mind works when you read—what your habits are, your preoccupations, your blind spots, what you do well and what you'd like to do better. Breaking the poem into parts is like putting the camera on slow motion—so you can see more clearly the details of how your mind gradually makes meaning out of words. Athletes often watch slow-motion pictures of how they function in order to learn to function better. (By the way, it's interesting to notice similarities and differences between how your mind works as you write and as you read.)

You can look at examples of this kind of writing on pages 301–304 of the "Readings" section of this workshop: reactions by students while reading Richard Wilbur's "The Writer" (printed on pages 300–301). What we are asking for is also the same as "movies of the reader's mind"—a method of giving feedback to fellow writers, which we explain and illustrate in a separate section of *Sharing and Responding* at the end of this book.

Share, Compare Notes, Create Meaning with Others

At this point it is useful and interesting to *share* your reactions with one or two others in the class. Indeed it also makes sense to do it earlier in the reading process, for example, even after people have read *only* the first stanza.

Most people find it interesting just to see how other people's minds work. In fact it's often a *relief* to see other people's "really rough drafts of reading." Sometimes we feel, "Oh dear, everyone else but me does it right," and it's fun to see that it's a messy, imprecise process for everyone. And it's common for students to think, "Teachers and critics have a magical ability to suck the meaning out of poems—whole and complete—but I don't have that ability." Just as with writing, it's a relief to discover that everyone's mind tends to be a mess at the early stages—no matter how skilled they are. Some people hide the mess more (sometimes even from themselves), but it's there. And it's interesting to see that everyone has different reactions and feelings, *even* when they happen to agree on the main outlines.

In addition we want to emphasize the collaborative dimension that is inherent in reading and the making of meaning. It's not that we usually read in groups; we usually read alone. But we usually discuss what we read with others if we have the chance. Lawyers and scientists and business people as well

For those of us
who were imprinted with fear
like a faint line in the center of our foreheads
learning to be afraid with our mother's milk
for by this weapon
this illusion of some safety to be found
the heavy-footed hoped to silence us
For all of us
this instant and this triumph
We were never meant to survive.

as literary critics usually reach conclusions about what something means and implies, on the basis of discussion with colleagues. Even when we can't *actually* discuss our reading with others, we often hold bits of mental discussion with them in our heads anyway. Besides, the meanings of all the words we are reading have been *negotiated* with others in the process of talking and listening. All meaning has a foundation in society and groups.

So find an occasion at some point to share your written reactions with others (though don't feel pressured to share any things that feel too private). The goal is to try to see the poem through their eyes. Then do a few more minutes of writing to record how their reactions and interpretations did or didn't affect how you see it. What new meanings, reactions, feelings, or thoughts come to you on the basis of hearing what others wrote? You may experience large changes or only tiny readjustments. Sometimes someone else's memory or association becomes prominent in your mind.

We're not saying you should try to *agree* with other readers (though agreement may indeed emerge). Just *use* other readers; *try out* their readings to help you find a meaning or interpretation of the poem that satisfies you. The goal is simply to see and understand the poem better.

Reading "Right" and "Wrong"—Reading with the Grain and against the Grain

It's important to realize that the goal here is not to read "right" but to read attentively and capture a record of how your mind makes meaning out of words. That is, every piece of writing implicitly asks us to become the *right* kind of reader for it, the reader who will go along and get the meanings and feel the feelings that the writing asks for. When we have difficulty reading something, it's really a case of "I can't—or won't—become the kind of reader that this piece asks me to be." Some women, for example, have called attention to how often pieces of writing ask the reader to take on a male point of view, sometimes even asking readers to take pleasure in the criticism of women. ("Wives take all the fun out of life!" is the feeling we're supposed to have.)

We're not asking you necessarily to go along with the poem—to become the kind of reader you feel this poem is asking you to become. It's fine to be a *resisting reader,* to read "wrong," or to read "against the grain." Notice in the "Readings" how Barbara Hales and Julie Nelson are resistant readers of Richard Wilbur's "The Writer": in their dialogue, one of the voices vehemently refuses to read the poem the way the poem seems to ask to be read. The only thing we ask is that you not *stop* reading: not stop with "Huh?" or "I hate this piece" or "I hate being the kind of person this poem asks me to be—or having the kinds of feelings it's asking me to have." Please stick with the poem and work out *a reading* even if it is only a description of what you sense the poem is trying to do to you and why you refuse and insist on having a completely different set of thoughts and feelings.*

Final Step: Learning about Yourself as a Reader

Read back over everything you have written so far and try to see what you can notice about how your mind and feelings work, about your habits as a reader. Notice which parts of the poem struck you most and which parts left you unaffected. How did your reactions differ from those of others? Think about which dimensions of your self or character played a role in your reacting and interpreting. Look in particular for life-themes and life-positions.

- *Life-themes.* Can you see any powerful experiences or interests or preoccupations that shaped your reactions? Here are some examples of life-themes that affect many people's reading: relations between parents and children, love, sex, divorce, eating, the outdoors, fighting, loneliness, adventure, or breaking free of obligations.
- *Life-positions.* We cannot step outside of the positions we occupy, and these positions tend to affect how we read. Can you see in your reading any effects of your age? your gender? the region where you live? your race? your nationality? your class? your sexual orientation? your occupation?

*We want to note, however, that we are not arguing for a universal principle that says, "You always have a duty to keep on reading whatever someone puts in front of you." We believe that it's important sometimes to refuse and say, "I don't think this reading is good or right for me."

PROCESS BOX

In the actual process of composition or in preliminary thinking, I try to immerse myself in the motive and *feel* toward meanings, rather than plan a structure or plan effects.

Robert Penn Warren

291

Interpretation as Response: Reading as the Creation of Meaning

And when the sun rises we are afraid
it might not remain
when the sun sets we are afraid
it might not rise in the morning
when our stomachs are full we are afraid
of indigestion
when our stomachs are empty we are afraid
we may never eat again
when we are loved we are afraid
love will vanish
when we are alone we are afraid
love will never return
and when we speak we are afraid
our words will not be heard
nor welcomed
but when we are silent
we are still afraid.

It's interesting to get a better picture of *who we are as readers*—what lenses we read through. There is no such thing as perfectly neutral reading. But insofar as we can get a sense of what lenses we read through, we can get a better sense of what kinds of things we might miss. Do you think, for example, that women read and notice and react differently from how men do? It can be interesting to share this last writing too—about yourself as a reader—but we think it's more important to write these things *for yourself.* Share only what you can.

 ## 2. INTERPRETATION AS RENDERING OR ANIMATION OR PERFORMANCE

Whenever you read something out loud, you interpret it. That is, you can't read something out loud without automatically deciding what the words mean, and that meaning will *show* in your reading (unless you just *pronounce* the words disconnectedly without any sense of meaning—but that's not what we mean by "reading out loud"). Often we don't have to figure out the meaning before we read out loud because the act of reading out loud in itself *leads us* to figure out the meaning of words that we had been stuck on—*puts* the meaning there on our tongue, as it were. The mouth can be smarter than the eyes about language. Thus, the minimal task we have in mind here is simply to *read the poem out loud* in such a way as to make the meaning as clear as possible to readers.

But don't settle for the minimal task. Critics have often noted that the best interpretation of a text may be a *rendition* or *performance* of that text. To figure out how to "render" a text out loud is usually the quickest and most insightful way to figure out an interpretation. If you read the words with any spirit or life or animation—if you don't cop out and use a timid monotone— you will convey much more than the meaning of the words. You will convey the spirit or tone of the words—the implications.

Just by trial and error—using your mouth and your ear—you can decide how a line or stanza or whole poem should *sound* (ditto for a short story). Once you work that out, you *have* interpreted it. Then you can explain your interpretation "in other words": you can explain the interpretation you have already enacted in sound. Most important, this interpretation based on voice and sound is usually more insightful and sophisticated than the interpretation you come up with if you go straight to "interpretation talk."

We suggest using groups to put on a rendering or animation or performance of the Lorde poem (or one of the poems printed in the "Readings" at the end of this workshop). It is fine for performances to be playful and even take some liberties with the poem. Here are some techniques that student groups have used for renderings of Richard Wilbur's "The Writer" (printed on pages 300–301).

- *Using more than one reader and alternating between readers.* You can just have the group read the whole thing together—trying to bring out different moods or tones for the different parts of the poem. But one group used the whole group for stanzas one, four, five, and eleven (the stanzas that seem the most "choral"); they used a single reader for the first line of the second stanza and the first two lines of the sixth (where there is an "I" speaking); they used a group of just two readers for most of the second and third stanzas (the extended image of the typewriter and the boat) and two readers for the extended story of the trapped bird.

- *Echoing or repeating lines.* One group had one person repeat certain lines after they were said the first time—quietly and intermittently in the background: this reader repeated "My daughter is writing a story" until the group got to "I wish her a lucky passage"; then he repeated that phrase intermittently until the group got to "I remember" and he kept on with that—and then stopped for the last stanza. Another group did an experiment where each reader started one line later than the previous reader. It was like singing a round. They only had three readers and the effect was interesting—almost like waves. The listeners understood more than they thought they would. But the goal wasn't to put across a clear understanding: it was to give "musical" or "sound" rendition.

- *Putting parts in different orders.* Some groups experimented by starting with the story of the bird, or the extended image of hearing the typewriter and the boat. When we hear things in a different order, we notice new relationships; we learn more about the text.

So it is better to speak
remembering
we were never meant to survive.

- *Using sound effects.* Some groups used the sound of a typewriter—either intermittently or throughout the poem. Another got the sound of a bird banging against the window. One group made some "abstract" or nonrepresentational sound effects to go with the rendering.

- *Staging and interpretive movements.* One group had someone "playing" the father—walking meditatively around; another person playing the daughter holed up in a room—struggling with writing; another person acting out the trapped bird in a kind of dance. All this while a couple of others read. Some groups always tried rendering pieces *entirely* with movement and sound—no words at all. This is interesting and fun. For remember, these performances are for people who already know the poem. For one enactment, a person who knew American Sign Language did a signed version while another person read the words; it was extraordinarily beautiful and moving.

- *Adding words—creating a dialogue with the poem.* One group added words for the daughter to speak. Some groups interjected some of their own interpretive responses, adding thoughts or memories or reactions of their own. In one performance, one person kept interjecting the phrase "Get a life, Dad!" (see Hales and Nelson in the "Readings"). There are limitless possibilities. Any strong reactions or even background material can be added to a performance in order to make it a *dialogue* between your voice and the voice of the poet.

After the renderings, do some freewriting about what you learned from working out your own rendering and seeing those of others.

This performative approach is helpful in thinking about the question of whether there is such a thing as a "right" interpretation. As you'll see from the performances of your classmates, most sets of words can be performed in more than one plausible way. But some texts lend themselves to a multiplicity of readings or interpretations (these are more "open" sets of words), while other texts seem more "closed" or determined and seem to ask for only a few or possibly only one interpretation. We can usually notice when a reading is implausible—and notice the various degrees of pressure when a reading is pulling the text where it doesn't seem to want to go. But sometimes a very talented reader or actor can show us a new reading we never would have dreamed of or would even have called absurd, and succeed in making it seem absolutely plausible. For the purposes of this exercise, however, the goal is not *right* readings but *variations* in reading. It can be helpful to push and pull and even distort the text. Sometimes even a very wrong reading—satiric or parodic—can show us something in the words that we hadn't noticed.

3. RESPONDING AS A WRITER: RESPONDING IN KIND

In schools and colleges people often assume that writing about literature means writing some kind of *analysis* or *interpretation* or *essay* about the work. But it doesn't have to work that way. When *writers* respond and write about a poem, their response often takes the form of another poem: some kind of answering poem that in some way relates to or "bounces off" the poem they read. The way they *appreciate* a poem is to do a piece of work that somehow shares the same thematic or formal space as the poem. They create a companion poem. Many of the famous poems we read and appreciate (and write essays about) are really in a way companion or response poems to previous poems that the poet found powerful and enabling. Virginia Woolf wrote that the best way to understand a book is "not to read, but to write; to make your own experiment with the dangers and difficulties of words." (See pages 306–307 for Bi Chen's poetry response to Sindy Cheung's poem.)

Perhaps you don't normally write poems—or even find it a bit scary to think about doing so. This is true for both of us. What helps most is to find a poem that we like and connect with, and then take some of its form or theme—most of all some of its spirit and energy—and try to ride on its coat-tails to make a poem of our own. (We've learned from Kenneth Koch, Charles Moran, and Theodore Roethke about many of these techniques.)

Here are some suggestions for writing a poem in response to the Lorde poem:

■ *Use the structural germs.* Write a poem where you start off the first line with the phrase "For those of us who" and use that same phrase two more times; then use the variation, "For all of us." Then start a line with "When"

PROCESS BOX

No matter how long I stare out of the window it still won't come to me. Thoughts, ideas—where are you? How should I start? If I look hard enough maybe it'll come or be sent to me.

Brainstorm! Quick, jot down everything you know before it leaves you. Elaborate later—you might forget the good stuff now.

Something, someone, anything please stimulate me. I have writer's BLOCK!

Student

six times. Then "But" and finally "So." (If it helps you to cheat a bit, do so; however it often helps people *not* to cheat—to tie themselves rigidly to these obviously arbitrary rules. This can jiggle open certain doors in the mind.)

■ *Use the images.* Write a poem where you use images of shoreline, doorways, bread, children, lines in the forehead, sun, morning, stomach, speak, silence. Use them in any order.

■ *Use the theme.* Write a poem where you explore fear and relive the feeling, but where you go on to talk about what it will be like or what will happen when you face up to the fear and decide not to let it rule you. *Or:* write a poem that is a message of courage to others or perhaps to yourself, based on the recognition of bad news. *Or:* write a poem about why you have been silent, what you have been silent about, and what you will say and what it will be like when you are no longer silent. (See "Quiet Until the Thaw" in the "Readings" for a very different poem about silence and speech.)

■ *Reply.* Write a poem of reply to Audre Lorde (or to the "we" in the poem). If it helps you get started, begin by bouncing off words from the poem, for example, "You say you were never meant to survive"—and then go on from there.

What's crucial for this process of writing a poem is to accept the fact that you will probably be very dissatisfied, perhaps embarrassed. You have to give yourself permission to do something just for the heck of it—to see where the process leads you. When we do this, we have to *force* ourselves to keep writing, almost like freewriting, so that much of what we put down is just junk or filler. We end up throwing away more than half of what we've written, but we didn't suffer to write it so it doesn't hurt. You have to be playful and not too reverent about the process of "writing a poem."

After you have a draft, you can make big changes so that no one would ever see any relation to the Lorde poem. (You can even remove some of those structural or scaffolding words that the "rules" told you to put in.) But there's nothing wrong with leaving very direct links to the Lorde poem. It's an act of respect to write a poem that has echoes of her poem. (If you have a hard time connecting to this poem, your teacher might allow you to write a poem in response to a different one that suits you better.)

 MAIN ASSIGNMENT

Perhaps your teacher will treat that poem as the main assignment. Or perhaps she will ask for an essay about your emerging understanding or interpretation of the poem. Such an essay might contain *both* your understanding or interpretation—what sense or meaning you make of all those words—*and* an account of how you came to understand or interpret it this way through the three response activities. (Don't forget about the role of other people.)

Before we leave this workshop we want to reassure you that we're not trying to persuade you to go through these extensive processes every time you read something. If you are reading quickly for pleasure, that's fine. But these processes we are demonstrating here, once learned, will *enrich* your fast, casual reading. And if you have an assignment to interpret a piece of literature for a class, you might indeed find it helpful to go through all the response steps we've set up. Poetry could be defined, in fact, as language that's rich and well built enough that it bears *re*reading and *re*sponding. The pleasures and the meanings in poems don't get "used up" in one reading; indeed the more the words are read again, the more interesting the reactions that emerge.

PROCESS JOURNAL AND COVER LETTER QUESTIONS

- What did you learn about you as a reader? About the effect of life-themes and life-positions on how you read?
- What did you learn about you from the process of rendering or performing the poem? How did this change your reading?
- Reflect on your process of trying to produce a poem. What would it take to get you to do this more often?
- How did you respond to the readings and interpretations of others? And they to yours? Do you tend to be a believer or doubter of what others say?
- Reflect on the similarities and differences between your writing process and your reading process.
- How have your prior school experiences with literature influenced how you read and respond to literature?

FEEDBACK QUESTIONS

- On a poem:
  —"What words and images linger, work, or have impact? what meanings, feelings, or associations do those words produce?"
  —"Compare the ideas, mood, and structure of my poem to the Lorde poem."
  —"What new ideas or insights does my poem give you on the Lorde poem?"
- On an essay:
  —"How do your reactions and understandings of the poem differ from mine?"
  —"What happened for you as you moved from activities to interpretation? How does that compare to the reactions I described?"

About the Artificiality of Our Exercise: Repeatedly Interrupting Your Reading and Asking You to Write

These exercises in the reading process might seem odd and artificial to you, so we want to spell out now why we are asking you to use them. Our goal is to illustrate both what you *already do* when you read—and also help you a bit with what you *should do* in the future.

The Exercise as a Picture of What You Already Do. Because we keep interrupting you in the middle of your reading and asking you questions to write about, we are clearly producing an artificial reading process. We may cause you to think of things that you never would have thought of, just reading quietly on your own.

But reflect a moment about these things "we made you think of" as you were reading. We didn't put anything in your mind that wasn't there already; we didn't add anything. Any "new" thoughts or memories were already in your mind anyway. We merely interrupted you and made you pause so that more of what was in your mind came to conscious awareness.

Our point is that these things were probably already influencing your reading in ways that are below the level of your awareness—*even if you read quickly without any interruptions.* What's new in our exercise are not the thoughts and memories, but your awareness of them.

For example, our "artificial" exercise may have triggered a memory about the shoreline—or about bread. That memory might not have come to mind during a fast reading, but it probably *influenced* that fast reading without your noticing it. Research on reading gives more and more evidence of how quick and active our thinking and remembering are when we read—how much goes on below the level of awareness. Since we don't "take in meaning," but rather "make meaning," we do that making on the basis of all the thoughts, feelings, and experiences already inside us—not just on the basis of words on the page.

Think about where meaning comes from. There are no meanings *in* words; only in people. Meaning is what people *bring* to words—and the meanings people bring are their own meanings—amalgams of their own individual experiences. When readers see the word *chat* for example, they will bring different memories and associations—all having to do with informal conversation. Some people may have a very warm cozy feeling about chat. Others, however might find the word irrevocably colored by an experience when a large powerful person said, "I think we'd better go to my office and have a little *chat."* And yet a *French reader* will bring to those same four letters, 'c-h-a-t', meanings having to do with cats.

We might assume that the reading of straightforward prose is "regular reading," while the reading of difficult stories and poems is "irregular" or "exceptional." With difficult literature we have to stop and puzzle things out; we get one idea and then we have to change it when we get to something that contradicts it. But in fact the process of reading difficult pieces simply shows us more nakedly the very same process that goes on quickly and subliminally in all reading. (We see the same kind of thing in physics: cars and billiard balls seem to behave "normally," while subatomic particles seem peculiar—for example, having ambiguous locations and becoming smaller as they move faster. But in fact *everything* behaves according to those peculiar rules of relativity; we just can't see it with cars and billiard balls because they are large and move slowly.)

The Exercise as a Picture of What You Should Do in The Future. If you engage now and then in this artificial exercise—going slowly, pausing, looking inside at memories and associations, making hypotheses—you will learn to be more active and imaginative in your fast reading. You will learn to pay more attention to the words on the page and their relationships with each other; and you will pay more attention to the richness—the meanings, reactions, and associations—that you already bring to words. By being more skilled at the active and exploratory process of making meaning, you will simply understand more: you will be better at seeing the meaning even in very difficult pieces of writing.

Readings

THE WRITER

Richard Wilbur

In her room at the prow of the house
Where light breaks, and the windows are tossed with linden,
My daughter is writing a story.

I pause in the stairwell, hearing
From her shut door a commotion of typewriter-keys
Like a chain hauled over a gunwale.

Young as she is, the stuff
Of her life is a great cargo, and some of it heavy:
I wish her a lucky passage.

But now it is she who pauses,
As if to reject my thought and its easy figure.
A stillness greatens, in which

The whole house seems to be thinking,
And then she is at it again with a bunched clamor
Of strokes, and again is silent.

I remember the dazed starling
Which was trapped in that very room, two years ago;
How we stole in, lifted a sash

And retreated, not to affright it;
And how for a helpless hour, through the crack of the door,
We watched the sleek, wild, dark

And iridescent creature
Batter against the brilliance, drop like a glove
To the hard floor, or the desk-top,

And wait then, humped and bloody,
For the wits to try it again; and how our spirits
Rose when, suddenly sure,

It lifted off from a chair-back,
Beating a smooth course for the right window
And clearing the sill of the world.

It is always a matter, my darling,
Of life or death, as I had forgotten. I wish
What I wished you before, but harder.

RESPONSE TO "THE WRITER": MOVIES OF THE MIND WHILE READING

Elijah Goodwin

[Written after reading only the first quarter of the poem.] The sea imagery gives the act of writing power. I feel as though his daughter is writing something passionate. I almost picture a ship in a storm or a ship crashing through large waves. She is adventuring and exploring through her writing. What she is writing is something that she believes in, is excited about, rather than an assignment or the like. The chain hauled over the gunwale represents the lifting of her mental anchor as she is free to write. It represents freedom of ideas and creativity. She has let go of the anchor that holds back the creativity.

[Written after reading only the second quarter of the poem.] Each moment in life is important and can be very incredible. Even though she is young, she has had a lot of experiences, good and bad, and she carries them with her. It is possible for a young person to have a more incredible meaningful life than an old person. Sometimes I feel that way myself. That if I died tomorrow, I would die contented, knowing I have lived a full life.

[After reading almost to the end of the poem.] It keeps reminding me of the subject that I have been thinking of, the struggle to live freely. We will continue to batter ourselves against the walls as the bird continues to struggle to make the wrong choices and to recover and try again. And perhaps we may make it to the freedom of flight before we hit that wall or window one too many times. To find that entry into the wide open.

[After finishing the poem.] The romance of the ocean has always held a place in my heart. When I was young and even now, I travel to the ocean often, so I reacted right away because of the powerful effect the ocean imagery had on me. Lately I have been almost obsessed with the idea of being free and exploring. Being open to experiences, opening my mind, taking my body to its physical limits. I have been looking for the ultimate sensory and mental overload. To experience things so purely that you threaten to just burn out. And this is the angle I approached this poem with. I pictured the girl freeing her mind from pre-conceived ideas and pressures and the blocks of society. It was easier for me to react to the poem in pieces than as a whole. It is because of the way I think. Quick, fleeting, powerful images, glimpses through a window at high speed. It is not a matter of attention span; it's just that simple is more powerful.

RESPONSE TO "THE WRITER": MOVIES OF THE MIND WHILE READING

Tassie Walsh

The first thing I do is picture the scene. At first I imagine a young girl, but as I am told she types, I picture her to be a teenager in high school. She has a sunny room with her window open and the lace curtains blowing. It is late afternoon in the late spring or early summer. Her room has old teddy bears, mirrors, and pictures.

Her father is middle aged. He wears slacks and a shirt and a sweater without sleeves. The stairwell goes up then turns left. The stairs are carpeted beige and there are old family pictures on the wall going up.

I don't want to be here [at school]. I want to be in my sunny room. I want my home. I want warmth. I want my room. I want my bears and my mirrors and pictures. I want my dad to be interested in what I am doing.

It is about a wish for life. He wants his daughter to fly. He wants her to keep trying. It will be hard, she will fall, but he wishes her a lucky passage.

COLLAGE DIALOGUE ON "THE WRITER"

Barbara Hales and Julie Nelson

The father is proud of his daughter who has chosen the solitude of her room to write a story. He's curious and thinks she's too young to be interested in writing. She's excited, can't sleep and started writing even before the dawn arrived. She doesn't want to be disturbed and has sent the message out to her world by shutting the door. The keys continue at a steady pace. She's driven to get her thoughts and feelings onto the paper. The father stops by her door to listen. He continues to wonder what could possibly entice her from sleep at that early hour.

ALL THIS NOISE OF CHAINS!
WHY CAN'T HE GET ON WITH HIS OWN THING AND STOP FUSSING ABOUT HIS DAUGHTER.
I SENSE HIM THERE—OUTSIDE THE DOOR—
I WANT TO BASH HIS FACE IN.

Her struggle for freedom reminds him of the day they together witnessed the hurt and fear of a starling caught in that very room. They assisted only by raising the sash and staying present to send their healing energy to the bloody bird. They were delighted to watch it regain its strength and fly to freedom.

YUCK
"HUMPED AND BLOODY"—COME ON, IT WOULD DIE OF SHOCK IF IT WAS
THAT BADLY OFF.
HOW ABOUT FATHER OWNING HIS OWN FEELINGS. HE IS ASSUMING THIS
STRUGGLE IN HIS DAUGHTER—IT MAY OR MAY NOT BE TRUE.
THIS ASSUMPTION ANNOYS ME.
I IDENTIFY WITH THE DAUGHTER WHO WOULD BE FURIOUS IF SHE
SENSED HER FATHER HOVERING OUTSIDE THE DOOR AND WOULDN'T BE
ABLE TO WRITE.

Life will present traumas—even small things will sometimes feel like a
matter of life or death. The father would like to protect her from the
harshness and pain of life's experiences. But from the wisdom of his years, he
knows wishing her a lucky passage is all we can ever do for another person.

. . . . *the concerned, supportive parent.* . . .

. . . . *the child fighting, albeit prematurely, for her independence.* . . .

. . . . *the eternal "generation gap".* . . .

. . . . *the eternal parent/child dynamic.* . .

SOME THOUGHTS ABOUT "THE WRITER"
ON THE OCCASION OF THE DEATH OF
ISAAC BASHEVIS SINGER

Laura Wenk

I read the poem "The Writer" by Richard Wilbur just after hearing of the
death of the great Yiddish writer, Isaac Bashevis Singer. My interpretation of
the poem is wound around the feelings I had at that moment.
    For me the poem is about the ways that, while the young and old cannot
always truly communicate—cannot be fully in each other's worlds—there can
be a knowing. There can be a true, felt sense about each other's lives that can
be gratifying, that can fill our hearts and give us hope. So, it is a poem about
connections, although imperfect ones. As such, it is also a poem about being
able to let go and feel oneself as separate.
    The father in the poem had given as much as he could to his daughter. He
had helped her build a solid sense of self and let her follow her own heart. To
my mind this means that, among other things, he must have given her a sense
of the past—of who she is as understood by what has happened to those who
came before her. For growth and understanding of self is connected to
understanding one's parents, and them their own parents—so a chain is built.
    In reading this poem, I became the daughter. Isaac Bashevis Singer became
the father. He stood watching through the door along with other people who
have been important in creating an atmosphere in which I could grow to be a

strong, independent person. I sat inside typing, secure enough in my past to feel the turbulence of the present and dream of the future.

Even though I must do my own writing, I want to know that I am not entirely alone. I want to know that there are people near me—people who have come before and will come after—who are thinking clearly and acting out of a place of conscience.

I want to feel a thread running from the past to the knot where I hold it and onward into the future. I want this thread to sometimes become a live wire. There have been people who can turn on the current for me. They tell me that, while I, like the starling in Wilbur's poem, must find my way through that window alone, they have opened the window wider for me and will watch my flight through it.

There have been writers, like I. B. Singer, who have helped make the world of my grandmothers real to me—that have let me look back through that window to understand just how I got into this room to begin with. There have also been family members, friends and political activists whose presence, stories and work have strengthened my understandings, and made solid the ground on which I walk. I mourn the death of each living link to this rich past, and worry that in their absence the looking back will become impossible—the thread will be severed.

My grandmothers formed another link to a much more personal history—a family history. Each in her own way helped me to see patterns woven by the threads of their sisters and brothers, parents and grandparents. They wove a nest from which it was safe for me to venture outward—no matter how tentative my starts.

I don't think I will ever understand how my grandmothers found the strength to test their own wings in an air so filled with blood—so many losses. What lampposts lit their way through pogroms and gas chambers? How did they manage to trust that I could have a "lucky passage"?

Elsie, you were brave to open a window for me that you were too frightened to look out yourself.

Gerti, I still plant columbine and violets for you, and the smell of linden brings me to your side.

QUIET UNTIL THE THAW*

From the Cree Indians

Her name tells of how
it was with her.

---

*This and the following are Cree Indian "naming poems." You can write a naming poem for yourself or someone else. It might help you get going to borrow the first line, "His/her name tells of how it was with him/her." (You can drop it later.)

The truth is she did not speak
in winter.
Everyone learned not to
ask her questions in winter
once this was known about her.
The first winter this happened
we looked in her mouth to see
if something was frozen. Her tongue
maybe, or something else in there.
But after the thaw she spoke again
and told us it was fine for her that way.
So each spring we looked forward to that.

RAIN STRAIGHT DOWN

From the Cree Indians

For a long time we thought this boy
loved only things that fell
straight down. He didn't seem to care
about anything else.
We were afraid he could only HEAR
things that fell straight down!
We watched him stand outside
in rain. Later it was said
he put a tiny pond of rainwater
in his wife's ear
while she slept, and leaned over
to listen to it.
I remember he was happiest talking
about all the kinds of rain.
The kind that comes off herons' wings
when they fly up from a lake. I know
he wanted some of the heron rain
for his wife's ear too!
He walked out in spring to watch
the young girls rub wild onion under their eyes
until tears came out.
He knew a name for that rain too.
Sad onion rain.
That rain fell straight down
too, off their faces
and he saw it.

I AM SORROW

Sindy Cheung*

Who will listen to my feeling?
Who will listen to a useless land?
After the war, my skin has been damaged,
There are craters in my body.
Although I was sad, sorry, and suffering
  Who will listen to my feeling?
I am sad, sorrow, and suffering
  Who will know my feeling?
I am not sad about my harmed body.
I am sorrow because of the people, who can't use me rightly.
Who will know my feeling?

WISHING IN THE DARK

Bi Chen†

Looking out of the window,
A maze of eyes I see,
They are little
Yet,
So bright. Each reveals
Thoughts that sneak through the mind
Leaving behind
An unknown face.

"I am sorrow,"
That voice of yours I heard.
Looking up to search,
I found nothing
But endless shiny stars.
Are they not gorgeous?
Are they not amazing?
Are they not
The brothers of life?

---

*Sindy Cheung is a high-school-age "boat person" from Vietnam living in a refugee camp in Hong Kong.
†Bi Chen, an eleventh grader in San Jose, California, wrote "Wishing in the Dark" in response to Sindy Cheung's "I Am Sorrow."

Sitting here miles away from you,
Holding the heart of yours
In the hands of mine,
Begging the stars
To take your sorrow away.
May you have to face
No more sorrow,
I pray.
Search for the brightest star
In the dark.
There, you will find
My warmest blessing.

SONNET 3*

Burt Hatlen

Because learning to love you is a little
like trying to write a poem. How I must
each day start again, hunting for the right
words, the small tenderness that will

touch you here and here. I can say love
but the word lies lumpish on my lips.
I'd rather watch how you lick the tip
of your finger, before you turn the page.

So, when I want to be a poet, I jerk,
spin and spin, asking this one and that
to tell me who I am. But there is another

thing I can do, most simple, most difficult:
like getting up at six thirty A.M.
today to start the coffee, write this poem.

One way to write a poem bouncing off this one is to use the first sentence using the first element in the equation ("learning to love you") or the second ("trying to write a poem"). Stick to sonnet form—or depart from it.

HOW POETRY COMES TO ME*

Gary Snyder

It comes blundering over the
Boulders at night, it stays
Frightened outside the
Range of my campfire
I go to meet it at the
Edge of the light.

SLIVER

Langston Hughes

Cheap little rhymes
A cheap little tune
Are sometimes as dangerous
As a sliver of the moon.
A cheap little tune
To cheap little rhymes
Can cut a man's
Throat sometimes.

ANALYSIS OF "SLIVER"

Randie Gay

After reading the poem "Sliver" by Langston Hughes several times, I came up
with the idea that he was truly disheartened by the endless racial injustices
he and his race suffered throughout his lifetime. Without referring in the
poem to a specific incident, feeling or a mention of race and the pitfalls that
accompany race, I felt a weariness in Langston Hughes that, in the end,
weighed heavily on me and forced me to reacquaint myself with my
Blackness.

---

*Try writing a poem with the same title—or perhaps change the second word of the title.

At first glance, I thought the poem "Sliver" another "Black" poem by a Black author who has released his anger at his Blackness through poetry. Because the poem is relatively short (eight lines) and has a simple rhyme scheme (lines two and four rhyme, as well as six and eight), I initially dismissed the poem as just that—a simple little rhyme.

However, after a second and even a third reading, I sensed something deeper than just a rhyme. I sensed a weariness, a desperation, almost a resignation in Hughes.

I have two interpretations of "Sliver." Both include eventual death because of race, one of a white man and the other of the African-American race. The first three lines evoke a memory of myself at the age of five or so. I was playing on the neighborhood playground with some other children and a little White boy ran past the swingset I was swinging on, chanting "eenie-meenie-miney-mo, catch-a-nigger-by-his-toe!" He chanted this over and over again until finally an older boy told him to shut up or get beat up. Fortunately, the little White boy and I were both children; he did not understand what he was chanting and I did not understand what he meant. However, had we been older, and perhaps wiser, the words would have had meaning and would most likely have induced a dangerous confrontation.

I am also reminded of the sixties and the civil rights movement. Not everyone who believed in civil rights believed in peaceful, silent, nonviolent protest and civil disobedience. A chant like this could incite many people to violence.

When I first interpreted the poem, the last three lines of "Sliver" conjured up visions in me of a White man in a predominately Black part of town. The White man taunts a group of Black men standing on a corner by calling the group of men derogatory names. After awhile, one of the men in the group walks over to the White man and mercilessly slits the man's throat. I think there may have been a time, or times, in Hughes' life when he wanted to do just that. This last effort of justice and revenge (murder) reflects the turmoil, the anger and even hatred that Hughes and many Blacks often feel towards their tormentors.

My second interpretation of the poem did not evolve until I had read the poem many times. I was so absorbed in thinking of the cruel treatment of African Americans by White Americans and feeling the humiliation African Americans must have felt at such unfair treatment. I was so absorbed in my first interpretation of "Sliver" that I could not see the forest for the trees! All at once, it dawned on me that perhaps Hughes was not referring in lines seven and eight to a person who could be killed for singing a cheap rhyme. Instead, lines seven and eight refer to a Black man's potential of self-destruction or suicide. Hughes is expressing weariness at the inequalities he and many others had to suffer simply because of their race. He is saying a person can only take so much torment before he is more than willing to remove himself from such pain.

This simple poem "Sliver" stirs a multitude of thoughts and emotions in me. It angers me that Hughes had to endure the injustices he endured. It saddens me that even now, eighty-nine years after the birth of Hughes, African Americans still suffer from the same ailments of racial inequality as the African Americans of the early nineteen hundreds. Though progress has been made in achieving racial equality, to African Americans it is never enough nor swift enough. If Mr. Hughes could endure such pain while remaining optimistic, so will I.

WORKSHOP

12

ARGUMENT

In this workshop we focus on argument, on points of view presented through careful reasoning. The main assignment for this workshop will be (1) an analysis of one of your previous papers or (2) an analysis of a published argument or (3) an argumentative essay.

In Workshop 8 on persuasion we celebrated short, informal pieces. We emphasized the central skill in persuasion as getting someone to *listen*—to open the door of his mind; we downplayed longer, formal, carefully reasoned arguments. But obviously there are certain situations where it *is* valuable to use a long, careful argument. That is what we turn to in this workshop. Our goal is to help you see through any essay to the skeleton of reasoning at its heart in order to evaluate better the arguments of others and to construct better arguments of your own.

We have another goal here too, namely, for you to become more sophisticated about the *nature* of arguments, to become more critical as you read and listen to arguments. That is, even though argument is a subject complex enough for a whole book—indeed for a whole discipline (called "logic" or "rhetoric")—we can give you substantial help with it in this workshop. We'll start by asking you to keep three important things in mind:

1. There is no single, magic *right* way to argue, with all other ways being wrong. In fact, the nature of argument differs from field to field.

2. There are powerful procedures for working on argument that don't depend on the formal study of logic. We'll show you some of these practical procedures in this workshop. If you are interested in the nature of argument, you can turn to "Ruminations and Theory" at the end of the workshop where we talk more about this age-old subject. You may even want, in the process of this workshop, to analyze *that* piece as an argument.

3. Good arguments don't have to be aggressive or confrontational. (For more about nonadversarial argument or rhetoric, see "Ruminations and Theory" at the end of this workshop.)

 ## AN ARGUMENT FOR ARGUMENT

Sometimes you are lucky enough to be writing to readers who *are* ready to listen. A few people are open-minded in general, and many people are open-minded about issues where they don't have a personal stake. But they won't accept your view unless you can give a good argument—for they are also listening to people who disagree with you.

When you write essays for most teachers—especially essays in subject-matter courses—they won't buy a short, informal burst of persuasion: they're usually asking for a full, careful argument. And teachers are not the only people you'll have to write to whose job is to look carefully at all sides of an argument. Perhaps you need to argue to a person or committee that has nothing against you but nothing *for* you either. Certainly in the world of work, one often has to write a report or position paper or memo that carefully marshals the best argument. We might generalize (recognizing there are important exceptions) that for friends and general readers we need to write short, informal pieces of persuasion; but as *professionals* we need to analyze and write more formal and explicit arguments. In the readings at the end of this workshop, there's an excerpt from a dental brochure whose aim is to convince people that dentistry need not be painful. Compare this with the advertisements included in Workshop 8: you'll see directly some of the differences between persuasion and argument.

We suggested in Workshop 8 that experience and feelings often influence us more than careful reasoning, but for that very reason, we need careful argument as an *antidote*. Experience and feelings can fool us: a powerful story, letter, essay, or editorial may win our hearts, capture our feelings, and thus lead us to do exactly the wrong thing. One of the glories of language, especially written language, is that it permits us to consider things more carefully—to help us see whether we *should* follow our feelings and experience where they lead us. Writing, in particular, permits us to figure out reasons carefully and fully—to stand back from them and consider them one by one. In short, we need to be able to analyze and build arguments in order to make our *own* minds work well.

And, finally, you might not care at all about persuading others, but just need to figure out some issue for yourself. Persuasive "seeds" are not what you need; you need the best reasons and evidence to help you make up your own mind.

But it's not an either/or choice between persuasion and argument. Even though you will now be working on longer, more careful argument, that's no reason to forget the skills you focused on in the persuasion workshop to get readers to listen and to try to make your position human.

ANALYZING AN ARGUMENT

Summaries of the rules of reasoning are common, but they (like summaries of the rules of grammar) tend to be wrong unless they are long and complex enough to describe many, many exceptions. Reasoning is too complicated; the effectiveness of reasons in *particular* arguments depends on too many variables. For this workshop, then, instead of trying to give you brief rules, we'll help you harness and extend your *tacit knowledge* (which is enormous and complex): that shrewd common sense you have built up over years of practical reasoning. We'll also help you harness the knowledge of fellow students by working collaboratively.

We present here then a simple but powerful method for working on reasoning or arguments. You can learn to use it best if you practice it first on a piece of someone else's writing. It is a tool for standing back and seeing writing with detachment, which is harder with your own writing since you are so close to it. After learning to use this method with the writing of others, you'll be able to apply it to your own writing.

You might practice this procedure on one of the arguments in the readings at the end of this workshop, on a piece of persuasive writing by a classmate from the persuasion workshop (Workshop 8), on the "Argument for Argument" we just gave in the previous section, on a piece your teacher will give you, or on a speech (either on television or "live").

There are really two different tasks implied by the word "analysis":

- *Breaking down* an argument into its parts. This is a *descriptive* task of learning how to identify and isolate the main elements of an argument: the claim, the reasons, the support for those reasons, the assumptions, and the implications about audience.
- *Assessing* the effectiveness of an argument. This is an *evaluative* task of deciding how effective the reasons, evidence, and assumptions will be with various audiences.

It helps to realize that the first task—seeing what the elements of an argument *are*—is actually more important and more feasible than the second task of trying to *evaluate* the effectiveness of those elements. People get bogged down arguing about the effectiveness of an argument—or even of a single reason or piece of evidence—and thereby get distracted from the main job of seeing the argument clearly. Evaluating an argument is usually a matter of unending and messy dispute, whereas seeing it clearly is something you can manage. You can often get agreement among readers about what a reason *is* and what supports that reason, even though they can't agree on how persuasive the reason is.

The Main Task: Seeing the Elements of the Argument

1. Look at Reasons and Support

a. Main Claim. Read through the argument of the piece you're analyzing, decide what the main claim is, and summarize it in one sentence. Perhaps the main claim is obvious right from the start ("I wish to argue in favor of bicycle paths on campus"; "This law is absurdly overbroad"). If you're analyzing a draft, the main claim may be unclear, perhaps because the author hasn't yet got the claim clear to himself. Even in a finished piece, there may be slippage between an early statement of the claim or thesis and the final summary statement.

Take care to summarize the main claim in the simplest sentence you can manage; wording counts a lot. For example, there's a crucial difference be-

---

PROCESS BOX

Anybody who finds himself in this situation of writing to a prescribed notion or to illustrate or to fill in what he already knows should stop writing. A writer has got to trust the act of writing to scan all his ideas, passions, and convictions; but these must emerge from the work, be *of* it.

E. L. Doctorow

tween saying "Terrorism can be countered without violence" and "Terrorism can be reduced if the democratic nations of the world take certain firm actions." Make a note if you find a problem determining the main claim: if, for example, the writer changes claims or if you think the real claim is different from what the writer says it is. You might end up deciding there are actually the "makings" for two slightly different arguments in the piece you're analyzing.

If it's hard to decide on the main claim, go on to the next step and then come back later.

b. Reasons. Read through the piece again and decide what you think are the principal reasons that argue for the main claim you have identified—or tentatively identified. It's possible to pick out reasons even when you're unsure of the main claim. Summarize each reason in a *simple short sentence*. A word or phrase won't do because a word or phrase doesn't *say* anything; it only points. You need a sentence because the sentence forces you to decide what is being said.

Don't be surprised if it's hard to decide just what is a "reason." For a three-page essay, you could choose three main reasons or ten. It's a question of how *closely* you want to examine the thinking. Use your judgment; try it out different ways.

Don't worry at this point about the order of these reasons. Just summarize them in the order you find them (or out of order if you suddenly notice one you missed on a previous page)—even if that makes a jumble. You can re-order them later if you want to examine the reasoning more carefully or if you are analyzing a piece of your own that you intend to revise.

c. Support. For each reason, what support is given? Support might take the form of evidence, illustrative examples, even other "smaller" subreasons that you didn't list as major reasons.

2. Look at Assumptions

What assumptions or unstated reasons does the argument seem to make? You probably noticed some of the assumptions as you looked at reasons and support, but to find important assumptions you need to read through the argument once more with only this subtle question in mind: what did the writer seem to take for granted? Assumptions are slippery and often insidious because the writer gets them into the reader's head without *saying* them. And if you share the writer's assumptions, you'll have an even harder time uncovering them. For example, the following assumptions might function as unstated reasons in an argument: "What is modern is better than what is old-fashioned"; "Saving time is always a good thing."

To find assumptions it helps to imagine what *kind* of person is making the argument—perhaps even make an exaggerated picture of him or her in your mind—and try to think of what that kind of person takes for granted. Finding assumptions in a piece of our own writing is particularly difficult because we usually don't realize we have them: they're just "there."

3. Think about Readers or Audience

What is the implied audience? Who does the writer seem to be talking to? to people who already agree or don't agree? to peers? professionals? teachers? to a large or a small audience?

How adversarial is the writer? Does he take an either/or stand: insisting that others have to be wrong if he's right? Does he use a lot of energy in showing that others are wrong?

And also, how does the writer *treat* the audience? What's his voice or stance? Is he respectful? talking down? distant? hesitant? What does the author seem to want you as a reader or audience to think or do? To get at this, two or more of you can read the argument aloud as we suggest in Mini-Workshop C. For additional help with these questions about audience, you may want to look at Workshop 17, which includes an extended discussion of audience.

The Secondary Task: Evaluating or Assessing

This step involves looking back at what you have figured out in the previous steps: the reasons, the supports, the assumptions, and the audience implications. For each one simply try to decide on its effectiveness. As we said, this is the messy and arguable part. There are no rules for what works and what doesn't. Different arguments and supports work for different readers. Some people, for instance, are impressed by tight logic; others are made suspicious by it. But at least you are looking at smaller elements, and so judgments are a bit more manageable. There are a few techniques that might help:

- Look for counterarguments, counterevidence, or attacks that could be made against each reason, support, or assumption. That is, play the "doubting game" with each element.
- Ask what kind of person would agree and what kind of person would disagree with each reason, support, or assumption. What kind of person would "do" or think what the writing seems to be urging? This is a "humanizing" kind of approach that sometimes opens doors.
- See Section 10 in *Sharing and Responding*, "Skeleton Feedback and Descriptive Outline," for an example of this procedure used on a sample essay.

If you have done a careful job with the main task of *summarizing*—and that is feasible—then the task of *evaluating* becomes more manageable—though still messy.

Collaborative Option

Analyzing arguments is an ideal job for a pair or a group. You can learn to use this process more quickly, better, and more enjoyably if you do it with others. There are various ways to collaborate. You can just work through the argument together, discussing each step as you go. Such a process gives you the opportunity to experience directly how productive it is to do joint thinking.

But each of you can do this on his or her own and then compare notes. Or you can even divide up the target essay, have each person work on one part or one task, and then put your analyses together. You may think of yet other methods.

Collaboration can go much farther than this of course. You and your partner (or even three or four of you) can decide to analyze a given argument separately and then write a collaborative paper which presents the similarities and differences observable in the separate analyses.

And you can always go the route of full collaboration: do all the work with one or more of your classmates and produce a jointly written analysis.

 REVISING YOUR OWN ARGUMENT

We advised you to practice this analytic procedure on the writing of others, but of course one of the main uses is for revising your own writing: to strengthen the argument in some exploratory writing or in an informal, persuasive piece. If you are revising, you can't just stop with deciding what's strong and weak in your piece; you need to figure out how to improve it.

Here are a few suggestions:

- When you list main reasons (step 1b), write each one on a 3 X 5 card or a half sheet of paper. That way you will find it easier to play with a different order of points or even to restructure the whole piece.
- Define your main claim. If you are not sure, it may take a bit more exploratory writing.
- Figure out, finally, the best order for your argument. If you still find this difficult, it helps to realize that even though an argument operates in the realm of "reasoning," this doesn't mean that there's some perfect order you have to find. There are always a host of possible organizations or sequences that could be effective.

It's an important psychological fact that arguments are not necessarily more effective if they present reasons step by step in the most logical sequence, as in a geometry textbook. Obviously it pays to hide the logic in a poor argument, but even a strong argument is sometimes clearer and more persuasive if presented differently from how a logician or geometry text would present it. So try different orders; you can start with the most powerful reason, or end with it, or give reasons in the order you thought of them (with a kind of narrative thread), or clump them by resemblance.

In short, don't feel you have to have mastered logic to be good at this process. Use your intuition; follow hunches. Our *nose* for reasoning is usually more acute than our conscious knowledge of reasoning, just as our ear for grammar is usually more acute than our conscious knowledge of grammar. Of course intuition alone can be wrong. That's why you need the two powerful tools we suggest here: an x-ray of the skeleton of reasons in the argument and an assessment of the effectiveness of these reasons. And don't forget the value of collaboration in doing all of this.

Mid afternoon. I see Hugh as I'm walking back from Ludlow. I'm working on my memo about the goals of the Bard writing program. Rained *hard* all morning and suddenly now it's steamy bright sun with no trace of cloud in the sky.

We're standing in the middle of the path because I decided on the spot to ask him for feedback on the draft of my memo. I stand there with my little canvas briefcase and umbrella between my legs and read my draft out loud to him.

He nods his head at certain points and I nod inwardly: yes, he likes these places; they are strong. But when he speaks I learn they are places he *doesn't* like. He returns to an objection he'd voiced last week when I'd been talking about goals in our meeting. (An objection to my being too pushy and dogmatic in stating goals—trying to claim too much.)

After he's spoken, I know my response immediately. I'm polite, I don't argue, but I know clearly that I want to do it *my* way. I'm not threatened but I'm not in the slightest willing to back down and do it the way he suggests.

Right afterwards I discovered I was missing a crucial page of an earlier draft with a bit I wanted to use. It must be lying in a wastepaper basket on the third floor of Ludlow. I go back, scared I might have lost it. (I am still sometimes hit by feeling that if I lose a piece of writing I've worked on I'll never be able to create it again—it will be a permanent loss of something precious.)

I go back and find it, and while I'm there at my desk, I decide to work on the piece a bit more. With some quick cleaning up I can xerox a few copies and get more feedback—for my session with Hugh made me feel more settled in my mind as to how I wanted it.

I start working—cleaning up and retyping messy bits—and suddenly I realize I need to back down from my position of stubbornness. Chagrined to realize not just that I need to but *want* to. Just what Hugh suggested. For now in reading my memo I can notice a kind of tightness or restrictedness or off-balance in my writing which stemmed from my attempts in the memo to be stubborn and pushy and claim so much. For some reason, I *had* a need to make that claim; for some reason I don't need to make that claim now—and can see it's better not to.

In a nutshell. I got feedback from Hugh; I was forced to see my words through his eyes; I felt secure in rejecting that way of seeing my words; but then in going back to the text with my own eyes, I could no longer see it as I had seen it.

Peter Elbow

Analyzing an Oral Argument

If you elect to analyze a speech, you'll want to tape it so that you can check your response. (You might also want to look back at Workshop 10 where we give some suggestions about taking notes while listening.) A speech often gives an impression of careful reasoning which doesn't stand up on second hearing. It's difficult to hold the details of an argument in your mind while continuing to listen to a speech. Speakers can actually rely on that difficulty and fudge their logic. On paper, you can see reasoning better—with more perspective or detachment—especially if it's not your own.

Arguments appear on radio and television in various forms. Sometimes stations air editorials and ask for the public to respond. Sometimes they provide time for elected officials to present pronouncements related to some important governmental issue. And, during elections, radio and television air political speeches and debates in full. But you need to keep in mind that what appears to be purely oral, often isn't. Speakers on television are often reading from a TelePrompter into which a previously written speech has been fed.

What radio and television have created is a genre of oral argument based on written scripts.

You can also attend public lectures (or lectures for a large audience at your school) in which speakers are trying to convince an audience of something. Be aware here too, though, that many public lecturers read from typed copy. Government officials and politicians usually distribute copies of their speeches before they actually deliver them. Maybe a courtroom is the one significant place today where oral arguments exist apart from written script. Certainly far fewer great orators exist now than in the past. If you have access to a courtroom, you may want to listen to a lawyer's summation in which she presents a summary of all the evidence supporting her side of the argument.

In Workshop 10, we focused on the importance of being a critical listener in school, particularly in large lecture classes where discussion is at a minimum. When listening to politicians and others making pronouncements about important public issues either live or on television, you also need a critical ear. This assignment can start you along that path.

While listening to the speaker you selected, you may want to take a few notes when and if you recognize main points, assumptions, evidence, subreasons, and so forth. But even if you don't do that, you should do some writing as soon as possible to record your initial reactions, to record some sense of what your final judgment would be under normal circumstances when you would probably not hear the speech again or read it. Later you can listen to your tape and reconsider your initial reactions.

Analysis of an oral argument is a good assignment to do collaboratively: it will give you a chance to see if others "hear" the argument the same way you do. It will also give you more insight into how speakers can mislead because listeners *cannot* refer back to what was said previously in the same speech. Sometimes two people talking about a speech they've both just heard seem not to have even heard the same talk.

 ## BUILDING AN ARGUMENT

Find an issue to write about that's not completely clear or decided in your own mind: an issue you still have some questions about. Write a dialogue between your own different opinions. For example, you might start off by writing, "Colleges put too much emphasis on competitive sports: some football and basketball teams might as well be professional." Another voice might answer, "Yeah, but athletics makes some kids get an education who wouldn't otherwise."

Remember that arguments don't by definition have two sides; you can have more than two voices in your dialogue. Another voice can pop in and say, "Sports are good for people: they help them to work cooperatively and keep their bodies in good shape." Once you get started, follow the conversation wherever it leads. We think it will lead you to complex thinking and interesting writing.

But perhaps you want to write an argument concerning an issue that you feel no confusion about. You're convinced you know what is right and you want to convince others. Obviously, there's no internal dialogue here. What you have to do is *imagine* someone who disagrees with you. Perhaps you can think about what kind of life experience would lead someone to feel differently than you do. Be careful not to characterize that person as stupid: you need someone intelligent and fair-minded if you're going to get a useful dialogue going. Of course, if you can find someone in your class who disagrees with you, you can write a collaborative dialogue. Make it a dialogue in which you listen to each other, not one where you just try to shoot one another down.

If you have trouble coming up with a subject, look back over the freewritings you've done for other workshops. Look particularly for language that is unusually vivid and resonant. Its subject is probably especially thought-provoking for you. Look too for issues that reappear; that's evidence that they're on your mind.

Your dialogue should help you come to a clear position on your issue. But a clear position doesn't necessarily have to be a definite pro or con position; you can still write a good argument for a position something like this: "We need to understand better the place of competitive sports in education." A clear position doesn't necessarily mean that your feelings are clear about all the issues.

Once you have your position, you can complete your draft—using material from your dialogue to support it. It's sometimes possible to produce an effective argument by smoothing your dialogue, removing digressions, elaborating on significant points, and providing transitions and an introduction and conclusion. In effect, you will be presenting a narrative of the development of your thinking.

If you're aiming for a more traditional essay, you can isolate significant points in your dialogue and build an informal outline before completing your draft. The points we set forth in the previous section for analyzing arguments can help you identify and evaluate various elements in your dialogue: reasons, supports, assumptions, intended audience, and counterarguments.

 MAIN ASSIGNMENT

For your main assignment, choose one of the following:

1. Write a paper that analyzes the argument in an essay (yours or someone else's) or the argument in a speech. An alternative would be a paper that compares the arguments in two essays or speeches. (See the "Readings" in this workshop for an analysis of one of the essays in Workshop 8.)

2. Revise a persuasive piece you've already written, with emphasis on strengthening the argument for a particular audience. The most likely one to revise is the persuasive letter you wrote for Workshop 8; you can think of your revision as an editorial rather than a letter. But you could revise an earlier essay if you prefer, since a number of them could be called persuasive. You could even—as a major revision—recast a *non*persuasive piece as an argument.

3. Write a new essay in which you build the best argument you can. Be sure to enlist the help of your classmates in subjecting this new essay to the argument-analysis process we describe in this workshop.

4. Develop some aspect of the activities in this workshop collaboratively. We presented some possibilities on page 314–317.

SHARING AND RESPONDING

If you write an analysis, you can ask others to go over it with you point by point, using the items listed on pages 314–317 for analyzing arguments. Section 10 of *Sharing and Responding* will give you the best information on your reasoning and structure. But perhaps—after all this emphasis on reasoning— you should get feedback on factors like voice or stance toward readers (Section 6 of *Sharing and Responding*). As always, "Movies of the Reader's Mind" (Section 7 of *Sharing and Responding*) tends to tell you the most.

If you write an argument of your own, "Skeleton Feedback and Descriptive Outline" (Section 10 of *Sharing and Responding*) will give you the best information on the reasoning itself. That's the process we've been using in this workshop.

You should try to give readers written texts of what you write—particularly for later drafts—because it's difficult for anyone to follow an argument or an analysis when they can't read it. It probably makes sense for them to give you feedback in written form too.

PROCESS JOURNAL AND
COVER LETTER QUESTIONS

- Do you find yourself more comfortable working with short, informal persuasive pieces or longer, more careful arguments? What was different for you about doing these two different pieces?
- If you analyzed one of your own pieces, what was hardest? How useful was this procedure for revision?
- When persuading or arguing (either orally or in writing), did you find yourself putting more emphasis on why your own view was better or on why the other views were wrong? How did this affect your writing for this workshop?

RUMINATIONS AND THEORY

Nonadversarial Argument
Reasoning and Grammar

Nonadversarial Argument

"Construct a thesis, state it forcefully, line up evidence to prove that your thesis is correct, prove that contrary opinions are wrong, conclude by restating your thesis." Is this the kind of directions you've received for writing an argument? Writing that is structured this way is often seen as the only valid kind of argument—at times, as the only valid kind of writing.

The model of persuasion and argument seems to be grounded in either/or, right/wrong, good/evil stances: "If I am right, you *have* to be wrong." Consider the result of these approaches: the reader who thinks differently has to define herself as wrong or stupid or bad before she can take your position seriously. This explains why most persuasive pieces and arguments are exercises in wasted energy and tend to become mere displays of ability to follow prescribed form. We'd like to push for a different conception of argument, a less aggressive, adversarial conception.

In truth, there may be a way in which writing by definition is monologic and authoritarian—after all, there's one voice speaking. And while you're reading what someone else has written, it has more power than you do because you can't answer it and argue with it and make it change its mind. This power can have two opposing results: either we can succumb and be submissive to what we're reading, not question it at all, or we can resist it—perhaps even overdo our resistance—because we resent our inability to express our opinion to the author. We can even have both of these reactions to the same piece. The more strongly the author presents opinions, the more likely we are to have these reactions. The question is: what effect then does the author's opinion have on us?

We would answer our own question by saying "very little." If that's the case, the writer has not accomplished much.

One way to encourage dialogue is to contextualize what you're arguing for. In Workshop 10 we spoke of the importance of contextualizing all research, of recognizing the limits within which all research functions and thus the limits to what one can conclude. This same strategy is important in argument too. Arguments which are absolute, "My point is true for all people in all situations at all times!" probably provoke the most resistance from readers. If you can set what you're arguing for in a context and acknowledge that what you believe is conditioned by certain circumstances and experiences and present those, you may provoke less resistance from a reader. A reader can enter into the dialogue by bringing up other circumstances and experiences.

Does this mean that you can't argue for something if you believe it's absolutely true: the existence of a supreme being, the necessity for preserving the natural environment, the value of loving others, and so forth? No, of course not. What it does mean, though, is that you're more likely to be genuinely listened to if you say something like "This is what I believe and this is why I believe it" rather than "I'm right, you're wrong, and this is why."

Another thing we're *not* saying here is that arguments of the traditional sort are always the wrong way to go. As one kind of argument, they're worth studying and mastering. What we *are* saying is that argument doesn't *always* have to be the aggressive sort which hits readers over the head forcefully. An argument for your point of view can be just as effective—perhaps even more effective—if you think of your reader as a partner in discussion and your aim as a desire for conversation which will result in both of you being better informed about your issue.

Argument can use its power to create a foundation from which both writer and reader can build knowledge. After all, knowledge is always the result of collaboration of some sort between people, even when those people are long dead and our contact with them is only through written words. The challenge is to write in such a way that a reader is neither passive nor resistant but encouraged to become part of a dialogue. You can show your awareness of opposing opinions, of opposing voices, without belittling them. Once you've set up a tone of dialogue, your reader is far more likely to listen to you. More and more we hear people resentful of being forced into either/or arguments, seeing them as a trap which leads to hopelessness. Consequently, they may just tune out.

All of us have a much better chance of being persuasive if we can present a train of thought which says, in effect, "I'm not asking you to give up your beliefs; you can think whatever you like." We might even go so far as to say, "I'll bet your beliefs or opinions make a lot of sense. Continue to think whatever you want. But let me show you some of my thinking that I'll bet you'll find useful and interesting. Don't worry about the fact that what I say seems to contradict what you think. We might both be right in some way that we can't yet understand." This approach invites dialogue.

Here's an example. Both of us, the authors of this textbook, think that multiple-choice tests not only are a poor way to test writing but may even be harmful. We could go into meetings with administrators and teachers in charge of testing programs and say something like "Multiple-choice tests of student writing are unsatisfactory because they don't ask students to produce language, they present a false picture of what it means to write, they emphasize form above ideas, they are not based on recent research findings," and so forth. But we've had more success getting people to listen to us when we go into these meetings and start the discussion by saying something like "We've been wrestling with the problem of how to test student writing for a long time" or "Like you, we're interested in finding the best way to test student writing, a way that gives us the information we need, is not too expensive, and satisfies teachers and administrators. Here are some ways other people have come up with that we can talk about."

Of course, if it's true that you want your opponent to listen to you, then you have to listen to him. While you're drafting an argument, you can create an opponent as we suggested in this workshop. Writing out his side of the issue will make you a better proponent of your position. Paradoxically, you have a greater chance of arguing successfully with others the more you can enter into *their* position. What you are trying to produce in readers is a glimmer of feeling that says, "Hey, this writer isn't crazy. I can really see why he feels that way." It can be scary for readers to enter into the skin of "the enemy" especially if they think that position is immoral, uninformed, or stupid. The scariness comes from the fear: "Well, if they are right, even a little bit right, then I must be wrong." But this isn't true. It often happens that two opinions or positions which *look* opposite—and which make people fight tooth and nail—can actually *both* be right in certain senses. In short, you can argue your position without having to argue that the other position is wrong.

To go back to our example. We often go into meetings of administrators who are talking about testing student writing and simply ask them what they are doing now and what they like and don't like about that. In a similar way, it's possible to start a good argument paper by simply describing the current situation you'd like to see changed. Often faults reveal themselves.

We know there will always be situations where a person has to argue for an absolute acceptance of her point of view and a complete refutation of every opposing opinion she can think of: a lawyer arguing against a death sentence for her client, for example. But even here we believe that the principles of nonadversarial argument are worth considering.

Reasoning and Grammar

To figure out what makes good argument is interestingly like the task of figuring out what makes good grammar. Indeed reasoning and grammar are deeply similar: grammar is a picture of the regularities in how people use *language;* reasoning is a picture of the regularities in how people use *thought.*

Take grammar. Though there are certain universals—certain regularities in how people use language whether they speak English or Chinese—for the most part grammar is a story of local peculiarities: different languages and different dialects are composed of different regularities. Grammar is largely an empirical business: there is nothing but "what native speakers do." That is because at its most basic level, grammar is what makes language possible. "Mistakes" are either momentary lapses or—what is more likely—not mistakes in grammar but mistakes in *usage.*

If we let grammar include matters of *usage* (such as whether you may split infinitives or begin sentences with "And" or "Hopefully"), grammar then becomes defined more narrowly: "what *prestige* native speakers *approve of* or call *appropriate for writing.*" At the level of usage, dictionaries may tempt you to think there are right answers, but dictionaries do nothing but record what natives (or prestige natives) do or approve of. Thus dictionaries continually change their minds as the years go by and as people change their habits. At any given moment (now, for instance), dictionaries disagree about the usage and even spelling of certain words.

But although there is no such thing as "correct grammar" built into the universe (or at least very little of it, and it won't help you choose between "who" or "whom"), if you want to get a good grade in most classes, get certain kinds of jobs, or persuade your readers, you have to get rid of what *your* audience will call "mistakes."

The same situation holds for logic or reasoning. Here too there seem to be a few universals. In *The Meno,* Plato stresses the universals, concluding that all humans seem to agree about the rules of geometry or mathematics. But most of our reasoning is *not* about geometry and mathematics, and it turns out that good reasoning in most realms (like good grammar at the level of usage) depends on what different groups of people *call* good reasoning—that is, upon conventions that are different in different cultures or disciplines. Recently a number of critics have posited differences between feminine and masculine ways of presenting points of view. To reason well is to learn the conventions of a particular community of writers within a particular area of knowledge or practical functioning.

Are we saying that grammar and reasoning are nothing but a set of random rules to memorize—like batting averages or the capitals of the states? No. There is a rational and orderly science of grammar that you can study and master. It's a lovely science—in a sense the science of the human mind. The same goes for reasoning. But fortunately we don't *have* to study and master the science of grammar to make our language strong (or to get rid of most of what others call "mistakes"). And so our point in this workshop is that we don't need to study the science of logic to get our reasoning strong (and get rid of our worst mistakes in thinking).

The reason why we can do well without studying and memorizing rules is that we've done so much talking, listening, discussing, and writing that we already have an enormous amount of *tacit* or *unconscious* knowledge of grammar and reasoning. Can we get good grammar and good reasoning just by putting pen to paper and writing? Don't we all wish! No. We can only benefit from all our tacit knowledge if we go about using it in the right way. In this workshop we suggest tools to *harness* our tacit knowledge of reasoning effectively—and, in doing so, to gain more control and conscious awareness of that tacit knowledge.

Here are steps to help you make the best use of your tacit knowledge of *grammar* in the process of writing.

1. Start off writing as naturally and comfortably as possible: *don't* think about grammar or about any minor matters of phrasing or spelling; think only about what you want to say. *Talk* onto the paper. In this way you are making the most use of your intuitive knowledge of grammar. The most tangled and "mistake-riddled" writing almost always results from slow and careful writing: You stop after every three or four words and worry about whether something's wrong—and then think about how to finish the sentence. Or you search a thesaurus for a different word or search the dictionary for a spelling. You lose track of the natural syntax in your head. If instead you can get yourself to *talk on paper* naturally and comfortably, you will have mostly clear and correct syntax to start with.

2. Next, by whatever revising process you find best, get your text to say *exactly* what you want it to say—but still without worrying about minor matters of phrasing, grammar, and spelling. Thinking about these things will just distract you from paying attention to what you are trying to *say*. And why fix up the grammar and spelling in a sentence you may well throw away or rewrite anyway?

3. Now turn your attention to phrasing, spelling, and grammar. Read your draft aloud slowly and carefully to yourself and see what improvements you can make and what mistakes you can eliminate. If you read it *aloud* to yourself—slowly and with expression—you will find even more ways to improve it.

4. Read your piece aloud to one or two listeners: for *their* help, yes; but also because their presence as audience will help you recognize more problems and think of more improvements.

5. Give your final, typed version to another person to copyedit. In Mini-

Workshop K we set out a structured method for getting this sort of help from others.

Thus we do *not* in this book summarize the rules of language or grammar or usage for you. You can easily find other books—handbooks—which do so. (Unfortunately, however, such handbooks tend to be wrong unless they are enormously long and complex. Any simple rule will have too many exceptions that depend on the context.) You will do a better job of strengthening your language and "fixing your writing" if you work in the more empirical (and more enjoyable) fashion we've just described. The strength of our approach comes from (1) using language unself-consciously in order to tap your tacit knowledge; (2) examining and revising in a self-conscious, systematic, and controlled frame of mind—what you've produced; and (3) collaborating with others.*

These same three steps can make your *reasoning* effective too: (1) write out your argument and its support by talking naturally and unself-consciously on paper; (2) examine and revise what you've written, in the self-conscious, systematic way we've outlined in this workshop; (3) get help from others. By going about writing an argument this way, you use both intuitive and systematic modes of thinking; exploiting them together leads to powerful argumentative writing.

---

*You will have a harder time at this task if you are not a native speaker or if you don't read a fair amount. But don't underestimate your ear: if you've heard a lot of radio and television, you've heard plenty of Standard English and developed a keen sense of the differences between levels of formality.

Readings

LETTER TO THE EDITOR*

To the Editor:

As a recent graduate of Columbia College myself, I was strongly tempted to dismiss "Batman and the Jewish Question" (Op-Ed, July 2) by Rebecca Roiphe and Daniel Cooper as the product of a pair of intellectually overheated, pretentiously affected and politically correct undergraduates straining to ferret out all the nonexistent sinister motives lurking deep within our decadent popular culture. Then I saw "Batman Returns" for myself. Although I acknowledge the pitfalls in reading an overintricate analysis into such things, I cannot in good conscience gainsay the Roiphe-Cooper observations. Please allow me to add a few of my own:

One of the Penguin's chief underlings—whose duties include driving the train on which the Penguin hopes to cart off Gotham City's first-born children—strongly resembles the stereotype of the haggling Jewish peddler, who holds nothing sacred save the making of a profitable deal. Certainly, Tim Burton's vision of the Penguin, with hooked nose, absurdly bloated body and plutocrat's attire, bears more than a passing resemblance to Nazi caricatures of manipulative Jewish financiers, down to the ghoulish, perverted lust for fair, fresh-faced gentile maidens.

Furthermore, Max Schreck, the putatively Jewish villain, complains that he suffers persecution merely for being an honest businessman—when he is a duplicitous manipulator, as anti-Semites assert Jews are. Schreck, of course, owns a major department store, through which he squeezes profit out of the innocent gentile community by selling them Christmas merchandise. He attempts to buy the crowd's loyalty at Christmas by throwing them a few free trinkets. Quite a creepy—and not particularly subtle—insinuation, given the number of department stores established by Jewish entrepreneurs.

Alone among the film's characters, Schreck uses Yiddish words ("schmo" for example) and speaks with an obvious caricature of a New York Jewish accent.

It amazes me that this vile motion picture could have been produced without anybody along the line noticing—or caring—about the gratuitous bigotry embedded in its script and characters. The most charitable explanation I can devise is that those responsible simply knew no better.

That my fellow Columbians noticed these shenanigans when professional film critics failed to do so is a resounding endorsement of a solid liberal arts

*See the Readings for Workshop 8 for another letter on this matter.

education. If nothing else, however, "Batman Returns" gives the lie to the shibboleth that Jews control the entertainment industry and use it to manipulate the American public.

—Nicholas Corwin, *New York Times,* July 20, 1992

AIMING A CANNON AT A MOSQUITO

Mona Charen

Tooling around town with a baby in a stroller gives one a new appreciation for the difficulties of the disabled. Poorly designed buildings, where the elevator takes you to the basement garage only to open upon a flight of stairs—even two or three steps can be impossible for a person in a wheelchair—are the most maddening. It's a small inconvenience for me. I can always take the baby in one arm and carry the stroller in the other. The wheelchair-bound are stuck.

No doubt some well-meaning Capitol Hill staffer had thoughts such as these when she got the idea for a new federal act protecting the "rights" of the disabled. The mental image was probably of a person in a wheelchair, asking only for a chance to work and contribute to society like everyone else.

As with so much liberal legislation, and it is liberal (remember that the next time President George Bush touts this as one of the accomplishments of his first term), this law is absurdly overbroad. It attempts to kill a mosquito with a cannon. And the cannon, aimed at American business, will undoubtedly hamper U.S. competitiveness.

The Americans with Disabilities Act is advertised as another in a long line of civil rights bills. But it's more than that. Most state governments already forbid discrimination against the handicapped. The ADA goes further, requiring businesses with 25 or more employees (and in two years, those with 15 or more will be included) to make "reasonable accommodations" for the disabled.

What that will mean—how "reasonable" will be interpreted by the courts— remains unknown. In some easy cases, "accommodation" will mean a simple device on a telephone to permit a handicapped person to use it, or an adjustment to a computer. But in other cases, it may mean having to rearrange work schedules, or hire an extra employee to help the disabled one.

Still, not many Americans would object to paying slightly higher prices for products if it means giving a chance to those who are handicapped. But physical handicaps afflict only 3.3 million Americans. This law is written to cover 43 million. How do they get that figure?

The good folks in Washington have thrown into the "disabled" category those who are morbidly obese ("in rare and limited circumstances" say the regulations), and those with mental and emotional problems.

It's the mental and emotional disorders part of the definition that really opens Pandora's box. For while mental disability is no less real than physical disability, it is far easier to fake.

Most unsettling of all, the law includes among the disabled those who are "in recovery" from drug or alcohol abuse. Not only is an employer forbidden to discriminate against those workers, but they may be forced to permit them to attend support groups or counselling during work hours. Employers may also—though this too remains to be seen—be required to cover their medical expenses.

The lesson of Paul Tsongas—that Democrats must learn to be pro-business if they are truly pro-jobs—remains unabsorbed. Mandating ramps and hearing aids is one thing; calling every alcoholic disabled is quite another.

ANALYSIS OF MY ARGUMENT IN "SHORT LETTERS"

Janine Ramaz

The main claim of my essay "Short Letters" [printed in the "Readings" for Workshop 8] is that the letter about mothers going on space flights is the most effective one. The essay supports my claim with a number of reasons and supporting evidence.

The first reason I give is that a letter directed to the "Letters" column of a newspaper must state its point quickly and briefly. I observe that all three of the letters do this, but I don't really support this by quoting from the letters. Furthermore, since all of the letters are brief and quick about this, this reason does not give particular support to my preference for a particular letter. If I were going to revise my piece I'd have to think about whether this idea should come at the beginning of my essay or more towards the end.

My next reasons are really reasons why the other two letters I looked at are not as effective as the one I preferred. I don't prefer the letter about advertising cigarettes because it is too long. The support for this reason is that ideas are repeated, but I don't really say what the repeated idea is. I also criticize this letter because I hear a whiny voice in it. I'm of course making an assumption that people don't like whiny voices, but I think that's a pretty good assumption.

I criticize the third of these three letters because I don't think the author follows through on his argument. My support for this is that he doesn't talk at all about banning all guns. My second support for the weakness of this letter is that he brings in a side issue: race. This really weakens his argument. But perhaps I was too quick to write off this letter because I'm not a gun supporter. The author may really be quite wise not to bring up larger issues of gun use. And he is also smart in bringing in the issue of race because that may well appeal to a whole different audience than the gun argument.

The other reason I give for stating which letter is best relates to its language. The first support for this is that there are no extra words. The second support is that the language is plain and simple: I quote something as evidence of this. I'm assuming that people like plain simple language, but perhaps I should be careful about that assumption. It's possible that some readers might see plain, simple language as evidence of less education and knowledge.

And my final reason is that the most effective letter is the one with the broadest audience appeal. I support this by talking about the possible audiences or non-audiences of the other two letters. But if I revised this essay, I think I'd want to reconsider this reason. After all, there's no particular reason why these letters should appeal to a broad audience. Letter writers may just want to appeal to particular audiences.

My essay is not adversarial at all. The main point doesn't even come until over half way through. And I don't really argue strongly against the other two letters. In fact, I start by mentioning a good point about both of them. And I often qualify my statements by words like "I think" and "To me," so I'm not making absolute statements. I'm not an adversarial person so if I revised this, I don't think I would change my approach very much—though perhaps I ought to think about the effects of phrases like "I think."

The weakest part of my essay is its lack of real audience. This is a paper I wrote for the teacher; I'm not sure why anyone else would think it was interesting. The only possible place where I seem to appeal to a broader audience is in the last paragraph. I do believe that more people care about children losing their parents than about feminist issues or gun support or non-support.

The audience issue would be most important if I revised this. If I rewrote it, I think I'd want to make it an essay which gives advice about how to write an appealing letter to the editor of a newspaper. I'd use these three letters as examples of what to do and what not to do. I think this would give the paper more focus and make it more interesting to readers besides my teacher.

TOO MUCH FOR TOO LITTLE

A Student

When was the last time you sat down and really enjoyed dinner, let alone any other meal in the cafeteria? Can't remember, can you? Neither can I. Don't you think you deserve better service and a higher grade of food? Most students believe they deserve better treatment, so why isn't anything being done? Most students on campus are paying large amounts of money for room and board and also tuition. And a large amount of this money goes towards each student's meal plan during each semester. There's an old saying, "You get what you pay for," but unfortunately we are not.

Did you ever realize how a good meal and quality service affect your attitude and motivation for the day. Sometimes it's the only thing people look forward to. But as of lately, most people are left aggravated and hungry after making a trip to the cafeteria. The management on campus is in disarray at the moment. Their poor decision making and actions cause a great deal of hold-ups and confusion. If waiting on a long line that moves once every ten minutes isn't bad enough, try finding a seat.

Let's get to the heart of the matter, the food. Lately the quality of the food has gone from mediocre to downright pathetic. Management should put a little variety in their choice of food. They should give students a few alternate choices. Part of the time dinner is cold and sometimes unidentifiable. To cover up they say it's Chinese food. But once you taste it you realize you are eating last week's leftovers. So you say to yourself, "Maybe I'll have a hamburger, they can't mess that up." Wrong again. The burgers are pretty close to hockey pucks, and there are no french fries. The two usually go together hand in hand, burger and fries. And to finish off dinner maybe one would like some dessert, a piece of cake let's say. Well let's just say when the fork started to bend I kind of figured this cake is not for me.

So when is it all going to change? The school says they improved their food program from the previous year. Well I guess I should consider myself lucky. If I take into consideration how the food is now, I can merely assess that last year the food was really terrible or that they just have not made much progress at all. Changes won't come over night, and they may not come at all. It's up to the students to make the choice and to decide what's right. I mean if you like the way the food is now, then by all means enjoy yourself. But I would prefer some better quality food. I'm not asking for shrimp and lobster, even though I wouldn't mind. But a little more efficiency in the kitchen may save a lot of aggravation.

Cover Letter

When picking a persuasive topic to write about, it is to the author's advantage to touch on a subject in which the majority of the readers are familiar with. The aim of the paper was to stir up some feelings and opinions on the student food plan on campus. I went about writing the paper through my own personal experiences in the cafeteria. Receiving no help from anyone, the paper may tend to be one sided.

GAS ANALGESIA

From a brochure in the offices of Jack H. Weinstein and
Ira H. Abel, 1811 Avenue U, Brooklyn, N.Y.

Fear of dentistry goes back many years to the days when anaesthesia was unknown, and the procedures involved in treating teeth were painful. Today, we have excellent anaesthetics that can successfully eliminate practically all pain involved in dentistry. Novocaine can do this very easily. However, novocaine cannot eliminate the nervousness, the tension and the apprehension of most people. Then too, most people fear the injection of the needle.

Today, people need not stay away from dentists for any reason whatsoever because we have, in addition *ANALGESIA*.

What is Analgesia?

It is a mild gas with a pleasant sweet odor. We call it *SWEET AIR,* which is inhaled thru the nose. It is pleasant and easy to take for both children and adults.

What Does *Sweet Air* Do for the Dental Patient?

1. It relaxes.
2. It eliminates fear, nervousness and tension.
3. It eliminates most of the pain involved in dentistry, and the rest is so dulled that you do not mind it.
4. It makes you feel WARM and SAFE.
5. It is similar to a light pleasant intoxication.
6. It works three ways, in that you find you are not nervous or fearful BE-FORE, DURING or AFTER your dental visit.
7. If an injection is needed, you will find you don't mind it at all with *analgesia.* It is like a good friend that is with you at all times, close at hand, ready to help you, right at the moment you need him.

There are no after effects, and you can get right out of the dental chair and go about your business immediately. It is a very safe procedure.

WITH ALL DELIBERATE SPEED: WHAT'S SO BAD ABOUT WRITING FAST?

William F. Buckley Jr.

If, during spring term at Yale University in 1949 you wandered diagonally across the campus noticing here and there an undergraduate with impacted sleeplessness under his eyes and coarse yellow touches of fear on his cheeks, you were looking at members of a masochistic set who had enrolled in a course called Daily Themes. No Carthusian novitiate embarked on a bout of mortification of the flesh suffered more than the students of Daily Themes, whose single assignment, in addition to attending two lectures per week, was to write a 500-to-600-word piece of descriptive prose every day, and to submit it before midnight (into a large box outside a classroom). Sundays were the only exception (this was before the Warren Court outlawed Sunday).

For anyone graduated from Daily Themes who went on to write, in journalism or in fiction or wherever, the notion that a burden of 500 words per day is the stuff of nightmares is laughable. But caution: 500 words a day is what Graham Greene writes, and Nabokov wrote 180 words per day, devoting to their composition (he told me) four or five hours. But at that rate, Graham Greene and Nabokov couldn't qualify for a job as reporters on The New York Times. Theirs is high-quality stuff, to speak lightly of great writing. But Georges Simenon is also considered a great writer, at least by those who elected him to the French Academy, and he writes books in a week or so. Dr. Johnson wrote "Rasselas," his philosophical romance, in nine days. And Trollope . . . we'll save Trollope.

□ □ □ □ □

I am fired up on the subject because, to use a familiar formulation, they have been kicking me around a lot; it has got out that I write fast, which is qualifiedly true. In this august journal, on Jan. 5, Morton Kondracke of Newsweek took it all the way: "He [me—W.F.B.] reportedly knocks out his column in 20 minutes flat—three times a week for 260 newspapers. That is too little time for serious contemplation of difficult subjects."

Now that is a declaration of war, and I respond massively.

To begin with: it is axiomatic, in cognitive science, that there is no necessary correlation between profundity of thought and length of time spent on thought. J.F.K. is reported to have spent 15 hours per day for six days before deciding exactly how to respond to the missile crisis, but it can still be argued that his initial impulse on being informed that the Soviet Union had deployed nuclear missiles in Cuba (bomb the hell out of them?) might have been the strategically sounder course. This is not an argument against deliberation, merely against the suggestion that to think longer (endlessly?) about a subject is necessarily to probe it more fruitfully.

Mr. Kondracke, for reasons that would require more than 20 minutes to fathom, refers to composing columns in 20 minutes "flat." Does he mean to suggest that I have a stopwatch which rings on the 20th minute? Or did he perhaps mean to say that I have been known to write a column in 20 minutes? Very different. He then goes on, in quite another connection, to cite "one of the best columns" in my new book—without thinking to ask: How long did it take him to write that particular column?

The chronological criterion, you see, is without validity. Every few years, I bring out a collection of previously published work, and this of course requires me to reread everything I have done in order to make that season's selections. It transpires that it is impossible to distinguish a column written very quickly from a column written very slowly. Perhaps that is because none is written very slowly. A column that requires two hours to write is one which was interrupted by phone calls or the need to check a fact. I write fast—but not, I'd maintain, remarkably fast. If Mr. Kondracke thinks it intellectually risky to write 750 words in 20 minutes, what must he think about people who speak 750 words in five minutes, as he often does on television?

The subject comes up now so regularly in reviews of my work that I did a little methodical research on my upcoming novel. I began my writing (in

Switzerland, removed from routine interruption) at about 5 P.M., and wrote usually for two hours. I did that for 45 working days (the stretch was interrupted by a week in the United States, catching up on editorial and television obligations). I then devoted the first 10 days in July to revising the manuscript. On these days I worked on the manuscript an average of six hours per day, including retyping. We have now a grand total: 90 plus 60, or 150 hours. My novels are about 70,000 words, so that averaged out to roughly 500 words per hour.

Anthony Trollope rose at 5 every morning, drank his tea, performed his toilette and looked at the work done the preceding day. He would then begin to write at 6. He set himself the task of writing 250 words every 15 minutes for three and one-half hours. Indeed it is somewhere recorded that if he had not, at the end of 15 minutes, written the required 250 words he would simply "speed up" the next quarter-hour, because he was most emphatic in his insistence on his personally imposed daily quota: 3,500 words.

Now the advantages Trollope enjoys over me are enumerable and nonenumerable. I write only about the former, and oddly enough they are negative advantages. He needed to write by hand, having no alternative. I use a word processor. Before beginning this article, I tested my speed on this instrument and discovered that I type more slowly than I had imagined. Still, it comes out at 80 words per minute. So that if Trollope had had a Kaypro or an I.B.M., he'd have written, in three and one-half hours at my typing speed, not 3,500 words but 16,800 words per day.

Ah, you say, but could anyone think that fast? The answer is, sure people can think that fast. How did you suppose extemporaneous speeches get made? Erle Stanley Gardner dictated his detective novels nonstop to a series of secretaries, having previously pasted about in his studio 3-by-5 cards reminding him at exactly what hour the dog barked, the telephone rang, the murderer coughed. He knew where he was going, the plot was framed in his mind, and it became now only an act of extrusion. Margaret Coit wrote in her biography of John C. Calhoun that his memorable speeches were composed not in his study but while he was outdoors, plowing the fields on his plantation. He would return then to his study and write out what he had framed in his mind. His writing was an act of transcription. I own the holograph of Albert Jay Nock's marvelous book on Jefferson, and there are fewer corrections on an average page than I write into a typical column. Clearly Nock knew exactly what he wished to say and how to say it; prodigious rewriting was, accordingly, unnecessary.

Having said this, I acknowledge that I do not know exactly what I am going to say, or exactly how I am going to say it. And in my novels, I can say flatly, as Mr. Kondracke would have me say it, that I really do not have any idea where they are going—which ought not to surprise anyone familiar with the nonstop exigencies of soap opera writing or of comic strip writing or, for that matter, of regular Sunday sermons. It is not necessary to know how your protagonist will get out of a jam into which you put him. It requires only that you have confidence that you will be able to get him out of that jam. When you begin to write a column on, let us say, the reaction of Western Europe to

President Reagan's call for a boycott of Libya it is not necessary that you should know *exactly* how you will say what you will end up saying. You are, while writing, drawing on huge reserves: of opinion, prejudice, priorities, presumptions, data, ironies, drama, histrionics. And these reserves you enhance during practically the entire course of the day, and it doesn't matter all that much if a particular hour is not devoted to considering problems of foreign policy. You can spend an hour playing the piano and develop your capacity to think, even to create; and certainly you can grasp more keenly, while doing so, your feel for priorities.

The matter of music flushes out an interesting point: Why is it that critics who find it arresting that a column can be written in 20 minutes, a book in 150 hours, do not appear to find it remarkable that a typical graduate of Juilliard can memorize a prelude and fugue from "The Well-Tempered Clavier" in an hour or two? It would take me six months to memorize one of those *numeros*. And mind, we're not talking here about the "Guinness Book of World Records" types. Isaac Asimov belongs in "Guinness," and perhaps Erle Stanley Gardner, but surely not an author who averages a mere 500 words per hour, or who occasionally writes a column at one-third his typing speed.

There are phenomenal memories in the world. Claudio Arrau is said to hold in his memory music for 40 recitals, two and a half hours each. *That* is phenomenal. Ralph Kirkpatrick, the late harpsichordist, actually told me that he had not played the "Goldberg" Variations for 20 years before playing it to a full house in New Haven in the spring of 1950. *That* is phenomenal. Winston Churchill is said to have memorized all of "Paradise Lost" in a week, and throughout his life he is reported to have been able to memorize his speeches after a couple of readings. (I have a speech I have delivered 50 times and could not recite one paragraph of it by heart.)

So cut it out, Kondracke. I am, I fully grant, a phenomenon, but not because of any speed in composition. I asked myself the other day, Who else, on so many issues, has been so right so much of the time? I couldn't think of anyone. And I devoted to the exercise 20 minutes. Flat.

WORKSHOP
13

RESEARCH

Research results from the desire to know something. What that "something" is determines the kind of research the researcher undertakes. Sometimes research questions lead you to seek information mainly from print sources: books, periodicals, and newspapers. At other times, research questions mainly lead you to observe and interview. Quite often, researchers need data and information from a variety of sources. In this workshop, our goal is to get you to undertake several kinds of research. We hope you'll begin to believe as we do that personal research and library research are equally valid; which to use depends on what you want to know.

Your main assignment for this workshop will be:

1. To develop a research topic out of a previous piece of writing you've done for this class.*
2. To design a research plan that calls for both personal research (interviewing and observing) and library or print research.
3. And then to write a research paper that combines this information. Your final paper will need to include appropriate documentation.

We're trying to get away from the old "research paper mentality" that makes you say, "Let's see, this is a research paper. Therefore, none of my own thinking belongs here. My job is to find a topic that lets me quote and summarize from the assigned number of books and articles. This is library work: filling out cards, making outlines, pasting it all together, and getting footnotes right." We're asking for a paper that grows out of your own thinking but which joins your thinking, not only to the thinking of others but also to what you can learn from observation and interviewing. In a sense your job is to create and carry forward a conversation: you'll bring the thinking you've already done together with the thinking and observations of others and get all this material talking together.

 DECIDING ON A TOPIC

Mainly, in the assignments we've given you so far, we've asked you to write material out of your own head with input from your teacher and classmates in your writing class and in other classes. We think it highly likely that you found—while writing on some of these topics—that you wished you knew more about them. This is your chance to revise an earlier paper on the basis of research: interviewing, observing, reading.

Set aside some time for looking back over all the pieces you've done for this writing course. (We hope that, in itself, will prove to be valuable and interesting.) As you read, jot down a list of possibilities for research. Perhaps you wrote your narrative about the neighborhood, town, or city where you grew up. Maybe you wrote a description of a frightening dream. We've read

---

We are grateful to Charles Moran, at the University of Massachusetts at Amherst, from whom we first learned of this sensible approach to library research.

quite a few persuasive and argumentative papers on the subjects of college food plans, campus security, and the pros and cons of ungraded courses. And we've read many, many analyses of newspaper editorials, advertisements, and all varieties of literature: poems, plays, novels, and so forth. All of these subjects can be developed into research topics.

To arrive at a topic, try setting up a question for yourself. For example, the student who wrote the argument paper on the college food plan (see readings for Workshop 12) might ask: "What kinds of food plans are provided by college campuses, and what are the benefits and problems of each?" A student who analyzed the Charon piece on rights of the disabled (see readings for Workshop 12) might ask: "What services for the disabled are available on my campus, and how much use is made of them?" The student who wrote the narrative on the ice-cream man (see readings for Workshop 2) might ask: "What goes into becoming an ice-cream vendor and what is the history of this tradition?" A student who interviewed an engineer for Workshop 6 might ask: "How much writing do various kinds of engineers do, and how prepared are they to do it?"

First Round of Freewriting

Once you've selected a topic and framed a question for your research to answer, reread what you've already said about the topic and do some focused freewriting or clustering about what more you'd like to know. It's quite likely that you'll have more than one topic that seems promising and interesting to you. If so, do some more freewriting or clustering on all of them as a way to discover which presents the greatest complexity and richness for you. If you still can't decide, share this freewriting with others in and outside the class. Their responses will help you decide on your final topic.

When you settle on your final research question, do more freewriting. Push yourself as much as you can to get down on paper what you already know and what your opinions on the subject are. Don't worry about whether what you write is "right" or not. The point is to make clear to yourself exactly where you're starting from. You may be surprised to discover that you actually know more than you think you do and have more opinions about your subject than you're aware of—or, not so positively, you may find out that you have strong opinions and nothing to back them up.

For instance, our meal-plan writer surely knows college regulations: the costs of various plans, the restrictions and privileges of each, his own experience with the food and the experiences of his friends, his observations of others in the cafeterias, and so forth. He probably also knows something about changes in the plan, both those which have already occurred and others being discussed by students and administrators. But he may discover that although he thinks the food and the service are awful, when he tries to find specific examples of that, he comes up short.

As you do this freewriting, interject questions as they come up: "Have the prices gone up recently? How much?" "What kinds of plans do other schools have?" "What provisions are made for those on special diets?" "Is there a profit? Who gets it?" "What is it students are really complaining about?" Later you can reread and highlight or underline these questions.

 ## DESIGNING A RESEARCH PLAN

For the purposes of this workshop, we're going to ask you to design a research plan which requires you to do both kinds of research: library and personal. This may seem arbitrary to you (in fact, it is), but we want you to get some sense of the full range of research strategies and the ways these strategies complement one another. And perhaps it's not as arbitrary as it might seem at first since most subjects can probably be profitably researched in both ways.

To get started on a plan, make a list of questions you've thought up, starting with your major research question.* If you have a chance to share your freewriting and your list, others will probably come up with additional questions. Decide which can best be answered by library research and which by observation and interview. Since we're asking you to do both sorts of research, make sure you have questions in both categories. Again, your classmates can help here.

Following through on one of our examples, the student who wrote about the ice-cream man might list the following questions:

For interviewing ice-cream vendors:

1. How does your business work? Are you paid by the hour, by the week, by commission?
2. What products are the most popular? bring in the most profit?
3. Do you stock different products for different neighborhoods?
4. How can you be sure your ice cream is good?

For interviewing people who buy from ice-cream vendors:

1. What's particularly good about what you're buying?
2. Do you ever worry about whether ice cream is good for you?
3. How do you feel about the prices? How do they compare with the prices and quality at stores like Carvel and Baskin-Robbins?

For observing:

1. Who buys ice cream from vendors?
2. Are people who buy ice cream mostly overweight?
3. Where do people eat the ice cream they buy?
4. Are most people who buy the ice cream in a group? or do they come alone?

---

*Notice how William Zinsser does this in the excerpt in the "Readings" at the end of this workshop. ("Surely mathematics was a world of numbers. Could it also be penetrated with words?" And "Could a lifelong science boob follow Einstein's train of thought?" And "How does someone write chemistry?")

5. How much time do people spend deciding what they want? Can I draw any conclusions about who's decisive and indecisive?
6. Who buys more ice cream from vendors: males or females? old or young? particular ethnic groups?

For the library:

1. Where did the name "Good Humor" come from?
2. Who are the people that drive these trucks? What statistics or case studies are available about them?
3. When did this business start? Who started it? Could I sketch in a history of it?

Once you have this bare-bones list of questions, you'll profit from talking them over with others. Get them to help you devise more questions and refine those you already have. And most important, get them to help you with questions for interviewing and observing. Then you're ready to decide more specifically how to go about your research: what to do first, next, and last.

For example, the student who wanted to find out more about the writing engineers do might go to the library and look for research studies specifically about this, or for more general studies which look closely at what different kinds of engineers actually do on their jobs. She could then design interview questions which seek to validate or extend this research. She might want to design a questionnaire for engineering undergraduates to see how aware they are of the place of writing in their future careers. Or she could reverse these tasks and observe and interview first, perhaps get permission to sit in several engineering classes and see what kinds of writing occur there—or even sit in an engineering office and observe. On the basis of these observations, she could design a questionnaire soliciting information about how students and professionals view the writing they're doing. She could then go to the library and see whether what she has observed and found out is substantiated by other research.

All topics are not alike; some may require that you do a particular kind of research first. The main thing in this workshop is for you to learn to have comfortable traffic back and forth between your own thinking and observing and the thinking and information that others have published. In most workshops we emphasize collaboration with fellow students. Here we want you to understand that you can also collaborate with people you know only through their published works or through interviewing them. What you'll probably realize as you work through this assignment is that you'll need to move back and forth between doing personal research and reading.

Before you actually begin to do whatever research you've laid out for yourself, we suggest that you write a quick version of some of the things you suspect your research will uncover. This may seem odd to you, but it often makes your research more exciting if you've already got some possible conclusions in mind. This quick version can be very sketchy. Just fantasize that you're someone who already knows all there is to know about your topic.

A note of caution: Students often think that research papers have to prove something. But (one of the lessons we stressed in Workshop 8) we can seldom prove things: all we can do is get people to listen. Except in rare cases, you're not going to be able to get a final answer to whatever question you pose for yourself. The best you can do is gather data which give you insight into a possible answer, one which can be valid within the limits you set for yourself. You can't come to any conclusions about what American college students think about campus food. But you can come to some conclusions about what undergraduates (or perhaps just freshmen or perhaps just male freshmen) on your particular campus think about campus food in particular cafeterias right now. You set up the limits, the context, in which you are doing your research. When you report it, you then let your readers know what that context is.

You can't claim anything beyond what your research shows, but that doesn't mean you can't make suggestions or hypothesize about larger issues. It just means you have to acknowledge what your data and information apply to and what they don't. Nor does it mean that your research isn't useful; we suspect that this sort of particularized research would be more interesting to the administrators at your school in charge of food services than more generalized research that might not apply so directly to the decisions they have to make.

Collaborative Option

Most researchers, aware of the limitations we wrote about in the last paragraph, know they need to pool their work in order to begin to think about definitive answers. You and another student or even your whole group may decide to focus on one topic, which you can research together. You can then integrate what you've done and turn this workshop into a collaborative writing task. This sort of project will give you a feel for the kinds of collaborative work so prevalent in the scientific and business world today.

If you decide to make this into a major collaborative project, you may want to go back and read over the sections on collaborative writing in Workshop 3.

 ## INTERVIEWING AND OBSERVING

Observing and interviewing are skills; you'll want to make sure you're doing them as well as possible. Before you begin your research-through-observing, map out where to observe and what sorts of activities to look for. The questions you draw up to further your research will be mainly questions you'll be addressing to yourself while you're observing. After a practice run, you may need to alter those questions. Most researchers build a practice run directly into their research plans, knowing that they can't always decide what to look for until they've started looking.

If you're going to design a questionnaire, make sure you try it out on friends or classmates first to uncover whatever glitches it may have. Researchers in the social sciences almost always do this. When you plan your interviewing, it's important to prepare a set list of questions if you're going to draw valid conclusions. You can do these activities in tandem also: first ask your informants to respond to a written questionnaire and then follow that up

I decided to write my essay as an informative piece on AIDS, because I feel that the AIDS crisis is a very serious issue that has to be exhausted until everyone begins to care and take precautions. The "Magic" Johnson tragedy really shocked me and instilled a fear in me that made me want to find out more about AIDS, and maybe allow others to learn from my essay. My main goal of this essay is education; to educate myself and others about AIDS.

I took the time to thoroughly read pamphlets and magazines on AIDS. Once I was knowledgeable about the subject I then conducted surveys on some Stony Brook students. I asked them one question; "how is AIDS transmitted?" Only the least knowledgeable (ignorant) students' responses were placed in my essay.

Student

by interviewing a random sample of those who responded. This is also an established research practice; it's done by the U.S. Census Bureau, for example. Also, before you start on your interviews, you may want to look back at some of the advice we gave in Workshop 6.

Your subject may be quite different from the ones we've been using as examples. We cannot include all possibilities here. Strategies for research are as varied as the questions which can be asked. But you should be able to lay out a plan of action for yourself—with the help of your teacher and your classmates. The important thing is to keep your task manageable, to make it into something you can handle within the time you have. Your teacher will let you know how much time that is.

 ## USING THE LIBRARY

If you're not familiar with your campus library, you'll want to set aside some time to become comfortable finding your way around it. Check to see whether there's a handout or some other printed introduction available. Many campus libraries set up group tours for students unacquainted with the facility. Sometimes writing teachers or teachers of other introductory courses set aside class time for a visit to the library.

Obviously you cannot "master" a college library on the basis of this one task, but the trick is not to feel intimidated. Few people who use libraries *ever* master them. Realize that it's legitimate to ask librarians for help; don't be afraid to ask "dumb" questions. Most librarians are happy to help as long as you treat your own questions as occasions for learning—not just as requests for them to do the work for you. Also, libraries are ideal places for wandering and browsing; people who like libraries let themselves pause and glance at books or documents that they are passing—read a few titles, pick up a book, look at the table of contents, and read a page. Libraries are good for serendipitous finds. Don't give in to the feeling that many people have: "I don't belong here if I don't know where to find what I want."

Here are some of the most promising places to look for information in a library:

- General encyclopedias (e.g., *Encyclopedia Americana* or *Encyclopaedia Britannica*).
- Specialized encyclopedias (e.g., *McGraw-Hill Encyclopedia of Science and Technology, International Encyclopedia of Higher Education,* or *The New Grove Dictionary of Music and Musicians*). There are specialized encyclopedias in many areas. Ask the librarian about your interest.
- Almanacs (e.g., *Universal Almanac* or *Facts on File*).
- Biographical dictionaries (e.g., *Dictionary of American Biography* or *International Who's Who*).
- General periodical indexes to short articles (e.g., *Readers' Guide to Periodical Literature* or *Book Review Digest*).
- Specialized periodical indexes (e.g., *Education Index* or *United States Government Publications*). There are many such specialized indexes.
- Abstracts. An abstract is a summary of a scholarly work. Reference rooms in libraries have volumes in various subject areas which include abstracts of articles that appear elsewhere, usually in periodicals. For example, there is a series of volumes titled *Psychological Abstracts*. Using this series saves you time because you can usually tell from the abstract whether a particular article is relevant to your research. You don't even have to spend time finding the article itself. Abstracts are also sometimes included at the beginnings of articles in certain journals and essay collections. These too can save you time by pinpointing which articles would help your research and which wouldn't.
- The subject index in the card catalog. Many libraries have replaced or are replacing card catalogs with computer catalogs. They're almost always quite easy to use; undoubtedly you'll find printed instructions available. If not, ask for help from a librarian. Computer catalogs cut research time immensely.
- On-line searches. Many libraries are now equipped with special computer programs which make it possible for researchers to probe an immense store of material. Generally, this is done by isolating and labeling three aspects of your project and feeding these labels into a computer. The computer then lists for you sources in which all three of these aspects come together. Usually the computer will print out possible sources for you. You will want to check your library to see if it has this capability and how you can go about using it.

Our list of reference sources is, of course, only illustrative. There are far too many to list here. (A full writing handbook or a textbook devoted to research papers will give more.) To see what's available—and you can often find a reference book that is just what you need—consult a guide like Eugene P. Sheehy's *A Guide to Reference Books* or ask the help of a librarian. The value of reference books is that they give you an overview of your topic and a range of books and articles you can track down.

The essential skill for doing library research is to learn a *different relationship with the printed word*. We tend to feel we have to *read* articles and books; but in research you need to learn to *glance, browse,* and *leaf* through print. You have learned the main thing if you can tell in a few seconds from a title or an abstract whether something is worth tracking down, then tell in a minute or two whether an article is worth reading, and in two or three minutes whether a book is worth spending an hour trying to "mine" (not necessarily read). To do this makes you feel insecure at first, but give yourself permission to keep on until you feel more comfortable with the process. Instead of feeling intimidated by the *weight* or *mass* of what might seem like everything that's ever been written, try to change gears and think of it as a vast collection of meeting rooms. In each room people are talking about a topic. Imagine that you have an invitation to poke your head into as many rooms as you want just for a moment or two: no one will be disturbed by your coming in for a few moments or by your leaving in the middle of the discussion. Just be sure to jot down a few notes about the conversation you've heard in each room after you leave it.

Of course you have to do some *careful* reading too. Think of it this way: you don't have much time for this research assignment, so you'll want to end up having browsed and dipped into a number of books and articles and having found 50 to 100 pages worth reading carefully for the light they throw on your topic. The main task is to *find* the best 50 to 100 pages to read carefully—not to waste your time reading the *wrong* 50 to 100 pages—though inevitably you will do some reading you won't use. This procedure should make you more skilled and comfortable when you have something you want to investigate further. Our goal is for you to feel that from now on you can wade in and make use of a library whenever you have something that merits the search— whether a school assignment or something you need to know in your life.

Remember too that you cannot say *everything* about any topic. You always need to limit what you say in some way. Your research is always more convincing and valid to the degree that you realize—and you show your reader that you realize—that you are not claiming to have read everything on the subject. This means that you can feel fine about acknowledging what you *haven't* done (instead of trying to hide it or be defensive about it). One of the most interesting parts of a research paper can be a section that talks about questions or material you *would* pursue if you were able to carry on with more research—or what you suggest for others who might want to carry the question further. Good researchers almost always do this.

As you read the 50 to 100 pages you've identified as best dealing with your topic in some central way (they probably won't be all in one book or one article), keep a dialectical notebook as we describe in Mini-Workshop B.

 EXPLORATORY DRAFT

Once you've done whatever tasks you set for yourself for the first segment of your research (either observing/interviewing or library study), you're ready to write an exploratory draft. Before beginning though, we recommend that you lay out all the notes and writing you've done so far and read through everything. After this perusal do some freewriting to record what you've learned and how you react to seeing all the material. Think particularly about whether you've discovered any patterns or recurrent themes in your writing and notes. Think about what parts of your research have been the most helpful.

You may discover at this point that you're not so interested in your original question any more, but in some other question which has arisen as you worked on this project. If this were a rigid assignment, you'd have to continue with your original questions, but we're not being rigid here. If you have come up with a more interesting question or discovered something more thought-provoking than what you started out to discover, we hope you'll change your project to follow up on it. (And we suggest that if in other classes you come up with something slightly different from the assignment, you ask your teacher whether you can adjust the assignment to what you've discovered. The worst she can say is "no." Many teachers will say "yes.")

What you need to do then before you start this draft is to write out clearly for yourself what you have discovered so far. This will help you decide what you want or need to know more about. You'll probably be able to include some of this writing in your paper. As you write this draft or after you've finished it, jot down questions for yourself to use as the basis of your next round of research, which may include a return to what you've already done to refine it or a move to the other form of research—either in or out of the library.

One of the fallacies about research is that researchers always use everything they find and all research notes they write up. This is simply not true. Remember that research is finding out about something. If you knew what that was going to be at the outset, you wouldn't need to do that research. But since you don't know, you'll read lots and write lots that won't be relevant at all to your finished research. Researchers almost always throw away more than they use. This doesn't mean that what they threw away was useless.

 MOVING TOWARD A FINAL DRAFT

Whenever you decide you have done as much research as you need to do, you are ready to write a full draft of your paper. Before beginning, you'll benefit from laying out the writing you've done so far and looking through it again. You may discover—perhaps for a second time—that you're not so interested in your original question any more. Your data may point to something far more intriguing to you. That will probably be fine with your teacher, but you should check with him.

Because the research process gives you lots of notes and rough writing, you may lose direction or perspective. Thus, you may want to make an outline before you start your full draft. Or you may decide instead to make an outline *after* you've written your draft. This can also work well. You could do both. Just don't agonize so long over your outline that you have too little time and energy to write the paper itself. You don't need to spend a lot of time on an outline. It can be as simple as this:

I'll start by stating why I was interested in my subject and what my original thinking was, move to how I went about doing the research, lay out some of what I found, and end with my conclusions.

Or you may want something as detailed as this:

1. Statement of question
2. Statement of methods of research and questions asked
3. Recounting of observations
   a. Engineers
   b. Classrooms
4. Recounting of interviews
   a. Engineers
   b. Undergraduates
5. Recounting of information gleaned from books and magazines
6. Reflections on if and in what ways the interviews, observations, and printed sources confirm one another
   a. Similarities
   b. Differences
7. Conclusions
8. Possible explanations of conclusions
9. What I learned and what it means to me
10. What I'd still like to know

An important thing to remember about outlines—whether generalized or specific—is that they're only outlines: you need not follow them like a robot. As you begin to write, you may discover some better structure. That may cause you to go back and revise your outline, although you needn't do this if you feel that the structure you're working with is satisfactory.

You can get help from others at this stage. Read or describe your bits of information and data to them and ask them for suggestions about what they see as central and organizing. There are no "right answers" as to how a paper should be organized; it's a question of what works best for readers.* You may want to try out two or three organizations.

A little aside: One way to structure your final paper is to present the story of your search. Tell how you started—including false starts—your original writing and thinking, early hypotheses, what was going on in your head as you worked through the series of steps we've led you through, the order in which you discovered things, what you did, partial conclusions you drew, and what you finally concluded. In other words, your paper could end up being a mixture of process writing and the results of that process. But in order to do this, you'll need to do process writing throughout. So we suggest that at the

---

*There are some important exceptions here: if you write a research paper for a particular discipline such as chemistry or sociology, there are some formats and customs for how it should be put together—just as there is a standard form for scientific articles in certain fields. But we assume that you will not be writing that kind of paper now.

The paper I recently sent off to the journal represents the most demanding and most satisfying work of my writing life so far. . . .

The project began two years ago, when for the sake of my own sanity I decided to focus on an interdisciplinary project—the interface of ecology and philosophy. I had been drowning in philosophy, condemned to be free. I had no moorings or orientation within philosophy, so I turned to my own experience and concerns to give me a foothold in reality. That allowed me the freedom to explore diverse aspects of philosophy without losing a basic sense of direction and purpose.

Slowly, I began to pull the ideas together. . . . Once in a while, I would try to draw my thoughts together into a self-definition, usually a short written statement. What am I doing? How? Why? Invariably my thought would break through that inadequate statement almost before my inadequate word-processor was done printing it. I kept reading and thinking and talking, biding my time.

Last January, I began a period of more focused research, with a paper topic in mind. I don't know when I finally settled on a title, but the topic *was* the title: "How Ecological Is Ecophilosophy?" I read intensively, and scribbled down notes as my thought developed.

At last the time was ripe to begin writing. It was March, almost April. Drawing it all together, making it *fit* was more difficult than I had ever imagined. I was dealing with a lot of material and thought: *patience* became my chief tool. On paper, or on my WP, I worked it through, forcing the thoughts into words, forcing the words into structured forms, on the paper.

Inspiration would strike at odd times. I had to keep pencil and paper handy, just in case I had a flash. . . .

During the summer, I ignored it. I told people that I'd buried it in the backyard for the earthworms to edit. When autumn came, the time was ripe once more. Exhumed and reconsidered, with more and more feedback, the paper changed again and again, passing through successive stages of order and disorder. It would arrive at equilibrium, but my thought would break through it, breaking it apart, and it would demand reintegration. . . .

A few weeks ago, I was satisfied with my paper: it was good enough to submit for consideration. All I had to do was polish it up. So I read it over and found a dozen things to revise; they were minor points really, but important enough. So I "fixed" them, and read it over again. I found a dozen things to revise. Again and again.

I foresaw no end to it but the slow demise of my paper. If I picked at it ad infinitum it would come apart again, and I doubted I had the energy or the time to rebuild it. My thought was already moving beyond it, to new things. The moment was propitious: I mailed it to the journal.

Bob Kirkman

end of each piece of your search, you do some writing in your process journal. Even if you don't decide to use it in your paper, it will be a valuable record for you.

 ## DOCUMENTATION

You'll need to make sure that you know how to document the information you've used in your paper. If you've used interviews, you must document these interviews. Your teacher will tell you what style of documentation she wishes you to use. She may also want to go over some of that technical information in class. If you've used a questionnaire, you should include it plus a tabulation of the answers.

Documentation of sources is particularly important in research papers—just as important for personal research as for library research. None of us has the right to claim credit for the ideas and words of others regardless of whether we read them or heard them in an interview. And, from a pragmatic point of view, documentation lends authority to your research paper. If people know that you feel safe in revealing your sources, thus giving readers the opportunity to check their validity, they're far more likely to give your words credit.

Quotations

It is possible to do lots of research and learn from the information and opinions of interviewees and published works and write a terrific paper of your own—without a single quotation or footnote. (Joyce has no footnotes in *Ulysses* for all the details he checked up on.) But for this assignment we are asking for some quotations and footnotes. You should integrate and internalize what you learn into your own thinking, but this is also an assignment in showing to readers that *others* have said things about your topic. Your reader should not feel he is in a closet with you having a dialogue but rather that he is in a large room with a number of people—other voices—involved in the issue. Quotations which allow these voices to come through to your readers will give them a feel for the texture of research on your issue.

For the format and use of quotations in your text, see Mini-Workshop I.

Footnotes Aren't Footnotes Any More

"Footnote" is the word that probably springs to mind when you think of how to document your sources: a *note* at the *foot* of the page. But we are following the recent Modern Language Association (MLA) guidelines for citing sources *without* footnotes. The new MLA citation system makes life easier for both writers and readers and is now standard for academic writing in most of the humanities. (You can still use footnotes for an aside to the reader, but try not to use too many since they can make a reader feel bumped around.)

The citation system that fits the social or natural sciences is the American Psychological Association (APA) system. A number of the essays in the readings in this book, as you've probably noticed, use the APA documentation style. At the end of our listing of examples in the MLA style, we'll list the major differences between MLA and APA.

Documentation procedure has two elements: the *parenthetical citation* in your text as you go along, and the *list of works cited* at the end. When you want to document a source—that is, to tell readers what article or book or interviewee you are quoting from or referring to—add a small parenthetical citation. Parentheses show readers where to look for the full information about the article or book in the final list of works cited without distracting your reader as much as old-style footnotes do.

Parenthetical Citations

Put in the parentheses only the information that readers need for finding the article or book in your list of works cited. Thus:

- Give *only* the page number(s) in your parentheses if you mention the author in your text. For example, your text might read as follows:

  > Murray writes of a pregnant waiting and silence that come before starting to write (377).

  Note that the parenthesis is *inside* the sentence's punctuation.

- If the author's name is not in your sentence, then add the name to the parenthesis. For example:

  > Some writers speak of the need for waiting and silence before writing (Murray 377).

  Note that there's no comma after the author. The last name alone is sufficient unless you are using two authors with the same name.

- If you cite more than one work by Murray in your essay, add the title (or shortened title) to your parenthesis, e.g., (Murray, *Learning by Teaching* 377–8). But you can skip the title if you mention it in your text. Note the comma after the author but not after the title.

Other conventions:

- Titles of articles or chapters are in quotation marks; book titles are underlined—with no quotation marks.
- If the work has more than one volume, specify which one you are citing, followed by the page number, e.g., (1:179).
- If citing a passage from a poem, give line numbers. If citing a passage from a play, give act, scene, and lines, e.g., (4.5.11–14).
- If there are two or three authors, give them; for more than three, give the first author and add "et al."

In APA style, always give the date of the work, but don't give page numbers unless it's a direct quotation. Thus our first example above, if changed to APA, would be simply: (1983). The second example would be: (Murray, 1983). Note the comma before the date.

Works Cited

This is a list that comes at the end of your paper on a separate sheet. The items are alphabetized by author and follow this general sequence: author, then title, then publisher. Here's the order in more detail:

- Author (last name first)
- Title of the work you're citing
- The title of any larger work or magazine or journal—if the work you're citing is contained in it
- Editor or translator
- Edition
- Number of volumes

- City of publication
- Publisher
- Year of publication
- Page numbers (if the work you're citing is only a portion of the larger publication)

Here are examples of the most common kinds of citations:

- Book:

> Aitchison, Jean. <u>The Articulate Mammal: An Introduction to Psycholinguistics</u>. New York: McGraw Hill, 1976.

Note that if Aitchison had been the editor rather than the author, her name would be followed by a comma and "ed."

- Essay from a professional journal:

> Flower, Linda, and John R. Hayes. "A Cognitive Process Theory of Writing." <u>College Composition and Communication</u> 32 (1981): 165-86.

Note that the second author's name is not reversed. Because the pages of this journal are continuously numbered throughout the year, we have "32 (1981): 365-86." If it were a journal where each issue started with page 1, the note would read "32.4 (1981): 17-38." (The "4" here means the fourth issue of that year.)

- Poem or essay in a book of poems or essays edited by someone else:

> Friebert, Stuart. "The Apron." <u>50 Contemporary Poets: The Creative Process</u>. Ed. Alberta T. Turner. New York: David McKay, 1977. 102.

- Book Review:

> Nilsen, Don. L. F. Rev. of <u>American Tongue and Cheek: A Populist Guide to Our Language</u>, by Jim Quinn. <u>College Composition and Communication</u> 37 (1986): 107-8.

- An interview:

> Jones, Rafael. Personal interview [or Telephone interview]. 7 July 1992.

- A personal letter:

> Trimbur, John. Letter to the author. 17 Nov. 1984.

- If it is an unsigned work (e.g., in an encyclopedia or newspaper), begin with the title. (Thus its place in your alphabetized list would be determined by the first letters of the title.) If it is an unsigned U.S. Government publication, however, begin with "United States," then the agency that puts it out, and then the title of the piece—as though the government were the author.

The punctuation in these citations is a bit sparse and counterintuitive—hard to remember: we ourselves have to look it up again and again. You could make a photocopy of these pages to keep handy. And we've printed this information inside the back cover for ready reference.

Note how citations have "hung margins." That is, the first line of each citation is "flush left" (all the way left), and succeeding lines of each citation are indented five spaces—as we have shown them. Our examples are single-spaced (as they usually are in published or printed matter), but on manuscripts like yours they should be typed double-spaced.

If you are using APA style, you will call the list of sources "References" rather than "Works Cited." The chief differences in style are that initials rather than first names are used, the date of the work appears immediately after the author's name, only the first word of the source is capitalized (although journal titles are capitalized in the conventional manner), and no quotation marks are used for journal articles. Thus, you would have the following:

```
Aitchison, Jean (1976). The articulate mammal: an in-
     troduction to psycholinguistics. New York: Mc-
     Graw Hill.
Flower, Linda, and John R. Hayes (1981). A cognitive
     process theory of writing. College Composition
     and Communication, 32, 365-86.
```

You'll notice also some minor differences in punctuation.

We have given here only the most common kinds of citations. You will have to consult a good handbook for more complicated ones, especially for using works from unusual sources (such as a television advertisement, record jacket, or map). On the other hand, few readers will care too much about deviations from correct form when it comes to seldom-cited kinds of sources.

 ## SUGGESTIONS FOR SHARING AND RESPONDING

For your early exploratory freewriting, you might use "Sayback" (*Sharing and Responding,* Section 3). This sort of feedback will help you figure out where you are going or want to go. Ask listeners to concentrate particularly on what they see as the implications of what you've written. In addition to "Sayback," here are some questions you may find helpful:

■ "What do you think I'm primarily interested in finding out?"
■ "Do you think that the task I'm setting for myself is feasible? And if not, how can I alter it?"
■ "How do you think I can go about answering my question or finding out what I want to know?"

For later drafts, you'll find "Sayback" valuable again. But you might also ask your readers to do "Skeleton Feedback" in Section 10 of *Sharing and Responding.*

We suggest too that you write out some questions you specifically want listeners and readers to give you feedback on. Here are some general questions you may find helpful at this stage of your project:

- "Have I accomplished what I led you to expect I was going to accomplish?"
- "Have I given you sufficient evidence to justify whatever conclusions I've drawn?"
- "Does my organization work? Does my paper seem to be a unified whole?"
- "What do you hear as my position or point of view or bias in this paper? Do you see me openly showing it or keeping it kind of hidden? Whatever my approach, how does it work for you? How do you react to the relationship between my opinion or feelings here and the information I present?"
- "Have I made clear the limits of my subject?"

PROCESS JOURNAL AND COVER LETTER QUESTIONS

What did you notice and what can you learn from:

- How you went about choosing a topic?
- Your first efforts in the library—especially if you had not used a library much before?
- Your success (or difficulties) with integrating your thinking and the thinking or information of others: did your thinking change much or not at all on the basis of your personal research? your library work?
- What advice can you give yourself for doing future research projects and papers?

RUMINATIONS AND THEORY

The Ongoing Conversation

> Imagine that you enter a parlor. You come late. When you arrive, others have long preceded you, and they are engaged in a heated discussion, a discussion too heated for them to pause and tell you exactly what it is about. In fact, the discussion had already begun long before any of them got there, so that no one present is qualified to retrace for you all the steps that had gone before. You listen for a while, until you decide that you have caught the tenor of the argument; then you put in your oar. Someone answers; you answer him; another comes to your defense; another aligns himself against you, to either the embarrassment or gratification of your opponent, depending upon the quality of your ally's assistance. However, the discussion is interminable. The hour grows late, you must depart. And you do depart, with the discussion still vigorously in progress. (Burke 45)

The usual thing we do when we need to know something is ask questions. Often what we need to know is very simple: what time is it? How do I get to the zoo? In these cases, we ask someone and that's usually the end of our research. (The fact that we may get the wrong answer is irrelevant since we won't realize that until later.) But once we've gotten an answer, we're in the position of passing it along to others. We can now, for instance, direct someone else to the zoo—and that person can direct another and on and on. And perhaps the person who gave us directions originally got them from someone else. So we're in the midst of a conversation whose beginning we were not present for and whose ending we're unlikely to be present for either.

But just as often what we need to know may be more complex: how have digital watches affected people's sense of time? Why do people go to the zoo? What do we get out of looking at animals? To get answers to these questions, we need to do more than ask one question of one person. We need to figure out how to ask questions, observe reactions, and draw conclusions. And often what we want to know may require us to seek out information in books and periodicals.

Just as often, though, we can't state precisely what we want or need to know. It may be so fuzzy in our minds that we don't know what questions to ask to start off our research. So, we have to do a fair amount of thinking, talking, writing, and reflecting in order to pinpoint and focus our purpose. We, in effect, put ourselves into conversation with ourselves and with others. In a sense, this too is research. More than one philosopher has noted that asking the right questions is often more meaningful than getting the right answers.

However we come to decide what our research will be and how best to do it, when we finally do report it to others, we continue the conversation we had joined when we began our research. In fact, whenever we use language, whether written or oral, we are joining an ongoing conversation—either with ourselves or with others. Oral conversations tend to move steadily forward since it's difficult for us to have access to what was spoken a year ago much less centuries ago. But written conversations can span centuries, continents, and even languages.

Almost as far back as we have written records, writers have been addressing issues of human relationships, power struggles, the meaning of life, proper behavior, and so forth. Not one of us can have access to all that has been written on subjects which interest us, but printed materials make possible such access. Still, we can digest only a portion of all that's available. Teachers point us to what our culture and traditions have labeled as the most significant of prior writings on any given subject. Even that changes over time as scholars uncover new documents, reconsider old documents, or understand better the significance of documents once considered unimportant.

When you do print-based research in a library, you are entering into a conversation with those who wrote centuries ago or thousands of miles away. But, in order to situate yourself within that conversation and to make valid contributions to it, you need to know what has been said in it. This is the basic purpose of most education: to help you find your place in the ongoing flow of history. Unless you show your familiarity with this conversation, most people will not give much weight to your contribution to it. In truth, they probably won't even listen to you. If, for example, you want to write about the role of economics in society, you should probably be familiar with canonical works on the subject: Malthus and Marx and others whom your economics teachers will identify for you. You'll also need to become familiar with what is currently being written on the subject. Knowing both what has been written on the subject and what is currently being written and said on the subject will enable you to make valuable contributions to this particular ongoing conversation. And, if you want to make some permanent impact on that conversation, you'll write your words down so they'll be available for future study. Writing thus allows all of us to talk both to the past and to the future as well as to the present.

But you can have an ongoing conversation with yourself also. That conversation will obviously draw part of its substance from what you've read and what you've heard from others. But a large part of its substance will come from interaction with what you've previously thought and said. This conversation may concern the same subjects as the historical conversations: the meaning of life, human relationships, and so forth. For instance, you probably often find yourself saying something like: "I used to think X about the difference between Republicans and Democrats, but I now think Y." Or: "I used to want to be an engineer, but now I think I'd rather be a teacher."

What we say to ourselves changes as we experience more of the world around us and as that world changes. And, for most of us, the conversation with ourselves is unrecorded. One of our aims in this book is to push you to record some of this personal conversation in your freewriting and exploratory writing. If you've done this, you've discovered how often such personal conversation can be interesting to others as well as to yourself. So often we've had students who moan that they have nothing to say. We think that they believe this because they haven't yet realized that their personal ruminations can be engrossing for others. A large part of the appeal of essays is that they foreground the workings of one mind as it treats a particular subject. We talk more about this in Workshop 9.

Why are we writing about this here in Workshop 13? Because we believe that research is a way of integrating our personal conversations with ourselves into our conversations with others across history and geography. Most research becomes both. In articles reporting scientific research, for instance, authors often begin with a review of the literature. Such a review is merely a summing up of the most important writing on a subject. Having done that, the authors move on to report their particular, personal research on that subject. In their conclusions, they often integrate what they've uncovered and what previous researchers have uncovered. These articles, in turn, will be used by future researchers who desire to join the conversation.

These sweeping conclusions may seem quite grandiose considering that we got to them from simple questions such as "What time is it?" and "How do I get to the zoo?" But we sincerely believe that most research begins simply and that all research is a combination of personal insights and an awareness of what others have contributed. This is what makes it a conversation. And similar qualities make most writing a conversation with others and with yourself about matters you and they wish to talk about.

Readings

WHEN A CHILD HAS CANCER

Kymberly Saganski

When a child is afflicted by cancer, the family members react differently as a result of the initial shock. In the case of my family, my parents experienced a typical preoccupation with the trivial things, a fear of death and worries about finances. My own reactions included fear, disorganization and even selfishness. These are all common among families dealing with a profoundly ill member.

The ultimate determination that a family member has cancer is never easy to accept, but it seems more difficult when the ill member is a child. At the age of fifteen, my younger brother was diagnosed as having acute lymphoblastic leukemia and lymphoma. In its advanced stages, "leukemic blood cells rapidly glut the bone marrow, pour over into the bloodstream, and invade the lymph nodes, the spleen, and such vital organs of the body as the liver, brain and kidneys" (Levitt and Guralnick 72). It seemed ironic that my father's first thoughts were of his son's high school sports career and the soon to be arriving hospital bills. My mother, having watched my grandfather die of the same rare combination of diseases, thought only of my brother's fifty percent chance for survival. In order to avoid the entire situation, I worried about the fact that I was getting behind in work at my Massachusetts school since my mother and I had joined my father and brother in New Jersey where they were living. Peter, my brother, was hospitalized immediately, and the bills started to accumulate from that moment forward.

After this initial hospitalization, the patient often feels lost, helpless and scared. Parents become frantic as they watch their son's or daughter's dreams for the future become unstable and begin to topple. The remaining children fight for their position in the reshuffled family. Although they are not decision makers, their needs are often considered when decisions are being made. Many times, even though there is nothing concrete that they can do to help the situation, the presence of other children is soothing in and of itself.

The patients, themselves, may react in a variety of ways. Sometimes they withdraw from everyone else, repressing their thoughts and emotions. Other times, they become bitter and resentful, blaming everyone and everything for their predicament. Barbara Rabkin, a scientific journalist for *Macleans* magazine, contends that the entire process of "coping with leukemia itself . . . is complicated by the lack of public understanding and acceptance of the disease" (54–5). There are a few patients who seem to accept their condition from the beginning and maintain an open mind and a positive attitude. These cases, however, are few and far between. According to Rabkin, this is the time when the support of other families is the most important. The family members dealing with the cancer need to have contact with unafflicted families in order to maintain their grasp on "real life" (55). I don't happen to agree with this rationalization.

My family dealt with the cancer as individuals. We each reacted in our own separate ways to my little brother's illness. My parents tried to be supportive, as I did, but Pete had decided that his best defense was anger. He was angry at his doctors for misdiagnosing his cancer as an allergy when he had first become sick eleven months earlier. He was angry at himself for not knowing his own body better, and he was angry at all of his friends and relatives for showing him sympathy, which he interpreted as pity. He decided then and there that he was going to hate this cancer until it left him alone.

I had no idea as to what I should do with myself. My brother seemed to resent the fact that I was up and around while he was hooked up to machines and lying flat on his back in a hospital bed. John Spinetta, writing for *Human Behavior,* contends that this resentment is a natural phase of the cancer acceptance cycle by the patient (49), but I couldn't deal with the rejection of my sympathy for my brother. Because I seemed so uncomfortable at the hospital, I was given the choice of missing school for a month and staying in New Jersey or returning to Cape Cod and living alone for an indefinite period of time. That was the least of the decisions that I was asked to assist in making. I delayed my return home in case I could be some help to my parents.

My brother had the option of three different kinds of chemotherapy. He refused to have any input whatsoever, so my parents asked me to put myself in my brother's position and try to imagine living with the various side effects of the different drugs. I had a lot of difficulty with this task, but I tried my best in order to take some of the pressure off my parents. I decided then that even though I seemed to be a comfort to my mother, her worries about my falling behind in school were just added troubles to her already heavy heart, so I returned to school. This return to an almost normal life helped me to deal with the situation, and the fact that I had the added responsibility of living by myself kept my mind from wandering back to Peter constantly.

I was surprised at the amount of time that the social workers on Peter's case spent with my entire family. I had never before realized that an illness such as cancer affects the whole family in such a complete way. Ann Brierly, a social worker at my brother's hospital, believes that the best way to ease the pain of a family illness is to educate all members about the nature of the illness. Once my parents were adequately informed concerning Peter's cancer, they were able to deal with it from a clinical point of view. When people inquire as to Peter's condition, I say that after all we have been through, he is what is so far considered cured. In my heart I feel like I should answer, "We survived," and I hope we will never have to live through such an ordeal again.

Works Cited

Brierly, Ann.   Telephone interview. 6 May 1985.

Levitt, Paul M., and Elissa S. Guralnick.   *The Cancer Reference Book.* New York: Paddington Press, 1979.

Rabkin, Barbara.   "Childhood Leukemia." *Macleans* 23 Apr. 1979: 54–5.

Spinetta, John.   "Childhood Cancer: Study of a Family Coping." *Human Behavior* May 1979: 49.

THE LIFE AND TIMES OF SHAG

Alan M. Beck

[1971]

It was still dark enough to see stars when I arrived at the Amalgamated Clothing Workers of America (ACWA) building near downtown Baltimore. I saw and heard nothing. I left the car, walked around the building, returned, checked the air temperature, and reported my findings into a tape recorder I always kept with me:

2 September 1970, 64 degrees F., clear and slightly windy, 4:20 a.m. No signs, garbage behind homesite from previous day now gone—probably collected. I will now wait for Shag, who I suspect is still in the shrubbery, left side of ACWA, Eutaw and McMechen.

Studying the stray dogs of Baltimore is my thesis project for a doctorate in ecology, and for the next few weeks I would be concentrating on Shag, a large, white, shaggy-haired male with black markings. I chose him from the study population because he was a truly ownerless stray. Ordinarily, owned and ownerless strays are indistinguishable, except at moments of owner-dog interaction, and both types serve as the feral dogs of the city environment.

Lately, Shag had been spending his nights in the shrubbery, although earlier in the summer he had found shelter in a house hallway. He would push the front door open to gain access and wait for someone leaving to help him get back to the streets, but his habit of "marking" the inside hall had led to his ouster by the building's residents. During the past two years, I discovered other stray dog den sites—in vacant buildings and garages, under porches and cars, and in garbage dumps. All provide protection against weather and people.

4:50 a.m. Barking now becoming apparent. The area is coming alive, but still no sign of Shag.

Waiting is a very real part of wildlife study. I welcome it, however, as it gives me time to plan future approaches and reflect on aspects just completed. I spent the first part of the summer of 1970 sampling the dog populations of selected areas around the city, mainly by photographing each stray dog and plotting the sighting on maps. One advantage of working in the urban ecosystem is the ability to locate the subject with remarkable precision by using street crossings and house numbers.

Another advantage of studying feral dogs is that their mixed heritage leads to wide variations in morphology and behavior, which enabled me to recognize individuals. I seldom encountered the monotony of pedigree breeds. As part of my studies, I photographed every stray dog I saw while traveling through a neighborhood. A dog photographed more than once is, in the terms of wildlife study, a recapture. Therefore, just as a wild bird population can be calculated from the number of banded birds recaptured, I was able to compute the city's stray dog population from the number of dogs rephotographed. Photographic recapture and other methods revealed a total population of 100,000 dogs, both owned and ownerless, in Baltimore, which is an increase of 25,000 animals over the city's dog population as estimated ten years ago by Dr. Kenneth Crawford, the state veterinarian.

Cities throughout the world are encountering such dog population explosions, including the half-million dogs each in New York, Mexico City, and Buenos Aires. In many cities, dogs appear to be increasing more rapidly than humans. Such populations have many ecological implications for a city. A study by New York's Environmental Protection Administration noted that the owners of dogs permit them to leave from 5,000 to 20,000 tons of excrement and from 600,000 to over 1 million gallons of urine on the streets each year. Even if Baltimore has only one-fifth of those estimates, what does it mean for this or any city? While my original objective was to establish the life history of the feral urban dog, I had to include such implications, for they are part of the ecology of the animal.

Ever-growing fecal depositions are a potential health hazard as well as an insult to the senses. There is the possibility of visceral larva migrans (VLM), a syndrome caused in humans when the eggs of *Toxocara canis* (dog worms) are ingested, usually by children playing in or eating infected dirt, often from under street trees where dogs may have defecated days earlier. Severe cases of VLM, characterized by enlargement of the liver and spleen, convulsions, and blindness, are very rare. One symptom, which often goes undetected, is a marke l increase in the number of eosinophil cells in the blood. Milder symptoms, such as coughing and fever, are so like other childhood diseases that VLM goes undiagnosed most of the time. Although there have been six child blindness cases reported at Baltimore's Johns Hopkins Hospital in the past ten years, there has been no record of VLM frequency in its less debilitating form.

Dog feces is a major factor in the breeding of house flies, which then possibly transmit such bacteria as *Salmonella* from dogs to man. In addition, rat eradication officials and residents of my study area have observed rats feeding on dog feces and, indeed, rats are most common in alleys with high fecal residues. Garbage, from cans knocked over by dogs, and dog feces are probably important components of the rat food chain.

At 5:22 a collie bolts out of an open doorway, which is then closed. Other dogs are now apparent, but still no sign of Shag.

This kind of pet release, before and after the usual workday, is one reason why dog activity is greatest in the mornings and evenings. Ownerless strays are also active during these periods, possibly because dogs are gregarious animals, initiating each other's activity, or because all dogs avoid activity during the heat of the day.

6:00 a.m. The sky is light blue and church bells are ringing. Shag and a male Doberman, Shag's constant companion, appear in the rear view mirror. Where in the hell did they come from?

Waiting was over, and I left the car to follow at a distance with tape recorder and camera. Because feral urban dogs are accustomed to the presence of man, their normal activities may be studied more easily than those of most wild animals. If the dogs gave any indication that I was altering their behavior by following them, I turned away or "tied" my shoelace, which was all that was necessary for them to lose interest in me. Anyone observing my behavior must have assumed that I was an unemployed photographer with particularly obstinate shoelaces.

Shag and Dobe headed for their usual feeding alley, where they were joined by several other dogs in going from garbage can to garbage can, sniffing and occasionally lifting off bags from the tops. Some of the cans had already been knocked over. It was 6:09 and still dark enough to observe rat activity. Dogs, cats, and rats all seemed to ignore each other, sometimes eating garbage within a foot of each other. But my presence chased away the rats. Garbage collection was on Mondays and Thursdays. As this was Wednesday, there was ample food. But even after collection on the following day, there would be enough residue left on the ground to attract dogs before the street sweepers removed it, so garbage collection day was not an environmental catastrophe. The residue persists to the evening and undoubtedly feeds the nocturnal rats, mice, and roaches. Subtle changes in canine presence and behavior do occur with food availability, so dogs can be used as indicators of urban environmental deterioration and can be correlated with trash and pest species.

By 6:20 Shag and Dobe returned to the alley beside the ACWA building, where, as usual, they found water under the air conditioner unit. They lay down in the median green, facing east. It is 59 degrees F. At 6:34 Dobe rose and left.

This was my day to be with Shag, so I waited, watching him as he slept. Five minutes later he stood, stretched, looked and sniffed in all directions, then immediately took off in the same direction as Dobe had. They were a true pack of two.

One-half of the dogs I observed were in the company of other dogs (as many as 17 in one pack), but few packs are stable in size and membership. Instead the packs form and dissolve over a period of minutes or hours, giving the impression of a loose social structure, more like that of people in the streets than wolves in the wild.

I followed Shag through several alleys, and at 6:45 we caught up with Dobe, who was feeding at the base of an overflowing apartment house dumpster.

Children, unable to open its heavy door, had left garbage bags at the base. The dogs left to continue their tour of the alleys and streets. Being large dogs they could often lift bags of garbage out of the cans without knocking them over. They would rip open paper and plastic bags by shaking them or running with them in their teeth. I am not sure whether they could smell the food through the plastic bags or had learned what they contained from previous encounters with open plastic bags.

At 7:00 a.m., the dogs are back on Madison and meet two small pet dogs that have just emerged from a doorway. Shag attempts a typical nose-anus greeting but is rebuffed by barks and snaps. No fight. Shag and Dobe cut across recently cleared field.

The new dogs, although considerably smaller, had a territorial advantage. The interaction between pet and nonpet stray has many implications for the pet owner concerned about disease and dog fights.

At 7:10 Shag found a garbage can on its side and pulled out wrappings frequently used for food take-out orders. He ate what appeared to be a portion of spaghetti with bread.

At 7:13 both dogs left the can, and I surveyed what remained of the "kill." Shag had finished all the spaghetti, bread, and sauce but had left prunes, raisins, and tobacco.

After more travel, through alleys and a playground, both dogs came to rest on the median strip a block away from the homesite. While on their stomachs they both stared intently at a building diagonally across the street. Fortunately, the median had benches and I could rest too. They were not sleeping but were waiting for something to happen, although I could not figure out what. . . .

WRITING MATHEMATICS*

William Zinsser

One day I got a letter from a woman named Joan Countryman, who is head of the mathematics department at Germantown Friends School in Philadelphia. She had heard about my interest in writing across the curriculum.

"For many years," she said, "I've been asking my students to write about mathematics as they learned it, with predictably wonderful results. Writing seems to free them of the idea that math is a collection of right answers owned by the teacher—a body of knowledge that she will dispense in chunks and that they have to swallow and digest. That's how most nonmathemati-

---

From Writing to Learn.

cians perceive it. But what makes mathematics really interesting is not the right answer but where it came from and where it leads."

The letter grabbed my attention. Surely mathematics was a world of numbers. Could it also be penetrated with words? Could a person actually write sentences that would lead him through a mathematical problem and suggest further questions—different questions from the ones the teacher might raise?. . . Yet here in the morning mail was a teacher who got her math students to write—a humanist in the world of fractions and cosines. Joan Countryman explained that she was one of a small but growing number of pioneers in her discipline, frequently invited to give workshops to introduce teachers to the idea of writing mathematics. I called her and asked if she would introduce the idea to me. . . . We made a date for me to come to Philadelphia and talk to her and attend one of her classes.

□ □ □ □ □

I put my first question to Joan Countryman as we settled down to talk in her late-Victorian house, a house I had been warmly admiring for its fanciful curves and angles and other eclectic design details.

"What is mathematics?" I asked.

"You've been talking about mathematics ever since you walked into this house," she said. "When you commented on the dormers and the staircase and the circular windows you were making mathematical points."

I said I thought they were aesthetic points. Like Molière's bourgeois gentleman, who was astonished to learn that he had been speaking prose all his life, I was surprised to learn that I had been speaking mathematics.

"Sure they're aesthetic points," she said, "but there are all sorts of interesting mathematics about the way the house is constructed and about the shapes you've been noticing. Unfortunately, most people don't see the world that way because they've been alienated from mathematics and told that it's something apart from what they're able to do."

"So what is mathematics?" I asked, still hoping for a definition.

"What are any of the disciplines but a way in which people try to make sense of the world or the universe?" she said. "Mathematics is one way of doing that, just as literature is, or philosophy, or history. Math does it by looking for patterns and abstracting—that is, by examining a specific case and generalizing from that. . . . I asked Joan Countryman when she began to think that there might be another language—writing—which could take students into the subject by a different route.

"When I started teaching math I was thirty," she recalled, "and I had been out working in the field of urban education as a program planner for the Philadelphia school district, so when I got into a classroom I had serious questions about the relationship between what one does in school and what one does in life. I didn't like the isolation of the process of learning math: You study it alone and you take your tests alone and you don't have much to do with other people. I immediately put the kids in groups and made them teach each other and take tests together. I was determined to get them away from the idea that their education is a private experience.

"I also wanted them to be less passive. Math is an active process, and you'll never know that if you sit and wait for the teacher to tell you, 'This is how to do long division—it's a set of specific steps.' The action should begin long before that, with the student initiating a question like 'I've got fifty-three of these things; how am I going to divide them among the people in the room?' Most kids think that the teacher has all the information and they don't have any. I don't like the implications of that—that you aren't capable of finding things out yourself.

"So from the start I got my students to write about what they were doing. My first idea was to ask them to write mathematics autobiographies. . . . Another format is for students to keep a journal with a running account of their work. "In a journal," Mrs. Countryman said, "I want them to suspend judgment—to feel free to ask questions, to experiment, to make statements about what they do and don't understand. At first they need help to learn to write without censoring their thoughts—to feel confident that nobody will criticize what they've written."

The following entry, written by a twelfth-grade student named Neil Swenson after a month's exposure to calculus, is typical of how the form lends itself to recording successive stages of thought:

> In my first journal entry I wrote that I believed that calculus is a way of finding solutions to problems that can't be solved with conventional math, by using abstractions. I was partially correct in that many parts of calculus do require abstract thinking. But that's not really what calculus is. Calculus is a way of dealing with motion. It's a way of finding out exactly how something is moving. Without calculus it was impossible for us to know what the instantaneous velocity of something was. We could only know the actual rate of change if it was changing at a constant rate; then its derivative or the slope of its tangent line is equal to the slope of the original line. When we had something that had a variable rate of exchange we tried to find the average velocity, but this was inaccurate. . . .

Listening to these examples, I saw that many of my beliefs about writing and learning also apply to mathematics: that we write to discover what we know and don't know; that we write more comfortably if we go exploring, free of the fear of not being on the "right" road to the right destination, and that we learn more if we feel that the work has a purpose. Motivation is as important in mathematics writing as in every other kind of writing. I asked Joan Countryman how she keeps alive the awareness that math is closely related to life.

"There's no dearth of topics for math papers," she said, "but often students seem to be just meeting an assignment instead of pursuing a genuine interest of theirs. I'm always looking for a connection between mathematics and social questions. . . .

□ □ □ □ □

Physiological note: I had been sitting in Joan Countryman's living room for two hours talking about mathematics. My pulse was steady, the hand that held my note-taking pencil didn't shake and wasn't even clammy. Where was that old math anxiety? I hadn't been at any loss for questions; they came to me naturally. Like the process of writing, the process of asking questions had been a form of learning, raising further questions and telling me what I wanted to know next. I was genuinely curious. It never occurred to me that this was a subject I wasn't supposed to be any good at. What did occur to me was that mathematics was not some arcane system of numbers; it was a language, a way of putting thoughts together. I might never master the language—my checkbook might still go unbalanced—but at least I had begun to glimpse what the language was trying to say and how it could help people to understand the world around them.

By extension, I thought, this must also be true of engineering, chemistry, biology and all the other special languages that have been invented to express special ideas. They can be at least broadly apprehended. What keeps us from trying is fear; the engineer is as frightened of my language (writing) as I am of his. . . .

How does someone write chemistry? Here are two explanations that I like, taken from *The Journal of Chemical Education.* Chemistry teachers are now beginning to insist on writing from their students, and these two women are obviously leaders of the trend.

The first professor, Estelle K. Meislich, of Bergen Community College, Paramus, New Jersey, begins her article by raising the most common bugaboo that science teachers worry about: "Is there some way of requiring good writing from students that will not diminish the science content?" The concern behind the question is twofold: that teaching writing will take time away from teaching chemistry, and that writing in the sciences is "not the same" as writing in the humanities.

Tackling the question, Professor Meislich writes: "Here is a method I have used successfully for the past eight years in courses for both chemistry majors and nonmajors. On every examination I ask at least one and often several questions that require a written response. Students are told that their answers must be written in 'acceptable' English for credit. If I decide that a scientifically correct response is poorly written, the student cannot get credit for the correct answer until it is rewritten in correct English.

"The student has one week to return the rewritten paper for credit. During this time students are encouraged to meet with a writing instructor for help in rewriting. (I send the writing instructor a copy of the examination with correctly written answers to prepare him or her for students' requests for help.) Of course incorrect answers, no matter how well written, cannot be rewritten for credit.

"A paper that requires a rewritten answer will have two grades. The first one is for the originally submitted examination. The second grade, shown in parentheses, is the one that the student will receive if an acceptable rewritten answer is returned on time. . . . Once students accept the fact that correct but poorly written answers are unacceptable, most of them write more carefully. Eventually very few of them have to rewrite at all. In this way, writing becomes an integral part of the course without diminishing the chemical content." . . .

WORKSHOP

14

TEXT ANALYSIS THROUGH EXAMINING FIGURATIVE LANGUAGE

Since there are a number of workshops on analyzing texts in this book, you've probably tried at least one approach already. Our aim in presenting these various approaches is to expand your options when you're asked to analyze a text.

In this workshop we specifically want to help you see the value of focusing on figurative language: metaphor, simile, image, and symbol. Figurative language is usually a center of intensified energy and meaning in discourse. It usually reveals what is *implied* in a text rather than what is *said*. You've undoubtedly focused on figures of speech in your English classes as a way of getting closer to the meaning of fiction or poetry. But attention to figurative language can also help you analyze expository writing such as essays and editorials. All this close looking at texts should make you more consciously aware of how words and phrases carry secondary as well as primary meaning.

Your assignment for this workshop is to write an analysis of a text based on its figurative language. Before we describe more specifically how to do that though, we're going to talk a bit about figurative language itself to give you background for your analysis.

 ## FIGURATIVE LANGUAGE

Metaphor

Metaphor is the most basic or universal "figure"—the paradigm of figurative language. A metaphor is a word or phrase used (to put it bluntly) "wrong" but on purpose—used in something other than its normal or usual fashion—used not literally but figuratively. If we say, "The farmer *plowed* the field," "plowed" is literal. But if we say, "The student *plowed* through his homework," "plowed" is figurative. To use a word metaphorically awakens us to new possibilities of meaning. By saying that the student "plowed" through homework, the speaker forces us to realize that "plowing" cannot mean what farmers do to fields. Therefore we are forced to create or remember a sense of plow that fits the sentence. ("Oh, I guess he went through his homework methodically and persistently.") We have probably heard the word "plow" in this metaphorical sense before so that we can't feel much "wrongness." We don't have to ask ourselves directly, "Let's see; what can you do to homework that is like what a farmer does to a field?" The tired metaphor doesn't waken us to many new possibilities of meaning.

When we hear a metaphor we've *never* heard before, however, we are forced to forge new meaning. "In her room at the prow of the house . . ." (writes Richard Wilbur in his poem "The Writer," printed in the "Readings" section of Workshop 11). Most of us probably haven't heard this metaphor before. This use of "prow" asks us to see a house in a new way—as a ship—and to sense one room as somehow forging forward. But the usage is not *so* odd— the meaning not so new—because we have probably heard "prow" used metaphorically for various things besides ships, if not for houses.

We have to work harder to make new meaning in these lines by Dylan Thomas in "Poem in October" about his thirtieth birthday:

> I rose
> In rainy autumn
> And walked abroad in a shower of all my days

The "wrongness" of the "shower of all my days" metaphor is not easy to interpret. Our hunch (given the context) is that the poet is inviting us to feel an October shower as also a shower of all our past days.

If we keep talking about people "plowing through" things, we will someday cease to experience that use of "plow" as a metaphor. We will call it literal. (Just as we probably experience "She *upset* me by being late for dinner" as equally literal with "He *upset* the glass of wine at dinner.") When that time comes, we will say that "plow" means something like "to cut methodically and persistently through something" just as literally as it means what farmers do to fields.

Though we can usually tell the difference between what is literal and metaphorical, there is no hard and fast way to decide in a fuzzy case—in the case of a metaphor that is so common that we can't decide whether to call it literal. Many of our literal meanings started out as metaphorical. Whether a word is metaphorical depends on whether people experience that usage as metaphorical—whether they experience any "wrongness" or "blockage of meaning" in the usage. Thus consider "leg of a table": is "leg" a metaphor or not? Probably not for most of us, but if you feel "leg" as a word that fits only living beings, not tables, then you will feel a "wrongness" that gives the word a metaphorical force. (In the nineteenth century, people sometimes put skirts on tables to cover their legs—showing perhaps that they experienced the animal or human connotations of legs.) Some people might even argue that "plow" is now literal in our "plowed through the homework" sentence.

Simile

We move from metaphor to simile when we use "like," "as," "seems"—or some similar word—to signal a comparison. Thus we can change Wilbur's metaphor to a simile by saying, "Her room, *like* the prow of a ship. . . ." In one sense the difference between metaphors and similes is trivial, just a matter of sticking in a "like" or an "as." But it's interesting to note that deep down, metaphors and similes represent different orientations to reality. Metaphors insist on bending reality or telling lies—and thus in a sense represent magical thinking: houses have no prow. Similes refuse to bend reality; they insist on being literal. They say only that the room is like a prow. Metaphors can thus be said to represent a different and more metaphysical view of reality. When we meet them in the flesh, however, metaphors and similes often don't function so very differently; similes can be just as startling or resonant, even magical, as metaphors: "I was like a tree in which there are three blackbirds." In fact the full sentence as Wallace Stevens wrote it grafts a metaphor onto the first element of the simile or comparison:

> I was of three minds,
> Like a tree
> In which there are three blackbirds.
> —from "Thirteen Ways of Looking at a Blackbird"

Image

Images need not be metaphors or similes at all; they need not involve any comparison or anything figurative. Images are simply picture-words—words which set something before our eyes. However, images are often involved in metaphors and similes. In fact critics often use the word "imagery" when they mean "metaphors, similes, and images." Critics say, "Let's look at the imagery of this poem," and they mean all the figures.

Another image.

> A pleasant apron with flowers and teacups all over. The kettle was singing. And steaming.
>
> —Stuart Friebert

This is just an image with no simile or comparison (though it contains the common metaphor of a kettle "singing"). Notice that the image is not just visual; it presents a kitchen scene which appeals to our ears and perhaps even to our tactile sense of the steam.

The distinguishing mark of an image then is that it appeals to our senses, not just our minds. It's a showing, not just a telling—a recreating of something palpable, not just a naming or explaining. Here too, of course, there is no firm dividing line between when something is shown versus told. Thus the following three phrases would probably not count as images for most people because they are scarcely more than naming:

> the notes of bells, the sounds of musical instruments, the noises of wind, sea, and rain. . . .

But you could argue that they are small images. Dylan Thomas continues his list, however, with three more items which, though short, are so artfully phrased as to bring a sound to almost any reader and thus make us count them as strong images:

> the rattle of milkcarts, the clopping of hooves on cobbles, the fingering of branches on a window pane. . . .

Let's look at Thomas's whole sentence—a long singing one—and notice how it combines the three figures we've talked about: image, simile, and metaphor. That is, the whole thing is an extended simile or comparison. Many of the compared items are images; and one of those images contains a metaphor, "fingering of branches." (He is speaking of his childhood experiences while reading.)

> And these words were, to me, as the notes of bells, the sounds of musical instruments, the noises of wind, sea, and rain, the rattle of milkcarts, the clopping of hooves on cobbles, the fingering of branches on a window pane, might be to someone, deaf from birth, who has miraculously found his hearing.

Symbol

The symbol is a word or phrase that *stands for* ("symbolizes") something. It presents a comparison but only an *implied* one, not a stated one: a comparison between x and y and only x is stated. The symbol symbolizes by virtue of *resembling or partaking of* what it stands for. Thus the circle has often been a symbol of infinity or perfection, the rose a symbol of beauty or of the Virgin Mary, the sun a symbol of reason. The symbol is inherently more magical or mystical than the metaphor or simile: it resonates with the life and significance of what it symbolizes.

Thus if we have a piece of writing where circles turn up frequently—not in metaphors or similes but just in literal description (for example, a dream poem where birds fly in perfect circles), and if we feel that the way the writer *uses* these circling birds is somehow *loaded* or *resonant*—such that the writing seems to point beyond mere birds flying in circles, then we could say that these descriptions are functioning as symbols and ask ourselves what their symbolic meaning might be. Perhaps we would conclude that they symbolize perfection. Remember, however, that symbols do not carry automatic symbolic meanings that you can look up in a dictionary. Admittedly there are dictionaries of symbols or of dream symbols, but you shouldn't trust them. They tell only what some alleged authority thinks or pronounces to be symbol-with-translation—for example, that whenever you dream of bread or houses you are dreaming of your mother. Sometimes yes, sometimes no. It depends on how symbols are used. Symbols give us a good glimpse of the values that a culture takes for granted. When Malcolm X looked up "black" in the dictionary, he noticed how it was taken to symbolize what is evil or inferior; and things that are soft, yielding, and passive have tended to symbolize women.

The Wallace Stevens poem we just quoted opens with what some readers might call a symbol:

Among twenty snowy mountains
The only moving thing
Was the eye of the blackbird.

Or later in the poem:

The river is moving.
The blackbird must be flying.

Others might say there are no symbols here, merely evocative literal state-ments. One cannot settle such arguments conclusively. The key is whether we sense a word or phrase *standing for* or *symbolizing* something—and doing so not arbitrarily but by virtue of its own nature and the way it relates to its linguistic context. Once we sense that, we try to get at *what* the word or phrase stands for or symbolizes. It's usually a mistake to try to translate a symbol. It makes more sense to talk about symbols causing additional mean-ings to hover over a text. For example, the moving eye of the blackbird among twenty white mountains might imply or symbolize a piercing awareness at the heart of no awareness. And the moving river linked to the flying blackbird might imply or symbolize change being everywhere and all changes somehow linked to each other. But of course this is arguable. Notice too that there is no metaphor or simile in either case. (The Sherwood Anderson story in the "Readings" is a literal story but it is heavy with resonance—with a sense of symbolic weight or of the hovering of additional meanings.)

To pinpoint a symbol we need to sense first that the language is heavy with meaning. Needless to say, not all readers are going to agree. And even where readers agree on the presence of a symbol, they will often disagree about what the symbol means. But we're all users of symbols. Virtually every dream we have is full of things that carry extra meanings hovering over them.

 ## A WAY TO ANALYZE BY FOCUSING ON FIGURATIVE LANGUAGE

What follows is a somewhat schematized procedure for writing an analysis of a text. We suggest these steps because writing analysis is hard, and there is a particular danger of jumping too soon into conclusions without examining enough evidence from the text. The power of the following steps for ex-ploratory writing is that they force you to do the bulk of your writing *before* figuring out what your main points are or how you will organize your final essay. When you do this noticing-and-exploring before you stop and work out what it all means, that working out is almost invariably more interesting and intelligent. It builds on richer thinking. (Be sure to do your exploratory writ-ing on only one side of the paper so that you can cut and paste later.)*

---

*We are indebted to the Bard Institute for Writing and Thinking for help in working out this ap-proach to analyzing a text.

This process is intended to help you with two goals that often seem to be at odds: to pay close attention to the language of the text you are analyzing, but also to relate what you see to your own experience and values—to build bridges between the text and yourself.

Reading the Text

Read the text you want to analyze at least a couple of times. Try to read it with pleasure—but also with care. Don't worry about analyzing it, just try to *immerse* yourself in it as much as you can. At this stage, the goal is not "figuring out" but *noticing*. Best of all is to read it out loud—trying out a few variations and hearing others try a few different readings. (See Mini-Workshop C on text rendering.)

Writing a Draft

1. Put the text aside and list the figurative words, phrases, or passages that come to you as memorable or important or intriguing. Don't worry about whether these are really figurative or about distinctions between various kinds of figurative language. Just list words or passages that seem especially alive or important. More often than not they will have figurative language.
2. Circle three or four phrases or passages that somehow seem the most important or intriguing.
3. Choose one—the one most interesting to you. Briefly describe it and go on writing about it—as much as you can—relating it to other parts of the piece but also to your own experience, memories, or values. How do you find yourself reacting to this passage? (You might want to look at the text again to see it freshly.)
4. To end this piece of writing, figure out the main thing you want to say about this passage.

PROCESS BOX

Stories tend to appear to me, not as formal ideas, but as metaphors, and these metaphors seem to demand structures of their own: they seem to have an internal need for a certain form. [Questioner: Can you say something more about these metaphors that your fiction grows out of?] They're the germ, the thought, the image, the idea, out of which all the rest grows. They're always a bit elusive, involving thoughts, feelings, abstractions, visual material, all at once. I suppose they're a little like dream fragments, in that such fragments always contain, if you analyze them, so much more than at first you suspect. But they're not literally that—I never write from dreams. All these ideas come to me in the full light of day. Some, when you pry them open, have too little inside to work with. Others are unexpectedly fat and rich. Novels typically begin for me as very tiny stories or little one-act play ideas which I think at the time aren't going to fill three pages. Then slowly the hidden complexities reveal themselves.

Robert Coover

5. Do the last two steps now for the other phrases or passages you circled.
6. Reread the whole text and then write about what these three phrases or passages have in common. What do they tell you about the text? How could you relate them to your own experience?
7. What's puzzling? What do the three passages *not* have in common? What other passages seem interesting or call for attention? How does your experience seem different or contradictory to the poem?
8. Now read or think back over what you have written and do some "So what?" writing. Figure out the main thing you want to say about how this text works—works in itself or works on you.

It helps to go through these activities in a class or workshop with others—not just for the encouragement and company but so that at various points you can share some of what you've written and hear some of what others have written.

Revising

Now you have already produced the makings or ingredients of a draft of an analytic essay. To revise, we suggest these steps:

- Look back over the text. Read it aloud again to see if you hear it any differently now.
- Look back over what you have written.
- Make up your mind now about what you really want to have for your main point. (Perhaps you've already done this in step 8.) In truth, there are good published works of literary analysis that consist of nothing but a succession of good but unconnected observations or insights. But most critics and teachers feel that you don't have a critical essay unless you reach some conclusion that ties together most of those smaller points.
- In the light of your main point, cut and paste the better parts of what you've already written into the order that makes the most sense.
- Now read over your cut-and-paste draft and wrestle with it to get it the way you want. Perhaps you'll have to make major structural changes—even change your mind about what you are saying; perhaps you'll just make smaller changes. (We discussed this in detail, of course, in Workshop 7 about revising.)

 SHARING AND RESPONDING

If you share a piece of first-stage writing—as in the eight steps—look for feedback that simply carries your thinking forward: "Summary and Sayback" and "Pointing and Center of Gravity" in *Sharing and Responding,* Sections 3 and 2, may help by tuning you into what is implied and almost said in your early draft. The following questions will help too.

- "Does my draft reach a conclusion, or is it just a collection of insights? If I have no conclusion, get me to keep talking until I find one, or tell me some points you hear implied."

■ "Do I manage to make you see the text as I do? Is my analysis convincing to you? What parts or aspects of the text do you feel I don't pay enough attention to?"

PROCESS WRITING OR COVER LETTER QUESTIONS

■ Was your reading of a text changed because you knew you'd have to analyze it or write about it? If so, what was gained? what was lost?
■ Did our sequence of steps help or get in your way?
■ Did the words and phrases that came to your attention seem to be figurative language? If not, what kinds of things made the language memorable or interesting?
■ Were you able to pay close attention to the language of the text and still relate the text to your own experience or values?

RUMINATIONS AND THEORY

Figurative Language as a Window on the Mind

People often believe that "regular language" says what it means and literature (especially poetry) has "hidden meanings" that only teachers and critics can find by some mysterious process. This is an unhelpful view of language. For "regular texts" aren't so regular, and literary texts aren't so esoteric.

If you think that figurative language occurs only in literature, you've been misled by the fact that people talk about it most in the study of literature. Figurative language is universal. Listen closely to any extended conversation. Better yet, record it so you can really examine the language. You'll find many metaphors, similes, and images in the words people speak as they go about their lives. You'll probably find even more in sports writing and political speeches. Slang is peppered (note the metaphor) with figurative language.

Figurative language appeals to the mind at a deep level—perhaps for many reasons. For one thing it's in the nature of the mind to see things as *like* other things or standing for other things. Indeed that's how we *do* see. It's virtually impossible to see any chair or person exactly in its uniqueness; we tend to see it as an instance of a type. Thinking could be defined as nothing but seeing things as like and unlike other things. This, remember, is how we tend to define something: by showing how it is both like and unlike related things. (See Lakoff and Johnson in the final reading in this workshop on how metaphor permeates our language and thinking.)

But it's not just a mistake. Literal language is a lens, and it distorts—like any lens. But we are so *used to* literal language that we think it is clear glass. Literal language is nothing but a lens that we don't notice anymore. But though we are used to literal language, most of us realize deep down that distortion is going on. We know there are things we aren't seeing—or saying— with the common lens, and that if we tried out other lenses, we'd see some new things. Most of us feel that we can't say things *just as they are* with our literal or regular language. Words don't ever seem to get quite accurately at what we are trying to say; there is always some slippage. So we all have the impulse to find other words (or other media) to capture things we cannot say quite right—in short to call things by the wrong name.

We cannot make up *new* words: no one will understand them. But we can use the old words in new ways, and *that does* bring out aspects of our experience that we cannot capture otherwise. A new lens brings new distortions, but it helps us notice what we didn't notice with the old lens. Thus we all use metaphor to make sense of things that are hard to make sense of.

And why images? If we see something that is powerful or important (or hear it or touch it), we have the impulse to put our experience in words—for ourselves and to tell others. We see this phenomenon most clearly when someone has been in a terrible accident or has experienced something frightening: he has an impulse to tell about it again and again. The same is true if something wonderful happens:

> "Did I tell you about what happened at third base? The ball bounced out of Schmitt's mitt and into the catcher's. You should have seen the look. . . ."

> "Yes, you've already told me three times."

The truth is we all *need* to talk about what is important—and tell it again and again. The telling helps us digest and make sense of our experience.

Thus if we find the metaphors and images in the conversation of a friend, we'll usually find the most interesting places, the places where his mind *reveals itself* the most. If these are *new* metaphors—metaphors he created (and people do it all the time)—they will represent the *making of new meaning:* places where he wasn't satisfied with the implications of words as others use them. These are usually places where his mind is the most in touch with what he wants to say.

If they are *used* metaphors—metaphors he found handy—they will represent places where you usually get the quickest and surest picture of the attitudes that he lives inside of—the meanings that shape his mind. For example, if someone says he "scored a touchdown on the physics exam" (or that he "scored" last night on a date), he is showing that at some level he thinks of school and dating as competitive games, where the object is to win. To find the metaphors in someone's language is to find the keys to how he understands the world.

If you find the places where someone lingers for a moment over a detail and gives a bit of an image for it—where he doesn't just say he went to a restaurant but tells how the candles looked or how the waiter spoke—you can find some of the experience that is probably the most felt and the most important to the person.

Passages of figurative language often have the strongest effect on listeners. If someone tells you, "For me, playing music is like flying over a spectacular landscape," this probably affects you more than if he said something literal like, "I am utterly involved in the excitement of playing music."

We are taking here a *cognitive* and *functional* approach to figurative language—not a *decorative* approach. That is, some critics talk as though figurative language is important because it "beautifies" thought. Some venerable theories of poetry say that the poet first finds her idea and then "clothes it" in "rich fabric" or in the "colors of rhetoric"—meaning figurative language. But though some writers work that way—and all of us sometimes stop and search for a colorful word when we want to dress up something we are saying—figurative language is much better understood as reflecting the way the mind works.

Therefore the quickest way to get to the heart of what's interesting and important in a conversation—or in a political speech, an advertisement, a story, novel, or poem—is to look at the figurative language.

Readings

MY MOTHER, THAT FEAST OF LIGHT

Kate Barnes

My mother, that feast of light, has always sat down,
Composed herself, and written poetry, hardly
Reworking any, just the way she used to
Tell us that Chinese painters painted; first they
Sat for days on the hillside watching the rabbits,
Then they went home, they set out ink and paper,
Meditated; and only then picked up their brushes
To catch the lift of a rabbit in mid-hop.

"If it didn't come out I would throw it away."
                                        Oh, she
Is still a bird that fills a bush with singing.
The way that she lifts her tea cup, the look she gives you
As you sit across from her, it is all a kind
Of essential music.
                    I also remember my father
Alone at the dining-room table, the ink bottle safe
In a bowl, his orange-red fountain pen in his big
Hand. The hand moved slowly back and forth
And the floor below was white with sheets of paper
Each carrying a rejected phrase or two
As he struggled all morning to finish just one sentence—
Like a smith hammering thick and glowing iron,
Like Jacob wrestling with the wonderful angel.

MY MOTHER, THAT BEAST OF BLIGHT

Amber Moltenbrey

The three pieces that I have picked out from the poem "My Mother, That
Feast of Light" all relate together in the image of a story. The story begins to
unravel with the line "If it didn't come out I would throw it away." This
sentence brings the introduction of the mother, that beast of blight. I imagine
the mother in the poem as a bottomless well of words, which she forms

together to produce a feast of interesting phrases—only, at the completion of a piece, to cast it aside as a reject of her own senses, a work that she has no desire to keep.

The sentence "I also remember my father/Alone at the dining room table . . ." brings to me a feeling of sorrow or pity, and leads me to side with the father in this tale of literary unrest. The father in the story is what starts my mind rolling. I do not see the father as a poet, or anything close to one, for that matter. I see him as a struggling businessman, trying to manage the farm efficiently, as he writes a letter to the local bank explaining a late payment.

In the line "As he struggled all morning to finish just one sentence. . . " the father seems to be performing a chore rather than a pleasant ritual. It is here that I see the father resenting the mother for her writing ability; and her, a blight to all of his efforts. This becomes the plot-thickening ingredient in the poem.

In the story I see the mother as very well respected by her children, writing poetry when the mood strikes her, only to abandon it as something she had never written. I see the father as a one-man-band in the family. The piece of the poem that states "the look she gives you/As you sit across from her . . ." makes me wonder why no one sits across from the father as he writes. Maybe a boost of confidence is all that is needed for the father to complete a piece of writing successfully. It seems it is a wondrous occasion when the mother writes (and only then to throw it away), but when the father writes it is a thankless task "to finish just one sentence. . . ." It is as though the father has no one to stand by him, no one to share his problem with, no one there to offer help. I feel that the father has been left out of a family secret, or something special that the whole family should share.

The story in my mind leads me to think about the literary unrest that occurs in the poem. The mother, having seemingly no problems producing a piece of writing, and the father struggling to construct a respectable sentence, create a symbolic contrast that gives the poem an added feature. This twist makes the story more intriguing and leads the reader to dig deeper into the meaning of the poem.

The aspects that have been neglected by my story are the ones that might prove that the mother has any sensitivity. The story of the Chinese painters gives a hint of sentimentality that I don't care to relate in my story, although it may very well be an important part of someone else's interpretation. Jacob wrestling the "wonderful" angel is not incorporated in my story either because of the "wonderfulness" of it. I don't see the children of the family ever relating their father to something "wonderful."

The effect of this piece of poetry has hit me like few others. I find it difficult to read and comprehend an average poem. This poem worked because of the many images that focused in my mind. Not only the ones I have written about, but other images that I didn't have time to develop. The figurative language in the poem adds color to the story. I also believe that the author leaves room for many interpretations in the poem by using the different methods of figurative language.

WRITING STYLES IN "MY MOTHER, THAT FEAST OF LIGHT"

Karen Daley

The poem "My Mother, That Feast of Light" by Kate Barnes is a comparison between two very different writing styles. Barnes poetically describes her parents while illustrating their unique methods for writing. Her mother is presented as a natural writer who has the ability to transform her thoughts and images onto paper. She spends a great deal of time just thinking through what she wants to write before she actually picks up her pen, allowing her words to flow freely onto her paper, not revising a single word. Her father has a much more tedious writing style. He knows what he wants to write, but the words that come out of his pen are much different, often awkward and unclear. He struggles with every word until his thoughts and images are presented in a creative manner.

As the poem begins you can see how Barnes illustrates her mother possessing such a creative and natural writing ability. "My mother, that feast of light" is a phrase that stands out, creating a positive view of her mother. A light is something that shows you the way in the dark, it is warm, bright, and alive. When it is used to describe her mother, the reader tends to develop a favorable opinion of her because the word "light" is associated with many positive images. Another phrase that eloquently presents her mother as a talented writer is "To catch the lift of a rabbit in mid-hop." The mother possesses the special ability to refer back to her own memory and create a vivid picture of a rabbit hopping, through the use of her carefully chosen words. The mother has this special ability due to the fact that she spends a great deal of time reflecting upon her vivid memories before she actually begins to write.

"I also remember my father alone at the dining-room table." The word *alone* stands out from the rest of the sentence. It conjures up negative feelings, forcing the reader to sympathize with the father. The phrase is written in common, everyday language lacking the imagination and creativity that was present in the first sentence describing the mother. Barnes seems to change her own style of writing when describing each parent. She describes her parents the way they might describe themselves: the mother who is very confident and expressive as opposed to the father who is unsure and always struggling with his words. Barnes writes with great detail and imagination, reinforcing the image of her mother as a talented poet. Her style changes when she describes her father. Her images become plain and uncreative, presenting her father as a struggling writer.

The idea that her father is a hard-working writer is reinforced once again. "The ink bottle safe in a bowl, his orange-red fountain pen in his big hand." Why is her father so persistent? It must be because he has ideas in his head that he wants to express on paper. Unfortunately he has a great deal of difficulty doing so. "The ink bottle is safe in a bowl" symbolizes the thoughts and images that are trapped in his head; he must struggle with them to get his ideas onto paper. Often the way he writes is awkward, which seems due to his large hand. We assume that the word *big* represents the difficulty he has with writing his thoughts down clearly. Fortunately, he does not allow his big hand to keep him from writing, although writing is much more of a struggle for him than for his wife.

Both of these writers are equally gifted, but go about writing in two totally different ways. Their thoughts are dreamlike (vivid but unreal) and until they reach paper their readers cannot see and feel the thoughts that they are trying so hard to share. The mother's method appears very carefree and simple, making her come across as a confident writer whom many readers may envy. The father struggles through his writing. His frustrations dealing with poetry are very common and familiar emotions that cause the reader to empathize with him. As you can see, Barnes uses her words not only to illustrate the two different writing styles but to force the reader to feel the same emotions that she, as a writer, is trying so hard to get across.

ONE ART*

Elizabeth Bishop

The art of losing isn't hard to master;
so many things seem filled with the intent
to be lost that their loss is no disaster.

Lose something every day. Accept the fluster
of lost door keys, the hour badly spent.
The art of losing isn't hard to master.

Then practice losing farther, losing faster:
places, and names, and where it was you meant
to travel. None of these will bring disaster.

I lost my mother's watch. And look! my last, or
next-to-last, of three loved houses went.
The art of losing isn't hard to master.

I lost two cities, lovely ones. And, vaster,
some realms I owned, two rivers, a continent.
I miss them, but it wasn't a disaster.

---

*Notice how this poem is answered by Adrienne Rich in the following one.

—Even losing you (the joking voice, a gesture
I love) I shan't have lied. It's evident
the art of losing's not too hard to master
though it may look like (*Write* it!) like disaster.

UNTITLED

Adrienne Rich

It's true, these last few years I've lived
watching myself in the act of loss—the art of losing,
Elizabeth Bishop called it, but for me no art
only badly-done exercises
acts of the heart forced to question
its presumptions in this world   its mere excitements
acts of the body forced to measure
all instincts against pain
acts of parting   trying to let go
without giving up   yes   Elizabeth   a city here
a village there   a sister, comrade, cat
and more   no art to this but anger

WEN-FU

Lu Chi (A.D. 261–303)

Taking his position at the hub of things, [the writer] contemplates
    the mystery of the universe; he feeds his emotions and his
    mind on the great works of the past.
Moving along with the four seasons, he sighs at the passing of
    time; gazing at the myriad objects, he thinks of the complexity
    of the world.
He sorrows over the falling leaves in virile autumn; he takes joy in
    the delicate bud of fragrant spring.
With awe at heart, he experiences chill; his spirit solemn, he
    turns his gaze to the clouds.
He declaims the superb works of his predecessors; he croons the
    clean fragrance of past worthies.
He roams in the Forest of Literature, and praises the symmetry of
    great art.

Moved, he pushes his books away and takes the writing-brush,
that he may express himself in letters.

At first he withholds his sight and turns his hearing inward; he is
lost in thought, questioning everywhere.

His spirit gallops to the eight ends of the universe; his mind
wanders along vast distances.

In the end, as his mood dawns clearer and clearer, objects, clean-
cut now in outline, shove one another forward.

He sips the essence of letters; he rinses his mouth with the extract
of the Six Arts.

Floating on the heavenly lake, he swims along; plunging into the
nether spring, he immerses himself.

Thereupon, submerged words wriggle up, as when a darting fish,
with the hook in its gills, leaps from a deep lake; floating
beauties flutter down, as when a high-flying bird, with the har-
poon-string around its wing, drops from a crest of cloud.

He gathers words never used in a hundred generations; he picks
rhythms never sung in a thousand years.

He spurns the morning blossom, now full blown; he plucks the
evening bud, which has yet to open.

He sees past and present in a moment; he touches the four seas in
a twinkling of an eye.

Now he selects ideas and fixes them in order; he examines words
and puts them in their places.

He taps at the door of all that is colorful; he chooses from among
everything that rings.

Now he shakes the foliage by tugging the twig; now he follows
back along the waves to the fountainhead of the stream.

Sometimes he brings out what was hidden; sometimes, looking for
an easy prey, he bags a hard one.

Now, the tiger puts in new stripes, to the consternation of other
beasts; now, the dragon emerges, and terrifies all the birds.

Sometimes things fit together, are easy to manage; sometimes
they jar each other, are awkward to manipulate.

He empties his mind completely, to concentrate his thoughts; he
collects his wits before he puts words together.

He traps heaven and earth in the cage of form; he crushes the
myriad objects against the tip of his brush.

At first they hesitate upon his parched lips; finally they flow
through the well-moistened brush.

Reason, supporting the matter [of the poem], stiffens the trunk;
style, depending from it, spreads luxuriance around.

Emotion and expression never disagree; all changes [in his mood]
are betrayed on his face.

If the thought touches on joy, a smile is inevitable; no sooner is
sorrow spoken of than a sigh escapes. . . .

THE BOOK OF THE GROTESQUE

Sherwood Anderson

The writer, an old man with a white mustache, had some difficulty in getting into bed. The windows of the house in which he lived were high and he wanted to look at the trees when he awoke in the morning. A carpenter came to fix the bed so that it would be on a level with the window.

Quite a fuss was made about the matter. The carpenter, who had been a soldier in the Civil War, came into the writer's room and sat down to talk of building a platform for the purpose of raising the bed. The writer had cigars lying about and the carpenter smoked.

For a time the two men talked of the raising of the bed and then they talked of other things. The soldier got on the subject of the war. The writer, in fact, led him to that subject. The carpenter had once been a prisoner in Andersonville prison and had lost a brother. The brother had died of starvation, and whenever the carpenter got upon that subject he cried. He, like the old writer, had a white mustache, and when he cried he puckered up his lips and the mustache bobbed up and down. The weeping old man with the cigar in his mouth was ludicrous. The plan the writer had for the raising of his bed was forgotten and later the carpenter did it in his own way and the writer, who was past sixty, had to help himself with a chair when he went to bed at night.

In his bed the writer rolled over on his side and lay quite still. For years he had been beset with notions concerning his heart. He was a hard smoker and his heart fluttered. The idea had got into his mind that he would some time die unexpectedly and always when he got into bed he thought of that. It did not alarm him. The effect in fact was quite a special thing and not easily explained. It made him more alive, there in bed, than at any other time. Perfectly still he lay and his body was old and not of much use any more, but something inside him was altogether young. He was like a pregnant woman, only that the thing inside him was not a baby but a youth. No, it wasn't a youth, it was a woman, young, and wearing a coat of mail like a knight. It is absurd, you see, to try to tell what was inside the old writer as he lay on his high bed and listened to the fluttering of his heart. The thing to get at is what the writer, or the young thing within the writer, was thinking about.

The old writer, like all of the people in the world, had got, during his long life, a great many notions in his head. He had once been quite handsome and a number of women had been in love with him. And then, of course, he had known people, many people, known them in a peculiarly intimate way that was different from the way in which you and I know people. At least that is what the writer thought and the thought pleased him. Why quarrel with an old man concerning his thoughts?

In the bed the writer had a dream that was not a dream. As he grew somewhat sleepy but was still conscious, figures began to appear before his eyes. He imagined the young indescribable thing within himself was driving a long procession of figures before his eyes.

You see the interest in all this lies in the figures that went before the eyes of the writer. They were all grotesques. All of the men and women the writer had ever known had become grotesques.

The grotesques were not all horrible. Some were amusing, some almost beautiful, and one, a woman all drawn out of shape, hurt the old man by her grotesqueness. When she passed he made a noise like a small dog whimpering. Had you come into the room you might have supposed the old man had unpleasant dreams or perhaps indigestion.

For an hour the procession of grotesques passed before the eyes of the old man, and then, although it was a painful thing to do, he crept out of bed and began to write. Some one of the grotesques had made a deep impression on his mind and he wanted to describe it.

At his desk the writer worked for an hour. In the end he wrote a book which he called "The Book of the Grotesque." It was never published, but I saw it once and it made an indelible impression on my mind. The book had one central thought that is very strange and has always remained with me. By remembering it I have been able to understand many people and things that I was never able to understand before. The thought was involved but a simple statement of it would be something like this:

That in the beginning when the world was young there were a great many thoughts but no such thing as a truth. Man made the truths himself and each truth was a composite of a great many vague thoughts. All about in the world were the truths and they were all beautiful.

The old man had listed hundreds of the truths in his book. I will not try to tell you all of them. There was the truth of virginity and the truth of passion, the truth of wealth and of poverty, of thrift and of profligacy, of carelessness and abandon. Hundreds and hundreds were the truths and they were all beautiful.

And then the people came along. Each as he appeared snatched up one of the truths and some who were quite strong snatched up a dozen of them.

It was the truths that made the people grotesques. The old man had quite an elaborate theory concerning the matter. It was his notion that the moment one of the people took one of the truths to himself, called it his truth, and tried to live his life by it, he became a grotesque and the truth he embraced became a falsehood.

You can see for yourself how the old man, who had spent all of his life writing and was filled with words, would write hundreds of pages concerning this matter. The subject would become so big in his mind that he himself would be in danger of becoming a grotesque. He didn't, I suppose, for the same reason that he never published the book. It was the young thing inside him that saved the old man.

Concerning the old carpenter who fixed the bed for the writer, I only mentioned him because he, like many of what are called very common people, became the nearest thing to what is understandable and lovable of all the grotesques in the writer's book.

From METAPHORS WE LIVE BY

George Lakoff and
Mark Johnson

Metaphor is for most people a device of the poetic imagination and the rhetorical flourish—a matter of extraordinary rather than ordinary language. Moreover, metaphor is typically viewed as characteristic of language alone, a matter of words rather than thought or action. For this reason, most people think they can get along perfectly well without metaphor. We have found, on the contrary, that metaphor is pervasive in everyday life, not just in language but in thought and action. Our ordinary conceptual system, in terms of which we both think and act, is fundamentally metaphorical in nature. . . .

Primarily on the basis of linguistic evidence, we have found that most of our ordinary conceptual system is metaphorical in nature. And we have found a way to begin to identify in detail just what the metaphors are that structure how we perceive, how we think, and what we do.

To give some idea of what it could mean for a concept to be metaphorical and for such a concept to structure an everyday activity, let us start with the concept ARGUMENT and the conceptual metaphor ARGUMENT IS WAR. This metaphor is reflected in our everyday language by a wide variety of expressions:

Argument Is War

Your claims are *indefensible*.
He *attacked every weak point* in my argument.
His criticisms were *right on target*.
I *demolished* his argument.
I've never *won* an argument with him.
You disagree? Okay, *shoot!*
If you use that *strategy,* he'll *wipe you out*.
He *shot down* all of my arguments.

It is important to see that we don't just *talk* about arguments in terms of war. We can actually win or lose arguments. We see the person we are arguing with as an opponent. We attack his positions and we defend our own. We gain and lose ground. We plan and use strategies. If we find a position indefensible, we can abandon it and take a new line of attack. Many of the things we *do* in arguing are partially structured by the concept of war. Though there is no physical battle, there is a verbal battle, and the structure of an argument—attack, defense, counterattack, etc.—reflects this. It is in this sense that the ARGUMENT IS WAR metaphor is one that we live by in this culture; it structures the actions we perform in arguing.

Try to imagine a culture where arguments are not viewed in terms of war, where no one wins or loses, where there is no sense of attacking or defending, gaining or losing ground. Imagine a culture where an argument is viewed as a dance, the participants are seen as performers, and the goal is to perform in a balanced and aesthetically pleasing way. In such a culture, people would view arguments differently, experience them differently, carry them out differently, and talk about them differently. But *we* would probably not view them as arguing at all: they would simply be doing something different. It would seem strange even to call what they were doing "arguing." Perhaps the most neutral way of describing this difference between their culture and ours would be to say that we have a discourse form structured in terms of battle and they have one structured in terms of dance.

This is an example of what it means for a metaphorical concept, namely, ARGUMENT IS WAR, to structure (at least in part) what we do and how we understand what we are doing when we argue. *The essence of metaphor is understanding and experiencing one kind of thing in terms of another.* It is not that arguments are a subspecies of war. Arguments and wars are different kinds of things—verbal discourse and armed conflict—and the actions performed are different kinds of actions. But ARGUMENT is partially structured, understood, performed, and talked about in terms of WAR. The concept is metaphorically structured, the activity is metaphorically structured, and consequently, the language is metaphorically structured.

Moreover, this is the *ordinary* way of having an argument and talking about one. The normal way for us to talk about attacking a position is to use the words "attack a position." Our conventional ways of talking about arguments presuppose a metaphor we are hardly ever conscious of. The metaphor is not merely in the words we use—it is in our very concept of an argument. The language of argument is not poetic, fanciful, or rhetorical; it is literal. We talk about arguments that way because we conceive of them that way—and we act according to the way we conceive of things.

The most important claim we have made so far is that metaphor is not just a matter of language, that is, of mere words. We shall argue that, on the contrary, human *thought processes* are largely metaphorical. This is what we mean when we say that the human conceptual system is metaphorically structured and defined. Metaphors as linguistic expressions are possible precisely because there are metaphors in a person's conceptual system. Therefore, whenever in this book we speak of metaphors, such as ARGUMENT IS WAR, it should be understood that *metaphor* means *metaphorical concept.*

Some Further Examples

We have been claiming that metaphors partially structure our everyday concepts and that this structure is reflected in our literal language. Before we can get an overall picture of the philosophical implications of these claims, we need a few more examples. In each of the ones that follow we give a metaphor and a list of ordinary expressions that are special cases of the metaphor. The English expressions are of two sorts: simple literal expressions and idioms that fit the metaphor and are part of the normal everyday way of talking about the subject.

Theories (and Arguments) Are Buildings

Is that the *foundation* for your theory? The theory needs more *support*. The argument is *shaky*. We need some more facts or the argument will *fall apart*. We need to *construct* a *strong* argument for that. I haven't figured out yet what the *form* of the argument will be. Here are some more facts to *shore up* the theory. We need to *buttress* the theory with *solid* arguments. The theory will *stand* or *fall* on the *strength* of that argument. The argument *collapsed*. They *exploded* his latest theory. We will show that theory to be without *foundation*. So far we have put together only the *framework* of the theory.

Ideas Are Food

What he said *left a bad taste in my mouth*. All this paper has in it are *raw facts, half-baked ideas, and warmed-over theories*. There are too many facts here for me to *digest* them all. I just can't *swallow* that claim. That argument *smells fishy*. Let me *stew* over that for a while. Now there's a theory you can really *sink your teeth into*. We need to let that idea *percolate* for a while. That's *food for thought*. He's a *voracious* reader. We don't need to *spoon-feed* our students. He *devoured* the book. Let's let that idea *simmer on the back burner* for a while. This is the *meaty* part of the paper. Let that idea *jell* for a while. That idea has been *fermenting* for years.

Understanding Is Seeing; Ideas Are Light-Sources; Discourse Is a Light-Medium

I *see* what you're saying. It *looks* different from my *point of view*. What is your *outlook* on that? I *view* it differently. Now I've got the *whole picture*. Let me *point something out* to you. That's an *insightful* idea. That was a *brilliant* remark. The argument is *clear*. It was a *murky* discussion. Could you *elucidate* your remarks? It's a *transparent* argument. The discussion was *opaque*.

Love Is Magic

She *cast her spell* over me. The *magic* is gone. I was *spellbound*. She had me *hypnotized*. He has me *in a trance*. I was *entranced* by him. I'm *charmed* by her. She is *bewitching*.

Love Is War

He is known for his many rapid *conquests*. She *fought for* him, but his mistress *won out*. He *fled from* her *advances*. She *pursued* him *relentlessly*. He is slowly *gaining ground* with her. He *won* her hand in marriage. He *overpowered* her. She is *besieged* by suitors. He has to *fend* them *off*. He *enlisted the aid* of her friends. He *made an ally* of her mother. Theirs is a *misalliance* if I've ever seen one.

WORKSHOP

15

VOICE

Do you underline a lot of words when you write? Do you like to use two or three exclamation marks or question marks at the end of sentences when you are excited—or end a sentence with !?#@!? when you are mad or happy? DO YOU SOMETIMES WRITE IN ALL CAPS WHEN YOU WANT TO EMPHASIZE SOMETHING? When you write by hand, do you sometimes use double and triple underlinings—or write words in giant letters?

Think for a moment about what we are doing when we use these visual effects in writing. Surely we are trying to get some of our voice into our writing, trying to make writing a little more like speaking, trying to get a few bits of emphasis, intonation, and drama down on the page.

But as you have no doubt learned, you mustn't put in these visual voice marks if you want to produce "good writing" or "careful writing" or "standard writing." (Peter Elbow always underlines "too many" words in his rough drafts, and so revising for him always involves getting rid of one after another after another.)

Are the conventions of literacy actually saying, "We don't want voice in writing"? Has our culture come to define literacy in such a way as to have less voice in writing than there could be? We suspect it has, but this is a debatable point.

What's not debatable, though, is that certain *kinds* of voice are frowned on in certain kinds of writing. That is, in the case of *highly formal writing* (such as we find in business reports and scholarly journals), readers and writers seem to want formal voices: quieter, more dressed up, well-behaved, and impersonal voices. "Don't raise your voice; keep it decorous; keep it genteel." In the case of *informal writing,* on the other hand (such as we find in newspaper feature stories and many magazine articles and literary essays), readers and writers seem to like informal voices: personal, lively, casual, idiosyncratic voices.

But notice that even in informal writing, we're supposed to create these lively, informal, personal voices *without* using typographical tricks and without too much underlining and double exclamation marks. Good writers are supposed to wangle that voice *into the words themselves*—not do it by using visual markers that tell us how the words are supposed to be spoken. (It's interesting to notice that musicians have come to welcome these markers that tell players how loud or soft to play and where to put emphasis. Early composers like Bach didn't put in dynamic cues like "allegro" and "forte" and little lines or dots to tell players to emphasize a note or make it short: but in the last few hundred years composers have put in more and more of these directions to "readers." The same with drama: early playwrights like Shakespeare gave no stage directions, but more recent playwrights have given more and more directions about how to say the words and stage the play.)

And how about writing in school and college? Is it formal or informal? Can it have a personal, lively, casual voice, or must it be dressed up and restrained? As all students know, teachers don't agree. Some teachers are happy to get an informal voice while others want a dignified, impersonal voice. What bothers many teachers is a *mixing* of voices: hearing the collision of a casual spoken voice with a formal academic one. The moral is obvious:

what students need is the ability to notice the voice in their writing and adjust it: to use different voices for different teachers or readers and to notice mixtures that don't work. We've designed the exercises in this workshop to help you with this goal.

But there's one more issue that many of you will raise sooner or later: "I want my writing voice to *fit me!* I don't just want it to fit my readers. If I adjust my voice to different audiences, I don't want to sound artificial or fake. I want to sound like me." This is a feasible goal too, one we can understand by looking at actual speech. That is, almost everyone's voice or way of speaking tends to change when they talk to different people or are in different situations. Think about how you can often tell who a friend is talking to on the phone just by the tone of voice he or she is using. But some people manage to sound "like themselves" even when they use different voices. They always sound real, not pretending. Other people sound like themselves only when they talk to *some* people; and they sound fake or artificial or unreal when they talk to others. Most people sound unlike themselves when they are nervous or afraid; but some people sound this way even if they aren't nervous— they have developed certain *roles* they use in certain situations or for certain audiences, and they don't sound natural in those roles.

We have designed the exercises in this workshop, then, to help you learn not only to vary your written voice as needed but also if possible to still sound like yourself.

The *main assignment* is to take a paper you have already written and revise it with special attention to voice. Probably the best choice would be a paper (or draft) that bothers you because of the voice—where, for example, you feel the writing is stiff, awkward, or artificial. But any paper will do: any paper that bothers you for some reason—or even a paper you'd simply enjoy playing with by writing it in a different voice.

We can also suggest an *alternative assignment:* write an essay that explores the voices you find in different pieces of your writing and in different speaking situations. Explore how they relate to each other and whether you think you have "*a* voice."

EXERCISES TO HELP YOU RECOGNIZE AND USE DIFFERENT VOICES ON PAPER

We spend lots of our life listening to people and noticing *how they talk*. From an early age we get skilled at noticing whether someone is mad at us or fond of us or is in a bad mood—just by listening to their voice (even if we are listening to them on the phone and voice is the only cue we have). We have many words that describe how people talk—words for tone of voice: cheerful, chirpy, sarcastic, breathy, haughty, scared, timid, flat. But when words are written instead of spoken, they just sit there silently on the page. We can't hear them; they don't speak to us. Plato criticized writing over speaking on just this score.

Yet writing *will* speak to us if we "listen" to it well enough—with our ear and our mouth. We may have to practice, however, to learn to apply our sophisticated voice-listening skills to writing. Here are four short exercises that will help you hear and understand and describe the voice in a piece of writing. These exercises are done best in pairs or small groups.

(1) *What does the voice in the writing actually* sound *like?* Enact the voice; render the passage out loud. That is, don't just "say" the words, but give them a reading that brings out the tone, mood, feeling, or character—the voice—that seems to fit best. (You practiced this activity if you did Workshop 11.)

Try to get two or three readings of the same passage to see if different readers bring out different voices. For of course readers are likely to disagree about the voice they hear—and rightly so since different voicings can be equally "in" the text (for example, the same passage could be read as sarcastic or straight). In addition, a single passage can *change* voices or tones as it goes along—for example, gradually building up to more excitement, or suddenly slowing down and becoming quietly meditative. Since the goal is to hear voices on the page—that is, to explore voice in written language—it's fine to play around, stretch, or even exaggerate a bit. Then you can discuss your reactions to these readings and try to decide when a reading fits the written words well and when it wasn't right for the words.

Here's a suggestion: many people have an easier time doing this exercise if they first visualize in their mind a *character* who is saying these words and a *scene* or *setting* where that character is speaking—and even how that character is standing or moving.

Here's a sample passage that we'll use to illustrate these exercises:

Fun. Fun. Did I say this was fun? A curse, that's what the computer is. In process. Nothing's ever done. You can always find a new way to rework things. Example: the ending. That came to me while I was working on another paper. It probably doesn't work, but hell, enough is enough. I've got shopping to do, cards to send, laundry, you name it. I'm calling it quits. OK, so I'll give it one more read tomorrow in school. (Deb DuBock, process writing, 12/91)

We can't illustrate out-loud renderings of this passage (unless we included a tape recording with the book), but we can talk about the voices we heard when we did readings of this passage ourselves and with students. Some people read it with a voice of cheerful, amused exasperation, while others heard and rendered a voice of serious heart-tearing frustration. One reader heard a kind of frenzied Dr. Strangelove voice in the passage and spit out those first two words ("Fun. Fun.") through tightly clenched teeth like a mad scientist going crazy. Notice the rich possibilities in those first two words: some people gave the second "fun" a very different mood or tone from the first one—more angry and sarcastic; others gave the second "fun" a tone of questioning as though it represented someone suddenly noticing what she had just said and questioning it. ("Fun. *Fun?*"—the second one saying, in effect, "Are you kidding?")

Quite a few people rendered changes in mood in midpassage. A number of people put in a big pause before that last "OK, so I'll give it one more read tomorrow in school"—some of them making it sound discouraged and dejected, others reading in a voice of amused self-mocking—the voice of someone who knows that she always gives in to the need for more work and has come to accept that fact about herself. What we see here is what all actors know: that the same words have a number of potential voices in them.

(2) *What kind of person talks this way?* Role-play the speaker in the passage, pretend to *be* that person, and then talk in "your voice" about "yourself." That is, tell us what kind of person you are and how you see things and how you go about doing things.

Here is one possible role-play of the voice in our sample passage:

Yes, I love my computer, I love writing. But sometimes I feel like I'm going crazy. But you know what? I love that feeling of going crazy. It's the only thing that gives me some excitement in life. I can't stand it when everything goes as planned. Don't you feel the same way? I pity you if you don't. On days when everything runs smoothly, I get scared that maybe my life will turn out empty.

You can do this role-playing either "live" (in speech) or on paper—perhaps both. Again, it can be helpful to imagine your person in a particular scene and posture.

(3) *How does this person or voice talk about other things?* Write something completely different—but in that voice. Pretend to be this person and write a little story or description or make a request—*as this person would write.* Here's an example of the kind of thing we have in mind, based on Deb DuBock's passage:

My mom called me last night. Saturday night! What made her think I'd be here. The nerve! But there I was. I thought it was going to be someone else and I answered all happy. I know she could hear my voice fall when she told me it was her. But what did she expect? She wants me to come visit next weekend. Next weekend! Give me a break. I'm not going, I'm just not going. I'm an adult, OK? I'm earning money. I'm taking care of myself. N. O. No. OK . . . so what are you making for dinner?

(4) *How would you describe the voice?* After you have enacted the voices in a piece of writing in these exercises, you will find it much easier to find explanatory language to describe the voices you hear in it. What is the tone, character, mood of this voice?

Here is one possible description of the voice Deb DuBock used:

> It's a voice of exasperation and frustration. But there's also a note in the voice of self-awareness—that this frustration is not the end of the world—a faint note even of amusement or enjoyment. And that last sentence has a smile of amused self-mocking underneath the discouraged giving in.

You don't actually need to be able to *describe* voices to be able to hear them, understand them, and use them well in writing and speaking. To describe them is a somewhat detached and analytic ability. Yet this is a useful and interesting ability—both for analytic school writing (especially in literature classes—see Workshop 11) and also for dealing with countless situations in life. ("I hate it when you are sarcastic with me!" "Oh, come on. Here we go again. I wasn't being sarcastic; I was just making a friendly joke.")

Now use these four exercises on one or more of these other sample passages:

(a) You see, there's a simple reason our elected officials consistently fail to function: They are stupid. (Not all. There are 17 who actually know what they are doing.) Please don't look for anything more complex. They are dumb, that's all. End of story.

As a matter of fact, if you take a close peek at them you will see a herd of peabrains who are today—this very moment—holding the best job they will ever have. And they're lucky to be employed because who would hire them?

You wouldn't put them behind the counter at the J&J Variety in Waltham be-

---

PROCESS BOX

[Toward the end of his life, Mark Twain started dictating his autobiography to a secretary—lying in bed each morning smoking cigars. He wrote about this method to William Dean Howells.] You will never know how much enjoyment you have lost until you get to dictating your autobiography; then you will realize, with a pang, that you might have been doing it all your life if you had only had the luck to think of it. And you will be astonished (& charmed) to see how like *talk* it is, & how real it sounds, & how well & compactly & sequentially it constructs itself, & what a dewy & breezy & woodsy freshness it has, & what a darling & worshipful absence of the signs of starch, and flatiron, & labor & fuss & the other artificialities! Mrs. Clemens is an exacting critic, but I have not talked a sentence yet that she has wanted altered. There are little slips here & there, little inexactnesses, & many desertions of a thought before the end of it has been reached, but these are not blemishes, they are merits, and their removal would take away the naturalness of the flow & banish the very thing—the nameless something—which differentiates real narrative from artificial narrative & makes the one so vastly better than the other—the subtle something which makes good talk so much better than the best imitation of it that can be done with a pen.

Selected Mark Twain

cause they steal. You couldn't have them wait tables at the Stockyard because they are so slow they could not remember a food order.

Pick up trash? Why, they take 12 months to do eight hour's work as it is now; your Christmas tree would still be at the curb on Decoration Day.

Park cars? You'd no sooner leave the lot than they would retain one of their idiotic cousins to handle the vehicle because they have this genetic defect that causes them to pack anything—a payroll or the front seat of a Ford Escort—with some relative who couldn't beat Lassie at Scrabble. (Mike Barnicle 21)

(b) The written word is weak. Many people prefer life to it. Life gets your blood going, and it smells good. Writing is mere writing, literature is mere. It appeals only to the subtlest senses—the imagination's vision, and the imagination's hearing— and the moral sense, and the intellect. This writing that you do, that thrills you, that so rocks and exhilarates you, as if you were dancing next to the band, is barely audible to anyone else. The reader's ear must adjust down from loud life to the subtle, imaginary sounds of the written word. An ordinary reader picking up a book can't yet hear a thing; it will take half an hour to pick up the writing's modulations, its ups and downs and louds and softs.

An intriguing entomological experiment shows that a male butterfly will ignore a living female butterfly of his own species in favor of a painted cardboard one, if the cardboard one is big. If the cardboard one is bigger than he is, bigger than any female butterfly ever could be, he jumps the piece of cardboard. Over and over again, he jumps the piece of cardboard. Nearby, the real, living female butterfly opens and closes her wings in vain. (Annie Dillard 17–18)

(c) Style is the physiognomy of the mind, and a safer index to character than the face. To imitate another man's style is like wearing a mask, which, be it never so fine, is not long in arousing disgust and abhorrence, because it is lifeless; so that even the ugliest living face is better. An affectation in style is like making grimaces. . . .

Every mediocre writer tries to mask his own natural style, because in his heart he knows the truth of what I am saying. He is thus forced, at the outset, to give up any attempt at being frank or naïve—a privilege which is thereby reserved for superior minds, conscious of their own worth, and therefore sure of themselves. What I mean is that these everyday writers are absolutely unable to resolve upon writing just as they think; because they have a notion that, were they to do so, their work might possibly look very childish and simple. For all that, it would not be without its value. If they would only go honestly to work, and say, quite simply, the things they have really thought, and just as they have thought them, these writers would be readable and, within their own proper sphere, even instructive. (Arthur Schopenhauer 60)

 EXERCISES TO EXPLORE YOUR OWN VOICES IN WRITING

Our goal here is to give you a better sense of the different voices that already exist in your writing. Poke around among all the different kinds of writing of yours that you can find—writing you've done in this course and writing you've done for other reasons—and try to find four or five passages with *different* voices or tones or moods. Short passages of just a couple of paragraphs will do just fine. You may think that you always write in the same voice, but if you look carefully (listen carefully), you'll find much more variety than you expected.

The different papers you've written here on different topics will probably show variations in voice. If you have old papers around, they may show you changes in your written voice over time. But don't just look at papers; there's lots more writing you do. Look at freewriting, early drafts, journal writing, personal notebooks, notebooks you keep for other classes (where you sometimes write notes to yourself or friends), notes to roommates, letters to friends or family, more formal letters you've had to write such as job applications. (If you contribute to computer networks or bulletin boards or use electronic mail, this is an interesting place to look at your voice. This new medium is particularly interesting because it is clearly *writing,* but people use it more as though they were speaking. Notice the little smiley faces and codes people also use to signal tone.)

But don't forget (and this may be the most important thing for this course) that you can often find different voices in just one paper. Papers often start off in one voice (sometimes a somewhat stiff or neutral or careful voice); they often change voices as the writer gets warmed up; and sometimes writers slide into yet other voices when they provide examples, give anecdotes, make asides or digressions (and you certainly better not forget to look at the tone of your parentheses).

Out of your four or five passages, try to see to it that one or two feel comfortable to you and somehow feel "like you"—sound the way you want to sound. Try also to get a passage or two that feels *uncomfortable*—to illustrate what happens to your voice when you somehow don't manage to sound like yourself. It can be helpful to get a friend to help you look for passages with different voices. Someone else can sometimes have an easier time noticing differences.

The goal now is to work on hearing and understanding those voices better and figuring out how they work. Get into pairs or small groups and apply the four exercises you did above, but this time to your own writing (perform the words to see what the voice sounds like; pretend to be the person that this voice implies and write about yourself; write in this voice about something else; describe the voice).

The biggest benefit from these exercises—and the biggest boost to your writing—will come from the first three exercises, and especially the *enacting* or *performing* activities. For the main way that you learn about voice and develop your voice or voices is not by analyzing but by getting voices into your ear and mouth and body—so that the voices just *come out of you.*

But it can feel a little uncomfortable or unsafe letting *other* people do these role-play exercises on your writing. Other people are likely to exaggerate or even slip into a bit of parody. So it's fine to do the first three exercises yourself and let others just *describe* the voices they hear in your passages. But if you feel brave and don't mind a little play or stretching of your voices, you will learn a lot from letting others do the first three exercises on your passages.

In any event, the goal is to find and bring to life the voice in your passages—and perhaps see the different voices and sounds in there. It helps to experiment and stretch. Remember your ultimate goal: the ability to use different voices in your writing, and the ability to find and use a voice that feels

I feel caught in between two cultures. When I have to write a letter to my family and friends back in Korea, I realize that I have lost the eloquence of my native language. In particular, I have forgotten lots of Chinese characters that are used frequently in written Korean. I hardly read or speak Korean these days since I have to write, read, and speak English everyday. While I feel sad about losing touch with my native tongue, I also strongly feel that as a foreigner living in this country I must master English in order to survive. Instead of feeling as though I am lost and split between these two cultures, I should feel enriched since I am bilingual and can enjoy both cultures.

I used to write poems when I was in college back in Korea. The colors that emerged from my poems were frequently black and white as I would write about darkness, human suffering, snow, and so on. I remember that I used to be afraid of darkness when I was little, but as I grew up, I became fascinated by the secrecy that darkness implied. While I, as a college student, searched for some meaning in life, black became my favorite color. I thought that black meant negation and nothingness, but it also could be thought of as a point of beginning from which all things can happen. Since I came to America, I have hardly written any poems. I used to feel inspired to write when I was younger. I wonder whether the reason that I stopped doing creative writing is because English is not my native language, or because I am getting older and don't feel inspiration anymore, or because I have to do academic writing all of the time.

I still dream in Korean even though I dream in English most of the time, now. Sometimes, I speak in English to my family in my dreams but I don't remember whether they understand me or not.

Eunsook Koo

right for you, that comes from a deeper part of you. When you get such voices, you and your listeners will often know it right away. They'll feel a click or resonance. Sometimes *you* won't hear that click and will resist. That is, sometimes readers say to a writer, "Yes, that's it; that's strong; that's you." And the writer says, "But that's not how I want to sound; that's not me." This is an interesting dilemma: no easy answers. In our experience, voices that are more "yours" are not necessarily ones you like, but rather ones that are powerful. When you use them, your writing is not "nice," but the meanings come through more forcefully. Teachers may not like them either.

Note that you are not necessarily trying to decide on *one right voice* for you. There probably is no such thing. You need different voices for different situations. Nevertheless, try to get a feel for when a voice feels right for you and when it doesn't. You may begin to get a sense of a *kind* of voice or *range* of voices that you recognize as yours—and other voices that seem definitely wrong or unfitting for you.

 ## MAIN ASSIGNMENT

Choose one of your papers that you would like to revise by changing the voice. It could be a finished paper, it could be a draft, or it could be a substantial fragment (for example, from your private writing or freewriting). Your teacher may direct you among these choices.

The exercises you have done will put you in a good position to do this assignment, but there is no right sequence of steps to follow. Perhaps you will start work on this paper with nothing but a sound in your ear and a feel in your mouth for the voice(s) you are trying for or some awareness of the voice(s) you don't like. Or perhaps you can start work by describing or explaining to yourself analytically what those voices are. Our only advice is to use both kinds of understanding: analytic, explanatory understanding and the understanding that consists of the sounds of words in your ear and the feel of words in your mouth. Use each kind of understanding as a check against the other.

As you do this assignment in revising voice, stay alert for impulses to change even the *ideas* or *content* of what you are saying. These may be faint impulses but they are important. For when you *use* a different voice, you are *being* a different person—or at least taking a different point of view or speaking from a different part of yourself. Naturally it will lead you to think different thoughts. Thus, you might think you are doing only what we called (in Workshop 7) second-level revising, or changing the muscles, but you will probably find yourself drifting into first-level revising, or changing the bones. When this happens, it's a good sign.

Alternative Assignment. Write a paper exploring your voice—that is, the different voices you find in your speaking situations and writing situations—and the question of whether there is a single voice in or underneath or behind them all: "your voice." Here are some questions that might help you write this paper:

■ What are your important voices? Think back to times when your speaking or writing voice was notable or important. Examples: (a) Think of a person you feel comfortable and easy talking to. What is your voice with this person? What does it tell about you? What side of you does it bring out? (b) Think of a time when you felt particularly awkward in talking—tongue-tied or artificial or "not you." What was your voice like then? Where did that "not you" voice come from? (c) Think of a time when you spoke with particular intensity and conviction. Perhaps you were mad or sad or excited. As you spoke, you could feel, "Yes. This is right. I'm saying what I really need to say and damn it, I'm saying it so my listener *has* to hear it." What was your voice like? What part of you was it bringing out? In short, think about how certain people or occasions bring out different voices in you. Role-play or freewrite conversations you might have with them. Just speak or write *your* words, not theirs. This can help you see your different voices. (These can make interesting pieces of writing too—where readers can half-imagine the situation. Comedian Bob Newhart has made a career out of creating these different voices where you hear only one side of a conversation.)

■ What are some of the voices you have *heard* that have been important in your life: (family, friends, teachers, coaches)? A bunch of friends who hang around together often start sounding similar. Most of our voices have been influenced even by voices of characters in public life, on TV or radio, in books, in church, in school—voices we hear often that carry weight or authority. Think of phrases that reverberate in your ear or your memory from some of these people. Listen to that phrase in your mind's ear—listen to *how* the person says it—and write about that voice and its meaning for you.

- Do you find yourself usually comfortable in your speaking and writing voice? However you answer, try to explain how your situation came about.
- What voices and parts of yourself do you show in speech but have a hard time using in writing? Are there parts of yourself that come out in writing but don't show in speech?
- Where would you put yourself on this continuum: at the one end are people who feel they have a single, "real" voice that represents their real self (despite variations in tone in different situations); at the other end are people who feel that none of the voices they use are more real or "theirs" than any others. In short, how do you relate to yourself the notion of "real self" and "real voice"?

As part of this paper or perhaps even as a separate project, you could make a collage of passages from your writing in different voices—or else create a collage where you write about the same topic in all the voices you find in your writing.

Collaborative Option: A collaborative essay comparing the voices of two or three of you. Start by each of you making a collage of passages of your own writing—passages that illustrate your different voices. This first step can be done individually, but it's interesting and helpful to enlist the aid of your partner(s) in choosing among possible passages and deciding what order to put them in. Then write your collaborative essay comparing the constellation of voices each of you has. Possible questions: Does one of you have a wider or narrower range of voices? What are the feelings that each of you has about various voices and about the range of them? How do the voices seem to relate to the person's identity—as seen by herself and seen by others? Do certain voices seem less legitimate? Do certain voices have a particular history?

 ## SHARING AND RESPONDING

- "Describe the main voice you hear in my revised version. How is it different from the voice of my piece before it was revised? Try describing the two voices in terms of clothing (jeans? baggy sweater? jacket and tie?)."
- "Describe any changes or variations of voice you can hear (for example, from confident to timid or serious to humorous). Do these changes or variations work, or are they a problem for you?"
- "Do you hear any echoes of outside voices—voices that are not mine? Have I 'made them part of my voice,' or do they seem undigested or unassimilated?"
- Alternative assignment: "Which parts of my essay are most interesting to you? What do you learn from my essay about voice as an issue?"

PROCESS JOURNAL AND
COVER LETTER QUESTIONS

- Talk about how you experienced the first four exercises: performing a voice? role-playing the person in the voice? writing something else in that voice? and describing the voice? What did you learn from the *process* of doing them (that is, apart from learning about voice)?
- When you were revising your paper for voice, what changes in content or point of view did you notice?
- Which parts of you are brought out by the voice you used in your revision?
- Note: The questions for the alternative assignment also make good process questions.

Readings

A COLLAGE OF PASSAGES ABOUT VOICE

With the people I know very well, I find that all of the emotion which would normally be expressed in the face is there in the voice: the tiredness, the anxiety, the suppressed excitement and so on. My impressions based on voice seem to be just as accurate as those of sighted people.
> —John M. Hull, from *Touching the Rock: An Experience of Blindness*

Ever since I was first read to, then started reading to myself, there has never been a line read that I didn't *hear*. As my eyes followed the sentence, a voice was saying it silently to me. It isn't my mother's voice, or the voice of any person I can identify, certainly not my own. It is human, but inward, and it is inwardly that I listen to it. It is to me the voice of the story or the poem itself. The cadence, whatever it is that asks you to believe, the feeling that resides in the printed word, reaches me through the reader-voice. I have supposed, but never found out, that this is the case with all readers—to read as listeners—and with all writers, to write as listeners. It may be part of the desire to write. The sound of what falls on the page begins the process of testing it for truth, for me. Whether I am right to trust so far I don't know. By now I don't know whether I could do either one, reading or writing, without the other.

My own words, when I am at work on a story, I hear too as they go, in the same voice that I hear when I read in books. When I write and the sound of it comes back to my ears, then I act to make my changes. I have always trusted this voice.
> —Eudora Welty, from *One Writer's Beginnings*

A dramatic necessity goes deep into the nature of the sentence. Sentences are not different enough to hold the attention unless they are dramatic. No ingenuity of varying structure will do. All that can save them is the speaking tone of voice somehow entangled in the words and fastened to the page for the ear of the imagination. That is all that can save poetry from sing-song, all that can save prose from itself.
> —Robert Frost, from "Introduction," *A Way Out*

That second voice—the distinctive mode of expression, the expected quirks and trademark tone, the characteristic attitude of writer toward reader and subject—has taken over as the meaning of *voice* in writing today. Hemingway had a voice: spare, selective, easily parodied because readily identifiable.

This is not necessarily the natural voice of the writer; for example, I knock myself out in these language pieces to adopt a scholarly breeziness, respectfully flip and deliciously tedious—a darting-about voice far different from my march-over-the-cliff, calumnious polemics on the op-ed page. Voice is not essence, but is essential to separate the writer from the pack. (That sentence is in a didactic, op-ed voice, and has no place in this light and airy space.)

—William Safire, from "The Take on Voice"

"Women's talk," in both *style* (hesitant, qualified, question-posing) and *content* (concern for the everyday, the practical, and the interpersonal) is typically devalued by men and women alike. Women talk less in mixed groups and are interrupted more often. By the late 1970s feminist sociologists and historians had begun to describe and contrast the private domestic voice of women with the public voice of men and to tie such differences in voice to sex-role socialization. And Carol Gilligan had begun to write about hearing "a different voice" as women talked about personal moral crises and decisions.

What we had not anticipated [when we began our book] was that "voice" was more than an academic shorthand for a person's point of view. Well after we were into our interviews with women, we became aware that it is a metaphor that can apply to many aspects of women's experience and development. In describing their lives, women commonly talked about voice and silence: "speaking up," "speaking out," "being silenced," "not being heard," "really listening," "really talking," "words as weapons," "feeling deaf and dumb," "having no words," "saying what you mean," "listening to be heard," and so on in an endless variety of connotations all having to do with sense of mind, self-worth, and feelings of isolation from or connection to others. We found that women repeatedly used the metaphor of voice to depict their intellectual and ethical development; and that the development of a sense of voice, mind, and self were intricately intertwined.

—Mary Belenky, Nancy Goldberger, Blythe Clinchy, Jill Tarule, from *Women's Ways of Knowing*

So poets have been considered unbalanced creatures. . . . They are in touch with "voices," but this is the very essence of their power, the voices are the past, the depths of our very beings. It is the deeper, not "lower" (in the usually silly sense) portions of the personality speaking, the middle brain, the nerves, the glands, the very muscles and bones of the body itself speaking.

—William Carlos Williams, from "How to Write"

I am writing a story in my journal. . . . I make my way through layers of acquired voices, silly voices, sententious voices, voices that are too cool and too overheated. Then they all quiet down, and I reach what I'm searching for: silence. I hold still to steady myself in it. This is the white bland center, the level ground that was there before Babel was built, that is always there before the Babel of our multiple selves is constructed. From this white plenitude, a voice begins to emerge: it's an even voice, and it's capable of saying things straight, without exaggeration or triviality. As the story progresses, the voice grows and diverges into different tonalities and timbres; sometimes, spontaneously, the force of feeling or of thought compresses language into metaphor, or an image, in which words and consciousness are magically fused. But the voice always returns to its point of departure, to ground zero.

—Eva Hoffman, from *Lost in Translation: A Life in a New Language*

SPEAK FOR YOURSELF

Susan Faludi

"I am at the boiling point! If I do not find some day the use of my tongue . . . I shall die of an intellectual repression, a woman's rights convulsion."
—ELIZABETH CADY STANTON, IN A LETTER TO SUSAN B. ANTHONY

"Oh, and then you'll be giving that speech at the Smithsonian Tuesday on the status of American women," my publisher's publicist reminded me as she rattled off the list of "appearances" for the week. "What?" I choked out. "I thought that was *at least* another month away." But the speech was distant only in my wishful consciousness, which pushed all such events into a mythical future when I would no longer lunge for smelling salts at the mention of public speaking.

For the author of what was widely termed an "angry" and "forceful" book, I exhibit a timorous verbal demeanor that belies my barracuda blurbs. My fingers may belt out my views when I'm stationed before the computer, but stick a microphone in front of me and I'm a Victorian lady with the vapors. Like many female writers with strong convictions but weak stomachs for direct confrontation, I write so forcefully precisely because I speak so tentatively. One form of self-expression has overcompensated for the weakness of the other, like a blind person who develops a hypersensitive ear.

"Isn't it wonderful that so many people want to hear what you have to say about women's rights?" the publicist prodded. I grimaced. "About as wonderful as walking down the street with no clothes on." Yes, I wanted people to hear what I had to say. Yes, I wanted to warn women of the backlash to our modest gains. But couldn't they just read what I wrote? Couldn't I just speak softly and carry a big book?

It has taken me a while to realize that my publicist is right. It's *not* the same—for my audience or for me. Public speech can be a horror for the shy person, but it can also be the ultimate act of liberation. For me, it became the moment where the public and the personal truly met.

For many years, I believed the imbalance between my incensed writing and my atrophied vocal cords suited me just fine. After a few abysmal auditions for school plays—my one role was Nana the dog in "Peter Pan," not, needless to say, a speaking role—I retired my acting aspirations and retreated to the school newspaper, a forum where I could bluster at injustices large and small without public embarrassment. My friend Barbara and I co-edited the high school paper (titled, interestingly, The Voice), fearlessly castigating all scoundrels from our closet-size office. But we kept our eyes glued to the floor during class discussion. Partly this was shyness, a genderless condition. But it was a condition reinforced by daily gendered reminders—we saw what happened to the girls who argued in class. The boys called them "bitches," and they sat home Saturday nights. Popular girls raised their voices only at pep squad.

While both sexes fear public speaking (pollsters tell us it's the public's greatest fear, rivaling even death), women—particularly women challenging the status quo—seem to be more afraid, and with good reason. We *do* have more at stake. Men risk a loss of face; women a loss of femininity. Men are chagrined if they blunder at the podium; women face humiliation either way. If we come across as commanding, our womanhood is called into question. If we reveal emotion, we are too hormonally driven to be taken seriously.

I had my own taste of this double standard while making the rounds of radio and television talk shows for a book tour. When I disputed a point with a man, male listeners would often phone in to say they found my behavior "offensive," or even "unattractive." And then there were my own internalized "feminine" voices: Don't interrupt, be agreeable, keep the volume down. "We're going to have to record that again," a weary radio producer said, rewinding the tape for the fifth time. "Your words are angry, but it's not coming through in your voice."

In replacing lacerating speech with a literary scalpel, I had adopted a well-worn female strategy, used most famously by Victorian female reformers protesting slavery and women's lowly status. "I want to be doing something with the pen, since no other means of action in politics are in a woman's power," Harriet Martineau, the British journalist, wrote in 1832. But while their literature makes compelling reading, the suffrage movement didn't get under way until women took a public stand from the platform of the Seneca Falls Women's Rights Convention. And while Betty Friedan's 1963 "The Feminine Mystique" raised the consciousness of millions of women, the contemporary women's movement only began to affect social policy when Friedan and other feminists started addressing the public.

Public speech is a more powerful stimulus because it is more dangerous for the speaker. An almost physical act, it demands projecting one's voice, hurling it against the public ear. Writing, on the other hand, occurs at one remove. The writer asserts herself from behind the veil of the printed page.

The dreaded evening of the Smithsonian speech finally arrived. I stood knockkneed and green-gilled before 300 people. Was it too late to plead a severe case of laryngitis? I am Woman, Hear Me Whisper.

I cleared my throat and, to my shock, a hush fell over the room. People were listening—with an intensity that strangely emboldened me. It was as if their attentive silence allowed me to make contact with my own muffled self. I began to speak. A stinging point induced a ripple of agreement. I told a joke and they laughed. My voice got surer, my delivery rising. A charge passed between me and the audience, uniting and igniting us both. That internal "boiling point" that Elizabeth Cady Stanton described was no longer under "intellectual repression." And its heat, I discovered, could set many kettles to whistling.

Afterward, it struck me that in some essential way I hadn't really proved myself a feminist until now. Until you translate personal words on a page into public connections with other people, you aren't really part of a political movement. I hadn't declared my independence until I was willing to declare it out loud. I knew public speaking was important to reform public life—but I hadn't realized the transformative effect it could have on the speaker herself. Women need to be heard not just to change the world, but to change themselves.

I can't say that this epiphany has made me any less anxious when approaching the lectern. But it has made me more determined to speak in spite of the jitters—and more hopeful that other women will do the same. Toward that end, I'd like to make a modest proposal for the next stage of the women's movement. A new method of consciousness-raising: Feminist Toastmasters.

VOICES I HEAR

Bryant Shea

Two years ago I read a Charlie Brown comic strip and the last frame read "The worst thing to have is a great potential." Boy can I relate to that. In four years of high school sports I never lived up to what anyone thought I could do, including myself. Freshman year it was great, "you have great potential" I would hear and even if I screwed up they would let me try again. By senior year though it was "He had so much potential." It was ridiculous; I was a two sport All-Star and had gone to the state finals or semifinal in three different sports. I started for all the teams I played on, but still I did not live up to my "potential." Every time I do poorly at something I hear that voice in my head "you had so much potential—if only you had worked harder." It rings in my head constantly "you had so much potential . . . you had so much potential." I really wish I could walk into something and have everyone think I sucked. At least this way it would be a surprise that I was good. Instead good is the expected, great is my "potential." Charlie Brown was right, "The worst thing to have is a great potential."

That is probably the most memorable voice that rings in my head, but there are others as well. Whenever I do anything stupid I hear my mom's voice saying "Oh Bryant, why?" No matter how old I get I still remember her saying that all the time when I made a stupid mistake. She did not get upset; she got disappointed, which I think was probably worse. The first time I can remember her saying that I was about five. I had gone outside and played in the mud wearing my school clothes. When I came in I knew that I had done something stupid and I was getting ready to get yelled at, but my mom just came in the room and said "Oh Bryant, why? you know better than that." It was worse than getting yelled at; I felt like I had really disappointed her. Now when I hear that voice I do not worry so much that my mom will be disappointed but rather that I have disappointed myself. Another voice that I constantly hear is that of my basketball coach. Whenever I am doing anything physically demanding and I want to quit, I hear his voice in my head saying "Come on Bryant you know you can do this, work it, work it." I think in the six years I knew my coach he said "work it" about a million times. When I first met my coach he was a basketball instructor at my camp. He used to push everyone to the limit and if you gave less than one hundred percent he got mad. By the end of the week we called him the "work it" man, because he used the phrase so much. Little did I know that I would have to hear it for four more years in high school. I will admit this though; his voice ringing in my head has pushed me along many times when I thought I was going to give up.

It is funny how you can translate people's voices into your own. The three voices that I talked about above were all from people I know, but when I hear them it is me talking. I get upset when I do not live up to my potential, I am the one disappointed when I do something stupid, and I am the one pushing myself to do better when I hear "work it." I guess that everyone has the same thing happen to them; it is part of growing up I would assume.

Along with these voices that I have of other people, my mind has its own voice. It is the voice that I talk to when I have to figure something out; it's the voice that right now is saying, "Okay think what else do I have to write about." This voice is my conscience and it is what I hear when I do something wrong. It says "Should I really be doing this" or "wow I didn't think you could be so mean." Everyone has a voice like this and without it we would probably be in a lot of trouble. This voice is what interprets the other voices that I hear and then says, "Listen to what they have to say." I think it would be great sometimes to hear what other people are saying to themselves when they're talking to you. The voice inside your head tends to be much more honest than the one that comes out of your mouth, and most of the time we would be better off listening to our inner voice.

A COLLAGE OF PASSAGES ABOUT SPLIT INFINITIVES FROM STYLE MANUALS

(A) SPLIT INFINITIVE.   The English-speaking world may be divided into (1) those who neither know nor care what a split infinitive is; (2) those who do not know, but care very much; (3) those who know & condemn; (4) those who know & and approve; & (5) those who know & distinguish.

1. Those who neither know nor care are the vast majority, & are a happy folk, to be envied by most of the minority classes; 'to really understand' comes readier to their lips & pens than 'really to understand', they see no reason why they should not say it (small blame to them, seeing that reasons are not their critics' strong point), & they do say it, to the discomfort of some among us, but not to their own.

2. To the second class, those who do not know but do care, who would as soon be caught putting their knives in their mouths as splitting an infinitive but have hazy notions of what constitutes that deplorable breach of etiquette, this article is chiefly addressed. These people betray by their practice that their aversion to the split infinitive springs not from instinctive good taste, but from tame acceptance of the misinterpreted opinions of others; for they will subject their sentences to the queerest distortions, all to escape imaginary split infinitives. [H. W. Fowler, *A Dictionary of Modern English Usage,* Oxford: Clarendon Press, 1926: 558.]

(B) *E3-d Do not split infinitives needlessly.*   An infinitive consists of *to* plus a verb: *to think, to breathe, to dance.* When words appear between its two parts, an infinitive is said to be "split": *to carefully balance.* If a split infinitive is obviously awkward, it should be revised.

> *If possible, patients*
> ~~Patients~~ should try to ~~if possible~~ avoid going up and down stairs.

Usage varies when a split infinitive is less awkward than the preceding one. To be on the safe side, however, you should not split infinitives, especially in formal writing. [Diana Hacker. *A Writer's Reference.* 2nd ed. Boston: Bedford of St. Martins, 1992, 40.]

(C) Our attitude toward split infinitives is the same as our attitude toward ending sentences with a preposition: we don't understand why anyone would care, since we can think of no way in which either affects anyone's ability to communicate written meaning. So, all we're going to do here is tell you what a split infinitive is. . . .

The truth about split infinitives is that you're not likely to write ones that seem awful to you. But if you need to satisfy a teacher who penalizes you for all split infinitives, you'll have to track them down. Our suggestion is that if you don't like what your sentence sounds like after you unsplit the infinitive, rewrite the entire sentence. [Pat Belanoff, Betsy Rorschach, Mia Oberlink, *The Right Handbook: Grammar and Usage in Context,* 2nd ed, Portsmouth NH: Boynton/Cook, 1993: 133–4.]

NOBODY MEAN MORE TO ME THAN YOU[1] AND THE FUTURE LIFE OF WILLIE JORDAN JULY, 1985

June Jordan

Black English is not exactly a linguistic buffalo; as children, most of the thirty-five million Afro-Americans living here depend on this language for our discovery of the world. But then we approach our maturity inside a larger social body that will not support our efforts to become anything other than the clones of those who are neither our mothers nor our fathers. We begin to grow up in a house where every true mirror shows us the face of somebody who does not belong there, whose walk and whose talk will never look or sound "right," because that house was meant to shelter a family that is alien and hostile to us. As we learn our way around this environment, either we hide our original word habits, or we completely surrender our own voice, hoping to please those who will never respect anyone different from themselves: Black English is not exactly a linguistic buffalo, but we should understand its status as an endangered species, as a perishing, irreplaceable system of community intelligence, or we should expect its extinction, and, along with that, the extinguishing of much that constitutes our own proud, and singular identity.

What we casually call "English," less and less defers to England and its "gentlemen." "English" is no longer a specific matter of geography or an element of class privilege; more than thirty-three countries use this tool as a means of "intranational communication."[2] Countries as disparate as Zimbabwe and Malaysia, or Israel and Uganda, use it as their non-native currency of convenience. Obviously, this tool, this "English," cannot function inside thirty three discrete societies on the basis of rules and values absolutely determined somewhere else, in a thirty-fourth other country, for example.

In addition to that staggering congeries of non-native users of English, there are five countries, or 333,746,000 people, for whom this thing called "English" serves as a native tongue.[3] Approximately 10% of these native speakers of "English" are Afro-American citizens of the U.S.A. I cite these numbers and varieties of human beings dependent on "English" in order, quickly, to suggest how strange and how tenuous is any concept of "Standard English." Obviously, numerous forms of English now operate inside a natural, an uncontrollable, continuum of development. I would suppose "the standard" for English in Malaysia is not the same as "the standard" in Zimbabwe. I know that standard forms of English for Black people in this country do not copy that of whites. And, in fact, the structural differences between these two kinds of English have intensified, becoming more Black, or less white, despite the expected homogenizing effects of television[4] and other mass media.

Nonetheless, white standards of English persist, supreme and unquestioned, in these United States. Despite our multi-lingual population, and despite the deepening Black and white cleavage within that conglomerate, white standards control our official and popular judgments of verbal proficiency and correct, or incorrect, language skills, including speech. In contrast to India, where at least fourteen languages co-exist as legitimate Indian languages, in contrast to Nicaragua, where all citizens are legally entitled to formal school instruction in their regional or tribal languages, compulsory education in America compels accomodation to exclusively white forms of "English." White English, in America, is "Standard English."

This story begins two years ago. I was teaching a new course, "In Search of the Invisible Black Woman," and my rather large class seemed evenly divided between young Black women and men. Five or six white students also sat in attendance. With unexpected speed and enthusiasm we had moved through historical narratives of the 19th century to literature by and about Black women, in the 20th. I had assigned the first forty pages of Alice Walker's *The Color Purple,* and I came, eagerly, to class that morning:

"So!" I exclaimed, aloud. "What did you think? How did you like it?"

The students studied their hands, or the floor. There was no response. The tense, resistant feeling in the room fairly astounded me.

At last, one student, a young woman still not meeting my eyes, muttered something in my direction:

"What did you say?" I prompted her.

"Why she have them talk so funny. It don't sound right."

"You mean the language?"

Another student lifted his head: "It don't look right, neither. I couldn't hardly read it."

At this, several students dumped on the book. Just about unanimously, their criticisms targeted the language. I listened to what they wanted to say and silently marvelled at the similarities between their casual speech patterns and Alice Walker's written version of Black English.

But I decided against pointing to these identical traits of syntax; I wanted not to make them self-conscious about their own spoken language—not while they clearly felt it was "wrong." Instead I decided to swallow my astonishment. Here was a negative Black reaction to a prize winning accomplishment of Black literature that white readers across the country had selected as a best seller. Black rejection was aimed at the one irreducibly Black element of Walker's work: the language—Celie's Black English. I wrote the opening lines of *The Color Purple* on the blackboard and asked the students to help me translate these sentences into Standard English:

You better not never tell nobody but God. It'd kill your mammy.
Dear God,
 I am fourteen years old. I have always been a good girl. Maybe you can give me a sign letting me know what is happening to me.
 Last spring after Little Lucious come I heard them fussing. He was pulling on her arm. She say it too soon, Fonso. I aint well. Finally he leave her alone. A week go by, he pulling on her arm again. She say, Naw, I ain't gonna. Can't you see I'm already half dead, an all of the children.[5]

Our process of translation exploded with hilarity and even hysterical, shocked laughter: The Black writer, Alice Walker, knew what she was doing!

If rudimentary criteria for good fiction includes the manipulation of language so that the syntax and diction of sentences will tell you the identity of speakers, the probable age and sex and class of speakers, and even the locale—urban/rural/southern/western—then Walker had written, perfectly. This is the translation into Standard English that our class produced:

> *"Absolutely, one should never confide in anybody besides God. Your secrets could prove devastating to your mother."*
> Dear God,
> I am fourteen years old. I have always been good. But now, could you help me to understand what is happening to me?
> Last spring, after my little brother, Lucious, was born, I heard my parents fighting. My father kept pulling at my mother's arm. But she told him, "It's too soon for sex, Alfonso. I am still not feeling well." Finally, my father left here alone. A week went by, and then he began bothering my mother, again: Pulling her arm. She told him, "No, I won't! Can't you see I'm already exhausted from all of these children?"
> (Our favorite line was "It's too soon for sex, Alphonso.")

Once we could stop laughing, once we could stop our exponentially wild improvisations on the theme of Translated Black English, the students pushed me to explain their own negative first reactions to their spoken language on the printed page. I thought it was probably akin to the shock of seeing yourself in a photograph for the first time. Most of the students had never before seen a written facsimile of the way they talk. None of the students had ever learned how to read and write their own verbal system of communication: Black English. Alternatively, this fact began to baffle or else bemuse and then infuriate my students. Why not? Was it too late? Could they learn how to do it, now? And, ultimately, the final test question, the one testing my sincerity: Could I teach them? Because I had never taught anyone Black English and, as far as I knew, no one, anywhere in the United States, had ever offered such a course, the best I could say was "I'll try."

He looked like a wrestler.

He sat dead center in the packed room and, every time our eyes met, he quickly nodded his head as though anxious to reassure, and encourage, me.

Short, with strikingly broad shoulders and long arms, he spoke with a surprisingly high, soft voice that matched the soft bright movement of his eyes. His name was Willie Jordan. He would have seemed even more unlikely in the context of Contemporary Women's Poetry, except that ten or twelve other Black men were taking the course, as well. Still, Willie was conspicuous. His extreme fitness, the muscular density of his presence underscored the riveted, gentle attention that he gave to anything anyone said. Generally, he did not join the loud and rowdy dialogue flying back and forth, but there could be no doubt about his interest in our discussions. And, when he stood to present an argument he'd prepared, overnight, that nervous smile of his vanished and an irregular stammering replaced it, as he spoke with visceral sincerity, word by word.

That was how I met Willie Jordan. It was in between "In Search of the Invisible Black Women" and "The Art of Black English." I was waiting for

Departmental approval and I supposed that Willie might be, so to speak, killing time until he, too, could study Black English. But Willie really did want to explore Contemporary Women's poetry and, to that end, volunteered for extra research and never missed a class.

Towards the end of that semester, Willie approached me for an independent study project on South Africa. It would commence the next semester. I thought Willie's writing needed the kind of improvement only intense practice will yield. I knew his intelligence was outstanding. But he'd wholeheartedly opted for "Standard English" at a rather late age, and the results were stilted and frequently polysyllabic, simply for the sake of having more syllables. Willie's unnatural formality of language seemed to me consistent with the formality of his research into South African apartheid. As he projected his studies, he would have little time, indeed, for newspapers. Instead, more than 90% of his research would mean saturation in strictly historical, if not archival, material. I was certainly interested. It would be tricky to guide him into a more confident and spontaneous relationship both with language and apartheid. It was going to be wonderful to see what happened when he could catch up with himself, entirely, and talk back to the world.

September, 1984: Breezy fall weather and much excitement! My class, "The Art of Black English," was full to the limit of the fire laws. And, in Independent Study, Willie Jordan showed up, weekly, fifteen minutes early for each of our sessions. I was pretty happy to be teaching, altogether!

I remember an early class when a young brother, replete with his ever present pork-pie hat, raised his hand and then told us that most of what he'd heard was "all right" except it was "too clean." "The brothers on the street," he continued, "they mix it up more. Like 'fuck' and 'motherfuck.' Or like 'shit.'" He waited. I waited. Then all of us laughed a good while, and we got into a brawl about "correct" and "realistic" Black English that led to Rule 1.

Rule 1: *Black English is about a whole lot more than mothafuckin.*

As a criterion, we decided, "realistic" could take you anywhere you want to go. Artful places. Angry places. Eloquent and sweetalkin places. Polemical places. Church. And the local Bar & Grill. We were checking out a language, not a mood or a scene or one guy's forgettable mouthing off.

It was hard. For most of the students, learning Black English required a fallback to patterns and rhythms of speech that many of their parents had beaten out of them. I mean *beaten*. And, in a majority of cases, correct Black English could be achieved only by striving for *incorrect* Standard English, something they were still pushing at, quite uncertainly. This state of affairs led to Rule 2.

Rule 2: *If it's wrong in Standard English it's probably right in Black English, or, at least, you're hot.*

It was hard. Roommates and family members ridiculed their studies, or remained incredulous, "You *studying* that shit? At school?" But we were beginning to feel the companionship of pioneers. And we decided that we needed another rule that would establish each one of us as equally important to our success. This was Rule 3.

Rule 3: *If it don't sound like something that come out somebody mouth then it don't sound right. If it don't sound right then it ain't hardly right. Period.*

This rule produced two weeks of compositions in which the students agonizingly tried to spell the sound of the Black English sentence they wanted to convey. But Black English is, preeminently, an oral/spoken means of communication. *And spelling don't talk.* So we needed Rule 4.

Rule 4: *Forget about the spelling. Let the syntax carry you.*

Once we arrived at Rule 4 we started to fly because syntax, the structure of an idea, leads you to the world view of the speaker and reveals her values. The syntax of a sentence equals the structure of your consciousness. If we insisted that the language of Black English adheres to a distinctive Black syntax, then we were postulating a profound difference between white and Black people, *per se.* Was it a difference to prize or to obliterate?

There are three qualities of Black English—the presence of life, voice, and clarity—that testify to a distinctive Black value system that we became excited about and self-consciously tried to maintain.

1. Black English has been produced by a pre-technocratic, if not anti-technological, culture. More, our culture has been constantly threatened by annihilation or, at least, the swallowed blurring of assimilation. Therefore, our language is a system constructed by people constantly needing to insist that we exist, that we are present. Our language devolves from a culture that abhors all abstraction, or anything tending to obscure or delete the fact of the human being who is here and now/the truth of the person who is speaking or listening. Consequently, *there is no passive voice construction possible in Black English.* For example, you cannot say, "Black English is being eliminated." You must say, instead, "White people eliminating Black English." The assumption of the presence of life governs all of Black English. Therefore, overwhelmingly, *all action takes place in the language of the present indicative.* And every sentence assumes the living and active participation of at least two human beings, the speaker and the listener.

2. A primary consequence of the person-centered values of Black English is the delivery of voice. If you speak or write Black English, your ideas will necessarily possess that otherwise elusive attribute, *voice.*

3. One main benefit following from the person-centered values of Black English is that of *clarity.* If your idea, your sentence, assumes the presence of at least two living and active people, you will make it understandable because the motivation behind every sentence is the wish to say something real to somebody real.

As the weeks piled up, translation from Standard English into Black English or vice versa occupied a hefty part of our course work.

> Standard English (hereafter S.E.): "In considering the idea of studying Black English those questioned suggested—"
>
> (What's the subject? Where's the person? Is anybody alive in there, in that idea?)
>
> Black English (hereafter B.E.): "I been asking people what you think about somebody studying Black English and they answer me like this:"

But there were interesting limits. You cannot "translate" instances of Standard English preoccupied with abstraction or with nothing/nobody evidently alive, into Black English. That would warp the language into uses antithetical to the guiding perspective of its community of users. Rather you must first change those Standard English sentences, themselves, into ideas consistent with the person-centered assumptions of Black English.

Guidelines For Black English

1. Minimal number of words for every idea: This is the source for the aphoristic and/or poetic force of the language; eliminate every possible word.
2. Clarity: If the sentence is not clear it's not Black English.
3. Eliminate use of the verb *to be* whenever possible. This leads to the deployment of more descriptive and therefore, more precise verbs.
4. Use *be* or *been* only when you want to describe a chronic, ongoing state of things.

    He *be* at the office, by 9. (He is always at the office by 9.)
    He *been* with her since forever.

5. Zero copula: Always eliminate the verb *to be* whenever it would combine with another verb, in Standard English.

    S.E.: She is going out with him.
    B.E.: She going out with him.

6. Eliminate *do* as in:

    S.E.: What do you think? What do you want?
    B.E.: What you think? What you want?

    Rules number 3, 4, 5, and 6 provide for the use of the minimal number of verbs per idea and, therefore, greater accuracy in the choice of verb.

7. In general, if you wish to say something really positive, try to formulate the idea using emphatic negative structure.

    S.E.: He's fabulous.
    B.E.: He bad.

8. Use double or triple negatives for dramatic emphasis.

    S.E.: Tina Turner sings out of this world.
    B.E.: Ain nobody sing like Tina.

9. Never use the *-ed* suffix to indicate the past tense of a verb.

    S.E.: She closed the door.
    B.E.: She close the door. Or, she have close the door.

10. Regardless of intentional verb time, only use the third person singular, present indicative, for use of the verb *to have,* as an auxiliary.

    S.E.: He had his wallet then he lost it.
    B.E.: He have him wallet then he lose it.
    S.E.: He had seen that movie.
    B.E.: We seen that movie. Or, we have see that movie.

11. Observe a minimal inflection of verbs. Particularly, never change from the first person singular forms to the third person singular.

S.E.: Present Tense Forms: He goes to the store.
B.E.: He go to the store.
S.E.: Past Tense Forms: He went to the store.
B.E.: He go to the store. Or, he gone to the store. Or, he been to the store.

12. The possessive case scarcely ever appears in Black English. Never use an apostrophe ('s) construction. If you wander into a possessive case component of an idea, then keep logically consistent: *ours, his, theirs, mines.* But, most likely, if you bump into such a component, you have wandered outside the underlying world-view of Black English.

S.E.: He will take their car tomorrow.
B.E.: He taking they car tomorrow.

13. Plurality: Logical consistency, continued: If the modifier indicates plurality then the noun remains in the singular case.

S.E.: He ate twelve doughnuts.
B.E.: He eat twelve doughnut.
S.E.: She has many books.
B.E.: She have many book.

14. Listen for, or invent, special Black English forms of the past tense, such as: "He losted it. That what she felted." If they are clear and readily understood, then use them.

15. Do not hesitate to play with words, sometimes inventing them: e.g. "astropotomous" means huge like a hippo plus astronomical and, therefore, signifies real big.

16. In Black English, unless you keenly want to underscore the past tense nature of an action, stay in the present tense and rely on the overall context of your ideas for the conveyance of time and sequence.

17. Never use the suffix *-ly* form of an adverb in Black English.

S.E.: The rain came down rather quickly.
B.E.: The rain come down pretty quick.

18. Never use the indefinite article *an* in Black English.

S.E.: He wanted to ride an elephant.
B.E.: He want to ride him a elephant.

19. Invariant syntax: in correct Black English it is possible to formulate an imperative, an interrogative, and a simple declarative idea with the same syntax:

B.E.: You going to the store?
You going to the store.
You going to the store!

Where was Willie Jordan? We'd reached the mid-term of the semester. Students had formulated Black English guidelines, by consensus, and they were now writing with remarkable beauty, purpose, and enjoyment:

"I ain hardly speakin for everybody but myself so understan that." —Kim Parks

Samples from student writings:

"Janie have a great big ole hole inside her. Tea Cake the only thing that fit that hole . . .

"That pear tree beautiful to Janie, especial when bees fiddlin with the blossomin pear there growin large and lovely. But personal speakin, the love she get from starin at that tree ain the love what starin back at her in them relationship." (Monica Morris)

"Love is a big theme in, *They Eye Was Watching God.* Love show people new corners inside theyself. It pull out good stuff and stuff back bad stuff . . . Joe worship the doing uh his own hand and need other people to worship him too. But he ain't think about Janie that she a person and ought to live like anybody common do. Queen life not for Janie." (Monica Morris)

"In both life and writin, Black womens have varietous experience of love that be cold like a iceberg or fiery like a inferno. Passion got for the other partner involve, man or woman, seem as shallow, ankle-deep water or the most profoundest abyss." (Constance Evans)

"Family love another bond that ain't never break under no pressure." (Constance Evans)

"You know it really cold/When the friend you/Always get out the fire/Act like they don't know you/When you in the heat." (Constance Evans)

"Big classroom discussion bout love at this time. I never take no class where us have any long arguin for and against for two or three day. New to me and great. I find the class time talkin a million time more interestin than detail bout the book." (Kathy Esseks)

As these examples suggest, Black English no longer limited the students, in any way. In fact, one of them, Philip Garfield, would shortly "translate" a pivotal scene from Ibsen's *Doll House,* as his final term paper:

Nora: I didn't gived no shit. I thinked you a asshole back then, too, you make it so hard for me save mines husband life.

Krogstad: Girl, it clear you ain't any idea what you done. You done exact what once done, and I losed my reputation over it.

Nora: You asks me believe you once act brave save you wife life?

Krogstad: Law care less why you done it.

Nora: Law must suck.

Krogstad: Suck or no, if I wants, judge screw you wid dis paper.

Nora: No way, man. (Philip Garfield)

But where was Willie? Compulsively punctual, and always thoroughly prepared with neatly typed compositions, he had disappeared. He failed to show up for our regularly scheduled conference, and I received neither a note nor a phone call of explanation. A whole week went by. I wondered if Willie had finally been captured by the extremely current happenings in South

Africa: passage of a new constitution that did not enfranchise the Black majority, and militant Black South African reaction to that affront. I wondered if he'd been hurt, somewhere. I wondered if the serious workload of weekly readings and writings had overwhelmed him and changed his mind about independent study. Where was Willie Jordan?

One week after the first conference that Willie missed, he called: "Hello, Professor Jordan? This is Willie. I'm sorry I wasn't there last week. But something has come up and I'm pretty upset. I'm sorry but I really can't deal right now."

I asked Willie to drop by my office and just let me see that he was okay. He agreed to do that. When I saw him I knew something hideous had happened. Something had hurt him and scared him to the marrow. He was all agitated and stammering and terse and incoherent. At last, his sadly jumbled account let me surmise, as follows: Brooklyn police had murdered his unarmed, twenty-five year old brother, Reggie Jordan. Neither Willie nor his elderly parents knew what to do about it. Nobody from the press was interested. His folks had no money. Police ran his family around and around, to no point. And Reggie was really dead. And Willie wanted to fight, but he felt helpless.

With Willie's permission I began to try to secure legal counsel for the Jordan family. Unfortunately Black victims of police violence are truly numerous while the resources available to prosecute their killers are truly scarce. A friend of mine at the Center for Constitutional Rights estimated that just the preparatory costs for bringing the cops into court normally approach $180,000. Unless the execution of Reggie Jordan became a major community cause for organizing, and protest, his murder would simply become a statistical item.

Again, with Willie's permission, I contacted every newspaper and media person I could think of. But the William Bastone feature article in *The Village Voice* was the only result from that canvassing.

Again, with Willie's permission, I presented the case to my class in Black English. We had talked about the politics of language. We had talked about love and sex and child abuse and men and women. But the murder of Reggie Jordan broke like a hurricane across the room.

There are few "issues" as endemic to Black life as police violence. Most of the students knew and respected and liked Jordan. Many of them came from the very neighborhood where the murder had occurred. All of the students had known somebody close to them who had been killed by police, or had known frightening moments of gratuitous confrontation with the cops. They wanted to do everything at once to avenge the death. Number One: They decided to compose personal statements of condolence to Willie Jordan and his family, written in Black English. Number Two: They decided to compose individual messages to the police, in Black English. These should be prefaced by an explanatory paragraph composed by the entire group. Number Three: These individual messages, with their lead paragraph, should be sent to *Newsday*.

The morning after we agreed on these objectives, one of the young women students appeared with an unidentified visitor, who sat through the class, smiling in a peculiar, comfortable way.

Now we had to make more tactical decisions. Because we wanted the messages published, and because we thought it imperative that our outrage be known by the police, the tactical question was this: Should the opening, group paragraph be written in Black English or Standard English?

I have seldom been privy to a discussion with so much heart at the dead heat of it. I will never forget the eloquence, the sudden haltings of speech, the fierce struggle against tears, the furious throwaway, and useless explosions that this question elicited.

That one question contained several others, each of them extraordinarily painful to even contemplate. How best to serve the memory of Reggie Jordan? Should we use the language of the killers—Standard English—in order to make our ideas acceptable to those controlling the killers? But wouldn't what we had to say be rejected, summarily, if we said it in our own language, the language of the victim, Reggie Jordan? But if we sought to express ourselves by abandoning our language wouldn't that mean our suicide on top of Reggie's murder? But if we expressed ourselves in our own language wouldn't that be suicidal to the wish to communicate with those who, evidently, did not give a damn about us/Reggie/police violence in the Black community?

At the end of one of the longest, most difficult hours of my own life, the students voted, unanimously, to preface their individual messages with a paragraph composed in the language of Reggie Jordan. *"At least we don't give up nothing else. At least we stick to the truth: Be who we been. And stay all the way with Reggie."*

It was heartbreaking to proceed, from that point. Everyone in the room realized that our decision in favor of Black English had doomed our writings, even as the distinctive reality of our Black lives always has doomed our efforts to "be who we been" in this country.

I went to the blackboard and took down this paragraph, dictated by the class:

" . . . YOU COPS!

WE THE BROTHER AND SISTER OF WILLIE JORDAN, A FELLOW STONY BROOK STUDENT WHO THE BROTHER OF THE DEAD REGGIE JORDAN. REGGIE, LIKE MANY BROTHER AND SISTER, HE A VICTIM OF BRUTAL RACIST POLICE, OCTOBER 25, 1984. US APPALL, FED UP, BECAUSE THAT ANOTHER SENSELESS DEATH WHAT OCCUR IN OUR COMMUNITY. THIS WHAT WE FEEL, THIS, FROM OUR HEART, FOR WE AIN'T STAYIN' SILENT NO MORE:"

With the completion of this introduction, nobody said anything. I asked for comments. At this invitation, the unidentified visitor, a young Black man, ceaselessly smiling, raised his hand. He was, it so happens, a rookie cop. He had just joined the force in September and, he said, he thought he should clarify a few things. So he came forward and sprawled easily into a posture of barroom, or fireside, nostalgia:

"See," Officer Charles enlightened us, "Most times when you out on the street and something come down you do one of two things. Over-react or under-react. Now, if you under-react then you can get yourself kilt. And if you over-react then maybe you kill somebody. Fortunately it's about nine times out of ten and you will over-react. So the brother got kilt. And I'm sorry about that, believe me. But what you have to understand is what kilt him: Over-reaction. That's all. Now you talk about Black people and white police but see, now, I'm a cop myself. And (big smile) I'm Black. And just a couple months ago I was on the other side. But see it's the same for me. You a cop, you the ultimate authority: the Ultimate Authority. And you on the street, most of the time you can only do one of two things: over-react or under-react. That's all it is with the brother: Over-reaction. Didn't have nothing to do with race."

That morning Officer Charles had the good fortune to escape without being boiled alive. But barely. And I remember the pride of his smile when I read about the fate of Black policemen and other collaborators, in South Africa. I remember him, and I remember the shock and palpable feeling of shame that filled the room. It was as though that foolish, and deadly, young man had just relieved himself of his foolish, and deadly, explanation, face to face with the grief of Reggie Jordan's father and Reggie Jordan's mother. Class ended quietly. I copied the paragraph from the blackboard, collected the individual messages and left to type them up.

Newsday rejected the piece.

The Village Voice could not find room in their "Letters" section to print the individual messages from the students to the police.

None of the tv news reporters picked up the story.

Nobody raised $180,000 to prosecute the murder of Reggie Jordan.

Reggie Jordan is really dead.

I asked Willie Jordan to write an essay pulling together everything important to him from that semester. He was still deeply beside himself with frustration and amazement and loss. This is what he wrote, un-edited, and in its entirety:

"Throughout the course of this semester I have been researching the effects of oppression and exploitation along racial lines in South Africa and its neighboring countries. I have become aware of South African police brutalization of native Africans beyond the extent of the law, even though the laws themselves are catalyst affliction upon Black men, women and children. Many Africans die each year as a result of the deliberate use of police force to protect the white power structure.

"Social control agents in South Africa, such as policemen, are also used to force compliance among citizens through both overt and covert tactics. It is not uncommon to find bold-faced coercion and cold-blooded killings of Blacks by South African police for undetermined and/or inadequate reasons. Perhaps the truth is that the only reasons for this heinous treatment of Blacks rests in racial differences. We should also understand that what is conveyed through the media is not always accurate and may sometimes be construed as the tip of the iceberg at best.

"I recently received a painful reminder that racism, poverty, and the abuse of power are global problems which are by no means unique to South Africa. On October 25, 1984 at approximately 3:00 p.m. my brother, Mr. Reginald

Jordan, was shot and killed by two New York City policemen from the 75th precinct in the East New York section of Brooklyn. His life ended at the age of twenty-five. Even up to this current point in time the Police Department has failed to provide my family, which consists of five brothers, eight sisters, and two parents, with a plausible reason for Reggie's death. Out of the many stories that were given to my family by the Police Department, not one of them seems to hold water. In fact, I honestly believe that the Police Department's assessment of my brother's murder is nothing short of ABSOLUTE BULLSHIT, and thus far no evidence had been produced to alter perception of the situation.

"Furthermore, I believe that one of three cases may have occurred in this incident. First, Reggie's death may have been the desired outcome of the police officer's action, in which case the killing was premeditated. Or, it was a case of mistaken identity, which clarifies the fact that the two officers who killed my brother and their commanding parties are all grossly incompetent. Or, both of the above cases are correct, i.e., Reggie's murderers intended to kill him and the Police Department behaved insubordinately.

"Part of the argument of the officers who shot Reggie was that he had attacked one of them and took his gun. This was their major claim. They also said that only one of them had actually shot Reggie. The facts, however, speak for themselves. According to the Death Certificate and autopsy report, Reggie was shot eight times from point-blank range. The Doctor who performed the autopsy told me himself that two bullets entered the side of my brother's head, four bullets were sprayed into his back, and two bullets struck him in the back of his legs. It is obvious that unnecessary force was used by the police and that it is extremely difficult to shoot someone in his back when he is attacking or approaching you.

"After experiencing a situation like this and researching South Africa I believe that to a large degree, justice may only exist as rhetoric. I find it difficult to talk of true justice when the oppression of my people both at home and abroad attests to the fact that inequality and injustice are serious problems whereby Blacks and Third World people are perpetually short-changed by society. Something has to be done about the way in which this world is set up. Although it is a difficult task, we do have the power to make a change."

Willie J. Jordan, Jr.
EGL 487, Section 58, November 14, 1984

Works Cited

1. Black English aphorism crafted by Monica Morris, a Junior at S.U.N.Y. at Stony Brook, October 1984.
2. *English Is Spreading, But What Is English?* A presentation by Professor S. N. Sridhar, Dept. of Linguistics, S.U.N.Y. at Stony Brook, April 9, 1985: Dean's Conversation Among the Disciplines.
3. Ibid.
4. *New York Times*, March 15, 1985, Section One, p. 14: Report on study by Linguistics at the University of Pennsylvania.
5. Alice Walker, *The Color Purple*, p. 11, Harcourt Brace, N.Y.

WORKSHOP

16

REVISION THROUGH
PURPOSE AND
AUDIENCE: WRITING
AS DOING THINGS
TO PEOPLE

The goal of this workshop is to help you learn to shape your writing better by thinking more pointedly about what you want your words to *do,* and to *whom*—that is, about purpose and audience. The main assignment is to revise a paper you wrote for some other workshop in this textbook. In Workshop 7, we laid out one way to go about revision. In this workshop, we're going to suggest other ways to work on revision.

We almost always have a *purpose* in mind when we speak. We may be just expressing ourselves ("Ouch!"), making contact ("Hello, how are you?"), conveying information ("It's 10 o'clock"), or persuading ("It's much too hot to work—come to the beach with us"). Even when we talk to ourselves, we probably have some purpose: to buoy our spirits ("C'mon, you can do it"), to keep from being frightened ("It's only the cat"), or to get something off our chest ("I hate him, hate him, hate him!").

In addition, we almost always have an *audience* in mind when we speak: maybe just anyone ("Help! I'm drowning!"), a good friend ("I've missed you"), a parent ("I've studied all week; can I use the car?"), a teacher ("Do you take off for misspelling?"), peers ("Let's do something different this weekend"). And of course we sometimes just speak to ourselves. Since writing usually takes more time and effort than speaking, we're even more likely to have a purpose in mind when we write compared to when we speak—even if the purpose is mostly to fulfill an assignment for a teacher.

Purpose and audience interact to influence what you say. In all likelihood, if you want to borrow a friend's car, you wouldn't persuade him by saying you had studied all week. You'd be more likely to say: "Are you really my friend?" If you're writing to convey information about the popular music scene to your teacher, you'd probably include more background information than if you were writing an article for your campus newspaper. When we write only for ourselves, though, we can use whatever language and approach we please—and say whatever we want—since there's no fear of hurting or annoying someone or getting a baffled look.

 ## AUDIENCE IN WRITING

Let's work up to purpose by way of audience. Sometimes you know who your audience is, for example, your parents or a particular committee or group of friends. Perhaps your audience is your classroom partner or group.

But sometimes you don't know your readers. You may have to write a letter to an organization or an application to a bureaucracy and not have a clue who will actually read it. You may be writing an essay of application to law school, medical school, or some other special program and have little sense of who the admissions people are and what they are impressed by. Sometimes you know *who* your readers are but not what they're *like.* That is, you may write something for a particular newspaper or magazine that gets all sorts of readers with all sorts of views and feelings. Or perhaps you have nobody-and-everybody in mind as your audience: you're writing about an issue for people in general or just for yourself.

There's nothing wrong with writing when you are unclear about your audience. Very good writing can be produced in that frame of mind. Besides, you often have no choice: you must write and you don't know the audience. But even when you are very clear about your audience, you may get confused when you think about them; in that case, it pays to forget about them and write your first draft to no one in particular or to a friendly audience. If your audience is not a problem, however, you can usually focus your thoughts and language better if you keep them in mind. (Notice how audience works—or doesn't work—in the Grace Paley story in the "Readings" for this workshop.)

Two Kinds of Audience Analysis

The obvious kind of audience analysis is to think about who your readers are and where they stand on the topic you are writing about. If you are writing something persuasive or argumentative, you will probably think most about where they *disagree* with you: after all that's why you're writing—to *change* their minds.

But watch out. Yes, you need to understand the points of disagreement, but your best hope of persuasion is usually to build from a platform of agreement or shared assumptions.* Your audience analysis needs to focus on figuring out some of those points of agreement. Even if your disagreement is very large, and even if you feel you are trying to persuade people who are deeply different from yourself, there are probably crucial *assumptions* that you share. (For example, die-hard pacifists and hawks in this country often agree about the desirability of democracy and individual freedom.) To put it another way, if you cannot find any shared agreement or feel some *kinship* with the "enemy," it's probably a waste of time writing to persuade them.

Often it's difficult and even boring to try to decide before you write what your audience is like and where it stands on a particular matter. You'll often discover much more about them if you get a draft written first—and then pretend to be your audience while you read it over: try to read through their eyes. You'll discover some of their feelings, ideas, and assumptions that you wouldn't otherwise have noticed. Even better, you can enlist other readers to help you read like your audience.

Whether you know your real audience or not, there's a second kind of audience analysis that helps in revising. That is, you can analyze the audience that your writing *implies*. For if you look closely at any piece of your writing, you can find clues about whom you were *unconsciously assuming* as reader. For example, does your piece have little touches that imply your readers are smart or dumb? informed or uninformed about the topic? likely to agree or likely to fight you? frivolous or serious?

The "implied reader" is a subtle dimension of a text (and an important, critical concept in literary criticism as well as composition). Most of us need

---

*Notice how the Charen article in the "Readings" in Workshop 12 starts from a shared experience of motherhood.

the help of responders to discover the implied reader in what we write. For example, sometimes a responder will show you that your text gives off contradictory audience cues. Perhaps at one point your writing implies that the readers are already interested in your topic, and at another point that they are uninvolved. Perhaps you can carry this off (somehow making it clear that you are writing to all readers), but the contradiction may undermine your writing by alienating *all* readers: everyone feels, "He's not talking to me."

One of the most common kinds of implied reader is a "reader in the head"—that is, some past reader who continues to be a powerful influence on you. For example, responders may show you that your letter to a newspaper is full of confusing qualifications because you are still unconsciously writing for a teacher who told you never to make a broad generalization when writing about a controversial subject. It's probably not suitable advice for this audience. Or your essay for an economics teacher is full of impressive verbal fanciness that had always won praise from English teachers, but it's inappropriate for this audience. We carry around audiences from the past in our heads, and we need readers to help us notice when we continue to write to them.

Digression on Teacher as Audience

Teachers read differently from most readers. They read not for pleasure or information, but because it's their job. They read as coach or director. Think about how a director watches a play she's directing—as opposed to how the audience watches it. The director is certainly a *real* audience; she is "really" watching the play, probably more carefully than the "real" audience. Yet, of course, the performance is not for her but for those who buy the tickets. They pay to see the play; she's being paid to watch and kibitz. She's not so much trying to tell the actors how *she* reacts to the play (she may be tired of it by now), but rather how she imagines the audience will react.

School writing situations are often comparable. For example, your writing teacher may specify an audience other than herself for a writing assignment (for example, the readers of the editorial page of the local newspaper). Or she may simply assume that the writing is not *only* for her but also for general readers or other students in the class. In either case you have some kind of *double-audience* situation—especially if you are graded on the piece.

It is rare that we write something *only* for the teacher. Notice the difference if you write a letter to her arguing for a change in your grade. Usually you write *for* the teacher and she is a kind of stand-in for other readers. Teachers occupy a trick role as readers. On the one hand, they try to read as coach or editor, telling you not so much how they react but how they think your real audience will react. But, on the other hand, of course, their own reactions will color their understanding of the reactions of others.

A "coach" or "editor" is a nice image for the writing teacher. For a coach or editor is an ally rather than an adversary. A coach may be tough on you, but she is not trying to be the enemy; she's trying to help you beat the real "enemy" (the other team). There's no point in fighting the coach or being

I used to have a teacher in elementary school who asked his students to keep a diary and who read his students' diaries in order to check whether they were keeping enough entries. Since I knew that he was going to read my diary, I used to make up events and people to fill up the pages instead of writing honestly about my everyday life. I was outraged by the fact that the teacher had the authority to read all of his students' diaries. I believed in the notion of privacy even at the age of eight. Whenever I had to write a diary entry at the end of the day just before going to bed, the face of my teacher used to appear in the back of my mind and hover over me as I wrote. I couldn't write honestly about my feelings so I decided to make up something instead. After a while, I got used to writing about my fictional life which was very different from my real life. Sometimes, I found that I had to keep from getting carried away lest the teacher suspect that my diary entries were not actual events in my life.

Eunsook Koo

mad at her, or for the coach to fight you. The better you and the coach work together, the better chance you both have of achieving your common goal of "winning" against a common adversary.

But you may have noticed that teachers can easily fall into being *grumpy* coaches. Sometimes it seems as though the only thing we teachers do is criticize your writing. One reason for our attitudes arises from the conditions under which we have to read student papers. As writing teachers we always read student writing in stacks of 25, 50, or 75 papers at a time. Have you ever thought about what a peculiar and unpleasant way of reading this is? Teachers naturally fall into what you might call "schematic" reading. After the tenth or fifteenth paper (especially if all the papers are on the same topic or in the same genre), we often develop a kind of "ideal paper" in our heads. Instead of just reading a paper itself to see what is there, we "check it against" that model—looking for certain points that need to be made or certain features that this assignment calls for. We fall into looking at each paper in terms of how well it fits or doesn't fit "what we are looking for." (Notice how we teachers often talk in terms of what we are "looking for," and how you students ask us, "What do you want us to do in this paper?") In "normal" reading conditions, the reader isn't checking what he reads for the presence of something he *already knows;* he's looking to find things he *doesn't* know.

We're not trying to blame teachers. This kind of reading is an inevitable consequence of the *role* of teacher and the conditions in which we read. A director can't enjoy a play in the way a paying audience can. Frankly, we think most writing teachers are overworked and underpaid. But the role and these reading conditions can lead teachers to be grumpy or to emphasize mistakes. That's why we urge you so much in this book to use your *fellow students* (in pairs or small groups) as another audience for your writing. Fellow students may not be as skilled in reading as your teacher, but they can read your writing as "real readers"—take it on its own terms and simply look for pleasure or usefulness—and not feel they are reading as a job or duty or to "teach" you.

In short, we want you to get the best of both audiences: use your teacher for her professional expertise in diagnosis and advice; use your fellow students for their ability to tell you what actually happens when real readers read your words. You get the *worst* of both worlds if you try to get your fellow students to give you professional diagnosis and advice and ask your teachers not to be critical. It is worth having some frank discussions about this tricky double-audience situation in school writing: for students to tell honestly how they experience the teacher as audience, and for teachers to talk honestly about how they experience their situation as readers. It is a painful area, but not one for blaming: there are no right answers here. It's a question of gradually seeing clearly something that, as far as we know, no one yet understands well.

 ## PURPOSE IN WRITING

We can highlight *purpose* in writing if we consider the interesting situations where writing itself undermines its very purpose. For example, sometimes you can persuade better by *not* writing: by sitting down with your reader and *talking*. If you write to him, that written document may put him off with its formality and distance. Indeed, sometimes the most persuasive thing you can do is not even to talk but to *listen*. Often your only hope of persuading someone is to show him that you respect his thinking and are in fact willing to adjust yours on the basis of what he's saying.

But, of course, sometimes writing is a better mode of persuasion than speaking. For in some situations and with some people, speaking just leads to fruitless arguments. A piece of writing can be less disputatious, less intrusive, calmer. Writing can give you a chance to express something quietly to the person without the need for him to answer back to you: a chance to plant a seed and avoid all arguing.

Does this sound like an odd digression—to question *whether* to write at all? Well, the digression highlights the practical and, as it were, nitty-gritty approach you need to take concerning purpose if you want to make an actual difference through your writing. If you really think about who your audience is and what you want to do to them, you may have to rethink a lot of things you took for granted. Most of us tend to stress what words *mean,* not what they *do.* But, of course, some of the best and most highly paid writers in our society—writers of advertisements—think very much in terms of what words do. There are a number of things that will help you to articulate your purposes more clearly in this concrete and specific way:

- Practice *responding* to writing by telling what the words actually *do* to you—that is, by giving movies of your mind as a reader. (See Section 7 of the *Sharing and Responding* part of this textbook.)
- Hear movies of the minds of readers as they read what *you've* written. (You'll get more chance for this later in the workshop.)
- Look at advertisements in print and on radio and TV, and analyze them for their purpose: what was the writer trying to make *happen* in us?

I have a really hard time with writing a diary or journal because I can never figure out who the audience is supposed to be. Is it me? Is it the teacher? I can't write just for myself when I know someone else is going to read it.

Student

■ Consider *examples* of specific statements of purpose—such as the following—and force yourself to come up with comparably specific statements for your own writing.

—To make readers *act* in a certain way (buy something, vote for someone, give a contribution, write a letter to their representative, and so forth).

—To make them feel a certain way (for instance, to feel sympathy for a particular person); or to give them a vicarious experience—that is, to make them feel as though they've actually been there (to "show" them, not just "tell" them).

—To make them trust you, or make them laugh.

—To impress readers (teachers?) that you've really learned a lot of material and thought things through.

—To convince readers that you are right.

—To make readers feel you understand how they see or feel things.

—To bowl readers over.

—Instead of wanting to bowl readers over (with the danger of making them feel threatened or making them want to fight against you), just to plant the seed of a difficult or alien view.

—To give readers information. (But notice that this is falling short of the task. No advertising writer would let herself stop there. *Why* are you giving readers information? What do you want the information to make them feel or do?)

An Extended Example: Our Purposes in Writing this Textbook

By way of further example, let us list here some of the specific purposes we've had in mind in writing the textbook you hold in your hands. Our audience is students. However, students will never read a course-oriented textbook unless it is chosen and assigned by their teacher. So it turns out we have the same tricky double-audience situation that you often have: teachers aren't our "real" audience, but they "really" are our audience.*

---

*Double audiences aren't as odd as you might think. A children's book must appeal to grown-ups before children get a chance to read it. You can't get an article or even a letter into the newspaper unless the editor thinks it's suitable. Every book must appeal to an editor before it can be published and be read by an audience. Indeed most books, even after they are published, won't get into many readers' hands unless they succeed at appealing to reviewers.

Our purpose is to make things happen in the world, to change behavior. We take our book as a very practical enterprise. Suppose, for example, that some reader should come up to us and say, "I just *love* reading your book. It's so interesting and entertaining. Of course, I never do any of those funny activities you describe; I just continue to write the way I always have." We might feel a glint of pleasure that this reader "loves" our book, but we'd have to admit that we'd *failed* in our main purpose of affecting behavior.

But we can't affect people's behavior unless we can affect their attitudes. We want to make teachers and students trust us. We want to make them think that we know a lot about writing and teaching and that we understand their problems. We want teachers to feel, "This is a smart, sensible book; it will make my teaching easier and more effective."

In the end our major purpose is to *help students become better writers.* Notice, however, that such a broad, pious statement of purpose is not specific enough to be of much use—for revising or helping readers give us feedback, for instance. Here are more down-to-earth statements of what we are trying to do to you to make you better writers:

- To get you over any nervousness or fear of writing you might have.
- To make you trust that you always have lots of words and thoughts available—and thereby make you more confident about writing.
- To get you to *like* writing and thus write a great deal. For we believe that you'll learn more in the end from writing a great deal than from advice or suggestions. And you won't write lots unless you like writing.
- To make you realize that when you have to write something, you have a number of different ways to go about writing it: to feel a sense of choices, options, power.
- To get you to be much more aware of your writing process, to *notice* the different gears you use and the funny tricks your mind and feelings play—and thereby help you end up with more conscious control over yourself as you write. (Students sometimes think process writing is odd or "merely theoretical" at first, but we want you to feel that it is practical: a method that can help you get unstuck and figure out the best way to tackle the writing task at hand.)
- To help you move comfortably back and forth between being loose and accepting in exploratory writing, and tough-minded and critical as you assess and revise.
- To help you work more independently, without always needing directions from the teacher or the book.
- To help you collaborate better with each other—in writing and responding to writing.

 MAIN ASSIGNMENT

The assignment for this workshop is to analyze audience and purpose in a piece of writing you have *already written,* and then to revise that piece on the basis of your analysis. You can choose any piece of writing to work on—

from a collage to a descriptive piece to an argument (though your teacher may ask you to work on one particular kind of writing). Here are the main questions you need to address in your analysis:

- *Audience.* Whom did you see then as your audience and whom do you see now?
- *Purpose.* Were you consciously trying to do something to readers when you were writing your piece? Can you now see any unconscious purpose you had? Would you specify a different purpose now?
- *Actual effects.* What actual effects does your writing seem to have on the readers in your group? What specific words or features seem to cause their reactions?
- If your group members are the "wrong" audience for this piece, what differences do you think there would be between their reactions and those of your "right" audience?
- *Advice for revising.* Finally, make sure your analysis includes some advice to yourself for revising.

The goal of this analysis is not to *judge* but to *describe*. That is, we're not trying to get you to congratulate or criticize yourself ("I tried to make them laugh but they sat there stony-faced!"), but rather to write a paper that describes *purposes* in writers and *effects* on readers—relating those purposes and effects to *specific* words and features on the page. In making this analysis, you might find it helpful to make references and comparisons to other pieces you've heard and discussed in your group.

Ways to Proceed

There are many ways to complete the assignment for this workshop, but here is a sequence of steps you will probably find helpful.

- Pick out the piece of your writing that you want to analyze. If your teacher gives you free choice, pick whatever piece intrigues you. Perhaps it's interesting because you are pleased with it and want to look more closely at something that worked for you. More likely, it's a piece that still troubles you and you want to revise it.
- Do some fast exploratory writing about the audience and purpose you had in mind in your original writing. Try to put yourself back into that situation. Do you have any different feelings now about audience and purpose for this piece? Can you now see any unconscious purpose you had? (For example, you might have been trying to persuade politely, but now you can see that unconsciously you were trying to make readers look silly.) Perhaps you were trying to get something off your chest in addition to having some effect on readers.
- Look at any response you got from your teacher on this paper and see what you can learn about the effects your words had on her.
- Share your piece with your partner or group and ask them to tell you in detail about the *effects* the writing had on them. Ask them to give you careful movies of their minds. It will help a lot if you make them stop periodically and report specifically what is happening to them as readers.

- Then, changing to a more analytic mode, ask them to relate these effects to specific features of the text. If a reader got bored or hostile, can they figure out what words or tone or structural feature in the writing caused it? You can join in on this analysis.

- Then ask your partner or group to talk about whom they see as the audience and what your text implies about audience. Does the text imply that readers are professional or amateur? emotional or cool? Can they see any old "audiences in your head" which lead you to shape your writing inappropriately? Again, you can join in.

- If your group is the wrong audience for your piece, ask them to speculate on any differences between their reactions and those of your intended reader. In this discussion, don't overestimate *differences* between readers. That is, if your intended audience is your teacher or a newspaper editor, your classmates are admittedly different; many of their reactions will be different from those of your teacher or the editor. But you can learn a great deal from seeing what your words did to the wrong readers. For example, your group might say they felt intimidated by your tone. Probably your teacher would not feel exactly intimidated, but there may well be something problematic about your tone. Perhaps it is smug.

- To complete your analysis, ask your classmates for advice about revising. Give yourself advice too: on the basis of what you have learned about audience, purpose, and effects, what changes do you plan for your revision?

- Revise your piece on the basis of your analysis. Show your revision to your group or partner and tell them what you have done and why. Ask them for any further suggestions.

We don't want to leave you with the impression that you need to go through all these steps in order to revise something you write and make its purposes clearer to your intended audience. But we do believe that good writers have an intuitive sense or "feel" of audience and purpose which guides them as they revise. Our hope is that if you consciously go through the steps we've suggested here, you'll discover how attentive you need to be to all this when you revise. As you develop into a more experienced writer, this sense of audience and purpose may go underground, but it will still be a source of intuition or "feel" for whether or not your words are matching your intentions. So whenever you're struggling as you revise, look back at the steps we recommend here, and this may get you going again. Take from our suggestions whatever helps you in a specific instance of revision.

Variations on the Assignment

1. Instead of actually revising an earlier paper, make your final piece for this workshop be a written *analysis* of that earlier paper. If you select this option, be sure to include an extended proposal for revision.

2. Revise an earlier paper *and* produce a written analysis of it. If you decide to do this, your discussion of specific revisions in the analysis essay need not be as extensive as for variation (1).

3. Instead of concentrating only on analyzing your essay, make your final piece a comparison of your writing with the writing of someone else in your group: the audience, purposes, and effects of *two* pieces of writing. (Sometimes analysis is easier when you have two pieces to compare.)

4. Make your final piece an essay about purposes and audience in *three or four* papers in the group. Obviously you can't write a full analysis of that many papers. Your analysis would have to center on one or two key issues of audience and purpose (for example, trying to get hostile readers on your side or trying to make readers experience a certain emotion), and explore that issue in terms of examples and illustrations from all the papers.

Collaborative Option

Write a collaborative essay with two or three people in your group whose writing is also being analyzed. This essay can take the approach of either variation (3) or (4) described previously.

 ## SHARING AND RESPONDING

In order to get material for your analysis and revision, you'll need to get feedback from classmates. You should already have some feedback on the paper you're analyzing if it's a paper you wrote for an earlier workshop in the textbook. See if you can locate that feedback. And make sure you get readers to give you emotional as well as logical reactions to the paper you plan to revise. "Movies of the Reader's Mind" (Section 7 of the *Sharing and Responding* part of this text) is probably the best technique for this.

If you are doing this workshop's assignment collaboratively, enlist others outside your group to give you feedback both on the paper(s) you're analyzing and on the essay you produce as a result of the analysis.

For feedback on your analysis, you'll find the following sections of *Sharing and Responding* particularly useful: "Summary and Sayback" (3), "Skeleton Feedback and Descriptive Outline" (10), and "Criterion-Based Feedback" (11), especially the criteria traditionally applied to expository writing.

In addition, you might ask your readers and listeners the following questions:

- "Do you agree with me about whom I have identified as the audience of the paper(s)? about what I have identified as purpose(s)?"
- "Do you understand what I would do if I did revise? What other suggestions would you make for revision?"

When sharing your revised paper, ask readers and listeners the following questions:

- "Have I taken my own advice from my own analysis of this paper?"
- "Whom do you now see as the audience for my paper, and what do you see as its purpose?"

PROCESS JOURNAL AND COVER LETTER QUESTIONS

- Do you usually have a definite audience in mind when you start to write? How do various audiences affect your writing? teachers? your writing group? Which audiences do you find most helpful and most problematic? Do you find it difficult to ignore audience?
- How do you see and experience the teacher as audience?
- Do you usually have some definite purpose in mind when you start to write? Or do you discover purposes after starting? How does purpose function for you as you write?

RUMINATIONS AND THEORY

Purpose, Genre, and an Overview of Rhetorical Terrain

Global Goals: Expressive, Transactional, and Poetic

Can We Forget about Purpose and Audience?

Purpose, Genre, and an Overview of Rhetorical Terrain

In Workshop 5 we emphasized genre; in this workshop we emphasize purpose. It's worth exploring how genre and purpose are similar and how they differ.

It seems as though certain genres are designed to accomplish certain purposes. If you want to persuade someone, you're likely to assume you should write a persuasive essay—not a poem or a story. (In this case the genre's name even carries the name of the purpose—to persuade.) And yet if you take it for granted that you shouldn't write a poem or story, you should think again. You would be putting too much stock in genre and not thinking concretely enough about purpose.

For really there is no *necessary* connection between genres and purposes. Poetry, for example, may seem to express personal emotion more often than informational essays do, but that's just a matter of how poetry has tended to develop since the romantic period in the nineteenth century. Essays can express personal emotion, and poems can convey information. (Until the romantic period, poetry was treated as an appropriate genre for conveying information—even scientific information. The first version of atomic theory came in a long Greek poem, "On the Nature of Things," by Lucretius. Alexander Pope wrote an important poem called "An Essay On Man"—which is, indeed, an essay.) The important practical point here is that the persuasive essay is not the only way to persuade. Stories, novels, poems, and letters can sometimes persuade better than essays. (We've mentioned the persuasive power of *Uncle Tom's Cabin* before the Civil War. See Levensky's use of a published letter to persuade in the "Readings" for Workshop 5.) And the essay can be a form of lyric or autobiography.

It turns out that the grading of writing is often linked to assumptions about genre. If someone says, "This is a poor persuasive essay," he may well mean that the piece violates what he expects of the persuasive essay genre; yet it may in fact persuade many readers. Or a teacher may say, "This is an excellent persuasive essay" (and even give it an A)—and yet not actually be persuaded by it.

Some writers don't care whether their pieces fit the traditional forms and conventions. That is, some story writers don't care if some readers say, "This is a very peculiar story—there's no real ending" (again, look at the Paley story in the "Readings" for this workshop), or "I can't figure out whether this is a story or an essay." Some business writers don't care if readers say, "This writer doesn't seem to know the rules for proper memos." Those writers simply want to have a certain *effect* on readers, and they have decided they can do it better by breaking certain "rules" or "conventions" about genres. Of course, they must recognize the risk in this approach: they will annoy those readers who don't like departures from genre, but it is through this process that genres change. For example, it's no longer clear that the story genre demands a climax or an ending that resolves all the loose ends.

Another way to say this is that there isn't a perfect genre for each purpose. You can do many things with any one genre—for example, you can use a story to amuse or to persuade or even to convey information. (Think about the purely informational qualities of novels like Arthur Hailey's *Airport* and James Michener's *Hawaii*.) The point is that you need to think concretely and realistically about purpose—and not take things for granted.

Let's stand back and look at the whole terrain referred to as *rhetoric*. We emphasized finding your topic in Workshop 4 ("Private Writing"); we emphasized genre and audience in Workshop 5 ("From Private to Public Writing"). Now we emphasize purpose and audience in this workshop. It is a good time to stand back and see how purpose, audience, genre, and topic are distinct, yet intertwined.

There is a traditional diagram called the "rhetorical triangle," or the "communications triangle," that sets out a schematic overview of what we might call the "rhetorical terrain":

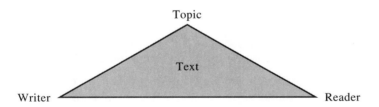

- To focus on purpose is to focus on people—what the *writer* intended and what happens to *readers* as they read.
- To focus on the *topic* is to focus on the world or the message.
- To focus on genre is to focus on the *text*—the form and the conventions used. (To think about conventions is also to think about the history of texts—for example, whether stories need to have tidy endings.)

When you focus on one dimension, you may leave other dimensions vague or ambiguous for a while. For example:

- We may get quite far in writing a poem about something (thus knowing genre and topic) but not be sure of audience or purpose. There's nothing wrong with proceeding in that manner.
- We may be engaged in writing a letter to someone (knowing genre and audience) but not be sure of the topic or purpose: we just know we want to write to them. Fine.
- We may start to write something entertaining about something (purpose and topic) but not be sure of the audience or genre.
- Indeed, we may know only that we want to write about a particular *topic* (e.g., an issue or a frightening experience), and remain vague about all three other dimensions: audience, genre, and purpose. We simply need to write in an exploratory way and see where it takes us.

Each rhetorical dimension is related to the other. Any change in one is likely to cause a change in the other. But as we have seen, the lines of connection are a bit rubbery. But *before you are finished* with any piece of writing, you should be sure of all four dimensions. Indeed, one way to check over a piece of writing and move toward revision is to make sure you are clear and consistent about audience, purpose, genre, and topic (or message).

Global Goals: Expressive, Transactional, and Poetic

In this workshop we've emphasized small nitty-gritty goals: what specific effects do you want your words to have on specific people? what observable changes would occur if your words worked? We've warned you against large global aims because they are fuzzy. But we don't mean to dismiss the value of talking in larger terms.

James Britton provides perhaps the most useful (and influential) statement of three *global* concepts for describing purposes in writing: "expressive," "transactional," and "poetic."

1. *Expressive writing* is writing that somehow expresses or pictures the writer. Expressive writing may be the pure "venting" of words which no one but the writer would ever understand—words which merely get what was inside outside, with no concern for a reader. Or they may be perfectly clear to readers: a clear and careful expressing of something in the writer.

2. *Transactional writing* is writing which makes something happen in the world. It informs, persuades, or—to give a crass but concrete example—produces a refund by return mail. When your aim is transactional, you are jumping into events and using words as a *participant* or as a way of *acting* on the world—trying to have an *effect*.

3. *Poetic writing* is writing that remains valuable for itself—apart from any expressive or transactional purpose. That is, poetic writing (in Britton's sense of the term) is worth saving and reading not because it expresses you or gets anything done (though it may do one or both these things) but because it is

pleasing for itself as language. Thus a "poem" (in the conventional sense of the term) is usually "poetic writing" in Britton's sense. That is, the poet is trying to make the language and the form so pleasing that you will value the poem even if you hate what it says. But, of course, a novel or an essay or any form of writing can be pleasing in itself, as language, and thus be an instance of poetic writing in Britton's sense.

These three terms are slippery since a piece of writing can have all three purposes: we may write a *poem* to *express ourselves* and thereby to *make something happen* in the world; for example, a poem to express how you feel that's designed to get someone to marry you. Nevertheless we can often clarify our goals for a piece of writing if we ask ourselves which of the three purposes, if we *had* to choose, is our main priority. Thus, if you *had* to choose, which do you care more about: succeeding in expressing how you really feel? ending up with a good poem? or getting the person to marry you? Or if you had to choose between getting a refund or having a splendid letter which magnificently pulverizes the store for incompetence, which would you choose? If your goal were transactional, you would take the refund and be willing to throw away the writing—or ruin the writing by making it dull or even servile—if that's what it took to get the refund. If your goal were poetic, you would be willing to skip the refund so long as you could make a wonderful, witty, or acerbic letter which perhaps you would save—even publish; but no refund.

It is helpful to bring the communications triangle to bear (pictured in the previous section). Expressive writing can be said to focus more on the writer, poetic writing more on the text and language, and transactional writing either more on the reader (persuading) or more on the topic and the world (explaining).

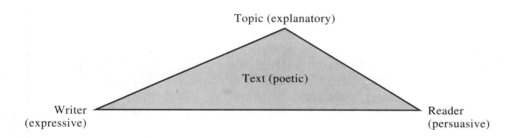

Topic (explanatory)

Text (poetic)

Writer
(expressive)

Reader
(persuasive)

But it doesn't pay to put too much faith in these neat schemata. If anything is neat, it probably doesn't fit the messy realities of language and communication very well. For instance, transactional writing may very well be expressive and put the focus on the writer: that is, we sometimes get our refund by expressing how we feel—not by cajoling the reader or explaining events. The same goes for poetic writing: sometimes our poem about a tree renders the tree by telling how things are with us.

It helps to think of expressive writing as coming first or being a foundation for the others (and this is Britton's point). That is, often we cannot find impersonal arguments for a refund or create an accurate picture of the tree until we first find words for our personal reactions concerning the refund or the tree. Britton argues that expressive writing (where you don't usually worry about audience, accuracy, or effect) underlies transactional and poetic writing even if all it does is help people *get going* on a piece of writing—even if it never makes any appearance in the finished piece.

Can We Forget about Purpose and Audience?

We have spoken of the value of thinking about audience and purpose; then we turn around and say it is sometimes useful to forget about audience and purpose if your hands are full just trying to figure out what *you* think (rather than worrying about how to convey what you think to others).

Does it sound as though we think you can just turn on and turn off all orientation toward audience and purpose—as with a mental faucet? It's important to acknowledge that in a sense one can never *avoid* orientation toward audience and purpose in any use of language: to open our mouths is to have the impulse to say something to someone for some reason. Our language is often shaped quite well by audience and purpose without our having any conscious awareness of who the audience is and what our purposes are.

But even if we can't get away from audience and purpose (or, putting this in its most general form, even if human intelligence is deeply social and human behavior is deeply purposive), there's still a big difference between *being* conscious of audience and purpose and *not* being conscious of them. There's also a big difference between trying to make your writing *fit* audience and consciously allowing your writing *not* to fit audience and purpose (for example, in exploring a topic). Thus, even if we can't get away from orientation toward audience and purpose, we *can* get away from trying to think about

---

PROCESS BOX

I don't consciously think of audience when I write. In writing for this course, I knew I was going to share my writing with the class but I didn't think of this or imagine them in some way. Right now, I guess I'm directing this writing to you but I'm not really thinking of that. Does this make any sense? I'm not sure where I go in my mind when I write. The feeling I have is of moving upward and sky, kind of out of body: a suspended state once I get moving and forgetting time. This is why I tend to write late at night. There are less interruptions and the time is more open ended. I do this weird consciousness thing even when I write letters. Then I have a person in mind but I direct the writing to their gut or heart and occasionally their mind. When I first fell in love with my old boyfriend, he was living far away. I wrote to him often and I remember imaging a kind of moving cloud or smoky essence that I directed my writing toward: the part of him I loved and wanted to connect with.

Nancy Blasi

them and plan for them. In short, there are advantages in trying to plan and know and control what we are doing, but also advantages in leaving quite a lot to intuition or the tacit dimension.

We recognized this same issue when we spoke of organization versus messiness in freewriting. Does doing fast and furious freewriting and not worrying at all about the organization mean you are getting away from organization? No, for it's impossible to get away from organization; everything has organization. But it does mean three important things:

- You are getting away from *thinking* about organization.
- You are inviting messy organization.
- You are inviting your *intuitive* or *tacit* power of organizing—your imagination. For we can often make a more interesting organization by intuition than by careful planning.

Thus, when we forget about audience and purpose, we invite writing that doesn't fit an audience or purpose. But we also invite writing that suits an audience and purpose more cleverly than we could have planned. So what it all boils down to is trying to learn to take the best advantages of *both* dimensions of the mind: careful conscious planning and intuition. For even though we are often more intelligent in our unconscious intentions than in our conscious ones, intuition can also lead us down the garden path. Therefore, *before we are finished with a piece of writing,* we do well to try to invoke the careful and conscious side of our minds: to become clear about audience and purpose and organization. For example, we may have to wrestle with a decision between conflicting aims that our intuition had allowed into our text. "Let's see. Now that I'm finishing this piece, who am I really writing to? What do I really want to do to them? Persuade, yes, but what things do I need to do to them to persuade them? Out of everything I've written so far, what would work best to achieve this purpose? What do I need to discard?"

Readings

IS PHOENIX JACKSON'S GRANDSON REALLY DEAD?*

Eudora Welty

A story writer is more than happy to be read by students; the fact that these serious readers think and feel something in response to his work he finds life-giving. At the same time he may not always be able to reply to their specific questions in kind. I wondered if it might clarify something, for both the questioners and myself, if I set down a general reply to the question that comes to me most often in the mail, from both students and their teachers, after some classroom discussion. The unrivaled favorite is this: "Is Phoenix Jackson's grandson really *dead?*"

It refers to a short story I wrote years ago called "A Worn Path," which tells of a day's journey an old woman makes on foot from deep in the country into town and into a doctor's office on behalf of her little grandson; he is at home, periodically ill, and periodically she comes for his medicine; they give it to her as usual, she receives it and starts the journey back.

I had not meant to mystify readers by withholding any fact: it is not a writer's business to tease. The story is told through Phoenix's mind as she undertakes her errand. As the author at one with the character as I tell it, I must assume that the boy is alive. As the reader, you are free to think as you like, of course: The story invites you to believe that no matter what happens, Phoenix for as long as she is able to walk and can hold to her purpose will make her journey. The *possibility* that she would keep on even if he were dead is there in her devotion and its single-minded, single-track errand. Certainly the *artistic* truth, which should be good enough for the fact, lies in Phoenix's own answer to that question. When the nurse asks, "He isn't dead, is he?" she speaks for herself: "He still the same. He going to last."

The grandchild is the incentive. But it is the journey, the going of the errand, that is the story, and the question is not whether the grandchild is in reality alive or dead. It doesn't affect the outcome of the story or its meaning from start to finish. But it is not the question itself that has struck me as much as the idea, almost without exception implied in the asking, that for Phoenix's grandson to be dead would somehow make the story "better."

It's *all right,* I want to say to the students who write to me, for things to be what they appear to be, and for words to mean what they say. It's all right,

---

*This is Eudora Welty's analysis of "The Worn Path," included in the readings for Workshop 2.

too, for words and appearances to mean more than one thing—ambiguity is a fact of life. A fiction writer's responsibility covers not only what he presents as the facts of a given story but what he chooses to stir up as their implications; in the end, these implications, too, become facts, in the larger fictional sense. But it is not all right, not in good faith, for things *not* to mean what they say.

The grandson's plight was real and it made the truth of the story, which is the story of an errand of love carried out. If the child no longer lived, the truth would persist in the "wornness" of the path. But his being dead can't increase the truth of the story, can't affect it one way or the other. I think I signal this, because the end of the story has been reached before old Phoenix gets home again: she simply starts back. To the question "Is the grandson really dead?" I could reply that it doesn't make any difference. I could also say that I did not make him up in order to let him play a trick on Phoenix. But my best answer would be: "*Phoenix* is alive."

The origin of a story is sometimes a trustworthy clue to the author—or can provide him with the clue—to its key image; maybe in this case it will do the same for the reader. One day I saw a solitary old woman like Phoenix. She was walking; I saw her, at middle distance, in a winter country landscape, and watched her slowly make her way across my line of vision. That sight of her made me write the story. I invented an errand for her, but that only seemed a living part of the figure she was herself. What errand other than for someone else could be making her go? And her going was the first thing, her persisting in her landscape was the real thing, and the first and the real were what I wanted and worked to keep. I brought her up close enough, by imagination, to describe her face, make her present to the eyes, but the full-length figure moving across the winter fields was the indelible one and the image to keep, and the perspective extending into the vanishing distance the true one to hold in mind.

I invented for my character, as I wrote, some passing adventures—some dreams and harassments and a small triumph or two, some jolts to her pride, some flights of fancy to console her, one or two encounters to scare her, a moment that gave her cause to feel ashamed, a moment to dance and preen— for it had to be a *journey,* and all these things belonged to that, parts of life's uncertainty.

A narrative line is in its deeper sense, of course, the tracing out of a meaning, and the real continuity of a story lies in this probing forward. The real dramatic force of a story depends on the strength of the emotion that has set it going. The emotional value is the measure of the reach of the story. What gives any such content to "A Worn Path" is not its circumstances but its *subject:* the deep-grained habit of love.

What I hoped would come clear was that in the whole surround of this story, the world it threads through, the only certain thing at all is the worn path. The habit of love cuts through confusion and stumbles or contrives its way out of difficulty, it remembers the way even when it forgets, for a dumfounded moment, its reason for being. The path is the thing that matters.

Her victory—old Phoenix's—is when she sees the diploma in the doctor's

437

Readings
Is Phoenix
Jackson's
Grandson
Really Dead?

office, when she finds "nailed up on the wall the document that had been stamped with the gold seal and framed in the gold frame, which matched the dream that was hung up in her head." The return with the medicine is just a matter of retracing her own footsteps. It is the part of the journey, and of the story, that can now go without saying.

In the matter of function, old Phoenix's way might even do as a sort of parallel to your way of work if you are a writer of stories. The way to get there is the all-important, all-absorbing problem, and this problem is your reason for undertaking the story. Your only guide, too, is your sureness about your subject, about what this subject is. Like Phoenix, you work all your life to find your way, through all the obstructions and the false appearances and the upsets you may have brought on yourself, to reach a meaning—using inventions of your imagination, perhaps helped out by your dreams and bits of good luck. And finally too, like Phoenix, you have to assume that what you are working in aid of is life, not death.

But you would make the trip anyway—wouldn't you?—just on hope.

ANALYSIS OF COVER LETTER FOR ADVERTISEMENT

(See "Readings" at the end of Workshop 8.)

An analysis of our cover letter for the advertisement we designed as an assignment for Workshop 8 shows us that we do not need to change our audience and purpose: we still need to write to the cereal company for the purpose of getting ourselves hired to produce ads for the new cereal. But we have realized that we need to think more about that audience in terms of our purpose.

When we wrote our original letter, we thought of our audience as people who wanted to make a profit from their new cereal and who were looking for a new advertising firm. After thinking more about this, we have begun to realize that the reader of this letter probably wants as wide an audience as possible for the new cereal. Our problem is that we are not sure whether the cereal company would be more likely to respond to a hard-sell approach—almost like an ad itself—or to a neutral descriptive approach, which is the one we have now except for a few adjectives like "vibrant" and "exciting." As we thought about this audience also, we thought that they are probably more sophisticated about magazines and other places to advertise than we are.

When we read our original letter to our group, they told us that the words "vibrant" and "exciting" stood out and they had a negative reaction to them—as though we were pushing too hard to look good. They also told us that they thought the second paragraph was good and described the ad well. But they reacted somewhat differently to the third paragraph because they thought the male figure could also be seen as someone who looks backward in his life rather than forward. They also wondered about why we assumed so quickly that the cereal could not be a family cereal.

We decided that when we revise the letter, we need to think a lot about the language and whether we should be hard sell or soft sell. We need to think about the sophistication level of our audience and how resistant they might be to advertising language. We also need to worry about how we could make the cereal more of a family cereal.

REVISION OF COVER LETTER

Mr. John Jones, President
Wilton Products
5555 Fifth Avenue
American City, American State 55555
Attn: Advertising Department

Dear Mr. Jones:

Your innovative new cereal, "Designer Breakfast," has the potential to appeal to Americans across the board; we are the advertising company which can make that potential realized.

Our young creative advertising team has designed a set of ads to demonstrate *our* potential to make your product a household word. We suspect that you examined these ads before you started reading our letter and have already realized how strong they are. We certainly don't need to tell you how these ads make their points: you're quite capable of seeing that yourself. If our ads cannot stand on their own, we don't deserve your account.

Therefore, in terms of explanation, we're just going to say a few words about how these ads could be manipulated to reach a variety of audiences. For instance, if we keep the same layout, we can change the male and female figures to children bounding out of their houses and heading for a school bus. The figures could also be those of an older man and woman dressed for hiking or golf or tennis. We can substitute figures from the artistic world—carrying musical instruments or canvases. The possibilities are almost endless. An ad campaign designed to alter the appeal within similar frameworks would undoubtedly reach consumers of all varieties. Needless to say, these figures could also be altered to different races and ethnicities.

We are certain we can sell your product. Our past successes attest to that. You probably know that it was our company which designed the highly effective campaign for Labova shoes and the award-winning ads for Lama's new line of soups. This same team can make your product just as successful as these are.
We look forward to talking to you about our ideas.

Sincerely,

Jason Multer
Antoinette Jajee
Martine Oxenham
Ngoyen Nong
Alex Ujibwa

From A CONVERSATION WITH MY FATHER

Grace Paley

My father is eighty-six years old and in bed. His heart, that bloody motor, is equally old and will not do certain jobs any more. It still floods his head with brainy light. But it won't let his legs carry the weight of his body around the house. Despite my metaphors, this muscle failure is not due to his old heart, he says, but to a potassium shortage. Sitting on one pillow, leaning on three, he offers last-minute advice and makes a request.

"I would like you to write a simple story just once more," he says, "the kind de Maupassant wrote, or Chekhov, the kind you used to write. Just recognizable people and then write down what happened to them next."

I say, "Yes, why not? That's possible." I want to please him, though I don't remember writing that way. I *would* like to try to tell such a story, if he means the kind that begins: "There was a woman . . ." followed by plot, the absolute line between two points which I've always despised. Not for literary reasons, but because it takes all hope away. Everyone, real or invented, deserves the open destiny of life.

Finally I thought of a story that had been happening for a couple of years right across the street. I wrote it down, then read it aloud. "Pa," I said, "how about this? Do you mean something like this?"

> Once in my time there was a woman and she had a son. They lived nicely, in a small apartment in Manhattan. This boy at about fifteen became a junkie, which is not unusual in our neighborhood. In order to maintain her close friendship with him, she became a junkie too. She said it was part of the youth culture, with which she felt very much at home. After a while, for a number of reasons, the boy gave it all up and left the city and his mother in disgust. Hopeless and alone, she grieved. We all visit her.

"O.K., Pa, that's it," I said, "an unadorned and miserable tale."

"But that's not what I mean," my father said. "You misunderstood me on purpose. You know there's a lot more to it. You know that. You left everything out. Turgenev wouldn't do that. Chekhov wouldn't do that. There are in fact Russian writers you never heard of, you don't have an inkling of, as good as anyone, who can write a plain ordinary story, who would not leave out what you have left out. I object not to facts but to people sitting in trees talking senselessly, voices from who knows where . . ."

"Forget that one, Pa, what have I left out now? In this one?"

"Her looks, for instance."

"Oh, Quite handsome, I think. Yes."

"Her hair?"

"Dark, with heavy braids, as though she were a girl or a foreigner."

"What were her parents like, her stock? That she became such a person. It's interesting, you know."

"From out of town. Professional people. The first to be divorced in their county. How's that? Enough?" I asked.

"With you, it's all a joke," he said. "What about the boy's father? Why didn't you mention him? Who was he? Or was the boy born out of wedlock?"

"Yes," I said. "He was born out of wedlock."

"For Godsakes, doesn't anyone in your stories get married? Doesn't anyone have the time to run down to City Hall before they jump into bed?"

"No," I said. "In real life, yes. But in my stories, no."

"Why do you answer me like that?"

"Oh, Pa, this is a simple story about a smart woman who came to N.Y.C. full of interest love trust excitement very up to date, and about her son, what a hard time she had in this world. Married or not, it's of small consequence."

"It is of great consequence," he said.

"O.K.," I said.

"O.K. O.K. yourself," he said, "but listen. I believe you that she's good-looking, but I don't think she was so smart."

"That's true," I said. "Actually that's the trouble with stories. People start out fantastic. You think they're extraordinary, but it turns out as the work goes along, they're just average with a good education. Sometimes the other way around, the person's a kind of dumb innocent, but he outwits you and you can't even think of an ending good enough."

"What do you do then?" he asked. He had been a doctor for a couple of decades and then an artist for a couple of decades and he's still interested in details, craft, technique.

"Well, you just have to let the story lie around till some agreement can be reached between you and the stubborn hero."

"Aren't you talking silly, now?" he asked. "Start again," he said. "It so happens I'm not going out this evening. Tell the story again. See what you can do this time."

"O.K.," I said. "But it's not a five-minute job." Second attempt:

Once, across the street from us, there was a fine handsome woman, our neighbor. She had a son whom she loved because she'd known him since birth (in helpless chubby infancy, and in the wrestling, hugging ages, seven to ten, as well as earlier and later). This boy, when he fell into the first of adolescence, became a junkie. He was not a hopeless one. He was in fact hopeful, an ideologue and successful converter. With his busy brilliance, he wrote persuasive articles for his high-school newspaper. Seeking a wider audience, using important connections, he drummed into Lower Manhattan newsstand distribution a periodical called *Oh! Golden Horse!*

In order to keep him from feeling guilty (because guilt is the stony heart of nine tenths of all clinically diagnosed cancers in America today, she said), and because she had always believed in giving bad habits room at home where one could keep an eye on them, she too became a junkie. Her kitchen was famous for a while—a center for intellectual addicts who knew what they were doing. A few felt artistic like Coleridge and others were scientific and revolutionary like Leary. Although she was often high herself, certain good mothering reflexes remained, and she saw to it that there was lots of orange juice around and honey and milk and vitamin pills. However, she never cooked anything but chili, and that no more than once a week.

She explained, when we talked to her, seriously, with neighborly concern, that it was her part in the youth culture and she would rather be with the young, it was an honor, than with her own generation.

One week, while nodding through an Antonioni film, this boy was severely jabbed by the elbow of a stern and proselytizing girl, sitting beside him. She offered immediate apricots and nuts for his sugar level, spoke to him sharply, and took him home.

She had heard of him and his work and she herself published, edited, and wrote a competitive journal called *Man Does Live By Bread Alone.* In the organic heat of her continuous presence he could not help but become interested once more in his muscles, his arteries, and nerve connections. In fact he began to love them, treasure them, praise them with funny little songs in *Man Does Live . . .*

> *the fingers of my flesh transcend*
> *my transcendental soul*
> *the tightness in my shoulders end*
> *my teeth have made me whole*

To the mouth of his head (that glory of will and determination) he brought hard apples, nuts, wheat germ, and soybean oil. He said to his old friends, From now on, I guess I'll keep my wits about me. I'm going on the natch. He said he was about to begin a spiritual deep-breathing journey. How about you too, Mom? he asked kindly.

His conversion was so radiant, splendid, that neighborhood kids his age began to say that he had never been a real addict at all, only a journalist along for the smell of the story. The mother tried several times to give up what had become without her son and his friends a lonely habit. This effort only brought it to supportable levels. The boy and his girl took their electronic mimeograph and moved to the bushy edge of another borough. They were very strict. They said they would not see her again until she had been off drugs for sixty days.

At home alone in the evening, weeping, the mother read and reread the seven issues of *Oh! Golden Horse!* They seemed to her as truthful as ever. We often crossed the street to visit and console. But if we mentioned any of our children who were at college or in the hospital or dropouts at home, she would cry out, My baby! My baby! and burst into terrible, face-scarring, time-consuming tears. The End.

First my father was silent, then he said, "Number One: You have a nice sense of humor. Number Two: I see you can't tell a plain story. So don't waste time." Then he said sadly, "Number Three: I suppose that means she was alone, she was left like that, his mother. Alone. Probably sick?"

I said, "Yes."

"Poor woman. Poor girl, to be born in a time of fools, to live among fools. The end. The end. You were right to put that down. The end."

I didn't want to argue, but I had to say, "Well, it is not necessarily the end, Pa."

"Yes," he said, "what a tragedy. The end of a person."

"No, Pa," I begged him. "It doesn't have to be. She's only about forty. She could be a hundred different things in this world as time goes on. A teacher or a social worker. An ex-junkie! Sometimes it's better than having a master's in education."

"Jokes," he said. "As a writer that's your main trouble. You don't want to recognize it. Tragedy! Plain tragedy! Historical tragedy! No hope. The end."

"Oh, Pa," I said. "She could change."

"In your own life, too, you have to look it in the face." He took a couple of nitroglycerin. "Turn to five," he said, pointing to the dial on the oxygen tank. He inserted the tubes into his nostrils and breathed deep. He closed his eyes and said, "No."

I had promised the family to always let him have the last word when arguing, but in this case I had a different responsibility. That woman lives across the street. She's my knowledge and my invention. I'm sorry for her. I'm not going to leave her there in that house crying. (Actually neither would Life, which unlike me has no pity.)

Therefore: She did change. Of course her son never came home again. But right now, she's the receptionist in a storefront community clinic in the East Village. Most of the customers are young people, some old friends. The head doctor has said to her, "If we only had three people in this clinic with your experiences . . ."

"The doctor said that?" My father took the oxygen tubes out of his nostrils and said, "Jokes, Jokes again."

"No, Pa, it could really happen that way, it's a funny world nowadays."

"No," he said. "Truth first. She will slide back. A person must have character. She does not."

"No, Pa," I said. "That's it. She's got a job. Forget it. She's in that storefront working."

"How long will it be?" he asked. "Tragedy! You too. When will you look it in the face?"

WORKSHOP

17

AUTOBIOGRAPHY AND PORTFOLIO

Our experience has taught us that writers learn the most by becoming students of their own writing processes. Thus, our major aim in this workshop is to get you to learn something about yourself and your writing process that will be useful when you are doing future writing tasks in school. But we also hope the activities of this workshop will help you see some role for writing in your life outside of school assignments. Along the way you should discover for yourself that writing leads to learning.

Your major assignment will be to create a portfolio of writing you have done throughout the semester and add to it an autobiography of yourself as a writer. And since you will be using writing you've done throughout the semester as a basis for your autobiography, this workshop will encourage you to look back on the term and assess honestly what happened to you and to your writing.

For most of you, this may be your final assignment of the term. It will help you solidify and benefit from what you have been learning all semester. Some of what you've learned you've been explicitly aware you were learning; but you have learned many other things in an intuitive, unconscious way. This autobiography will help you see and consolidate *all* you have learned. It needn't be too much work, yet you can discover much about your own learning and how it has affected the way you write.

The theme of your autobiography is the theme of the course: *the writing process.* The autobiography will help you see the writing process in detail and empirically—not just settle for generalizations. The *facts* about what you actually do when you write are probably somewhat different from what you *think* you do. Discovering these facts almost always makes your writing easier and better.

 CREATING YOUR PORTFOLIO

Your teacher may have asked you at the beginning of the term to start a portfolio and keep everything you write in it. Or she may have asked you to put only certain things in it. Perhaps she has looked at it—even evaluated it—once or twice already. In our classes we like our students to put a wide variety of kinds of writing in their portfolios: some journal pieces, freewritings, exploratory writings, responses to readings, drafts, peer responses, and process writing, as well as finished pieces. We like also for students to put into their portfolios other pieces of writing we haven't asked for that they may be particularly proud of: pieces written for other classes and even pieces written for pleasure.

Your teacher will tell you what she would like you to include in your portfolio. Chances are that if she is going to use the portfolio to help decide your grade for the term, she won't want everything in there and will ask you to make some selections either with or without help from her and your classmates. These pieces will serve as a basis for your autobiography, which in turn will serve as a kind of cover sheet for your portfolio.

Your first task for this workshop then is to assemble the portfolio your teacher asks for. Once it's all together, read back over it and do some freewriting about what you see there.

 ## POSSIBLE INGREDIENTS, ISSUES, OR THEMES FOR YOUR AUTOBIOGRAPHY

Following are methods and topics to help you bring together material for your autobiography. Some of these issues you've already written about in your process journal throughout the term. Perhaps you've already reread your journal as you were assembling your final portfolio. If not, you should now look back through your journal and identify these passages. The freewriting you did after preparing your portfolio will probably touch on a number of these issues also. Other topics we suggest in the list that follows you will not have written on. You should begin writing on any or all of the topics on the following list and see what happens. Looking at the contents of your portfolio may help you come up with specific ideas and examples. For right now, the important thing to remember is that you're not trying to draw conclusions: you're still in the data-collection stage.

Moments. What important incidents do you remember from past writing experiences?

Stages. Intuitively divide your life as a writer into a few stages or periods; then ask yourself what characterizes each of those stages.

Kinds. What kinds of writing have you done in the past and what kinds do you do now? Remember that there are many more kinds of writing than those you've done in school: making lists is writing; so is graffiti. What is different about your experience with different kinds of writing?

In-School versus Out-of-School Writing. Do you go about both of these the same way? Differently? Do you feel the same way about both? Why or why not?

Audience. Who are the important people you have written for? (Not just teachers.) What effects have these different audiences had? on your feelings? on your writing? Which audiences helped you the most or held you back? How often do you feel yourself to be the only audience of what you are writing? (Don't forget "ghost audiences" or audiences we carry around in our heads and unconsciously try to please—usually left over from experiences with past audiences.) Many people remember bad audiences more than good ones. Is that true of you? Why?

Physical. Where do you write? When? How fast or slow? What are the effects of using pen, pencil, typewriter, or word processor? How do you hold and move your body? Do you feel tense or relaxed after a session of writing?

Tell everything that could be figured out from a *complete video recording* of your writing from start to finish.

Process.   Can you isolate specific ingredients in your writing process: that is, generating words and responses, copyediting, publishing? Nonwriting counts too: sitting and thinking, talking to people. Which of these give you the most trouble? the least? the most satisfaction? the least? Why?

Intervention.   In what ways have others intervened in your writing? ("Here, let me show you!" "Do it this way." "You must start by making an outline." "You must start by freewriting"—and so forth.) How has intervention affected your writing?

Response and Feedback.   What kinds of response and feedback have you gotten—and not just from teachers? What effects did this feedback have on you? (Don't forget no response and nonverbal response—silence and laughter.)

Writing for Other Classes versus Writing for This Class.   If you've written papers for other classes this term, what's different about how you went about it? Did you do any freewriting, produce a draft which your teacher responded to either verbally or in writing, revise one or more times, copyedit? Compare the total effort involved in that project and the total effort involved in writing a piece for this class. Pay attention too to any differences in feelings or attitudes toward the two pieces of writing. If you did not use the techniques we've been stressing in this book, do you think you could have or should have? Why or why not?

Problems.   Stuck points and breakthroughs. What's hardest for you or what gets in the way most? How have you made or not made progress? Where have you made the greatest progress?

Myths.   What are some of the feelings or ideas that you've had about your writing (or that most people seem to have) that you now see are *false?* Where did these myths come from? What purposes did they serve and what effect have they had on you? What follows from abandoning them?

The Word "Writer."   Who do you think of as a writer? What are the characteristics of a writer? Can you think of yourself as a writer? If not, why not?

Temperament or Character.   Do you see any relation between your writing process and your temperament, character, or feelings? Does your writing process show you to be "loose" or "tight," vulnerable or confident? In general, do you think that someone's writing process reflects her character?

 MAKING A DRAFT

You should now have much raw material—some developed, some just bits. Read through all of this *and* through all your process writing from the semester. (You probably have more than you realize; some of your assignments have been process writing or include bits of it. You'll find other bits here and there. Some will be in notebooks for other subjects.) Mark the bits that are interesting and useful. You can probably use some of this process writing as part of your paper if you choose and cut well.

Next, consider what all this process writing is telling you. Do some freewriting or outlining or note jotting to figure out what your autobiography might focus on.

Two additional things we consider particularly important in any writer's autobiography: one is a mini-study or close look at *one* specific piece of writing, and the second is an analysis of how your present writing process differs from the way you used to write. We could have included both of these in our earlier list, but we wanted to give them special emphasis.

1. For your mini-study, choose something that you wrote this term. Choose that piece which—as the psychologists say—you "cathect" most: that piece you have the strongest feelings about or feel the strongest connection with. You can learn most from looking honestly and in detail at such a piece. You might also, however, simply pick the piece which you happen to have the most process writing for—the most evidence as to what actually was going on as you wrote. Evidence maximizes learning. Spend some time reconstructing how you wrote this piece from beginning to end in as much detail as possible; look at the writing itself, the various drafts, and see what they tell you. Select specific passages which you can quote and comment on. Do some freewriting, outlining, and jotting about what you figure out as you study this piece.

2. Think back on the writing you did *before* this course. (Some of your process writing will be about that too. You might have included it in the collage you did early in the semester about your writing history.) What does that early writing tell you? Many of you have probably saved copies of papers written in high school. You might want to look at these and see how much you can remember about writing them. This should lead you to some conclusions about the similarities and differences between how you used to write and how you write now. This, in turn, should make clearer the effects of this term's work on your writing.

Now you have the ingredients for producing a draft. You can do some cutting and pasting and arranging, but make sure to let this draft making be a process of *new discovery*—not just an assembling of what you already have. Look at all this material that you now suspect belongs in your draft. What does it mean? What does it add up to? What emphasis, claim, focus, shape, approach, spirit do you want your case study to have? If you keep these questions in mind, you will find new answers as you write and paste.

In making your draft, you are finally ready to ask the practical question: what useful advice or suggestions can you give yourself for future writing? What are the *dangers* for you as a writer? What do you wish someone would whisper in your ear as you undertake writing tasks in the future?

A good writer's autobiography can be structured like a story or like an essay. That is, you can build it around *either* of the two major structural impulses for writing:

- Narrative, temporal. ("And then, and then, and then . . ."—with scattered "so what's" that tell the *point* of the story.)
- Expository, conceptual. ("Here's what I'm trying to tell you, and here's what it means or why it's important.")

If you choose the story mode, make sure there is enough "so what." Don't let it be *just* a story. If you are clever, you can make *some* of the "so what"—the significance—be implied or unstated. But some of it has to be explicit too. Of course, there's nothing wrong with "just a story"—*as* a story—but this assignment asks you to spell out some of the meaning or significance. If you choose the essay or expository mode, don't let it get too dry, abstract, or generalized. Keep the life in it by using specific examples, telling mini-stories, and incorporating descriptions—including particulars and quotations from writing you did, feedback you got, and so forth.

Try to emphasize for yourself that this task can be fun, not just work. Remember:

- You are the authority on you.
- You've done lots of writing and thinking this semester about yourself as a writer. What has been the most interesting and useful to *you?*
- Your audience is not just your teacher but also yourself: what you can figure out for yourself is really more important than what you can figure out for your teacher. Your classmates are an additional audience. Your teacher will probably give you a chance to share your autobiography, but if not, find a way; autobiographies are almost always a treat to read and hear.

 MINIMAL GUIDELINES

Make certain your autobiography includes at *least* the following. Undoubtedly you'll want to do more; this is just a foundation for you to check your draft against.

1. Examination of your writing both *before* taking this course and *during* this course. That is, the autobiography should function somewhat as a way of talking about how this course affected or did not affect how you write.
2. Examination of one piece or episode of writing in some detail. Indeed, you could center the *whole* autobiography around your examination of one piece of writing, bringing in the other parts of your autobiography in *relation* to this piece.
3. Quotations from your writing. Show how these examples of words-on-the-page illustrate (or do not illustrate) what you are saying about your writing process. That is, explain the relationship between your process and your product—between *what*'s on the page and *how* it got there.
4. Examination of comments or feedback by others. Comments can be from teachers, friends, or classmates, from this course or other courses.

5. A bit of advice for yourself: on the basis of all this exploration, what suggestions can you give yourself to make your writing go better in the future? Give your autobiography a *practical* dimension. Make it something that you will find useful to read over in the future when you are engaged in writing.

 SHARING AND RESPONDING

The most useful feedback is probably what's produced by using the techniques in Section 3, "Summary and Sayback," and Section 2, "Pointing and Center of Gravity," in the *Sharing and Responding* part of this book. But you may also want to get some comments on how your structure is coming across—especially when you've gotten to the final-draft stage. To get some feedback on this, you can use the *Sharing and Responding* sections grouped under structural responses.

Here are some more specific questions to use, but the important thing is for you to ask for the kind of feedback *you* feel most useful.

- "What changes do you see in me as a writer? What do you think I've learned during this term? What do you think I need to work on most? What do I seem most confident about? least confident about?"
- "Do you think some of what I've recorded contradicts any conclusions I've drawn? Do you feel gaps—something missing that would make the picture of me as a writer more complete?"
- "What do you find the most surprising or unique about my autobiography?"
- "What did you find helpful for *yourself* as a writer from my autobiography? What did you learn from me that *you* find the most valuable?"

PROCESS JOURNAL AND
COVER LETTER QUESTIONS

As always, these are merely suggestions. In fact, you may even want the last segment of your autobiography to consist of comment on and analysis of what it was like writing it.

- How did you feel about this assignment *before* you started it? Did you think you would enjoy doing it? find it a bore? feel unable to come up with enough material? What were your feelings when you were finished?
- Were you able to come up with genuine advice for yourself—advice that you think will be truly useful?
- If you had a chance to hear or read the autobiographies of others, what were your reactions? Did you sense mainly similarities or differences between theirs and yours?
- Do you think *how* you write makes a difference? Why or why not?
- Do you think writing is or will be important to you? What evidence do you have for your answer?

From *A Case Study of Myself*

The funny thing about the feedback that I received in this course is that I don't think I ever immediately understood what it was saying. The typed feedback letters were immensely helpful. But, I've realized after reading back through them all that what I read and what you wrote in the first place are two different things entirely!

For example, there are sentences which I swear I never read before, suddenly appearing on the page when I go back two weeks later to read it. Also, it seems that what I took your point to be—what you were trying to emphasize—when I first read the feedback and what I understand your points to be now are not the same, either.

I think that I have come up with an explanation for this phenomenon. It seems to me that a piece is very important to me when I write it, when I hand it in, when I get feedback on it, and for about one week afterward, because a piece of writing in this class is sort of representative of just where I am in the class right then—how I'm feeling.

The feedback is sort of like an affirmation that what I wrote was valid or "good." I guess that I've been trained this way. And even though I know that your feedback doesn't aim to say "yes" or "no," "good" or "bad," I still can't help reading it that way. So the feedback sheet comes to me and I say, "Did he like it?" instead of just taking in what you've said.

Because of this, when I get a sheet back and interpret what you've written, I almost end up changing your intention. The words on the page get translated through my own agenda (read: did he like it?) and I lose (or even fail to see!) what you're actually saying. Going back and reading through the sheets, it seems that many things that I took to be negative weren't. They just weren't worded in that "yes, this is an A or this is very good" way that I was expecting.

This, to me is shocking. I've always thought of myself as a person who takes constructive feedback of any sort exceptionally well. But now I realize that I don't take *any* type of feedback well, except for the sort of polar feedback that grades or extreme "yes" or "no's" produce. I used to think that I was an open-minded student, evidenced by the fact that I enjoy getting specific, negative feedback almost more than I enjoy positive feedback. I was proud of this.

But now I realize that I *like* that feedback because when I get it, it's spelled out for me—"what I did wrong." I don't have to evaluate myself or question my writing at all. I just have to take the expert's word for it. And this is easy.

I used to think, being a prospective teacher (sort of), that giving meaningful feedback would be simple: just be specific. But now, having evaluated my own responses to feedback, I wonder: Will being specific with feedback and asking for revisions make for a better writer, or just make for a better paper? And which is more important?

Victoria Malzone

 ## RUMINATIONS AND THEORY

Autobiography and Metacognition

Writing autobiography is a form of metacognition. Perhaps you've seen the word "metacognition" before you started this course—maybe in a psychology or education class. "Meta" is a prefix which comes to us from Greek; one of its meanings is "going beyond" or "higher." Thus "metacognition" literally means "going beyond" cognition or knowing; metacognitive theories, then, are those which consider our ability to know what we know.

Kenneth Burke, a modern rhetorician (we used some of his words to start the "Theory and Ruminations" section in Workshop 13), writes in *Permanence and Change* of the trout who, having escaped once from a hook embedded in bait, is afterwards warier. The trout may miss out on some genuine food because something about it looks like what almost caught him. And the trout may also fall for bait offered in some other way. No matter, the trout's behavior has changed.

Human beings, Burke goes on to say, can go one step farther than a trout, for we "can greatly extend the scope of the critical process"; we are the only species "possessing an equipment for going beyond the criticism of experience to a criticism of criticism. . . . we may also interpret our interpretations." The "equipment" which allows us to criticize our criticism and interpret out interpretations is language. And writing, we add, allows us to physically see that criticism and those interpretations. It allows us to observe our observations.

Recent research suggests that our unconscious mind is both cognitive and emotional. Events we have not perceived can affect how we behave. In extreme cases, they may lead to psychosis that can be eradicated only if the patient becomes aware of the unconscious roots of the psychosis. We don't want to suggest that writing is psychosis, but we do believe that our unconscious affects how we write also. No one teaches any of us how to put the words "round," "big," "box," and "green" in the right order, but as native speakers we are going to come up with "big round green box" unless we're deliberately seeking a particular effect. (And even that proves our point because we wouldn't get that particular effect if readers didn't automatically "know" the usual order.) Our unconscious mind stores much complex "knowledge" we don't quite understand but can learn to tap into. But our unconscious can lay traps for us too which we may also not understand. Analyzing our own writing behavior and actual pieces of our own writing can help us understand the ways in which our unconscious helps and hinders. This too is a way of knowing what we know.

Metacognition is not just valuable for mental activities. Athletes and their coaches are well aware of the power of metacognition, of studying and analyzing physical behavior. Football teams watch videos of prior games as a way to improve performance. Often when teams have had a particularly disastrous day, a coach will sit them down immediately after the game and insist that they "replay" crucial moments while they're still fresh in their minds—even before they take showers. The coach does this to show them not just what they did wrong but how they can do better the next time. Video technology has developed to the point where gymnasts' movements can be digitalized on a screen so that athletes and their coaches can analyze them minutely. Ballet dancers practice before mirrors so that they can see themselves. Exercise therapists even tell us that exercise is more effective when the person exercising thinks about what she is doing, thinks about the movements of the muscles and limbs. When you write, you're exercising a muscle. We believe that a muscle becomes stronger if you look at its actual movements on a regular basis.

Students sometimes become bored with process writing: they've told us so; their teachers have told us so. But we are not dissuaded. We continue to believe that if you can learn what process writing really is—not just mechanically going through the questions in every workshop, but actually probing the steps of your own writing—your writing will improve. The Russian psychologist and learning theorist Lev Vygotsky concluded after years of observing children learning that human beings are far more likely to move to higher learning if they understand what they've already learned, if, that is, they know what they know.

Thus we think that you can best come to conclusions about ways to improve *your* writing process by studying *your* writing process—by collecting as much information as you can about it and drawing conclusions about it *only* as a result of discovering patterns in it. This is the philosophy that lies behind the assignment for this workshop. We use our students' autobiographies as guides to helping us design our courses and assignments. Obviously we cannot design a course for one individual, so we seek common elements in the autobiographies we read. In other words, we generalize in an effort to come to conclusions which are valid for many student writers. Despite this, however, we recognize that each student's writing process is slightly different. We recognize, that is, the importance of specific data even as we make attempts at generalizations. But your task (at least right now) is different from ours. Your concern is to improve *your* writing. Thus, your autobiography needs to focus solely on you and to draw conclusions solely from your personal experiences and your specific interactions with others in a variety of writing environments.

We'll conclude this section and the main body of our textbook with a quotation from the *Notebooks* of Samuel Taylor Coleridge, who has much to say about imagination and creativity:

> Consciousness . . . mind, life, will, body, organ (as compared with machine), nature, spirit, sin, habit, sense, understanding, reason: here are fourteen words. Have you ever reflectively and quietly asked yourself the meaning of any one of these, and asked yourself to return the answer in *distinct* terms, not applicable to any of the other words? Or have you content yourself with the vague floating meaning that will just save you from absurdity in the use of the word, just as the clown's botany would do, who knew that potatoes were roots, and cabbages greens? Or, if you have the gift of wit, shelter yourself under Augustine's equivocation, "I know it perfectly well till I am asked." Know? Ay, as an oyster knows its life. *But do you know your knowledge?*

Readings

AUTOBIOGRAPHY OF MYSELF AS A WRITER

Barbara Smith

It is only recently that I have come to think of myself as a writer. As a student, of course, I have done a lot of writing, but I would think of this only as a method of communication, that is, to make the teacher aware of my grasp of the material. I have often used writing as therapy. Once a disturbing thought is recorded, it seems I can put it aside with the assurance that I can always retrieve it if the disturbing thought or once-repressed declaration should ever become an immediate, pressing issue. Even then, though, I didn't see myself in terms of a "writer" any more than I considered myself a "phone caller" or a recording secretary. Writing was one of many activities which I employed as a tool in my role as student and in my life as a functioning human being.

When I think of my writing as it was before I began my graduate work three years ago, I understand how my perception of myself as a writer has changed. In my previous academic writing experiences, I was carefully molded; I allowed this to happen because the path of least resistance seemed to be that of a teacher pleaser. I did well in high school and as an undergraduate because of this attitude. I was eager to share my papers with whoever was interested enough to want to read them, and was pleased when some of my pieces were displayed or presented in school publications. I never experienced the "highs and lows," the fears and passions that I sometimes do now. I realize now that this was because while I was given the satisfaction of external validation of my work, my own standards were held off, somewhere distant, and undeveloped. I was successful according to other people's standards. I now realize that it made little difference whether those standards were high or low; they simply were not mine. Writing was a game more than it was an intensely personal experience. The better I got at playing it, the more comfortable I felt. Any negative feelings that I can now recall, were, at the time, suppressed. Finally, I became aware that insensitivity and passionless writing were too high a price for the comfort and security of teacher pleasing. I am now able to find value in game playing, but I have to be master of the game—harness the rules to work for me as an exercise or an adventure into new experiences.

The major events which eventually led to my identity as a writer were spread out over a long period of time. The first significant event was as an undergraduate. I had one instructor who eased the transition from learning to write for teachers to learning to write for myself as well. He made this a painless process by stressing that pleasing myself was an important element in pleasing him. For the first time, feedback was actually helpful. I learned how to say what I wanted to say better. I reached a new plateau in that class, but I still didn't feel like a writer.

Soon after graduation, I stopped writing anything. It was a dark period for me. I was living in Connecticut then, and could feel something strange happening to me. For years I felt a vague uneasiness that defied identification. My self-esteem had plummeted to new lows. I now believe that this is why I stopped writing. Nothing I had to say would be important enough to commit to paper. And, now that I was out of school, there was no one to please. I tried to analyze what this new world of mine was like, what the cause of this ineffable lack of self-awareness was. The answer came through writing.

One Sunday while reading the theater section of the *Times,* I came upon a review of a new play in which a woman was victimized by perpetrators who committed a "series of little murders." There was nothing subtle about the effect that phrase had on me. It struck me as a lightning bolt, and I began to write. This frenetic writing session lasted for weeks. I would allow very few interruptions as I enumerated and expanded on what I for the first time perceived as the victim of a "series of little murders." I began to feel as though my brain had been invaded. As I thought and wrote about my writing experiences, I began to see them as a microcosm of my larger world. My extreme compliance and submissiveness led me to become dependent on other people's acceptance of my writing (and myself). Rather than face the tension that was caused between pleasing others and pleasing myself, I simply stopped writing, and for all intents and purposes, stopped being; I had never felt less alive. I saw myself as a victim, and finally realized that I alone allowed it to happen. The spark of self-recognition generated by that phrase ignited an untapped source of power and self-awareness; if I permitted it, I could also forbid it, and for the first time I felt great control—over myself, my writing, my life.

For a long time I would not show any of this writing to anyone. I came to understand that this atypical behavior (insistence on privacy) was the result of producing a piece of writing that was mine. Showing it was revealing myself. I was not yet prepared to do that. But here was writing that was important, articulate, precious, and mine.

Soon after, I could articulate precisely what I perceived a few short weeks ago as merely vague and disturbing, and I knew what I needed to do about it. I truly believed that my survival was at stake. We moved back to New York (my roots), away from a stifling environment, and I began my graduate work at Stony Brook.

I attacked writing projects with vigor, and refused to be "thrown." Once I discovered the power in writing, I wanted to explore every facet of it. I wanted to study literature, to understand the power and skill of great writers. And I wanted to develop my own skills and style.

As I continue to understand myself better, and become more at peace with who I am, I try to harness my bitter reactions to a formerly repressive writing (and living) atmosphere. The wildness and abandon which were so productive for me during that frenetic burst of writing and explosion of truth sometimes must be tamed in later revisions. But I try to keep the life there, and the power.

If the subject of a paper I am writing excites me, I can infuse even term papers with life and power. I usually generate the best of this kind of writing early on, when I'm just writing to get started, to state the thesis as best as I can, and to support it based on what is already in my head. The paper then gets drier, more "scholarly" as I refer to the text I am studying or to critical material. I must channel my thoughts and discipline myself to focus on goals set by professors. But the processes involved in meeting those goals have been ones of my own devising. I think of myself as a writer now. I try to "sprinkle" those sentences that reflect my excitement throughout the paper when I revise, so that I as the writer come through, and so that I don't wind up with a paper that is separated into halves by tone.

When I'm not engaged with the topic, the paper is usually a disaster. I feel that old "forced" feeling, the need to write for teachers only, to write the "right" things, to guess at what they want, because what I want has no meaning or relevance if I can't muster up some feeling for the subject. In these cases I don't think of myself as a writer (well, perhaps some kind of diminutive one). I feel more like a secretary who has been instructed to write a letter in regard to some specific matter. I can do it, but I remain detached, and the paper suffers. What I've learned from all this is that choosing a topic that fascinates me is a crucial first step that could lead to my best writing. Unlike my earlier writing stages, I am now cautious about sharing my writing; first I must trust the reader. I take this as a good sign—I am in that piece, this is me that is being perused, not an inanimate response to an assignment. It is a stage to be worked through, although I suspect the apprehension will never completely subside. I have developed a strong resistance to writing to please others and yet am still a bit anxious about saying, in effect, "Here I am." It is a concern that I'm pleased finally to be able to recognize, and one which I hope one day to celebrate as the beginning of a healthy self-consciousness as a writer.

I suppose that writing, like any art form, is best when it is a mode of unadulterated self-expression. But there seems to be a problem of inconsistency in how we value self-expression. The problem involves great risk; if the artist is good, self-expression is celebrated. If she is merely adequate, it is tolerated; and if poor, it is ridiculed. Writing, like life, can be kept "safe" from public scrutiny. But I have learned that being "safe" may be dull and boring, and for me, boredom is far more destructive than risk taking. Sharing this paper is a risk, but it is also a thrill—a dangerous, exhilarating exposition. I know too, that the reason for my positive attitude is that I trust my audience. What I haven't figured out yet, is how to write with this degree of investment—vulnerability, actually—for an audience I don't trust or even know—how to put what I am into my writing, and not what I think I should be. Of course, it's easier to walk a tightrope when you know there is a net beneath you. Taking risks is safer then. No net, less tricky stuff. Less tricky stuff, less risk—less risk, more safety—more safety, more boring. Boring = no growth, and no growth = no life. I guess what I'm saying is that risks are crucial. And writing which is powerful because of the assurance that it will remain private, often (ironically) is the very writing that ought to be shared. This is the paradox that I am in the process of working out.

CASE STUDY*

Mitchell Shack

I hate to start out on a negative comment, but I feel I must say that I don't like to think of this as a case study. It makes me feel as if I am preparing a report for a doctor or psychiatrist. Actually I would like to think of it as simply an expression of my feelings about my accomplishments and struggles of being a writer.

In order to write such a paper, I must remember not only works I have written this semester, but also ones that I have written in the past years. Remembering the latter bunch is not such an easy task; not just because of the time difference between now and when they were written, but because I would rather not remember some of the papers. The papers were not actually bad, but I have bad memories of my writings in those days. What I mean is that those papers were written because I was forced to write them; not because I wanted to write them. The papers accomplished the task that they were supposed to do, but they did little more. They were quite boring and uninspired works. Actually the word "works" is an accurate description of those writings because that's exactly what I thought of them—as doing work.

Most of my writings—correction—all of my writings, were assignments in high school, usually English essays. These papers were usually about a book we read in class, or an essay on a test. My style of writing was simple. I just stated the facts, one right after another, and somehow linked all these facts together to form an essay. There was little creativity at all and it was amazing that the teacher didn't doze off before reaching my closing paragraph.

Well, that's how I stood coming into this class, and I anticipated little change in my attitude upon completion of this class. As a matter of fact, I thought that I was going to hate writing even more than I already did, if that was even possible. Much to my surprise my attitude took a complete reversal during the span of this course. "What brought about that change?" you may ask. I think it is because I began to write about things that I wanted to write, not things that other people wanted me to write. I began to even enjoy my

---

In the first edition of this textbook, we used the label "Case Study" for this workshop. Mitchell Shack and others (particularly Pam Moore at Stony Brook) convinced us to drop it and use "autobiography" instead.

writing; something that was previously all too painful just to think about. My writings have drastically improved because of this change in attitude. My papers have become more creative and not just a list of facts anymore. My style of writing has become more natural. It has become smoother and I have "opened up" more so that I can get what I'm thinking in my head down on the paper. That may not seem like a big task to some people, but it would have seemed almost impossible to me just a few months ago. My papers have changed from simply stating what happened to explaining how I felt when it happened. I have also learned new techniques and methods of writing which I will pick up on later.

So far I have been telling you about changes that have come as a result of taking this course, so I think I should give some examples of these changes to prove my point. The paper that I like the best was a descriptive narrative about my favorite person of my childhood, the ice-cream man, so I think it's only fair to talk about that piece. I enjoyed this piece because I was able to open up and explain how I felt and what I was thinking at that time and not just give a plot summary. For example one line from the story says, "The truck from far away looked like an old bread truck, but it would not have mattered one bit if it looked like a garbage truck, just as long as it sold ice cream." The same line written before this class would have probably looked more like "The truck was white and looked like a bread truck." I changed from just putting down facts to putting down feelings along with those facts. This brightens up my papers greatly, gives a more personal feel to it, and makes it much more interesting and entertaining to read. I accomplished this task in an "Image of an Ice-Cream Man," and that is why I feel this paper is a representative of not only one of my better papers, but also of my improvements in writing over previous years.

There are many techniques that I learned which I can attribute to my change in writing. One such thing is the use of freewriting. I have never before used freewriting, and early in the semester I just thought it was a waste of time. In looking back over my papers and some of the freewriting I did that led to those papers I realized I was mistaken. Many of my ideas came as a result of freewriting; some of which I may not have thought of if I just sat down and wrote the paper. I used freewriting in the "Image of an Ice-Cream Man," and the paper benefited from its use. For example I wrote, "I watched him as he was making it, and my mouth watered just looking at all the ice cream, lollipops, bubble gum, chocolate bars. Italian ices, and other candy I saw inside the truck." This line and many of the others were taken right out of my freewriting. The freewriting allowed me to open up and "look back" in my mind and remember things that I have forgotten over the years. In the line above, using freewriting allowed me to remember in my mind exactly what the truck looked like and what I saw when I looked in it. Another thing that I like about freewriting is that I am not restricted to a topic or an idea. I can let my mind wander and go where it wants to go. I don't even have to worry about punctuation, grammar, or anything else that can inhibit my thinking. The result is usually writing that "flows" and seems natural, and this type of writing can enhance any paper.

Another useful technique which I learned is the loop writing process. I only used this process for one paper, and I must admit that what resulted was one of my weakest papers. This was not because of the loop writing process, but it's because of what I did in actually writing the paper after using the loop writing process. To tell you the truth, the loop writing process worked too well. The process consisted of using all different ways of thinking about a topic to get ideas on that topic. This included my first thoughts, prejudices, dialogues, lies, stories, and portraits about the topic. I used this process in writing "How Death Motivates Us in Life," and my problem was that I came up with too many ideas about the topic. The loop writing process allowed me to think of so many different aspects of the topic and for each aspect come up with several ideas pertaining to it. The problem came when I tried to write an essay which incorporated all these ideas in them. I mentioned all these ideas, but because of the great number of them, I didn't go into any single one in great detail. This resulted in a lot of superficial ideas, but no depth to my paper. What I should have done was pick out the ideas that proved my point the best and go into depth with those items. What I am trying to get across is that the loop writing process is very helpful, especially with topics that you seem short on ideas to pursue. But I have to be careful and not get carried away with myself and try to fit every single idea that I come up with into my paper.

So far I have been talking about methods I learned which aided me in my writings, but I haven't really talked about how I go about using these methods in actually creating a piece. Believe it or not, my favorite way of writing is to compose my paper directly on my computer. This may seem odd or difficult to some people, but to me it works fine. Actually I usually start by freewriting on the topic, or using the loop writing technique if I'm short on ideas. Next I usually make a rough outline of what I am going to say. I try to think about how I want my paper organized and in what order each point should go, and then I create the basic form of an outline. I then go back and jot down a few examples under each argument to prove it. I don't write in sentence form; I just scribble down a few key words and later on when I actually write my paper I look over these key words and then write about them.

This is the part when my computer comes into play. I load up my word processor, set my margins, and start writing. I like using the computer rather than a typewriter or pen and paper because I can edit directly as I go along. I can switch sentences around, delete words, add phrases, and do many other operations immediately. The words look on screen as they will on paper so I can see the structure forming and know how the finished product will look. I can go back and change my paper three weeks or three months later without having to retype it since it is saved on disk. Also my word processing program contains a spelling checker which I find very useful since I am far from being the world champion in spelling bees, and it contains a thesaurus so I can have some place to turn to if I get stuck. . . .

One thing that I haven't already mentioned and I feel is a major reason why I enjoyed taking this course is that I was actually able to tell a story. I was able to relate an experience that over the years didn't seem important enough to tell anybody. This year I got the chance and just being able to do that has made this course worthwhile for me.

From HUNGER OF MEMORY

Richard Rodriguez

At school, in sixth grade, my teacher suggested that I start keeping a diary. ("You should write down your personal experiences and reflections.") But I shied away from the idea. It was the one suggestion that the scholarship boy couldn't follow. I would not have wanted to write about the *minor* daily events of my life; I would never have been able to write about what most deeply, daily, concerned me during those years: I was growing away from my parents. Even if I could have been certain that no one would find my diary, even if I could have destroyed each page after I had written it, I would have felt uncomfortable writing about my home life. There seemed to me something intrinsically public about written words.

Writing, at any rate, was a skill I didn't regard highly. It was a grammar school skill I acquired with comparative ease. I do not remember struggling to write the way I struggled to learn how to read. The nuns would praise student papers for being neat—the handwritten letters easy for others to read; they promised that my writing style would improve as I read more and more. But that wasn't the reason I became a reader. Reading was for me the key to "knowledge"; I swallowed facts and dates and names and themes. Writing, by contrast, was an activity I thought of as a kind of report, evidence of learning. I wrote down what I heard teachers say. I wrote down things from my books. I wrote down all I knew when I was examined at the end of the school year. Writing was performed after the fact; it was not the exciting experience of learning itself. In eighth grade I read several hundred books, the titles of which I still can recall. But I cannot remember a single essay I wrote. I only remember that the most frequent kind of essay I wrote was the book report.

In high school there were more "creative" writing assignments. English teachers assigned the composition of short stories and poems. One sophomore story I wrote was a romance set in the Civil War South. I remember that it earned me a good enough grade, but my teacher suggested with quiet tact that next time I try writing about "something you know more about—something closer to home." Home? I wrote a short story about an old man who lived all by himself in a house down the block. That was as close as my writing ever got to my house. Still, I won prizes. When teachers suggested I contribute articles to the school literary magazine, I did so. And when I was asked to join the school newspaper, I said yes. I did not feel any great pride in my writings, however. (My mother was the one who collected my prize-winning essays in a box she kept in her closet.) Though I remember seeing my byline in print for the first time, and dwelling on the printing press letters with fascination: RICHARD RODRIGUEZ. The letters furnished evidence of a vast public identity writing made possible.

When I was a freshman in college, I began typing all my assignments. My writing speed decreased. Writing became a struggle. In high school I had been able to handwrite ten- and twenty-page papers in little more than an hour—

and I never revised what I wrote. A college essay took me several nights to prepare. Suddenly everything I wrote seemed in need of revision. I became a self-conscious writer. A stylist. The change, I suspect, was the result of seeing my words ordered by the even, impersonal, anonymous typewriter print. As arranged by a machine, the words that I typed no longer seemed mine. I was able to see them with a new appreciation for how my reader would see them.

From grammar school to graduate school I could always name my reader. I wrote for my teacher. I could consult him or her before writing, and after. I suppose that I knew other readers could make sense of what I wrote—that, therefore, I addressed a general reader. But I didn't think very much about it. Only toward the end of my schooling and only because political issues pressed upon me did I write, and have published in magazines, essays intended for readers I never expected to meet. Now I am struck by the opportunity. I write today for a reader who exists in my mind only phantasmagorically. Someone with a face erased; someone of no particular race or sex or age or weather. A gray presence. Unknown, unfamiliar. All that I know about him is that he has had a long education and that his society, like mine, is often public *(un gringo)*.

"What is psychiatry?" my mother asks. She is standing in her kitchen at the ironing board. We have been talking about nothing very important. ("Visiting.") As a result of nothing we have been saying, her question has come. But I am not surprised by it. My mother and father ask me such things. Now that they are retired they seem to think about subjects they never considered before. My father sits for hours in an armchair, wide-eyed. After my mother and I have finished discussing obligatory family news, he will approach me and wonder: When was Christianity introduced to the Asian continent? How does the brain learn things? Where is the Garden of Eden?

Perhaps because they consider me the family academic, my mother and father expect me to know. They do not, in any case, ask my brother and sisters the questions wild curiosity shapes. (That curiosity beats, unbeaten by age.)

Psychiatry? I shrug my shoulders to start with, to tell my mother that it is very hard to explain. I go on to say something about Freud. And analysis. Something about the function of a clinically trained listener. (I study my mother's face as I speak, to see if she follows.) I compare a psychiatrist to a Catholic priest hearing Confession. But the analogy is inexact. My mother can easily speak to a priest in a darkened confessional; can easily make an act of self-revelation using the impersonal formula of ritual contrition: "Bless me, father, for I have sinned. . . ." It would be altogether different for her to address a psychiatrist in unstructured conversation, revealing those events and feelings that burn close to the heart.

"You mean that people tell a psychiatrist about their personal lives?"

Even as I begin to respond, I realize that she cannot imagine ever doing such a thing. She shakes her head sadly, bending over the ironing board to inspect a shirt with the tip of the iron she holds in her hand. Then she changes the subject. She is talking to me about one of her sisters, my aunt, who is seriously ill. Whatever it is that prompted her question about psychiatry has passed. . . .

What did my father—who had dreamed of Australia—think of his children once they forced him to change plans and remain in America? What contrary feelings did he have about our early success? How does he regard the adults his sons and daughters have become? And my mother. At what moments has she hated me? On what occasions has she been embarrassed by me? What does she recall feeling during those difficult, sullen years of my childhood? What would be her version of this book? What are my parents unable to tell me today? What things are too personal? What feelings so unruly they dare not reveal to other intimates? Or even to each other? Or to themselves?

Some people have told me how wonderful it is that I am the first in my family to write a book. I stand on the edge of a long silence. But I do not give voice to my parents by writing about their lives. I distinguish myself from them by writing about the life we once shared. Even when I quote them accurately, I profoundly distort my parents' words. (They were never intended to be read by the public.) So my parents do not truly speak on my pages. I may force their words to stand between quotation marks. With every word, however, I change what was said only to me.

"What is new with you?" My mother looks up from her ironing to ask me. (In recent years she has taken to calling me Mr. Secrets, because I tell her so little about my work in San Francisco—this book she must suspect I am writing.)

Nothing much, I respond.

I write very slowly because I write under the obligation to make myself clear to someone who knows nothing about me. It is a lonely adventure. Each morning I make my way along a narrowing precipice of written words. I hear an echoing voice—my own resembling another's. Silent! The reader's voice silently trails every word I put down. I reread my words, and again it is the reader's voice I hear in my mind, sounding my prose.

When I wrote my first autobiographical essay, it was no coincidence that, from the first page, I expected to publish what I wrote. I didn't consciously determine the issue. Somehow I knew, however, that my words were meant for a public reader. Only because of that reader did the words come to the page. The reader became my excuse, my reason for writing.

It had taken me a long time to come to this address. There are remarkable children who very early are able to write publicly about their personal lives. Some children confide to a diary those things—like the first shuddering of sexual desire—too private to tell a parent or brother. The youthful writer addresses a stranger, the Other, with "Dear Diary" and tries to give public expression to what is intensely, privately felt. In so doing, he attempts to evade the guilt of repression. And the embarrassment of solitary feeling. For by rendering feelings in words that a stranger can understand—words that belong to the public, this Other—the young diarist no longer need feel all alone or eccentric. His feelings are capable of public intelligibility. In turn, the act of revelation helps the writer better understand his own feelings. Such is the benefit of language: By finding public words to describe one's feelings, one can describe oneself to oneself. One names what was previously only darkly felt.

I have come to think of myself as engaged in writing graffiti. Encouraged by physical isolation to reveal what is most personal; determined at the same time to have my words seen by strangers. I have come to understand better why works of literature—while never intimate, never individually addressed to the reader—are so often among the most personal statements we hear in our lives. Writing, I have come to value written words as never before. One can use *spoken* words to reveal one's personal self to strangers. But *written* words heighten the feeling of privacy. They permit the most thorough and careful exploration. (In the silent room, I prey upon that which is most private. Behind the closed door, I am least reticent about giving those memories expression.) The writer is freed from the obligation of finding an auditor in public. (As I use words that someone far from home can understand, I create my listener. I imagine her listening.)

My teachers gave me a great deal more than I knew when they taught me to write public English. I was unable then to use the skill for deeply personal purposes. I insisted upon writing impersonal essays. And I wrote always with a specific reader in mind. Nevertheless, the skill of public writing was gradually developed by the many classroom papers I had to compose. Today I *can* address an anonymous reader. And this seems to me important to say. Somehow the inclination to write about my private life in public is related to the ability to do so. It is not enough to say that my mother and father do not want to write their autobiographies. It needs also to be said that they are unable to write to a public reader. They lack the skill. Though both of them can write in Spanish and English, they write in a hesitant manner. Their syntax is uncertain. Their vocabulary limited. They write well enough to communicate "news" to relatives in letters. And they can handle written transactions in institutional America. But the man who sits in his chair so many hours, and the woman at the ironing board—"keeping busy because I don't want to get old"—will never be able to believe that any description of their personal lives could be understood by a stranger far from home.

From A CASE STUDY OF MYSELF AS A WRITER

Jean Shepherd

When I begin writing, I compose the first sentence in my head. As I put pen to paper, words begin to rush into my mind. For a few seconds, I can hardly write fast enough to get them all down, but after a brief period, maybe after several sentences, I pause and read what I have written. Possible revisions of words and phrases occur to me, and I write them anywhere I can—to the side, above, or below appropriate sections of the text, often with arrows pointing to their future positions. I reread once more to get the sound of my writing in my head, and then I'm off again in a frantic race with my mind to get the words on paper before they are gone. I use this write, stop, read, revise, read, start again process until I am through writing or until I come to a good stopping place.

At this point, my paper looks like a plate with words and arrows spilled over it in different directions. No one else could ever read this draft, and if I wait a day, I won't be able to read it either. Therefore, I must begin immediately to copy over, selecting words and phrases out of the choices I have given myself on the previous writing. Sometimes new word options and ideas occur to me as I rewrite; during this stage I seem to be more aware of sentence rhythms, and I try to write more slowly this time so I will put the endings on my words. The result of this stage is what I call my rough draft. If I get too caught up in rewriting and again write too fast, I may have to copy it over a second time.

The rough draft often contains ideas that never occurred to me before I wrote. It is obvious that during the first stages of writing I move pen on paper, think of words, spell words, punctuate, see relationships between ideas, invent new ideas, hear the sound of my words, read, and revise all at the same time. The pen becomes an extension of my mind, and unfortunately, my fingers can never move as quickly as my thoughts come, so I am always in a race to the end of a sentence. While producing this rough draft, I am unaware of anything around me. My body is tense with concentration as I rush to record my ideas. During this stage, my thinking is almost unconscious.

The next step of writing, the first revision, is a more conscious stage, and I am more relaxed as I progress. At this point, I correct sentences and sometimes continue to add ideas. I may mark out phrases or entire sentences to avoid wordiness. I change forms of subordination, usually making dependent clauses into phrases, and check coordination to see if it should remain as it is or if it should become subordination. At this point, I am very aware of sentence rhythms and variety, and I try to avoid awkward repetitions of words. I have the poor speller's habit of avoiding words I can't spell, so at this stage, I make a conscious effort to use whatever word I really want. Sometimes, when I get toward the end of the paper, I will think of words to add at the beginning, so I go back and put them in the margin. When I have gone over my paper once this way, I read again, making a few more minor adjustments, and then my first revision is complete.

For the next revision, I am calm and quite relaxed. This is the mechanical stage. I go through the paper and check all punctuation. Then I go back for my most hated task, checking spelling. I underline every word that may not be spelled correctly. Then I look up each one in a word book or dictionary. Oddly enough, I still may change some words or add a phrase even at this stage; I always seem to be aware of the sound of my writing. When this stage is complete, I am ready for the last step, typing.

My evaluation of what I've written is constantly changing as I go through all of these stages. During the first two steps of my rough draft, I feel excited.

I'm sure that everything I am saying is clever and imaginative. I am convinced that I've written something that everyone will enjoy and admire. If I am writing for a class, I am sure that I will make an A and that my paper will be the best in the class. When I begin the first revision, my heart sinks. I am embarrassed by my own words and feel confident that anyone else who reads it will laugh and think me a fool. If I am writing for a class, I am sure that I will fail. I have to force myself to go on and not throw the paper out, telling myself that I have to turn in something and that I don't have time to begin again.

After I type a paper, it seems very separate from me. When I read it over, I find words and ideas that surprise me. I can't remember having written such words or having conceived of such thoughts. At this point, I become pleased with parts of my writing, but I have no idea how it will seem to someone else. I have never turned in an assignment with any notion of what grade it may earn.

A LOOK INSIDE: CASE STUDY OF MYSELF AS A WRITER

Greg Teets

Mind—Before

In the beginning thoughts were formless and void, often misguided.

For semester's term paper I have a list of possible topics. They range from a comparison of Shakespeare's tragedies to an evaluation of Greek poetry.

Purpose was unclear.
Structure was unthought of.

Follow the guidelines given on page 427 of the *Warriner's* text book.

Ideas moved randomly colliding with each other, destroying each other.

A discussion on the economic problems in *Hamlet.*

Among the good thoughts garbage drifted adding to the confusion. In the last minute rush for perfection, junk was pulled out and used instead of the good.

The paper is due tomorrow. I haven't started. This sounds good.

From the start, order was
plain, passive, and predictable. Methodically, ideas
and lessons were communicated.

For this essay we will be
using the five paragraph
format.

Emotion did not exist. All
subjects were treated with
cold, formal objectivity.

Remember, this is a
formal essay. Be object-
ive and don't use slang
or contractions.

Feelings that were suddenly
displayed were quickly
covered-up.

Your feelings on the
subject are not relevant
to the meaning of the
story.

When he finished he looked
and saw that it was not
pleasing to his eyes.

New System

Freewriting: A technique
used to remove the garbage
from one's head and get real
ideas flowing.

Artists. Paintings,
sculpture, poetry. They
work magic. Their
fantasies become reality
because they do it.

Exploratory Draft: A piece
of writing in which one
discovers how they feel and
what they know about a topic.

Artists are interesting
people. They have
learned to place their
intangible into tangible
objects.

Rough Draft: An organized
and structured revision of
an exploratory.

Artists are magical
people. They can put
their ideas into things
like sculpture, poetry,
or paintings.

Final Copy: The end result
of the three processes above.
Usually, it is radically
different from all previous
versions.

Artists are magical
people. They have
learned to direct their
intangible thoughts into
tangible objects like
poetry, sculpture, or
painting.

Mind—After

In the beginning thoughts are always vague, unexplored. What do I write the essay on?

Freewrite. Go. Unconnected thoughts. Don't worry about grammar, structure, punctuation. Take a snapshot of your thoughts.

Gradually, things move together. Look over freewriting. See the natural connections. Don't box yourself in.

Exploratory. Begin to pull thoughts together. Get a feel for the topic. Add a little structure.

The purpose is to tell a story. Who is my audience? What do they need to know? Communicate with them.

Rough Draft. Organize. Make ideas cohesive. Show them your insight.

Reread essay. Is this really what I want to say? Do I make my point? Will the reader understand what I am saying? Check mechanics of the paper.

Add emotion. Add depth. Final Draft. No contractions. Does this feel right? Am I happy with the end product? Yes.

Process Journal:

"The piece moved and grew like it was alive.

"I'm beginning to think that nothing is ever finished . . . unless it's written down.

"The 'felt sense' clicked and it became easy to express my emotions on paper and I wasn't ashamed or afraid.

"The 'invisible' writing makes me focus on what is popping up in my head, not what's happening around me.

"Now, I find writing fun and relaxing.

"[I]t seems like there is a lot of garbage in my head. I can write it down and it goes away.

"I've discovered that I am a very spontaneous thinker. The momentary ideas are usually the best.

"For days I've been
trying to think of a
narrative, but nothing satisfied me.
Finally, boom, big revelation,
bingo!

   "Now, I am able
to release my thoughts.
Instead of trying to
structure them and
then write them down
I do the reverse.
The 'Doty'* system
works much better
than my old system."

Genesis

In the beginning, God created
the heavens and the earth.

And the earth was formless
and void,

Blank paper, pen, ink,
blank screen, keyboard,
mouse, blank mind.

God said, "Let there be light."

Alphabet.
c,m,p,g,n,x,n,q,y.

And God separated the darkness
from the light.

Syllable, word, phrase.
Sentence, paragraph,
essay.

God created man in his own
image.

Final paper, hidden
meaning, my mirror,
myself.

And God saw that it was good.
It was very good.

Eugene Doty was this student's teacher.

MINI-
WORKSHOPS

MINI-WORKSHOP

A

WRITING SKILLS QUESTIONNAIRE

In order to help you get more out of our text and take more control over your own learning, we've made a list of specific skills we are attempting to teach. Filling out the questionnaire will help you notice better what you are learning and not learning—and help us teach you better.

You will benefit most from this questionnaire if you fill it out three times—at the beginning, middle, and end of the course. This way you'll be able to see more about what changes are taking place. (The second and third times you use this form, you may want to cover your previous answers.)

Use the numbers 1 through 4 to stand for these four responses: "Yes," "Fairly well," "Not very well," and "No." If you don't know the answer—which may often happen at the start of the course—use a question mark.

When you complete the questionnaire at the beginning of the course, fill in the *left-hand* column of blanks. In the middle of the course, use the *middle* column of blanks. At the end use the *right-hand* column of blanks.

— — — Do you enjoy writing?

— — — In general do you trust yourself as a person who can find good words and ideas and perceptions?

— — — Do you think of yourself as a writer?

GENERATING

— — — On a *topic of interest to you,* can you generate lots of words fairly quickly and freely—not be stuck?

— — — Again on a topic of interest to you, can you come up with ideas or insights you'd not thought of before?

— — — On a topic that *doesn't* much interest you (perhaps an assigned topic), can you generate lots of words fairly quickly and freely—not be stuck?

— — — On a topic not of interest, can you come up with ideas or insights you'd not thought of before?

— — — On a topic where you start out not knowing what you think, can you write or think your way through to a conclusion?

— — — On a topic where you start out with your mind made up, can you write or think your way into actually *changing* your mind?

REVISING

— — — Can you revise in the literal sense of "resee"—thus rethink and change your mind about major things you have said?

— — — Can you find a main point in a mess of your disorganized writing?

— — — Can you find a *new* shape in a piece of your writing which you had previously organized?

— — — Can you find problems in your reasoning or logic and straighten them out?

— — — Can you make your sentences clear—so they are clear to readers on first reading?

— — — Can you get your sentences lively? Can you give them a human voice?

— — — Can you get rid of *most* mistakes in grammar, spelling, punctuation, and so on, so most readers would not be put off?

— — — Can you get rid of virtually *all* such mistakes?

— — — Can you guess how most readers will react to something you've written?

— — — Can you adjust something you've written to fit the needs of particular readers?

FEEDBACK

— — — Can you enjoy sharing with friends a draft of what you've written?

— — — Can you read out loud to listeners a draft of your writing so that it is really clear and "given," that is, not mumbled and "held back"?

— — — Can you openly listen to the reactions of a reader to your writing and try to see it as she sees it, even if you think her reactions are all wrong?

— — — Can you give noncritical feedback—telling the writer what you like and summarizing or reflecting what you hear the words saying?

— — — Can you give "movies of your mind" as a reader—a clear story of what was happening in your mind as you were reading someone's writing?

— — — Can you give "criterion-based feedback"—telling the writer how the draft matches up against the most common criteria of good writing?

COLLABORATION

— — — Can you work on a task collaboratively with a partner or a small group: pitch in, share the work, help the group cooperate, keep the group on the task?

AWARENESS AND CONTROL OF WRITING PROCESS

— — — Can you give a *detailed* account of what is going on when you are writing: the thoughts and feelings that go through your mind and the things that happen in the text?

— — — Do you notice problems or "stuck points" in your writing and figure out what the causes are?

— — — Can you make changes in the way you go about writing based on those things you noticed?

— — — Can you vary the way you go about writing depending on the situation: the topic, audience, type of writing, and so on?

MINI-WORKSHOP

B

DOUBLE-ENTRY OR DIALECTICAL NOTEBOOKS

All there is to thinking . . . is seeing something noticeable which makes you see something you weren't noticing which makes you see something that isn't even visible.
—Norman Maclean, *A River Runs Through It*

One of the goals of this book is to help you pay more attention to the *way* you write—what actually goes on as you put words down—how you make meaning and change meaning. Thus all the process writing.

It turns out to be just as useful to pay attention to the way you *read*—and interestingly enough the central activities are the same: making meaning and changing meaning. In this mini-workshop we will show you a simple and practical way to take notes on what you are reading. In the short term, a double-entry notebook helps you understand better the particular piece you are reading; in the long term, it improves your skill in reading. There will be more about the theory in the "Ruminations and Theory" section.

KEEPING A DIALECTICAL
OR DOUBLE-ENTRY NOTEBOOK

477

Double-Entry or
Dialectical
Notebooks

Let us quote Ann Berthoff, who devised this procedure:

> I ask my students (all of them: freshmen, upperclassmen, teachers in graduate seminars) to furnish themselves with a notebook, spiral bound at the side, small enough to be easily carried around but not so small that writing is cramped. . . . What makes this notebook different from most, perhaps, is the notion of the double-entry: on the right side reading notes, direct quotations, observational notes, fragments, lists, images—verbal and visual—are recorded: on the other (facing) side, *notes about those notes,* summaries, formulations, aphorisms, editorial suggestions, revisions, comments on comments are written. The reason for the double-entry format is that it provides a way for the student to conduct that "continuing audit of meaning" that is at the heart of learning to read and write critically. The facing pages are in dialogue with each other. (44)

That's all there is to it. But if you do this regularly, you will notice how that dialogue—that continuing audit of meaning—gradually helps you read more accurately and more creatively and thus helps you get more out of your reading.

Try it (1) on a piece of reading, then (2) on a piece of your experience.

1. Choose a piece of reading that you can learn from and reflect on—not just something you read to pass the time. Start reading it, and as you do, pause to write down (on the right side of your notebook) words, details, images, or thoughts that strike you. You're not "taking notes." Don't clench and try to capture or summarize everything; just encourage yourself to note words and ideas and reactions that draw your attention—to muse and speculate about your reading. If you find yourself reading more than a few pages without any notations, stop and ask yourself what you noticed in those pages you just read—or how you were reacting. At the end make a few more notations to capture quickly what's in your head as you finish reading.

Now read over these entries slowly. As you do, jot down on the left side of your notebook whatever comes into your mind as you read the right side. There is no "right" way to do this, but here are some suggestions of entries you could make:

- Second thoughts. What further ideas do your recorded notes suggest?
- How do your notes relate to other parts of your life—to your deepest concerns or interests?
- Reactions to your reactions. What do your notes tell you about how your mind works or what you are interested in?
- Dialogue with the author. What do *you* have to say? How would he or she reply?
- Who do you want to talk to about these things? What would you tell or ask them?
- Summary. What's the most important thing you notice about your notes as you read them over? What kinds of connections can you find in your

notes? What conclusions about your reading do your notes make possible? What parts now seem particularly important or unimportant? (It's wise to consider carefully what *seems* unimportant: something about it attracted your attention.)

Don't worry about the exact difference between what to write on the right and on the left. There's no rigid difference. Mainly it boils down to time: as you are reading something for the first time, whatever you write goes on the right side. As you read this over, whatever additional thoughts you have go on the left. Thus the important thing about this process is to get your *thoughts to be in dialogue with each other.* The dialectical notebook makes it possible for you to exploit the advantages of being two people at once—having two different viewpoints or having discussions with yourself. (Thus it is like our exercises in writing dialogues.)

2. Try the same thing with a recent experience: an important conversation, argument, or interchange with someone; a walk that was important to you (perhaps in a beautiful place or at a time when you needed to think something over); an activity that was important to you (such as being in a deciding game, taking a crucial exam, surviving a harrowing ordeal, or being invited to a party with new friends). On the right side, put down first-stage notes: what you can remember, what you notice. Then go on to write second-stage reflexive *notes on those notes* on the left side of your notebook.

If possible, share both sides of your notebook with others and listen as they read theirs. This will give you some hints about the ways others read, ways you may want to try out. Others will learn from you in the same way.

 RUMINATIONS AND THEORY

Dialectical Notebooks and the Parallel between Reading and Writing

The dialectical or double-entry notebook reinforces the *parallel* between reading and writing. The central activity in both is the *making of meaning.* We tend to think that "meaning" is "out there," that our task in reading and writing is to discover it—not to make it. But even though it *looks as though* writers "have" meanings which they "put into the words"—and then readers "take the meaning out" at the other end—this is an illusion. We don't have a meaning until we have words for it. But even this does not encompass the complexity: words cannot "have" or "contain" meanings—only people can; words are only meaningful insofar as people *attribute* meanings to them. In short, words cannot transport a writer's meanings into our heads; they can only give us a set of directions for creating our own meanings in our own heads—meanings which, *if all goes well,* will resemble what the writer had in mind.

It's as though the writer has movies in her mind and she wants to *give* us her movies. But in truth she cannot. She has to hope that she has been clever enough to create a set of directions that leads us to create movies in our minds that are like the ones in hers. Needless to say, that's hard. This little allegory explains something we all know about language: that it's hard to make people truly understand what we have in mind.

This view of language and communications as *complex* shows us something important about reading (or listening): reading is not finding meaning but *making meaning*—not hunting for messages that are already there, but building messages. If you have the wrong idea of reading, you tend to feel (if things go well), "Oh goody, I found it"—as in an Easter egg hunt. And if things don't go well you feel, "Oh dear, where did they hide it?" When you are having difficulty in reading, it's counterproductive to think of it as a problem in finding a pesky little hidden packet; it's better to think of it as a problem in building or creating.

We're not going so far as to say (as Humpty Dumpty did to Alice) that words can mean anything—that we can build any meaning we want out of a set of someone else's words. There are *rules* for doing this building which people have to obey, or they build all wrong. We all know the difference between being involved in successful communication and unsuccessful communication, though most of us would be hard put to articulate *how* we know this. The trouble is that the rules for building meanings out of words are *unstated,* and they are *continually in the process of negotiation.* For that's a picture of a natural language (such as English): a game played by a large number of people where they follow unspoken rules which (because they are unspoken) are continually in the process of slight change. Can you remember games like "Pass the Scissors" where you join in and play before you know the rules—and the process of playing is the process of trying to learn the rules? That's how it is with language. And that's why critics and ordinary readers are able to find new meanings even in much-studied classics such as *Hamlet.*

Therefore to help us read better—particularly when we are reading something difficult or our reading is not going well—we need to pay more attention to the *process by which we build meanings out of other people's words.* A dialectical notebook helps us do that. It can help you assess what happens when you engage in *making meaning* from a text. Do you have strong feelings about the subject matter? or about the writer? Are you bored by it? What associations jump to mind as you read? How does this writing relate to other things you know and other things in your life? Do you tend to create mental images as you read or relate what you're reading to other things you have read? Do you attend mainly to ideas or to the way something is written? What things impress you? What things do you tend to overlook? We cannot know the *rules* for building meaning—almost no one does—but we can watch more closely as we go about building meaning. We can learn to be more sensitive and insightful as we read—and perhaps learn to detect what doesn't fit the meaning we're gradually building up. (What doesn't fit often provides clues to the need for us to shift our sights a bit.) We *can* learn something about *how* and *why* we construct the meanings we do construct. All this we can do instead of just saying, "Where is the meaning? Where did the writer hide it?"

☐ ☐ ☐ ☐ ☐

This mini-workshop draws heavily on Ann Berthoff's "A Curious Triangle and the Double-Entry Notebook; or How Theory Can Help Us Teach Reading and Writing." The notebook is her idea. But see also Peter Elbow's "Methodological Doubting and Believing" in *Embracing Contraries* (151–53).

MINI-WORKSHOP C

BREATHING LIFE INTO WORDS: TEXT RENDERING OR READING OUT LOUD

It's an old principle that the best *interpretation* of a text is a good *performance* of it: a good reading of it out loud. Whether your goal is the enjoyment of a text or the practical goal of having to work out a full interpretation (perhaps for an essay assignment), the fastest and most satisfying way to learn what a text means and how it works is to read it out loud.

But first, we want to speak for a moment to any misgivings you may have about reading out loud. It may be that you *hate* it. Many students do: when we make them do it, they feel we are punishing them. There are many reasons you may feel this way:

- You may feel self-conscious when you read out loud: as though you are "making a spectacle of yourself" or "sticking out"—or even "making a fool of yourself."
- You may be bad at it.
- It may in fact have been "punishment" in school when everyone had to take a turn reading aloud from the book—and if you were bad, you had to read more.
- You may even hate having someone read aloud *to* you, feeling as though the enjoyment is "babyish" (even though you undoubtedly loved it as a child).

But we find that once we give students practice in reading aloud, most of them appreciate it: partly for the practical benefits that we stress here, but also for the pure pleasure of making words alive instead of dead. There are some important guidelines we've learned, however, for overcoming bad feelings about it:

- If you're not used to reading out loud, it's best to start with your *own* writing. Then you have the best reason to read out loud: your text is probably handwritten, perhaps marked up with corrections and revisions, so that others would have a hard time reading it. But you know how it should sound, and you have a reason to want to get it across to others. (We hope you've already done lots of this reading in sharing sessions.)
- When we push someone to render something he didn't write, we always give him some time to practice reading it aloud to himself: to whisper privately or speak it out loud in his head. This gives him a chance to stumble and experiment, to check out the pronunciation of unfamiliar words, and to figure out what the piece means and how to express it. It's not fair either to the reader or to the listeners to push someone to read something out loud they can't read decently. (After someone has practiced, we help him with his shyness by insisting that he come out with it forcefully.)

 TRYING IT OUT

The main thing is practice. Following are four slightly different ways of practicing text rendering as interpretation.

1. Text rendering as figuring out the *literal meaning*. Suppose you are faced with a text that is difficult to understand. You look at it and it looks odd; you start reading it over silently and can't figure out what it's saying (even if you know most of the words and phrases). Perhaps it is a modern poem—perhaps one without any punctuation—or an experimental short story or novel, or something with older language like Chaucer or Shakespeare used.

Try reading it out loud. Force yourself to *say* the words—trying to feel out the best way to phrase them. If the language seems odd or difficult, sound it out tentatively and listen for how it "goes": where the words seem to speed up, pause, or stop; where the stresses appear; where your voice rises and falls in pitch. Your instinct can guide you as you proceed. Of course you may stumble a bit and need to try a line one way and then another. You may find yourself repeating a particularly difficult spot. But you'll be surprised at how often your *voice* and your *ear* find sense in a passage of words where your eye was lost. Your voice and ear have better instincts than your eye about rhythm, intonation, and syntax.

Here is a poem that seems difficult when read silently, but becomes clearer (if not completely clear) when you read it out loud. You need to give yourself a chance to stumble and experiment as you try it out. Don't just go through it once and give up; don't allow yourself to get bogged down by trying to interpret it as you read. Give your voice and ear freedom. Read it through five, six, seven times—however many times it takes to go from beginning to end fluidly.

SPRING AND FALL:
To a Young Child

Márgarét, are you gríeving
Over Goldengrove unleaving?
Leáves, líke the things of man, you
With your fresh thoughts care for, can you?
Áah! ás the heart grows older
It will come to such sights colder
By and by, nor spare a sigh
Though worlds of wanwood leafmeal lie;
And yet you wíll weep and know why.
Now no matter, child, the name:
Sórrow's spríngs áre the same.
Nor mouth had, no nor mind, expressed
What heart heard of, ghost guessed:
It ís the blight man was born for,
It is Margaret you mourn for.

—*Gerard Manley Hopkins*

2. Tex⁺ rendering or making the meaning *live*. Reading is no fun, however, if it's only figuring out the plain meaning—as though it were a puzzle. What makes reading worthwhile is when the meaning seems alive and jumps from the page to your mind—and lives in your mind. Text rendering helps here too more than anything else. When language works at its best, the "inner dimension" (meaning) and the "outer dimension" (sound, rhythm, emphasis, and tone) all work together. This is what it means for words to have life or breath. Try reading the Hopkins poem again—but this time make your task not just to figure out the literal meaning; try to read the text aloud in a way that can help *make the meaning clear to a listener who has never heard the words before and has no text to look at.* In fact, when you first read it to someone, she should *not* have the text before her.

We're not trying to imply that text rendering is only for poetic or creative texts. You can take any text—or passage from a text—that you simply want to understand better. Practice saying the text until you can say it so that listeners *hear* or *experience* the meaning. That's all. But it's not easy. The process will make you not just understand the text but get inside it so that you can *mean* the words as you say them. For that's the central act in reading something out loud so it works: *you* have to succeed in feeling or experiencing the meaning in the words. Listeners can tell when you are asleep at the switch, when you are just going through motions and reciting something you haven't gotten inside of. This is just as necessary when reading expository prose as when reading fiction or poetry. If you are reading a physics textbook and having trouble, you can solve much of the problem (perhaps not all) by forcing yourself to read it out loud.

Try working out a reading of the following passage from William James until you can really experience what he is saying, until you can say it so that a listener will get the meaning.

> The Empirical Self of each of us is all that he is tempted to call by the name of *me*. But it is clear that between what a man calls *me* and what he simply calls *mine* the line is difficult to draw. We feel and act about certain things that are ours very much as we feel and act about ourselves. Our fame, our children, the work of our hands, may be as dear to us as our bodies are, and arouse the same feelings and the same acts of reprisal if attacked. And our bodies themselves, are they simply ours, or are they *us*? Certainly men have been ready to disown their very bodies and to regard them as mere vestures, or even as prisons of clay from which they should some day be glad to escape.

You will sometimes feel a kind of click when you get something to sound right—and when you do, you will immediately understand better what the piece is about and how it works.

It is helpful to hear different readings of the same passage by two or more people (and the readings will differ even if the passage is a plain and straightforward piece of prose). Listeners can simply tell which parts of which readings *came through* most clearly. If you then discuss individual reactions, the discussion will inevitably lead you to the relationship of the form and the meaning and to questions of how words work on readers—and thus lead you right to the heart of the most important questions for interpretation.

Notice that you are trying to *act* or *perform* or *dramatize* here: you are trying to let the meaning find its way into sound. Have you noticed that good readers of poetry often don't act at all? Sometimes there is no "personality" in their readings. Sometimes they sort of chant or intone the words, searching *not* for performance but for the *sound* of the meaning-in-language.

3. Text rendering or interpretation as *finding the right voice, tone, stance.* When we discuss the interpretation of a story, essay, or poem, or when we are writing an essay of interpretation, one of the main doorways in is through voice, tone, or stance. We may argue, for example, about whether words are ironic or sarcastic or straight. To answer such questions is central to interpretation—yet difficult. And arguments about such questions are notoriously hard to settle. Probably the best way to deal with these issues is to work out

your own reading and then compare alternative readings by others. Again, your voice and ear often *tell* you the tone before you even need to think about the question in theoretical terms. And instead of letting two people argue on and on, have them each *read* the text as they think it should sound. That sometimes settles things, and when it does not (after all, texts do invite different readings), it usually makes the discussion much more fruitful and down to earth.

By the way, don't assume that you can use this approach only on short poems or short pieces—just because we have used such pieces here for convenience. If you are working on a long essay or story, even a novel, you can pick out passages that seem most interesting or perplexing or passages that seem to illustrate the main voices or tones in the piece—and work out readings. Once you can say and hear an important passage right, you can often hear the interpretation of the whole piece.

For example, if you are trying to discuss how *The Adventures of Huckleberry Finn* works, you could center the whole discussion on the task of figuring out how its opening passage should *sound*—how it should be read. Try out different readings and talk about which attempts *sound* right. The discussion will probably boil down to figuring out what kind of person Huck is and how he relates to Twain. The best way to deal with that slippery theoretical discussion is with the ear as you try out different voices.

> You don't know about me, without you have read a book by the name of "The Adventures of Tom Sawyer," but that ain't no matter. That book was made by Mr. Mark Twain, and he told the truth, mainly. There was things which he stretched, but mainly he told the truth. That is nothing. I never seen anybody but lied, one time or another, without it was Aunt Polly, or the widow, or maybe Mary. Aunt Polly—Tom's Aunt Polly, she is—and Mary, and the Widow Douglas, is all told about in that book—which is mostly a true book; with some stretchers, as I said before.

4. Text rendering or interpretation as *hearing other voices:* play, distortion, exaggeration, parody, deconstruction. Sometimes the best way to discover what's in a text is by a process of elimination; see what's not there and what's almost, sort of, marginally there: try out distorting lenses. Read a text aloud in a way that deliberately exaggerates or parodies it. Obviously you'll discover what's not in the text, but the striking thing about this playing around is how it surprises you: you keep discovering that what you assumed was all wrong and a complete violation of the text manages in fact to capture a subtle note that's really there. When you do a hysterical reading of some staid essay, you'll catch a glimpse of some below-the-surface hysteria; or a tragic reading of a comic piece may show you a bit of darkness lurking there. There is often a bit of rightness in that "wrong" voice, tone, or stance.

You can try this playfully "foolish" approach on any of the preceding examples. Or try it on the opening passage of *Pride and Prejudice.*

> It is a truth universally acknowledged that a single man in possession of a good fortune must be in want of a wife.

However little known the feelings or views of such a man may be on his first entering a neighborhood, this truth is so well fixed in the minds of the surrounding families, that he is considered as the rightful property of someone or other of their daughters.

Try it on an advertisement or a political speech.

Try it on the essay or story you are currently writing: you'll discover some rich hints and possibilities you didn't know were in your own text. Sometimes you'll decide to get rid of this underlying tone or voice: maybe you uncover a hint of whining or self-pity which you know undercuts your meaning. But sometimes you'll decide to emphasize one of these faint notes, bring it more to the foreground and out of obscurity. For example, you may uncover in your serious essay a humorous strand that is worth bringing out. It's not so uncommon to uncover a tone of uncertainty and doubt you didn't know was there. You'll feel the impulse to get rid of it; maybe it undermines your position. But think again. More often than not your piece will be stronger if it *acknowledges* that doubt better and allows itself to be somewhat *about* the uncertainly you were hiding from yourself.

Here then is a way to find the richness of implications in almost any set of words. All these exercises in breathing life into words are ways of learning to read better.

MINI-WORKSHOP

D

WRITING WITH A WORD PROCESSOR

 ADVANTAGES OF USING A WORD PROCESSOR*

The two main cognitive skills needed for writing well are the ability to *make* a mess and to *clean up* that mess. That is, you can't have *good* words unless you have more to choose from than you can use—which means a mess. Yet in order to write well, you also need the opposite mental skill: the ability to doubt, reject, and change, that is, to clean up that fertile mess. It turns out that the word processor is ideal for both these mental operations.

The word processor helps you get more down quicker. When you're trying to get started—which is usually the hardest part of writing—you can start anywhere, often in the middle. You just start with an idea that you feel confident of, one you know you will want in there somewhere. This gets you going.

---

*See Elbow's freewriting on this subject in Workshop 4.

You can add other ideas later—before, after, or in the middle of what you've already written. It's much easier to find those missing ideas once you've gotten rolling.

When you are writing on a word processor and your mind jumps to something new (a problem about what you're writing, or a different idea, or an idea about how to organize the piece), you can get it down before you forget. You don't have to try to remember it or jot it on a different piece of paper. You can zip to the beginning or the end of the file and put it there. Or you can write it right where you are: just start a new line or write in caps or indent the whole passage—so it's obvious later that it's an interruption. You don't have to worry about finding the right place for it now; you can move it later. Or if you run out of energy on a particular topic or phase of your project, you can drop it and go on to another idea without worrying about a transition or about effective sequencing of your ideas. You can figure out the structure later—and good ideas for structure often pop into your head when you are steaming along. *Because* you know you can correct and rearrange later, you have more permission to make a mess—but a fruitful, creative mess.

Most of all, the word processor makes it easy to revise. You suddenly see a new idea or new arrangement when you're almost done, and you can wade in and try it. Or you've finished and you're reading it over and you discover something awkward or problematic. Before you would have had to retype the whole thing; now you can quickly make the change and print it again.

The processor even encourages you to experiment with multiple possibilities that you wouldn't have been able to compare using pen or typewriter. You can save a file of what you have and then start revising. Meanwhile you have the original for comparison just in case the experiment makes it worse or—what's more likely—it makes part better and part worse. Being able to revise this way makes it easier for revising to be what it ought to be: movement back and forth between generating and refining, between creating a mess and cleaning up.

We've stressed how word processors help you make a mess, but they turn out paradoxically to be just as useful in cleaning up messes. They make it easy to come up with neat copy: to throw away what you don't want, change and rearrange bits, and fix words and spellings.

PROCESS BOX

I just crossed out a passage on the paper that I couldn't make myself cross out when I was trying to edit it on screen. I suddenly realized that I felt more secure drawing a line through the passage on paper because, despite that line, the passage was *still there*. For me to make that deletion on screen, I have to actually "delete" it. It disappears. That makes me feel nervous; I want to hang on to it. (Of course I could delete it to a "dump file"—and in fact I often do that when I'm revising on screen. Deleting it on paper is easier, more psychologically feasible. And once I've crossed it out on paper and seen that it's better this way, then I'm happy to delete it on the file.

Peter Elbow

Spelling and grammar have always been superficials of writing, but they've always unduly influenced readers and unduly weighed on writers. Snobbery enters in: just as some people look down on others and ignore what they say on the basis of *accent,* even more people do the same thing on the basis of *spelling* and *grammar.* This may be unfair, but there is a level of deviation from accepted norms which becomes intolerable to almost everyone. Word processing programs with spelling checkers and so-called grammar checkers can detect many (but not all) mistakes for us.

The word processor also makes it easier to share with readers—sometimes for feedback and sometimes just for the sense of audience. You can quickly print out a copy to try on readers. Even if your piece is at an early stage, you can still have it neat and easy to read. Indeed you can give them a disk and let them comment on the document—or even revise for you. Thus the processor is great for collaborative writing: one person writes a very rough draft and gives a copy of the disk to the other person to revise it through to the next stage; and then the first person revises it again. This is the procedure we've used in writing this book. Before long we couldn't remember who started, who put in what: neither of us feels it as *his* or *her* piece—it feels like *ours.*

Some of you may have the opportunity to experience the collaborative possibilities of word processing more directly by using special software programs. These programs make it possible for a group to all read, respond to, and suggest revisions on the same piece at the same time. Alternatively, these programs permit students to "log in" at any time, "bring up" another student's paper or comments, and respond to them whenever they have time. Quite a few of these programs also permit "conversational" exchanges through the computer: I type in a message which can be read as I'm typing it and responded to immediately. These conversations can be "compacted" and printed out so that writers can read them over when they get around to revising. When computers are set up with modems, students can correspond with others on campuses throughout the world. We're convinced that this technology is still young, that the collaborative potential of computers will turn out to be their most valuable trait.

NEW ATTITUDE, NEW POWER

The most important effect of using a word processor is probably on one's *attitude* toward writing. It often leads to a subtle but deep change: it can make writing feel more like play, experimentation, even fooling around—less sacred and "heavy." Once you see how easy it is to do away with words on the screen, you no longer think of ideas as permanent just because they've been put into words. Though good writers are often reverent about writing, they are equally adamant about the necessity to play and juggle. Writing with a word processor can get rid of that feeling of anxiety and indelibility about writing—the fear of "putting it down in black and white."

Paradoxically the word processor has a way of convincing you of the power of writing too. You type something and think, "I don't want anyone to read that." You erase it immediately. But somehow it stays with you and affects you as you continue to write—even though it no longer exists anywhere in print. Suddenly you realize that anything you take the trouble to shape into writing assumes a certain independence or power it didn't have before.

An even subtler matter of attitude: it's as though the word processor is a kind of bridge or intermediary between our minds and the paper. Our minds are fluid—and usually messy; writing is static—and supposed to be well organized. The difficulty in writing is trying to bridge this gulf between what is fluid and what is static—what is messy and what is coherent. The word processor can serve as a bridge: it's both mindlike and paperlike. When you get used to writing on a computer, you come to feel as though the words you are writing are half in your mind and half on paper. The computer functions as a second mind and as a second piece of paper.

Like your mind, it is easily changed, fluid, easily emptied; and you can't look at all of it at once. Admittedly you have more distance from what's on the screen than you do from what's in your mind. The computer gives you a bit of leverage, but not as much as you get when you see something on paper. Thus it gives you a second mind that you have more control over.

But when you print out something you are writing, you've moved that "sort of in-mind" document to something that's "sort of on-paper." It's *on* paper— still and quiet—no longer fluid and changeable; you can get a mind scan. Yet it's nevertheless so easily changeable; it's still "wet," and you are never *stuck* with it.

 ## DANGERS

Losing What You've Written. When people start using a computer, they often proceed very gingerly for fear of hurting this delicate machine by pressing the wrong button. Though you can easily hurt it by dirt, smoke, or spilling something on it, it's hard to do harm by pressing wrong buttons. *But you can harm what you've written*—harm it out of existence. It's fine to start in writ-

---

PROCESS BOX

My writing habits have changed radically [because of using a computer]. I used to spend most of my time preparing to write—reading, meditating, taking notes, jotting down at least a rough outline of what I was going to say, discussing my problems with colleagues, doing some more reading to fill in the gaps, and then fiddling around with a lot of inconsequential and irrelevant activities just to postpone the awful moment when I would have to sit down and put some words on paper. . . . Now more than ever, the act of putting words down is part of the invention process for me. I am likely now to start out with only a vague idea of what I want to say in a discourse and to discover what I want to say . . . and how I want to say it by simply laying words out on the monitor's screen.

Edward P. J. Corbett

ing before you have much mastery over your computer or your word processing program, but don't write anything that *matters* until you're good at saving
what you've written. Make sure you save onto a backup file every ten to twenty minutes—and onto a backup disk every time you end a spell of work.

Premature Editing. It's so easy to fix mistakes or make changes with a word
processor—indeed it seems like fun—that you may find yourself tempted to
stop and go back and make a correction every time you mistype, misspell, or
change your mind about a word. Learn to block that impulse. Learn to keep
on writing and leave the mistakes there. If you think of a better word or
phrase, write it where you are, but don't go back and remove the old one.
(You may find later that the old one is better or that you want to scrap the
whole section—why waste all that time and trouble on something you may
later reject?) You may even be tempted to spend lots of time playing formatting games—on a paragraph or section you later decide to discard. All this
can disrupt what may be a productive spurt of idea generation.

If you find you have trouble keeping yourself steaming along—too distracted perhaps by your environment, problems with other things you have to do,
or anxiety about word choice, grammar, and spelling—try "invisible writing":
turn your screen down. When you can't see what you write, you are *forced* to
keep steaming ahead—forced to concentrate intensely on what you are trying
to say. Invisible writing becomes easy if you just try it a few times. At first
you may be disoriented not to see your words; but if you keep at it, you may
find it exhilarating to be almost totally free from words as graphic symbols
and totally caught up in words as carriers of meaning.

Too Much Fluidity. Sometimes you can be tempted into *overutilizing* the
computer's potential for change: you write it this way, then change it to that,
then try it a different way, then a fourth. (This can happen from the word
level to the section level.) Suddenly your head starts to swim, and you feel you
are sinking into quicksand. Some people even get addicted to small-scale *fiddling* with the text and end up spending *more* time than if they were writing
with a quill on parchment. The cure shows how this problem is related to that
of premature editing: sometimes you have to just force yourself to keep writing and writing in the direction you're going, forbidding yourself to make any
changes—pretending you are writing in ink. Once you have a whole draft—or
more or less the makings of a draft—then the playing with changes doesn't do
so much harm. The danger is when you let it interrupt you at early stages.

Wordiness. The "kitchen sink" syndrome. It's good that word processors
make people write more (and research shows that they do), but it's not so
good that word processors tempt people to leave too much in the final document. It's so tempting to keep everything you've written. You can just clean it
up, find the most logical place in the document, and electronically paste it
right in there. If you had to copy the whole piece over again, you'd think
twice about keeping that extra word, phrase, paragraph, or section! Perhaps
the best cure is to force yourself to read the whole thing over *out loud*—so

you are forced to experience it as a reader experiences it. Another possible cure is to make one paper into two or even three. This may well have the benefit of making each paper effectively focused.

The Seduction of Neatness. No matter what you write, you can print it out in lovely neat letters, paragraphs, and pages—perhaps even with all the words spelled right (thanks to a spelling checker). Yet it may be awkward to read, repetitive, and incoherently organized. (And those correctly spelled words may be the wrong ones.) Nothing makes readers feel better treated than to give them a neat document; yet when that neatness serves to cover up messy or careless thinking, those same readers are sometimes even madder at you than if you had handed them something that honestly revealed itself as work in progress. The best cure is the same as before: to force yourself to read over out loud what you have written before giving it to someone. Of course, you can also warn your readers—orally or in writing—that, even though the piece *looks* neat, it is really quite an early draft.

Trying to Revise or Edit on Screen. It may seem as though it's a waste of time to print out a "hard" copy and edit on paper: it takes time to print it out, and you have to make changes on paper and then transfer those changes to the file. It's tempting to think you can save time if you just read your piece off the screen and make any editing changes there. But the truth is that it's hard to revise well on screen because you can't see enough of the document on the screen. Since you can't get a picture of the whole thing, you lack perspective on the structure and shape of your thinking.

Trying to revise on screen leads to an overload in your own head—makes you slow, tired, and confused. With printed copy, you'll find you can proceed much more crisply and quickly—and with a clearer head. If you worry about consistency of thought, for instance, you can put three passages side by side and work on all three at once. You can't do this on the computer. Thus it's often worth printing a copy to revise from unless you are making *only* tiny changes at the word level—and even here most people find it easier to spot misspellings, typos, and other small mistakes on paper than on screen. (Frequent printing for the sake of revising is also insurance against *losing* what you've written through a mistake or disk error.)

 LEARNING TO MASTER YOUR WORD PROCESSOR

Word processing programs can be cheap or expensive, limited or powerful in what they can do, simple or complex to use, poorly explained or well explained. And those factors don't always correlate. We're not experts on this, but we know that you don't have to pay top money to get one that is powerful, well explained, and relatively simple to use. If you are in the position to buy one, take plenty of time and get *lots* of expert advice. And, if possible, devote some time to trying each one out.

More often than not, unfortunately, the instructions are not clear. They tend to be written by technicians and to be "COIK": "Clear Only If Known." You can negotiate the instructions better if you have a sense of what you *need* to know. Here's our experience of what's important.

Most Important. Naming, renaming, copying, and saving files; moving the cursor quickly and comfortably all around the file (it's worth learning any tricks early); moving and copying blocks, efficient deleting (by word, line, sentence, paragraph—or however your program lets you); printing.

Also Important. (Some programs won't do all these things.) Using place markers so you can move quickly here and there in a file; using "windows" (if that's a capability) so you can consult notes or a different file; playing with formatting and reformatting (such as using different margins and page lengths); "hang paragraphing," where you indent a whole paragraph 5 or 10 spaces; and creating and having easy access to footnotes.

MINI-WORKSHOP

E

MIDTERM AND END-TERM RESPONSES TO A WRITING COURSE

As teachers we don't benefit much from students' telling us we are terrific or awful teachers. But when a student can give us a specific picture of what she's learned and noticed and of what our various teaching activities have made her think and feel, that's pure gold. You may not realize how much in the dark we teachers are about the effects of our teaching. The essential principle in responding to teaching is the same as that in responding to writing: instead of trying to *judge* or to give objective evaluations or God-like verdicts, it's much more helpful to give *honest and accurate information about what happened,* that is, to tell about the effects of the teaching on you.

Another essential principle from writing also fits teaching: the person *giving* feedback learns as much as the person *getting* it. Think of the responses you write for this mini-workshop, therefore, as being for your benefit as much as for the benefit of your teacher. People don't usually learn unless they are reflective and thoughtful about their experiences. Thus the best way to increase learning in schoolwork is to reflect back on *what* you've learned, *how* you've learned it, and what it *means.*

As teachers we always try to build into our courses some quiet retrospective moments to help students pause and reflect on their learning. We find that these moments help students get in the habit of being more reflective about their learning in all areas. And it turns out that our students' reflections on their learning are usually the most useful kind of feedback for us as teachers.

NOT JUST AT THE END OF A COURSE BUT IN THE MIDDLE TOO

Traditionally teachers ask for these kinds of responses at the end of a course. But we've found that they are also helpful—in some ways more so—at the middle point in a course. Of course, you cannot judge the whole course when it's only half over, but at the midpoint there's still time to *talk* to students about something in our teaching that may be confusing and time to make adjustments in our teaching. Many issues come out in midsemester responses, and they need talking about. Sometimes they can lead to a change of procedure; sometimes they show us that we need to discuss and clarify something we had been taking for granted. Almost always they help.

Turning from the teacher's benefit to your benefit, if you pause at midsemester for some retrospective reflections on the weeks that have gone by, you may notice a habit of yours that is getting in your way. Perhaps you realize that you tend to be preoccupied while writing with whether you will please the teacher. As you reflect on those feelings, you will probably see more clearly how much they get in the way of doing your best writing. Or perhaps this midcourse writing will help you reflect on your dissatisfaction with the course. You may realize that your dissatisfaction is indeed justified. But your reflections may also help you realize that you only have two choices: learning something despite the dissatisfaction or not learning anything. It all depends on how you deal with your dissatisfaction. Your midcourse explorations may show you how to get the best out of a bad situation instead of just letting *yourself* pay the penalty because someone else isn't meeting your needs or expectations.

Here then are questions to help you write responses that will be useful both for yourself and for your teacher. We've given far more questions than you can use for a short document. Perhaps your teacher will specify certain ones you should answer—or leave the choice up to you. Probably your teacher would like to see some of these responses, but it is helpful to write them with utter honesty for yourself first—leaving until later the question of which ones you will show to others.

QUESTIONS FOR RESPONSE

1a. Which *moments* come to mind when you think back over the class? good moments? bad moments? perplexing moments? Quickly sketch in a small handful of such moments. Two or three sentences can easily sketch a moment; often one sentence will do (indeed you can sometimes point with just a phrase to a moment that your reader will obviously remember—e.g., "That morning you lost your temper about people coming in late"). Just take the moments that come to mind.

1b. What do these moments tell about you as a student, about the teacher, and about the course?

2. What are you most proud of about your own effort or accomplishment in the course? What are you not satisfied with, or what do you want to work on improving?

3. What are the most important strengths or skills you brought to this course?

4. What's been the greatest challenge for you?

5. Tell about the effects of the course on your writing. Talk about:
Changes or lack of change in the quality of *what* you write
Changes or lack of change in *how* you write
Changes or lack of change in your attitudes and feelings about writing

6. What have you learned other than about writing—perhaps about yourself or about people or about learning?

7. What has been the most important thing you've learned? If you wish, you can just circle something you've already written.

8. What do you most need to learn next?

9. What was the most and the least helpful about:
In-class activities
Homework assignments
Group work
Comments on papers
Readings
Conferences
Grading procedures
How the course is structured
How the teacher operates

10. What aspects of you has the course brought out? What aspects did it leave untapped or unnoticed?

11. Imagine this course as a journey: where is it taking you?

12. Imagine it as a detour or setback in some larger journey: explain.

13. Describe the climate and weather of the course. Has it remained the same or gone through cycles?

14. Describe the course as a machine, as a living organism, as a slow-acting poison, as a *Mission: Impossible* script.

15. If you could start over again, what would you do differently? What have you learned about how to learn better?

16. Do you have any suggestions about how the course could be made more helpful?

 OTHER FORMAT FOR WRITING RESPONSES

A Letter to Your Teacher. The questions are helpful because they pinpoint many important issues and permit relatively short answers. But you may find it more helpful to *read through* the questions slowly and then write a letter to your teacher. There's something powerful about starting off on a blank piece of paper with "Dear————." To write a letter is to be faced with the best question of all: "What do *I* need to *say* to this person?" Because it's a letter and because you are writing very much *to* her, you cannot help treating your teacher as a person (not just a role or an authority figure), and this awareness may lead you to certain insights you wouldn't get from "answering a questionnaire."

 STILL ANOTHER FORMAT FOR WRITING RESPONSES*

It's useful to build evaluation directly into classroom activities so it's ongoing. Teachers who think this way may develop several strategies. A simple one concentrates not on judging what either you or the teacher is doing but on making suggestions for changes. For instance, the teacher can distribute a form like the following and ask you to draw a directional arrow on each line:

Students should be less involved in class.	—|—|—|—|—|—	Students should be more involved in class.
We should do more group work.	—|—|—|—|—|—	We should do less group work.
I'd like to do more reading.	—|—|—|—|—|—	We're asked to do too much reading.
We should be able to choose more of our own topics.	—|—|—|—|—|—	I'd rather be given more assigned topics.
The teacher should write fewer comments on our papers.	—|—|—|—|—|—	The teacher should write more comments on our papers.

*This form and the procedures connected to it are based on one developed by Bob Boice and Lyle R. Creamer.

Teacher's comments should be less directive.	— | — | — | — | — | —	Teacher's comments should be more directive.
We should do less in-class freewriting.	— | — | — | — | —	We should do more in-class freewriting.
There should be more attention to grammar.	— | — | — | — | — | —	There should be less attention to grammar.

Your teacher may ask you to respond to a form such as this several times during the semester, and may even ask each of you at some time to work with several others in compiling the results of the form and leading a discussion based on these results at the next class.

MINI-WORKSHOP

F

THE SENTENCE AND END-STOP PUNCTUATION

Look at the following groups of words and decide whether or not each one is a sentence. Don't agonize over the decision; just read each one quickly *out loud* and let your instincts tell you yes or no.

Sitting on the doorstep.
Go.
With careful analysis and painstaking research.
Stupid!
To the door.
The people at the end of the block who have been living there for years.
Jane and John were the kind of people who remained good friends even if you hadn't seen them for ten years.
Jennifer and her mother.
Come and visit with us whenever you can find the time.
John lost.
Let's go.

All the way around the block, into the building, up the stairs, and into the apartment.

Because it's dark.

But only if you have finished your work.

While all of us were sitting on the beach, watching the sun sprinkle sparkling lights on the calm waters of the inlet and feeling far away from everyday cares.

And then there were none.

After you've decided which of these are sentences, check to see if others agree.

We started off this workshop asking you to do this exercise because linguists tell us that native speakers of a language recognize complete sentences in their language. In fact, many linguists believe that children as young as two have intuitive knowledge of what a sentence is. Our beginning exercise is a way of testing this premise. We suspect that you and your classmates agreed on almost all your responses. In other words, we believe that linguists are right: native speakers of a language do "know" what a sentence is. They "know" in the sense that they can intuitively produce and recognize sentences.

If what we're saying is true, why do so many native speakers have problems with incomplete and run-on sentences? We can think of two important reasons.

First, knowing what a sentence is doesn't mean we know how to demonstrate that information when we write. This is one way in which spoken and written language differ greatly. Our voice punctuates our speech so that others can understand it; on paper we have to use punctuation marks. That is, we often need to turn intuitive knowledge into conscious knowledge. That may sound easy; it usually isn't. Second, no sentence exists in a vacuum; sentences always have a context. In speech that context includes the words we have already spoken, but it also includes our physical surroundings and our own gestures. If you're sitting on a beach, watching a beautiful sunset, you can gesture toward the setting sun and say "Beautiful!" Anyone listening will consider that a complete sentence because of the context which allows them to fill in the missing words: "The sunset is beautiful." Or in conversation, if someone says, "Why are you leaving?" and you answer "Because I'm hungry," anyone listening will consider your words a complete sentence because they can fill in the missing words: "I'm leaving because I'm hungry."

These are called fragments—understood words are missing—and in writing they are often called *wrong*, even though they are fine in speech. That's what causes trouble. Most teachers and editors would consider the following wrong:

The senators refused to withdraw their proposal to ship wheat to the drought-stricken countries. A proposal unpopular with the chairperson.

Even though most of us would agree on mentally inserting the words *this was* before *a proposal*, this agreement isn't enough in a piece of writing; most teachers probably want the words to be there on the page.

Maybe you think this is being picky, but it really isn't. We think everyone who reads our piece will automatically insert the intended words, but sometimes we're wrong. In speaking we can see our audience and tell whether they "get" our omitted words, but in writing we don't know how our reader is doing. If we're wrong, our reader may either find our writing incoherent or—what may be worse—misconstrue our meaning.

Nonetheless, good writers use fragments, and you can too, provided you don't confuse your readers. If you want to make sure that none of your fragments are confusing or awkward to readers, always ask a couple of people to read what you write before you hand it in. Ask them to let you know if they're confused. If it's a fragment that's causing the confusion, you'll probably want to fix it. Keep in mind, however, that your friends may not notice fragments that are *not* confusing—fragments that *function* as complete sentences even though they're missing an explicit subject or a verb. It's a good idea to find out how your teacher feels about fragments such as these.

Let's reconsider the "test" we started with. When linguists say that all native speakers know what a sentence is, they mean that native speakers can recognize sentences when *spoken* and in *context*. You may have had some disagreement on the "test"—and perhaps even some downright "mistakes"—because (1) it's harder to tell what's a sentence if it's not spoken, and (2) it's difficult to deal with any set of words which have no context since such a condition doesn't match our own experience. (In extended pieces of writing, the issue is even more complicated. The sentences are in a context, but for the sake of punctuation we have to act as if they are not—act as if the sentences stand alone even though they don't. This runs counter to our intuition.) Still, it needn't take much for you to learn to *adapt* the sentence-knowing skills you have to these harder conditions.

Fragments earn their name because they lack words that complete them. Run-ons display the opposite fault: they contain too many words, enough words, in fact, for two sentences. Run-ons are never a feature of the spoken language of native-born speakers. We all indicate sentence division in speech by pitches and pauses. This being true, we can correct written run-ons by reading aloud. The only problem is to decide what mark of punctuation to use at the point of sentence division: an end mark, a semicolon, a colon, or a conjunction with a comma. Thus you can use your intuition to avoid run-ons only up to a certain point. Beyond that, you're going to have to know some of the rules.

 ## SOME PRACTICE AND SOME RULES

Grammar books usually define a sentence as a group of words which contains a subject and a verb and a complete idea. The problem with "complete idea" is that it's often difficult in practice to decide what a complete idea is, where it starts, and where it ends. "A sentence is a group of words that can stand alone" probably works better as a definition because it allows you to rely on your implicit knowledge of what a sentence is. Thus once you decide that a group of words can stand alone, you need look only at whether it has an explicit subject and verb.* The only kind of English sentence that doesn't need a subject is an order ("Come here, please") since the understood subject of all orders is "you," and our grammar doesn't require us to make this "you" explicit.

Here are a few exercises you can do to make you think explicitly about the use of end marks in written prose.

1. Read through the following paragraph and decide where end marks should go; that is, decide which groups of words make complete sentences.

> The essayist does not usually appear early in the literary history of a country he comes naturally after the poet and the chronicler his habit of mind is leisurely he does not write from any special stress of passionate impulse he does not create material so much as he comments upon material already existing it is essential for him that books should have been written, and that they should, at least to some extent, have been read and digested he is usually full of allusions and references, and these his reader must be able to follow and understand and in this literary walk, as in most others, the giants came first: Montaigne and Lord Bacon were our earliest essayists, and, as yet, they are our best.

After you've completed this exercise, compare the way you did it with the way others in your group did it and arrive at a consensus about each punctuation mark. If there's class time for more comparisons, all the groups in the class can compare results and work toward a class consensus.

2. Pick out a paragraph from a piece you're currently working on and give an unpunctuated copy of it to someone else. Ask him or her to follow along as you read the passage aloud, and insert appropriate punctuation marks. When you've finished reading, you and your listener can compare the two copies and work out whatever discrepancies exist. But don't argue if you disagree.

When you and your partner have made your decisions about what to agree and disagree about, bring your paper to your entire group for possible resolution of differences. What your group cannot resolve to the satisfaction of everyone, you can save for a full-class discussion. At this point you may also want to consult a grammar book or handbook for help.

Remember that—in disputed cases—you are the author and should make the choice that seems best to you. Not everything is hard and fast, even in the world of grammar. There are exceptions to many usage rules, and choices can depend on context.

One of the most important things you'll discover from doing this exercise

---

*If you have difficulty identifying subjects and verbs, you'll need to spend some time with a grammar book. Try to find one which identifies parts of speech by position (for example, a noun is a word that can replace the x in the following: The x is here) and by form (for example, a verb is a word that can take the following as endings: s or es, d or ed, and ing).

is that your voice can help you make decisions about punctuation. As you listened to others read, you undoubtedly heard their voices drop in pitch at the ends of sentences and then pause briefly before continuing.

3. Decide whether you think the following groups of words, all punctuated as sentences, are in fact sentences. One way to do this is to read the passage aloud and force your voice to take its cues from the punctuation. That is, let your voice drop off in pitch whenever you see a period and then pause before continuing with the next sentence.

> I knew I couldn't think. All I knew then was what I couldn't do. All I knew then was what I wasn't, and it took me some years to discover what I was.
>
> Which was a writer.
>
> By which I mean not a "good" writer or a "bad" writer but simply a writer, a person whose most absorbed and passionate hours are spent arranging words on pieces of paper. Had my credentials been in order I would never have become a writer. Had I been blessed with even limited access to my own mind there would have been no reason to write. I write entirely to find out what I'm thinking, what I'm looking at, what I see and what it means. What I want and what I fear. Why did the oil refineries around Carquinez Straits seem sinister to me in the summer of 1956? Why have the night lights in the bevatron burned in my mind for twenty years? *What is going on in these pictures in my mind?*

After you've made decisions about the end marks in the excerpt, talk with your group members about their decisions. There are fragments in this passage. Did you have problems with them? Did others?

 SUGGESTIONS

If you have trouble marking sentence endings in writing, you're going to have to do a fair amount of extra work. We suggest the following approach:

1. Read your piece of writing backward (that is, read what you take to be the last sentence, then the preceding one, and so on). That sounds strange, we know. But sentences in a piece of writing often sound complete to us because we are in possession of whatever information prior sentences have given us. Thus we read individual sentences in the context of what precedes them. This is, of course, exactly what we should be doing, but it can blind us to the grammatical incompleteness of a particular sentence. Reading backward makes it impossible for us to apply previously given information to a sentence.

Start by reading the last sentence of your piece. When you've made a decision about that, go to the second-to-final sentence and read that, and so on. If certain sentences are problematic for you, write them out on a separate piece of paper and give them to someone else to read. This way they'll have to deal with the sentence in isolation—and for this purpose, that's exactly what you want them to do.

2. Check a good handbook for the rules on punctuation. We think the following rules are crucial:

- Complete sentences can end with a period, a semicolon, a colon, a question mark, or an exclamation point.
- If you use a semicolon after a complete sentence, make sure that a complete sentence follows the semicolon also.
- Do not use a comma to separate complete sentences. Most teachers will not approve. This error is usually called a "comma splice" or a "run-on." (Such creatures regularly appear in published prose, but they are often considered unacceptable in academic writing.)

MINI-WORKSHOP

G

COMMAS

Comma rules are the hardest of all. We'll give you some rules, but almost all commas rules have exceptions. Effective use of commas requires you not only to know the requisite rules but also—at least some of the time—to make decisions.

Rule 1. Use a comma before the conjunction in a compound sentence:

This is the first clause in a compound sentence, and this is the second clause.

There are two exceptions:

If the clauses in a compound sentence are short, you can omit the comma:

That is short and this is too.

If both clauses in a compound sentence have the same subject—and there is no chance for misreading—you can omit the comma.

This clause is independent and it's short too.

Rule 2. Use a comma after introductory words, phrases, and clauses:

After these introductory words, you should use a comma.

Second, you need a comma here also.

When a sentence begins with a dependent clause, put a comma after the clause.

There is an exception:

If the introductory segment is short—and there is no chance of misreading—you can omit the comma:

After this you don't always need a comma.

But beware of skipping the comma and ending up with a sentence that leads the reader to say it wrong:

After this writing will never be the same.

Rule 3. Use a comma to separate items in a series:

A series can be made up of any items that are parallel: sentences, clauses, phrases, or words.

Note that the final comma—the one after *phrases*—is optional, but you should be consistent.

Rule 4. Use a comma to separate nonrestrictive or nonessential parts of a sentence from the main part of the sentence.

An embedded clause, which is what this is, can be either restrictive or nonrestrictive.

An embedded clause which is restrictive should not be set off by commas.

Commas and Pausing

These rules don't quite cover all comma use because sometimes we sense the need for a comma in a certain spot just because we "feel" a pause in the structure or rhythm of a sentence. This usually means that if we read our piece aloud, we'd pause at this spot. The pause we make as we *speak* helps our listeners understand our words. The comma performs the same function in written language. Even when we're reading silently and not physically hearing words, we often "feel" pauses, and it's reassuring to see commas in these spots. Conversely, when we see a comma at a spot where neither structure nor meaning requires a pause and where a pause would disrupt meaning, we're confused. Our comprehension of what we're reading then suffers.

So the best advice we can give you about commas is to read what you've written aloud and notice where there are pauses. You can then examine each spot to see if a comma is advisable. Another way to do this is to give someone else a copy of your writing and let them mark the text wherever you pause. In this way you won't break the flow of your words by stopping to mark pauses. Still another way to do this is to read your piece into a tape recorder and then mark the pauses yourself as you listen to the playback. These are particularly good exercises to use if you tend not to use enough commas.

Workshop

oh god she tells me
to unpunctuate
unstructure
and my stomach
jellies
for years
i've been comfortable
with commas tight
as rosary beads
circling my throat
with semi-colons stuffing
my nostrils like cloudy incense
with periods clinging like black robes

blocking my eyes
how the hell
can i get this old
boulder off my back
without some skin
coming with it
it's been grooved to the wings
of my shoulders
if i throw it off
i will be weightless
lighter than air
a red balloon
floating over paris

Barbara Hoffman

Another tactic is to read aloud your writing and pause slightly at each comma (or ask someone else to read it aloud this way). This is probably the best tactic if you tend to overdo comma use. If commas (and periods and semi-colons, for that matter) match the speaking voice and sentence structure, your readers (even a diligent teacher!) will probably find no fault. In fact, research studies have shown that teachers are unlikely to notice mechanical errors of any kind if what they read truly engages their interest. So that's the main advice we can give you: make your writing interesting to your readers.

A Historical Note

Historically commas (and other punctuation marks) developed to mirror certain qualities of oral language which convey meaning but are not represented by recording the sounds of words. These qualities include pauses and variations of pitch and stress. At the end of a sentence, for instance, we usually pause and slightly lower the pitch of our voices. Periods in written language are the equivalent of these speech features. At the spots where commas appear, we often pause (although this pause is usually shorter than that at the end of a sentence), but pitch usually stays the same. Read the following excerpt aloud, and you'll get some sense of how this works:

Of course we're here an hour before the game starts. I don't mind, though. Now I can see all the other crazy Syracuse Orangemen basketball fans beside me! My brother and I sit down, taking the whole scene in. The Carrier Dome is a massive building with a white, balloon-like roof. It can hold a 100-yard football field, but today there is a blue curtain cutting the area into two parts. One half has vendors selling refreshments and Syracuse University paraphernalia. There is also a stage with two men singing, tables with important patrons clad in orange, and a giant-sized screen which will show the game for the unfortunate fans sitting behind the blue curtain.

When written language began to be considered as important as spoken language (or more important), punctuation began to have quite a different function: *to show the grammatical structure of sentences.* Quite a few rules came into existence to do this, but through the years this list has usually been reduced to the four we listed at the beginning of this mini-workshop.

These two systems of punctuation now exist side by side: to guide us in pausing and to show the grammatical structure of sentences. But usually they do not conflict. It's easy to see why, since the structure of sentences has a great deal to do with where a speaker pauses. In fact, the two systems often work harmoniously together. We often decide whether to use a comma after introductory words on the basis of whether we "hear" a pause:

In August, I'll go.
In August I'll go.

There really is no right or wrong here, but the two sentences shouldn't sound alike when read aloud.

Here's a paragraph (from the essay on page SR-57 of *Sharing and Responding*). See if you can put in commas and give a reason for each one. You can then check what you've done against the writer's punctuation.

As the washing machine fills itself with water the rushing sound starts me drifting away again. As I begin to dream about all of the money I am going to win in the lottery I am rudely interrupted by footsteps. "Please God let that be the man of my dreams tall dark and rich." I am anxiously awaiting the entrance of Michael Jordan. The footsteps are getting closer closer closer I sit up and cross my legs. I put a big sensual smile on my face; then he enters. I do not know who that beast is but it is a far cry from Michael Jordan or even Mr. Rogers. It is the cleaning lady.

Once you've practiced on this paragraph, you can select one of your own and do the same thing. Perhaps your teacher will give you a chance to do this in class so that you can work with others. If all the members of your group punctuate at least one paragraph written by each group member, you'll have the basis for a lively and profitable discussion about commas.

Note.   There are a number of fine points about commas—tiny rules and exceptions which we have chosen not to include in this short treatment. You need to check a comprehensive handbook for difficult cases. But if you really master the main things we treat here, you will seldom get into trouble.*

---

*For fun with comma rules, see the Stein piece in Workshop 5.

MINI-WORKSHOP

H

APOSTROPHES

The apostrophe is a peculiar punctuation mark. No language except English uses it. Basically it performs two functions in written language: it takes the place of deleted letters, and it shows possession. The first of these functions usually causes no problems for most writers:

she[i]s = she's
I[ha]ve = I've
can[no]t = can't

But the use of the apostrophe to show possession causes problems for most inexperienced and even for some experienced writers. Speech is no help at all: we can't *hear* the difference between *boys, boy's,* and *boys'.* We use *context* to tell us what the sounds mean.

The boys left early.
The boys left hand is stronger than his right.
The boys left hands were tied behind their backs.

Speech thus trains us to use context to determine the meaning of the s sound at the end of words. Having learned this, we tend to transfer this strategy to written language and allow the context to guide us here also.

But, standard written English requires that we use apostrophes even though they may be unnecessary for meaning. That's probably why apostrophes are so hard. You *do* need to get them right though, because whether we like it or not, teachers and most other people regard someone who makes mistakes with apostrophes as an illiterate.

Apostrophes to Show Possession

The basic rules seem simple. An apostrophe indicates that the preceding word possesses something: *boy's* indicates that *a boy* possesses something: *boys'* indicates that *boys* possess something. One way to help yourself is to use an *of* phrase to test whether the apostrophe is appropriate:

The boy's left hand is stronger than his right.

The "left hand of the boy" is what "boy's left hand" means, so the apostrophe is appropriately placed.

The boys' left hands are tied behind their backs.

The left hands of the boys is what *the boys' left hands* means, so again the apostrophe is correctly placed.

Look at the following paragraph and see if you can get apostrophes where they belong:

I wholeheartedly believe in the value of education, but sometimes it seems to be more trouble than its worth. I transferred to this school from a small college upstate in order to get a better education and to extricate myself from a situation I felt I had to reassess. (That, however, is a different story!) Since my parents home is an hour and fifteen minute drive from Stony Brook, the logical thing for me to have done was to get some form of housing nearer to school. This I proceeded to do, by moving into an apartment that was way beyond my means, and glibly signing a years lease in the bargain. My roommate was a good friend from high school who was dying to get out of her mothers house. We received countless warnings on the dangers of friends living together, but we brushed off those of little faith, knowing it would be different for us.

▢ ▢ ▢ ▢ ▢

As it turned out, there *had* been a mistake, and I would get the loan, but only after reapplying for it, as the computer had erased me. "It will only take eight to ten weeks to process," the polite voice informed me sweetly.

"Oh, no, thats not possible," I laughed airily. "You see, my rents due next week, and theres nothing in the house to eat, and. . . ."

Im sorry," she interrupted firmly, "That is the length of time it takes to process a loan."

"But I havent even bought my books yet!" I said desperately.

"Im sorry," she replied crisply, and hung up.

▢ ▢ ▢ ▢ ▢

Our friendship definitely benefited from the situation. Since weve been home, theres no tension over who *always* has to clean the bathroom, and over who used up the last of the mayonnaise and didn't get more. Were almost on the same footing as when we moved in together, which makes us both very happy. The commuting isnt too bad either, as I enjoy driving. Who knows? Maybe next year Ill live at home and use my loan for updating my wardrobe.

You can check what you did against what the writer did by turning to the end of the section on apostrophes.

Apostrophes for Other Uses

It's only fair to warn you that apostrophes do appear in other sorts of places also. Some handbooks advise using them for plurals of letters and numbers:

> I cannot read her 7's.
> The 1960's are both praised and maligned.
> I particularly like the A's on that sign.

Other handbooks, however, prefer no apostrophes in these sentences:

> I cannot read her 7s.
> The 1960s are both praised and maligned.
> I particularly like the As on that sign.

We also want to warn you that the apostrophe is not always an indicator of true possession. *An hour's stay* doesn't really mean the hour possesses the stay, but the test we suggested above still works: *an hour's stay* equals *a stay of an hour.*

If you have real problems with apostrophes, you're going to have to do some hard, rather tedious proofreading which will require you to check every *s* that comes at the end of a word. We do think, though, that if you do this conscientiously for a while, you'll find yourself beginning to put the apostrophe in with greater regularity *as* you're writing.

Note. We haven't done a survey, but we bet most apostrophe errors occur with *its* and *it's*. Just remember that *it's* equals *it (i)s* and *its* is a possessive. That last one seems contradictory—since we associate the apostrophe with possessives—but *hers* and *theirs* and *his* don't have apostrophes either. The it's/its conundrum is similar to two others:

> *who's (who* plus *is)* and *whose*
> *they're (they + are)* and *their*

Apostrophes as the Writer Used Them

> I wholeheartedly believe in the value of education, but sometimes it seems to be more trouble than it's worth. I transferred to this school from a small college upstate in order to get a better education and to extricate myself from a situation I felt I had to reassess. (That, however, is a different story!) Since my parents' home is an hour and fifteen minute drive from Stony Brook, the logical thing for me to have done was to get some form of housing nearer to school. This I proceeded to

do, by moving into an apartment that was way beyond my means, and glibly signing a year's lease in the bargain. My roommate was a good friend from high school who was dying to get out of her mother's house. We received countless warnings on the dangers of friends living together, but we brushed off those of little faith, knowing it would be different for us.

□ □ □ □ □

As it turned out, there *had* been a mistake, and I would get the loan, but only after reapplying for it, as the computer had erased me. "It will only take eight to ten weeks to process," the polite voice informed me sweetly.

"Oh, no, that's not possible," I laughed airily. "You see, my rent's due next week, and there's nothing in the house to eat, and. . . ."

"I'm sorry," she interrupted firmly, "That is the length of time it takes to process a loan."

"But I haven't even bought my books yet!" I said desperately.

"I'm sorry," she replied crisply, and hung up.

□ □ □ □ □

Our friendship definitely benefited from the situation. Since we've been home, there's no tension over who *always* has to clean the bathroom, and over who used up the last of the mayonnaise and didn't get more. We're almost on the same footing as when we moved in together, which makes us both very happy. The commuting isn't too bad either, as I enjoy driving. Who knows? Maybe next year I'll live at home and use my loan for updating my wardrobe.

MINI-WORKSHOP

I

QUOTATION AND THE PUNCTUATION OF REPORTED SPEECH

Quotat on marks are the primary way to show in writing *exactly* which words were said or written by someone other than you.

Notice how this works:

Elizabeth Kinney, a student who read an earlier draft of our book, said about it, "I think the idea of considering all of us as writers is absurd, and I don't think any student really takes that notion seriously."

The quotation marks tell you exactly which words are Elizabeth Kinney's and which are ours.

THE CONVENTIONS FOR USING QUOTATION MARKS

The conventions for using quotation marks can be tricky, but if you master them and end-stopping (getting periods where they are needed and keeping your reader from shouting "sentence fragment!" or "run-on sentence!"), you have mastered 95 percent of what you need to know about punctuation. (Colons and semicolons are infrequent and easy; commas are hopelessly arguable.)

1. *Periods and commas go* INSIDE *quotation marks.* If the *quoted* sentence doesn't end where you end your quotation, you should include four dots with spaces between them to show that you stopped quoting before the person finished her sentence:

> Elizabeth Kinney, a student who read an earlier draft of our book, said, "I think the idea of considering all of us as writers is absurd. . . ."

(Notice that the first dot has no space before it. Note also that many British editors use an alternative style: they put periods and commas outside quotation marks. Perhaps you've observed this practice in some books. We think it best to follow the style used by American editors, since that is probably what your teacher will prefer—though, of course, you can ask her.)

If you omit words in the middle of a sentence you're quoting, use only three dots, with a space before the first dot and after the last one:

> "I think . . . considering all of us as writers is absurd. . . ."

2. *Semicolons and colons belong* OUTSIDE *quotation marks.* To show what this looks like, we've rewritten our original excerpt slightly.

> Elizabeth Kinney, a student who read an earlier draft of our book said, "I think the idea of considering all of us as writers is absurd"; then she went on to disagree with us further.

3. *Question marks, exclamation points, and dashes sometimes go inside and sometimes outside.* They go *inside* the quotation marks if they're part of the quotation and *outside* if they're not.

> Do you think she was right when she said, "[C]onsidering all of us as writers is absurd"?

The question is ours, not Kinney's, so the question mark belongs outside the quotation marks. (The *C* is in brackets because it wasn't capitalized in the original.)

> We had to think about our position again when Kinney asked, "Do you really want all students to think of themselves as writers?"

This time the question was hers, and so the question mark belongs inside.

4. *Quoted material which blends directly into your words needs no extra punctuation mark.*

Elizabeth Kinney said our idea of treating students as writers "is absurd."

5. *When you use a phrase of attribution (for example,"she said" or "John insisted on announcing"), you need a colon or comma after the phrase of attribution.* Generally colons appear before formal statements and commas before informal ones. Levels of formality are difficult to assess though. What you should keep in mind is that using a comma before a quotation suggests less formality to your readers. If that's what you want, the comma is probably correct. In other words, the choice is mostly a stylistic one. Thus both of these are correct; the comma in the first passage keeps the tone slightly informal:

> A student reader of our text said, "I think the idea of considering all of us as writers is absurd, and I don't think any student really takes that notion seriously."

> She went on to say: "Even if you define a writer as anyone who writes, the public thinks of a writer as a professional who is capable of writing and doing a good job of it."

6. *If the phrase of attribution follows the quotation, a comma is needed—* unless, of course, the quotation ends with an exclamation point or a question mark.

> "When you propose that all students can think of themselves as writers, it sounds patronizing," said Elizabeth Kinney.

> "When you propose that all students can think of themselves as writers, it sounds patronizing!" said Elizabeth Kinney.

7. *If you have a quotation-within-a-quotation, use regular quotation marks for the main quotation and single quotation marks for the inner quotation.*

> She went on to say: "Even if you say 'a writer is anyone who writes,' the public thinks of a writer as a professional who is capable of writing and doing a good job of it."

8. *If you quote a long passage—three lines or more—it's usually clearer if you indent ten spaces from your left margin and* OMIT *the quotation marks.* Precede the quotation with a colon. Thus:

```
Here is a comment from a student who used an earlier
draft of our book:

        Even if you say a "writer is anyone who
        writes," the public thinks of a writer as a
        professional who is capable of writing and
        doing a good job of it. When you propose that
```

`all students can think of themselves as writ-`
`ers, it sounds patronizing.`

Now that you've read over these conventions, we suggest that you look closely at the student and professional interviews in Workshop 6 and analyze these writers' use of punctuation relative to quotations. Have they followed the conventions?

Practice

Bring in a paragraph you're working on (even if it isn't from a final draft) which contains a fair quantity of quoted words. Put in punctuation and then read through the paragraph with a classmate or two explaining to them why you used each mark. Since class time may be limited and your teacher will want to use most of it for substantive matters (like discussing content, organization, tone, etc.), you may not have time for in-class work on these conventions. But you can still get feedback—from a friend, classmate, family member, or tutor in your school's writing center. If something's particularly problematic, you may want to check it with your teacher.

MINI-WORKSHOP

J

SPELLING

Spelling, like punctuation, is solely a feature of the written language. And for many it's a very important feature. Many people—not just teachers—will think you are not just illiterate but stupid if your spelling is poor. In fact, research studies have demonstrated that spelling has little to do with intelligence. But it's also true that spelling is highly tied to reading; we get our sense of correct spelling from *seeing* words, not from hearing them. Thus if you do a lot of reading, you're more likely to spell more words correctly. Consequently readers tend to think that anyone whose spelling is poor has not read much; that is, he's illiterate.

Nor do we want you to think we're minimizing the importance of spelling. If each of us spelled our own way, writing would become totally chaotic. Misspelled words can block communication. And most readers—including us—get annoyed by misspellings. Our annoyance causes us to get mad at the writer, and this hostility blocks our intent to focus on meaning. We react this way because we feel that if someone really wanted to communicate with us, he or she would take the trouble to spell correctly.

English is basically a phonetic language. What this means is that written English words represent sounds, not things. For example, *house* represents the spoken word "house," which in turn represents a building or structure people live in. The symbol ⬟, on the other hand, would represent the building or structure directly. (Despite this phonetic base, most of us probably do not need to hear the word *house* when we read it in order to know what it means: we probably go directly from the marks on the page to the idea of "house.") In some languages of the world, like Chinese, written words are not a record of the spoken language. Chinese characters represent things without reference to the way a speaker would represent them.

Even though English is phonetically based, it is not *purely* phonetic. The letter *A* in English represents *various* sounds. And conversely the sound that in the International Phonetic Alphabet is represented as /e/ and pronounced like the vowel sound in *say* is represented in a number of different ways in written English.

Why has English slipped from being fully phonetic? Evidence suggests that our writing was once totally phonetic. Old English scribes probably recorded, or tried to record, the sounds of the language directly. We know this because scribes from different regions spelled words differently—depending on the accent or dialect of that region. When printing was introduced in England during the fourteenth century, printers began to feel the need for standardization of spelling. The *sounds* of the spoken language continued to change, but the *spelling* of words did not. And so, today, for example, the word *says* is pronounced more like *sez,* but you don't see it written like that except in special circumstances.

All this explains why our spelling can cause difficulty, but it is of no help at all as you seek to deal with that difficulty. Some people seem to be chronically poor spellers (even if they do read a lot), and others seem to be good spellers without much effort. Most of us fall somewhere in between. Certain words give us trouble and other words—usually those we use all the time—give us no trouble at all. Consequently all we need to do is to look up new words when we want to use them.

But for those of you who are poor spellers, dictionaries are often not much help because you just don't know which words to look up. And, needless to say, looking up all the words you use would be enormously onerous. Some handbooks and secretarial manuals give lists of frequently misspelled words, and there are some special spelling dictionaries which help you find words even if you look them up under the wrong spelling. But these do not solve all one's problems. So what do you do?

Our best suggestion is to learn to use a word processing program on a computer and equip your computer with a spelling checker. (Or use a typewriter with a built-in spelling checker.)

Nevertheless you'll still need to check for "correctly spelled mistakes" such as using *effect* for *affect* or *except* for *accept.* You'll want to gradually compile a list of these homophones (sound-alikes) that trip you up, and make your spelling checker flag them for you—along with those special words that you have difficulty with which may not be built into the spelling checker itself. Also, beginning to appear on the market now are credit-card-sized spelling checkers which look like small calculators and can contain up to eighty thousand words. Buying one of these may be a good investment for anyone who is a chronically poor speller.

Our second best suggestion is to enlist the aid of a friend, roommate, or family member who is a good speller and ask him to read through whatever you plan to submit for grading. All he needs to do is mark the misspelled words. It is your job to look them up. This may be a lot to ask of someone, particularly if you are a really bad speller. But perhaps there's something you can do for this person to return the favor. Even if you just read through whatever he writes and give him your reactions to it, you'll be doing something important for him.

There's something sociable and communal about getting help from a friend, but there's also something attractive about *not* getting help from a friend. That means spending money. *Some* typists are skilled spellers and will simply fix all your spelling. You may have to pay a bit extra. But look long and hard enough—perhaps insist on references—until you find one who really *is* expert.

Frankly, other than that, we can't give you much help. We do believe that the more you write and the more you look up words, the better speller you'll become. But you may never become good enough to give up relying on help.*

Finally we *may* be able to help you somewhat with the following account of the major spelling problems. We suggest that you keep a special spot in your notebook and see if you can group your spelling errors according to the following list. Undoubtedly you'll also need to set up some personal categories—plus a list which gathers together the uncategorizable words. This may help you gain some control over the problem even if you can't eliminate it. Furthermore, such lists may also prove to you that you're not making a lot of errors, just some of the same errors over and over.

Here are special areas of difficulty for most poor spellers:

1. Doubling Letters

This causes the most difficulty when you're adding endings to words. The basic rule is to double the final letter of a word before adding a suffix if it meets the following three conditions:

a. The ending to be added to the main word must begin with a vowel: *-ing, -es, -ed, -y.*

b. The word must either be a one-syllable word (such as *sit, tap, slip*) *or* end with an accented syllable (such as *admit, begin,* and *prefer*).

c. The word must end with a single consonant that is preceded by a single vowel. (For example, *occur* ends in a single consonant that is preceded by a single vowel, so we get *occurred* and *occurring*. The word *creep*, on the other hand, ends in a single consonant, but that consonant is not preceded by a single vowel, so we get *creeping*.)

---

*Note: *For testimony to this, see the Levinsky letter in the Readings for Workshop 5.*

Exceptions:
- *qu* is considered one consonant sound, so *equip* + *ing* = *equipping*.
- *x* is a double consonant sound since *x* is really the two sounds *k* and *s*, so *fox* + *es* = *foxes*.
- Think of both *y* and *w* as vowels, so *toy* + *ing* = *toying*.

Test yourself: add *-ing* to *forget* and *compel*; add *-ed* to *shop* and *drape*; add *-y* to *cat*; add *-er* to *plan*; add *-ance* to *remit*; add *-ent* to *repel*. (Answers are at the end of this mini-workshop.)

2. Dropping the Silent *E* before Adding Endings

The basic rule is to *drop* a silent *e* when adding a suffix that begins with a vowel: *bite* + *ing* = *biting*.

Exception: Keep the silent *e* which occurs after *c* or *g* if the added ending begins with an *a* or *o*: *change* + *able* = *changeable*. (This exception grows out of the pronunciation rules of English. Most of the time we pronounce the *g* or *c* before *a*, *o*, and *u* differently from the way we pronounce it before *i* or *e*: *gin* and *gone*; *necessary* and *case*.)

Other exceptions are *dyeing* (meaning to change color), *acreage*, *mileage*, *truly*, *judgment*, *acknowledgment*, *ninth*, *wholly*.

Try some: *outrage* + *ous*; *manage* + *able*; *love* + *able*; *race* + *ed*. (Answers are at the end of this mini-workshop.)

3. Adding *ify/efy*

Verbs are formed by adding *ify*: *classify*, *justify*, *amplify*. There are only four exceptions: *liquefy*, *stupefy*, *rarefy*, *putrefy*.

4. Words Ending in *sede/ceed/cede*

a. Only one word ends in *sede*: *supersede*.
b. Only three words end in *ceed*: *exceed*, *succeed*, *proceed*.
c. All other words ending with the "seed" sound, end in *cede*: for example, *concede*, *precede*, *recede*.

5. *ie/ei*

The old jingle is probably the most helpful:

I before *e* except after *c* or when sounded like *ay* as in *neighbor* or *weigh*.

Thus *priest* and *niece*, but *ceiling* and *perceive*.

Exceptions: *neither*, *either*, *leisure*, *seize*, *weird*, *sheik*, *financier*, *foreign*, and *conscience*.

Try these: *theif* or *thief*, *deceit* or *deciet*, *piece* or *peice*, *consceince* or *conscience*, *frieght* or *freight*. (Answers are at the end of this mini-workshop.)

6. Adding *able* or *ible*

The rules here are so complex that they're more confusing than helpful. Your best tactic is simply to keep a list. In general, common words add *able*: *eat-*

able, readable, comfortable. Less common words usually use *ible: admissible, ineligible, accessible.* There are many exceptions though, such as *possible.*

7. Adding *ance* or *ence*
Again, just keep two separate lists.

> ANCE: abundance, acquaintance, appearance, brilliance, endurance, guidance, ignorance, importance, maintenance, reassurance, remembrance, repentance, significance, tolerance

> ENCE: absence, audience, coincidence, conference, confidence, consequence, competence, convenience, correspondence, dependence, difference, essence, excellence, existence, experience, inference, influence, intelligence, magnificence, occurrence, patience, permanence, preference, presence, reference, severence, residence, sentence, violence

8. Words Ending in *ary* or *ery*
Only two commonly used words end in *ery: cemetery* and *stationery* (meaning the stuff you write letters on).

9. Changing *y* to *i* before Adding Endings
a. Change *y* to *i* before adding to any ending *not* beginning with *i.* Thus *happy + ly = happily; jolly + er = jollier; pity +ful = pitiful;* but *pity + ing = pitying.*
b. Keep the final *y* if it is preceded by a vowel: *play + er = player.*
c. Exceptions occur when adding *ness, ship, like,* or *ly: shyness, citylike, ladyship, slyly.*

> Try some: *beauty + ful; marry + ing; fly + er; history + cal; ninety + eth; lonely + ness; copy + ing; victory + ous; delay + ed; dry + ness.* (Answers are at the end of this mini-workshop.)

10. Learn to Look for Homonyms—Words That Sound Alike but Have Different Meanings or Use, Such as *berth* or *birth*
Any good grammar book or handbook will have lists of these words, usually under some heading like "Words commonly confused."

Final Word. Spelling can psychologically discombobulate some people more than any other dimension of writing. The thing to keep in mind if you are troubled by spelling is that it is *not* necessary to know spelling. It is only necessary that for certain important pieces of writing *you must—by hook or by crook—get the spelling right.*

Think of it like typing. When you submit writing to someone, often it *must* be typed. That doesn't mean *you* must type it. There's nothing morally wrong with hiring a typist to do it for you. However it's nicer and cheaper if you can type; you don't feel dependent on others. This is exactly how it is with spelling.

1. forgetting, compelling, shopped, draped, catty, planner, remittance, repellent
2. outrageous, manageable, lovable, raced
5. thief, deceit, piece, conscience, freight
9. beautiful, marrying, flier, historical, ninetieth, loneliness, copying, victorious, delayed, dryness

MINI-WORKSHOP

K

COPYEDITING AND PROOFREADING

Bring to class a typed copy, or copies, of the final draft of a paper you plan to hand in. Another student will copyedit and proofread your paper, and you will do the same for her. If there's time, you will want to exchange papers with at least two people. Your teacher may allow time for this in class, or she may ask you to do this work at home.

Read your classmate's paper *very carefully,* and pencil in any corrections you think appropriate. You are looking for *all* errors in mechanics or typing (capitalization, underlining, abbreviations, and so forth) and *all* violations of the rules of standard written English. What you'll want to check particularly are spelling, punctuation, sentence structure, subject-verb agreement, and pronoun reference. If you aren't sure about a change you've made, put a question mark by it. If a sentence doesn't sound right to you, but you can't pinpoint exactly what's bothering you, just draw wiggly lines under it. Be sure to sign your name to the paper as editor. Your teacher may want to collect all edited copies of each paper in order to pinpoint particular students' problems.

When you're finished, select two of the corrections you've made and write a rule for each. Don't look up the rule in a handbook; just state the rule in a way that explains why you made the correction. Here's more of the essay we quoted from in Workshop 7, with copyediting changes added, as well as two rules written by the student-editor:

Upon entering, the bar is to the person's immediate left and a few steps below is the dance floor. By the way, the steps are notorious killers since many, under the influence of alcohol, forget they exist. On the other side, there is the seating area consisting of dozens of tables and black velvety, cushiony, re-cliner-type chairs. They are the type of chairs ~~you~~ *one* lose ~~yourself~~ *one*self in.

There's a lower level which is reached by descending a flight of wooden stairs. This staircase is actually wooden slat/s bound together, which allows heels to get caught. Many-a-times, there's *are* men standing below it waiting for damsels to (decend,) preferably those wearing skirts. This lower level is a very quite *sp* and intimate dwelling (designated) for ?
those couples who want to leave their inhibitions behind.

Rule: Don't use "you" in an essay.
Rule: Use commas after introductory words.

Once you get the copies of your paper back, you'll need to make a decision about each correction or comment made by your editor(s). If you're sure they're right (perhaps your mistake was carelessness or poor typing), make the correction neatly in ink on your good copy. If you're sure they're wrong, don't erase the change; leave it, so that your teacher will know what you've made a decision about. If you're not sure one way or the other, you'll have to check in a handbook. If your teacher hasn't recommended one for you to buy, you should ask her for a recommendation.* If you can't find what you need in your book, you'll need to find some other authority: a classmate, your roommate, a family member, your teacher, or a tutor in the Writing Center.

Sometimes the best strategy for dealing with problems you can't clearly define is to rewrite the problem sentence in a different way. Try to think yourself back into the idea you had when you wrote the sentence, and see if you can write it in a way that matches your idea more clearly. Say what you mean aloud to yourself, talk it through—then try writing it again. You may want to rewrite the sentence several ways. You'll probably recognize which one is the best one. If you do rewrite an entire sentence, you should reread the paragraph it's in to make sure you haven't disrupted the flow of the ideas and language. If, when you've made decisions about all suggested changes, you discover you've made so many that it's hard to read your paper, ask your teacher if she'd like you to retype it. If you do retype it, remember it needs proofreading again. (This is one advantage of writing on a computer.)

If your teacher gives you additional class time, you can share your findings and problems with others in the class. All of us store rules about language in our heads, even though we may not be consciously aware of them. If we didn't have such rules, we couldn't talk or write at all. If you can become consciously aware of the rules you use, you can discard or alter those that are unacceptable (as defined by your teacher or the grammar book you are using) and sharpen those that are valid. Class discussion will make you aware of which you should keep and which you should discard.

If you make a relatively high number of usage errors, you'll need to do some extra work. Set aside several pages in your journal or notebook to list the errors you make. In this way, you can discover which errors recur and concentrate on avoiding them. What you'll probably discover is that you're not making many different errors, but the same errors over and over. Your teacher may, of course, expect you to do some extra work to begin clearing up your particular set of errors.

Your teacher probably won't be able to provide time in class for you to proofread and copyedit every paper you hand in. But *you* should find the time for it. You may be able to make arrangements with classmates to do this outside of class. Otherwise, you can ask your roommate, a friend, or a family member. You can even hire a tutor to help. Very few of us are able to edit ourselves; most of us can do a better job on someone else's paper than on our own. (Every published writer gets help copyediting from editors—as we did on this book.) Typographical and usage errors can destroy the best piece of writing; once you've spent a lot of time getting your thoughts straight and in good order, it's foolish not to take a little extra time to make them readable. Surface flubs can make readers decide not to read at all—or to read in a hostile mood.

For help with understanding how grammatical and usage rules work, see The Right Handbook.

MINI-WORKSHOP
L

THE DIFFERENCE BETWEEN GRAMMATICAL CORRECTNESS AND A FORMAL, IMPERSONAL VOICE

Many students confuse *correctness* and *formality* and so when something has to be *correct,* they try to write in a formal voice and their writing becomes stiff, awkward, artificial—and often their thinking gets cramped and uninteresting too. In this mini-workshop we will try to show you two simple principles that can have a big effect on your final drafts: (1) Writing can be correct without having to be formal and impersonal; (2) writing can be formal and impersonal without being stiff or artificial.*

For this workshop you need a short passage of casual, informal, comfortable writing with plenty of mistakes in spelling, grammar and usage. A half page or a couple of paragraphs will do. It's fine to use a piece of journal writing or exploratory draft writing or freewriting you already have on hand. Or you could now do ten minutes of freewriting about something that's interesting to you. (Of course *some* fast freewriting *doesn't* have a comfortable casual voice: sometimes freewriting gets tangled and garbled. But don't use a passage like that; find one that really is informal and comfortable.)

 EXERCISE ONE

How to make your writing correct without having it be formal or impersonal? That is, how to get rid of all the mistakes and still keep your writing personal or informal?

Go through your passage and make whatever changes are necessary to get it clear; get rid of all the mistakes in grammar and usage, *but make as few changes as you can!* Therefore, when you find a mistake or a place that doesn't make sense or doesn't say what you want, don't rewrite the whole passage. Just make the smallest change you can and use as much of the original, comfortable language and voice as possible. (You might get a fellow student to look for mistakes you've missed.) What you should end up with is a passage that is *absolutely correct* but completely *informal, casual, personal,* and *comfortable* in voice. It will have no mistakes in what we call "Standard Written English."

Peter Elbow did this exercise with a piece of his informal, private freewriting. Here is a passage from his original, fast, casual writing (the full piece is in the "readings" for Workshop 4):

> Screen is something halfway between mind and paper.
>
> Mind is a mess: paper supposed to be neat. When I'm writing on screen, it feels like it's sort of—half—still in my mind. It's a second mind—It's not stll partly *in* me. Like my mind I can't look at all of it at once, I can only put my attention on one bit at a time. I don't yet have complete detachment from it til I print it out. It gives me a second mind.
>
> Another mind. Sometimes I make such a mess that I feel in a swamp—too many options—once I remember feeling Oh I wish I were writing in ink on expensive velum so I would just choose a word and be done. Not feel like I have to keep revising and changng. I want something *final* (must find that process piece I wrote when I was in that situation.
>
> Sometimes I try to revise too much on screen. Too much chaos in the mind.

---

*We lump "formal" and "impersonal" together as categories, but we acknowledge that, strictly speaking, there is a difference. That is, you could use informal language yet have no personal references at all; or use formal language, but use that language to refer to yourself and to personal experiences. Most of the time, however, formality and impersonality go together. Indeed, the very use of casual, informal language tends to give a personal flavor.

When he did minimal revising in order to get rid of mistakes and get the passage clear—but make as few changes as possible—here's what he came up with:

> What's on the screen is halfway between thoughts and feelings in my mind and writing on paper. Mind is a mess; writing is supposed to be neat. But when I'm writing on screen, the words seem half in my mind. The computer is a kind of second mind. The words are still partly *in* me. The computer text is also like my mind because I can't look at it all at once. I can only put my attention on one screen at a time. I don't have complete detachment from it till I print it out.
>
> Another mind. Who says two minds are better than one? Sometimes I make such a mess with my two minds that I feel in a swamp—too many options. Once when this happened I remember feeling, "Oh, I wish I were writing in ink on expensive velum so I would just have to choose each word and be done. Not feel as though I have to keep revising and changing. I want something *final.*" I still have some process writing I did when I was in that situation.
>
> Sometimes I try to revise too much on screen. This makes for too much chaos in the mind.

The point we are trying to make is that correct writing doesn't have to be formal or impersonal or stiff in any way. When a teacher says, "I want your paper to be absolutely correct," you may think that she hates an informal, personal voice—whereas all she hates is *mistakes.* In such a situation (and this is also the situation for most magazine and newspaper writing and many committee reports), your best route is the one you take in this exercise: write in your most comfortable voice and then correct and clarify it afterwards. Of course you can't use slang or ungrammatical constructions if the audience wants correctness, but you can keep an informal personal style nevertheless: there is *no conflict* between writing in an informal voice and writing *correctly.*

By the way, here is Peter's process writing—reflecting on the choices he made in trying to get rid of mistakes but keep the informal voice he started with:

> Plenty of the decisions were easy. I felt easy about keeping contractions. I consider them definitely correct: no conflict with what we think of as "Standard Written English"—though I know that some teachers or stylists disagree. I also felt clear that I had to change "feel *like* I have to keep revising" to "feel *as though* I have to keep revising." "Feel like" sounds like a definite mistake to me and to most English teachers, though plenty of literate people let it go by these days as correct informal writing.
>
> I felt pretty clear about keeping my two-word, verb-less sentence ("Another mind."). It's not awkward and it doesn't sound like a mistake. But plenty of teachers would disagree with me about it. Language is a matter of social negotiation, and "rules" about what is correct are slowly but constantly shifting like the coastline.
>
> I *would have* changed the other sentence without a verb ("Not feel as though I have to keep revising and changing") except that it was in quotation marks: it was a quotation from me talking to myself in my head. As a quotation of reported speech, it seemed acceptable; as a regular sentence I would judge it not acceptable for Standard Written English.

EXERCISE TWO

529

Grammatical
Correctness and
a Formal,
Impersonal Voice

We can carry the same principle farther now and show you that writing can even be formal and impersonal without being stiff, awkward, or artificial. It can still sound like you.

Sometimes teachers or other readers don't just ask for correctness, they ask for writing that is impersonal and formal. (In fact, when some teachers ask for correctness, they really mean "make it formal.") And when you set out to produce formal or impersonal writing, you often write language that feels awkward and artificial. But that's not necessary. You can have formal, impersonal writing that still seems comfortable and sounds like you—if you go about producing it in the right way.

The crucial process here is to *start out* your piece informally in a voice that feels comfortable for you. Don't worry about correctness or the need for formality. *After* you've written it, go through and remove *only* the personal and informal features (just like you removed *only* the mistakes in the earlier exercise). You will end up with something quite *formal* that is not dead; it will still have your voice in it. But if you start off trying to *write* it in a formal voice, your language will often feel very stiff and uncomfortable.

Here is what Peter Elbow came up with when he removed the personal, informal elements.

What's on the screen is halfway between the thoughts and feelings in our minds and writing on paper. Mind is a mess; writing is supposed to be neat. But when we write on screen, the words still seem half in mind. The computer is a kind of second mind.

The computer text is also like our minds because we cannot look at it all at once. We can put our attention on only one screenful at a time. We don't have complete detachment from what we've written until we print it out.

Are two minds really better than one? Sometimes we make such a mess with our two minds that we feel caught in a swamp. We can feel as though we have too many options. We can wish we were writing in ink on expensive velum so we simply have to choose each word and be done with it. When we feel we have to keep revising and changing, we wish for something *final.*

Revising too much on screen can make for too much chaos in the mind.

Here is Peter's process writing—reflecting on the choices he made:

When I looked for informal or personal elements to remove I came up with these: contractions; dashes as punctuation; sentences without a verb; conversational words like "till" and "bit"; conversational expressions like "just have to choose" (changed to "simply have to choose").

It was also informal to write in the first person ("I") and refer to my own individual experience. I decided I could make it fairly formal and impersonal by changing to first-person *plural* ("we"). Perhaps others would disagree.

I could have made my language more definitely formal and impersonal by talking about "people" instead of "we," but that seemed needlessly stiff and stuffy.

I got interested in my question, "Who says two minds are better than one?" It gives a personal flavor because it is addressed directly to the reader. First I changed it from a question to a statement ("Conventional wisdom tells us that two minds are better than one"), but that also felt needlessly stuffy. I decided I could keep it as a question if the question isn't pointed so directly at the reader ("Are two minds really better than one?"). That seems a way to have a kind of formality and impersonality while still keeping things livelier and closer to my voice.

Our point then in this mini-workshop is that your writing (and your sanity) will benefit enormously if you remember these distinctions. You can have writing that is perfectly correct, but is still personal and informal. And you can have writing that is *impersonal* and *formal* but is still lively and sounds more or less like you, not stiff, awkward, and dead.

Therefore, here is our advice: Always start off writing in a way that feels comfortable for you—in a voice that feels like the right voice for you (unless you are actually trying to mimic someone else's voice). Don't worry about correctness or level of voice. *Afterwards* you can go through and do the minimal revising needed for correctness—or perhaps even for formality. If you try to start off writing in a formal voice, you will often get tangled and artificial language.

On the other hand if you really want to sound like someone different from yourself—someone with a completely different character (perhaps someone older or more formal or more authoritative), *then* it may pay to start out trying to *use* that voice from the beginning. Try to imagine and see that person in your mind's eye and hear them talk in your mind's ear. Try a bit of speaking as that person would speak. Role-play that character a bit: how would the person sit or stand or walk or hold his or her head? Try to *enter* the role and *be* the person—and then write from within that role. But you *don't* need to pretend to be someone else just to write something correct or formal.

One additional piece of advice: When it comes to correctness, formality, and voice, a great deal depends on the first few paragraphs or the opening page of a piece of writing. If you can start by establishing the voice and the level of formality that you want, many readers will not notice differences in the rest of the piece. And readers are a bit more forgiving about mistakes if the first page or two are clean. In short, if you get the beginning right, you have more leeway in what follows. Look around, for example, at formal pieces of writing (perhaps scholarly essays or business memos), and you'll see that they often establish their formality in the first page or so and then actually lapse into some real informality afterwards. When the informality is in the beginning, readers say, "This writer can't write formal prose." When the informality comes later on, many readers say, "This writer has a real facility with formal writing."

SHARING AND RESPONDING

CONTENTS

Cover Letter   SR-5

Summary of Kinds of Responses   SR-8

Procedures for Giving and Receiving Responses   SR-13

Full Explanations of Kinds of Responses—With Samples   SR-18

    1. Sharing: No Response or Responses from the Self   SR-18

    2. Pointing and Center of Gravity   SR-19

    3. Summary and Sayback   SR-22

    4. What Is Almost Said? What Do You Want to Hear More About?   SR-25

    5. Reply   SR-27

    6. Voice   SR-29

    7. Movies of the Reader's Mind   SR-31

    8. Metaphorical Descriptions   SR-38

    9. Believing and Doubting   SR-41

   10. Skeleton Feedback and Descriptive Outline   SR-44

   11. Criterion-Based Feedback   SR-50

Sample Essays   SR-57

COVER LETTER

Dear Students and Teachers,

In this *Sharing and Responding* guide we present a variety of methods for sharing your writing and getting helpful responses. First we'll give a brief overview of the methods; then we'll explain them in more detail and illustrate their use on two sample essays.

Our goal is to help you become comfortable and skilled at asking for feedback and giving it. We think this may well be the most valuable part of the *Community of Writers* workshop course, that is, the part you are most likely to use after the course is over.

 ## SUGGESTIONS FOR USING *SHARING AND RESPONDING*

There are more techniques here than you can use on any one occasion. But we want you to try them all out in order to learn the wide range of options you have for feedback. Then you will be in a position to ask for the kind of feedback that is right for you, depending on your preferences or temperament, the kind of piece you're working on, and the stage it's at. Many people don't like getting feedback on their writing because they feel they are "on the chopping block." They don't realize how many options they could ask for, and so they end up helplessly putting themselves in the hands of readers. *Sharing and Responding* will help you *take charge* of the process of getting responses.

We also urge you to try out these techniques in order. They go from quicker to more time-consuming, from easier to harder, and from safer to riskier. This progression builds a feedback situation of support and trust. Don't assume though that the later kinds of responding are *better:* some of the earliest ones remain the most useful despite being quick and easy.

 ## OUR UNDERLYING PREMISES AND CONVICTIONS

We find that most students are reluctant to judge or evaluate each other's writing and give advice about how to improve it. We think they are right. Evaluation and advice are *not* what writers need most. What writers need (and fortunately it's what all readers are best at) is *an audience:* a thoughtful, interested audience rather than evaluators or editors or advice-givers. In the long run, you will learn the most about writing from feeling the *presence of interested readers*—like feeling the pressure or weight of a fish at the end of the line. You can't trust evaluations or advice. Even experts on writing usually disagree with each other. And even when they agree about what is weak, they often disagree about how to fix it.

Therefore we urge you to follow a crucial principle for feedback: don't let anyone give you evaluation or advice unless they also give you the perceptions and reactions it is based on, that is, unless they describe *what they see* and *how they are reacting*. For example, if a reader says, "The organization is confusing in your piece," make sure she goes back and describes the sequence of parts in your piece as she sees them, and/or the sequence of her reactions as she was reading: When did she first start feeling confused, and what kind of confusion was it? What was going on in her mind and feelings at different points?

Many students have never written except in school, never given their writing to anyone but a teacher, and always gotten some kind of evaluative response. But it's hard for writers to prosper unless they give their work to a variety of readers (not just teachers) and get a variety of responses (no response, nonevaluative responses, evaluative responses). The suggestions here will give you the variety of audience relationships you need to develop a more productive sense of audience.

You will improve your writing much faster if you let us and your teacher help you build a community in your classroom: a place where people hear clearly even what is mumbled, understand what is badly written, and look for the validity even in what they disagree with. Eventually you will learn to write to the enemy—to write surrounded by sharks. But you will learn that necessary skill better if, for a while, you practice writing to allies and listening to friends.

 ## TWO PARADOXES OF RESPONDING

First paradox: the *reader* is always right; yet the *writer* is always right. That is, readers get to decide what's true about their reactions—about what they see or think or feel. It's senseless to quarrel with readers about their experience of what's happening to them (though you can ask them to explain their experience more fully).

Nevertheless, you as the writer get to decide what to *do about* any of this feedback from readers: what changes to make, if any. You don't have to follow their advice. Just listen openly and swallow it all. You can do that better if you realize that you get to take your time and make up your own mind.

Second paradox: the writer must be in charge; yet the writer must sit quietly and do nothing. As writer, you must be in control. It's your writing. Don't be passive or helpless. You get to decide what kind of feedback, if any, you need. Are you trying to improve this particular piece? Or perhaps you don't care so much about working on this piece any more but just want feedback on it to learn about your writing in general. Or perhaps you don't want to work on anything but just enjoy sharing this piece and hearing what others have to say. Don't let readers make these decisions for you. Ask for what you want and don't be afraid to stop them if they give you the wrong thing. For example, sometimes it's important to insist, "I'm still very tender about this piece. I just want to hear what it sounds like for now and not get any feedback."

Nevertheless you mostly have to sit back and just listen. If you are talking a lot, you are probably blocking good feedback. For example, don't argue if they misunderstand what you wrote. Their misunderstanding is valuable, and you need to understand it in order to see how your words function. If they want to give you feedback you didn't ask for—or not give you what you ask for—they may have good reasons. If you aren't getting honest, serious, or caring feedback, don't blame your readers. You may not have convinced them that you really want it.

 ABOUT HOW WE WROTE
SHARING AND RESPONDING

In our first drafts of the *Community of Writers* book, we put all our sharing and responding suggestions in the workshops themselves. But then we ran into a dilemma. We realized that we wanted to give students and teachers lots of choice of which workshops to use and what order to use them in. Yet we *didn't* want to give that much choice about which feedback techniques to use and which order to use them in. For it's crucial to us that you go through a progression that gives the best learning and builds the most trust. Because of this dilemma, we hit on the plan of having a separate *Sharing and Responding* guide (though we have also kept a few suggestions in each workshop).

Also, this part in the first edition of our textbook was too complicated: too many kinds of response were arranged in groupings which were too complex. We realize now that as we worked out this book for the first time, we built too much of our background thinking *into* the structure itself. Writers often speak of the principle of "scaffolding": structures put up in order to help construct the building in the first place—but which can be taken down after the building is done. We had too much scaffolding in the first edition. You'll find the same thing sometimes happens to you. You'll write something and it comes out complicated; but once you've got it written, you finally understand it better and you can then revise to make it simpler.

Peter Elbow
Patricia Belanoff

SUMMARY OF KINDS
OF RESPONSES

Here is an overview of eleven different and valuable ways of responding to writing—and a few thoughts about when each kind is valuable. We will explain them more fully later and illustrate their use on sample essays. After you have tried them out, you can glance back over this list when you want to decide which kind of feedback to request.

1. SHARING: NO RESPONSE

Read your piece aloud to listeners and ask: "Would you please just listen and enjoy?" You can also give them your text to read silently, though you don't usually learn as much this way. Simple sharing is also a way to listen better to your *own responses* to your own piece, without having to think about how others respond. You learn an enormous amount from hearing yourself read your own words—or from reading them over when you know that someone else is also reading them.

No response is valuable in many situations: when you don't have much time, at very early stages when you just want to try something out or feel very tentative, or when you are completely finished and don't plan to make any changes at all—as a form of simple communication or celebration. Sharing gives you a nonpressure setting for getting comfortable reading your words out loud and listening to the writing of others.

2. POINTING AND CENTER OF GRAVITY

Pointing: "Which words or phrases or passages somehow strike you? stick in mind? *get through?*" Center of gravity: "Which sections somehow seem important or resonant or generative?" You are not asking necessarily for the *main points* but rather for sections or passages that seem to resonate or linger in mind or be sources of energy. Sometimes a seemingly minor detail or example—even an aside or a digression—can be a center of gravity.

These quick, easy, interesting forms of response are good for timid or inexperienced responders—or for early drafts. They help you establish a sense of contact with readers. Center of gravity response is particularly interesting for showing you rich and interesting parts of your piece that you might have neglected—but which might be worth exploring and developing. Center of gravity can help you see your piece in a different light and suggest ways to make major revisions.

3. SUMMARY AND SAYBACK

Summary: "Please summarize what you have heard. Tell me what you hear as the main thing and the almost-main things." (Variations: "Give me a phrase as title and a one-word title—first using my words and then using your words.") Sayback: "Please say back to me in your own words what you hear me getting at in my piece, but say it in a somewhat questioning or tentative way—as an invitation for *me to reply* with my own restatement of what you've said."

These are both useful at any stage in the writing process in order to see whether readers "got" the points you are trying to "give." But sayback is particularly useful at early stages when you are still groping and haven't yet been able to find what you really want to say. You can read a collection of exploratory passages for sayback response. When readers say back to you what they hear—and invite you to reply—it often leads you to find exactly the words or thoughts or emphasis you were looking for.

4. WHAT IS ALMOST SAID? WHAT DO YOU WANT TO HEAR MORE ABOUT?

Just ask readers those very questions.

This kind of response is particularly useful when you need to *develop* or enrich your piece: when you sense there is more here but you haven't been able to get your finger on it yet. This kind of question gives you concrete substantive help because it leads your readers to give you some of *their ideas* to add to yours. Remember this too: what you imply but don't say in your writing is often very loud to readers but unheard by you—and has an enormous effect on how they respond.

Extreme variation: "Make a guess about what was on my mind that I *didn't* write about."

5. REPLY

Simply ask, "What are *your* thoughts about my topic? Now that you've heard what I've had to say, what do *you* have to say?"

This kind of response is useful at any point, but it is particularly useful at early stages when you haven't worked out your thinking yet. Indeed, you can ask for this kind of response even before you've written a draft; perhaps you jotted down some notes. You can just say, "I'm thinking about saying X, Y, and Z. How would you reply? What are your thoughts about this topic?" This is actually the most natural and common response to any human discourse. You are inviting a small discussion of the topic.

 ### 6. VOICE

(a) "How much voice do you hear in my writing? Is my language alive and human? Or is it dead, bureaucratic, unsayable?" (b) "*What kind* of voice(s) do you hear in my writing?" Timid? Confident? Sarcastic? Pleading?" Or "What kind of person does my writing sound like? What side(s) of me comes through in my writing? Most of all, "Do you trust the voice or person you hear in my writing?"

This kind of feedback can be useful at any stage. When people describe the voice they hear in writing, they often get right to the heart of subtle but important matters of language and approach. They don't have to be able to talk in technical terms ("You seem to use lots of passive verbs and nominalized phrases"); they can say, "You sound kind of bureaucratic and pompous and I wonder if *you* actually believe what you are saying."

 ### 7. MOVIES OF THE READER'S MIND

Ask readers to tell you honestly and in detail what is going on in their minds *as* they read your words. There are three powerful ways to help readers give you this kind of response. (a) Interrupt their reading a few times and find out what's happening at that moment. (b) Get them to tell you their reactions in the form of a *story* that takes place *in time*. (c) If they make "it-statements" ("It was confusing"), make them translate these into "I-statements" ("I felt confused starting here about . . . ").

Movies of the reader's mind make the most sense when you have a fairly developed draft and you want to know how it works on readers—rather than when you're still trying to develop your ideas. Movies are the richest and most valuable form of response, but they require that you feel some confidence in yourself and support from your reader, because when readers tell you honestly what is happening while they are reading your piece, they may tell you they don't like it or even get mad at it.

 ### 8. METAPHORICAL DESCRIPTIONS

Ask readers to describe your writing in terms of clothing (e.g., jeans, tuxedo, lycra running suit), weather (e.g., foggy, stormy, sunny, humid), animals, colors, shapes.

This kind of response is helpful at any point. It gives you a new view, a new lens; it's particularly helpful when you feel stale on a piece, perhaps because you have worked so long on it. Sometimes young or inexperienced readers are good at giving you this kind of response when they are unskilled at other kinds.

9. BELIEVING AND DOUBTING

Believing: "Try to believe everything I have written, even if you disagree or find it crazy. At least *pretend* to believe it. Be my friend and ally and give me more evidence, arguments, and ideas to help me make my case better." Doubting: "Try to doubt everything I have written, even if you love it. Take on the role of enemy and find all the arguments that can be made against me. Pretend to be someone who hates my writing. What would he or she notice?"

These forms of feedback obviously lend themselves to persuasive essays or arguments, though the believing game can help you flesh out and enrich the world of a story or poem. Believing is good when you are struggling and want help. It's a way to get readers to give you new ideas and arguments and in fact improve your piece in all sorts of ways. Doubting is good after you've gotten a piece as strong as you can get it and you want to send it out or hand it in— but first find out how hostile readers will fight you.

10. SKELETON FEEDBACK AND DESCRIPTIVE OUTLINE

Skeleton feedback: "Please lay out the reasoning you see in my paper: my main point, my subpoints, my supporting evidence, and my assumptions about my topic and about my audience." Descriptive outline: "Please write *says* and *does* sentences for my whole paper and then for each paragraph or section." A *says* sentence summarizes the meaning or message, and a *does* sentence describes the function.

These are the most useful for essays. They are feasible only if the reader has the text in hand and can take a good deal of time and care—and perhaps write out responses. Because they give you the most distance and perspective on what you have written, they are uniquely useful for giving feedback *to yourself.* Both kinds of feedback help you on late drafts when you want to test out your reasoning and organization. But skeleton feedback is also useful on early drafts when you are still trying to figure out what to say or emphasize and how to organize your thoughts.

11. CRITERION-BASED FEEDBACK

Ask readers to give you their thoughts about specific criteria that you are wondering about or struggling with: "Does this sound too technical?" "Is this section too long?" "Do my jokes work for you?" "Do you feel I've addressed the objections of people who disagree?" And of course, "Please find mistakes in spelling and grammar and typing." You can also ask readers to address what *they* think are the important criteria for your piece. You can ask too about traditional criteria for essays: focus on the assignment or task, content (ideas, reasoning, support, originality), organization, clarity of language, and voice.

You ask for criterion-based feedback when you have questions about specific aspects of your piece. You can also ask for it when you need a quick overview of strengths and weaknesses. This kind of feedback depends on skilled and experienced readers. (But even with them you should still take it with a grain of salt, for if someone says your piece is boring, other readers might well disagree. Movies of the reader's mind are more trustworthy because they give you a better picture of the personal reactions *behind* these judgments.)

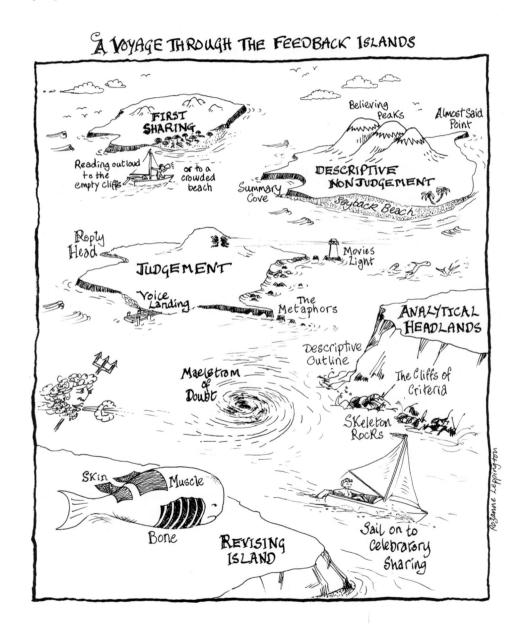

A VOYAGE THROUGH THE FEEDBACK ISLANDS

PROCEDURES FOR GIVING AND RECEIVING RESPONSES

We've briefly summarized your choices among *kinds of response*. Now we want to emphasize that you also have important choices among *procedures for getting responses*. It's important to test these out too—in order to see which ones are the most helpful for you in different situations.

EARLY OR LATE DRAFTS?

Responses are helpful on both early and late drafts: indeed, it's a big help to discuss your thinking even *before* you have written at all. (For very early drafts, these response modes are particularly helpful: pointing, center of gravity, summary, sayback, almost said, and reply.) At the other extreme, it can be helpful and interesting to get feedback even on *final drafts* that you don't plan to revise any more: you will learn about your writing and about how readers read. When poets and fiction writers give readings, the goal is pleasure and celebration, not feedback. (Keep your eye out for notices of readings by poets and writers in local schools, libraries, and bookstores. They can be fun to attend.)

PAIRS OR GROUPS?

On the one hand, the more readers the better: readers are different, and reading is a subjective act so you don't know much if you only know how one reader reacts. On the other hand, more readers take more time and you *can* learn a lot from one reader if she is a good one—if she can really tell you in detail about what she sees and what goes on in her head as she reads your words. Also it's easier to build an honest relationship of trust and support between just two people. (If you know you are working on something important and will want to get feedback at various stages, you can use your trusted readers one or two at a time.)

You can have it both ways too—getting the multiple perspectives of groups and the trust and support of pairs—by first getting brief feedback from a group and then dividing into pairs for fuller responses (or vice versa).

NEW FACES OR THE SAME OLD FACES?

If you change readers, you get variety and new perspectives. But good sharing and responding depend on a climate of safety and trust. Certain things can't occur until reader and writer have built up trust, and that takes longer than you might think. Most writers find one or two trusted readers or editors, and rely on them over and over.

SHARE OUT LOUD OR GIVE READERS COPIES ON PAPER?

The process of reading out loud brings important learning: you can feel strengths and weaknesses physically—in your mouth as you pronounce your words and in your ear as you hear them. And you can tell about the effects of your words by watching your listeners. Reading out loud is more alive. But if your piece is very long or time is short, you will need to give paper copies. Paper texts give readers more time to read closely and reflect on your writing—especially if the material is technical. Remember, however, that if listeners can't follow your piece as you read it out loud, it is probably not clear enough.

Perhaps the most efficient way to get the most feedback in the shortest time is to circulate paper copies around a group: at every moment, everyone is reading someone's paper and writing feedback. (You have the choice of whether to let readers see how previous readers responded.) But efficiency is not everything; this method is not very sociable. You can also combine the two modalities by reading your paper out loud but giving listeners a copy to follow. (Computers and photocopy machines make it easier to create multiple copies—and don't forget about good old carbon paper.)

Writers have always used the mail to share writing with readers and get responses, but electronic mail and fax machines have encouraged lots more people to "meet" across hundreds and thousands of miles. Some people use these media not just for transmitting pieces of writing and responses but even for more or less "real time" conversation about the writing.

ABOUT READING OUT LOUD

You need to read your piece twice. Otherwise listeners can't hear it well enough to give helpful responses. But if you don't want to read it twice in a row (which can feel embarrassing), there is a good solution. Have each person read once for no response; then have each person read again for response. Listeners need a bit of silence after each reading to collect their thoughts and jot down a few notes; this way no one will be too influenced later by hearing the responses of others.

Also, it can be interesting and useful to have the second reading given by someone other than the writer. This way listeners get to hear two different "versions" of the words. When someone reads a piece of writing out loud, that in itself constitutes feedback: it reveals a great deal about what the reader sees as the meaning, emphasis, implications, and voice or tone of the piece. Some critics and writers say that a set of words is not "realized" or "complete" until read out loud—that words on the page are like a play script or musical notes on a page: mere ingredients for the creation of the real thing, which is a performance.

Some writers get others to give both readings, but we think that's sad because you learn so much from reading your own words. If you feel very shy or even afraid to read your writing, that means it's even more important to do so.

 ## RESPONDING OUT LOUD OR ON PAPER?

Both modes are valuable. Spoken responses are easier to give—more casual and social. And it's interesting for responders to hear the responses of the others. Written responses can be more careful and considered, and the writer gets to take them home and ponder them while revising.

There's an easy way to combine written and spoken responding. First, all group members give copies of their paper to everyone else. Then members go home and read *all* the papers and take a few notes about their responses to each one. But each member has responsibility for giving a careful written response to only *one* paper. When the group meets for sharing responses, the person who wrote out feedback starts by reading what he wrote (and hands his written feedback to the writer), but then the others chime in and add responses on the basis of their reading and notes. This method is particularly useful if there isn't much time for group work or if the pieces of writing are somewhat long.

 ## HOW MUCH RESPONSE TO GET?

At one extreme, you'll benefit from no response at all—that is, from private writing where you get to ignore readers for a while, and from mere sharing where you get to connect with readers and feel their presence but not have to listen to their responses.

At the other extreme, it's crucial sometimes to take the time for extended and careful response—perhaps in writing—from at least one or two readers. We urge you to create some occasions where you ask a reader or two to take your paper home and write out at least two or three pages that provide these things: (a) a description of what they see (skeleton or descriptive outline, description of voice, and so forth); (b) a description of how they reacted (movies of their minds—what the words *do* to them); (c) what they see as strengths and weaknesses of your paper and suggestions for improving it. If your teacher asks for this extensive approach to feedback, she will probably ask you to write out your reactions to those responses—in particular whether you think their evaluation and advice make sense or not and why.

A middle course is to get two to four minutes of response from each reader. This won't give you the complete story of the readers' perceptions or reactions, but it will give you the most powerful thing of all: the leverage you need to *imagine what your piece of writing looks like through someone else's eyes.* Sometimes just one tiny remark is all you need to help you suddenly stop seeing your words *only* from your own point of view and start experiencing how *differently* they sound to someone else.

WAYS TO HELP RESPONSE PAIRS OR GROUPS WORK BETTER

When it comes to people working together on difficult activities (and nothing is more "difficult" than showing your own writing), there are no magic right methods. But there are some helpful rules of thumb.

First, remember that even though *you* may feel naked or vulnerable in sharing your writing, especially if it is an early draft, *readers* will be just as naked and vulnerable if they give you good feedback. To give accurate movies of the mind is a generous gift: honest readers are willing to be guinea pigs and let you see inside their heads. And this kind of honesty goes against many habits and customs of student life. Classmates won't give you this gift unless you treat them with great respect—*and* are very assertive about insisting that you really want good feedback. (As teachers, we used to shake our fingers at students who weren't giving much feedback and try to cajole them into being "more responsible responders." But that never seemed to help. We discovered we could get better results by turning back to the *writer* and saying: "Are *you* willing to put up with not getting feedback? *We* can't make them do it. Only you can.")

Try to avoid arguments—whether between responders or between writer and responder. Arguments waste time, and they make responders less willing to be honest. But most of all, you usually *benefit* from having different and unreconciled points of view about your text. Don't look for a "right answer" but for how your writing looks through different sets of eyes. And when readers disagree, that brings home the central principle here: *you* get to make up your *own* mind about how to interpret the feedback, how seriously to take it, and what changes to make, if any.

When working in groups, always make sure someone agrees to watch the time so that people at the end don't get cheated.

Spend some time talking about how the feedback process is working. Try taking a few moments now and then to write out informal answers to these questions.

- What works best in your group?
- What is not working well?
- Do you wish members were more critical of your work? Less critical?
- Which has been the most helpful to you, oral or written responses?
- Does your group work best with detailed instructions? with little guidance?

- Is there someone who always seems to take charge? or who doesn't participate much? How do you feel about this?

You can share these responses yourselves and identify problems and discuss ways to make things work better. You can make these comments anonymous if you wish by giving them to another group to read to you. Your teacher may ask for these responses and use them as a basis for full-class discussion.

 FINAL NOTE

Does this seem too complicated? All these kinds of responses and ways of giving them? (Believe it or not, we've made it simpler than in the first edition.) There is, in fact, a lot to learn if you want to get useful responses and give them. But *after* you and your friends have tried out all these techniques and built up a relationship of trust, you can make the whole feedback process become simple. You don't *have to* decide on any particular kind of feedback to ask for; you can just say, "Tell me about your responses" or "Just write me a letter." You can trust them to give you what is most valuable. But if you leave it wide open this way *before* readers have practiced all these responding techniques, you often get nothing—or even get something hurtful or harmful. It won't take you too long to try out the eleven kinds of feedback—especially since you can sometimes use more than one in one session.

FULL EXPLANATIONS
OF KINDS OF RESPONSES—
WITH SAMPLES

 ### 1. SHARING: NO RESPONSE OR RESPONSES FROM THE SELF

If you've never done freewriting before—writing without stopping and not showing your words to anyone at all—it can feel peculiar. But most people quickly find it comfortable and helpful. Similarly, if you've never done sharing before—reading your words to someone without getting any response at all—that too can feel peculiar. When you read your words aloud (or give people a copy of your writing), you probably have an urge to ask them how they *liked* it—whether they thought it was any *good.* Because all school writing is evaluated, we sometimes assume that the *point* of writing is to be evaluated. But when we speak to someone, do we immediately ask them how good our words were? No. We want a *reply,* not an evaluation. We speak because we are trying to *communicate* and connect.

With sharing we're emphasizing writing as communicating and connecting rather than performing for a judgment. You'll find that it's a relief to give your writing to others (aloud or on paper) just to communicate, just for the fun of it—just so they can hear what you have to say and learn from you. It's a relief to say (on some occasions, anyway), "The hell with whether they liked it or agree with it. I just want them to *hear* it." If you practice sharing in the right spirit, you will soon find it as natural and helpful as freewriting.

And what is the right spirit? In sharing, the goal is for writers to *give* and for listeners to *receive.* Writing is gift giving. When you give someone a gift, you don't want her to criticize; you want her to use it and enjoy it. If you happen to give someone a gift he doesn't like, do you want him to complain? No, you want him to thank you all the same.

We stress reading your words aloud here, especially at first, because you learn so much by using your mouth and ears. And there is a special psychological benefit from learning to *say* your words aloud: you get over the fear of making a *noise* with your written words. But it is also useful to share silently, by giving readers a copy of what you've written. Many teachers periodically create a class magazine. Sometimes they set this up officially with a lab fee to cover costs; sometimes they just ask everyone to bring in multiple copies of a piece. If you single-space your piece, you can often fit it on one sheet, back-

I felt good about reading my piece of writing to the response group yesterday. It was good for me to be in control, by being able to specify what kind of response I wanted to receive. One thing that frightens me as a writer reading my stuff, is that once it's out there, I'm terribly vulnerable. It is often like sharing a secret part of myself. Or like giving birth. As long as the idea stays within me, it is protected, but once it is "born," it is vulnerable. I think of getting my Shakespeare paper back from M. with the *B+* and the marks all over it. I had a very hard time starting the next paper. I didn't trust my ability. I felt the unseen censor's heavy presence. I know that his intentions were to help me to improve my writing, but my problem was to get past the roadblock of my damaged ego. . . . I can't change how the world deals with my writing, so maybe the key is in working on my own attitude toward the criticism I get.

Jo Ferrell

to-back. Also, you'll find it a pleasure to make a little magazine at the end of the course of your favorite three or four pieces of your own writing (with a nice cover), and give copies to a handful of friends and family.

We suggested earlier that as you try out different kinds of feedback, you might try out more than one kind in one session. But don't combine sharing with feedback (not at first, anyway). The whole point of sharing is to get *no* response. Even if it feels odd at first, try to notice the benefits of it.

Guidelines for the Writer Who Is Sharing Aloud

- Take a moment to look at your listeners, relax, and take a deep breath. Say a few introductory words if that helps.
- Read slowly, clearly. *Own* your writing; read it with authority even if you are not satisfied with it. Concentrate on the meaning of what you're reading. Don't worry about whether listeners like it.
- Take a pause between paragraphs. Let people interrupt to ask you to repeat or go slower, but don't let them give you any feedback. Just go on to the next person.

Guidelines for Listeners

- Your job is to receive without comment. Give no feedback of any kind.
- If the writer is racing or mumbling so you can't understand, interrupt him appreciatively but firmly, and ask him to read more slowly and clearly.
- When the writer has finished reading, thank her and go on to the next person. If there is time after everyone has read, you might want to hear the pieces again—especially the more complex ones. Or you might agree to discuss the *topics,* but don't let the discussion turn into feedback on each other's writing.

2. POINTING AND CENTER OF GRAVITY

These two kinds of feedback fit well with two readings of your piece: after the first reading, listeners can *point* to the words and phrases that struck them or seemed most memorable. This is a way of letting a writer know which bits of his writing got through or made the strongest impression.

Then after each person's second reading, listeners can tell where they sense any *centers of gravity:* spots they sense as generative centers or sources of energy in the text. They might *not* be main points. Sometimes an image, phrase, detail, or digression seems a point of special life or weight in the piece.

When you read, don't rush—even though you might feel nervous. Allow a bit of silence after each reading. Give listeners time to collect their impressions.

Why Would Anyone Want Wholly Descriptive Feedback without Criticism or Advice?

This and the next two kinds of response ("Summary and Sayback" and "What Is Almost Said?") ask for description without evaluation or suggestions. If this feels odd, consider the following reasons:

- We benefit most from feedback on *early* drafts, but it doesn't make sense to evaluate an early draft. When we put off feedback until after we've slaved over something, it's hard to revise because we've invested too much sweat and blood. Nonjudgmental feedback gives us early feedback and new ideas and simply ignores the fact that, of course, there are obvious problems in our early draft. It makes readers into allies rather than adversaries while they help us *see* our still evolving text better and give us new insights.
- Perhaps we're trying out a new kind of writing or an approach that we're weak at: we're trying to break out of the rut of what we can already do well. Or we're working on something so difficult but important that we don't want criticism yet. We just need some *perspective* on our piece. We need a reader to trust us, to trust that *we* can see faults ourselves and work through them. And frankly we also need some encouragement and support in seeing what's *right* or *strong* in the piece.
- We may want feedback from someone who is a good reader but who can only criticize. It's her only gear. We need her perceptions but not her knife. Asking for descriptive responses is a way to nudge her out of her judgmental rut.
- We often need to *give* feedback to a weak or inexperienced writer or to a writer in a rut. Often we sense that criticism and "helpful advice" are *not* what he needs. Sure, his writing has serious problems, but what he needs is encouragement and confidence. We often sense, in fact, that the very thing that's been *undermining* his writing is too much criticism: he's been clenching too hard; he's been criticizing and rewriting every phrase as he writes it—until all the energy and clarity are gone from his writing. He'll write better when he trusts himself better. Nonjudgmental feedback will help.

SAMPLES OF FEEDBACK: POINTING AND
CENTER OF GRAVITY

SR-21

Kinds of
Responses—
2. Pointing and
Center of Gravity

The sample essays will be found on page SR-57–SR-60.

"The Laundry Room"

Pointing

One Reader:

Pastel green walls
Personally the rinse cycle is my favorite
Curses the heavens
Deafening silence

Another Reader:

Laundry room. Sanger. Cycles. Downy fabric softener. Dynamic temperature. Hot, cold. Twenty-five minute journey inside my head. Does Keith really like me, or is he just using me for my mind. Another machine coming to a violent halt. (Like deafening silence at the end.) Please God let that be the man of my dreams. Closer, closer, closer. Cross my legs, sensual smile. Mr. Rogers. Draining water from the machine (I can hear it). Cannot stand my guts. Perfume, White linen. *Fifty dollars!* Shannon.

The whole bit with the guy and your comments: very vivid for me; and especially the joke about sticking it in when he wants to. Same for the little overheard conversation: very dramatic; captures my attention and interest.

Personally the rinse cycle is my favorite. Nervous anticipation—I wonder how it will come out. I'm not particularly fond of drying. Bored yet stupid and intelligent enough. I take my clothing and leave.

Center of Gravity

One Reader:

When the man comes running in
When you put the fancy perfume in and are a bit embarrassed when the girl comes in who doesn't like you

Another Reader:

Even though you only mention it briefly, the center of gravity seems to appear at the beginning of the second paragraph, when you wonder about Keith. I sense some uneasiness about your relationship, and it is echoed by the fight that the couple outside is having a few paragraphs later. I can't quite get my mind off the possibility that you're in a troubled relationship, and it seems that everything you see and hear is filtered through a feeling of anxiety coming from that relationship.

"The Greek Decision"

Pointing

One Reader:

Cherry at the top of an ice cream sundae
Swished through the nylon net

Smote us with a silver sword
Small, bone-chilling planet of Pluto

Another Reader:

Greek decision. Please consider. You. Helping out in Special Olympics. Climbing Mount Everest without a harness. God was a figment of society's imagination. Assistant treasurer. The recruiter will think I'm the cherry on a sundae. Shoot the final shot. You must now be responsible for the actions of all the members. Losing a friend. Wanting to sock the girl in the face. Weigh the positives and negatives.

Center of Gravity

One Reader:

When you were embraced by your teammates
When you were being embarrassed by the brother in front of his overweight girlfriend
When you talk about the friend you lost

Another Reader

The paragraph about basketball, and playing on a team, summarizes what fraternity life is all about, at least in the context of this essay. The ball swishing through the net is probably at the center of the bigger center of gravity; it is such a crucial, triumphant sentence that it creates a whole new dimension to everything else. The game, and the ball going through the hoop, is an analogy for the life of the fraternity member.

A Third Reader:

Addressing us directly ("you"): seriously trying to grab hold of us and making us listen and affecting our thinking.

The problems: being responsible for what others do; losing a friend; not liking a guy and wanting to punch his girl friend—especially this last bit.

 ## 3. SUMMARY AND SAYBACK

These two kinds of response are similar. Try them both and see which one feels more useful to you (or perhaps work out some combination of the two). If your piece is not too long or complex, you can get summary feedback after the first reading and sayback after the second. (If your piece is long or complex, you need two readings even for summary feedback.)

Summary is a way to find out how readers understand your words—whether your message got through. Many needless misunderstandings come about because readers are arguing about the strengths or weaknesses of someone's ideas without realizing they have different interpretations of what the piece is saying. The procedure is simple: just ask readers for a one-sentence summary, a one-phrase summary, and a one-word summary. (You can even ask for two versions of these summaries: one version that uses words from your writing and one where listeners must use their own language.) Another way to ask: "Give me a couple of titles for this piece."

Sayback (or active listening) is a simple but subtle variation. The author reads and the listener "says back" what she hears the writer "getting at." But she says it back in a slightly *open, questioning* fashion in order to *invite the writer to restate* what she means. In effect the listener is saying, "Do you mean . . . ?" so that the writer can say, "No, not quite. What I mean is . . . ." Or "Yes, but let me put it this way: . . . ." Or even—and this is pay dirt—"Yes, I *was* saying that, but *now* I want to say . . . ." Sayback helped her move past her original thinking.

In short, sayback is an invitation to the writer to find *new* words and thoughts—to *move* in her thinking. Sayback helps the writing continue to cook, bubble, percolate. It helps the writer think about what she *hasn't yet said* or even thought of.

Thus, though sayback is useful any time, it is particularly useful at an early stage in your writing when you have only written in an exploratory way and things haven't jelled yet.

Here's an important variation: *Sayback to help you figure out what you are doing.* Get your listener to tell what he senses as your *goals* (the effects you want your writing to have) and your *strategies* (how you want to achieve those effects with language). Use his guesses as a springboard to help *you* talk out your goals and strategies for this piece. The best thing for revising is to get clearer in your mind what you're trying to accomplish and what language strategies you want to use. Take plenty of time to talk and take notes.*

To the Listener Giving Sayback

- Don't worry about whether you like or don't like something: that's irrelevant here. Listen and get engaged with what you hear.
- After listening, try to sum up in a sentence or two what you feel the writer is *getting at.* For sayback, say your response in a mildly questioning tone that invites the writer to respond. Think of yourself as inviting the writer to *restate* and thereby *get closer* to what she really wants to say.

To the Writer Asking for Sayback

- Listen openly to the listener's sayback. If the listener seems to misunderstand what you have written, don't fight it. Use this misunderstanding as a spur to find new words for what you are really trying to say. The process of listening to a misunderstanding and then saying what you really mean often helps you find new key words and phrases that get right to the heart of the matter and prevent future misunderstanding.

---

*We are grateful to have learned about the use of sayback responding from Sondra Perl and Elaine Avidon of the New York City Writing Project.

Group work is really interesting now. I never liked sharing before I took this class but now I even look forward to it. English was always not one of my better subjects, especially writing anything other than letters to my friends or opinion papers. I never wanted to share my writing because I felt stupid and like I wasn't a good writer.

It's really easy to share my work now and I met great people in the class. Sharing and working together is a way to get to know people better and gives you a group of people that you can feel comfortable with and even become close friends with.

A Student

■ Don't feel stuck with what you've already written; don't defend it. Keep your mind open and receptive: think of this as help in *shifting, adjusting, refining your thinking.*

SAMPLES OF FEEDBACK: SUMMARY AND SAYBACK

"The Laundry Room"

<u>Summary</u>

One Reader:

You're telling us what happened during the period of time you were in the laundry room, what you did, what others around you did.

Another Reader:

You go in to do your laundry. You hear footsteps and think you're going to meet someone special, but you meet no one but a girl who doesn't like you, a guy who's a jerk, and overhear another jerk talking to his girl friend. But you get very involved in your own different reactions to the different stages in the laundry cycle.

A Third Reader:

Two-Phrase Summary: Around and around in the laundry room: a collage of thoughts and images
One-Word Summary: Annoyance

<u>Sayback</u>

One Reader:

You're telling me that things are different from the real world when you're in the laundry room? You think that most of the people in the dorms are unfriendly? You're saying that you're having some trouble with a man in your personal life?

Another Reader:

I hear you telling a story about the richness and drama of crummy dull reality. Am I right in hearing you imply that because you have this rich life inside your head, all these ordinary or even stupid parts of life (such as the jerks) seem interesting? I hear a strong theme of *cycles.* Things go round and round. Also a theme of fantasy: meeting fabulous men and becoming fabulously rich. But a theme that of course we'll never ever get our fantasies—but with a mood of humorous acceptance.

"The Greek Decision"

Summary

One Reader:

You're giving the pros and cons about fraternities, though you lean more to the pros. You refer to your own experience as proof.

Another Reader:

Sentence: Fraternities are a good thing, though they also present serious drawbacks. (Actually I feel you saying both things—feel a conflict between the main point at the beginning and at the end.)
    Phrase, your language: Considering the positives as well as the negatives.
    Phrase in my words: Pleasures and pains of fraternities.

Sayback

One Reader:

You're giving the reasons why you decided to become a member of a fraternity and acknowledge that all the reasons are not on one side of the argument. You talk about the social service activities of the fraternity and the feeling of belonging. You also talk about the negatives: a friend you lost as a result and a person in the fraternity you don't like.

Another Reader:

You're saying fraternities don't deserve the bad reputations they've been getting? Being in a fraternity will help me get a job? You're saying that being a fraternity member is like being on a team? You think that fraternity life requires sacrifices? You want me to join a fraternity?

 ## 4. WHAT IS ALMOST SAID? WHAT DO YOU WANT TO HEAR MORE ABOUT?

This response technique moves slightly away from what's in the text. No text can ever tell readers everything they need for understanding it; all texts assume that readers already know some of what the writer knows. Literary theorists speak of what's not there as "gaps." When readers respond to a piece of writing by telling you *what's almost said or implied,* they are telling you how they are filling in your gaps: what they feel hovering around the edges, what they feel you have assumed.

A surprisingly helpful and playful variation is to ask readers to guess what was on your mind that you *didn't* write about. This kind of feedback often gets at an undercurrent or mood or atmosphere that is only faintly present in your writing but which has an important subliminal effect on your readers.

SAMPLES OF FEEDBACK: WHAT IS ALMOST SAID?
WHAT DO YOU WANT TO HEAR MORE ABOUT?

"The Laundry Room"

What Is Almost Said?

One Reader:

That a laundry room is a little world of its own where, if you stay long enough, you'll run into just about everything

That you have big plans for yourself that don't connect directly into what you're doing at school

Another Reader:

You seem anxious about something. I can't help wondering whether it has to do with your friend, Keith. There's a current of tense uncertainty throughout your essay, and its origin is never really addressed.

A Third Reader:

Life is always going to be disappointing and dull and ordinary; I'll never get rich; guys will always be jerks. So what else is new? But I can still have fun.

What Do You Want to Hear More About?

One Reader:

I'd like to hear more of your mind wanderings and reflections on the people who come in while you're there. I guess too it would be nice to have more of a description of the place if it didn't go on too long and become boring.

Another Reader:

If I were talking to you I'd like to hear more about those almost-said feelings. But I'm not anxious to get you to put that into your writing. That is, I love how they are so faintly not-quite-said. I guess I'd enjoy hearing more about you and your love life—but again, not in *this* particular piece of writing—and how Shannon got to be mad at you. I'll bet you said something a little zinging to her. I'll bet I'd have to learn to joke back at you—so as not to feel zinged by your wit.

"The Greek Decision"

What Is Almost Said?

One Reader:

That you still have doubts about whether you made the right decision, that you have a strong need to feel you belong.

Another Reader:

I don't have any serious doubts about fraternities, but my teacher has told me that a persuasive paper always has to consider the opposite arguments, so I'm doing it here. But once I do it, I'm really surprised at how strong those drawbacks are. I wonder if I did the right thing in joining?

A Third Reader:

I actually have mixed feelings a lot of the time about my fraternity. I'm glad I'm a part of a brotherhood, but I really do regret having sacrificed my friendship with that person I mentioned. It really disturbs me a lot.

I want to fit in more than anything else. I think everyone does. In a fraternity, I can easily feel how I fit in with a group of people, which is nice. I don't like to sit around by myself or with one other person all the time; I want to be part of the gang. So far, it's working.

What Do You Want to Hear More About?

One Reader:

The loss of your friend, whether you think this is the right decision for everyone or just for you, and whether you would make the same decision today if you had it to do over again.

Another Reader:

The friendship that you lost. What kind of friendship it was, what kind of contacts existed afterwards. Did he (she?) get mad at you and not want to see you? Did you get mad at him/her for how s/he felt? Or did you just drift apart?

The incident where you wanted to punch the girl; I was bothered because you said you didn't like him, yet you wanted to punch her. Sounds kind of awful, but I'm curious whether she did things that made you mad at her.

 ## 5.   REPLY

When you ask readers to reply to what you have written, you are asking for the most human and natural kind of response. And you are also asking readers to treat your writing in the most serious way: to *engage with it* at the level of substance. In effect, you are saying, "Please take my writing and my thinking seriously enough to reply to *what* I have said—instead of ignoring or sidestepping my ideas and just talking about how clearly or well I have presented them. Reply to my text as a human, not as a helper, teacher, evaluator, or coach." When you ask for a reply, you are really inviting your listeners to enter into a discussion with you about the topic. You are thus also inviting them to leave your writing behind as they get involved in the issues themselves. Nevertheless, such a discussion can be one of the most helpful things of all for your writing. Since you are inviting a discussion, you should feel free to jump in and take full part. For this kind of feedback, you don't need to hold back and mostly listen.

SAMPLES OF FEEDBACK: REPLY

"The Laundry Room"

One Reader:

There are times in everyone's life when she (or he) has to sit somewhere and just wait—in doctors' offices, in train stations, and so forth—and it helps to pass the time if you can tune into the other people around you, make up stories about them perhaps, or just figure out what their lives might be like. It's better than just

I spent a long time writing a good draft of a memo to teachers in the writing program. I was making suggestions for an evaluation process I wanted them to use. (I wanted them to write reflectively about their teaching and visit each other's classes.) I worked out a plan very carefully and at the end I really *wanted* them to do this—realizing of course that some would not want to. The more I thought about it, the more I felt I was right. I ended up putting it very strongly: they *have* to do it.

I read my draft out loud in a staff meeting to Pat, Bruce, Jeff, Aaron, and Cindy. Wanted feedback. People were slow to bring up that final bit (that they *have* to do it), but finally Cindy brought it up bluntly as a problem. Some disagreed and said, in effect, "Yes, we've got to insist." But Bruce and Jeff thought the way I wrote it went too far—would get readers' backs up unnecessarily. (I don't want to be inflammatory," I said, and Aaron replied, "But you seem to want to make a flame.")

I wanted to defend what I wrote, but I held back; but the impulse to defend kept recurring. Finally I saw that I *could* make my point more mildly—and it would get my point across *more* effectively. I could see it was better the milder way. Finally, I ended up feeling, "That's what I *wanted* to say."

I tell the story—it came to me this morning as I woke up early—as a paradigm of how feedback can and should work; of writing as a potentially collaborative social process. That is, it now strikes me that I *needed* to write those things; I needed to punch it to them. But by having the chance to read it out loud to this surrogate audience rather than the real one—an audience with whom I felt safe—peers—I could as it were "get it said." And then listen; and finally hear.

By the end, I felt comfortable and grateful at the outcome—even though of course some little part of me still experienced it as having to "back down and "accept criticism." Yet by the end, it didn't feel like backing down and "doing it their way." By the end it was what *I* wanted to say.

In short, the process of reading a draft to a safe audience and getting feedback wasn't just a way to "fix" my draft. The main thing was that *it allowed my mind to change.* My intention ended up being different from what it had been.

Peter Elbow

frustrating yourself with being impatient. I know lots of people who write in journals when they're stuck like this, but I think it's nice just to fantasize as you did.

Another Reader:

Yes, we (I'm writing as a man) can be jerks in our dealings with women, but women sometimes bring out our best. We're struggling nowadays to re-define our ways of dealing with women—*and with ourselves.* Something important is happening between the sexes. I don't mind you ridiculing us when we are ridiculous, and zapping us when we are selfish or cruel; but please help us out too. We'll try to help you.

"The Greek Decision"

One Reader:

Yes, fraternities and sororities can make people feel as though they belong. But they're also exclusionary—often in terms of race and ethnic background, sometimes in terms of religion. And they blackball people and hurt their feelings and often the healing takes a long time. Also, usually the groups are ranked in some way: one fraternity or sorority is the best, others not so good, and down the line.

There's enough of that in our society already without adding fuel to the fire. And certainly there are plenty of groups around for students to join if they want to do some social good.

Another Reader:

I joined a fraternity when I was in college. I wanted to be in a good one. I didn't want to be left out. But once I was in, I didn't enjoy it. I didn't like the mumbo jumbo; and it felt kind of artificial—everyone pretending to be buddies; it bothered me. I quit. Later I joined with some others to make a proposal to the board of trustees to get rid of fraternities. I guess I am a negative reader of your paper—and yet, I like the fact that you are explicitly trying to address your comments to people who have negative views.

A Third Reader:

This was interesting for me to read, because I really don't know anything about fraternities. I was really surprised when you started talking about the Special Olympics—which goes against all the stereotypes of what a fraternity is.

I can't help thinking that there's no way to really understand what it's all about unless you live it. I imagine a fraternity as a large family. It seems like it would be a lot of fun, yet also quite a drag sometimes, especially when someone gets into trouble. It must be tough to be identified with a fraternity; as you say, you become responsible for others' actions. But there must be a big reward coming the other way for you to put up with all the trouble that can be involved. You certainly mapped out the benefits in your essay.

I can only wonder what it means to be so close-knit to a large number of people. I don't know if I could do it. It seems suited to you, however, even though I don't know you. I wouldn't be surprised if you consider yourself a fraternity brother, in at least some fashion, for the rest of your life.

 ## 6. VOICE

Voice is a large, rich concept that you can explore more fully in the workshop we devoted to it in the *Community of Writers* text (Workshop 15). But to get feedback about voice you can ask two questions that get at two dimensions of voice in writing: (a) "*How much* voice do you hear in my writing? Is my language alive, human, resonant? Or is it dead, bureaucratic, silent, unsayable?" (b) "*What kind* of voice or voices do you hear in my writing? Timid? Confident? Sarcastic? Whispering? Shouting? Pleading?" There are some interesting variations on the second question: "What kind of *person* does my writing sound like?" Or "What kind of person do I become in my writing?" Or "What side of me does my writing bring out?" Keep in mind that there are often *several voices* intertwined in a piece of writing. If you listen closely, you may hear someone move back and forth between being confident and uncertain, between being sincere and sarcastic. The writing may draw out the various sides of the writer. Multiple voices need not be a problem; we all have multiple voices. The issue is whether they work well together or get in each other's way. In the case of essays, it's important to ask, "Do you trust the voice or person you hear in my writing?"

Responses about the voice or voices in a piece of writing are remarkably interesting and useful. They go to the heart of what makes writing work for readers, since our response to writing is often shaped by our sense of what kind of voice we are hearing. And voice gets to the heart of how we as writers come up with words, for we often write best when we feel we are "giving voice" to our thoughts; and we often revise best when we sense that the voice doesn't sound right and change it to get closer to the voice we want. In short, our *ear* may be the most powerful organ we have for both reading and writing. But some readers need a bit of practice in learning to hear and describe the voices in writing.

Make sure, as always, that everyone's piece gets two readings—perhaps by having one read-around and then a second reading for response.

Feedback about voice lends itself particularly to what is one of the most useful forms of feedback: *rendering* or *enacting* your words. You might get a listener to do your second reading—or even two listeners to do both readings. Or get listeners to read short bits where they hear a voice. It's interesting and fun to ask readers to *bring out* the voice or voices as they read. They'll have an easier time if you are willing to invite them to exaggerate or play around a bit—to read it *as if* they were whining or arrogant or depressed, or whatever the voice suggests to them. This can lead to some parody and silliness, so you mustn't take offense. The goal is to help you *hear* the various voices and potential voices in your words. If you are willing to invite this kind of performance, it will become the most lively and *enjoyable* of all forms of feedback.

SAMPLES OF FEEDBACK: VOICE

"The Laundry Room"

One Reader:

The writer sounds like she wants to have a conversation with the reader. She feels sour about a lot of people, and isn't afraid to say it. She isn't in the greatest mood, either. The reader can tell that she is pretty annoyed as she writes this—but she's enthusiastically annoyed, and wants to let the reader in on everything that pops into her mind. Nothing seems fake about her writing. The events she describes are spontaneous and her attitudes toward them are extremely personal.

Another Reader:

How much voice? Throughout I hear a lot of voice in this piece: it isn't just "thoughts" or "ideas"—but a kind of spoken voice in your head. And you have a number of quotations here—most of them "spoken" thoughts in your head—and they are particularly alive and voiced.

What kind of voice. Now that I think about voice, I realize that your first sentence is an "essay voice": an explaining voice, talking to *us*—"making a point." But as soon as you get to the next sentence, it becomes the voice of you talking/thinking to yourself. We are overhearing. We are taking a ride or going along with you as these thoughts happen to you—everything is in the present tense. I like this kind of voice. (It makes me think you could just cut that first sentence.)

It's often a kind of inner quiet meditative voice ("entered a different world; ruled by cycles"). Your mind and feelings wander from thing to thing—your feelings about different parts of laundry. But there are these loud noises of machines. And your voice gets more pointed and zingy with other people ("it's just the cleaning lady; cannot stand my guts; acting like such a baby; if he can't stick it in when he wants to"). But then back to the calm again; then the fighting couple again. And it ends with that very quiet meditative voice.

"The Greek Decision"

One Reader:

Your voice sounds very bureaucratic in the opening sentences. As I start to read this, I feel like a computer has been programmed to say these things to me. Soon, however, your voice becomes quite personal and much more interesting. Your voice never quite becomes conversational, partly because you force all those metaphors on yourself (the cherry on the sundae, etc.) which reminds me that this is an essay that was written for a class.

The last sentence felt bizarre to me—a bureaucratic-personal hybrid that catches me off guard. It sounds like you want to be ALMOST threatening, as if you were advertising for the Marines. I can, however, imagine someone saying this and believing it.

At times you sound pleading, unsure. If I exaggerated, I'd call it whining at points. But then at other times you sound confident and solid.

Another Reader:

Your voice seems personal in many ways: open, informal, even slangy at times ("bad rap")—and you give lots of particular examples from your experience and talk about your reactions and feelings. But also, again and again, I hear what ends up being a kind of *impersonal* voice since it is a voice of popular expressions that are just "in the air"—rather than your particular voice or language (e.g., all walks of life, unique in his own little way, both sides of the fence, second to none, east, west, north, and south, reap immediate rewards, swished through the net, shriek in victory). Some of these phrases are really very colorful (e.g., smite us with a silver sword, trip to the bone chilling planet, as big as a large oil tanker, mean as a cobra). But some of them sound kind of corny (e.g., beautiful human being's face, bustling college men, climbing to the peak of Mt. Everest, cherry at the top of the sundae).

Your voice feels to me more trustworthy when you talk about the problems than when you sing the praises.

I heard your friend's voice for a moment when you talked about "neglecting our year long friendship for a bunch of superficial friendships that would be limited to partying." I liked hearing this different voice.

7. MOVIES OF THE READER'S MIND

What we need most as writers is not evaluation of the quality of our writing or advice about how to fix it, but an accurate account of what goes on inside readers' heads as they read our words. We need to learn to *feel* those readers on the other end of our line. When are they with us? When are they resisting? What kind of resistance is it—disagreement or annoyance? When are their minds wandering?

Movies of the reader's mind is the form of response that really underlies all other forms—the foundation, the mother of all feedback. After all, everything

Note: Our normal method of collaborating on the first edition was for one of us to start a unit—do a very rough draft—and give it to the other to work on. The second person would just take it over—make it his or hers—make extensive changes—especially because the first version was often still quite unformed. Then what that second person produced would go back to the first person for more revision. All this usually on disks rather than on paper.

In this way we often lost track of who started something and who "owned" a section or an idea. We pretty much drifted or fell into this method: we were in a hurry, we knew we had a lot to write, and we didn't have time or energy to "protect" everything we wrote. Most of all we trusted each other. It worked remarkably well.

But for this particular unit we proceeded differently. Peter had worked out a fairly full outline and I took on the job of writing a draft from that outline. Then, instead of Peter taking it over from there—as we normally did—he wrote marginal feedback and gave it back to me to revise. (Peter was working on a couple of other units.) Thus we drifted into a problematic arrangement for this unit: I was writing a unit which felt like "Peter's"—and getting feedback from him about how to revise what I'd written.

I'm revising according to feedback and angry. Why doesn't he write the damn thing himself if he knows so surely what he wants? It's insulting—giving it back to me to do *his* way. I can't do it. I feel as though I'm not into it, not into the ideas—just into superficial stuff, trying to make it what someone else wants it to be. I'd like to just give it back to him and say that: "Here, you have such a sure idea about what this should be, why give it to me to do? I'm not a typist." Does he think I'm inept? stupid? Maybe he's right. Maybe I'm no good at this and he's saying these things so he won't have to say that. He doesn't think "Life is unfair" is good. But I like it and I'll keep it. He wants this to be mainly a paper handed in to a professor in some other class, not an explanation for the self of something difficult. But I prefer the latter. So I kept trying to make the unit into what he wanted, while still thinking my idea was good.

But somehow (because he's a nice guy I guess) I kept on working with the suggestions. And as I wrote, I got caught up in thinking about getting students to see something two different ways: for themselves and for others. An interesting problem presented itself to me for solution. Could I make it work out that way? I began to explore, and suddenly it was *my* idea; although it wasn't suddenly—just my realization of what had happened seemed sudden. Apparently I was writing according to the feedback, and the idea became mine. I saw an interesting way to develop it, potential for the unit I hadn't seen before, ideas I had never written before. I got excited about it because it was good. Then I could write again without anger or resistance.

The feedback was gone; I really didn't look at any more of the marginal comments because they no longer mattered. I had my own way to go. I just forgot the way it had been done. When I finished up and polished it a bit, I looked back and who'd believe it! I had—on my own—come to saying almost exactly the same thing he said later on in the part of the feedback I hadn't even read. That's eerie! This must be an instance of authentically situated voice—somehow using the words and ideas of others and forging them in the furnace of my own word hoard. The ideas I got caught up with seemed to begin to write themselves out. But they also produced an interesting intellectual challenge to me. And there was something very satisfying about discovering that the two of us had been on the same wavelength—or close anyhow. His good ideas had fertilized my good ideas, and we ended up with something that was undoubtedly better than anything either of us could have done alone. It has been worth working through the anger.

Pat Belanoff

anyone might say about a text grows out of some reaction. Suppose, for example, that someone reads your essay and says she doesn't agree with your main point or doesn't like your voice in this piece. You need to ask her to back up and give you the movies of her mind that *led to* this conclusion: what did she understand your main point or your voice to be? Her movies may reveal to you that she *doesn't* disagree with you or dislike the voice; she *misunderstood* them. Therefore the cure (if you decide you want to adjust the piece for this reader) would *not* be to change your point or your voice but to make them *stronger* so that they are not misunderstood.

It's not so easy to give good movies of the mind. For example, a reader might tell you he feels your tone is too aggressive and wants you to soften it. But what were his *reactions*—the movies of his mind—that led to this reaction? Perhaps at first he can't tell you. ("I don't know. I was just bothered; that's all.") But if you ask him to try to ferret out those too-quick-to-notice reactions behind that conclusion, he might be able to tell you that he felt a bit irritated or provoked by what he thought were some sly digs you were making about people you disagree with. Once you learn what was actually happening in this reader, you can draw your own conclusions instead of just having to buy or resist his conclusion. After getting back to his reactions, you may decide that the problem was not the "digs" themselves but the slyness. You might well decide that the solution you need is not to remove or soften what he felt as sly digs but to make your disagreement with others much more frank and blunt.

Movies of a reader's mind can be confusing until you are used to them. They consist of nothing but facts or raw data, not conclusions; and the same piece of writing causes different things to happen in different minds. What you get is messy. But movies gradually help you develop your sensitivity to what your words are likely to *do* inside readers' minds.

Movies do not require experts. In fact, sometimes you get wonderfully clear and helpful movies from children or very naive readers. Sometimes sophisticated readers have a hard time getting behind their judgments and conclusions to the feelings and reactions that led to them. You need honesty and trust.

Here are some ways to help readers learn to notice and describe their reactions while reading:

- *Serialize or interrupt your text.* Read your writing to listeners one section at a time (or hand them your text one section at a time). At each interruption, get them to tell you what's going on in their heads right at that moment. These "stop-frame movies" are particularly important near the beginning of your piece—after about a paragraph—so that you can find out how your opening affects readers. In particular, you need to know whether your opening has made them resist you or go along with you. That is, readers' reactions to the rest of your piece often depend on whether they became friendly or unfriendly during the first few paragraphs. For the rest of your piece, either they are pedaling with you and helping you along—or they are dragging their heels and seeing every possible problem. If you give them a written version of your piece to read at home, persuade them to interrupt their reading at least two or three times and take a few notes of what's actually happening in their minds at the time of each interruption. This technique helps them capture their reactions "on the fly."

■ *Get their responses in story form.* Get readers to tell you their responses in the form of a story: that is, "First I felt this, then I thought that," and so on. The story form prevents them from falling into useless global generalities like "I enjoyed it" or "It was exciting" or "I was bored."

■ *Get "I-statements."* If a reader says, "You should change this word or move that paragraph," you don't know what was happening to him: was he bored, confused, or in disagreement? Get readers to tell their reactions in sentences starting with "I."

We have held off movies of the reader's mind until now—until you've tried other kinds of feedback and, we hope, developed trust in yourself and a relationship of trust and support with your readers—because movies are not always easy to listen to. If readers tell you honestly what went on as they were reading your words, you may well hear something like, "I was getting madder and madder because I felt lost—starting in the first paragraph. And I felt your voice was arrogant too, and so I wanted to quarrel with everything—even when I agreed with your actual points." It's hard to benefit from responses like that unless you feel them coming from a friend or ally.

When a reader gives you movies of reactions that are very critical, remember that she is not trying to be fair or impartial (as in "evaluating by criteria," which comes later in our sequence). She is just trying to tell you accurately what was occurring in her. She is not pretending to be God making an objective judgment. These are just *her* subjective reactions, and they might be different from those of most other readers.

Here are some other suggestions for getting movies of readers' minds:

■ Don't make apologies or explanations of your writing before they hear or read it and respond, because these will heavily influence how they react.

■ Don't quarrel with what a reader says—even if he's utterly misunderstanding what you wrote. You're not trying to educate readers about your text; you're trying to get *them* to educate *you* about your text.

■ Invite exaggeration or parody. This can be scary, but also a big help if your readers are having trouble telling you what's happening as they read or if they seem to be beating around the bush. For example, readers might feel vaguely bothered by something in your writing but be unable to explain what they feel. "It's OK," they'll say. "I pretty much liked what you wrote." But you can feel some hesitation or reservation. If you feel brave enough to invite them to *exaggerate* their reaction, they will often find words for what's going on and say something like this: "If I were to exaggerate, I'd say you are beating me over the head here." You need to feel fairly secure before you ask for exaggeration because it may lead to a strong statement. But an element of play or humor can keep things from getting too sticky. For example, another helpful question is this: "What would a *parody* of my paper look like?" They might then reply: "Well, I guess it would be a three-page soap box rant that's all one breathless sentence." You can reassure them that you know this is not an *accurate* or *fair* picture of your piece, but this distorted picture captures a *tendency* in your piece.

- Movies of the mind requires honesty from readers and reveals as much about them as about your writing. If you aren't getting honesty, perhaps you haven't convinced your readers that you really want it.

SAMPLES OF FEEDBACK: MOVIES OF THE READER'S MIND

"The Laundry Room"

One Reader:

Right from the start I sense that you're going to tell me that the laundry room was not boring. I'm not quite sure I understand how the smell of fabric softener or detergent can be calming; they get in my nose. I like the way the journey is "inside" your head like the clothes are inside the machine. I do see how the rushing sound could start someone daydreaming; that can be soothing. It's good that you're daydreaming about money and then switch your daydreams to reality with the wish that the footsteps might be some rich guy. I can almost see you there all prepared to make an impression. I wonder what the cleaning lady thought? I didn't quite understand the linking of Michael Jordan and Mr. Rogers. Is Mr. Rogers supposed to represent someone who would never interest you?

I can't imagine anyone having a personal favorite cycle on the washing machine. I smiled a bit at that. I can't quite figure whether the words you quote are said aloud or not—I guess not, because there's no one there to say them to. (What happened to Shannon?) But then perhaps you were talking to yourself. If you said these words aloud, the man might react unpleasantly. I can sort of imagine the man's behavior when he realizes others are there and have been watching his performance. I've done things like that and then realized how stupid I must look.

I can't quite understand "nervous anticipation" about what clothes are going to look like when they come out of the machine. I like the way others keep interrupting your thoughts and your description of what you're doing. That seems so realistic to me; after all, you can't really plan when others are going to break in. I didn't get a sense that you were going to go crazy; you seemed to actually be enjoying yourself in the laundry room.

Another Reader:

Boy, I'm getting bombarded with images! I like the way you switch from dreaming about the lottery to fantasizing that Michael Jordan is about to enter. I'm thrown for another loop when it turns out to be the cleaning lady. This whole essay is becoming very unpredictable, and I think this kind of randomness adds an extra vitality and spark to what you're doing.

I think the encounter with Shannon is funny. Reading about the guy who kicks his laundry machine right after reading about Shannon conveys some kind of appropriate logic. I start to feel surrounded by hostile figures as I read this entire paragraph.

I find the sentence about the guy who "can't stick it in when he wants to" extremely bitter and ill-conceived. I think the "woman/machine" phrase belongs in a psychology textbook, not here.

I can't believe that you're actually experiencing "nervous anticipation" because you don't know how your clothes are going to come out.

I think it's a little odd to end a paragraph with "now I can get out of here . . . ." while beginning the next one with "I cannot leave yet . . . ."

I think the last thought, about making money on laundry, is well-placed and effective, especially when you conclude that you would be a billionaire.

I like the last two sentences a lot. "Deafening silence" makes me stop, think and realize that I understand exactly what it means, even though it's an oxymoron. With the machine and essay stopping in the last sentence, I see myself just like you: we're both leaving the laundry room. It's a graceful way to finish, and it makes sense.

A Third Reader:

Perhaps at first I had a bit of response that said, "What a boring place to write about," but I can't remember it because really quite early—from the moment you say, "I just entered a different world"—I *enjoy* this idea of really zeroing in on this world. I am intrigued and often attracted to laundry rooms. And partly it's a literary matter: I love the idea of zeroing in on a little world and making it a universe. Makes me think of the Arnold Wesker play about a restaurant kitchen as the whole universe.

I'm confused by "dynamic temperature" for a moment—and then you explain it and I'm intrigued by that. Makes me think about swimming in a pond when you come to cold spots and warm spots.

I enjoy the way you play with me on "Does Keith really like me or is he just using me for my mind." First I read it wrong—according to the stereotype—a guy only liking a girl for her body. And then I woke up to the fact that you were saying the opposite. And when I straighten it out in my mind, I enjoy how a little untold story pops into my mind—about Keith who studies with you and keeps getting you to help him with homework and tests and helping him write papers.

I like sweet smelling soap and perfume. I enjoy your pleasure in it. I get confused about the fifty dollars. Is there fabric softener that expensive? Perhaps you're just exaggerating. Oh, I get it, I guess you are just putting in some actual perfume? Really? I never heard of it—but I like the idea—as a piece of wildness.

Gradually I realize that I'm spending more of my time thinking about the details of the laundry than the story itself. But Shannon's dirty look and the guy running in make me start reacting to the story. I get involved in his behavior and I really laugh at your witty and somewhat wicked remark about guys when they can't stick it in—the surprising link between laundry and sex. Although now that I think of it, the laundry/sex link has been there all the time: how clever. Did you realize this as you were writing?

Laundry room as scene of continual drama. I love it. Always something going on. But now I'm back to laundry. Your nervous anticipation. And I like it that you have such strong feelings about the different parts of the cycle: you like this part, and don't like that part. I guess I'm feeling now that this whole piece is about cycles. I like that. Life as cycles. Relationships; sex; laundry.

And then again a little implied story—micro drama. And again it's about guys sticking it in. I could get defensive. Do I feel I'm being attacked as a man? Is that how I am with women? I hope not, but it's a little close for comfort, yet I identify more with you—with the speaker—than with "men in general." And even though you are a little cutting in your perceptions about men, I feel a friendly kindly spirit throughout that I like: a person who enjoys living a playful fantasy life in her head. Enjoying the little dramas in one's head and in the laundry rooms of life.

And I love the ending; waking up; it's over; time to go home. I like the element of imagination and the literary. Kind of a frame for the story. The pleasure of seeing very everyday reality through a transforming lens—what is ordinary is not just ordinary. Makes me think of how *Taming of the Shrew* is really just a dream that Shakespeare puts inside the head of the guy who falls asleep at the beginning of the play and wakes up at the end. You give me the pleasure of re-seeing the ordinary and dramatic as fun and witty.

"The Greek Decision"

One Reader:

I'm turned off pretty much by the first sentence because the social scene I associate with fraternities is out-of-control machoism and too much drinking. I'm going to have to force myself to be charitable.

It's good to put this nice thing about retarded kids right at the beginning, but it looks like grabbing at straws to me, struggling to find something noble in the fraternity world. I'm unconvinced. Yes, maybe there are people from all sorts of geographical areas—but was their skin all one color? Were any of them a different religion? But it's good that the writer didn't just join unthinkingly. That makes me feel a bit more positive about the argument he's making.

Surely many organizations would give the writer the chance to be a treasurer; it's possible that the person who interviews him might have been blackballed from a fraternity and couldn't care less about the experiences gained in them. And surely students can be involved in sports without being in a fraternity. This doesn't seem like a strong argument to me.

I respond fairly positively to the writer's presentation of the negatives. I think the lesson learned as a result of one of the members being a vandal is a good one and makes me realize that a fraternity can be a kind of family. A person can be embarrassed by a family member in much the same way.

I get the sense there's more to losing the friend than the writer is saying; I feel sadness there. The friend sounds like he might have been a good friend. I get a sense that the writer is pretty vulnerable. But then I shouldn't fuss so much; I was a member of a college sorority and the sense of belonging it gave me was important. I'm just not terribly proud of that affiliation any more.

I don't believe the decision will affect anyone's life until the day they die—that's really overglorifying fraternity life. Shows me that his perspective isn't that hot. All in all, I'm a pretty hostile reader of this paper.

Another Reader:

I feel like I've heard, or read, most of the stuff in the first paragraph before. I know that fraternities are supposed to be valuable institutions, and that fraternity brothers usually disagree with those who say that the Greek system is worthless.

I wasn't really captured by the paragraph involving diversity. It seemed so general to me that I assumed it could have been a lie.

I thought the "cherry at the top of an ice cream sundae" bit was a little silly. It seemed to me that you were forcing yourself too hard to come up with a clever analogy for yourself, simply because you were writing a paper.

I found the basketball story compelling. I can remember being in a similar situation. A fraternity is a team on and off the court, and I'm glad you implied this without saying it outright.

I find that the next paragraph, about negatives, fits right in with your anecdote about basketball. I keep thinking about the fraternity as a team in this paragraph, and that makes it more effective for me.

For some reason, I found the word "sacrifice" in the third-to-last paragraph disconcerting. It's such a nasty word in some ways. I get a feeling of fatalism and inevitability from your description of losing a friend. I get the idea that you think it had to happen, and that you were powerless to stop it. I'm not talking about your actual friendship, but about the way you accounted for its end.

I found the similes in the second-to-last paragraph a bit too abundant. I also thought your description of the ogre fraternity brother and his girlfriend was a little too meanspirited and vengeful. I am, however, getting a firmer grip on your personality; the personal tone in this paragraph is a little unexpected, and more interesting at least than the brochure-like opening paragraph.

A Third Reader:

When you start speaking of problems, I feel your voice most real and convincing. I feel you *thinking* most then; or perhaps what I love is that I hear a lot of genuine *questioning*—not just being sure of yourself. I always love that—and I tend to resist writing when it seems too sure of itself. At the end, because of how strongly you speak of the negatives, I want you to reconsider your fervent loyalty and sound a bit more divided.

I get disturbed when you say you wanted to punch out your "brother's" girlfriend. Both before and after you mention that, you say how much you don't like *him*—and so I can't figure out why you want to punch her. It sounds a little violent and makes me think of the violence associated with fraternities.

 8. METAPHORICAL DESCRIPTIONS

It turns out that you can usually see a faint star better out of the corner of your eye than when you look at it directly. The same thing happens in the middle of the night when you try to see the faint luminous dial of the bedside clock: a squint from the corner of your eye usually shows you more. So too, we can often capture more of what we know about something if we talk *indirectly*—through metaphor—than if we try to say directly what we see. For metaphorical feedback, get readers to describe what you have written in some of the following terms:

Weather(s).   What is the weather of the writing? sunny? drizzling? foggy? Try noticing different weathers in different parts of the writing.

Clothing.   How has the writer "dressed" what he has to say? In faded denims? In formal dinner wear? In a carefully chosen torn T-shirt?

Shape.   Picture the shape of the piece—perhaps even in a drawing.

Color(s).   If the writing were a color, what would it be? Different colors at different spots?

Animal(s).   Ditto.

Writer-to-reader relationship.   Draw a picture or tell a story with the writer and the reader in it. See what kind of relationship seems to get implied between writer and reader.

In order to give metaphorical feedback, you must enter into the game. Don't strain or struggle for answers: just relax and say the answers that come to mind—even if you don't understand them or know why they come to mind. Some of the answers may be "off the wall," and some of the good ones will *seem* so. Just give answers and trust the connections your mind comes up with.

The writer too must listen in the same spirit of play: listen and accept and not struggle to figure out what these answers mean. The writer, like the responder, needs to trust that there is useful material in there—even if it's mixed with things that aren't so useful. An owl swallows a mouse whole and trusts her innards to sort out what is useful and what's not. You too can eat like an owl: listen in an attitude of trust that your mind will use what makes sense and ignore what does not.

There's a side benefit to this kind of feedback. It highlights an important truth for almost all feedback: that we are not looking for "right answers." We're looking for individual perceptions—ways of seeing. And it all works best if there is a spirit of play and trust.

SAMPLES OF FEEDBACK: METAPHORICAL DESCRIPTIONS

"The Laundry Room"

One Reader:

Weather.   It's waves, cycles. Calm sea, little ocean waves, interspersed with big waves, and finally ending calm.

Clothing.   It's old jeans and an old stretched tee-shirt—but it magically transforms itself into a gauzy, romantic ballet costume, and then back at the end to the jeans and shirt.

Animal.   The writing is a lazy, graceful, purring, friendly cat—but as I play with her, she shows her claws a bit and I get a tiny scratch.

Picture of writer-reader relationship.   You meet a stranger in a diner and decide to tell her about things that go on in your mind that you never tell anyone—completely openly—because you assume you'll never see her again. She's driving across country and only stopped off for coffee. You are sad but glad she's leaving.

Another Reader:

Weather(s).   Heat, humidity, dark clouds. Occasional rumbles of thunder, accentuated by violent flashes of lightning. Pounding rain at times.

Clothing.   A gray sweatshirt that feels very heavy, probably because it's a little bit wet from the rain.

Shape.

Color(s).   Dark gray and pastel green, with just a hint of light blue. These colors permeate the entire piece.

Animal(s).   A fish, swimming slowly through murky water.

Picture of writer-to-reader relationship.   The writer is yelling. We're both standing next to loud machines in the laundry room, and she's trying to tell me what's happening. She's yelling because she wants to be heard over the noise of the machines, but she's also aggravated, and would probably be yelling even if the machines were turned off.

"The Greek Decision"

One Reader:

Weather.   Cloudy, gloomy with streaks of distant thunder and lightning.

Clothing.   Casual, but a kind of studied casualness, neat and perhaps preppy.

Shape.   Square.

Color.   Sickly green, brown with streaks of red or yellow here and there.

Animal.   A woodchuck or a chimpanzee.

Writer-to-reader relationship.   Somewhat distant at the beginning; in places the voice is a bit pleading as though the writer needs me to see his point; in places the voice is more casual and story-telling-ish; then the voice goes back to the more distant one, then to story-telling again, then to distance.

Another Reader:

Clothing.   It's comfortable denims; a clean white shirt; a bright flowered tie.

Animal.   It's a skittish cat playing with catnip.

Picture of writer-reader relationship.   We start to have a conversation in the classroom. We know each other from the class, but not well. Then you say, "Come on, let's go to a bar and really talk about this." And we go and sit in a corner booth and you start telling me stories. You speak more freely. As we have drinks, you loosen up and start confiding in me more and more and start revealing your doubts.

A Third Reader:

Weather(s).   Bright sun, light wind, temperature around 75 degrees. Sometimes the clouds block out the sun for up to three minutes at a time.

Clothing.   A t-shirt with the name of the fraternity on it. It's a little bit worn, but not so much that the name of the fraternity is illegible.

Shape.

Color(s).   Bright blue, bright red, bright green.

Animal(s).   An excited dog, running up some stairs.

Picture of writer-to-reader relationship.   We're both standing in the Campus Center; you're wearing a suit. You're talking to me, over the din of the crowds, looking straight into my eyes. For all your excitement, you act very calm and reasonable.

9. BELIEVING AND DOUBTING

SR-41

Kinds of
Responses—
9. Believing
and Doubting

This kind of response zeros in on the content or ideas in your writing. It invariably gives you more ideas, more material. The obvious place to use it is on essays, but if you ask readers to play the believing and doubting game with your stories, you'll get interesting feedback too.

Believing

Simply ask readers to believe everything you have written—and then tell you what they notice as a result of believing. Even if they disagree strongly with what you have written, their job is to *pretend* to agree. In this way, they will act as your ally: they can give you *more* reasons or evidence for what you have written; they can give you different and better ways of thinking about your topic.

Doubting

Now ask readers to pretend that everything you've written is false—to find as many reasons as they can why you are wrong in what you say (or why your story doesn't make sense).

Here are some techniques that help with doubting and believing:

- Role-play. Instead of being yourself, pretend to be someone else who *does* believe or doubt the piece, and think of the things this person would see and say. It's a game; just pretend.

PROCESS BOX

Why can't I deal with this? The feedback from both of them is enormously useful, but it makes me uncomfortable and mad. I'm all stirred up. It leaves me upset and unable to sleep or relax. I think the crucial factor is that it doesn't feel like it's coming from an ally. I feel I have to fight. That's the main response: Wanting to fight them. Energized for fight. Aggression. Unable to relax. Unable to put it aside. Caught.

I guess you could call that useful. It certainly triggers a piece of my character that is strong. I'm a fighter. My intellectual life is, in a way, a fight. (Perhaps I should talk about this in the Believing essay. I'm in combat.) But it's so exhausting always to be in combat. Yes, it is energizing; it keeps one going. But is it really the best way to go? I wonder if it brings out the *best* thinking.

Thinking with my dukes up too much?

Compare the effect of this feedback with the effect of the feedback I got from Paul on the same draft. It was so energizing and comforting. But not sleepy comforting. It made me go back to my thoughts and ideas. It got me *unstuck* from the adversarial defensive mode where I'm trying to beat these guys. It sent me back into my thoughts and simply had me explore what I had to say.

The comparison casts an interesting light on the public and private dimensions of writing. Feedback from ———— and ———— keeps me fixated on *them*—on audience. I want to beat them. Paul's feedback sends me back into myself and helps me forget about audience.

Peter Elbow

- Imagine a different world where everything that the piece says is true (or false): enter into that make-believe world and tell what you see. Or tell the story of what a world would be like where everything that the piece says is true (or false).

Usually it makes the most sense to start with the believing game. So first, ask your readers to find all the possibilities and richness in what you have written: build it up before tearing it down. But if readers have trouble believing, they might need to start with the doubting game. This can get the doubting out of their system or satisfy that skeptical itch, and afterward they might find themselves freer to *enter into* a way of thinking that is foreign to them.

You don't necessarily need to get both kinds of feedback. In fact, if you are working on an early draft—or if you feel very fragile about something you have written—it can be very useful to get *only* believing responses. This is a way to ask people frankly to support and help you in making your case or imagining the world you are trying to describe. Conversely if you have a late draft that you feel confident about and are trying to prepare for a tough audience, you might ask only for doubting.

Readers will benefit from a spirit of play in giving this kind of response, and you will too as writer, especially when you are listening to the doubting response. People can get carried away with the skeptical wet-blanket game. (School trains us to doubt, not to believe.) You might hear lots of reasons why what you wrote is wrong. Taken as a game, doubting needn't bother you. What's more, this play dimension helps you take *all* feedback in the right spirit. For feedback is nothing but help in trying to see what you have written through various lenses—to see what you can't see with *your* lens.

SAMPLES OF FEEDBACK: BELIEVING AND DOUBTING

"The Laundry Room"

Believing

One Reader:

The laundry room is a place to reflect and daydream; it's hard to do homework there because you keep getting interrupted by having to put in softener and so forth. So it's best to just sit and think about what you want out of life. But, no matter where you are, the world has a way of interrupting reflections. You have several interruptions here. I think if I were in there I might also reflect on what it means to constantly be rewashing the same clothes, what it looks like to see rows of exactly alike machines and how that contrasts with the different kinds of people who come in to use them. A laundry room is not very glamorous; something goes on there that just keeps life going; the activities there maintain life: they don't change it. But, then, of course, if you met the man you eventually married there, you would be able to see that the laundry room had changed your life.

Another Reader:

The laundry room really is a different world. I can't imagine a better place for you to relate to the reader the sense that it really is a completely different environment from everywhere else.

The laundry room is exactly the kind of place where someone tries to drift off to sleep and gets interrupted by people. It's so easy to be doing something embarrassing in a university laundry room—and then to have people discover you doing these embarrassing things—because it's such an informal and unpopulated environment. You feel like you can get away with anything sometimes, because the room is usually empty.

You never know what's going to happen in that kind of place. What makes this essay so effective is its depiction of a public place, where anything might occur. Randomness is the key word here, and it is delivered in abundance. The couple fighting outside is believable, too, partly because I've heard such arguments myself while waiting in the laundry room. The laundry room in most dorms is located right off a hallway that connects with other rooms, so the sound of people talking outside, or fighting, is almost guaranteed.

Doubting

One Reader:

This entire piece is fiction. There is no way that all of this happened at once, and most of it is hopelessly exaggerated.

You did not put on a big, sensual smile before the cleaning lady entered. You only imagined that you did. If you had, the cleaning lady would have looked at you strangely, and you would have mentioned it.

The couple arguing outside the room never said anything that you claim they did. The boy never admitted to cheating on his girlfriend. Boys don't do that. Sure, they were having a fight, but it wasn't quite so clear what they were fighting about. It never is.

A person cannot be stupid and intelligent at once. The person who invented the dryer was a genius, but that person never made any money from it.

You do not account for the fact that you often study in the laundry room. Everyone does. You weren't just sitting there by yourself, thinking. You either had a friend with you, or you had some studying to do. Please be straight with your readers next time.

Another Reader:

I find myself doubting whether these things could all have happened during one visit to the laundry room—didn't anything ordinary happen there? I find it hard to believe that you would waste expensive perfume in the washing machine. I also doubt that the time would have seemed to pass that quickly. After all, most washing machines take about a half hour to get clothes clean; there wasn't a half hour of description here. And I do have a lot of trouble believing that those smells would be calming. Laundry rooms usually smell pretty bad: a damp intermixing of all kinds of smells which don't blend well together. Also laundry rooms usually aren't very attractive and not very conducive to daydreaming.

No, you can't get all that drama and meaning into this dirty, noisy little room. And your world leaves out the essential thing in the world: *actual* drama (not just observed drama)—really *connecting* with people, not just observing them.

"The Greek Decision"

Believing

One Reader:

Well, it will help to remember back to my college days. I was insecure and in need of reassurance and acceptance. The sorority gave me that. I too was an officer and it gave me one of my earliest chances to practice leadership. It also gave me the opportunity to solidify my opinions about the ways some people judged others. It made me see how superficial some of this was. And I had some good friends in the sorority with whom I had lots of fun. Members respected me. Campuses (particularly on big schools) can be very alienating. Greek organizations can give students a sense of somewhere to feel at home; this probably keeps some students from dropping out. There is a sense of family too in that there has to be some joint responsibility for maintenance of property. For many students this may be the first time they've had to clean and so forth on their own initiative rather than being pushed by parents.

Another Reader:

Yes, fraternities are an artificial structure, but they help people really live and work together in a community. That's how humans function best. We are at our worst when we are solitary and lonely. We need the safety and security of a community in order to take the risks of being most human. In groups where we pledge to help and respect each other, we can do good things for others as well. And on a college campus, we have plenty of contact with others too—so it's not too exclusive. But my loyalty to fraternities does not blind me to the genuine dangers: I insist on confronting them, not closing my eyes to them. Therefore I can work on avoiding them as much as possible. I'm not a blind fanatic.

Doubting

One Reader:

Fraternities are an excuse for underachieving students to get drunk every day. No one in a fraternity ever does anything worthwhile. You even admit to a vandalism committed by members of your own fraternity. You provide the evidence for my own argument.

There is no diversity in fraternities. You are lying. I've seen all-black fraternities, as well as all-white ones. I've never seen anything in between.

Fraternities are overloaded with people who want to make trouble. This is obviously true, since you dedicate roughly half of your essay to specific, bad fraternity members (the vandals and the "ogre"), and don't dedicate any space, at all, to specific people in the fraternity who actually engage in productive activity. You are, in essence, admitting that everyone around you is a troublemaker—but I knew that was true in the first place. The evidence in your essay betrays your own argument.

Another Reader:

You say you are a fan of fraternities and that they are a good thing, but really, you present the drawbacks more strongly than the advantages. I don't believe your main thesis. I think this ought to be an essay that expresses your uncertainty: on the one hand your pleasures in being in a fraternity and on the other hand your sense that perhaps they are a bad idea.

10. SKELETON FEEDBACK AND DESCRIPTIVE OUTLINE

In literature classes we tend to *describe* what is going on in a story, poem, or novel, rather than judge it or find mistakes. Inherent in such an approach is *respect for the text* as a way to see the text better—allowing the text to speak on its own. You will benefit from asking for the same kind of respect for your writing, and from showing that kind of respect to the writing of others. We suggest here two ways for describing a text.

Skeleton Feedback

A good way to analyze the reasoning and the structure in almost any essay is to get readers to answer the following questions:

- What do you see as the main point/claim/assertion of the whole paper?
- What are the main reasons or subsidiary points? It's fine to list them as they come—in any order.
- Taking each reason in turn, what support or evidence or examples are given for it—or could be given?
- What assumptions does the paper seem to make about the topic or issue? That is, what does the essay take for granted?
- What assumptions does the paper seem to make about the *audience*? That is, who or what kinds of readers does the writer seem to be talking to (and how are they most likely to react to the ideas in the paper)? How does the writer seem to *treat* the readers, for example, as enemies? friends? children? That is, what is the writer's stance toward the audience?
- Finally, what suggestions do you have? About the order or organization? About things to add or drop or change?

It probably makes the most sense for readers to answer these questions in writing and at leisure—with the text in hand. However, you *could* get this kind of feedback orally if you have a group that will cooperate in working out shared answers to the questions.

Descriptive Outline

This procedure (developed by Kenneth Bruffee) involves a sustained process of analyzing the *meaning* and *function* of discourse. You can't really do a descriptive outline unless you have the text in hand and take time: this is a kind of feedback that needs to be written.

The procedure is to write a *says* sentence and a *does* sentence for each paragraph or section, and then for the whole essay. A *says* sentence summarizes the meaning or message. A *does* sentence describes the *function*—what the paragraph or piece is trying to do or accomplish with readers (for example, "This paragraph introduces the topic of the essay by means of a humorous anecdote" or "This paragraph brings up an objection that some readers might feel, and then tries to answer that objection").

The key to writing *does* sentences is to keep them different from the *says* sentences—keep them from even *mentioning* the content of the paragraph. Thus, you shouldn't be able to tell from a *does* sentence whether the paragraph is talking about cars or ice cream. Here is a *does* sentence that slides into being a *says* sentence: "This paragraph gives an example of how women's liberation has affected men more than it has women." To make it a real *does* sentence, remove any mention of the ideas or content and talk only about function: "This paragraph gives an example" would do. Or perhaps better, "This paragraph gives an example designed to surprise the reader."

The power in both skeleton feedback and descriptive outlines comes from the distance and detachment they provide. Thus, they are useful for *giving yourself* feedback—particularly when you feel all tangled or caught up in your piece from having worked long and closely on it.

SAMPLES OF FEEDBACK: SKELETON FEEDBACK AND DESCRIPTIVE OUTLINE

"The Laundry Room"

Skeleton Feedback

One Reader:

Basically this is a narrative, moving from going into the laundry room, doing the various things one does to get laundry washed and dried, but recording also the thoughts and reflections that occur when the author is just waiting until the next routine needs to be done. She puts the laundry in, reflects, is interrupted by someone coming in and so forth. This pattern goes on throughout the piece which ends with reflections that the reader knows will probably be interrupted again although there is somewhat more of a sense of peace at the end, that maybe there will be time for a longer reflective period now. There is no overall assertion or explicit main point.

Descriptive Outline

One Reader:

First Paragraph
- *Says:* that the writer is going into the laundry room and will be there for 25 minutes.
- *Does:* sets the scene both physically and emotionally. Or introduces.

Second Paragraph
- *Says:* that the writer puts clothes in the washing machine and thinks about her boyfriend.
- *Does:* prepares the reader for alternate description of activities and reflection.

Third Paragraph
- *Says:* that the writer would like to be swept off her feet by someone rich and handsome.
- *Does:* makes a bit of fun of the writer's reflections; shows that she doesn't take herself too seriously.

Fourth Paragraph
- *Says:* that the writer continues with doing what she has to do to get the laundry done, but is interrupted (and embarrassed) by someone she doesn't like and by someone who gives her a chance to reflect amusingly on male behavior.
- *Does:* describes the actual world the writer is in and shows how she reacts to it.

Fifth Paragraph
- *Says:* that the writer is mostly focusing on her laundry, but that concentration is broken by voices from outside. Her calm is disappearing; she wants the job to be over.
- *Does:* the tone changes a bit.

Sixth Paragraph
- *Says:* that the writer is worrying about how her clothes will come out, but then starts to relax and daydream again. Again the daydreaming is disturbed. She's finished with her laundry.
- *Does:* returns to the point where she started and again demonstrates that the real world and the fantasy world can exist in the same place, though the real world usually wins out. Also this paragraph concludes the time sequence.

For the whole essay
- *Says:* (not actually stated): that life is outwardly dull and just going around in meaningless circles, yet it is completely absorbing if you get good at observing and fantasizing.
- *Does:* entertains; but more than that, it tries to demonstrate a surprising fact of life by actually *giving* us the experiences that would "prove" it—that is, by taking us on a journey of experience.

SR-47

Kinds of
Responses—
10. Skeleton
Feedback and
Descriptive Outline

"The Greek Decision"

Skeleton Feedback

One Reader:

Starts with a general statement about fraternities and the recognition that many don't approve of them. He presents one argument with an example, then a second argument with some back-up reasoning, then another argument with an example, then something about the fraternity and sports. Then he moves to negatives: gives one and an example, another and an example, and a third and an example. Closes with a balanced statement about the decision to join.

Another Reader:

Main Claim
Although there are some drawbacks involved, fraternity life is a valuable asset for college students.

Reasons and Support
- Fraternity members become involved in community and national services and events. (Support: Special Olympics anecdote.)
- Fraternity members can get involved with others who come from different cultures or environments. (Support: Description of diversity.)
- Members can learn about decision making. (Support: I am assistant treasurer; in charge of taxes.)
- Members are responsible for each other; they're a team. (Support: Basketball anecdote; after-effects of vandalism.)
- Someone who wants to join a fraternity has to be ready to make sacrifices or compromises. (Support: I lost touch with my friend.)
- There can be antagonism between some fraternity brothers. (Support: Hostile fraternity brother.)

Assumptions
- It is good to be part of a group or brotherhood.
- Diversity creates a productive atmosphere.

Readers and Audience
He could be talking to high school seniors, or prospective students; however, he is really only speaking to those who are already interested in joining a fraternity. No

one who really doesn't want to join one will want to read about the negative aspects of becoming a fraternity brother.

People who are already fraternity members will appreciate what he says about nearly everything. Those who find fraternities aversive will try to disagree with what he's saying, except for the parts where he admits to negative aspects.

He treats the reader nearly as an equal, but there is a feeling that he's writing for people who are slightly younger than him, with less of an idea of what they want to do in college.

A Third Reader

<u>Main Claim</u>
Fraternities are a good thing.

<u>*Main Points*</u> (as they occur) and *Support, Evidence, Examples*

- Fraternities are important for many students. You give no support at this point.
- They are often criticized. No reasons at this point—but later on, good examples.
- Fraternities do good things that often aren't recognized. You support this with an interesting personal example. But the logic is tricky here. Guys don't have to be in a fraternity to do this kind of volunteer work. However you *could* have told us that fraternities get the kinds of guys doing volunteer work who wouldn't normally do it.
- Fraternities have all sorts of people in them—not just a narrow range. No support.
- I learned about decision making and got valuable practice as assistant treasurer. Supported by interesting personal example. But I wonder whether everyone gets this kind of experience. Seems like you *could* have talked about everyone having to take part in self-governance (if that's true)—and how few people get much experience at that.
- Being in a fraternity helps me be close to fellow members—especially in sports. Supported by interesting personal example. Illustrates and convinces me of the point.
- But as a member I am held responsible for the actions of fellow members. A vivid example. Illustrates and convinces me of the point.
- Fraternities cut people off from some parts of the university population. Supported by interesting personal example. Illustrates and convinces me of the point.
- Fraternities make you associate with some people you don't like. Supported by interesting personal example. And yet the example backfires because it gives the picture of you wanting to punch out a girl just because she is the friend of someone you don't like and laughed at you and you find her unattractive. Makes you sound like a "fraternity punk."
- People better think carefully about whether to join a fraternity. This is said very clearly, and it seems a good conclusion given the strongly balanced points you were making. For some reason, I missed it on my first readings and assumed you were more gung-ho at the end than in fact you are. Was this just my bad reading or is there something about the way you make this non-gung-ho point?

<u>Assumptions</u>
- We need to be individuals; but we need to fit in.
- If we just "look at both sides of the issue" we have done enough: we don't have to figure out how they relate to each other.
- Our only choice is joining or not joining. You don't consider the possibility of "fraternal" groups or clubs other than fraternities or colleges *without* fraternities.

SR-49

Kinds of
Responses—
10. Skeleton
Feedback and
Descriptive Outline

Suggestions

I didn't realize till I did the skeleton feedback that your opening main statement (fraternities are good) is different from the closing one (you have to make up your own mind). Now I'm not sure where you really stand. I feel you have to decide which is your main point. I'd opt more for the tone of the ending one—and make the whole thing more questioning, less gung ho. Or work through the conflict more.

Descriptive Outline

One Reader:

First Paragraph

- *Says:* that many people view fraternities negatively and he wants his readers to keep an open mind and listen to what he has to say.
- *Does:* asks people to consider changing their minds about his topic.

Second Paragraph

- *Says:* that fraternities work with handicapped people.
- *Does:* appeals to readers' social conscience.

Third Paragraph

- *Says:* fraternities are made up of people from diverse backgrounds.
- *Does:* counters one of the most prevalent arguments against his subject.

Fourth Paragraph

- *Says:* discusses how a fraternity allowed him to have the sort of experience which would help him in the job market.
- *Does:* gives a bread-and-butter sort of reason for readers to see his subject favorably.

Fifth Paragraph

- *Says:* through participating in fraternity sports teams, the author felt he fit in.
- *Does:* gives another positive aspect of his topic.

Sixth Paragraph

- *Says:* how being a member of a fraternity can sometimes cause others to connect you with an undesirable member.
- *Does:* shows a negative side of his decision (although I don't think this is necessarily a negative).

Seventh Paragraph

- *Says:* that deciding to join a fraternity caused him to lose a good friend.
- *Does:* gives another negative side of his decision.

Eighth Paragraph

- *Says:* he has to associate sometimes with members he doesn't like.
- *Does:* gives another negative side of his decision.

Ninth Paragraph

- *Says:* that anyone deciding whether or not to join a fraternity should look at all sides because this is an important decision.
- *Does:* ends with a conclusion that seems more open minded or less partisan than much of the essay.

Another Reader:

For the whole essay

- *Says:* I feel a conflict of messages: fraternities are good; the problems are very serious.
- *Does:* I feel a conflict of functions: trying to persuade us to agree with you; telling us to make up our own mind.

- *Says,* first paragraph: Keep an open mind about deciding whether to join a fraternity.
- *Does,* first paragraph: Establishes the topic in an extremely general manner.

- *Says,* second paragraph: Fraternities engage in productive activities, for example, the Special Olympics.
- *Does,* second paragraph: Attempts to surprise reader and supply insight into the general topic.

- *Says,* third paragraph: The final factor that made me want to join the fraternity was diversity.
- *Does,* third paragraph: Supplies further insight into the topic.

- *Says,* fourth paragraph: The skills I have gained in decision making will help me in the job-hunting process.
- *Does,* fourth paragraph: Gives the reader an idea of my duties; uses an analogy to make a point.

- *Says,* fifth paragraph: I won a basketball game for my team.
- *Does,* fifth paragraph: Describes feelings of camaraderie. Implies that these feelings apply to the overall message.

- *Says,* sixth paragraph: Everyone is responsible for each other.
- *Does,* sixth paragraph: Addresses the negative side of the topic and explains it.

- *Says,* seventh paragraph: I had to sacrifice a friendship for my fraternity.
- *Does,* seventh paragraph: Continues the work of paragraph six; reveals some private aspects of my own character.

- *Says,* eighth paragraph: Some people in the fraternity are antagonistic.
- *Does,* eighth paragraph: Describes a confrontation; continues to address negative aspects.

- *Says,* ninth paragraph: Be careful when you decide whether or not to enter a fraternity.
- *Does,* ninth paragraph: Gives the reader a warning.

 ## 11. CRITERION-BASED FEEDBACK

You may well have been getting a bit of this kind of feedback all along. No matter what kind of response you are asking for, it's hard not to ask your readers a few questions about aspects of your writing you feel uncertain about. "I've been trying to get this complicated piece clearly organized and easy to follow. Have I succeeded for you?" "I've done a lot of cutting. Does it feel too choppy?" "I want this to be fun to read, not a chore. Have I succeeded with you?"

The piece of writing itself will suggest certain of its own criteria—usually depending on function. For example, the main job might be to *convey information*. Or as the writer, you can specify the criteria you consider most important, for example, tone or voice.

The criteria traditionally applied to essays or nonfiction or expository writing are these:

■ *Focus on task.* If the piece is written in response to an assignment, question, or task, does it squarely *address* it?

■ *Content.* Are there good ideas, interesting or original insights? Are the ideas supported with reasons, evidence, examples?

■ *Organization.* It's important to realize that even unconventional organization can be successful. The *real* questions about organization are always these: Does the *beginning* serve as a good way to bring readers in? Do the *middle parts* lead readers successfully where they need to go? Does the *ending* give a satisfying sense of completion or closure? Notice, for example, that many successful essays begin with an anecdote or example such that readers don't even know what the essay will be about, much less what it will be saying. The opening is successful because the anecdote *works* to get readers involved—such that they don't mind not knowing where they are going.

■ *Coherence among sentences.* Do sentences seem to follow satisfactorily from each other?

■ *Clarity of language.*

■ *Voice.* What is the voice or persona—and the stance toward the reader—and do they work well?

■ *Mechanics.* Spelling, grammar, punctuation; proofreading.

The criteria that are traditionally applied to *imaginative writing,* such as fiction or narrative, are these:

■ *Plot.* Is it a believable, interesting, or meaningful story?

■ *Character.* Do we find characters real or interesting?

■ *Description, vividness of details.* Do we *experience* what's there?

■ *Language.* Not just "Is it clear?" but "Is it alive and resonant with meaning—perhaps through imagery and metaphor?"

■ *Meaning; "So what?"* Is there a meaning or impact that makes the piece seem important or resonant?

Specifying Criteria Helps in Giving Feedback to Yourself

Criteria give you a kind of leverage or perspective, and help focus your attention on things you might otherwise miss when you read over what you've written. Before reading over a draft, you can pause and consciously ask yourself, "What criteria are the most important for this piece of writing?" or "What features of writing do I especially need to be careful about?" This will help you see more.

To Readers

You can make your criterion-based responses more valuable in two ways:
- Be specific: point to particular passages and words which lead you to the judgments you make.
- Be honest and try to give the writer the movies of your mind that lie *behind* these judgments. That is, what *reactions in you* led to these judgments? For example, if you felt the organization was poor, were you actually feeling lost as you read, or just somewhat distracted or merely disapproving?

SAMPLES OF FEEDBACK: CRITERION-BASED FEEDBACK

"The Laundry Room"

One Reader:

- *Plot.* Believable and interesting. The only place where I had trouble was where you said when the machine stopped that you could get out of there and then in the very next paragraph you said you couldn't leave. That didn't flow well for me.
- *Character.* The writer's character comes across as strong and believable. She has a good sense of herself and an active, inquiring mind that makes the best of a situation. She is also a bit of a romantic dreamer.
- *Description.* I could use a bit more here; I'd like to see the laundry room better. I do like the use of smell though and the description of the room as being half hot and half cold. That sort of sets me up for the alternations you make between reality and daydreaming. I don't think I want descriptions of the people who come in and out though. They seem mostly important as objects to reflect on. Though it might be interesting to see Shannon a bit better, especially if you were a bit unpleasant in describing her.
- *Language.* Mostly the language works well for me. "She cannot stand my guts" seemed a little slangy to me, but I have no suggestion for changing it. Perhaps it's because "guts" is such a strong word. Also I was a bit startled by the word "beast" in reference to the cleaning lady. It seemed a bit nasty. I liked the idea of comparing the journey inside your head with the spinning of the washing machines. I liked "defensively" to describe the man leaving—it seemed like just the right word. And I like "deafening silence": an oxymoron.
- *Meaning.* I see this as a slice-of-life vignette. It helps me understand that life is always equally everywhere if you keep your eyes open and have an inquiring mind. It even makes me think that someone could write a whole book just about what goes on in a laundry room. For me the "so what" is that whether life is boring or exciting has much more to do with the inside of a person's head than with where she (or he) actually is physically.

Another Reader:

- *Description.* Good. Many descriptions are just adequate while a few—like "deafening silence"—really surprise.
- *Sense of the writer.* Very good. I feel very much in touch with the writer, and her attitudes toward others. The sense of the writer is what this work conveys most successfully.
- *Language, clarity.* Okay. Sometimes quotes are put around sentences for no reason. It basically makes sense sentence by sentence, however.

- *Meaning.* Weak. There really isn't one. There's no focus. (Of course, I don't know what the assignment was.)
- *Insights, understanding.* The writer seems to understand a lot, but doesn't really want to bother with insights too much. More insight would help.
- *Mechanics.* The writer often uses commas where semicolons might be better. And it's "Michael," not "Micheal." "A lot" is two words. The writer needs to check some apostrophes too.

A Third Reader:

- *Character and voice.* They are the same thing here. I find the character—which is the voice—the consciousness—to be interesting and imaginative: it pulls me in.
- *Meaning.* I love the way there is this rich but only implied meaning: laundry room as universe; life and existence as continuous cycles; the vicissitudes of human relationships. And all in the humdrum reality of a laundry room. This is the strength of the piece.
- *Humor, wit.* A definite strength.
- *Mechanics.* A couple of times you use two quoted sentences in a row and I can't tell whether it's two people or one—and who is talking/thinking.

"The Greek Decision"

One Reader:

- *Focus on task.* The author starts by saying he knows fraternities have a bad reputation, but he wants his readers to keep an open mind about them. I have a little trouble with this because he obviously thinks fraternities have more good than bad (after all, he joined), but by the end he's just saying people should weigh both sides.
- *Content.* I'm not sure I see any original insights here. Before the author revises, he might want to talk about the subject more and see if he can come up with less obvious good and bad points.
- *Organization.* The organization seems pretty good; each paragraph deals with either one reason against or one reason for. The author might (since he starts off on a kind of negative note) want to think about whether or not putting the negatives first might be more effective—in other words, get the negatives out of the way and end on a more positive note.
- *Coherence among sentences.* The sentences flow well.
- *Clarity of language.* I understood everything. Some of the metaphors are a bit shocking ("climbing to the peak of mount Everest without a harness on," "smite us with a silver sword"); I'm not sure they worked too well with me as they seemed too extreme for the ideas they were connected to.
- *Voice.* I do have some problems here because the voice is fairly formal right at the beginning and at several places in the body of the paper and again at the end, but in other places it becomes folksy sounding. Sometimes the voice is sort of whining and pleading; other times it seems more sure of itself. In the part describing the basketball game, it becomes a little bit too informal for me. I find it difficult to take that part seriously.
- *Mechanics.* Pretty good, but I notice some problems with apostrophes.

Another Reader:

- *Focus on task.* Excellent. You do not waver from your original purpose, which is to explicate the pros and cons of joining a fraternity.
- *Content.* Your understanding of the subject is abundant. You know what a fraternity is all about. Your reasoning, while not particularly weak, depends on your subjective point of view. There is very little irreducible logic here, but the subject is probably not suited to that.
- *Clarity.* The visual analogies are a little too clear.
- *Organization.* The first paragraph is very weak because it has no focus. I could start with the second paragraph, describing the benefits of being in a fraternity, and know exactly what I'm reading about. Your argument is weakened when you save all the negative aspects for the end; the reader will be thinking about the drawbacks involved in fraternity life. The structure, overall, basically makes sense, with examples to back up your main claim.
- *Sense of the writer.* Your enthusiasm is contagious. It becomes a little bit over-done when you use metaphors (sundae, Pluto, cobra) that I can't believe you would really use in regular speech.

Extended Response: Selecting and Blending Types of Feedback

Now that you and your classmates have practiced all these kinds of feedback, you should be able to choose which to use whenever you respond. Not all of these kinds are equally useful for all pieces of writing. Nor is it necessarily useful to keep the varieties separate, as we've asked you to do so far.

We suggest that now you practice giving each other extended written responses using whatever types of feedback seem right for the paper you're reading. Following are samples of this extended sort of feedback.

LETTERS AS FEEDBACK

"The Laundry Room"

Dear Ngozi:

I just finished reading your essay "The Laundry Room"; I really liked it. What it made me realize is that there are all these pieces of time in life when you just have to sit and wait for some reason. Time will pass much faster if you can get involved in the surroundings, be observant.

I like when you talk about "the cycles of the washing machine" because it made me think of life-cycles, particularly the alternation between busy and not-busy periods. It also fits in well with the alternation of your mental activity which you give details of: first daydreaming, then observing and commenting on actual events, then back to daydreaming and so forth.

I didn't particularly like the word "beast" in reference to the cleaning lady; it seemed a bit mean and insensitive. But I loved your reaction to the arrival of Shannon and the scene with the guy kicking the machine. There you seemed to have a good sense of yourself and others: what makes you and them tick. I particularly liked how you could tell a little joke on yourself.

I did have some problem at the beginning of the last paragraph because you had just told me you could get out of the laundry room and then you tell me you have to stay. That didn't flow well for me.

And I liked your ending.

Pat Belanoff

"The Greek Decision"

Dear Jeremy:

These are a few thoughts about your essay which I just finished reading. I hope they'll help as you're revising it into a final draft.

In truth, I don't know how good a reader I am for your piece since I'm not much of a believer in fraternities and sororities. You did give some good reasons though which I think you could build up a bit more: when you talk about your experience as treasurer, you might want to add something about how you have to work closely with others in something approaching what the business world is like. I think the metaphor you use there (the "cherry at the top of an ice cream sundae") trivializes what you are saying and doesn't really fit since the cherry is just something added that's nice. It's not really anything of substance.

And when you talk about the guy in the fraternity you didn't like, you might want to add something about how getting along with unpleasant people is something everyone has to learn and when the unpleasant person is a member of your fraternity you have to find some way to deal with him because you can't just walk away.

You speak of having to deal with being connected to someone bad (the thief), but I think that's both a negative and a positive. You might be considered undesirable by some because you are in the same fraternity; on the other hand, the situation forces you to assert yourself more to make people realize who *you* are. That could be seen as character building.

I like the fact that you don't preach at me and don't hit me over the head with the positives you see in fraternity life. That does make me more ready to listen to you. But I do think you might want to look at your focus more closely. Part of the essay seems directed to the topic "Why a Fraternity Has Been Good for Me" and part of it seems directed to the topic "Being Open-Minded about Whether or Not to Join a Fraternity." I wasn't sure which point was your central focus.

I'm curious about the friend you lost; it seems to me that bothers you more than you say. Maybe you could strengthen that part of your essay.

Pat Belanoff

EXTENDED WRITTEN FEEDBACK (by another reader)

"The Laundry Room"

What I see here is a little story or meditation about all the things that happen to you during a short stay in the laundry room. It's all in a small place: in the room; in your head. An ordinary mundane crummy place. But full of the richness and drama of life. I see you very subtly implying lots of interesting themes: life as a cycle; cycles of washing, rinsing, perfuming, drying; cycles of human relationships—falling in love, having fights; getting dirty, getting clean; cycles of going back and forth between going inside your head (meditating on the cycles of washing machines) and coming out of your head and watching human dramas. Also there's the theme that life *is* kind of crummy and ordinary—but that one can make it interesting by looking at it with amused detachment.

I enjoy being pulled into your world. I definitely get pulled back and forth very much between being interested in how the washing machine "story" is going (the mystical cycles of reality) and interested in the human dramas.

I get quite interested in the way the paper digs at men and how they treat women. I feel this works well: subtle but pointed.

Suggestions for revising? There were two places that somehow didn't work as well—didn't get me to identify: where you imagine Michael Jordan walking in and where you imagine getting rich. Is it that these were slightly corny? Or could they have been handled better? Most of what you have is very subtle—and these places seem more heavy-handed and obvious—too much like an obvious move in a TV show.

"The Greek Decision"

What I see is someone starting out being enthusiastic about fraternities. Then you consider the difficulties, and you seem to get in touch with some powerful reasons and experience—and I feel your writing and language stronger. And you end up with a less enthusiastic mood or point of view.

I get attracted by your strong, direct, open voice starting at the end of the first paragraph. But then bothered by your being a bit too gung-ho and cheery. But then I am attracted by your serious exploration of the difficulties—the sense that you are not just going through the motions of "considering the opponent's point of view"—but really *feeling* those objections. And I like the open, non-pushy way you end. Though in fact, I am left hungry because I want to hear you think more about what *you* make of this interesting mix of advantages and disadvantages. A bit of a cop out ending.

When you revise, figure out how to handle the business of the guy and his girl friend. You let yourself "blurt" something that works against you.

Suggestions. You will get help in revising as you notice the gradual change in your thinking or mood or emphasis over the course of the essay. The obvious thing would be to make the whole paper reflect your final position that is more even-handed. But another option would be to *build in the change* to the very paper. Allow the paper actually to tell the story of how you are being forced to reconsider your enthusiasm. Let the paper be a bit of an open, conscious story of your exploring. This would make it dramatic.

SAMPLE ESSAYS

 "THE LAUNDRY ROOM" BY NGOZI EFOBI*

At first glance a laundry room might seem an insignificant or even a boring place to be. As I step into the laundry room in Sanger, it feels as if I have just entered a different world—a world where I am ruled by the cycles of the washing machine and not by my wrist watch. My body becomes one with the pastel green walls. I suddenly feel calm because each breath that I take is filled with a potent smell of Downy fabric softener or some equally capturing smell like detergent. The dynamic temperature in the room keeps my body alert. One side of the room is hot because of the dryer, while the other side is a little on the cold side because of the washing machines. After my body learns to adjust to the temperatures, I can begin my twenty-five minute journey inside my head.

As I prepare to load the washing machine, my mind begins to wander: "Does Keith really like me, or is he just using me for my mind?" Then I am forced back to reality by the sound of another washing machine coming to a violent halt. I have finished putting my clothing in, now I add the detergent. I set the washer for a permanent press cold water wash, then I take a seat.

As the washing machine fills itself with water, the rushing sound starts me drifting away again. As I begin to dream about all of the money I am going to win in the lottery, I am rudely interrupted by footsteps. "Please God let that be the man of my dreams, tall dark and rich." I am anxiously awaiting the entrance of Micheal Jordan. The footsteps are getting closer, closer, closer, I sit up and cross my legs. I put a big sensual smile on my face; then he enters. I do not know who that beast is, but it is a far cry from Micheal Jordan or even Mr. Rogers. It is the cleaning lady.

The machine is now in the automatic cool down cycle. This cycle is identified by the sound of water draining from the machine. The machine stops for about two minutes, then starts again. It is now time for the rinse cycle. Personally the rinse cycle is my favorite because I get to add sweet smelling perfume to the water. Today, I think that I will add White Linen perfume. Just as I start adding some perfume to the wash, who comes in? Shannon, a girl who

---

*Both of these essays are mid-process drafts ready for final revising.

cannot stand my guts. Shannon thinks that I am conceited. It is just my luck that she walks in when I am doing a silly thing, like putting fifty dollar perfume into my wash. Shannon gives me a dirty look, and I shoot a cold look back her way. All of a sudden a guy comes running into the laundry room hysterically, ready to add the fabric softener. He realizes that he has just missed the rinse cycle by about two minutes; he throws a fit. First he vociferously curses the heavens, then he kicks the machine three times. "Look at that, a big grown up man acting like such a baby." "That is so much like a guy, if he can't stick it in when he wants to, then that means that there is something wrong with the woman/machine." When he finally realizes that he is not alone, he defensively picks up his fabric softener and leaves.

By now, the calm feeling that I had in the beginning is slowly being replaced by nervous anticipation. "I wonder how my clothing is going to come out." "I have been in this laundry room long enough." The spin cycle finally begins. Only five more minutes, then I can leave. The silence in the room is broken by the sound of a couple fighting outside. Did these people think that they were alone, or did they want the entire world to be in their business? "How could you do that to me," she asked. "Maria, I am sorry but I was lonely; she was not that good anyway." Wow, this guy had alot of nerve; was he kidding, or did I just miss something? Thank God my machine stopped; now I can get out of here before I go crazy.

I cannot leave yet because now I have to put my clothing into the dryer. I am not particularly fond of drying my clothing in the machine because they never come out quite the same as they went in. If I am not careful my size nine jeans will come out of the dryer as a size two. I put my clothing in and relax. I start to wonder about who invented the dryer. Who was so bored yet stupid and intelligent enough to think up something like a box that blows hot air and spins? "Why could'nt I have come up with that?" I would have made so much money! Think about it: at seventy five cents a load, and about ten thousand students per college, each doing an average of eighteen loads a semester . . . I would be a billionaire. I am shoved back into my world by the deafening silence. The machine has stopped; I take my clothing out and leave.

Process Writing for "The Laundry Room"

I never imagined that putting together a story could be so hard. It was very difficult for me to write a narrative piece because of the confusion of the voice and who is speaking. In my first draft, my teacher told me that I was jumping in and out of a narrative and that I should try to keep things more organized. My group in class told me that I should make my piece a little clearer. They suggested that I tell the story in the first person: this was good advice. I followed their suggestions and found that it made my task a little easier.

I liked my idea about using a laundry room; it was very original. I actually wrote my paper in a laundry room because if I tried to remember everything that I was thinking and doing and then attempted to write it down at a later time, it would be very difficult if not impossible to recall. I worked very hard on this paper and enjoyed writing it too, even though I felt like giving up at times.

Fraternities supply the social life for many students in the United States. For more than a century they have been home to numerous amounts of bustling college men. Over the years many people have looked at fraternity people as a real nuisance. Many people who have been in the gray area whether to get involved have been shunned away because of the way the Greek area is perceived in the community. When looking into the social scene at a university you must make a concerted effort to examine the fraternity system. When making the decision whether to get involved or not, please consider the positives as well as the negatives. Keeping an open mind and listening may give you a better sense of what the Greek area is actually about.

Fraternities have gotten a bad rap over the many years of their existence. In reality, a fraternity does many things which they don't get any credit for. While I was a brother at the Pike chapter in Colorado, the brotherhood worked with the Special Olympics on an annual basis. We would work with mentally handicapped people at a local ski resort, helping them race through gates on the mountain. The feeling you get when helping a person with a handicap is like climbing to the peak of mount Everest without a harness on. The look on these beautiful human beings' faces when they finished the ski race was second to none. Being involved in the fraternity system has allowed me to get involved in events such as working with these people.

While pledging Pike two years ago, I was unsure if I really wanted to be associated with the system. I thought that if I joined I would be giving up on finding friends that were diverse. What I found out was that a fraternity has people from all walks of life. There were people from the east, west, north and south, and all were somewhat different in their individual way. There were people who believed in God and others who felt that God was a figment of society's imagination. There are many other things that made each person unique in his own little way. This was the deciding factor that pushed me to the house because I could have my own identity and I could still get involved.

Being active in the fraternity has allowed me to gain some very important knowledge about decision making. I am the assistant treasurer and in charge of the taxes for the Theta Mu chapter and its employees. This will give me something to make the recruiter want to hire me when I am applying for a job. The recruiter will think that I am the cherry at the top of an ice cream sundae and will hire me over another less qualified individual. There are many great opportunities to get ahead in the future by actively working for the house, today. Working for the house will reap immediate rewards because results will be seen as soon as the work is completed. Chipping in to get a goal accomplished will help you in group decision making in the future.

Since moving to the University of Massachusetts I have been involved in sports through the fraternity. This has allowed me to get close to some guys that I may have never come in contact with, otherwise. When playing in a tight game, my brothers and I had to work as a team to win. They selected me to shoot the final shot to win the game. My heart went into my throat, but I wasn't going to let my team down. When the shot went up, the only thing I could think of was what if I missed and the other team was victorious. When the shot finally swished through the nylon net I let out a shriek in victory as my teammates embraced me, giving me the feeling that I fit in. These types of stories remind me about how positive a fraternity setting can be.

The negatives that are associated with a fraternity are very real and must be factored in when choosing whether or not to join. When joining a house you must now be responsible for the actions of all the members. A member of my house was arrested for vandalism a few years ago leaving the reputation that our whole house was a bunch of punks and anytime we mentioned that we were members, people wanted to smite us with a silver sword. The members must work very hard to regain the confidence in the community due to the actions of just one member.

Fraternities can be very diverse in the make up of a single house, but in joining a house you are cutting up the university population and entering into only one piece of the pie. Joining Pike opened up many doors for me, but I lost a very important relationship due to my association with the Greek system. My friend felt that I was neglecting our year long friendship for a bunch of superficial friendships that would only be limited to partying. You must sacrifice something in order to gain something else if that something else is more important to you. I'm not saying that I am glad about losing this friend, but it is a choice I had to make.

The relationships formed in the fraternity are not always peaches and cream like some outsiders perceive. Of course, you join a fraternity because you like the brotherhood, but there are always certain individuals who you would like to see take an eternal trip to the small, bone chilling planet of Pluto. When I was a pledge at the house at the University of Colorado there was a brother who was as big as a large oil tanker and as mean as a cobra. He would always go out of his way to make me look like a bumbling idiot. At parties he would call me over to where he was standing and verbally abuse me in front of his overweight girlfriend. She would laugh and all I wanted to do was sock her in her distorted face. This guy is someone that I still dislike today and if this was the individual I met first while pledging I might have decided to remain an independent. These ogres that aren't pleasant may ruin it for their fraternity and may ruin it for me, the pledge.

When making a decision whether to join the Greek system or remain independent you must weigh the positives and negatives. Once you have looked carefully at both sides of the fence, then you should make an educated decision. This decision will effect your life until the day you die.

WORKS CITED

Anderson, Sherwood. "The Book of the Grotesque." *Winesburg Ohio,* New York: Viking Penguin, 1919.

Austen, Jane. *Pride and Prejudice.* New York: Penguin, 1981.

Bacon, Francis. *Francis Bacon: A Selection of His Works.* Ed. Sidney Warhaft. Indianapolis: Odyssey,1965.

Balaban, John. "South of Pompeii the Helmsman Balked." *College English* 39 (1977): 437–441.

Barnicle, Mike. "It Beats Going Home." *Boston Globe* 5 Jan. 1993: 21.

Bashō. *A Haiku Journey: Bashō's "The Narrow Road to the Far North" and Selected Haiku.* Trans. Dorothy Britton. New York: Harper and Row, 1974.

Beck, Alan M. "The Life and Times of Shag." *Ants, Indians and Little Dinosaurs.* Ed. Alan Ternes. New York: Scribner's, 1975.

Belanoff, Pat, Betsy Rorschach, Mia Oberlink. *The Right Handbook: Grammar and Usage in Context.* 2d ed. Portsmouth, NH: Boynton Cook, 1991.

Belenky, Mary, Nancy Goldberger, Blythe Clinchy, Jill Tarule. *Women's Ways of Knowing.* New York: Basic Books, 1986. (We quote from pp. 17–18.)

Berthoff, Ann. "A Curious Triangle and the Double-Enrty Notebook, or How Theory Can Help Us Teach Reading and Writing." *The Making of Meaning: Metaphors, Models, and Maxims for Writing Teachers.* Portsmouth, NH: Boynton Cook, 1981. 41–47.

Birke, Lynda. *Women, Feminism, and Biology.* Hempstead, England: Harvester-Wheatsheaf, 1986.

Bishop, Elizabeth. "One Art." *The Complete Poems: 1927–1979.* New York: Farrar, Straus Giroux, 1982. 178

Blau, Sheridan. "Invisible Writing: Investigating Cognitive Processes in Composition." *College Composition and Communication* 34 (1983): 297–312.

Boice, Robert, and Lyle R. Cramer. Appendix to Peter Elbow's "Making Better Use of Student Evaluations of Teachers." *Profession 92.* New York: Modern Language Association, 1992: 42–48.

Britton, James, et al. *The Development of Writing Abilities, (11–18).* Urbana, IL: NCTE, 1975.

Buckley, William. "With All Deliberate Speed: What's So Bad about Writing Fast?" *New York Times* 4 Feb 1986.

Bullough, Vern L. "American Experience." *The Subordinate Sex.* Urbana: University of Illinois Press, 1973.

Burke, Kenneth. *Rhetoric of Motives.* Berkeley: University of California Press, 1950. (We quote from p. 45.)

Charen, Mona. "Aiming a Cannon at a Mosquito." *Newsday* 29 July 1992.

Chen, Bi. "Wishing in the Dark." *Shattered Reflections: An Anthology of Poetry from Independence High School, San Jose, California.* Ed. Ky Dang. San Jose: San Jose Center for Literary Arts, San Jose State University, 1991.

Cheung, Sindy. "I Am Sorrow." *Shattered Reflections: An Anthology of Poetry from Independence High School, San Jose, California.* Ed. Ky Dang. San Jose: San Jose Center for Literary Arts, San Jose State University, 1991.

Chi, Lu. "Rhymeprose on Literature: The *Wen Fu* of Lu Chi." Trans. Achilles Fang. *Harvard Journal of Asiatic Studies* 14 (1951): 527–566.

Clemens, Samuel L. *Selected Mark Twain-Howells Letters: 1872–1910.* Ed. Frederick Anderson et al. Cambridge, MA: Belknap Press, 1967. (In a Process Box in Workshop 5, we quote from pp. 102–103; in a Process Box in Workshop 15, we quote from pp. 370–371.)

———. *Adventures of Huckleberry Finn.* New York: Dodd, Mead, 1984.

Coleridge, Samuel Taylor. *Notebooks.* Ed. Kathleen Coburn. New York: Pantheon, Bollingen series, 1957.

Conrad, Joseph. Preface. *The Nigger of the Narcissus.* New York: Doubleday, 1954.

Coover, Robert. "An Interview with Robert Coover." *Anything Can Happen.* Ed. Tom LeClair and Larry McCaffery. Urbana: University of Illinois Press, 1983. 63–78.

Corbett, Edward P. J. "My Write of Passage: From the Quill Pen to the Personal Computer." *Computers and Composition* 8.1 (1990): 84–85.

Corwin, Nicholas. Letter to the editor. *New York Times* 20 July 1992; A14.

Cree Indian Naming Poems. *The Wishing Bone Cycle: Poems from the Swampy Cree Indians.* Gathered and translated by Howard A. Norman. New York: Stonehill Publishing, 1976.

Darwin, Charles. *Autobiography of Charles Darwin.* Ed. Nora Barlow. New York: Norton, 1969.

Dillard, Annie. *The Writing Life.* New York: Harper and Row, 1989.

Doctorow, E. L. "An Interview with E. L. Doctorow." *Anything Can Happen.* Ed. Tom LeClair and Larry McCaffery. Urbana: University of Illinois Press, 1983. 91–105.

Dudley, Louise P. Letter to the editor. *New York Times* 12 Oct. 1992; A18.

Dunn, Stephen. "An Interview with Stephen Dunn" by Jonathan L. Thorndike. *AWP Chronicle,* Oct./Nov. 1992: I, 14–16.

Durso, Joseph. "Knight Has a Whirlwind Week." *New York Times* 1 June 1986: 53.

Elbow, Peter, ed. *Nothing Begins with an 'N': New Investigations of Freewriting.* Carbondale: Southern Illinois University Press, 1991.

———. "Methodological Doubting and Believing: Contraries in Inquiry." *Embracing Contraries: Explorations in Learning and Teaching.* New York: Oxford University Press, 1986. 254–300.

———. *Writing with Power.* New York: Oxford University Press, 1973.

———. *Writing without Teachers.* New York: Oxford University Press, 1981.

Faludi, Susan. "Speak for Yourself." *New York Times Magazine* 26 Jan. 1992: 10.

Federman, Raymond. "An Interview with Raymond Federman." *Anything Can Happen.* Eds. Tom LeClair and Larry McCaffery. Urbana: University of Illinois Press, 1983. 126–151.

Fowler, H. W. *A Dictionary of Modern English Usage.* Oxford: Clarendon Press, 1926.

Frost, Robert. "Introduction." *A Way Out.* New York: Seven Arts Press, 1917.

"Gas Analgesia." Brochure from offices of Jack H. Weinstein and Ira H. Abel.

Gendlin, Eugene. "Experiential Phenomenology." *Phenomenology and the Social Sciences.* Ed. M. Natanson. Evanston, IL: Northwestern University Press, 1973.

———. *Focusing.* 2d ed. New York: Bantam, 1981.

Gilbert, Sandra M, and Susan Gubar. "A New World beyond Snow White." *New York Times* 1 April 1992: A25.

Gordimer, Nadine. *The Essential Gesture: Writing, Politics, Places.* Ed. Stephen Clingman. New York: Knopf, 1988.

Gosse, Edmund. "The Essay." *Encyclopaedia Britannica.* 11th ed. New York: Encyclopaedia Brittanica, 1910.

Gray, Francine du Plessix. "I Write for Revenge against Reality." *New York Times Book Review* 12 Sept. 1982: 3

Hacker, Diana. *A Writer's Reference.* 2d ed. Boston: Bedford of St. Martins, 1992.

Hailey, Arthur. *Airport.* New York: Doubleday, 1968.

Hardwick, Elizabeth. "Its Only Defense: Intelligence and Sparkle." *New York Times Book Review* 14 Sept. 1986: 1.

Hatlen, Burton. "Sonnet 3." *I Wanted to Tell You.* Orono: University of Maine, 1988. 135.

Herman, Judith, and Lisa Hirschman. *The Signs Reader.* Ed. Elizabeth Abel and Emily K. Abel. Chicago: University of Chicago Press, 1983.

Hikmet, Nazim. "Autobiography." *Selected Poetry.* New York: Persea Books, 1986.

Hoagland, Edward. "Essay: What I Think, What I Am." Letter to the editor. *New York Times, Book Review.* 27 June 1976; 35.

Hoffman Eva. *Lost in Translation: A Life in a New Language.* New York: Penguin, 1989. (Quote from pp. 275–276)

Hopkins, Gerard Manley. "Spring and Fall: To a Young Child." *Poems of Gerard Manley Hopkins.* London: Oxford University Press, 1930.

Hughes, Langston. "Sliver." *Selected Poems of Langston Hughes.* New York: Knopf, 1959: 267.

Hull, John M. *Touching the Rock: An Experience of Blindness.* New York: Pantheon, 1990.

Hyre, Meg. "Some Reflections on Not Voting in Presidential Elections." *Catholic Worker* Sept. 1992: 5.

James, William. *The Variety of Religious Experience.* New York: Penguin, 1982.

Jordan, June. "Nobody Mean More to Me than You and the Future Life of Willie Jordan." *On Call: Political Essays.* Boston: South End Press, 1985. 123–139.

Lakoff, George, and Mark Johnson. *Metaphors We Live By.* Chicago: University of Chicago Press, 1980. (We quote from pp. 3–9 and from pp. 46–49.)

Lemonick, Michael D. "What's a Short, Bald-Headed, Potbellied Guy to Do? The List of Risk Factors for Heart Disease Grows Even Longer." *Time* 8 Mar. 1993: 60.

Levensky, Mark. "A Letter." *Elementary English.* Jan. 1972: 83–84.

Lorde, Audre, "A Litany for Survival." *Black Unicorn: Poems.* New York: Norton, 1978. 31–32.

Lucretius. "The Nature of Things." Trans. F. O. Copley. New York: Norton, 1977.

McCormick, Katheryn. "Tackling Racism in the Mystery Novel." *Newsday* 1 Feb. 1993: 35.

Maclean Norman. *A River Runs Through It.* Chicago: University of Chicago Press, 1976.

Macrorie, Ken. *Searching Writing.* Rochelle Park, NJ: Hayden, 1980.

———. *Writing to Be Read.* Rochelle Park, NJ: Hayden, 1968.

Mathews, Laura. "Books." *Glamour.* May 1993.

Michener, James A. *Hawaii.* New York: Random House, 1959.

Moffett, James. "On Essaying." *Forum: Essays on Theory and Practice in the Teaching of Writing.* Ed. Patricia Stock. Portsmouth, NH: Boynton Cook, 1981.

Montaigne, Michel de. *Montaigne: Essays.* Trans. J. M. Cohen. New York: Penguin, 1959.

Moran, Charles. "Reading Like a Writer." *Vital Signs.* Ed. James. L. Collins. Portsmouth, NH: Boynton Cook, 1989. Earlier version: "Teaching Writing/Teaching Literature." *College Composition and Communication* 32 (1981): 21–30.

Moran, Kay. Editorial. *Hampshire Daily Gazette* (Northampton, MA). 11 May 1993: 6.

Murray, Donald. "The Feel of Writing—And Teaching Writing." *Reinventing the Rhetorical Tradition.* Ed. Aviva Freedman and Ian Pringle. Canadian Council of Teachers of English, 1980.

New York Daily News. Unsigned letter to the editor. 20 March 1986.

The New Yorker. "Robert Bingham (1925–1982)." 5 July 1952: 100.

Paley, Grace. "A Conversation with My Father." *Enormous Changes at the Last Minute.* New York: Knopf, 1972.

Perl, Sondra, and Nancy Wilson. "Guidelines for Composing." Appendix A. *Through Teachers' Eyes: Portraits of Writing Teachers at Work.* Portsmouth, NH: Heinemann, Boynton Cook, 1986. 165–169.

Pope, Alexander. "An Essay on Man." *Pope: Poems and Prose.* New York: Penguin, 1985.

Rich, Adrienne. "16." *Your Native Land, Your Life.* New York: Norton, 1986. 98.

Rodriguez, Richard. *Hunger of Memory.* Boston: Godine, 1981.

Safire, William. "The Take on Voice." *New York Times Magazine* 28 June 1992: 14.

Schopenhauer, Arthur. *Parerga und Paralipomena.* Excerpted in *Best Advice on How to Write.* Ed. Gorham Munson. New York: Hermitage House, 1952: 61–77.

Schultz, John. *Writing from Start to Finish.* Portsmouth, NH: Boynton Cook, 1982.

———. *Writing from Start to Finish: The 'Story Workshop' Basic Forms Rhetoric-Reader.* Portsmouth, NH: Heinemann, Boynton Cook, 1990.

———. "Story from First Impulse to Final Draft." Videotape. Portsmouth, NH: Heinemann, Boynton Cook, 1992,

Sheehy, Eugene P. *Guide to Reference Books.* Chicago: American Library Association, 1986.

Snyder, Gary "How Poetry Comes to Me." *No Nature: New and Selected Poems.* New York: Pantheon, 1992. 361.

Stafford, William. "A Way Out." *Writing the Australian Crawl.* Ann Arbor: University of Michigan Press, 1978: 17–20.

Stein, Gertrude. *Lectures in America.* New York: Random House, 1957.

Stevens, Wallace. "Thirteen Ways of Looking at a Blackbird." *Harmonium.* New York: Knopf, 1950. 158.

Stokes, Rebecca. Letter to the editor. *New York Times* 20 July 1992: A14.

Stowe, Harriet Beecher. *Uncle Tom's Cabin.* New York: Bantam, 1981.

Twain, Mark. *See* Clemens, Samuel L.

Vogel, Ludwig R. Letter to the editor. *New York Times* 1 Nov 1992.

Warren, Robert Penn. Interview. *Paris Review Interviews.* 1st Series. Ed. Malcolm Cowley. New York: Viking, 1958. 183–208.

Welty, Eudora. "A Worn Path." *A Curtain of Green and Other Stories.* New York: Harcourt Brace, 1954.

———. "Is Phoenix Jackson's Grandson Really Dead?" *The Eye of the Story: Selected Essays and Reviews by Eudora Welty.* New York: Random House, 1978.

———. *One Writer's Beginnings.* Cambridge, MA: Harvard 1984. (We quote from pp. 11–12.)

Wideman, John. "The Divisible Man." *Life* Spring 1988: 116.

Wilbur, Richard. "The Writer." *The Mind Reader.* New York: Harcourt Brace Jovanovich, 1971.

Williams, William Carlos. "How to Write" (1936). Ed. J. Laughlin. *New Directions Fiftieth Anniversary Issue.* New York: New Directions, 1986. 36–39.

Woolf, Virginia. "Sunday (Easter) 20 April." *The Diary of Virginia Woolf.* Vol. I: 1915–1919. Ed. Anne Olivier Bell. New York: Harcourt Brace, 1977.

Zinsser, William. "Writing Mathematics." *Writing to Learn.* New York: Harper and Row, 1988.

ACKNOWLEDGMENTS*

p. 2: Excerpt from *The Autobiography of Charles Darwin*, edited by Nora Barlow. Reprinted by permission of Harcourt Brace and A. D. Peters & Co., Ltd.

p. 28: "Robert Bingham (1925–1982)" from *The New Yorker,* July 5, 1982. Copyright © 1982 The New Yorker Magazine, Inc. Reprinted by permission.

p. 29: Excerpt from "The Feel of Writing—And Teaching Writing" by Donald Murray in *Reinventing the Rhetorical Tradition*, edited by Aviva Freedman and Ian Pringle (Conway, AR: L & S Books for the Canadian Council of Teachers of English and Language Arts, 1980). Copyright © by the Canadian Council of Teachers of English and Language Arts.

p. 39: Line by Bashō from *A Haiku Journey: Bashō's "The Narrow Road to the Far North" and Selected Haiku,* translated by Dorothy Britton. Copyright © 1974. Reprinted by permission of HarperCollins Publishers.

p. 55: "A Worn Path" from *A Curtain of Green and Other Stories* by Eudora Welty. Copyright 1941, renewed 1969 by Eudora Welty. Reprinted by permission of Harcourt Brace.

pp. 70, 314, 371: Excerpts by Raymond Federman, E. L. Doctorow, and Robert Coover from *Anything Can Happen,* edited by Tom LeClair and Larry McCaffery. Published by the University of Illinois Press and reprinted with their permission.

p. 101: Excerpt from "Sunday (Easter) 20 April" from *The Diary of Virginia Woolf,* Vol. I: 1915–1919, edited by Anne Olivier Bell. Copyright © 1977 by Quentin Bell and Angelica Garnett. Reprinted by permission of Harcourt Brace.

p. 101: "Guidelines for Composing" from *Through Teachers' Eyes* by Sondra Perl and Nancy Wilson. Published by Heinemann Educational Books, Inc. Used by permission of Sondra Perl.

p. 108: "Knight Has a Whirlwind Week" by Joseph Durso from *New York Times,* June 1, 1986. Copyright © 1986 The New York Times Company. Reprinted by permission.

p. 109: "A Way of Writing" by William Stafford first appeared in *Field.* Reprinted by permission of the Estate of William Stafford.

p. 119: "Experiential Phenomenology" by Eugene Gendlin, from *Phenomenology in the Social Sciences,* Vol. 1, edited by Maurice Natanson. Copyright © 1973 by Northwestern University Press. All rights reserved. Reprinted by permission of the publisher.

p. 144: "A Letter" by Mark Levensky from *Elementary English,* January 1972. Copyright 1972 by the National Council of Teachers of English. Reprinted with permission.

p. 145: Excerpt from *Lectures in America* by Gertrude Stein. Copyright 1935 and renewed 1963 by Alice B. Toklas. Reprinted by permission of Random House, Inc.

p. 146: From "Autobiography" in *Selected Poetry* by Nazim Hikmet, translated by Randy Blasing and Mutlu Konuk. Copyright © 1986 by Randy Blasing and Mutlu Konuk. Reprinted by permission of Persea Books.

p. 149: "What's a Short, Bald-Headed, Potbellied Guy to Do?" by Michael D. Lemonick from *Time,* March 8, 1993. Copyright 1993 Time, Inc. Reprinted by permission.

p. 170: "Tackling Racism in the Mystery Novel" by Kathryn McCormick from *Newsday,* February 1, 1993. Used by permission of the author, *Newsday,* and Los Angeles Times Syndicate International.

p. 193: "Drafts and Revisions of an Editorial for the *Daily Hampshire Gazette*" by Kay J. Moran. Reprinted by permission of Kay J. Moran, Editorial Page/Business Editor of the *Daily Hampshire Gazette.*

*Every attempt has been made to locate the copyright holders. Should any changes in copyright lines be necessary, please notify the publisher.

p. 328: "Aiming a Cannon at a Mosquito" by Mona Charen from *Newsday,* July 29, 1992. By permission of Mona Charen and Creators Syndicate.

p. 331: "Gas Analgesia" excerpted from a brochure in the offices of Drs. Jack H. Weinstein and Ira H. Abel.

p. 332: "With All Deliberate Speed: What's So Bad about Writing Fast?" by William F. Buckley, Jr., from *New York Times,* February 9, 1986. Copyright © 1986 by The New York Times Company. Reprinted by permission.

p. 358: "The Life and Times of Shag" by Alan M. Beck. With permission from *Natural History* (10/71). Copyright, the American Museum of Natural History 1971.

p. 361: "Writing Mathematics" from *Writing to Learn* by William Zinsser. Copyright © 1988 by William Zinsser. Reprinted by permission of HarperCollins Publishers.

p. 368, 370: Excerpts from "Thirteen Ways of Looking at a Blackbird" by Wallace Stevens from *The Collected Poems of Wallace Stevens.* Copyright 1923 and renewed 1951 by Wallace Stevens. Reprinted by permission of Alfred A. Knopf, Inc.

p. 379: "One Art" from *The Complete Poems 1927–1979* by Elizabeth Bishop. Copyright © 1979, 1983 by Alice Helen Methfessel. Reprinted by permission of Farrar, Straus & Giroux, Inc.

p. 380: Excerpt from Lu Chi, "Rhymeprose on Literature: The *Wen-Fu* of Lu Chi," translated by Achilles Fang from *Harvard Journal of Asiatic Studies* 14 (1951), 527–566. Reprinted by permission of the publisher.

p. 380: Part 16, "It's true, these last few years I've lived" from *Contradictions: Tracking Poems,* reprinted by *Your Native Land, Your Life: Poems by Adrienne Rich.*

p. 382: "The Book of the Grotesque" from *Winesburg, Ohio* by Sherwood Anderson. Introduction, Malcolm Cowley. Copyright 1919 by B. W. Huebsch. Copyright 1947 by Eleanor Copenhaver Anderson. Used by permission of Viking Penguin, a division of Penguin Books USA, Inc.

p. 384: Excerpts from *Metaphors We Live By* by George Lakoff and Mark Johnson, pp. 3–9, 46, 49. Reprinted by permission of The University of Chicago Press and the authors.

p. 392: Excerpts from *Selected Mark Twain–Howells Letters: 1872–1910,* edited by Frederick Anderson et al., Belknap Press, 1967. Published by Harvard University Press and reprinted by their permission.

p. 399: Excerpt from *One Writer's Beginnings* by Eudora Welty. Copyright © 1983, 1984 by the President and Fellows of Harvard College. Reprinted by permission of the publishers, Harvard University Press, Cambridge, Mass.

p. 400: Excerpt from *Women's Ways of Knowing* by Mary Field Belensky et al. Copyright © 1986 by Basic Books. Reprinted by permission of Basic Books, a division of HarperCollins, Inc.

p. 401 "Speak for Yourself" (Hers Column) by Susan Faludi appeared in the *New York Times Magazine,* January 26, 1992. Copyright © 1992 by Susan Faludi and reprinted by permission of the Sandra Dijkstra Agency.

p. 406: "Nobody Mean More to Me than You and the Future Life of Willie Jordan, July 1985" by June Jordan. Copyright © June Jordan. Reprinted by permission of the author.

p. 436: "Is Phoenix Jackson's Grandson Really Dead?" from *The Eye of the Story: Selected Essays and Reviews* by Eudora Welty. Copyright © 1978 by Eudora Welty. Reprinted by permission of Random House, Inc.

p. 440: "A Conversation with My Father" from *Enormous Changes at the Last Minute* by Grace Paley. Copyright © 1972, 1974 by Grace Paley. Reprinted by permission of Farrar, Straus & Giroux, Inc.

p. 461: Excerpt from *Hunger of Memory* by Richard Rodriguez. Copyright © 1981 by Richard Rodriguez. Reprinted by permission of David R. Godine, Publisher.

p. 478: Excerpt based on "A Curious Triangle and the Double-Entry Notebook: Or How Theory Can Help Us Teach Reading and Writing" from The Making of Meaning: Metaphors, Models, and Maxims for Writing Teachers. Boynton/Cook, 1981. Used by permission of the publisher, Heinemann Educational Books, Inc.

p. 490: Excerpt from *Computers and Composition* by Edward P. J. Corbett, Vol. 8.1, November 1990, pp. 84–85. Reprinted by permission of the author.

AUTHOR/TITLE INDEX

"About Being a Man: Essay Developed from Private Writing" (Miller), 148

"Aiming a Cannon at a Mosquito" (Charen), 328

"American Experience" (Bullough) (excerpt), 272

"Analysis of Cover Letter for Advertisement" (Multer, Jajee, Oxenham, Nong, and Ujibwa), 438

"Analysis of My Argument in 'Short Letters'" (Ramaz), 329

"Analysis of 'Sliver'" (Gay), 308

Anderson, Sherwood, "The Book of the Grotesque," 382

"Autobiography" (Hakmit), 146

"Autobiography of Myself as a Writer" (Smith), 455

Barnes, Kate, "My Mother, That Feast of Light," 376

Be Brave Sweet Sister: Essay Developed From Open-Ended Writing" (Fogel), 142

Beck, Alan M., "The Life and Times of Shag," 358

Belenky, Mary, Nancy Goldberger, Blythe Clinchy, and Jill Tarule, *Women's Ways of Knowing* (excerpt), 400

Bianco, Salvatore, "Interview," 169

Birke, Lynda, "Reductionism and Biological Determinism," 269

Bishop, Elizabeth, "One Art," 379

"Book of the Grotesque, The" (Anderson), 382

Bresnan, Kristan, "Portrait of My Mother as a Writer," 166

Buckley, William F., Jr., "With All Deliberate Speed: What's So Bad about Writing Fast?" 332

Bullough, Vern L., "American Experience" (excerpt), 272

"Case Study of Myself as a Writer, A" (Shepherd) (excerpt), 464

"Case Study" (Shack), 458

"Caye Ocho Beach" (Foucard), 53

Charen, Mona, "Aiming a Cannon at a Mosquito," 328

Chen, Bi, "Wishing in the Dark," 306

Cheung, Sindy, "I Am Sorrow," 306

"Chronic Releasing: A Collage" (Ludvino), 36

Clark, Steve, "Collage about Myself as a Writer," 33

Clinchy, Blythe, Mary Belenky, Nancy Goldberger, and Jill Tarule, *Women's Ways of Knowing* (excerpt), 400

"Collaborative Collage about Writing a Collage" (Corry, Goodwin, Ludvino, Morey, and Walsh), 92

"Collage about Human Differences" (Vignali), 90

"Collage about Myself as a Writer" (Clark), 33

"Collage Dialogue on 'The Writer'" (Hales and Nelson), 302

"Collage of Passages about Split Infinitives from Style Manuals, A," 404

"Collage of Passages about Voice, A," 399

Conversation with My Father, A (Paley) (excerpt), 440

Corry, Laura, Elija Goodwin, Matt Ludvino, Denise Morey, and Tassie Walsh, "Collaborative Collage about Writing a Collage," 92

Corwin, Nicholas, "Letter to the Editor," 327

Cree Indians:
"Quiet until the Thaw," 304
"Rain Straight Down," 305

Daley, Karen, "Writing Styles in 'My Mother, That Feast of Light'," 378

Depina, Manuel, "Process Log about Using the Open-Ended Process," 114

"Divisible Man—As Published in *Life* Magazine" (Wideman), 208

"Divisible Man—Early Draft" (Wideman), 205

"Drafts and Revisions of an Editorial for the *Daily Hampshire Gazette*" (Moran), 193

"Drafts and Revisions of Two Short Book Reviews for *Glamour Magazine*" (Mathews), 197

Elbow, Peter, "Example of Writing with the Perl Guidelines," 116

"Essay, The" (Gosse), 244

"Essay: What I Think, What I Am" (Hoagland), 249

"Example of a Student's Freewriting" (anonymous student), 27

"Example of Open-Ended Writing Process" (Fogel), 112

"Example of Writing with the Perl Guidelines" (Elbow), 116

Faludi, Susan, "Speak for Yourself," 401

"Father-Daughter Incest" (Herman and Hirschman) (excerpt), 265

"Feel of Writing—and Teaching Writing, The" (Murray), 29

"Felt Sense" (Gendlin), 119

Fogel, Melissa:
  "Be Brave Sweet Sister: Essay Developed from Open-Ended Writing," 142
  "Example of Open-Ended Writing Process," 112

Foucard, Isabelle, "Caye Ocho Beach," 53

Frost, Robert, "Introduction," *A Way Out* (excerpt), 399

"Gas Analgesia" (from a brochure in the offices of Weinstein and Abel), 331

Gay, Randie, "Analysis of 'Sliver'," 308

Gendlin, Eugene, "Felt Sense," 119

Gilbert, Sandra M., and Susan Gubar, "A New World beyond Snow White," 275

Goldberger, Nancy, Mary Belenky, Blythe Clinchy, and Jill Tarule, *Women's Ways of Knowing* (excerpt), 400

Goodwin, Elija:
  "Response to 'The Writer': Movies of the Mind while Reading," 301
  and Laura Corry, Matt Ludvino, Denise Morey, and Tassie Walsh, "Collaborative Collage about Writing a Collage," 92

Gosse, Edmund, "The Essay," 244

Graham, Kimberly:
  "The Graham Report—Final Draft," 192
  "The Graham Report—Middle Draft," 190
  "The Male Bashing Stereotype—Early Draft," 188

"Graham Report—Final Draft, The" (Graham), 192

"Graham Report—Middle Draft, The" (Graham), 190

"Great Person-Hole Cover Debate, The" (Van Gelder), 226

Gubar, Susan, and Sandra M. Gilbert, "A New World beyond Snow White," 275

Hakmit, Nazim, "Autobiography," 146

Hales, Barbara, and Julie Nelson, "Collage Dialogue on 'The Writer'," 302

Hammond, Lynn, "Loop Writing about Teaching Writing," 84

Hatlen, Burt, "Sonnet 3," 307

Herman, Judith, and Lisa Hirschman, "Father-Daughter Incest" (excerpt), 265

Hirschman, Lisa, and Judith Herman, "Father-Daughter Incest" (excerpt), 265

Hoagland, Edward, "Essay: What I Think, What I Am," 249

Hoffman, Eva, *Lost in Translation: A Life in a New Language* (excerpt), 401

"How Poetry Comes to Me" (Snyder), 308

"How to Write" (Williams) (excerpt), 400

Hughes, Langston, "Sliver," 308

Hull, John M., *Touching the Rock: An Experience of Blindness* (excerpt), 399

Hunger of Memory (Rodriguez) (excerpt), 461

Hyre, Meg, "Some Reflections on Not Voting in Presidential Elections," 227

"I Am Sorrow" (Cheung), 306

"Ice-Cream Man, An" (Shack), 51

"Image of Ice-Cream Man" (Shack), 50

"Interview" (Bianco), 169

"Introduction," *A Way Out* (Frost) (excerpt), 399

"Is Phoenix Jackson's Grandson Really Dead?" (Welty), 436

Jajee, Antoinette, Jason Multer, Martine Oxenham, Ngoyen Nong, and Alex Ujibwa:
  "Analysis of Cover Letter for Advertisement," 438
  "Letter to a Product Producer," 224
  "Revision of Cover Letter," 439

Johnson, Mark, and George Lakoff, "Metaphors We Live By" (excerpt), 384

Jungwirth, Darci, "Loop Writing Collage," 87

Klinko, Eleanor:
  "Untitled 1," 242
  "Untitled 2," 243

Kolnicki, Gary:
  "What Keeps an Airplane Up? Version for General Readers or Students in the Writing Class," 277
  "What Keeps an Airplane Up? Version for Teachers or for People Who Know a Bit about Physics," 280

Lakoff, George, and Mark Johnson, "Metaphors We Live By" (excerpt), 384

Lemonick, Michael D., "What's a Short, Bald-Headed, Potbellied Guy to Do?" 149

"Letter, A" (Levensky), 144

"Letter to the Editor" (Corwin), 327

"Letter to a Product Producer" (Multer, Jajee, Oxenham, Nong, and Ujibwa), 224

Levensky, Mark, "A Letter," 144

"Life and Times of Shag, The" (Beck), 358

"Look Inside: Case Study of Myself as a Writer, A" (Teets), 466

"Loop Writing about Teaching Writing" (Hammond), 84

"Loop Writing Collage" (Jungwirth), 87

Lost in Translation: A Life in a New Language (Hoffman) (excerpt), 401

Lu Chi, "Wen-Fu," 380

Ludvino, Matt:
"Chronic Releasing: A Collage," 36
and Laura Corry, Elija Goodwin, Denise Morey, and Tassie Walsh, "Collaborative Collage about Writing a Collage," 92

"Male Bashing Stereotype—Early Draft, The" (Graham), 188

Mathews, Laura, "Drafts and Revisions of Two Short Book Reviews for *Glamour* Magazine," 197

"Meditation" (anonymous student), 151

"Metaphors We Live By" (Lakoff and Johnson) (excerpt), 384

Miller, Charles, "About Being a Man: Essay Developed from Private Writing," 148

Moffett, James "On Essaying," 247

Moltenbrey, Amber, "My Mother, That Beast of Blight," 376

Moran, Kay J., "Drafts and Revisions of an Editorial for the *Daily Hampshire Gazette*," 193

Morey, Denise, Laura Corry, Elija Goodwin, Matt Ludvino, and Tassie Walsh, "Collaborative Collage about Writing a Collage," 92

Mosley, Walter, "Tackling Racism in the Mystery Novel," 170

Multer, Jason, Antoinette Jajee, Martine Oxenham, Ngoyen Nong, and Alex Ujibwa:
"Analysis of Cover Letter for Advertisement," 438
"Letter to a Product Producer," 224
"Revision of Cover Letter," 439

Murray, Donald, "The Feel of Writing—and Teaching Writing," 29

"My Mother, That Beast of Blight" (Moltenbrey), 376

"My Mother, That Feast of Light" (Barnes), 376

Nelson, Julie, and Barbara Hales, "Collage Dialogue on 'The Writer'," 302

"New World beyond Snow White, A" (Gilbert and Gubar), 275

New York Newsday, "Tackling Racism in the Mystery Novel" (interview with Mosley), 170

New Yorker, The, "Robert Bingham (1925–1982)," 28

"Nobody Mean More to Me Than You and the Future Life of Willie Jordan, July, 1985," 406

Nong, Ngoyen, Jason Multer, Antoinette Jajee, Martine Oxenham, and Alex Ujibwa:
"Analysis of Cover Letter for Advertisement," 438
"Letter to a Product Producer," 224
"Revision of Cover Letter," 439

"On Essaying" (Moffett), 247

"One Art" (Bishop), 379

One Writer's Beginnings (Welty) (excerpt), 399

Oxenham, Martine, Jason Multer, Antoinette Jajee, Ngoyen Nong, and Alex Ujibwa:
"Analysis of Cover Letter for Advertisement," 438
"Letter to a Product Producer," 224
"Revision of Cover Letter," 439

Paley, Grace, *A Conversation with My Father* (excerpt), 440

"Parts of Speech and Punctuation" (Stein) (excerpt), 145

"Portrait of My Mother as a Writer" (Bresnan), 166

"Process Log about Private Writing" (Wong), 115

"Process Log about Using the Open-Ended Process" (Depina), 114

"Process Notes about Collaborative Writing (excerpts)" (Reckendorf), 95

"Quiet until the Thaw" (from the Cree Indians), 304

"Rain Straight Down" (from the Cree Indians), 305

Ramaz, Janine:
"Analysis of My Argument in 'Short Letters'," 329
"Short Letters," 223

Reckendorf, Kathy, "Process Notes about Collaborative Writing" (excerpts), 95

"Reductionism and Biological Determinism" (Birke), 269

"Response to 'The Writer': Movies of the Mind while Reading" (Goodwin), 301

"Response to 'The Writer': Movies of the Mind while Reading" (Walsh), 302

"Revision of Cover Letter" (Multer, Jajee, Oxenham, Nong, and Ujibwa), 439

Rich, Adrienne, "Untitled," 380

"Robert Bingham (1925–1982)" (published in *The New Yorker*), 28

Rodriguez, Richard, *Hunger of Memory* (excerpt), 461

Safire, William, "The Take on Voice" (excerpt), 400

Saganski, Kymberly, "When a Child Has Cancer," 356

Shack, Mitchell:
   "Case Study," 458
   "An Ice-Cream Man," 51
   "Image of Ice-Cream Man," 50

Shea, Bryant, "Voices I Hear," 403

Shepherd, Jean, "A Case Study of Myself as a Writer" (excerpt), 464

"Short Letters" (Ramaz), 223

"Sliver" (Hughes), 308

Smith, Barbara, "Autobiography of Myself as a Writer," 455

Snyder, Gary, "How Poetry Comes to Me," 308

"Some Reflections on Not Voting in Presidential Elections" (Hyre), 227

"Some Thoughts about 'The Writer' on the Occasion of the Death of Isaac Bashevis Singer" (Wenk), 303

"Sonnet 3" (Hatlen), 307

"Speak for Yourself" (Faludi), 401

Stein, Gertrude, "Parts of Speech and Punctuation" (excerpt), 145

Student, anonymous, "Example of a Student's Freewriting," 27

Student, anonymous, "Meditation," 151

Student, anonymous, "Too Much for Too Little," 330

"Tackling Racism in the Mystery Novel" (*New York Newsday* interview with Mosley), 170

"Take on Voice, The" (Safire) (excerpt), 400

Tarule, Jill, Mary Belenky, Nancy Goldberger, and Blythe Clinchy, *Women's Ways of Knowing* (excerpt), 400

Teets, Greg, "A Look Inside: Case Study of Myself as a Writer," 466

"Too Much for Too Little" (anonymous student), 330

Touching the Rock: An Experience of Blindness (Hull) (excerpt), 399

Ujibwa, Alex, Jason Multer, Antoinette Jajee, Martine Oxenham, and Ngoyen Nong:
   "Analysis of Cover Letter for Advertisement," 438
   "Letter to a Product Producer," 224
   "Revision of Cover Letter," 439

"Untitled" (Rich), 380

"Untitled 1" (Klinko), 242

"Untitled 2" (Klinko), 243

Van Gelder, Lindsy, "The Great Person-Hole Cover Debate," 226

Vignali, Amy, "Collage about Human Differences," 90

"Voices I Hear" (Shea), 403

Walsh, Tassie:
   "Response to 'The Writer': Movies of the Mind while Reading," 302
   and Laura Corry, Elija Goodwin, Matt Ludvino, and Denise Morey, "Collaborative Collage about Writing a Collage," 92

Way Out, A, "Introduction" (Frost) (excerpt), 399

Welty, Eudora:
   "Is Phoenix Jackson's Grandson Really Dead?" 436
   One Writer's Beginnings (excerpt), 399
   "A Worn Path," 55

"Wen-Fu" (Lu Chi), 380

Wenk, Laura, "Some Thoughts about 'The Writer' on the Occasion of the Death of Isaac Bashevis Singer," 303

"What Keeps an Airplane Up? Version for General Readers or Students in the Writing Class" (Kolnicki), 277

"What Keeps an Airplane Up? Version for Teachers or for People Who Know a Bit about Physics" (Kolnicki), 280

"What's a Short, Bald-Headed, Potbellied Guy To Do?" (Lemonick), 149

"When a Child Has Cancer" (Saganski), 356

Wideman, John Edgar:
   "Divisible Man—As Published in *Life* Magazine," 208
   "Divisible Man—Early Draft," 205

Wilbur, Richard, "The Writer," 300

Williams, William Carlos, "How to Write" (excerpt), 400

"Wishing in the Dark" (Chen), 306

"With All Deliberate Speed: What's So Bad about Writing Fast?" (Buckley), 332

Women's Ways of Knowing (Belenky, Clinchy, Goldberger, and Tarule) (excerpt), 400

Wong, Irene, "Process Log about Private Writing," 115

"Worn Path, A" (Welty), 55

"Writer, The" (Wilbur), 300

"Writing Mathematics" (Zinsser), 361

"Writing Styles in 'My Mother, That Feast of Light'" (Daley), 378

Zinsser, William, "Writing Mathematics," 361

SUBJECT INDEX

able/ible, 520–521
Abstracts, 344
Accuracy in quotation, 163
Advertisements, 214–215
Agreement, in collaboration, 76–78
Almanacs, 344
Alphabet:
   International Phonetic, 518
   letters of (*see* Letters, alphabetic)
American Psychological Association (APA) system, 349, 350, 352
Analysis:
   of arguments, 313–319
   of audience, 421–422
   based on figurative language, 366, 370–372
Analytic essays, 131, 370–372
ance/ence, 521
APA (American Psychological Association) system, 349, 350, 352
Apostrophes, 509–512
Arguments:
   analyzing, 313–319
   audience for, 222, 312–313, 316, 421
   building, 319–320
   formal vs. informal persuasion, 212, 213
   formal extended, 222
   importance of, 312, 313
   informal, persuasion as, 212–215
   nonadversarial, 312, 321–324
   reasoning and grammar in, 321–326
   revising, 317–319
   seeing elements of, 314–316
   (*see also* Persuasion)

ary/ery, 521
Assignments, writing, 3, 7, 12
Assumptions, in arguments, 315, 421
Attitude toward writing:
   effect of word processors on, 489–490
   toward collaborative writing, 79
Attribution, phrases of, 515
Audience:
   analysis of, 421–422
   for arguments, 312–313, 316, 421
   as focusing device, 138–139
   for formal arguments, 222
   for interview, 161
   purposes and, 420–424, 431, 434–435
   in rhetorical terrain, 431–432
   teacher as, 422–424
   trying out, 124–126
   varying, 71
   writing and, 122, 124–126, 137–139, 264, 420–424
Autobiographies, 447–454

Bad writing, 22
Beliefs, 130
Biographical dictionaries, 344
Book citations, 351
Book review citations, 351

Careful writing, 15, 22, 68
Catalogs, library, 344
cede/ceed/sede, 520
Changes of topics, 123–124
Character, in autobiography, 448
Citations, 348–352
   (*see also inside back cover*)
Claims, main, 314–315
Clauses, introductory, 506

Clustering (mapping), 13
Collaboration:
   interpretation through, 289–290
   for interviews, 155
Collaborative writing, 15
   agreement in, 76–78
   attitude toward, 79
   of collages, 74–77
   of description, 43–44
   of dialogue, 64–66, 70–71, 76
   of essays, 75–77
   loop writing for, 74–78
Collage, 18–19
   about collages, 24–26
   collaborative, 74–77
   for drafts of interviews, 160–161
   focused collage, 72, 74–76
   open collage, 72, 75, 76
Colons, 504
   quotation marks and, 514, 515
"Comma splice," 504
Commas, 504, 505–508
   quotation marks and, 514, 515
Communications triangle, 431–432, 433
Community, term, 2
Community of Writers, A (Elbow and Belanoff), 1–4
   purpose for writing of, 425–426
   structure of, 7
Compare-contrast essays, 131
Composing guidelines, Sondra Perl's, 100–104, 110–111
Composition courses, need for, 263–264
Compound sentences, 505
Content, starting with, 140–141
Contractions, 509
Contradictions, 123
Contrast-compare essays, 131

Control, emotional, and writing, 47

Conversation
  and dialogue, 64, 65
    (*see also* Dialogue)
  ongoing, research as, 353–355
Copyediting, 178, 523–525
Cover letters, 16–17

"Dangerous method," 80–82
Dashes, quotation marks and, 514
Definition, essays of, 131
Descriptions, 40–45, 49, 126–127
Dialectical notebooks, 476–480
Dialogue:
  argument building through, 319–320
  collaborative, 64–66, 70–71, 76
  description of genre, 128–130
  persuasive writing through, 218
Digressions, 123–124
Disciplines, writing in, 254–264
Discourse, 262
Discussion draft, 78
Documentation of sources, 348–352
    (*see also inside back cover*)
Double-audience situation, 422
Double-entry notebooks, 476–480
Doubling letters, 519–520
"Doubting game," 316
Drafts:
  of analytic essays, 371–372
  of autobiography, 448–450
  discussion draft (collaborative writing), 78
  exploratory, for research papers, 345–346
  of interviews, 160–161
  for persuasive writing, 218
  of research papers, 345–348
  for writing in disciplines, 257–258

e, silent, ending words, 520
Editing:
  copyediting and proofreading, 178, 523–525

premature, 491
    (*see also* Revising)
Editors, letters to, 213–214, 217–218
efy/ify, 520
ei/ie, 520
ence/ance, 521
Encyclopedias, 344
End-stop punctuation, 499–504, 514, 515
End-term responses to writing courses, 494–498
English, Standard, 186–187, 527
Errors, in loop writing, 71–72
ery/ary, 521
Essays, 232–241
  analytic, 131, 370–372
  citations for, 351
  collaborative, 75–77
  compare-contrast essays, 131
  of definition, 131
  expository, 131–132, 232–241
  five-paragraph, 132
  impersonal, 234–235, 239–240
  loop writing for, 74, 75–76
  personal (*see* Personal essays)
  persuasive, 130–131
  process essays, 131–132
  purposes of, 430
  reading of, 237
  research essays (*see* Research essays/papers)
Excitement, and writing, 47–48
Exclamation points, 504
  quotation marks and, 514
Expectations, 286
Experience, description and, 40, 42, 43, 49
Experiential writing, 69
Exploratory writing:
  content of, starting with, 140–141
  in drafts for research papers, 345–346
  private (*see* Private writing)
Expository essays, 131–132, 232–241
Expository writing, 69, 450
Expressive writing (global concept), 432, 433

Extended formal argument, 222

Feelings, in description, 42
Felt sense:
  private writing and, 102, 103, 110–111, 122
  revising and, 183
Fiction, 126
Figurative language, 366–370, 373–375
  text analysis based on, 366, 370–372
First thoughts, in loop writing, 67–69
Five-paragraph essays, 132
Focused collage, 72, 74–76
Focused freewriting, 12–13
Footnotes, 349
Form, starting with, 141
Formal argument:
  extended, 222
  informal persuasion vs., 212, 313
    (*see also* Arguments)
Formal voice, 388
  vs. grammatical correctness, 526–530
Foundations for writing, 100
Fragments, sentence, 500–501
Freewriting, 12, 104–105
  for expository essays, 232–235
  focused, 12–13
  importance of, 21–23
  for persuasive writing, 217–218
  for research papers, 339–340
  revising and, 179
  for writing in disciplines, 257
Freshman composition courses, need for, 263–264

Genres:
  definition of, 126
  descriptions of, 126–135
  as form or content, 140–141
  purposes and, 430–432
  in rhetorical terrain, 431–432
Global concepts for purposes, 432–434
Grammar, 324
  correctness of, vs. formal voice, 526–530

Grammar (*cont.*)
  reasoning and, 324–326
  revising and, 186–187
Grammatical structure of
  sentences, 499–503
Guessing, in interpretation, 286
Guidelines:
  minimal, for autobiography,
    450–451
  for MLA documentation (*see
    inside back cover*)
  Sondra Perl's composing,
    100–104, 110–111

Homonyms, 521
Homophones, 518
"Hung margins," 352

ible/able, 520–521
ie/ei, 520
ify/efy, 520
Imagery, 368
  (*see also* Figurative language)
Images, 40–45, 368–369, 374
Impersonal essays, 234–235,
  239–240
Implied readers, 421–422
Indentation (*see* Margins)
Informal argument, persuasion
  as, 212–215
Informal persuasion, 212, 222, 313
Informal voice, 388
  grammatical correctness and,
    527–528
Inspiration, 48
International Phonetic Alphabet,
  518
Interpretation, 286–296,
  298–299, 479–480
  reading out loud for, 292–295,
    481–486
Interviews:
  about writing, 154–164
  audience for, 161
  choosing person for, 154–155
  citation for, 351
  collaboration for, 155
  first 157–158
  notes after, 158–159
  observing and, for research,
    340–343

practice for, 155–157
second, 159–160
writing up, 160–163
Introductory words, phrases, and
  clauses, 506
Invisible writing, 13–14

Journal, process, 19–20

Knowledge, and writing in
  disciplines, 261–263

Language:
  in disciplines, 259, 262–263
  figurative (*see* Figurative
    language)
  literal, 373–374
  natural language ability, 4
  social, 2
Letters, 14–15
  citations for, 351
  cover letters, 16–17
  persuasive, to editors,
    213–214, 217–218
Letters, alphabetic:
  doubling, 519–520
  plurals of, 511
Library research, 341, 343–345
Lies, in loop writing, 71, 72
Listening:
  persuasion and, 213
  and writing in disciplines, 255
Literal language, 373–374
Literal meaning, 482–483
Logic, 212, 312, 324
Loop writing, 66–72, 73, 83
  for collaborative writing, 74–78
  "dangerous method" and,
    80–82

Main claims, 314–315
Mapping (clustering), 13
Margins:
  "hung," 352
  indented for long quotations,
    515–516
Meaning:
  figurative language and, 374
  interpretation of, 286–298,
    479–480
  (*see also* Interpretation)

literal, 482–483
  in narrative (story), 45
  reading out loud and, 482–484
Meditations, 133–134
Metacognition, 24, 452–454
Metaphor, 366–367, 374
Midterm responses to writing
  courses, 494–498
Modern Language Association
  (MLA) guidelines, 349–352
  (*see also inside back cover*)
Moments, in loop writing,
  69–70

Narrative (story), 42, 43, 45,
  127–128, 450
  in loop writing, 69–70
Natural language ability, 4
Nonadversarial argument, 312,
  321–324
Notebooks, double-entry or
  dialectical, 476–480
Notes:
  after interview, 158–159
  for writing in disciplines,
    255–256
Numbers, plurals of, 511

Observing and interviewing,
  340–343
Obsessions, 124
On-line searches, 344
Ongoing conversation, 353–355
Open collage, 72, 75, 76
Open-ended writing process,
  104–105
Opinions, 130
Outlines, 346–347
  (*see also* Clustering)

Papers, research (*see* Research
  essays/papers)
Parenthetical citations, 350
  (*see also inside back cover*)
Parody, 132–133
Pausing and commas, 506–507
Perception, 286
Performance (*see* Reading out
  loud)
Periodical indexes, 344
Periods, 504

Periods (*cont.*)
quotation marks and, 514
Perl composing guidelines, 100–104, 110–111
Personal essays, 239–240
expository, 234–235
grammatical correctness in, 527–528
meditations, 133–134
Persuasion, 130–131, 212–218
evaluation of, 216–217
formal argument vs., 212, 313
informal, 212, 222, 313
as informal argument, 212–215
letters to the editor, 213–214, 217–218
persuasive essays, described, 130–131
(*see also* Arguments)
Phonetics, 517–518
Phrases:
of attribution, 515
introductory, 506
resonant, 369
Plurals of letters and numbers, 511
Poems (*see* Poetry)
Poetic writing (global concept), 432–433
Poetry:
citations for, 351
genre, description of, 126, 134–135
interpretation of, 293–295
interpretation through, 295–296
purposes of, 430
Portfolios, 446–447
Portraits:
genre, description of, 126–127
loop writing for, 69–70
(*see also* Descriptions)
Possession, apostrophes for showing, 509, 510
Practice interview, 155–157
Preconceptions, in loop writing, 69
Prejudices, in loop writing, 68–69
Premature editing, 491
Private writing, 100

open-ended process for, 104–105
Perl's composing guidelines for, 100–104, 110–111
for public writing, in general, 122–124
purpose of, 107–109
for specific genres, 124–135
"Process Boxes," 16
Process essays, 131–132
Process journal, 19–20
Process writing, 15–16, 20
importance of, 23–24
Procrastination, 81
Proofreading, 178, 523–525
Prose, 126
Public writing:
informal, 14
private writing for, in general, 122–124
specific genres, 124–135
Punctuation:
apostrophes, 509–512
commas, 504, 505–508, 514, 515
dashes, 514
end-stop, 499–504, 514, 515
quotation marks, 513–515
systems of, 508
Purposes, 420, 424–426, 431
audience and, 420–424, 431, 434–435
genre and, 430–432
global concepts for, 432–434
of paragraphs, revising and, 181
in rhetorical terrain, 431–433
specific statements of, 425
in writing *A Community of Writers,* 425–426

Question marks, 504
quotation marks and, 514
Questionnaires:
for research, 341–343, 348
for response to writing courses, 494–498
on writing skills, 473–475
Questions, in expository essays, 131

Quotation marks, 513–515
omitted in long passages, 515
periods and commas and, 514, 515
question marks, exclamation points, and dashes and, 514–515
semicolons and colons and, 514
single, 515
Quotations:
from interviews, 162–163
long, indenting, 515–516
punctuation of, 513–515
within quotations, 515
in research papers, 349

Reading:
of essays, method for, 237
process of, and interpretation, 286, 287–292, 298–299, 479–480
and writing, parallel between, 478–480
Reading out loud:
for collaborative writing, 78
interpretation through, 292–295, 481–486
recognizing voice through, 390–391, 484–486
for writing in disciplines, 255
"Readings" sections, 16
Reasoning, grammar and, 324–326
Reasons, in arguments, 315
Reference books, 344
References, list of (*see* Works cited)
Rendering text (*see* Reading out loud)
Research, 338, 340–345
documentation of, 348–352 (*see also inside back cover*)
as ongoing conversation, 353–355
Research essays/papers, 132, 338
choosing a topic for, 338–339
documentation of sources for, 348–352

Research essays/papers (*cont.*) (*see also inside back cover*)
  drafts for, 345–348
  freewriting for, 339–340
  revising, 348
Reseeing and rethinking, 177–180
Reshaping and reworking, 178, 180–183
Resonance, and symbolism, 369
Responding, and purpose, 424
  (*see also* Interpretation)
Responses to writing courses, 494–498
Rethinking and reseeing, 177–180
Revising, 15, 176–187
  of analytic essays, 372
  of arguments, 317–319
  of dialogue, 65–66
  first-level, 179–180
  grammar and, 186–187
  of interviews, 161–162
  levels of, overview, 177–178
  putting perspective on, 184–186
  of research papers, 348
  resources for, 184
  second level, 180–184
  word processors and, 488,492
Reworking and reshaping, 178, 180–183
Rhetoric, definition of, 312
Rhetorical terrain, 431–433
Rough drafts (*see* Drafts)
"Ruminations and theory" sections, 7
Run-on sentences, 501, 504

Satire, 132–133
Sayings, in loop writing, 72
sede/ceed/cede, 520
Seeing, in interpretation, 286
  (*see also* Images)
Semicolons, 504
  quotation marks and, 514
Sentence fragments, 500–501
Sentences, 499–503, 508
  compound, 505
  definition of, 501–502
  run-on, 501, 504

Sharing and Responding section, 7
Silent *e* ending words, 520
Simile, 367–369
Social language, 2
Sondra Perl's composing guidelines, 100–104, 110–111
Sources, documentation of, 348–352
  (*see also inside back cover*)
Spelling, 517–522
Spelling checkers, 186–187, 489, 518–519
Standard English usage, 186–187, 527
Story (*see* Narrative)
Structure:
  for autobiography, 450
  of sentences, 499–503
  for writing in disciplines, 259
Students, good, definition of, 4
Summary guidelines for MLA documentation (*see inside back cover*)
Summing-up, in private writing, 104–105
Support, for arguments, 315
Symbols, 369–370

Tape recorder, 163
Teachers as audience, 422–424
Temperment, in autobiography, 448
Text analysis based on figurative language, 366, 370–372
Text rendering (*see* Reading out loud)
Thoughts, first, 67–69
Time, varying, 71
Topics:
  changes of, 123–124
  choice of, for research papers, 338–339
  in rhetorical terrain, 431–432
Transactional writing (global concept), 432, 433

Vocabulary, for writing in disciplines, 259
Voice, 388–395
  in collaborative essays, 77

grammatical correctness and, 526–530
reading out loud and, 390–391, 484–486

Word Processors:
  advantages of using, 487–490, 518
  dangers of using, 490–492
  mastering, 492–493
  writing with, 487–493
Wordiness, 491–492
Words:
  breathing life into (*see* Reading out loud)
  ending in silent *e,* changing, 520
  ending in *y,* changing, 521
  introductory, 506
Works cited:
  in *A Community of Writers,* guidelines for list of, 350–352
  (*see also inside back cover*)
Workshops, 3, 7
Writer(s), 3–4
  autobiography of self as, 447–451, 454
  varying, 71
Writing:
  analysis based on figurative language, 366, 370–372
  attitude toward, 79, 489–490
  audience and, 122, 124–126, 137–139, 264, 420–424
  bad, 22
  careful, 15, 22, 68
  collaborative (*see* Collaborative writing)
  descriptive, 40–45, 49, 126–127
  in disciplines, 254–264
  experiential, 69
  (*see also* Experience)
  exploratory, 140–141, 345–346
  (*see also* Private writing)
  expository, 69, 131–132, 232–241, 450
  expressive (global concept), 432, 433
  foundation for, 100

Writing (*cont.*)
  freewriting (*see* Freewriting)
  interview about, 154–164
  of interviews, 160–163
  invisible, 13–14
  kinds of, 12–17
  knowledge and, and writing in
      disciplines, 261–263
  learning from, 3
  of letters (*see* Letters)
  loop (*see* Loop writing)
  narrative, 42, 43, 45, 127–128,
      450
  open-ended process for,
      104–105
  persuasive (*see* Persuasion)
  poetic (global concept), 432–433
      (*see also* Poetry)
  private (*see* Private writing)
  process writing, 15–16, 20,
      23–24
  processes for, 12–17
  public (*see* Public writing)
  purposes of (*see* Purposes)
  reading and, parallel between,
      478–480
  sharing, 3
  tasks of, 12–17
  transactional (global concept),
      432, 433
  view of, 5–6
  with word processors, 487–493
Writing assignments, 3, 7, 12
Writing courses, midterm and
    end-term responses to,
    494–498
Writing processes, 12–17
Writing skills questionnaire,
    473–475
Writing tasks, 12–17

y, changing words ending in, 521